THE PATHOLOGY
OF
MENTAL RETARDATION

THE PATHOLOGY

OF

MENTAL RETARDATION

By

L. CROME, *M.C.*, M.R.C.P. (Ed.), M.C.Path.

Pathologist, Queen Mary's Hospital for Children,
Carshalton, Surrey

and

J. STERN, Ph.D.

Biochemist, Queen Mary's Hospital for Children,
Carshalton, Surrey

With 129 Illustrations

J. & A. CHURCHILL LTD.
104 Gloucester Place, London, W.1.
1967

John F. Kennedy Institute

First Edition . . 1967

To H.C. and D.J.S.

PRINTED AND BOUND IN ENGLAND BY
HAZELL WATSON AND VINEY LTD
AYLESBURY, BUCKS

PREFACE

THANKS to the many advances in the field of mental retardation and the new interest commanded by this subject, many workers in wards and laboratories face more often hitherto unfamiliar problems of diagnosis and management. Since it is often difficult to muster the widely scattered published data we have thought it useful to assemble in one volume the basic facts on the pathology of mental retardation, interpreting 'pathology' rather widely, to include aetiology, morphology, biochemistry and laboratory diagnosis. In doing so, we have of necessity leaned heavily on our own experience at the Fountain Hospital and, later, at Queen Mary's Hospital for Children, Carshalton, Surrey. This experience and limitation of space influenced greatly our choice of material. We say little about conditions not normally dealt with in the context of mental deficiency as practised in this country, e.g. Friedreich's ataxia, paying more attention to other disorders, such as Down's disease and undifferentiated mental retardation. On the other hand, we deal at greater length than their incidence warrants with certain rare diseases, such as the lipidoses and other neurometabolic disorders, because they are of practical importance from the viewpoint of differential diagnosis. In quoting references we have tended to cite the more recent and comprehensive sources in preference to the historically important ones. We cannot expect all readers to share our views and bias, and are ourselves conscious of at least one major gap in our text. We say little about adults compared to infants and children. This reflects not only our personal experience and ignorance but to some extent also those of others. Regrettably, little research has been done on the pathology of older retarded individuals. We hope that this book will be of interest to pathologists, psychiatrists, paediatricians, medical officers of health, school medical officers and, perhaps, also other readers who, like ourselves, remain perennially fascinated by the brain-mind relationship.

As mentioned, it has been our good fortune to have been members of the team at the Fountain Hospital and Queen Mary's Hospital for Children, and we owe a great debt to our colleagues there, past and present. We have drawn freely upon their studies and records, and have learned even more from them in informal discussions. This close contact has enabled us to achieve a surprising degree of unanimity on many controversial problems. The views we express are hence not only our own but, largely, also those of our colleagues. It would be difficult to mention all who have helped us in this and other ways, but no one has done more than Dr. Brian Kirman, the Director of Research at the Fountain Hospital, and we are happy to acknowledge our heavy indebtedness to him. Other colleagues who have often assisted us are Dr. L. T. Hilliard and Dr. J. M. Berg. Dr. Magda Erdohazi and Dr. Joan Bicknell have given us staunch support and advice in the preparation of the book and proof reading. In a sense, this book is a rewritten and greatly expanded version of the pathological part of Hilliard and Kirman's textbook

'Mental Deficiency', to which one of us has contributed and from which we reproduce a number of illustrations. We are grateful to Dr. Hilliard and Dr. Kirman for permission to do so. It is also a pleasant duty to acknowledge the financial aid given to us and our colleagues over the years for research purposes by the National Society for Mentally Handicapped Children, the Jewish Aid Committee, The League of Friends of Queen Mary's Hospital for Children, and the South West Metropolitan Regional Hospital Board.

A number of colleagues have read and helpfully criticised portions of this book. Mr. Norman Le Page has helped us greatly by preparing many photographs and we wish to record our appreciation of his skill and kindness.

Lastly, the task could well have proved beyond our power without the ever-willing assistance of the secretarial staff in our department. Mrs. Margaret Lane prepared many successive drafts of the typescript and the bibliography. Mrs. E. Hardy has prepared the Index of Authors and took part with Mrs. J. Buck and Mrs. J. Wheeler in the rest of the clerical work.

THE AUTHORS

CONTENTS

CHAPTER 1

THE GENETIC CAUSES OF MENTAL RETARDATION

Introduction

THE identification of the causes of mental retardation has been slow compared with the progress in other branches of medical and biological science. Traces of events and processes in the prenatal past of the patient and his ancestors leading to abnormal brain development or functioning are often overgrown and irretrievably obscured, while prospects of treatment, in the conventional sense of this word, have been and still remain discouraging. Moreover, other and more urgent medical problems, such as infections and the effects of malnutrition, have been making their claims upon the always limited resources of the medical services. Recently, however, the amount and scope of research have been expanding and the former outlook is rapidly changing. Many causes of mental retardation have become known, and retardation due to some of these may be preventable. Moreover, some of the progress, as in cyto- and biochemical genetics, is of great general interest and is stimulating study in many fields only remotely related to mental retardation. New knowledge comes therefore from far-flung lines of research.

Nevertheless, it is still true that the decisive cause of mental defect is ascertainable in only a minority of cases. Thus, in a survey of 800 severely subnormal patients admitted during a 10 year period to the Fountain Hospital, specific aetiological factors or distinct syndromes could be established in only one-third of the cases (Berg, 1961). Since many of these patients had been examined, often repeatedly, at leading London hospitals, it is reasonable to assume that the standard of investigation in Berg's series was as high as anywhere. Furthermore, the cases considered by him were severely subnormal; the uncertainty in regard to causation is even greater in higher-grade persons.

Pathological and Social Factors

It is convenient to present separately two sets of aetiological factors, the pathological and the social, although they are interdependent. The pathological factors are harmful biological or physical agents responsible directly for the onset of some encephalopathy or neural dysfunction. Adverse social factors may prevent, on the other hand, the full utilization of the curtailed abilities of the affected individual. Social adversity, such as poverty, overcrowding and malnutrition, also enhances the risk of exposure to some harmful pathological agents. The two sets of factors can operate in this complex way to result in all levels of defect. Nevertheless, in general, pathological factors, causing gross abnormality of the nervous system, are more important in the production of severe cases of mental subnormality, and social factors— in the determination of feeblemindedness and educational subnormality. While some of the social factors will be mentioned as occasion calls in the text below, no detailed consideration of the social background of mental deficiency can be attempted in this book. Readers requiring further information on this subject are referred to Kirman (1965).

When known, pathological factors leading to brain abnormality are best considered in terms of the diseases or syndromes which they produce. However, as already mentioned, most cases of mental retardation are not readily classifiable in this way and it is therefore also necessary to discuss causes in general terms. It seems appropriate to do so in chronological order, i.e. in accordance with their time of action in ontogenesis. Such a presentation can, of course, be only approximate so long as many causes remain unknown. Further, agents, such as infection, irradiation or malnutrition, are known to have widely different results when acting at different periods of ontogenesis.

In most cases of severe subnormality cerebral changes are already present at birth, while a minority acquire lesions in early post-natal life. The precise ratio of congenital to acquired cases is not known, but severe congenital malformations seem to involve the nervous system more frequently than any other part of the body. Many attempts have been made to estimate the incidence of somatic and neural malformations (Lamy and Frézal, 1960; McKeown, 1960). In countries where mortality due to infection has declined most, all congenital malformations account for some 15–20 per cent of neonatal and infantile mortality. Carter (1963) states, for example, that in Britain anencephaly has an incidence of 2 per thousand and spina bifida 3 per thousand of total births. In most countries, congenital malformations of the nervous system take second place after those of the cardio-vascular system. However, the neural malformations listed in the published surveys include only the grosser of the readily recognisable forms, such as marked hydrocephalus, gross microcephaly, Down's disease, anencephaly and spina bifida cystica. Most brain anomalies associated with mental retardation are much less obvious and the true incidence of neural malformation has therefore been considerably underestimated.

Inheritance in Mental Retardation

Familial Incidence

Certain distinct conditions associated with mental retardation conform to recognized patterns of inheritance. These are considered briefly on p. 8 in this chapter and, in greater detail, with the special syndromes. The question of the rôle of inheritance in other forms of mental retardation is, however, more controversial, and has always loomed large in discussions of this subject. That some of the old assertions amounted to little more than guess-work is at once evident from the table compiled by Tredgold (1952). This shows different authors assigning to heredity from 29 to 90 per cent of all cases of mental deficiency.

The most important survey in the field is probably still the Clinical and Genetic Study of 1,280 cases of Mental Defect by Penrose (1938). Some material is also available in the evidence included in the Report of the Departmental Committee on Sterilization (1934). Many newer valuable surveys have been published in recent years (e.g. Äkesson, 1961; Jastak, MacPhee and Whiteman, 1963). They do not alter, however, the conclusions outlined below.

Penrose found that the frequency of mental defect among the parents and sibs of his patients was 7 to 9 per cent, which compares with a figure for the population in general of approximately 1 per cent. The incidence among the patients' own children was even higher. He also observed, like the Departmental Committee, that familial incidence was greater among the higher-grade patients. The incidence in the grandparents of patients, however, did not exceed the figure for the general population. A correlation was demonstrated between the grade of the defect in the patient and that in the families; idiots, for example, though less likely to have affected relatives than the feebleminded, tended to have relatives who were also idiots (see, however, p. 9). Again, certain diseases were found more frequently in the relatives of patients with the same condition than among the relatives of other patients. This was the case in endocrine disorders, epilepsy, psychopathy and Down's disease.

These findings are comparable with many others not mentioned here, and constitute a strong *prima facie* case for heredity being one of the important factors in mental deficiency. But it must not be forgotten that families share not only a genetic background but also a large number of other factors in their biological and social environment.

The Study of Twins

The study of twins has yielded interesting information. The usual method has been to compare concordance and discordance for mental defect in monozygotic and dizygotic twins, on the assumption that the former are genetically identical, while the others show no more than ordinary fraternal similarity. In a series studied by Smith (1929), quoted by Böök (1953), 14 out of 16 uniovular twins were thus concordant compared with only 4 out of 50 binovular twins. In a later series, all of 60 pairs of uniovular and only 76 out of 168 binovular twins (Juda, 1939, quoted by Böök, 1953) were concordant for mental deficiency.

The above figures must be interpreted with caution. In the first place, twins, and particularly uniovular twins, are at a greater disadvantage in regard to mental development than singletons (Berg and Kirman, 1960). Many twins are premature, and thus exposed to special dangers associated with prematurity, such as retrolental fibroplasia and icterus. Secondly, intrauterine environment, events at birth and post-natal circumstances need not be identical even for uniovular twins. The occurrence of a microcephalic and a normal sib among uniovular twins has been described, for example, by Hinden (1956) and by Brandon, Kirman and Williams (1959). One of uniovular twins reported by Penrose (1937) had congenital syphilis. Similar discordance also occurs in respect of other congenital disease, e.g. of the heart (Forsyth and Uchida, 1951). Even uniovular twins suffering from the same enzymatic defect may exhibit striking individual differences. Thus, the 21-year-old phenylketonuric, uniovular, monochorionic but diamniotic twins described by Herlin (1962) showed, despite common rearing, very appreciable differences in intelligence, nature of epilepsy and E.E.G. tracings. Twin studies also provide ample evidence of the operation of environmental factors. For example, Newman, Freeman and Holzinger (1937) found that the correlation coefficient between the I.Q.'s of uniovular twins reared together was about $+ 0.91$, and ranged from $+ 0.67$ to $+ 0.73$ in uniovular twins reared separately.

Down's disease has also been studied in twins. Slater (1938), quoting the work of Rosanoff and Siegert, states that 64 recorded pairs were either uniovular and concordant, or binovular and discordant for Down's disease. There was, in addition, another case of Down's disease in one of a pair of allegedly monozygotic twins, and several similar instances have since been observed (Fanconi, 1962). This indicates that genetic factors play a major causal part in this condition and is in accordance with the recent findings of a chromosomal abnormality (p. 15). The incidence of Down's disease is, however, also related to increased parental age and, hence, environmental factors (p. 50).

For a balanced and very readable review of the problem of twin studies readers are referred to the books by Newman (1940) and Kallmann (1953).

Consanguinity

Very occasionally mental defectives are the issue of incestuous relations, but the rôle of consanguinity in mental defect is usually considered in terms of marriage between first or second cousins. First-cousin marriages are significantly commoner among the parents of known defectives than in the general population. It was found, for example, that ten of 800 consecutive admissions to the Fountain Hospital (1·25 per cent) had parents who were first cousins. This compared with about 0·4 per cent for the general population (Berg—unpublished observations). The incidence of consanguinity is also high in certain specific conditions, such as phenylketonuria, the lipidoses and some of the other metabolic disorders. This conforms to the theory of recessive transmission of these conditions, the chances of a child acquiring two pathological genes and being thus homozygous for an abnormal character increasing in the case of the marriage of near relatives. Estimations of the rate of consanguinity form a major part of the statistical studies of many genetic diseases. This has to be borne in mind in genetic counselling.

The 'Subcultural Group'

It is necessary to deal next with a few of the older hypotheses which continue to be re-stated in texts and reviews in spite of being largely outdated.

A glance at the distribution curve of intelligence in a community as measured by psychometry shows that it is not quite symmetrical (Fig. 1), the individuals in the asymmetrical portion at the low I.Q. end of the scale comprising the grossest cases of mental retardation. The majority of the higher-grade mentally handicapped are found in the symmetrical part of the Gaussian curve. It has been suggested by Lewis (1933) that these higher-grade defectives constitute a special 'subcultural' group as contrasted with the 'pathological' group, which contains the lower-grade cases. It has also been suggested that the chief cause of mental retardation in the subcultural group is 'normal' biological variation, as, for example, in stature, conditioned by the operation of polygenes, with social adversity playing a contributory rôle (Breg, 1962).

The usefulness of the above classification has been frequently challenged, and the problem was one of the objects of a study by Berg and Kirman (1959). It is true of course, that the bulk of the higher-grade cases are not yet classifiable

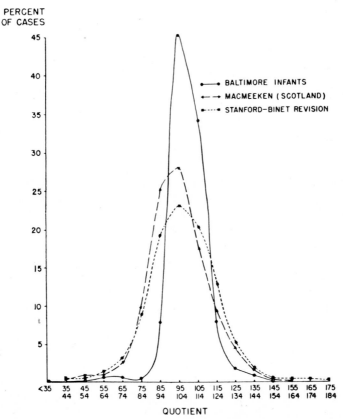

FIG. 1. Distribution of intelligence quotients. (Reproduced by kind permission of Professor Hilda Knobloch.)

in specific aetiological terms, but to say that their backwardness is due to 'biological variation' is begging the question of the reasons for such variation. Berg and Kirman found that some of the individuals with a relatively high I.Q., who were eligible in some respects for inclusion in the 'subcultural group', were in fact sufferers from a 'diluted' form of a disease such as phenylketonuria, tuberous sclerosis or residual kernicterus, conditions giving rise in other instances to some of the grossest forms of mental subnormality. There are further similar conditions and, as knowledge increases, more will undoubtedly be discovered. It may well be that many of the known and as yet unknown aetiological factors, genetic and environmental, will prove to have wide ranges of effect, extending from the grossest idiocy to full normality. Berg and Kirman observe that "if the biological variation is of such a degree as to produce seriously impaired intelligence, which does not permit the individual to cope with his environment, then the condition must be regarded as pathological. Similarly, it seems reasonable to suppose that many of the pathological lesions responsible for cases of mental defect are one of the means whereby biological variation operates".

In the light of these considerations it does not seem very useful to classify, as is done by Breg, approximately one-third of all admissions to institutions for the retarded and more than 60 per cent of the retarded in the community as 'subcultural'. If the distinction between the 'subcultural' and the 'pathological' is to be maintained, it cannot be on grounds of aetiology.

Twofold Manifestation of Heredity in Mental Defect

Another hypothesis similar to the above division of defectives into the 'subcultural' and 'pathological' has been advanced to explain some of the statistical features in the distribution of mental defect. As indicated already, there is some evidence that heredity plays a part in an increasing proportion of cases with the approach to the more normal ranges of intelligence. Or, in other words, the more normal the person the more he tends to resemble other members of the family. A possible explanation of the phenomenon, if real, is that heredity manifests itself in two different ways in the lower and in the higher ranges of intelligence. This is how the thought is expressed by Fraser Roberts (1950). "The greatest single advance in the understanding of the causation of oligophrenia came with the recognition that there are two kinds: a hypothesis now very generally accepted. The first kind depends upon a continuously graded character, general intelligence, and may be taken to comprise the bulk of high-grade oligophrenia. This metrical character, as measured, has heritable and non-heritable components, and the heritable portion of the variation is determined by polygenes. The second kind, comprising the great bulk of low-grade oligophrenia, is a highly diverse collection of entities: sometimes genetically determined, and when this is so, by major genes (or super genes); sometimes environmentally determined; sometimes by the interaction of genetic and non-genetic influences."

In practice, it is seldom possible to distinguish between the heritable and the non-heritable components of 'general intelligence' and to place particular persons into either of the above categories. Further, the hypothesis seems to exaggerate the difference in the pathogenesis of the two groups. As already stated, pathogenic agents often have a wide range of effect on intelligence and the difference between parent and child must increase with the degree of such manifestation. The increased rates of abortion, miscarriage, stillbirth, neonatal and later mortality among the severely affected would tend to enhance statistically the intellectual resemblance between parent and child among the less severely affected survivors.

These reflections are in keeping with the results of the study by Brandon

(1957). She investigated the offspring of 73 higher-grade institutionalized defectives and found that the loss from 150 pregnancies by miscarriage, stillbirth and later death was considerably higher than the national average. The medical condition of the dead children could be ascertained in only a few instances. The conditions detected were, rather significantly in the context of the present discussion, such gross neural malformations as anencephaly, hydrocephalus, microcephaly and a large swelling of the head. The average I.Q. of the 109 live children was 89·1 and the correlation of the mother's intelligence with that of the children was rather low. Ninety-nine or 91 per cent of the surviving children were apparently mentally normal. Brandon's series was not, perhaps, large enough to be fully conclusive, but the results certainly throw considerable doubt on some of the previously expressed views.

The Example of Microphthalmia

The complexity of genetical problems and the hazards of dealing with loose nosological categories are well illustrated by the example of microphthalmia, a condition frequently associated with mental retardation. Microphthalmia denotes smallness of one or both eyes. Its degree varies; in extreme cases there is total absence of the eyes—anophthalmia. Morphologically, the condition is usually divided into three groups; (1) Simple microphthalmia in which the eyes are small but otherwise normal; (2) microphthalmia associated with coloboma, and (3) microphthalmia without coloboma but with other ocular defects. Sjögren and Larsson (1949) found that mental deficiency was present in 58 of their 137 microphthalmic cases. The genetic basis of the condition has received much attention. Since James Briggs (1813–26, quoted by Sorsby, 1934) first reported its occurrence in a London family there have been many contributions on its familial incidence. It is usually said to be transmitted as a recessive Mendelian character (Kallmann, Barrera, and Metzger, 1940). It was thought to be sex-linked in the series of Fraser Roberts (1937) and of Stephens (1947), but behaved as an ordinary dominant in the cases of Leydhecker (1938). Sjögren and Larsson thought that it occurred sometimes as a dominant character having a low degree of penetrance.

Microphthalmia also occurs spontaneously in animals and can be produced experimentally. This was done in the chick embryo by Ochi (1919), who injected saline, distilled water or air into the albumen of an egg close to the blastoderm. Piglets develop this abnormality if their mothers are kept on a vitamin-A-free diet for some time before and after mating. Related eye abnormalities were also produced in rats by Warkany and Schraffenberger (1944) by keeping the pregnant animals on a vitamin-A-free diet. Foetal anophthalmia and microphthalmia follow likewise the experimental application of X-rays at certain early stages of gestation (Hicks, 1958). For a full up to date review of the experimental production of these abnormalities readers are referred to Lopashov and Stroeva (1964).

Thus, the hereditary basis of the condition is far from clear in spite of some of the earlier assertions. It is now known that human microphthalmia is one of the abnormalities which can be produced by maternal rubella (Gregg,

1941). The Swiss workers, Mutrux, Wildi and Bourquin (1949) have estimated that of 479 published cases of rubellar embryopathy 52 had microphthalmia. Microphthalmia may also occur in association with coloboma and limb deformities in 'thalidomide babies' (Gilkes and Strode, 1963). The condition has been described as one of the anomalies associated with chromosomal trisomy of the 13–15 group, and yet another cause is retrolental fibroplasia, which may be, in its turn, the result of different factors: environmental and genetic (p. 78). Furthermore, it should not be assumed that the presence of microphthalmia is always easy to establish and estimate. The range of micro-phthalmia extends, as said, from absence of the eyes to barely perceptible reduction in size, and its recognition becomes progressively more uncertain the milder the defect. Thus, since those cases which are difficult to identify, are probably also the most numerous, statistical and aetiological accuracy is easily vitiated.

Specific Transmission of Defect

It is thus clear that the time has come to abandon the attempts to assess the general significance of heredity in mental retardation and to turn instead to its precise rôle in more accurately defined conditions. Greater attention has re-cently been paid to these problems, and with help from vastly improved bio-chemical techniques many new diseases and syndromes have been recognized in which heredity plays a major part, and in which transmission is consistent with one of the main classical genetic patterns, i.e. autosomal recessive, dominant or sex-linked. This applies particularly to diseases caused by inborn errors of metabolism. Many of these are frequently, or even always, accom-panied by mental retardation and they are listed in Table 4. Others which may also be transmitted in well-defined genetic patterns, are not included in the table because their relation to possible metabolic defect remains uncertain. It is quite possible, for example, that some of the spino-cerebellar atrophies, such as Friedreich's disease, or certain forms of muscular dystrophy are caused by still unidentified metabolic errors, since these conditions may be transmit-ted in a sex-linked or autosomal recessive manner. Dominant transmission can be demonstrated in familial cases of tuberous sclerosis, neurofibromatosis and Huntington's chorea. Unequivocal evidence of sex-linkage in metabolic disorders usually associated with mental retardation has been more difficult to establish. Pitressin-resistant diabetes insipidus is largely confined to males and transmitted by unaffected females, and so is Lowe's syndrome and the undesignated condition described by Menkes *et al* (1962) (see Table 4, p. 214). A form of sex-linked hydrocephalus has been recently described by Edwards (1961) and Edwards, Norman and Roberts (1961) have demonstrated that the hydrocephalus was associated with stenosis of the cerebral aqueduct in another similar case. However, it has not been definitely proven that the cases of Edwards were in fact hydrocephalic, even though their heads were slightly enlarged and abnormal in shape. Moreover, since hydrocephalus is one of the commonest congenital malformations of the brain, its occasional presence in several male members of a family with unaffected females might be fortuitous.

A sex-linked form of gargoylism has also been described (see Table 6 and p. 230). Other instances of less specific forms of mental retardation apparently confined to males and transmitted by unaffected females have been recorded from time to time (Dunn et al, 1963).

Although the conditions considered here are already numerous and their number is likely to increase still further, all are rare and their total contribution to the prevalence of mental retardation is unlikely to be large. For example, of 800 consecutive admissions to the Fountain Hospital considered by Berg (1961), phenylketonuria, cretinism, lipidosis, galactosaemia and hypoglycaemia accounted for only 22 cases. In a comparable series of 2,081 mentally retarded individuals investigated in Northern Ireland, Carson and Neill (1962) found 49 cases of phenylketonuria, 2 of argininosuccinic aciduria, 1 case of Lowe's syndrome, 3 of galactosaemia, 3 of gargoylism, 1 of Lignac-Fanconi syndrome, 1 of an abnormality in cystine metabolism, 2 of homocystinuria and 2 severe, and 36 moderate cases of generalized aminoaciduria. It is possible, of course, that many of the aminoacidurias in this series were incidental and not causally related to mental retardation. Some evidence has been accumulating recently that homocystinuria will prove to be much more common than hitherto believed (see Table 4 and p. 278).

Other considerations are also relevant. Only a few cases of many of these conditions have been described and it is hence too early to be certain of their mode of transmission. Some of them occur not only in families but sporadically, when they are, perhaps, less likely to be diagnosed. Thus amaurotic idiocy is more easily recognized if it occurs in families and shows typical retinal changes so that due weight is not given to the sporadic and atypical cases in discussing aetiology. The same applies, no doubt, to other metabolic defects. The diagnosis of the first case in a family is likely to lead to a particularly thorough search for other affected members. Again, the diagnosis of tuberous sclerosis is weighted in favour of the more severe cases, so that an affected parent with a mild form is only likely to be diagnosed if he has a child with the fully developed condition.

It should also be mentioned that some conditions formerly described as heritable are not homogeneous entities. Thus cretinism comprises an endemic form caused by iodine deficiency as well as non-endemic variants caused by congenital absence or hypoplasia of the thyroid or by biochemical abnormalities of thyroid metabolism (Trotter, 1960; McGirr, 1960; Kitchin and Evans, 1960). 'True microcephaly', formerly regarded as an autosomal recessive condition, is also not a uniform group (Brandon, Kirman and Williams, 1959; Cowie, 1960), neither is deaf-mutism nor, probably, congenital diplegia.

According to genetic theory heritable disorders of metabolism owe their origin to a change (mutation) occurring in one of the genetic units of a chromosome. This change is discrete. It can be described as a point mutation and is very different from the grosser abnormalities in the number and structure of chromosomes (see below). In a number of cases a point mutation may result in the functional absence or deficiency of an essential enzyme in a metabolic pathway. Metabolites accumulate 'above' the block and there is usually a parallel deficiency or absence of products below the block. The harmful action of the enzymopathy may hence be ascribed to a lack of some essential metabolic product, the toxic action of metabolites above the block or a combination of the two sets of factors. The site of the metabolic block and the nature of the abnormal substances have in fact been clarified in many conditions, although it is still not always clear how these abnormalities impair intelligence (p. 89).

Chromosomal Anomalies

Another mechanism in the causation and transmission of certain diseases came to light with the discovery that relatively gross numerical and structural chromosomal anomalies occur in man, their occurrence in plants and animals having been known for some time. This phenomenon, first observed in Down's disease, was followed at once by a search for similar anomalies in other conditions, and subsequent observations have yielded a good deal of new information. The search is still on, and new findings are being constantly recorded. The field has been reviewed by a number of workers, as, for example, Polani (1962) and Warkany *et al* (1964), and it is safe to predict further publications on this subject.

The normal diploid number of human chromosomes is 46. This includes a pair of sex chromosomes, XX in the female and XY in the male. Autosomal chromosomes vary in size and form; it is possible to distinguish 7 groups according to certain criteria agreed upon by a study group which met for this purpose at Denver, Colorado (Fig. 2). These groups include the following consecutively numbered chromosomes: 1–3, 4–5, 6–12, 13–15, 16–18, 19–20, and 21–22, which are often designated consecutively by the letters A to G. *Trisomy* denotes a surplus of one chromosome over the normal pair. Thus if the total diploid number of chromosomes is 47 instead of 46, there must be a trisomy of one of the autosomal chromosomes, or abnormal duplication of one of the sex chromosomes. Chromosomal anomalies fall into 2 groups: autosomal and those of sex chromosomes.

The commonest chromosomal anomaly is the presence of *aneuploidy*, i.e. excess or lack of one or more chromosomes in the diploid cell. This usually results from failure of one of the chromosomes to separate (disjoin) properly during one of the two meiotic divisions preceding the formation of the ovum or sperm, or during one of the early divisions of the zygote. In most cases all cells of the affected individual are equally aneuploid, but in certain instances *mosaicism* may be present, viz. a mixture of normal and aneuploid cells or of two (or, indeed, more) different kinds of aneuploidy. It has been suggested that mosaicism may occur in the gonads or even parts of the gonads, the rest of the organism having a different chromosomal constitution—gonosomic mosaicism.

Another important event in the causation of some conditions is *translocation* of chromosomes. This term denotes the breakage of two chromosomes with subsequent reciprocal exchange and reunion of the fragments.

Whatever the nature and time of origin of the chromosomal anomaly, provided that the germ cells are involved and that the affected cells are viable, the change is transmissible to the progeny of the patient. But if only one ovum or sperm is affected in the parent, subsequent siblings will probably be normal.

Another relevant phenomenon in cytogenetics is *nuclear sex*. In normal females a single chromatin mass is demonstrable on the inner side of the nuc-

CLASSIFICATION OF HUMAN CHROMOSOMES

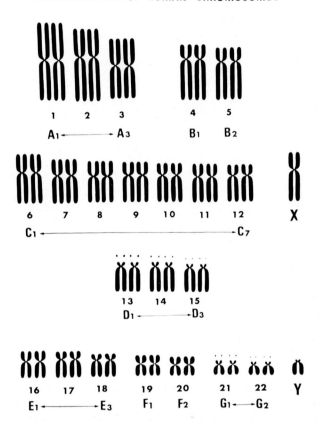

FIG. 2. This diagram shows two methods of classifying chromosomes: the Denver and the Patau (or London) systems. Under the Denver system autosomal chromosomes are numbered consecutively from 1–22. These figures are shown in the upper of the two lines under the chromosomes. Under the Patau system chromosome groups are classified by letters A–G. The sex X chromosome is morphologically similar to 6–12 (C) group, and the Y chromosome—to the 21–22 (G) group.

lear membrane of certain cells or in the form of a 'drumstick' attachment in leucocytes. It is absent in normal males. Chromosomal studies have shown that abnormalities of nuclear sex depend on certain abnormalities of the sex chromosomes. For example, some females having two chromatin masses (Fig. 3) have a sex formula of XXX instead of the normal XX and hence a total of 47 chromosomes, and abnormal chromatin-negative females may have a sex formula of XO instead of XX, with a total number of 45 instead of 46 chromosomes. Differently expressed, the number of chromatin bodies equals *n* minus 1, where 'n' is the number of X chromosomes in the cell. A recent and full review of the large amount of work done on sex chromatin is by Mittwoch (1964).

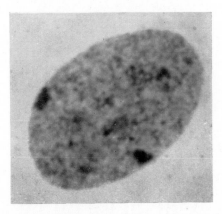

FIG. 3. Cell from buccal mucosa of a patient with the XXX syndrome showing two chromatin masses instead of the single one usual in females. (*By courtesy of Dr. Ursula Mittwoch*)

Anomalies of Sex Chromosomes

Klinefelter's Syndrome. In this condition the testes remain small after puberty and normal spermatogenesis does not occur. The body build is said to be somewhat eunuchoid and there may be gynaecomastia, although, in practice, there seems to be a great deal of variation in body build. The condition is often associated with mental retardation, frequently of mild degree, and is relatively common, its frequency having been estimated at 1 in 400 males. The patients are usually chromatin positive; their chromosomes number 47 and the sex formula is XXY (Fig. 4), but a few examples of mosaicism have been reported, usually of the XXY/XX type. Another few cases presented two nuclear masses in buccal smears and had 48 chromosomes with a sex formula-XXXY. Other variants and related anomalies have also been described. For example, a mentally retarded boy with a divided scrotum, a penis, congenital heart disease and renal malformation had 49 chromosomes with an apparent trisomy of chromosomes 8 and 11, and an XXY sex formula (Fraccaro, Kaijser and Lindsten, 1960). Another mentally deficient male described by Bray and Josephine (1963) had 49 chromosomes with an XXXYY sex chromosome karyotype.

Other Anomalies of the Sex Chromosomes. Following non-disjunction, an ovum may contain a pair of X chromosomes instead of a single one. If the sperm adds another one, the zygote will contain 47 chromosomes with an XXX sex formula—'triple-X' females (Fig. 3). Most instances of this condition were found in mentally defective women, who did not present any other distinctive features. The clinical and epidemiological aspects of this anomaly are discussed by Day, Larson and Wright (1964). Two mentally defective women reported by Carr *et al* (1961) had 48 chromosomes with an XXXX karyotype. Spermatogenesis rather than oogenesis may be implicated in the origin of some anomalies. This is suggested by abnormalities with multiple Y chromosomes, as in the case of XXYY constitution reported by Waterman, London, Valdmanis, and Mann (1966).

What amounts perhaps to another distinct condition has been discovered among male delinquents, some of whom are high grade mental defectives (Annotation, 1966). Their sex chromosomes are XYY, XXYY or a mosaic—

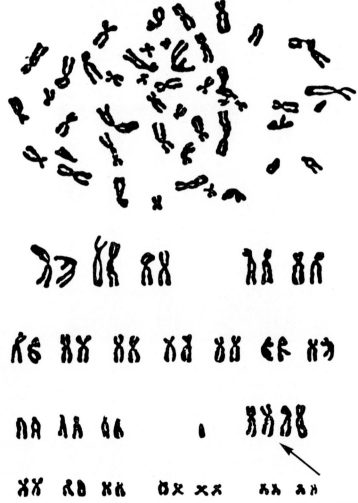

Fig. 4. The karyogram in a case of Klinefelter's syndrome showing an XXXXY formula. The X chromosomes are arrowed.

XXY/XY. Many of these individuals are unusually tall but present no other special diagnostic feature.

For other, presumably rarer, abnormalities of the sex chromosomes readers must be referred to fuller reviews and original case reports.

Ovarian Dysgenesis. This is a rarer disease affecting females, who may be mentally retarded, although the intellectual deficit is usually mild. The ovaries are very rudimentary. There may be associated visceral malformations, some retardation of growth and webbing of the neck—and the condition is then known as *Turner's syndrome* (Fig. 5). The secondary sex characters usually

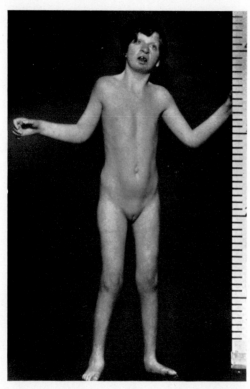

FIG. 5. Girl aged 14 years with Turner's syndrome. This patient showed stunted growth, webbing of the neck, delayed sexual development and mental retardation.

fail to appear and there is primary amenorrhoea. Some suffer from oedema of the legs, but this tends to disappear in the course of adolescence. Lymphan-giography has shown that these patients have hypoplasia or aplasia of the superficial lymphatic vessels of the legs (Benson, Gough and Polani, 1965). Most of these patients are chromatin negative, showing 45 chromosomes and an XO sex karyotype, but a few instances of mosaicism of the XO/XX, XO/XY and XO/XYY type have been observed. Some patients are, on the other hand, chromatin positive, in which case they may have mosaicism, other diverse chromosomal anomalies, or be, in a few as yet inexplicable cases, chromosomally normal. Examples of isolated gonadal dysgenesis have been described. These women are not dwarfed and have no somatic malformation, showing only ovarian hypoplasia. They may be chromatin negative or chromatin positive. The chromatin negative cases have had an XY sex formula with 46 chromosomes, and the chromatin positive had an XX formula with a normal number of autosomes. Turner's syndrome or, as the author prefers, 'Turner phenotype' has also been described in males (Heller, 1965). The affected individuals showed mental retardation and some of the following signs: gonadal agenesis or dysgenesis, webbing of the neck, cubitus valgus with some dwarfism, ocular deformities and cardiac malformation. However, chromosomal anomalies appear to be rare in such persons, only one of the cases having shown a mosaic with a strain of normal 46-XY patterned cells, and another a karyotype in which one chromosome of the 6–12 group was missing and there was an extra abnormal autosome in the 21–22 group.

Autosomal Anomalies

Down's Disease. Possibly the most important and interesting outcome of chromosomal study in the field of mental retardation remains the original demonstration of aneuploidy in Down's disease. Cells of affected persons usually show 47 chromosomes with trisomy for No. 21 (Fig. 6). However, in some cases of Down's disease the karyotype is 46 chromosomes with one abnormally long chromosome which may be a member of either the 13–15, 16–18 or the 21–22 group. The most plausible explanation offered for this phenomenon is that a translocation has taken place between one of the No. 21 chromosomes and another one, which usually belongs to the 13–15 group or the 21–22 group. Despite the normal chromosomal number there is in these cases a substantive trisomy for No. 21, the abnormally large chromosome containing the translocated fragment. In such cases one of the patient's parents may be a carrier of the condition, his or her karyotype being 45 with a monosomic No. 21 and an abnormally long chromosome in one of the other groups. Such a carrier does not manifest the disease because the karyotype is balanced: No. 21 is substantively disomic, i.e. normal, and there is thus substantive euploidy despite the appearance of aneuploidy. A germ cell produced by such a carrier may contain both the abnormally long chromosome and No. 21 and should another 21 be added on fertilization, the zygote will become trisomic for that chromosome and have Down's disease of translocation type. This is, at least in part, the explanation of 'repeat Down's disease', i.e. its occurrence in siblings, particularly when these are the children of young mothers (see p. 159).

In addition to regular Down's disease (simple trisomy of No. 21) and the translocation forms, mosaicism of the trisomy 21/normal type has been observed, as well as the occurrence of trisomy 21 together with a sex chromosome anomaly. Of three siblings with Down's disease described by Day and Miles (1965) two presented with no apparent chromosomal anomaly and the third with 47, of which one was a chromosomal minute. The mother had 45 normal chromosomes and a chromosomal minute. The authors suggest that translocation of No. 21 material with an undetected recipient chromosome

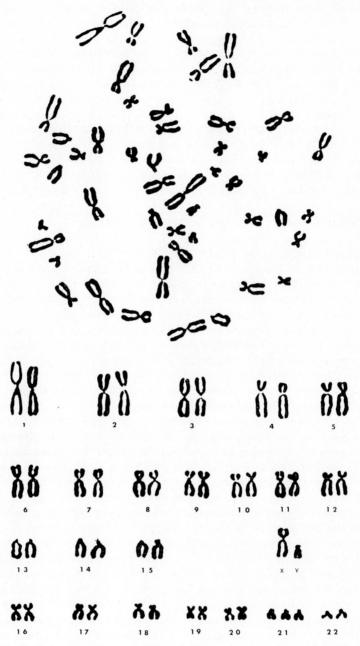

FIG. 6. The karyogram of a case of Down's disease showing trisomy of the No. 21 chromosome.

had in fact occurred in the two children with apparently normal karyograms. In a case reported by Cowie and Kahn (1965) the karyogram showed an extra F chromosome (group 19–20) and a deleted G(21/22) chromosome. The father carried a reciprocal F/G translocation. Instances of other rare anomalies in cases of Down's disease have also been recorded (Richards, 1964). The usual pattern of different chromosomal anomalies in cases of Down's disease may be gauged by the findings of Chitham and MacIver (1965) who investigated 105 unselected cases of this condition. Ninety-seven were found to be of standard type, i.e. trisomic for chromosome 21. Five cases showed translocation: three of (13–15/21) type, one of 21/22 and one of (16–18)/21 type. Three cases were mosaics.

It is believed that oogenesis rather than spermatogenesis is at fault in the causation of regular Down's disease. The main reasons are as follows: The parents in such cases are chromosomally normal. The abnormality must hence originate during one of the meiotic divisions or the early cleavage of the zygote. Since increased maternal and not paternal age is correlated with the incidence of Down's disease, it is reasonable to attach greater weight to maternal influence.

In the few recorded cases of females with Down's disease giving birth, about half of the children were themselves affected. This is what would be expected from cytogenetic considerations, the germ cells of such a mother tending to have 2 or 1 of the group 21 chromosomes in equal proportions.

The time of origin of the translocation responsible for some forms of Down's disease is, of course, inconstant. In a given case of overt Down's disease, the change may have occurred in any of the direct ancestors. Since some of them and their blood relations would have been carriers, it is likely that a family tree would show also some instances of the overt disease in the earlier generations. This has in fact been found by Johnston and Jaslow (1963).

Other Autosomal Anomalies. Other autosomal anomalies appear to be much less frequent as a cause of mental retardation. Two more or less specific complexes of multiple congenital malformations have been described in association with trisomies of the 16–18 (E) and the 13–15 (D) groups, but the patients so affected were usually stillborn or have died in early infancy. It is now thought that the chromosome concerned in 16–18 trisomy is No. 18. The average survival time of infants with 16–18 trisomy has been, for example, 3·7 months according to Ozonoff, Steinbach and Mamunes (1964). However, two older children with 13–15 trisomy observed by Beçak, Beçak and Schmidt (1963) were mentally retarded and suffered also from generalised congenital analgesia. Arhinencephaly, prosencephaly (Fig. 7) and ectopic tissue in the cerebellum occur frequently in association with 13–15 trisomy (Miller *et al.*, 1963; Snodgrass *et al.*, 1966). Occasional anomalies have also been reported in older mentally retarded children. For example, Warkany *et al.* (1962) described a boy with intellectual impairment, motor incoordination, absent patellae and other malformations. The patient showed mosaicism of the 46/47 type; the extra chromosome was thought to belong to the 13–15 group. Delhanty and Shapiro (1962) reported an instance of idiocy associated with unilateral microphthalmia and hydronephrosis. The karyotype of this case revealed an abnormally long arm of one of the 13–15 group. A self-per-petuating ring chromosome has been found in a mentally defective female with a 45 cell line of XO constitution (Fisher, 1965). (For a review of the ano-malies associated with E_1 trisomy, i.e. group 16–18, readers may be referred to the report by Rohde, Hodgman and Cleland, 1964.)

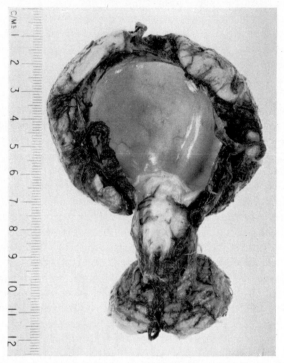

FIG. 7. Extreme prosencephaly in a case of 13/15 (D) group trisomy. The prosen-cephalon has not paired and there is no division into cerebral hemispheres. The ventricular cavity is single.

In addition to trisomy various other anomalies may be associated with mental retardation. These have been recently discussed by Grouchy (1965). Clarke, Stevenson, Davies and Williams (1964) have described a family showing translocation between the No. 3 chromosome and one of the 'X–6–12' or 'C' group. The family was identified by a propositus who was mentally defective and had skeletal anomalies. Chromosomal anomalies sometimes associated with the De Lange syndrome are considered on p. 325.

A new syndrome has recently emerged and may come to be known as Le-jeune's or *'cri du chat' syndrome* (McCracken and Gordon, 1965; Milunsky and Chitham, 1966). The cytogenetic anomaly with which it is associated is partial deletion of the short arm of one of the No. 5 chromosomes. The affect-ed children are mentally subnormal and have a peculiar weak mewing cry which is thought to be due to weakness and underdevelopment of the upper larynx. It has been suggested by some workers (but not accepted by others) that the facies of the patients is characteristic: the face is round, there is epicanthus, the eyes are wide-set and show an antimongolian slant, the ears are low-set and the lower jaws are small. There is marked hypotonia. Microcephaly and transverse palmar creases were present in some of the cases. The brain of a personal case with this syndrome showed total bilateral arhinencephaly and marked optic nerve agenesis. Colobomata were present in the eyes. As more cases are published, it is becoming evident that the clinical picture of patients with partial deletion of the short arm of one of the 4–5 group chromosomes is not homogeneous (Berg *et al.*, 1965). On the other hand, an infant with a clinically rather characteristic *cri du chat* picture has been found to have a somewhat different chromosomal anomaly—a ring-shaped No. 5 chromosome (Rohde and Tompkins, 1965).

Other, apparently rare, instances of different chromosomal anomalies have been and will, no doubt, continue to be reported. However, it is unlikely, perhaps, that chromosomal anomalies detectable by present methods will prove to be involved in the causation of further numerically substantial categories of mental defect. On the other hand, radical improvement in cytogenetic techniques may well lead to the demonstration of more subtle chromosomal abnormalities in many other conditions, particularly those with hereditary patterns of transmission and persistent and widespread biochemical abnormalities.

A promising new development of applied cytogenetics is the demonstration that amniotic cells obtained by *amniocentesis* of the pregnant woman are foetal in nature and that some of them can be used for chromosomal study (Steele and Breg, 1966). In this way the sex of the foetus becomes demonstrable and, no doubt, also chromosomal anomalies. It is possible that further improvement of these techniques will enable the diagnosis of some embryopathies to be made at an earlier stage of pregnancy.

The Mechanism and Possible Causes of Hereditary Change

The spectacular recent progress in molecular genetics brought with it an explanation of some of the empirically gathered data. The only known carrier of genetic information in higher animals is deoxyribonucleic acid (DNA). This substance is found in the nuclei of cells. A gene is therefore a functional unit of DNA controlling the production of a specific substance. A molecule of DNA is built like a pair of twisted strands (double helix) which are held together by transverse ladder-like bases (Fig. 8). The helical strands are formed by the sugar deoxyribose and phosphate (Fig. 9). The bases are either purines or pyrimidines. The two purines are adenine and guanine, and the pyrimidines —thymine and cytosine. Along the plane of the helical axis the bases of the two strands meet and are held together by hydrogen bonds (Fig. 10). Prior to the replication of a DNA molecule the bases separate and each strand is then united with a newly formed strand by similarly stacked bases. All enzymes are proteins, and these are produced in the organelles of the cytoplasm (ribosomes) according to information derived from the nuclear DNA. The information must therefore be carried from the nucleus to the cytoplasm by some substance. This substance is a ribonucleic acid, messenger RNA (m-RNA). Two further types of RNA, soluble or transfer RNA (t-RNA) and ribosomal RNA (r-RNA), also participate in enzyme synthesis (Dixon and Webb, 1964). An essential difference between proteins is the identity and position of their constituent amino acids. It has been shown that the position of each of the 20 known amino acids in the polypeptide chain of proteins is determined by the sequence of the four nucleotide bases in the DNA molecule. The actual coding

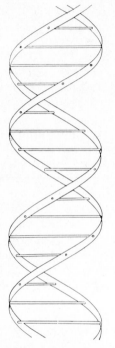

Fig. 8. The double helical strands of a DNA molecule held together by transverse ladder-like bases, according to Crick and Watson.

unit is the sequence of 3 of the 4 available bases—the 'triplet code' (for a full review see Zamenhof, 1963).

A point mutation can hence be understood as a change in the sequence of the nucleotide bases resulting later in the insertion of a wrong amino acid in the end-protein. Such a wrong protein cannot perform its proper enzymic rôle. Severe damage may destroy a DNA molecule entirely or in part. To constitute a mutation, the change must imply an interference with the sequence of the nucleotide bases which is still compatible with continued DNA replication. In fact, this change of sequence must occur during replication since there is no known enzyme which could effect a substitution of one base for another in a static DNA molecule. During replication a purine may be replaced by another purine, a pyrimidine by another pyrimidine, or alternatively, a purine may be replaced by a pyrimidine and *vice versa*. Another mechanism of mutation has been demonstrated in the phenomenon of 're-combination' of two DNA

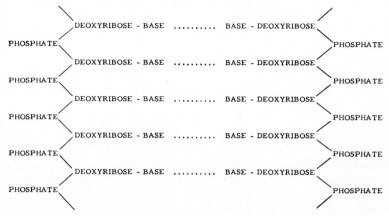

FIG. 9. The constituents of a DNA molecule, according to Crick and Watson.

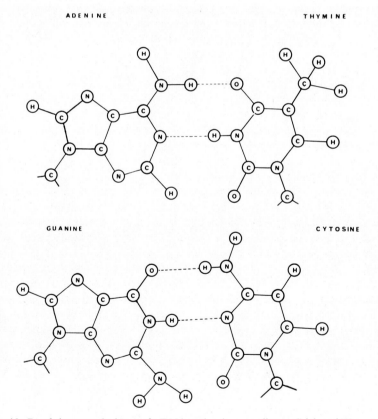

FIG. 10. Bonds between the bases of a DNA molecule, according to Crick and Watson.

strands. When such an event takes place a 'crossing-over' may occur between triplet coding units, with the result that the original code is altered.

Environmental Causes

Considerable knowledge has accumulated about the environmental causes of mutations and gross chromosomal anomalies in plants and animals, including mammals (Russell, 1962), and there is no reason to think that the causes in humans are fundamentally different.

Mutations may be spontaneous or induced. The term 'spontaneous' is really misleading, since such mutations are also determined by mutagenic agents, which are, however, constantly present in the environment in 'normal' amounts. Induced mutations result from the action of larger doses of similar mutagens or from artificially added non-naturally occurring factors. The primary effect of all known mutagens is to accelerate the mutation rate. It has not yet proved possible to produce a specially desired mutation—directed mutation, but this is the object of much of the current experimental work.

Known mutagens include all forms of ionizing irradiation, viz. cosmic rays, radioactive elements in the earth and atmosphere, and X-rays. Other known experimental mutagens are rapid oscillation of heat and cold, ultraviolet rays and many chemical substances, such as the alkylating or esterifying agents, nitrous acid, ferrous iron, hydroxylamine, deuterine (heavy water) and some of the nucleoside base analogues, e.g. 5-bromouracil, 5-iodouracil and 5-chlorouracil.

Spontaneous or induced gross chromosomal anomalies, including some resembling those found in man, have also been observed in animals. Experimental procedures used to produce such anomalies include X-rays, exposure to nitrogen mustard, colchicine (or better, its derivative 'Colcemid'), cold and heat, and mating delayed to the end of oestrus. (It has been recently suggested by Townes, DeHart and Ziegler (1964) that preconceptional x-ray irradiation may be a factor in the production of human 17–18 trisomy.)

The biochemical sequelae of the grosser chromosomal anomalies might be expected to be different from those resulting from point mutations. The loss or excess of relatively large masses of chromosomal material imply massive changes in the amount of genetic information with possible marked changes in the cellular economy. It is perhaps noteworthy in this connection that in many of the human conditions associated with point mutations there is a persistent inborn error of metabolism manifested by detectable specific biochemical changes while no such specific changes have been so far demonstrated with certainty in association with the grosser chromosomal anomalies, such as in Down's disease. This could mean that the major biochemical consequences of the gross chromosomal anomalies have a tendency to be more time-limited than in the case of point mutations. They may act, for example, only during certain phases of intrauterine life, such as the period of morphogenesis. However, it is also possible that some of the genes controlling the production of certain enzymes may be located upon the extra chromosomes and that this may cause a surplus in the amount of these enzymes. Thus some workers have suggested that the gene responsible for the production of the leucocyte alkaline phosphatase is located on chromosome 21, as the level of this enzyme is raised by a factor of approximately 3/2 in Down's disease (trisomy-21) and reduced in myeloid leukaemia in which one chromosome 21 is partially deleted. The interpretation of such biochemical findings is, however, uncertain (p. 160), particularly as the maldevelopment of certain organs in cases of gross chromosomal anomaly can itself result in secondary biochemical changes. Other workers have made similar observations in respect of genes influencing the alkaline-phosphatase activity of polymorphs. The meaning of these observations is also obscure (vide p. 163). However, secondary biochemical changes caused by the maldevelopment of certain organs in cases of gross chromosomal anomaly can certainly occur. Thus, failure of gonadal development in persons with Turner's or Klinefelter's syndromes can lead to changes in endocrine metabolism.

Can germ cells be injured by environmental agents and give rise later to mental defect in ways other than mere acceleration of the mutation rate or induction of the grosser chromosomal anomalies? This was regarded as likely in the last century. Some authors thought that mental defect could be the result of parental general ill-health, alcoholism, malnutrition, lead poisoning, and so on. Early animal experiments attempting to prove this hypothesis were, however, unsuccessful, and further enquiry along similar lines was discouraged by the wide acceptance of Weismann's (1893) views on mutation. This is, perhaps, unfortunate. A history of ill-health or general adversity prior to conception is often given by the parents of mentally defective children. It was reported, for example, that women kept in concentration camps during the last war showed in later years an increased incidence of abnormality among their children (Klebanow, 1949). He found 58 instances, or 4 per cent. of congenital abnormality among 1,430 such children. Involvement of the central nervous system was particularly common: the series included 12 cases of Down's disease, 5 hydrocephalics and 4 anencephalics. Similarly, a correlation of some of the grosser neural malformations, such as spina bifida, hydrocephalus and anencephaly, with lower income of the parents has been clearly demonstrated in some areas (Edwards, 1958). The adversity in such cases may operate both before and after conception. Russian workers, discouraged for some years from medical genetical studies, have also explored this field and observed frequent association of parental ill-health before conception with subsequent neural abnormality (Klosovskii, 1962).

Difficulties of Interpretation

The interpretation of these findings is fraught, however, with many difficulties. Leaving aside the possible methodological pitfalls of these investigations in human populations, such as scarcity of material, lack of homogeneity, absence of controls, sampling errors, statistical artefacts, and so on, the fact remains that no mechanism of hereditary change other than by involvement of the nucleic acids has as yet been demonstrated. As mentioned already, induced genetic change can be produced experimentally, and it is thus impossible to exclude the possibility that human adversity acts in a similar way. On the other hand, many of the human abnormalities observed under such circumstances have been of a kind not usually associated with recognized genetic patterns of transmission.

Another note of caution should also be sounded. Although the developments of the genetic theory outlined above have received wide and enthusiastic recognition, some questions are far from settled. A good deal of lasting change and adaptation occurs in the cells of a multicellular organism upon the background of a relatively constant genotype. Obvious examples are cellular specialization and differentiation during growth and development, the production of antibodies and other immunity processes, and the storage of memory traces in neural tissue. If such adaptation in response to altered environmental conditions is mandatory, failure of adequate adaptation must be regarded as pathological. This may well apply to germ as to other cells. Also, it must not be forgotten that no replication of the nucleic acids can take place without the mediation of cellular proteins—enzymes, and that the rôle of cellular proteins, cytoplasmic and nuclear, as well as of the cellular membranes may be as fundamental in the total behaviour of cells and organisms as that of the nucleic acids. Explanations of certain genetic phenomena are thus possible in terms of such integrated cellular responses from the standpoint of Neo-Lamarkianism, and this is part of the critique to which the recent views have been subjected by Dean and Hinshelwood (1963). They state, among other observations: "Our contention is that intensive work on individual fragments of a complex machine is not only incomplete but also may be misleading unless attention is paid to the way in which the parts fit together. Coding, information, messengers and carriers are all perfectly valid conceptions: so also are various kinds of enzyme-mediated condensation reactions. But these terms have in themselves little explanatory value and present-day ideas will only achieve maximum fruitfulness when so combined that they are not left simply to describe bits of a machine without anything to make it work." In the circumstances it appears to be legitimate to continue speculating on the possibility of the normal metabolism and development of germ cells being impaired in some as yet undiscovered way by a failure of full adaptation to their parental environment and of such pathogenesis not necessarily operating by a primary involvement of the nucleic acids.

REFERENCES

ÄKESSON, H. O. 1961). Epidemiology and Genetics of Mental Deficiency in a South Swedish Population. Uppsala: Boktryckeri Aktiebolag.
ANNOTATION (1966). Lancet, 1, 583.
BEÇAK, W., BEÇAK, M. L., and SCHMIDT, B. J. (1963). Lancet, 1, 664.
BENSON, P. F., GOUGH, M. H., and POLANI, P. E. (1965). Arch. Dis. Childh., 40, 27.
BERG, J. M. (1961). Proc. 2nd Internat. Congr. on Mental Retardation, Vienna. Basel: Karger. Part I, p. 170.
BERG, J. M., DELHANTY, J. D. A., FAUNCH, J. A., and RIDLER, M. A. C. (1965). J. ment. Defic. Res., 9, 219.
BERG, J. M., and KIRMAN, B. H. (1959). Brit. med. J., 2, 848.
BERG, J. M., and KIRMAN, B. H. (1960). Brit. med. J., 1, 1911.

Böök, J. A. (1953). In Sorsby, A. 'Clinical Genetics', London: Butterworths, p. 322.
Brandon, M. W. G. (1957). *J. ment. Sci.*, **103**, 710 and 725.
Brandon, M. W. G., Kirman, B. H., and Williams, C. E. (1959). *J. ment. Sci.*, **105**, 721.
Bray, P., and Josephine, Sz. A. (1963). *J. Amer. med. Ass.*, **184**, 1
Breg, W. R. (1962). *Quart. Rev. Pediat.*, **17**, 9.
Carr, D. H., Barr, M. L., and Plunkett, E. R. (1961). *Canad. med. Ass. J.*, **84**, 131.
Carson, N. A. J., and Neill, D. W. (1962). *Arch. Dis. Childh.*, **37**, 505.
Carter, C. O. (1963). In Norman, A. P., 'Congenital Abnormalities in Infancy,' Oxford: Blackwell.
Chitham, R. G., and MacIver, E. (1965). *Ann. hum. Genet.*, **28**, 309.
Clarke, G., Stevenson, A. C., Davies, P., and Williams, C. E. (1964). *J. med. Genet.*, **1**, 27.
Cowie, V. (1960). *J. ment. Defic. Res.*, **4**, 42.
Cowie, V. A., and Kahn, J. (1965). *Lancet*, **2**, 58.
Day, R. W., Larson, W., and Wright, S. W. (1964). *J. Pediat.*, **64**, 24.
Day, R. W., and Miles, C. P. (1965). *J. Pediat.*, **67**, 399.
Dean, A. C. R., and Hinshelwood, C. (1963). *Nature*, **199**, (4888), 7.
Delhanty, J. D. A., and Shapiro, A. (1962). *J. ment. Defic. Res.*, **6**, 38.
Departmental Committee on Sterilization (1934). Report, London: H.M.S.O.
Dixon, M., and Webb, E. C. (1964). 'The Enzymes,' London: Longmans.
Dunn, H. G., Renpenning, H., Gerrard, J. W., Miller, J. R., Tabata, T., and Federoft, S. (1963). *Amer. J. ment. Defic.*, **67**, 827.
Edwards, J. H. (1958). *Brit. J. prev. soc. Med.*, **12**, 115.
Edwards, J. H. (1961). *Arch. Dis. Childh.*, **36**, 486.
Edwards, J. H., Norman, R. M., and Roberts, J. M. (1961). *Arch. Dis. Childh.*, **36**, 481.
Fanconi, G. (1962). *Helv. paediat. Acta*, **17**, 490.
Fisher, G. W. (1965). *J. ment. Defic. Res.*, **9**, 39.
Forsyth, C. C., and Uchida, I. (1951). *Arch. Dis. Childh.*, **26**, 582.
Fraccaro, M., Kaijser, K., and Lindsten, J. (1960). *Lancet*, **2**, 2, 899.
Gilkes, M. J., and Strode, M. (1963). *Lancet*, **1**, 1026.
Gregg, N. McA. (1941). *Trans. ophthal. Soc. Aust.*, **3**, 35.
Grouchy, J. de. (1965). *J. Pediat.*, **66**, 414.
Heller, R. H. (1965). *J. Pediat.*, **66**, 48.
Herlin, K. M. (1962). *Acta paediat.* (*Uppsala*) Suppl. **135**, 88.
Hicks, S. P. (1958). *Physiol. Rev.*, **38**, 337.
Hinden, E. (1956). *Brit. med. J.*, **1**, 333.
Jastak, J. F., MacPhee, H. N., and Whiteman, M. (1963). 'Mental Retardation, its Nature and Incidence,' Delaware: University of Delaware Press.
Johnston, A. W., and Jaslow, R. I. (1963). *New Engl. J. Med.*, **269**, 439.
Kallmann, F. J. (1953). 'Heredity in Health and in Mental Disorder,' New York: Norton.
Kallmann, F. J., Barrera, S. E., and Metzger, H. (1940). *Amer. J. ment. Defic.*, **45**, 25.
Kirman, B. H. (1965). In Hilliard, L. T., and Kirman, B. H. 'Mental Deficiency,' London: Churchill, p. 57.
Kitchin, F. D., and Evans, W. H. (1960). *Brit. med. Bull.*, **16**, 148.
Klebanow, D. (1949). *Dtsch. med. Wschr.*, **74**, 606.
Klosovskii, B. N. (1962). *Vestnik Akad. med. Nauk.*, **10**, 32.
Lamy, M., and Frézal, J. (1960). In 'First Internat. Conf. on Congenital Malformation,' Philadelphia and Montreal: Lippincott, p. 34.
Lewis, E. O. (1933). *J. ment. Sci.*, **79**, 29.
Leydhecker, F. (1938). *V. Graefe's Arch. Ophthal.*, **139**, 97.
Lopashov, G. V., and Stroeva, O. G. (1964). 'Development of the Eye. Experimental Studies,' Jerusalem: Israel Program for Scientific Translations.
McCracken, J. S., and Gordon, R. R. (1965). *Lancet*, **1**, 23.
McGirr, E. M. (1960). *Brit. med. Bull.*, **16**, 113.
McKeown, T. (1960). In 'First Internat. Conf. on Congenital Malformation,' Philadelphia and Montreal: Lippincott, p. 45.
Menkes, J. H., Alter, M., Steigleder, G. K., Weakley, D. R., and Sung, J. H. (1962). *Pediatrics*, **29**, 764.
Miller, J. Q., Picard, E. H., Alkan, M. K., Warner, S., and Gerald, P. S. (1963). *New Engl. J. Med.*, **268**, 120.

MILUNSKY, A., and CHITHAM, R. G. (1966). *J. ment. Defic. Res.*, **10**, 153.

MITTWOCH, U. (1964). *J. med. Genet.*, **1**, 50.

MUTRUX, S., WILDI, E., and BOURQUIN, J. (1949). *Schweiz. Arch. Neurol. Psychiat.*, **64**, 369.

NEWMAN, H. H. (1940). 'Multiple Human Births,' New York: Doubleday, Doran & Co.

NEWMAN, H. H., FREEMAN, F. N., and HOLZINGER, K. J. (1937). 'Twins: A study of heredity and environment,' Chicago: University of Chicago Press.

OCHI, S. (1919). *Brit. J. Ophthal.*, **3**, 433.

OZONOFF, M. B., STEINBACH, H. L., and MAMUNES, P. (1964). *Amer. J. Roentgenol.*, **91**, 618.

PENROSE, L. S. (1937). *Lancet*, **1**, 322.

PENROSE, L. S. (1938). 'A Clinical and Genetic Study of 1,280 Cases of Mental Defect,' London: H.M.S.O.

POLANI, P. E. (1962). In Richter, D., Tanner, J. M., Lord Taylor, and Zangwill, O. L. 'Aspects of Psychiatric Research,' London: Oxford University Press, p. 154.

RICHARDS, B. W. (1964). *Develop. Med. Child Neurol.*, **6**, 175.

ROBERTS, J. A. F. (1937). *Brit. med. J.*, **2**, 1213.

ROBERTS, J. A. F. (1950). In 'Congrés Internat. de Psychiatrie,' **6**, Paris: Hermann & Co., p. 74.

ROHDE, R. A., HODGMAN, J. E., and CLELAND, R. S. (1964). *Pediatrics*, **33**, 258.

ROHDE, R. A., and TOMPKINS, R. (1965). *Lancet*, **2**, 1075.

RUSSELL, L. B. (1962). In 'Progress in Medical Genetics,' vol. II, Eds. Steinberg, A. G., and Bearn, A. G., New York and London: Grune and Stratton, p. 230.

SJÖGREN, T., and LARSSON, T. (1949). *Acta psychiat. (Kbh.)* Suppl. **56**.

SLATER, E. T. O. (1938). *J. Neurol. Psychiat.*, **1**, 239.

SNODGRASS, G. J. A. I., BUTLER, L. J., FRANCE, N. E., CROME, L., and RUSSELL, A. (1966). *Arch. Dis. Childh.*, **41**, 333.

SORSBY, A. (1934). *Brit. J. Ophthal.*, **18**, 469.

STEELE, M. W., and BREG, W. R. (1966). *Lancet*, **1**, 383.

STEPHENS, F. E. (1947). *J. Hered.*, **38**, 307.

TOWNES, P. L., DEHART, G. K., and ZIEGLER, N. A. (1964). *J. Pediat.*, **65**, 870.

TREDGOLD, A. F. (1952). 'A Textbook of Mental Deficiency,' London: Bailliere, Tindall and Cox, p. 22.

TROTTER, W. R. (1960). *Brit. med. Bull.*, **16**, 92.

WARKANY, J., and SCHRAFFENBERGER, E. (1944). *Proc. Soc. exp. Biol. (N.Y.)*, **57**, 49.

WARKANY, J., RUBINSTEIN, J. H., SOUKUP, S. W., and CURLESS, M. C. (1962). *J. Pediat.*, **61**, 803.

WARKANY, J., WEINSTEIN, E. D., SOUKUP, S. W., RUBINSTEIN, J. H., and CURLESS, M. C. (1964). *Pediatrics*, **33**, 290 and 454.

WATERMAN, D. F., LONDON, J., VALDMANIS, A., and MANN, J. D. (1966). *Amer. J. Dis. Child.*, **III**, 421.

WEISMANN, A. (1893). 'The Germ Plasm: A Theory of Heredity,' London: Scott.

ZAMENHOF, S. (1963). *Amer. J. Med.*, **34**, 609.

CHAPTER 2

DISORDERS OF GESTATION

The Embryo and Foetus

IT is now well established that diverse abnormalities, somatic and neural, can result from physical, chemical and biological agents acting upon the embryo and foetus. The evidence is only in part clinical or epidemiological since it is often impossible to ascertain conclusively the suspected factor. This is because many of the teratogenic agents cause little or no overt maternal disease, while, on the other hand, even serious maternal disease may not disturb normal gestation. Much information has been obtained from experimental studies with animals, though these are, of course, of only limited application to man. The physiological and pathological factors concerned in the maldevelopment of the foetus, involving as they do also the mother and placenta, are exceedingly complex and many are imperfectly understood. Probably the richest single source of information on this subject is the book by Morison (1963).*

Human gestation can be divided into two periods: embryonic and foetal. The embryonic period lasts to the end of the eighth week following fertilization of the ovum. By that time the product is 24 mm. long and has developed the rudiments of all organs (Millen, 1963a). During the later—foetal—period, organs and tissues grow rapidly in size and undergo further differentiation. The nervous system is particularly slow to mature and its full development is not complete till well after birth.

To produce most of the grosser malformations, teratogenic agents must act before the termination of the embryonic period. Because many organs appear at about the same time during embryogenesis, developmental disturbances often result in multiple malformations. Indeed, no known teratogenic agent is fully specific for its target organ. It must also be understood that when a certain abnormality, such as for example, cleft palate, is reported with some regularity following certain experimental procedures, this does not necessarily exclude the concomitant presence of other malformations. Experimental workers usually employ screening procedures designed to show up only a limited number of defects; few attempt to examine all tissues and organs. In most instances only the more conspicuous malformations are reported, and of these only such as are already evident at birth.

Some agents, especially in larger doses, will, of course, kill the embryo, and this may happen even before the mother becomes aware of the pregnancy. This is always a complicating factor in epidemiological studies. A further difficulty is that manifestations of the teratogenic effect can be often delayed, and this impairs the accuracy of the retrospective timing of the disturbance. When studying particular malformations, it is often possible to say that the cause must have acted before the termination of a certain stage of development; one can never be certain of the earliest possible date of its operation.

* For more recent studies see *Brit. med. Bull.* 1966, **22**, Number 1; *Pediat. Clin. N. Amer.* (1965), **12**, Number 3, and *Pediat. Clin. N. Amer.* (1966), **13**, Numbers 3 and 4.

Several morphological mechanisms can be implicated in teratogenesis. The development of certain structures may cease entirely or remain incomplete (agenesis, aplasia, hypoplasia). Excessive growth may occur (hyperplasia). There may be aberrant development or faulty differentiation of tissues, as in hamartoma. Some structures undergo degeneration in the course of their normal development but may persist if development is faulty. Others, already formed, may degenerate as a result of the disease.

A disturbance occurring during the foetal period will not usually result in gross malformation, since the main organs are already present at that time. It may, however, arrest or retard further development and tissue differentiation. Reactive changes, secondary to injury or infection, also develop at this time. It is sometimes stated that no malformations originate during the foetal as opposed to the embryonic period, but this is a matter of definition. The brain is particularly slow to mature; the full differentiation of some of its parts, such as the cerebral and cerebellar cortex, and full myelination end very late compared to that of other mammals. Many forms of congenital encephalopathy and maldevelopment in man seem to be certainly of foetal rather than embryonic origin. This is probably so in the case of microgyria (p. 109), some forms of porencephaly, ulegyria and lobar sclerosis (p. 118). There is also no doubt that congenital hydrocephalus can commence after the embryonic phase of gestation.

Maternal Diet

Experimental dietary deprivation or, rather, dietary imbalance has proved a useful tool in the hands of experimental teratologists. Many malformations, especially of the central nervous system, can be produced in the offspring of animals kept during pregnancy on a diet deficient in certain constituents, particularly vitamins. Many of the conditions produced in this way are analogous to human ones, e.g. hydrocephalus, microcephaly, rachischisis, prosencephaly, exencephaly, and so on. Some workers have studied the effect of vitamin A deprivation (Millen and Woollam, 1960). This causes hydrocephalus, ocular defects and a wide range of somatic and skeletal malformations in such animals as the pig, rabbit and guinea-pig. Excess of vitamin A is likewise harmful (Kalter and Warkany, 1961), but no such teratogenic effect has been so far observed with other vitamins. Among the defects observed in experimental animals subjected to hypervitaminosis A was absence of one of the umbilical arteries, and this anomaly has its counterpart in human pathology (Benirschke and Bourne, 1960). Hypervitaminosis A is influenced by many factors; its adverse effect is, for example, enhanced by cortisone and methylthiouracil and reduced by thyroxine. Insulin given concurrently with vitamin A has a protective effect. Deprivation of the various substances comprising the vitamin B group has also been studied by a number of workers, notably Professor Giroud and his colleagues in Paris. They employed both techniques of selective elimination of the vitamins from the diet and the administration of various vitamin antagonists. In this way they were able to produce a large variety of neural and somatic defects (Giroud, Lefèbvres and Dupuis,

1952; Giroud and Martinet, 1954; Giroud and Lefèbvres, 1957). The teratogenic effect of vitamin E deficiency has been demonstrated by Cheng and Thomas (1953) and of general starvation by Runner and Miller (1956). For a fuller general review of experimental teratogenesis by dietary deprivation and similar techniques readers are referred to Kalter and Warkany (1959).

It seems possible that maternal diet deficient in other constituents, such as trace elements, might be harmful, but the only available information is in regard to copper. Deficiency of copper is a factor in the aetiology of swayback —a form of congenital encephalopathy in lambs which resembles some human cases of encephalomalacia.

In contrast to the ample experimental evidence of the teratogenic effects of dietary imbalance, clinical information relating to this problem is rather scanty and inconclusive. This is, perhaps, understandable since it is always difficult to separate malnutrition in man from the other adverse social and biological factors with which it is so commonly associated. An increased incidence of hydrocephalus, spina bifida and anencephaly has been shown, for example, to be correlated in Scotland with a lower income of the family by Edwards (1958), but malnutrition is, of course, only one of the baleful consequences of poverty. A connection between the incidence of anencephaly and maternal malnutrition is suggested by the observations of Coffey and Jessop (1958) in Dublin. The effects of wartime starvation on the human foetus during the siege of Leningrad have been described by Antonov (1947) and in occupied Holland by Smith (1947). In the Australian population studied by Pitt and Samson (1961) deficiency of vitamin B seems to have been significant. In one of the earliest nutritional studies, Murphy (1947) claimed to have demonstrated that the mothers of malformed children had had diets deficient in phosphorus, calcium and vitamins. The rôle of iodine deficiency in the production of endemic cretinism is widely known, but it is unlikely that such deficiency leads to irreversible changes during intrauterine life since the onset of this form of cretinism is largely preventible by the addition of iodine to the diet of the newborn children. Some other forms of cretinism may be prevented by the timely administration of thyroid gland extract.

It seems unlikely that maternal dietary insufficiency is a very significant factor in the aetiology of mental retardation in industrially developed countries, but the position may be quite different in under-developed countries, where anaemias of pregnancy, syndromes associated with protein and vitamin deficiencies as well as rank malnutrition are still very prevalent. In their review of the causes of mental subnormality Knobloch and Pasamanick (1962) mention, for example, several studies dealing with the effect of supplementing the diet of poor pregnant women with protein and vitamins. This has the result of decreasing the prematurity rate, and prematurity is a significant factor in the causation of mental retardation (p. 48). The I.Q.'s of children of poor Negro women whose diet was supplemented by vitamins and iron in the second half of pregnancy were found to be higher than those of controls (Harrell, Woodyard and Gates, 1956).

On the other hand, conditioned dietary deficiency is probably an important factor in all countries. Thus, relative maternal malnutrition may follow excessive vomiting and toxaemia of pregnancy, and it has been suggested that incomplete utilization of vitamin A is an important teratogenic factor in cases of maternal diabetes mellitus and pre-diabetic conditions (Hoët, Gommers and Hoët, 1960). Absorption or utilization of vitamin B might be impaired in certain conditions. In a recent study Hibbard and Smithells (1965) demonstrated defective folate metabolism, as shown by the Figlu (formiminoglutamic acid) excretion test, in the mothers of malformed children. This test was performed as soon as the malformation of the infant was recognised, i.e. shortly before or after delivery. The number of Figlu-positive excretion tests was about 5 times higher than in controls, i.e. mothers of normal infants.

Irradiation

The action of ionizing irradiation upon germ cells and their precursors has already been mentioned. Ionizing irradiation is also teratogenic when applied during gestation, and exposure to it of pregnant animals is another frequently used experimental procedure (Millen, 1963b). Numerous deformities have been produced in this manner. From the viewpoint of mental defect, the most interesting studies are those dealing with the effect of irradiation on the developing nervous system. The immediate and acute neural sequelae of irradiation in rats have been described by Hicks (1958). The usual dose is 150–200 r. given at various stages of gestation. The embryos are then removed surgically at successive intervals. By this method, irradiation at the earliest stages (but not before the eighth day of gestation) results in severe derangement of the brain, eyes and head. At the four somite stage, the animals remain virtually normal, save for the absence of the eyes, optic nerves and optic tracts. Severe forebrain defects occur after irradiation prior to the four somite stage. Histologically, there is necrosis of the radio-sensitive neural cells, but a good deal of restitution is also taking place. At the 18–24 somite stage, the range of defects includes 'outpocketing' of the roof of the third ventricle and this may be associated with dilatation of the lateral ventricles. Later irradiation gives rise to many complicated patterns of defect including micrencephaly, abnormality in the corpus callosum, heterotopic formations of grey matter, and cerebellar defects. Experimental irradiation reveals 'critical periods' for certain defects, i.e. such deformities are most numerous with a constant dose applied at definite stages of gestation. An even more significant report from the viewpoint of mental retardation is that of Cowen and Geller (1960) who have studied the brains of rats who were allowed to survive for prolonged periods after intrauterine irradiation with 250 r. at different stages of gestation. They found that rats irradiated on the 18th, 19th and 20th day showed the greatest incidence of microcephaly and micrencephaly. As in most human cases, the micrencephaly was chiefly accounted for by a decrease in the size of the cerebral hemispheres and there was also an associated dilatation of the lateral ventricles. The cerebellum was reduced in size in a number of rats irradiated on and after the 17th day (the gestation of rats lasts about 21 days). Microphthalmia was common in rats irradiated between the 15th and 21st day. Many of the smaller brains showed cytoarchitectonic and myeloarchitectonic disturbances, absence of the corpus callosum and the presence of heterotopic formations of grey matter. The latter have been also reported in irradiated rats by Riggs, McGrath and Schwartz (1956) and are, perhaps, of particular interest since they represent a disturbance in the migration of primitive cells from the periventricular matrix to the periphery. This is analogous with human microgyria, pachygyria and nodular ectopia (p. 109) which are often found in cases of severe mental subnormality. A distinct deformity designated as 'the interhemispheric third ventricle'—a combination of agenesis of the corpus callosum with unroofing of the third ventricle and its abnormal upward extension into the interhemispheric space—occurred in rats irradiated on the 15–17th day. Hydrocephalus was observed in only 4 of the 270 rats examined and was not thought to be the result of prenatal irradiation.

In medical practice it has long been known that X-rays may cause sterility, but the vulnerability of the foetus to them was not fully appreciated till Murphy's (1929 and 1947) publication of the outcome of 625 pregnancies in women subjected to irradiation before and after conception. Of 74 infants born after irradiation *in utero*, 33 were unhealthy and 25 of these had congenital abnormality, particularly microcephaly, which was present in 17 cases. In the same year Goldstein and Murphy (1929) recorded a case of microcephaly following radium treatment of cervical carcinoma in a pregnant woman. Such microcephaly seems to be frequently associated with congenital ocular defects (Goldstein, 1930). Many similar cases have since been recorded (Pitt, 1962a). Nevertheless, prenatal therapeutic or occupational irradiation is probably only a rare cause of human malformation. It has been estimated, on the basis of experimental work, that exposure required to produce malformation is at least a hundred times that employed in diagnostic X-ray photography. That new methods of using ionizing irradiation may carry their own danger, is seen from the accidental induction of hypothyroidism in babies whose mothers had been treated with radioactive iodine before becoming aware of their pregnancy (Fisher, Voorhess and Gardner, 1963).

Only a few patients with defects attributed to prenatal irradiation appear to have been examined at autopsy. One, reported by Johnson (1938), had received an estimated total of 400 r. during treatment given to the mother on the 17th, 24th and 32nd day of pregnancy. The child was microcephalic and microphthalmic and died at 6 months. The brain weighed 225 g., the cerebral cortex showed neuronal paucity, the third ventricle was small, and there was maldevelopment of the corpus callosum and of some subcortical formations. The eyes were small. Another case described by Courville and Edmondson (1958) was a stunted microcephalic patient who died at 13 years. X-rays had been used to terminate this pregnancy by weekly doses given between 3–8 months. The cerebrum and the cerebellar folia were small, and the cerebral cortex showed simplification of the gyral pattern and some paucity of nerve cells. The writers thought that the histological features indicated progressive cortical degeneration. Another 2 cases presented by Miskolczy (1931) and van Bogaert and Radermecker (1955) showed cerebellar microgyria, marked micrencephaly and a heterotopic structure. A large glioma was also present in Miskolczy's case. Gross and Kaltenbäck (1958) mention 2 cases of encephalopathy possibly caused by prenatal irradiation. One showed microcephaly with a marked cerebellar cleft, the other—diffuse cerebral atrophy.

Populated areas differ from each other in the amount of their background radiation. It may be thought that the incidence of congenital malformations might vary and be higher in areas of greater radiation. However, attempts to demonstrate this have so far been inconclusive (Gentry, Parkhurst and Bulin, 1959; Knobloch and Pasamanick, 1962).

It must also be mentioned that the atomic bombing in Japan has confirmed the teratogenic effects of ionizing irradiation on the human foetus (Plummer, 1952; Yamazaki, Wright and Wright, 1954; Hollingsworth, 1960). Pregnant women within 1,200 metres of the centre of the explosion had offspring with a significantly higher incidence of neonatal death, morbidity, mental retardation and microcephaly. In another study Miller (1956) described the findings in 33 microcephalic children who had been exposed to atomic bomb irradiation in Hiroshima. The incidence of the defect was related to the intensity of the radiation and to the gestational age of the foetus at the time of exposure. Most of the children seem to have been irradiated at the 7th to the 15th week of gestation. Fifteen of the 33 microcephalic children were mentally retarded, and the occurrence of mental retardation was related to the distance at which the mother happened to be from the centre of the detonation. The effects of irradiation on the developing nervous system have been comprehensively reviewed by Yamazaki (1966).

Drugs and Intrauterine Hypoxia

To assume that certain drugs could harm the developing embryo seems scarcely more than common sense, but it took the thalidomide disaster to drive home fully the realization of this danger. Thousands of severely malformed babies were born to mothers who used this drug during early pregnancy, the estimated total of deformed children in England and Wales born alive between the beginning of 1960 and the end of August, 1962 being between 200 and 250 (Rep. publ. Hlth. med. Subj., 1964). When attention was thereafter focused on the dangers of medication during pregnancy, it soon became evident that the available knowledge was fragmentary and imprecise (Robson, 1963a). More recently the embryopathic action of drugs has been fully discussed at a symposium devoted to this subject (Robson, Sullivan, and Smith, 1965).

It had been known for some time that many malformations could be induced in the offspring of animals exposed during pregnancy to the action of various chemical substances (Murphy, 1960; Tuchmann-Duplessis and Mercier-Parot, 1960; Giroud, 1960). These agents include the so-called *cytotoxic drugs* which interfere with normal cell metabolism, such as the hypoglycaemic sulphonamides, nitrogen mustard, ethylenediaminetetraacetic acid and aminopterin. Among other substances which have been used in experimental teratogenesis are galactose, 2-deoxyglucose; certain antibiotics, such as actinomycin-D, tetracycline; azo-dyes, such as trypan blue, Evans blue, Niagara blue (Kalter and Warkany, 1959); caffeine, urethane, lead nitrate, phenyl mercuric acetate, and aminobenzene derivatives. Some of the experimental teratogenic drugs are commonly used in clinical practice, e.g. sodium salicylate produces many congenital defects in rats while nicotine and imipramine is teratogenic in mice (Robson, 1963b). A suggestion that anti-histamine preparations may be similarly dangerous has been made by West (1962).

Short of producing gross malformation, drugs and hormones administered during gestation might, perhaps, be responsible for subtler changes in the behaviour of the offspring. This appears to be so from recent work employing conditioning techniques for the testing of behaviour in laboratory animals (Werboff and Gottlieb, 1963; Werboff, 1962–63; Werboff and Kesner, 1963). It was found, for example, that administration of thyroid and pituitary growth hormones to pregnant rats led to a certain improvement in maze-learning in the offspring, while barbiturates, alcohol, and sodium bromide had a reverse effect.

Experimental results are not necessarily applicable to man; the toxicity and critical dosage may, for example, vary greatly in different species. The mode of pharmacological action must be also considered. Some drugs act directly upon the embryo, and others primarily on the placenta or the maternal organism. Thus, 5-hydroxytryptamine probably disturbs placental function, perhaps by inhibiting some of its active transport mechanisms (Robson, 1963a). This particular substance occurs naturally in the body, and may be present in excess in cases of so-called carcinoid tumours, since the latter are formed by cells which normally secrete 5-hydroxytryptamine. It is therefore of interest that Robson mentions a case of a woman with carcinoid syndrome giving birth to children with gross defects. It is further suggested by Robson (1963a) that drugs such as iproniazid and other amine oxidase inhibitors, in experimental animals, act primarily upon the mother, possibly by inhibiting pituitary function.

The clinical teratogenic effect of drugs is, of course, much more difficult to demonstrate. Quinine, ergot and lead are some of the drugs used in clandestine abortions. It seems likely that in some of these cases the foetus may not be killed and expelled outright but remain permanently injured. A history of an unsuccessful abortion is, indeed, not uncommon in cases of children with various congenital defects, and Belkina (1963) has reported on such an association in the case of quinine. The same may be true of some of the chemical contraceptives in use although no precise information is available. An attempt to use aminopterin as a systemic contraceptive was soon abandoned after the birth of several children with congenital malformations (Thiersch, 1956; Emerson, 1962). Even antibiotics, such as some of the sulphonamides, penicillin and the widely used tetracyclines, may not be quite safe (Brit. med. J., 1965a; Carter and Wilson, 1965).

The possibility that *maternal alcoholism* might harm the foetus has often been considered. Most experiments have been negative but Klosovskii (1962) mentions Russian work by Dulneva and by Barashnev which supported a harmful effect. Other drugs act by interfering with maternal endocrine function and these will be mentioned below (p. 40). A case of mental retardation with goitre following administration of iodides during pregnancy has been reported by Black (1963).

Experimental *anoxia* and *hypoxia*, usually produced by lowering the air-pressure, is another commonly employed teratogenic procedure (Kalter and Warkany, 1959; Kiseleva, 1963). In clinical practice, embryonic or foetal anoxia may arise from uterine haemorrhage, placental insufficiency, severe anaemia, administration of anaesthetics and carbon monoxide poisoning. In an experimental study, Kato (1957) has demonstrated that fuel-gas inhaled by pregnant mice resulted in many defects of the offspring, viz. pseudoencephaly, brain hernia, hydrocephalus, and so on. Human cases of congenital defects and mental retardation from similar causes have been also reported (Black, 1962; Gross and Kaltenbäck, 1958; Csermely, 1962) but it is often difficult to be certain of the aetiology in such circumstances. Mental retardation and congenital cerebral defects following suicidal or accidental maternal carbon monoxide poisoning have been mentioned by several other authors (Neuberger, 1935; Brandler, 1940; Hallervorden, 1949; Muller and Graham, 1955).

Although the use of thalidomide has been discontinued, it is perhaps worth returning to this subject briefly because it is still of more than mere historical interest. The use of *thalidomide* (synonyms are 'Distaval' and 'Asmaval', and the substance is an ingredient of the preparations 'Tensival' and 'Valgraine') has resulted mainly in agenesis or maldevelopment of the limbs—phocomelia and ectromelia (Speirs, 1962; Smithells, 1962; Mellin and Katzenstein, 1962). It is thus a drug which is fairly specific in its teratogenic action, but many other anomalies have also been reported in these cases, including absence of the external ears, intestinal atresias, congenital heart abnormalities and ocular defects (Gilkes and Strode, 1963). When used experimentally, the drug has very different effects in various species of animals, and some workers have failed entirely to demonstrate any teratogenic action with the dosage and animals employed by them. It is therefore clear that new drugs have to be tested for possible teratogenesis in many species. Lastly, thalidomide is clinically a mild sedative and hypnotic which was widely held to be non-toxic (although a few cases of peripheral neuropathy following its use had been reported in 1961). This must be remembered when prescribing for pregnant women, especially, new and relatively untried drugs. It seems best, indeed, to avoid all medication during pregnancy unless this is overridingly indicated.

Intrauterine infection

In general, the developing foetus seems to be well protected against infection. It is rare, for example, to find congenital cases of tuberculosis, malaria and other infections which are relatively common in the expectant mother. However, there are also notable exceptions and these are considered below.

Syphilis is easily transmitted through the placenta and in the past accounted for many abortions and stillbirths. It was also held to be responsible for a considerable number of cases of mental retardation, for example, 50 out of 1,280 cases (4 per cent) in the Colchester series of Penrose (1938). Congenital and juvenile cases of syphilis are certainly rare now in many countries, only 48 persons under 15 years having been dealt with for the first time in England and Wales in 1961. Of the 1,900 mental defectives at the Fountain Hospital, London, studied by Berg and Kirman (1959) 8 had congenital syphilis. Three of these were classified as taboparetic and 2 as meningovascular, leaving 3 whose mental defect was not definitely attributable to syphilis. It is possible that transplacental infection including syphilis accounts for a greater share of foetal losses and mental defect in poorer under-developed countries, but precise information on this point is lacking.

The only known protozoal foetal infection in this country is *congenital toxoplasmosis*, which is caused by *Toxoplasma gondii*. This condition may lead to early intrauterine death or result in severe neonatal disease, the salient features of which are choroidoretinitis, encephalitis with cerebral calcification, hydrocephalus, enlargement of the liver and spleen, and neonatal jaundice. Survivors may show severe mental retardation, paralysis, blindness and epilepsy. The pathological features of this infection have been fully described by Wolf and Cowen (1959). Although this disease is of considerable theoretical and practical interest, it is probably not responsible for many cases of mental retardation, no certain case having been found in several extensive surveys of institutional defectives. On the other hand, the disease is not always severe, and the milder cases are much more difficult to recognise. The later in life the disease is discovered, the larger the proportion of persons with normal intelligence (Couvreur and Desmonts, 1962). Most affected adolescents seem to have only ocular lesions. Couvreur and Desmonts consider that the most dangerous period is for maternal infection to occur between the 2nd and 6th month of pregnancy. However, toxoplasmosis acquired during pregnancy does not necessarily result in foetal infection, and even when this does occur, the foetus may develop normally.

A large proportion of the population develops in the course of time serological immunity to toxoplasma and this applies also to mental defectives (Burkinshaw, Kirman and Sorsby, 1953). Positive serological tests cannot serve therefore as evidence of active disease, and must be interpreted cautiously.

That *maternal rubella* may cause foetal malformation was first observed in Australia by Gregg (1941). This discovery was an important landmark in the study of human teratology and mental retardation. Although it was previously known that certain forms of maternal infection, such as syphilis or smallpox, could be transmitted to the foetus, malformations were usually still regarded as manifestations of abnormal heredity. Rubella was therefore almost the first specific instance of an environmental cause of malformations in man. Gregg's observations were soon confirmed in Australia and other countries. It was thought at first that the risk to the foetus in such cases is very high, sufficient in fact to justify therapeutic abortion. This pessimistic view was based on retrospective studies, but later experience showed the real risks to be considerably lower. Of the many reports on rubellar embryopathy, among the most instructive are those dealing with prospective studies: in Britain by Manson, Logan and Loy (1960), and in Sweden by Lundström (1962). The salient points of these reports have been admirably summed-up by Jackson (1963). Very interesting reports are also beginning to be published about the effects of the more recent American outbreak of the disease in 1964 (see below).

Maternal rubella is most dangerous to the foetus if it occurs during the first 3 months of pregnancy, but there is some evidence that deafness may develop in the affected child following a somewhat later maternal infection. It is not yet definitely established whether the foetus may be affected if the mother herself does not suffer from an overt form of the disease.

The most frequent result of foetal rubella is severe perceptive deafness, which occurred, for example, in about 31 per cent of the 57 children studied by Jackson and Fisch (1958). Unlike some of the other signs of the embryopathy, such deafness may not be detected until some years after birth. The other common anomalies are congenital heart disease—especially patent ductus arteriosus, microphthalmia, cataracts, choroidoretinitis, retinal pigmentation, dacryostenosis and mental retardation. (The distribution of intelligence appears to have been normal in the prospective follow-up series of children studied by Sheridan, 1964.) Somewhat less common are microcephaly, meningomyelocele, cryptorchidism and delayed dentition. Abnormal pigmentation of the retina has been observed relatively frequently, but this condition, unlike retinitis pigmentosa, is not progressive and seems to have little effect on vision (Stark, 1966). Many other malformations have been described in affected children, but not with statistically significant frequency. In addition, the proportion of abortions, stillbirths and premature births is raised. In 1964 a severe epidemic of rubella occurred in the U.S.A. About 10 per cent of infants born to affected mothers showed evidence of embryopathy. In addition to the signs observed in earlier epidemics, some infants showed thrombocytopenia, hepatosplenomegaly, meningoencephalitis, low birth weight, bulging anterior fontanelles, abnormal areas of radiological translucency in the metaphyses of the long bones, myocardial necrosis, jaundice, and interstitial pneumonitis (British Medical Journal, 1965c; Korones et al., 1965; Plotkin et al., 1965). Rubella virus has also been isolated in an English infant with microcephaly and giant-cell hepatitis who died at 7 weeks (Stern and Williams, 1966). It has been suggested that the dissimilar combinations of defects in individual cases and epidemics may be due to the fact that exanthematous rashes resembling those of rubella might be caused by several other viruses, e.g. Coxsackie A7 (Grist, Landsman and Ross, 1961), but this view has not yet been confirmed.

An important problem is the advice to be given to a pregnant woman contracting the disease or having contact with it. This must rest on a correct estimate of the overall risk of foetal damage at a particular stage in pregnancy. Jackson (1963) published data (Table 1) summarizing the outcome in a hundred pregnancies, compiled on the basis of the available British figures of cases in which maternal rubella had occurred before the 12th week of pregnancy. This is compared with controls (p. 37).

He comments as follows—" . . . for every 100 mothers who have had rubella in the first 12 weeks of pregnancy there will be 70 infants who survive without serious congenital defects although about 10 of these are likely to have some degree of deafness. The excess of foetal and postnatal deaths in the rubella group over the controls is only 9 and the excess of children who survive with major defects is only 11 although it is true that a few of these children will have multiple disabling defects such as blindness and deafness. The social

Table 1. ESTIMATED RISKS TO INFANTS FOLLOWING MATERNAL RUBELLA

	Maternal Rubella 0–12 weeks	Controls
Abortion	5·0	2·4
Stillbirth	4·5	2·4
Postnatal death under 2 years	6·9	2·4
Survivors with severe defects	13·0	1·5
Survivors with no severe defects	70·6	91·3
	100	100

tragedies caused by rubella in pregnancy are the excess of postnatal death and surviving children with severe defects over the normal risk. These amount to 16 cases in 100. If, for the sake of the mother's mental state, therapeutic abortion is recommended on the basis of these potential tragedies, 70 children with a good chance of normal life will be sacrificed in every 100 abortions induced."

This is one view and, no doubt, an informed one. Nevertheless, there is no certainty that all epidemics entail equal risks. There are, for example, considerable differences in the incidence of malformations and mental defect in the English and American prospective series considered respectively by Sheridan (1964) and Tartakow (1965). It is, of course, also impossible to predict the outcome in any individual case. It seems reasonable therefore that affected women should have the right to decide for themselves on the basis of their personal and family situation and the best medical advice whether to continue with or terminate the pregnancy. This is lawful in some countries but not in Britain.

If pregnancy is continued, the risk to the foetus may be reduced by passsive immunization. The following dosage is recommended by J. C. McDonald (1963): 1,500 mg. of gamma-globulin in cases of close contact in the first 6 weeks of pregnancy; 750 mg. from 6–12 weeks, and none later.

Within recent years the virus of rubella has been isolated by tissue-culture techniques and much headway has been made in the diagnosis of doubtful cases by the demonstration of the virus itself or of antibodies to it. It was also shown that immunological tolerance does not develop in cases of foetal rubellar infection, and rubella antibody has been demonstrated in affected infants aged six months to ten years (Dudgeon, 1965). Moreover, rubella virus has been recovered from foetuses and organs of infants who died with rubella-syndrome defects (Brit. med. J., 1965b; Monif et al., 1965) as well as from the nasopharynx of affected children as late as a year after birth (Dudgeon, 1966). Thanks to this advance it is quite realistic to expect that methods of active immunization against the infection will not be long delayed.

In the past it has been difficult to estimate the share of maternal rubella in the causation of mental retardation. Seven (0·9 per cent) of 791 severely subnormal children were thought to be caused in this way by Kirman (1955).

Disappointingly little is known about the cerebral or neural changes in cases of mental retardation caused by maternal rubella, but it seems unlikely that these are uniform. As mentioned already, some of the severe cases have presented spina bifida cystica, hydrocephalus and microcephaly. The brain of a case reported by Friedman and Cohen (1947) was small and showed agenesis of the corpus callosum. Microcephaly with external hydrocephalus was present in two instances studied by Mutrux, Wildi, and Bourquin (1949). Microscopically, there was perivascular fibrous gliosis of the white matter and slight cortical cytoarchitectonic anomalies. A subependymal cyst was present in the lateral ventricle of one of the cases. In his beautiful atlas of neuropathology Malamud (1957) describes two cases of rubellar embryopathy. The first one was retarded from birth and had spasticity with athetoid movements and, also, patent ductus arteriosus. The brain weighed 1,090 g. (age not stated) and there was a suggestion of pachygyria in most areas, and of microgyria in the occipital, temporal and frontal poles. The second case was a microcephalic mental defective with bilateral cateracts. His brain showed complete agenesis of the corpus callosum. Widespread gliosis of the cerebral and cerebellar white matter was present in both brains.

Since, as mentioned, deafness is another of the serious complications of rubellar embryopathy, its anatomical substrate is of obvious interest. Published observations on such changes have however been few and dissimilar. These reports together with the results of their personal study are reviewed by Friedmann and Wright (1966). It appears that haemorrhage is frequently present in the inner ear and that the vascular stria of the inner ear shows marked inflammatory change which may be followed by degeneration in the cochlear duct and organ of Corti.

The rôle of transplacental virus infection in the production of embryopathy has been fully reviewed by Töndury (1962). After discussing the experimental evidence the author reports his own histological findings in numerous human embryos obtained by spontaneous or induced abortion in cases of maternal infection. Definite lesions were found not only in cases of rubella, but also in those of infective hepatitis, chicken pox, vaccinia, mumps, influenza and poliomyelitis. The changes consisted of haemorrhage, necrosis of cells— particularly of the endothelium, myocardium, neural tissue, inner ear and enamel organ of teeth. The lens was frequently affected and giant cells occurred often in all organs. In the brain, liquefaction of tissue with formation of cysts was commonly seen in the so-called transitional zone of His, i.e. the site of the future white matter of the cerebral hemispheres, particularly in cases of poliomyelitis. 'Completed' malformations were observed in the hearts and lenses. In view of these observations and in spite of the equivocal statistical evidence the author regards the embryopathic effects of the above-named viruses as established.

The experience with maternal rubella has stimulated a search for other possible teratogenic viruses. As mentioned already, there is no doubt that many viruses can cross the placenta in individual cases and kill or infect the embryo. Suggestive cases and surveys have been reported since 1941, e.g. encephalitis of unknown origin by Roback and Kahler (1941), hydrocephalus in the case of maternal epidemic hepatitis (Kåss, 1951), and the possible placental transmission of the virus of epidemic encephalomyelitis by Medovy (1943). In a Norwegian survey undertaken by Grönvall and Selander (1948) 5 malformed infants were found among the children of 34 women who had suffered from mumps in pregnancy. Grönvall and Selander also studied the effect of other virus infections complicating pregnancy in a series of 20,000 births. The incidence of spontaneous abortion was found to be raised but, save for rubella and mumps, there was no evidence of a significant rise in the rate of congenital malformations. Some of the viral causes and their relation to metabolic embryopathies have been considered by Hoët, Meyer-Doyen, and Meyer (1958). In the already mentioned prospective British survey by Manson, Logan and Loy, maternal measles was followed by a 7·1 per cent incidence of congenital defects, compared with 2·3 per cent in the general population.

The commonest epidemic viral infection is probably *influenza*, and considerable interest has therefore been taken in its possible teratogenic danger. Use was made of an anticipated outbreak of an epidemic of Asian influenza in Dublin to prepare for a prospective study of its possible teratogenic effects (Coffey and Jessop, 1959). They followed up 663 pregnant women who were believed to have contracted the infection and found that the incidence of congenital defects in their children was 2·4 times greater than in controls. The defects were almost entirely of the central nervous system, the commonest being anencephaly. In a more recent communication, Coffey and Jessop (1963) described the results of the re-examination of the affected children and controls after an interval of about 3 years. As expected, a larger number of anomalies became apparent with time, and at re-examination 15·2 per cent of the affected and 10·1 per cent of the controls had defects compared with 3·6 per cent and 1·5 per cent in the earlier study. The preponderance in the influenza group over the controls was reduced from a factor of 2·4 to 1·5. However, serious defects of the nervous system, such as anencephaly, spina bifida, encephalocele and meningocele showed the same distinct preponderance in the influenza group and the same significant relation to the stage of maternal illness as at birth. Other studies elsewhere have not confirmed Coffey and Jessop's observations (Doll, Hill and Sakula, 1960), and their work and interpretation of the results have also been criticised on methodological grounds. It would seem that while the teratogenic danger of influenza is not high, it may be higher in some areas than in others (Saxén *et al.*, 1960; Hardy *et al.*, 1961). In a recent study of three major epidemics of influenza caused by A2 Asian virus in Birmingham, Leck (1963) found a slight increase of oesophageal and anal atresia, cleft lip and exomphalos in the post-influenzal births.

Poliomyelitis in pregnancy has also been studied by several workers, and the prevailing view is that its possible teratogenic effects are not demonstrable.

It may, however, produce abortion, and the infants of mothers who develop poliomyelitis in early pregnancy tend to be sub-normal in weight. Neonatal poliomyelitis is, on the other hand, a real danger in cases of later maternal infection (Horn, 1955).

Another mechanism of viral teratogenesis has been mooted by Stoller and Collmann (1965 and 1966), who demonstrated in Australia a connection between raised incidence of Down's disease and epidemics of *infective hepatitis* occurring 9 months earlier. They suggest that the virus may invade the ovum causing non-disjunction or translocation of chromosomes.

Cytomegalic inclusion body disease also shows occasional transplacental transmission. This infection is caused by the so-called salivary gland virus. The changes in the affected tissues are very characteristic, some of the cells being enlarged and containing marked nuclear and cytoplasmic inclusions. The generalized disease in infants is usually acquired neonatally and runs a very severe course. The most common presenting signs are anaemia with erythoblastosis, thrombocytopenic purpura with petechiae and bleeding from the gums and gut, hepatosplenomegaly, oedema and ascites. The head may be normal, microcephalic or hydrocephalic; convulsions occur, and the infant is often drowsy and has a 'cerebral cry'. Periventricular calcification is sometimes demonstrable by radiography. Survivors may be mentally retarded. Intrauterine transmission has been demonstrated in some cases. This results in cerebral malformation—microgyria and porencephaly (Fig. 11) (Crome, 1961).

Another infection is due to *Coxsackie B virus*. Most of the cases have occurred in maternity homes (Montgomery *et al.*, 1955; Javett *et al.*, 1956; Hosier and Newton, 1958). The clinical findings in this condition have been reviewed by Babb, Stoneman and Stern (1961). While the infection is mostly post-natal in onset, there is also evidence of occasional transplacental transmission (Kibrick and Benirschke, 1958). In infants the virus seems to attack characteristically the brain and the heart and the condition is therefore aptly described as encephalomyocarditis (Fig. 12). Although usually fatal, some of the infants have survived and showed residual mental retardation.

It may be reasonable to conclude this section by repeating that the only infection consistently associated with a relatively high risk of teratogenesis is maternal rubella. But this does not mean that the rôle of other intrauterine infections is negligible. It has been shown that foetal damage may be inflicted by a very mild, easily forgotten or entirely inapparent infection. The importance of infection as a causative agent lies in its ultimate preventibility. This may be achieved by the total elimination of a particular infection in the community, as seems possible in the case of syphilis, its early recognition and treatment in individual cases, passive and active immunization when this is practicable, and therapeutic abortion when all else fails.

Endocrine Causes

It would seem almost self-evident that correct hormonal balance is indispensable for the successful maintenance and issue of pregnancy. A very large number of 'endocrine procedures' have in fact been used experimentally to produce congenital malformations in animals. The main methods have included surgical removal of the tested gland, administration of different hormones or their equivalents, and the use of 'anti-hormones', such as alloxan to produce diabetes, or thiouracil to inhibit thyroid function. A useful account of some of these studies is contained in Kalter and Warkany's (1959)

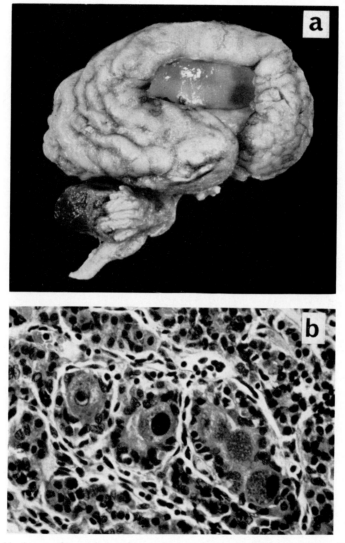

FIG. 11. A case of transplacental transmission of cytomegalic inclusion body disease showed micrencephaly and porencephaly (above, a). Microgyria was present but cannot be clearly seen in this photograph. The distended cells and large intranuclear and smaller cytoplasmic inclusions in the cells of the pituitary of this case are shown in the photograph below, b (Haematoxylin and eosin x 525).

survey. It is perhaps fair to sum up the results of all this work as indicating that any hormonal imbalance can be teratogenic in most species under certain conditions of dosage and duration. However, a relatively high tolerance to artificial hormonal fluctuation is amply demonstrable, while some 'beneficial' results have also been reported (see p. 43). It may be mentioned here that congenital defects have been produced in the offspring of mice exposed during pregnancy to excessive noise (Ishii and Yokobori, 1960) and it has been suggested that this agent acts by upsetting the endocrine balance of the animal.

From the viewpoint of human development the most important endocrine disorders are maternal diabetes mellitus and dysthyroidism.

In the pre-insulin days *maternal diabetes* invariably entailed high foetal loss.

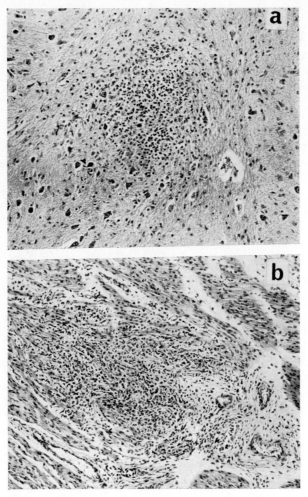

FIG. 12. The brain of a newborn infant thought to be on good but not fully conclusive evidence to have been infected with Coxsackie B virus showed encephalitis, (above), and myocarditis, (below). (Haematoxylin and eosin x 125).

While matters have certainly improved, the risks still seem high despite treatment (Stevenson, 1956; Harley and Montgomery, 1965). The incidence of
congenital defects in the children of diabetic mothers is raised to 8·6 per
cent according to Oakley (1953), and somewhat similar estimates have been
made by Mayer (1952), Dekaban and Magee (1958), Hiekkala and Koskenoja
(1961), and Gordon (1962). In a carefully controlled study in Copenhagen
Pedersen, Tygstrup and Pedersen (1964) found that overall frequency of
major congenital malformations in newborn infants of diabetic mothers was
about three times that in the general population. However, these high estimates
are not universally accepted. Farquhar (1959), for example, regards some of
them as grossly exaggerated. In his own series there was no significant difference in the incidence of congenital malformations between the children of
diabetic and normal women. This difference of opinion may depend partly
on the definition of 'congenital malformation'. Taking the broadest view of
the fate of the product, pre- and post-natal, there is little doubt of the increased hazards incurred by the children of diabetic mothers (Dekaban and
Baird, 1959; Dekaban, 1959). The post-natal development of these children
has been studied by Barashnev (1963), who found that they were often mentally
retarded and presented various neurological abnormalities.

In recent years attention has been directed to so-called 'prediabetes of
pregnancy' (Hoët, Gommers and Hoët, 1960). This condition is characterized
by lowered glucose tolerance in the absence of overt glycosuria. It occurs during
pregnancy and may be followed in subsequent pregnancies by frank diabetes.
It is associated with a raised incidence of foetal loss and malformations, which
may, it is said, be prevented by the administration of insulin during pregnancy.

The precise form taken by diabetic embryopathy is not uniform. Gellis and
Hsia (1959) reported that 104 of 721 liveborn infants of diabetic mothers in
their series died in early infancy, and the results of autopsies on 95 of these
children were subsequently described by Driscoll, Benirschke and Curtis
(1960). The birth weight of their cases was not excessive since most were
delivered electively before term. Gross malformations were present in 23
infants. These malformations did not appear to constitute any specific syndrome or pattern of anomalies. Six of the infants had major birth injury with
massive cerebral haemorrhage and 32 had slighter cerebral haemorrhage, but
no details of any neuropathological study were given. Seventy-one had hyaline
membrane disease of the lungs, and 24-pneumonia. Forty-six of the 57
infants whose pancreases were examined histologically showed hyperplasia of
the islets of Langerhans. The 4 cases described by Dekaban and Magee (1958)
were microcephalic idiots with severe diplegia. A fifth showed multiple congenital malformations, and in a separate publication Dekaban (1959) reported
a case of arhinencephaly in an infant of a diabetic mother. Another case
possibly caused by maternal diabetes is mentioned by Gross and Kaltenbäck
(1958). This was a tetraplegic idiot showing widespread cystic degeneration of
the cerebral white matter. Two children of diabetic mothers have come to
autopsy at Queen Mary's Hospital for Children in Carshalton. One showed

microcephaly with cortical gliosis, pseudolaminar cerebral necrosis, and some neuronal depletion in the cerebellar granular layer. Multiple areas of stenosis and atresia were present in the intestines. The second infant showed intestinal stenosis but no cerebral abnormality. It is impossible, of course, to be certain that maternal diabetes was in fact the sole cause of the embryopathy in the above cases.

The precise mechanism of diabetic embryopathy remains to be established. Hypoglycaemia, ketosis, hyperlipaemia, hormonal imbalance and faulty vitamin A metabolism may each play a part. The babies of diabetic mothers also tend to be heavier than others, even in the not infrequent instances of their being born before term. On account of their relatively large heads, they run a greater risk of birth injury. Furthermore, many of the children develop *in utero* a compensatory hyperplasia of the islets of Langerhans. Adjustment to new independent existence may not be sufficiently rapid and hypoglycaemia may be produced by the excessive insulin.

Maternal hypoglycaemia may be also teratogenic. Wickes (1954) recorded a case of a mentally defective child born to a schizophrenic woman who had had insulin treatment during pregnancy. He also reviewed some of the previously reported similar cases, showing that insulin given before the 10th week of pregnancy entails a definite risk to the infant. Furthermore congenital abnormalities have followed the exposure of the foetus to the hypoglycaemic drug—tolbutamide (Larsson and Sterky, 1960; Campbell, 1961; Ghanem, 1961).

Experimental evidence relating to the teratogenic rôle of *excess of thyroid hormone*, or of its *deficiency*, is rather scarce and somewhat contradictory. Tusques (1956) found that the administration of thyroid had an effect on the maturation of the brain, especially the cerebellum. There is also no doubt that experimental deficiency of thyroid leads to profound changes in the central nervous system, such as reduction in the weight of the brain, retardation in the development of the cortical neuropil (the neurones remain smaller and more closely set than in the normal cortex), and increased capillary permeability. Most of the experimental work has been, however, with new born animals rather than foetuses *in utero* (Eayrs, 1960).

Maternal thyroid disorders, viz. Graves' disease and hypothyroidism, have been studied by many workers. The incidence of congenital cretinism in endemic areas and among children of hypothyroid mothers is high. It can be prevented in some cases by the administration of iodine to mothers during pregnancy (Warkany and Wilson, 1954). A study of the outcome of pregnancy in cases of thyrotoxicosis has been recently undertaken by Yankova (1963). Only 327 of 585 such pregnancies terminated in a normal delivery (some had had induced abortion), and of these 7 were stillborn and another 7 died during the first 5–7 days of life. Many of the survivors were later examined and a large proportion of them showed various developmental defects, ranging from slight functional nervous changes to organic defects, such as pareses, hyperkinesia, sensory disturbances or, even, microcephaly, myxoedema, and, rather surprisingly—Down's disease. Yankova found that treatment of the thyrotoxicosis reduced considerably the risk to the foetus, but, she does not specify the nature of that treatment. Some of the drugs used in the treatment of thyrotoxicosis are known to be themselves dangerous to the foetus. Elphinstone (1953) has listed 10 previously recorded cases in which thiouracil was thought to have caused congenital foetal defects. In her own case such a baby had had hypothyroidism at birth, from which she recovered spontaneously, her mental development remaining however, retarded. In another instance reported by Morris (1953), the child developed hydrocephalus.

In a further study of 26 children with congenital myxoedema Yankova ascertained that 14 of their mothers had suffered from thyrotoxicosis during pregnancy.

Surprisingly little has been written about the morphological changes in human cases of dysthyroid embryopathy. Gross and Kaltenbäck (1958) described congenital dislocation of the hips and true porencephaly in a child whose mother had suffered from Graves' disease during pregnancy.

That maternal auto-immunization to thyroid may be an occasional cause of athyreotic cretinism has been recently suggested by Blizzard et al., (1960). They found that thyroid antibodies were present more frequently in the sera of cretins than in controls.

Little has been written about the possible teratogenic properties of *cortisone* and *ACTH* in clinical practice, although these drugs have been very widely used in experimental work. Black (1962) mentions that cortisone may cause abortion, stillbirth, prematurity and neonatal adrenal failure.

The effects of *maternal pituitary disorders*, including pituitary tumours, on the offspring have been studied by Sazonova (quoted by Klosovskii, 1962). She is said to have found that affected children showed acceleration or, conversely, retardation of growth, frequent nutritional and endocrine disorders, behaviour and personality changes, enuresis and convulsions. It is also stated that the mothers of 75 per cent of children suffering from hypothalamo-hypophyseal dysfunction, such as obesity, growth disorders and hypogenitalism, had themselves suffered from endocrine disturbances during pregnancy. However, 'pituitary disorders' are so heterogeneous and difficult to define that the result of any studies, unless well controlled, would be of doubtful validity.

Hormonal preparations are now increasingly used as *contraceptives*, and the results so far suggest that they are usually effective and safe. However, there is a good deal of evidence that some steroid hormones may pass the placental barrier. This is so in the case of various androgen preparations which are sometimes given during pregnancy for their progesterone-like action. Many cases of gonadal changes in the children of these mothers have been reported. These have usually been in the direction of masculinization of female infants (Nellhaus, 1958; Dubowitz, 1962). Such masculinization may be induced, paradoxically, by oestrogenic preparations (Cohlan, 1963). It would thus seem possible that should the oral contraceptives fail in their primary purpose, normal development of the embryo might be endangered. (Other theoretically possible hazards mentioned in the discussion of these preparations are impairment of subsequent fertility, an increased liability to thrombosis and later malignant disease.)

Maternal Ill-Health

In addition to the conditions already mentioned in connection with the endocrine disorders and dietary deficiencies during pregnancy (pp. 28 and 40), other maternal diseases may also disturb normal foetal development, and some might be more dangerous in this respect than others. Unfortunately, little precise information is available on this problem. Most of the attempts to clarify it were by retrospective studies, and these are notoriously unreliable in cases of mental retardation and congenital malformations.

A record of *toxaemia of pregnancy* is frequent in the antenatal history of mental defectives. Maternal renal disease has been also mentioned with relative frequency in such cases. On the other hand, Pitt (1962a) found no significant evidence of the rôle of maternal disease, other than diabetes, in the causation of malformation in his, rather small, Australian series of 400 malformed infants. The clinical picture in cases of mental retardation attributable to maternal toxaemia is, of course, variable (Schachter, 1964).

The relationship of *hydramnios* to foetal wastage and congenital malformations in Belfast was considered by Stevenson (1960), who found that hydramnios had been associated with 36 per cent of malformations, particularly anencephaly, with 15·6 per cent of stillbirths and with 6·7 per cent of all births.

Little is known of the rôle of *gynaecological abnormalities*, in general, in relation to mental defect. Holmes (1956) mentions, however, that the incidence of congenital abnormalities in the infant rises to 3 per cent in cases of uterine malformations in the mother.

Physical trauma during pregnancy, such as a heavy fall or a blow, is sometimes mentioned in the antenatal records of defective children, but it is, again, difficult to estimate its real significance. Very few of these cases appear to have been published (Hinden, 1965). It may represent a greater hazard in cases of twin pregnancy (Ostertag, 1956). As one of the rarest of possible causes Gross and Kaltenbäck (1958) mention 2 cases of micrencephaly with ulegyria born to mothers who were struck by lightning during pregnancy. Cerebral haemorrhage was found in a foetus whose mother died following status epilepticus during the sixth month of pregnancy (Solcher, 1964).

Prospective studies would seem to offer more hope in identifying teratogenic maternal disease. A study of this kind was undertaken by McDonald (1962). She was able to follow-up for some years about 3,300 women first seen and questioned by her during early pregnancy in Watford and St. Albans. In this series there were 122 congenital defects; 50 classified as major and 72 as minor. In addition, there were 68 spontaneous abortions and 74 stillbirths or neonatal deaths without congenital defect. She found that chronic disease was slightly more common among mothers of infants with major defects, and that this was due to an excess of pulmonary tuberculosis and anaemia. There was, further, a statistically significant excess of acute febrile illnesses, mostly respiratory, in the mothers of infants with major defect. There was also a suggestive relationship between acute maternal illnesses, febrile and non-febrile, and both abortions and stillbirths. Lastly, an excess of mothers of infants with major defects had been engaged in work which they described as heavy— especially laundry work.

To be really instructive, prospective studies of this kind must cover a large enough number of pregnancies and, since the work is very time-consuming, it is probably best undertaken as a collective project involving many centres and workers. Such a project is now afoot in the U.S.A. under the auspices of the National Institute of Neurological Disease and Blindness in Bethesda, and may be expected to yield most interesting information.

Emotional Stress

It may be thought that sudden emotional shock or prolonged anxiety experienced in pregnancy, especially during its early stages, may adversely influence foetal development. In theory, such stress could act by upsetting the hormonal balance of the mother, impairing her appetite and nutrition, or disturbing some of the lesser known mechanisms of neurosomatic regulation. As mentioned already, noise has been shown to be a teratogenic factor in experimental animals (p. 42) and it was suggested that this might be regarded as a kind of emotional trauma. Experimental anxiety produced in rats by using a buzzer, which had been previously reinforced by electric shocks, was also followed by a somewhat abnormal behaviour in the offspring (British med. J., 1964). Claims to have demonstrated the teratogenic effect of stress in human pregnancies have been also made (Stott, 1957, 1958, 1959, and 1961) but are not generally accepted. Among the conditions which Stott found associated with prenatal stress is Down's disease, and this is difficult to reconcile with the present views on the causation of that condition. Some support for the view that preconceptual emotional stress might be important in the causation of Down's disease, particularly in the children of older mothers, has come, however, from a later study in Edinburgh (Drillien and Wilkinson, 1964) and the discussion cannot be therefore regarded as concluded. Many other observations, including some personal ones, on the rôle of emotional factors upon prenatal development are mentioned by Ferreira (1965), but his 'psychosomatic' approach to this problem will be accepted by only some readers.

It seems almost impossible to separate emotional stress from other possible adverse factors, such as illegitimacy, toxaemia of pregnancy, excessive vomiting, inadequate prenatal care, and so on. The problem of mental stress has been also considered by Pitt (1962b), who found that a history of severe stress in early pregnancy was given by 9 of 129 mothers of children with congenital defects. This compared with 5·5 per cent in the controls, the difference being scarcely significant.

In order to demonstrate convincingly the teratogenicity of such emotional stress it would first be necessary to define it satisfactorily and then to show its effect prospectively in a large number of pregnancies. This remains to be done.

Prematurity

The effects of prematurity have been studied by many workers, and it is agreed by all that, as a group, premature infants are handicapped in both physical and mental development, although many develop perfectly normally. Statistically, retardation is demonstrable at all levels of intelligence. Thus, prematurity is significantly associated with gross malformations (Pitt, 1962b). Premature infants show a raised incidence of cerebral palsy, epilepsy and other forms of neurological defect with mental retardation (Knobloch et al., 1956). It may be mentioned that the population studied by Knobloch and her colleagues in Baltimore, U.S.A., included both white and negro children, the latter showing greater handicap. This difference disappears, however, when allowance is made for a higher frequency and degree of prematurity present in the negro children. In a prospective longitudinal study, Douglas (1960) found that premature children attending primary schools did worse than controls on mental testing and in scholastic achievement. The results of a prolonged and continued follow-up by Drillien (1959a and b) have also revealed that premature children tend to suffer more from general ill health, and are on the whole less intelligent. Prematurity may be associated with ophthalmic abnormality, such as retrolental fibroplasia, cataracts, and nystagmus (Kerr and Scott, 1954; McDonald, 1962), and this imposes a further strain on mental development (p. 78). More interesting information on the sequelae of prematurity has been published later by A. D. McDonald (1963). Of the 1,081 children weighing less than 1,800 g. at birth 6·5 per cent developed cerebral palsy, and of these 81 per cent presented 'spastic diplegia' as defined by her.

The study of prematurity has been greatly helped by standardization—any baby weighing less than 2·5 kg. is regarded as premature, and this convention has no doubt been a factor in the relative unanimity expressed by different workers. Matters are quite different, however, when attempts are made to incriminate a specific mechanism associated with prematurity in the causation of mental retardation. Thus, it has been suggested that cerebral haemorrhage, to which premature infants may be more prone, is the real cause of the retardation. However, prematurity may also be associated with many other factors, e.g. toxaemia of pregnancy, placental insufficiency, placenta praevia, infection, and so on. Many of these events may injure the brain or eyes of the premature child, while his later adjustment to the new milieu must unavoidably be more difficult and hazardous than in the case of a full-term child.

This complexity has been well summed-up in the following statement of Brown (1962)—"Statistical surveys do not bring out the fact that any large sample of small premature infants is inevitably a heterogeneous group; some are abnormal from the moment of conception; some have suffered damage from noxious agents in their intrauterine development; some have suffered perinatal cerebral injury from birth trauma or asphyxia; some are abnormally small and wasted as a result of 'placental insufficiency' and thereby rendered particularly susceptible to the harmful effects of asphyxia; some of these infants undoubtedly suffer from hypoglycaemia as a result of stress, probably because their glycogen reserves are exhausted; some suffer from cyanotic attacks and respiratory distress which lead to harmful biochemical disturbances; and some develop severe jaundice which is liable to damage their brain."

Working-class women have more premature babies than middle-class women (Department of Health for Scotland, 1943), and the association of prematurity with poverty, and hence limited social and cultural stimuli in postnatal rearing, has also been mentioned by Knobloch and Pasamanick (1962) and Kincaid (1965). It might therefore be thought that mental backwardness in premature children could be explained by poverty or be due to similarly correlated variables. However, this is certainly not the whole explanation. Douglas (1956) was able to match 407 premature babies with non-premature controls for sex, position in family, mother's age, social group, degree of overcrowding and place of residence. These pairs were given tests for reading, graded vocabulary and picture relationship. The premature group scored significantly less in all tests. They were most handicapped in reading which suggested that they tended to lack concentration. The handicap was only slight for the group. Compared with the general population, 1 in 17 of those whose scores fell into the lowest tenth was prematurely born against an expectation of 1 in 25.

It is very difficult to express numerically the actual size of the prematurity handicap, since this has varied greatly in the reported series, depending on the degree of prematurity studied, the length of the follow-up period and the screening methods employed. The summary of Knobloch et al., (1956) conveys perhaps more concisely than some of the more elaborate statements an impression of the risk involved. They observed 500 single-born premature infants and 492 controls. The incidence of abnormality increased with the fall in the birth weight. At 40 weeks of age the overall incidence of serious abnormality in the prematures was 9·4 per cent compared with 1·6 per cent in the controls. The rate of mental retardation was 3·6 per cent in the prematures and 1·6 per cent in the controls. About 50 per cent of infants weighing less than 1,501 g. at birth had a neurological or intellectual defect, and some also had an ocular defect. About 27 per cent of all prematures compared with 12·8 per cent in the controls showed some departure from normal development.

It is clear from the above that many different forms of encephalopathy can be associated with prematurity. Nevertheless, two types of change are specially frequent in fatal cases of prematurity; intraventricular haemorrhage and periventricular degeneration with breakdown of the white matter (Banker and Larroche, 1962; Larroche, 1964). It is possible that milder lesions of a similar kind account for the mental handicap in some of the survivors.

Birth Order, Parental Age and Twins

The risk of being born malformed and of remaining mentally retarded is not the same for all members of a sibship. All *firstborns* and the younger children in large families seem to run a greater risk. The additional hazards are, however, not very high (Penrose, 1963), and the pathogenetic mechanisms are uncertain. Since it is known that first confinements tend to be more difficult and prolonged than later ones, some of the danger in the case of firstborn children may be from birth injury (see p. 60). However, primogeniture is also a factor in the aetiology of conditions which cannot be attributed to birth injury, e.g. anencephaly and spina bifida (Pitt, 1962b; Penrose, 1963).

Maternal age is a well-known factor in the aetiology of certain conditions. Thus Down's disease, especially its 'regular' trisomic form, is more frequent in the children of older mothers. This tendency is also present in some cases of hydrocephalus, spina bifida and anencephaly. The estimated excess in the incidence of various malformations in children of mothers aged more than 40 years over the average varied between two- to threefold in different reported series. In the group of about 400 malformed infants studied by Pitt (1962b) the mean maternal age of all infants with major malformations was 27·67 years compared with 26·74 years, which was the general mean for hospitals. Further analysis showed that this was due to preponderance of mothers over 41 years. There is also a considerably increased risk for very young mothers— under 15 years (Hendricks, 1955).

The *father's age* appears to be much less important, but this view may well be modified with increased knowledge. According to Blank (1960), there is a slight correlation of acrocephalosyndactyly (Apert's syndrome) with advanced paternal age. Higher paternal age may be also significant in the aetiology of the 21/22 translocation form of Down's disease (Penrose, 1963). The possibility that congenital abnormalities, including cerebral ones, may be due to ano- malous spermatozoa has been mooted on a number of occasions. No definite proof is yet available but some of the recent work has supported such a hypo- thesis (Spector, 1964).

Most of the workers who investigated the relation of *twins* to mental retar- dation agree that this is a significant aetiological factor. In the series studied by Berg and Kirman (1960), for example, twins were more common among de- fectives, both in institutions and living at home, than among the general population, the figures being about 5 per cent compared with an expected 2·1 per cent. In an Ohio series considered by Hendricks (1955) the malformation rate per thousand live births was 9·2 in twins and 7·2 in singletons. The same would probably apply to triplets and other multiple births but it would be more difficult to obtain confirmatory data. Dunn (1965) reports on a careful prospective study of the perinatal period of 358 twins among 4,754 infants delivered at the Birmingham Maternity Hospital in 1960–1961. He found that congenital malformations were at least twice as frequent in twins as in singletons, and malformations causing perinatal deaths eight times as fre- quent. He suggests that intrauterine deprivation and growth retardation was an important factor in the increased incidence of mental and physical retardation and cerebral palsy in twins. The respiratory distress syndrome was the most important complication of prematurity in this series being responsible for most of the neonatal deaths. Other complications of prematurity which may predispose twins to brain damage are cold injury, hypoglycaemia, particularly in dysmature twins (Cornblath, 1965), jaundice and haemorrhage.

Seasonal Fluctuations and Geographical Distribution

The *season* of birth has been shown to be related to the incidence of certain congenital defects. For example, anencephaly, hare-lip, patent ductus ateriosus and congenital dislocation of the hip occur a little more frequently in children born during the winter (Edwards, 1961). The mortality rate of infants with congenital malformations has been shown by Buck (1955) in Canada to be higher between November and March than at other times of the year. This problem has been discussed by Knobloch and Pasamanick (1958 and 1962), who have considered their own and other studies dealing with the relation of mental retardation to the season of birth (Pintner and Forlano, 1943). It appeared, again, that children born in the winter were more frequently mentally retarded. Knobloch and Pasamanick suggest that the significant factor may be the hot weather during the early organogenetic stage of gestation. The heat, they think, might upset metabolism in certain vulnerable individuals.

The *geographical distribution* of some congenital deformities also presents certain interesting features. Anencephaly, spina bifida and hydrocephalus are, for example, more frequent in Western countries, such as Ireland, England and Western France (Giroud, 1960). Phenylketonuria is believed to be more common in the westernmost part—the so-called 'celtic fringe'—of Europe. These observations must be treated with caution since the methods of epidemiological study on which they are based are yet to be fully standardized.

The same applies, even more forcefully, to the reported *'racial' differences* in the incidence of certain forms of mental retardation. For example, most of the infants suffering from the recently described condition "spongy degeneration of the brain" have been Jewish (Banker, Robertson and Victor, 1964). It is also often stated that amaurotic family idiocy, Niemann-Pick disease or the infantile form of Gaucher's disease are more common among Jews. According to Groen (1964) Gaucher's disease occurs only in the descendants of the tribes of Judah and Benjamin (*sic*).

The pitfalls inherent in such statements can best be illustrated by reference to the epidemiology of Tay-Sachs disease, exhaustively studied at the Albert Einstein Research Institute in New York (Aronson, 1964). Data were obtained on 296 patients; but it proved impossible to obtain adequate family histories in 35 cases. Of the remaining 261 children 151 came from New York and its suburbs (142 Jewish and 9 non-Jewish), and 110 from other parts of the U.S.A., mainly Massachusetts and California (84 Jewish and 26 non-Jewish). From 89 cases collected in New York in 1951–60 Aronson deduced an incidence of Tay-Sachs disease of $2 \cdot 3 \times 10^{-4}$ for Jews and $2 \cdot 6 \times 10^{-6}$ for non-Jews. An earlier attempt was made by Myrianthopoulos (1962) to compute the gene frequencies by screening the death certificates of mentally retarded children and exploring the case notes when there was reason to suspect that the child had suffered from Tay-Sachs disease. He concluded that the condition was approximately a hundred times commoner in Jews than non-Jews.

Aronson (1964) thought of a number of reservations in regard to these figures. First, 'Jews' are not a genetically homogeneous group. In fact as far as can be ascertained from such data as those on genes determining blood group frequencies the genetic pattern of Jews is far closer to that of their Gentile neighbours than to that of other Jewish populations. Second, Tay-Sachs disease is often missed or misdiagnosed. This is more likely to happen in non-Jews as many clinicians mistakenly believe that the disease is largely confined to Jews. The incidence in Gentiles is therefore likely to be even more grossly underestimated.

Of some interest are studies of the incidence of Tay-Sachs disease in various Jewish communities. Goldschmidt (1956, quoted by Aronson, 1964) working in Israel found in a series of 31 cases that the gene frequency among Eastern European Jews appeared to be 20 times higher than in the rest of the population. He found no cases amongst Asian and North African Jews. Aronson states that in New York a much higher than expected percentage of the grandparents of Jewish children with Tay-Sachs disease came from four Polish-Russian provinces: Grodno, Vilno, Suwalki and Kovno, the homeland of many Jewish immigrants to that city.

Such a high local concentration of a lethal gene would be difficult to explain either by an inordinately high local mutation rate, by a selective physiological advantage of the heterozygote or by 'genetic drift' (Aronson, 1964). This leaves a sampling artefact as the most plausible explanation of the data.

It is sometimes said that phenylketonuria is exceedingly rare among occidental Jews. This also needs verifying.

In theory and by anology with other species it may be expected that local concentrations would occur of relatively 'new' hereditary diseases or of those held in positive balance by certain geographical factors. In human societies such a diversifying tendency would be counteracted by the levelling forces of outbreeding, physical mobility and public health measures.

The differences in the incidence of various congenital defects and mental retardation between coloured and white people in the U.S.A. have been shown by Knobloch and Pasamanick (1962) to be entirely accounted for by such factors as poverty and malnutrition.

REFERENCES

ANTONOV, A. N. (1947). *J. Pediat.*, **30**, 250.
ARONSON, S. W. (1964). In Volk, B. W., 'Tay-Sachs Disease,' New York: Grune and Stratton.
BABB, J. M., STONEMAN, M. E. R., and STERN, H. (1961). *Arch. Dis. Childh.*, **36**, 551.
BANKER, B., and LARROCHE, J. -CL. (1962). *Arch. Neurol. (Chic.)*, **7**, 386.
BANKER, B. Q., ROBERTSON, J. T., and VICTOR, M. (1964). *Neurology (Minneap.)*, **14**, 981.
BARASHNEV, YU. I. (1963). In Klosovskii, B. N., 'The Development of the Brain and its Disturbance by Harmful Factors,' Oxford: Pergamon, p. 167.
BELKINA, A. P. (1963). In Klosovskii, B. N., 'The Development of the Brain and its Disturbance by Harmful Factors,' Oxford: Pergamon, p. 184.
BENIRSCHKE, K., and BOURNE, G. L. (1960). *Amer. J. Obstet. Gynec.*, **79**, 251.
BERG, J. M., and KIRMAN, B. H. (1959). *Brit. med. J.*, **2**, 400.
BERG, J. M., and KIRMAN, B. H. (1960). *Brit. med. J.*, **1**, 1911.

BLACK, J. A. (1962). *Practitioner*, **189**, 99.

BLACK, J. A. (1963). *Arch. Dis. Childh.*, **38**, 526.

BLANK, C. E. (1960). *Ann. hum. Genet.*, **24**, 151.

BLIZZARD, R. M., CHANDLER, R. W., LANDING, B. H., PETTIT, M. D., and WEST, C. D. (1960). *New Engl. J. Med.*, **263**, 327.

BOGAERT, L. VAN, and RADERMECKER, M. A. (1955). *Rev. Neurol.*, **93**, 65.

BRANDLER, T. (1940). *Acta paediat. (Uppsala)*, **28**, Suppl. 1, 123.

BRITISH MEDICAL JOURNAL (1964). Annotation, **1**, 1064.

BRITISH MEDICAL JOURNAL (1965a). Annotation, **1**, 743.

BRITISH MEDICAL JOURNAL (1965b). Annotation, **1**, 541.

BRITISH MEDICAL JOURNAL (1965c). Annotation, **2**, 1382.

BROWN, R. J. K. (1962). *Develop. Med. Child Neurol.*, **4**, 543.

BUCK, C. (1955). *Canad. med. Ass. J.*, **72**, 744.

BURKINSHAW, J., KIRMAN, B. H., and SORSBY, A. (1953). *Brit. med. J.*, **1**, 702.

CAMPBELL, G. D. (1961). *Lancet*, **1**, 891.

CARTER, M. P., and WILSON, F. (1965). *Develop. Med. Child Neurol.*, **7**, 353.

CHENG, D. W., and THOMAS, B. H. (1953). *Proc. Iowa Acad. Sci.*, **60**, 290.

COFFEY, V. P., and JESSOP, W. J. E. (1958). *Irish J. med. Sci.*, Sixth Series, No. 393, 391.

COFFEY, V. P., and JESSOP, W. J. E. (1959). *Lancet*, **2**, 935.

COFFEY, V. P., and JESSOP, W. J. E. (1963). *Lancet*, **1**, 748.

COHLAN, S. Q. (1963). *J. Pediat.*, **63**, 650.

CORNBLATH, M. (1965). *Lancet*, **1**, 524.

COURVILLE, C. B., and EDMONDSON, H. A. (1958). *Bull. Los Angeles Neurol. Soc.*, **23**, 11.

COUVREUR, J., and DESMONTS, G. (1962). *Develop. Med. Child Neurol.*, **4**, 519.

COWEN, D., and GELLER, L. M. (1960). *J. Neuropath. exp. Neurol.*, **19**, 488.

CROME, L. (1961). *Wld. Neurol.*, **2**, 447.

CSERMELY, H. (1962). In 'Proc. of IVth Internat. Congr. of Neuropathology, 1961, Munich,' Stuttgart: Georg Thieme, **3**, 44.

DEKABAN, A. S. (1959). *J. Pediat.*, **55**, 767.

DEKABAN, A., and BAIRD, R. (1959). *J. Pediat.*, **55**, 563.

DEKABAN, A. S., and MAGEE, K. R. (1958). *Neurology (Minneap.)*, **8**, 193.

DEPT. OF HEALTH FOR SCOTLAND. (1943). 'Infant Mortality in Scotland,' Edinburgh.

DOLL, R., HILL, A. B., and SAKULA, J. (1960). *Brit. J. prev. soc. Med.*, **14**, 167.

DOUGLAS, J. W. B. (1956). *Brit. med. J.*, **1**, 1210.

DOUGLAS, J. W. B. (1960). *Brit. med. J.*, **1**, 1008.

DRILLIEN, C. M. (1959a). *Arch. Dis. Childh.*, **34**, 37.

DRILLIEN, C. M. (1959b). *Arch. Dis. Childh.*, **34**, 210.

DRILLIEN, C. M., and WILKINSON, E. M. (1964). *Develop. Med. Child Neurol.*, **6**, 140.

DRISCOLL, S. G., BENIRSCHKE, K., and CURTIS, C. W. (1960). *Amer. J. Dis. Child.*, **100**, 818.

DUBOWITZ, V. (1962). *Lancet*, **2**, 405.

DUDGEON, J. A. (1965). *Develop. Med. Child Neurol.*, **7**, 196.

DUDGEON, J. A. (1966). *Proc. roy. Soc. Med.*, **59**, 1084.

DUNN, P. M. (1965). *Develop. Med. Child Neurol.*, **7**, 121.

EAYRS, J. T. (1960). *Brit. med. Bull.*, **16**, 122.

EDWARDS, J. H. (1958). *Brit. J. prev. soc. Med.*, **12**, 115.

EDWARDS, J. H. (1961). *Ann. hum. Genet.*, **25**, 89.

ELPHINSTONE, N. (1953). *Lancet*, **1**, 1281.

EMERSON, D. J. (1962). *Amer. J. Obstet. Gynec.*, **84**, 356.

FARQUHAR, J. W. (1959). *Arch. Dis. Childh.*, **34**, 76.

FERREIRA, A. J. (1965). *J. nerv. ment. Dis.*, 141, 108.

FISHER, W. D., VOORHESS, M. L., and GARDNER, L. I. (1963). *J. Pediat.*, **62**, 132.

FRIEDMAN, M., and COHEN, P. (1947). *Amer. J. Dis. Child.*, **73**, 178.

FRIEDMANN, I., and WRIGHT, M. I. (1966). *Brit. med. J.*, **2**, 20.

GELLIS, S. S., and HSIA, D. Y.-Y. (1959). *Amer. J. Dis. Child.*, **97**, 1.

GENTRY, J. T., PARKHURST, E., and BULIN, G. V. (1959). *Amer. J. publ. Hlth.*, **49**, 497.

GHANEM, M. H. (1961). *Lancet*, **1**, 1227.

GILKES, M. J., and STRODE, M. (1963). *Lancet*, **1**, 1026.

GIROUD, A. (1960). In Wolstenholme, G. E. W., and O'Connor, C. M. Ciba Foundation Symposium on 'Congenital Malformation,' London: Churchill, p. 199.

GIROUD, A., LEFÈBVRES, J., and DUPUIS, R. (1952). *Rev. internat. Vitaminol.*, **24**, 420.
GIROUD, A., and MARTINET, M. (1954). *C. R. Soc. Biol. (Paris)*, **148**, 1742.
GIROUD, A., and LEFÈBVRES, J. (1957). *Ann. Nutr. (Paris)*, **11**, 15.
GOLDSCHMIDT, E. (1956). Quoted by Aronson, S. W. in 'Tay-Sachs Disease,' New York: Grune and Stratton.
GOLDSTEIN, L. (1930). *Arch. Neurol. Psychiat. (Chic.)*, **24**, 102.
GOLDSTEIN, L., and MURPHY, D. P. (1929). *Amer. J. Obstet. Gynec.*, **18**, 189.
GORDON, H. H. (1962). *Amer. J. med. Sci.*, **244**, 129.
GREGG, N. MCA. (1941). *Trans. ophthal. Soc. Aust.*, **3**, 35.
GRIST, N. R., LANDSMAN, J. B. L., and ROSS, C. A. C. (1961). *Brit. med. J.*, **1**, 965.
GROEN, J. J. (1964). *Arch. intern. Med.*, **113**, 543.
GRÖNVALL, H., and SELANDER, P. (1948). *Nord. Med.*, **37**, 409.
GROSS, H., and KALTENBÄCK, E. (1958). *Wien. klin. Wschr.*, **70**, 853.
HALLERVORDEN, J. (1949). *Allg. Z. Psychiat.*, **124**, 289.
HARDY, J. M. B., AZAROWICZ, E. N., MANNINI, A., MEDEARIS, D. N., and COOKE, R. E. (1961). *Amer. J. publ. Hlth.*, **51**, 1182.
HARLEY, J. M. G., and MONTGOMERY, D. A. D. (1965). *Brit. med. J.*, **1**, 14.
HARRELL, R. F., WOODYARD, E. R., and GATES, A. I. (1956). *Metabolism*, **5**, 555.
HENDRICKS, C. H. (1955). *Obstet. and Gynec.*, **6**, 592.
HIBBARD, E. D., and SMITHELLS, R. W. (1965). *Lancet*, **1**, 1254.
HICKS, S. P. (1958). *Physiol. Rev.*, **38**, 337.
HIEKKALA, H., and KOSKENOJA, M. (1961). *Ann. Paediat. Fenn.*, **7**, 17 and 32.
HINDEN, E. (1965). *Arch. Dis. Childh.*, **40**, 80.
HOËT, J. P., DE MEYER-DOYEN, L., and DE MEYER, R. (1958). *Rev. médicale de Liège*, **13**, 112.
HOËT, J. P., GOMMERS, A., and HOËT, J. J. (1960). In Wolstenholme, G. E. W., and O'Connor, C. M. Ciba Foundation Symposium on 'Congenital Malformation,' London: Churchill, p. 219.
HOLLINGSWORTH, J. W. (1960). *New Engl. J. Med.*, **263**, 481.
HOLMES, J. A. (1956). *Brit. med. J.*, **1**, 1144.
HORN, P. (1955). *Obstet. and Gynec.*, **6**, 121.
HOSIER, D. M., and NEWTON, W. A. (1958). *Amer. J. Dis. Child.*, **96**, 251.
ISHII, H., and YOKOBORI, K. (1960). *Gunma J. med. Sci.*, **9**, 153.
JACKSON, A. D. M. (1963). *Practitioner*, **191**, 152.
JACKSON, A. D. M., and FISCH, L. (1958). *Lancet*, **2**, 1241.
JAVETT, S. N., HEYMANN, S., MUNDEL, B., PEPLER, W. J., LURIE, H. I., GEAR, J., MEASROCH, V., and KIRSCH, Z. (1956). *J. Pediat.*, **48**, 1.
JOHNSON, F. E. (1938). *J. Pediat.*, **13**, 894.
KALTER, H., and WARKANY, J. (1959). *Physiol. Rev.*, **39**, 69.
KALTER, H., and WARKANY, J. (1961). *Amer. J. Path.*, **38**, 1.
KÅSS, A. (1951). *Acta paediat. (Uppsala)*, **40**, 239.
KATO, T. (1957). *Folia psychiat. neurol. jap.*, **11**, 301.
KERR, J. D., and SCOTT, G. I. (1954). *Arch. Dis. Childh.*, **29**, 543.
KIBRICK, S., and BENIRSCHKE, K. (1958). *Pediatrics*, **22**, 857.
KINCAID, J. C. (1965). *Brit. med. J.*, **1**, 1057.
KIRMAN, B. H. (1955). *Lancet*, **2**, 1113.
KISELEVA, Z. N. (1963). In Klosovskii, B. N. 'The Development of the Brain and its Disturbance by Harmful Factors,' Oxford: Pergamon, p. 125.
KLOSOVSKII, B. N. (1962). *Vestnik Akad. med. Nauk.*, **10**, 32.
KNOBLOCH, H., and PASAMANICK, B. (1958). *Amer. J. publ. Hlth.*, **48**, 1201.
KNOBLOCH, H., and PASAMANICK, B. (1962). *New Engl. J. Med.*, **266**, 1045, 1092, 1155.
KNOBLOCH, H., RIDER, R., HARPER, P., and PASAMANICK, B. (1956). *J. Amer. med. Ass.*, **161**, 581.
KORONES, S. B., AINGER, L. E., MONIF, G. R. S., ROANE, J., SEVER, J. L., and FUSTE, F. (1965). *J. Pediat.*, **67**, 166.
LARROCHE, J. -CL. (1964). *Rev. Neuropsychiat. infant.*, **12**, 269.
LARSSON, Y., and STERKY, G. (1960). *Lancet*, **2**, 1424.
LECK, I. (1963). *Brit. J. prev. soc. Med.*, **17**, 70.
LUNDSTRÖM, R. (1962). 'Rubella During Pregnancy. A Follow-up Study of Children Born

After an Epidemic of Rubella in Sweden, 1951, With Additional Investigations on Prophylaxis and Treatment of Maternal Rubella.' *Acta paediat. (Uppsala), suppl.* **133**.

MALAMUD, N. (1957). 'Atlas of Neuropathology,' Berkeley and Los Angeles: University of California Press.

MANSON, M. M., LOGAN, W. D. P., and LOY, R. M. (1960). 'Rubella and Other Virus Infections During Pregnancy,' London: H.M.S.O.

MAYER, J. B. (1952). *Z. Kinderheilk.*, **71**, 183.

MCDONALD, A. D. (1962). *Brit. med. J.*, **1**, 895.

MCDONALD, A. D. (1963). *Arch. Dis. Childh.*, **38**, 579.

MCDONALD, J. C. (1963). *Brit. med. J.*, **2**, 416.

MEDOVY, H. (1943.) *J. Pediat.*, **22**, 308.

MELLIN, G. W., and KATZENSTEIN, M. (1962). *New Engl. J. Med.*, **267**, 1238.

MILLEN, J. W. (1963a). *Develop. Med. Child Neurol.*, **5**, 343.

MILLEN, J. W. (1963b). *Practitioner*, **191**, 143.

MILLEN, J. W., and WOOLLAM, D. H. M. (1960). *Proc. Nutr. Soc.*, **19**, 1.

MILLER, R. W. (1956). *Pediatrics*, **18**, 1.

MISKOLCZY, D. (1931). *Arch. Psychiat. Nervenkr.*, **93**, 596.

MONIF, G. R. G., AVERY, G. B., KORONES, S. B., and SEVER, J. L. (1965). *Lancet*, **1**, 723.

MONTGOMERY, J., GEAR, J., PRINSLOO, F. R., KAHN, M., and KIRSCH, Z. G. (1955). *S. Afr. med. J.*, **29**, 608.

MORISON, J. E. (1963). 'Foetal and Neonatal Pathology,' London: Butterworths.

MORRIS, D. (1953). *Lancet*, **1**, 1284.

MULLER, G. L., and GRAHAM, S. (1955). *New Engl. J. Med.*, **252**, 1075.

MURPHY, D. P. (1929). *Amer. J. Obstet. Gynec.*, **18**, 179.

MURPHY, D. P. (1947). 'Congenital Malformation. A Study of Parental Characteristics With Special Reference to the Reproductive Process.' Philadelphia: University of Pennsylvania Press.

MURPHY, M. L. (1960). In Wolstenholme, G. E. W., and O'Connor, C. M., 'Ciba Foundation Symposium on Congenital Malformation,' London: Churchill, p. 78.

MUTRUX, S., WILDI, E., and BOURQUIN, J. (1949). *Schweiz. Arch. Neurol. Psychiat.*, **64**, 369.

MYRIANTHOPOULOS, N. C. (1962). In Aronson, S. M., and Volk, B. W., 'Cerebral Sphingolipidoses,' New York: Academic Press, p. 359.

NELLHAUS, G. (1958). *New Engl. J. Med.*, **258**, 935.

NEUBERGER, F. (1935). *Beitr. gerichtl. Med.*, **13**, 85.

OAKLEY, W. (1953). *Brit. med. J.*, **1**, 1413.

OSTERTAG, B. (1956). 'Missbildungen'. In Lubarsch, O., Henke, F., and Rössle, R. Handbuch der speziellen pathologischen Anatomie und Histologie, **13**, Ed. Scholz, W., Pt. 4, Berlin: Springer, p. 283.

PEDERSEN, L. M., TYGSTRUP, I., and PEDERSEN, J. (1964). *Lancet*, **1**, 1124.

PENROSE, L. S. (1938). 'A Clinical and Genetic Study of 1,280 Cases of Mental Defect.' London: H.M.S.O.

PENROSE, L. S. (1963). 'The Biology of Mental Defect,' London: Sidgwick and Jackson.

PINTNER, R., and FORLANO, G. (1943). *Psychol. Bull.*, **40**, 25.

PITT, D. B. (1962a). *Med. J. Aust.*, **1**, 82.

PITT, D. B. (1962b). *Aust. N.Z. J. Obstet. Gynec.*, **2**, 23.

PITT, D. B., and SAMSON, P. E. (1961). *Aust. Ann. Med.*, **10**, 268.

PLOTKIN, S. A., OSKI, F. A., HARTNETT, E. M., HERVADA, A. R., FRIEDMAN, S., and GOWING, J. (1965). *J. Pediat.*, **67**, 182.

PLUMMER, G. (1952). *Pediatrics*, **10**, 687.

REPORT ON PUBLIC HEALTH AND MEDICAL SUBJECTS No. 112. (1964). 'Deformities caused by thalidomide,' London: H.M.S.O.

RIGGS, H. E., MCGRATH, J. J., and SCHWARTZ, H. P. (1956). *J. Neuropath. exp. Neurol.*, **15**, 432.

ROBACK, H. N., and KAHLER, H. F. (1941). *J. nerv. ment. Dis.*, **94**, 669.

ROBSON, J. M. (1963a). *Proc. roy. Soc. Med.*, **56**, 600.

ROBSON, J. M. (1963b). *Practitioner*, **191**, 136.

ROBSON, J. M., SULLIVAN, F. M., and SMITH, R. L. (1965). A symposium 'Embryopathic Activity of Drugs,' London: Churchill.

RUNNER, M. N., and MILLER, J. R. (1956). *Anat. Rec.*, **124**, 437.

SAXÉN, L., HJRLT, L., SJÖSTEDT, J. E., HAKOSALO, J., and HAKOSALO, H. (1960). *Acta path. microbiol. scand.*, **49**, 114.

SAZONOVA, N. S. (1962). Quoted by Klosovskii, B. N., in *Vestn. Akad. med. Nauk.*, **10**, 32.

SCHACHTER, M. (1964). *Ann. paediat.*, **202**, 32.

SHERIDAN, M. D. (1964). *Brit. med. J.*, **2**, 536.

SMITH, C. A. (1947). *J. Pediat.*, **30**, 229.

SMITHELLS, R. W. (1962). *Lancet*, **1**, 1270.

SOLCHER, H. (1964). *Arch. Psychiat. Nervenkr.*, **205**, 165.

SPECTOR, R. (1964). *Develop. Med. Child Neurol.*, **6**, 523.

SPEIRS, A. L. (1962). *Lancet*, **1**, 303.

STARK, G. (1966). *Arch. Dis. Childh.*, **41**, 420.

STERN, H., and WILLIAMS, B. M. (1966). *Lancet*, **1**, 293.

STEVENSON, A. C. (1960). In Wolstenholme, G. E. W., and O'Connor, C. M., 'Ciba Foundation Symposium on Congenital Malformation,' London: Churchill, p. 241.

STEVENSON, A. E. M. (1956). *Brit. med. J.*, **2**, 1514.

STOLLER, A., and COLLMANN, R. D. (1965). *Lancet*, **2**, 1221.

STOLLER, A., and COLLMANN, R. D. (1966). *J. ment. Defic. Res.*, **10**, 84.

STOTT, D. H. (1957). *Lancet*, **1**, 1006.

STOTT, D. H. (1958). *J. psychosom. Res.*, **3**, 42.

STOTT, D. H. (1959). *Vita hum. (Basel)*, **2**, 125.

STOTT, D. H. (1961). *Vita hum. (Basel)*, **4**, 57.

TARTAKOW, I. J. (1965). *J. Pediat.*, **66**, 380.

THIERSCH, J. B. (1956). 'Proc. of the 5th Internat. Conf. on Planned Parenthood,' Tokyo. In *Acta endocr. (Kbh.)*, Suppl., **28**, 1.

TÖNDURY, G. (1962). In 'Pathologie und Klinik in Einzeldarstellungen' by Hegglin, F., Leuthardt, F., Schoen, R., Schwiegk, H., and Zollinger, H. U., Vol. **11**, Embryopathien, Berlin: Springer.

TUCHMANN-DUPLESSIS, H., and MERCIER-PAROT, L. (1960). In Wolstenholme, G. E. W., and O'Connor, C. M., 'Ciba Foundation Symposium on Congenital Malformation,' London: Churchill, p. 115.

TUSQUES, J. (1956). *Biol. med.*, **45**, 395.

WARKANY, J., and WILSON, J. G. (1954). In 'Genetics and the Inheritance of Integrated Neurological and Psychiatric Patterns,' **33**, Baltimore: Williams and Wilkin, p. 76.

WERBOFF, J. (1962–63). In 'Research Reviews 1962–63,' Ed. Carrick, D. J. E. L., London: Medical News Ltd., p. 122.

WERBOFF, J., and GOTTLIEB, J. S. (1963). *Obstet. gynec. Surv.*, **18**, 420.

WERBOFF, J., and KESNER, R. (1963). *Nature*, **197**, 106.

WEST, G. B. (1962). *J. Pharm. Pharmacol.*, **14**, 828.

WICKES, I. G. (1954). *Brit. med. J.*, **2**, 1029.

WOLF, A., and COWEN, D. (1959). *J. Neuropath. exp. Neurol.*, **18**, 191.

YAMAZAKI, J. N. (1966). *Pediatrics*, **37**, 877.

YAMAZAKI, J. N., WRIGHT, S. W., and WRIGHT, P. M. (1954). *Amer. J. Dis. Child.*, **87**, 448.

YANKOVA, M. F. (1963). In Klosovskii, B. N., 'The Development of the Brain and its Disturbance by Harmful Factors,' Oxford: Pergamon, p. 161.

CHAPTER 3

BIRTH INJURY

ONE of the most controversial subjects in the aetiology of mental retardation is the rôle of birth injury. A century ago, Little (1862), who described the condition bearing his name in which mental deficiency is associated with paralysis, contractures of the limbs and epilepsy, suggested that almost all such cases were caused by some mishap at birth, particularly anoxia. He wrote: "even the want of a few breathings, if not fatal to the economy, may imprint a lasting injury upon it"; and further: "there is, however, an epoch of existence, viz. the period of birth, during which, at first sight, we might consider that the foetal organism is subjected to conditions so different to those of its earlier and its prospective later existence, that any untoward influences applied at this important juncture affect the economy in a manner different to the influences at work during the periods ordinarily characterized as those before birth and after birth." These views were seriously challenged towards the end of the century by Sigmund Freud, who thought that most instances of cerebral palsy could be accounted for by congenital malformations of the brain. Opinion has since swung between these two extremes.

Diagnostic Difficulties

The term 'birth injury' has no constant, generally agreed, well defined, meaning. Some workers have stressed the mechanical effects of tearing, compression and haemorrhage, others incriminated anoxia, asphyxia, oedema, vascular disturbances or thrombosis. The presence or absence of 'birth injury' is, however, difficult to determine with certainty. Neonatal distress, asphyxia, convulsions, apnoea, have all been treated as criteria of birth injury, whilst others have concentrated on factors such as prolonged or instrumental labour.

The very numerous reported studies have, on the whole, pursued three lines of enquiry: follow-up of children born after a complicated confinement or showing signs of neonatal distress; secondly, retrospective analysis of confinements and the neonatal state of children showing later mental retardation and associated conditions, and, thirdly, pathological examination of the brains in cases of suspected or certain birth injury.

Both the prospective and the retrospective studies have demonstrated clearly that complicated labour and neonatal distress are associated with a raised incidence of subsequent mental retardation. Thus, to take one of the latest reports, Lebedev and Barashnev (1963) followed up 298 children born in Moscow in a state of blue or white asphyxia. Of these 29 died soon after birth and 269 were discharged from the maternity home in a satisfactory condition. The authors were able to re-examine 113 of those discharged from the maternity home when they were 7–10 years old. Of these, the confinement had been described as normal in 94 cases and complicated in 19 (by toxaemia, eclampsia, anaemia, and so on). Three mothers had contracted pelvis, and the babies presented by the breech in 18 cases. Labour had lasted over 24 hours in 28, and forceps were used in 7 cases. Thirteen were premature. At a later examination, neurological abnormalities were found in 30, and some mental retardation in 27 of the children. Many of the others showed slight behaviour and character defects: "in a family with several children, the parents could always pick out the child who was asphyxiated at birth." Other studies could be quoted in which the authors have used the same or similar criteria of 'birth injury', e.g. length of labour, degree of prematurity, use of instruments, use of drugs and abnormal presentation. The results were usually as above—that is, complicated deliveries and neonatal distress were associated with an increased incidence of subsequent mental impairment. Although some contrary views have been also expressed (Campbell, Cheeseman and Kilpatrick, 1950), the bulk of evidence strongly favours the view that 'birth injury' is a factor in the aetiology of mental retardation and related conditions. However, it is also known that children with congenital anomalies, especially cerebral ones, are much more likely to be distressed at birth, and that the same underlying cause (e.g. infection, prematurity or toxaemia) may be responsible for both the dystocia and the cerebral defect. To add to the difficulty, obvious birth injury, such as cerebral haemorrhage, is sometimes found in children born after a perfectly normal confinement, whilst, conversely, both dystocia and neonatal distress are not necessarily followed by encephalopathy and retarded development.

Cerebral Haemorrhage and Softening

One of the chief protagonists of the view that birth injury is very prevalent is the German pathologist, Philip Schwartz, who has recently reviewed and summarized his own previous publications and those of many others (Schwartz, 1961). He has examined numerous brains of infants dying at varying intervals after birth, often with a history suggestive of birth injury. As a result, he concludes that injury at birth is not only frequent but is associated with, and can be recognized, by the presence in the brain of certain characteristic lesions. The initial lesions are, according to him, haemorrhage and/or softening. The latter may be either complete or incomplete. Schwartz uses the terms 'dissolution' (Auflösung) and 'loosening' (Auflockerung) for these processes. These changes develop in time into a combination of cysts and scars, ranging from small focal lesions to almost total involvement of the brain, as in encephalomalacia and lobar sclerosis. In considering the mechanisms of the injury, Schwartz stresses particularly the differential pressure effect in the presenting part of the head. After rupture of the membranes, the presenting part is subjected only to atmospheric pressure, while the rest of the foetus is exposed to the additional pressure of uterine contractions. He postulates as a result a shift of the blood and fluid towards the presenting part with increased risk of congestion and haemorrhage, particularly in the territory drained by the vein of Galen.* Other authors have added to the list of possible traumatic, vascular or chemical mechanisms of damage at birth, (Malamud, 1959; Courville, 1950). Prematurity, for example, appears to increase the risk of haemorrhage, from the more fragile cerebral vessels. In some cases, there is sinus and venous thrombosis, subdural or intraventricular haemorrhage and arterial embolism or thrombosis. It is, indeed, common to find cerebral haemorrhage in infants dying soon after birth (Claireaux, 1959; Coutelle, 1960). The petechiae may be large and rupture, a considerable amount of blood escaping into the subarachnoid or subdural space. Intraventricular haemorrhage seems to be particularly common in premature infants. In other cases the haemorrhage may be massive, arising from one of the venous sinuses, as in tears of the falx cerebri or the tentorium cerebelli, when the contiguous parts of the brain itself are also frequently lacerated. However, such hae-morrhages seem to be mostly fatal and are probably not responsible for many cases of mental retardation. Subdural haematoma originating perinatally is another occasional cause of retardation (Christensen and Husby, 1963). An injury which seems to have been seldom mentioned is ping-pong ball-like indentation without frank fracture of the skull caused by some obstruction in the birth passage, instrumental delivery or impaction against a twin. If pro-longed and uncorrected the brain may be severely damaged in such cases. The factors involved in the production of this injury have been recently con-sidered by Axton and Levy (1965). Encephalopathy in at least two of 500 cases of severe subnormality examined pathologically at the Fountain Hospital was probably caused in this way.

A brain injury can also easily upset the function of the respiratory and vasomotor centres, leading to anoxia and circulatory disturbance after birth, which would tend, in their turn, to aggravate the damage. Oedema may be an additional factor. It is hence likely that several factors act in combination with each other.

Schwartz held that a great many neonatal and later disturbances such as convulsions, kernicterus, tetany, paralysis, epilepsy and coma, are attributable to birth injury. Such claims cannot be accepted uncritically, since many of the morphological changes described by him are now known to be caused in other ways, such as by infection or metabolic disease. Moreover, some of the gliotic encephalopathies described by him as sequelae of birth injury have been seen occasionally in stillborn infants.

Multiplicity of Factors

As already indicated, the term birth injury should not be interpreted nar-rowly. Pathogenic factors include disproportion of the head, prolonged

---

* If this theory were generally valid one would expect perhaps more complications to follow the use of the vacuum extractor (ventouse) applied to the presenting head of the child. But this procedure is usually quite safe (Chalmers, 1964) although accidental injury may occur if a fault develops in the mechanism of the air-extractor or pressure-gauge system of the instrument (Bajwa, 1965; Chamberlain, 1965).

labour, trauma, precipitate delivery, compression of the umbilical cord, use of instruments, inhalation of fluid, asphyxia, anoxia, effect of drugs, and prematurity, all of which may be involved in the causation of paranatal encephalopathy. In view of this complexity, it would be unreasonable to expect a uniform clinical or pathological picture as a sequel of birth injury. Yet some changes are, perhaps, characteristic of it. For example, Norman (1958) considers certain forms of ulegyria, rarefaction of tissue, and, less constantly, status marmoratus (marbling) of the cerebral cortex and basal ganglia, as being characteristic, and some, viz. cavitation of tissue at the lateral angle of the cerebral ventricles, as even a 'hall-mark' of birth injury. He may well be right, but the evidence is, for reasons expounded above, far from conclusive. Other neuropathological aspects of birth injury have also been reviewed by Norman and Urich (1959).

However produced, all definite evidence of birth injury disappears in time, and the brains of older mental defectives with a history compatible with damage at birth may present only the unspecific changes of gliosis, cavitation and, more rarely, hypermyelination. These are, however, merely suggestive and cannot prove that birth injury has really occurred.

A possible result of birth injury which has received attention in recent years, is the so-called 'incisural sclerosis'. This is a form of gliotic scarring affecting the hippocampus ascribed by Earle, Baldwin and Penfield (1953) to vascular obstruction during the delivery of the head. It has been suggested by them that the blood vessels supplying this part of the brain are compressed during delivery against the rim of the tentorium cerebelli and that the resulting ischaemia and congestion are the cause of sclerosis and, later, of 'temporal lobe epilepsy'. It is well known, that the hippocampus is often scarred in all forms of epilepsy, but the origin of this abnormality is still debatable (p. 74). Earle, Baldwin and Penfield have not really supported their hypothesis by conclusive evidence. This criticism is in agreement with the views expressed by Falconer, Serafetinides and Corsellis, (1964), who have reviewed this problem on the basis of data from temporal lobectomy performed in 100 cases of epilepsy.

It thus seems fair to sum up by suggesting that while birth injury is an important cause of mental retardation, it is impossible, as matters stand, to make more than an approximate estimate of its incidence. A tentative assessment at the Fountain Hospital based on clinical history, neurological status, exclusion of other known causes, and post-mortem findings, indicates that birth injury may account for 2–5 per cent of low-grade mental deficiency. Moreover, minor degrees of neural damage at birth may be more common than generally realized. For example, a little blood in the C.S.F. has been found in 7–13 per cent of all newborn infants (Sharpe and Maclaire, 1925). This being so, some of the mildest cases of mental impairment may also be due to injury at birth. We may therefore expect that improving antenatal and obstetric care will lower not only the incidence of mental deficiency, but help also in eliminating one of the contributory causes of other minor forms of intellectual impairment.

Experimental Work

Another ground for optimism is that the problem is at last yielding to experimental study; it is, perhaps, the dearth of such experimental work which has been largely responsible for the obscurity and confusion surrounding birth injury. The effect of anoxia on the cortex of mice and rats subjected to neonatal anoxia has been studied by Hicks, Cavanaugh and O'Brien (1962). The main sequelae were, apparently, retardation of the development of the neuronal dendritic processes and of the formation of intraneuronal ribonucleic acid. Jilek and collaborators (1964) studied the effect of hypoxia and oligaemia following ligation of both common carotids on the C.N.S. of the rat. They found that resistance to hypoxia decreased as the C.N.S. developed; the immature nervous system also showed greater powers of recovery when hypoxic changes had taken place. While in the younger rats functional and histopathological changes were concentrated in the phylogenetically oldest parts of the brain, in older animals the youngest parts of the brain suffered most. The very young but not the older animals could utilise the endogenous glycogen reserves of the brain when subjected to hypoxia. Glucose and, in the very young animals, lactic acid and sodium lactate had a protective effect in hypoxia.

Of even greater interest are the studies of scientists working under the auspices of the National Institute of Neurological Diseases and Blindness in Bethesda, U.S.A., who have begun to test the effects of anoxia on newborn monkeys. The animals were subsequently observed clinically and shown to present various forms of neurological and electroencephalographic abnormality. The brains of animals killed soon after the experiments showed symmetrical areas of degeneration and atrophy, particularly in the brainstem. Animals killed at 290 days of age showed, on the other hand, a somewhat different distribution of lesions, which then involved the cerebellum and cerebrum in addition to the brainstem (Windle et al., 1962). This work is continuing and more information will certainly become available. It is interesting, however, to note already that the lesions in the monkeys are in some respects very different from those attributed in the past to birth injury in man.

Another consequence of the experimental work is that it has become possible to assess objectively the effect of the early treatment of neonatal asphyxia. Thus, infusion of alkali and glucose in monkeys asphyxiated at birth reduces the incidence and extent of permanent brain damage (Dawes, Hibbard and Windle, 1964; Adamson, Behrman, Dawes, James and Koford, 1964).

Perinatal Mortality Survey

A revealing, if oblique, light has been shed on problems connected with birth injury, by the already mentioned survey of perinatal mortality in the United Kingdom, the first results of which have been published (Butler and Bonham, 1963). Information relating to 7,117 stillbirths and neonatal deaths has been collected throughout the country and analyzed centrally. These deaths occurred during three consecutive months in 1958, and pathological examination has been carried out in 5,248 of the cases. The survey is the largest of its kind ever undertaken, and its results cannot be summarised briefly. In general, the findings confirmed and added precision to many conclusions derived from other sources. Some of these have been discussed already in this chapter. Low income, birth order and maternal age were found to be aetiologically significant. So was geography, perinatal mortality being worse in the north and west and better in the south and east. Past history of abortion, stillbirth and birth of premature infants increases the risk. Babies born in hospitals after proper antenatal care and under the supervision of trained specialists fare better than those born at home or in General Practitioner Units. Toxaemia, bleeding during pregnancy, malposition, dystocia, instrumental birth and caesarean section are all associated, as might be expected, with higher perinatal mortality.

The main pathological findings were congenital malformations, especially of the brain and spinal cord, and evidence of antepartum and intrapartum anoxia with or without birth trauma. Other frequent lesions included pulmonary atelectasis, hyaline membrane of the lungs, intraventricular haemorrhage, and evidence of isoimmunization (almost entirely due to Rhesus factor). The relative incidence of these lesions differed, of course, depending on whether the infant was stillborn or died after birth. Infection became, for example, increasingly frequent in later neonatal deaths.

Since the main object of the survey was to determine the causes of deaths, it is impossible to transpose unreservedly the conclusions to problems of the causation of mental retardation. However, it seems reasonable that similar but less severe processes might permanently injure the brains of some of the survivors. Evidence cited in this chapter suggests that this is so with many agents. One of the more unexpected findings of the survey was the frequency of evidence of ante- and intrapartum anoxia with or without birth trauma in fatal cases. This cause was held responsible for almost 1 in 3 of all perinatal deaths. This suggests that lesser degrees of anoxia and circumstances leading up to it might be similarly significant in the causation of mental retardation.

REFERENCES

ADAMSON, K., BEHRMAN, R., DAWES, G. S., JAMES, L. S., and KOFORD, C. (1964). *J. Pediat.*, **65**, 807.
AXTON, J. H. M., and LEVY, L. F. (1965). *Brit. med. J.*, **1**, 1644.
BAJWA, R. (1965). *Lancet*, **1**, 630.
BUTLER, N. R., and BONHAM, D. G. (1963). 'Perinatal Mortality,' Edinburgh: Livingstone.
CAMPBELL, W. A. R., CHEESEMAN, E. A., and KILPATRICK, A. W. (1950). *Arch. Dis. Childh.*, **25**, 351.
CHALMERS, J. A. (1964). *Brit. med. J.*, **1**, 1216.
CHAMBERLAIN, G. (1965). *Lancet*, **1**, 632.
CHRISTENSEN, E., and HUSBY, J. (1963). *Acta neurol. scand.*, **39**, 323.
CLAIREAUX, A. E. (1959). *Guy's Hosp. Rep.*, **108**, 2.
COURVILLE, C. B. (1950). *Bull. Los Angeles neurol. Soc.*, **15**, 99, 129, 155.
COUTELLE, C. (1960). *Z. Geburtsh. Gynäk.*, **156**, 19.
DAWES, G. S., HIBBARD, E., and WINDLE, W. F. (1964). *J. Pediat.*, **65**, 801.
EARLE, K. M., BALDWIN, M., and PENFIELD, W. (1953). *Arch. Neurol. Psychiat. (Chic.),* **69**, 27.

FALCONER, M. A., SERAFETINIDES, E. A., and CORSELLIS, J. A. N. (1964). *Arch. Neurol.* (*Chic.*), **10**, 233.

HICKS, S. P., CAVANAUGH, M. C., and O'BRIEN, E. D. (1962). *Amer. J. Path.*, **40**, 615.

JILEK, L., FISCHER, J., KRULICH, L., and TROJAN, S. (1964). In W. A. and H. E. Himwich, 'The Developing Brain,' Amsterdam: Elsevier.

LEBEDEV, B. V., and BARASHNEV, YU. I. (1963). In Klosovskii, B. N., 'The Development of the Brain and its Disturbances by Harmful Factors,' Oxford: Pergamon, p. 131.

LITTLE, W. J. (1862). *Trans. obstet. Soc. Lond.*, **3**, 293.

MALAMUD, N. (1959). *J. Neuropath. exp. Neurol.*, **18**, 141.

NORMAN, R. M. (1958). In Greenfield, J. G., 'Neuropathology,' London: Arnold, p. 300.

NORMAN, R. M., and URICH, H. (1959). In Fleming, G. W. T. H., and Walk, A., 'Recent Progress in Psychiatry,' London: Churchill, **3**, p. 185.

SCHWARTZ, P. (1961). 'Birth Injuries of the Newborn. Morphology, Pathogenesis, Clinical Pathology and Prevention,' Basel: Karger.

SHARPE, W., and MACLAIRE, A. S. (1925). *J. Obstet. Gynaec. Brit. Emp.*, **32**, 79.

WINDLE, W. F., JACOBSON, H. N., RAMIREZ, R., DE ARELLANO, M. I., and COMBS, C. M. (1962). In 'Mental Retardation,' Proc. of the Assoc. for Research in Nervous and Mental Disease, **39**, London: Baillière, Tindall and Cox, p. 169.

CHAPTER 4

POST-NATAL CAUSES OF MENTAL RETARDATION: GENERAL CONSIDERATIONS

Infection

INFECTION of the central nervous system, especially meningitis, is still the commonest single cause of acquired mental deficiency. Thus, of 800 consecutive admissions to the Fountain Hospital, 22 cases (2·75 per cent) were caused by *meningitis* (Berg, 1962). The infection was tuberculous in 11 of these. This is noteworthy, since this form of meningitis was considered to be invariably fatal prior to the introduction of chemotherapy. It is curable now but not always completely, and tuberculous meningitis might hence be regarded as a new 'man-made instance' of mental retardation. For example, in a 3½–14 years follow-up of 65 streptomycin-treated cases in Liverpool, Todd and Neville (1964) found some physical defect, such as incoordination of a limb, epilepsy or deafness in about a third of the cases. Abnormal E.E.G. records were obtained in 47 patients. Intelligence was assessed as normal in 40, dull normal in 13, borderline defective in six and defective in another six of the cases. From such developments it is sometimes argued that the effect of more enlightened attitudes and of improved treatment is to increase the number of the handicapped and weak in society. This is certainly wrong. The following are, for example, some of the reported sequelae of meningitis treated by modern methods. Nyhan and Richardson (1963) record a mortality of 13 per cent and a high incidence of sequelae such as deafness and intellectual deficit in the U.S.A., but Heycock and Noble (1964) state that such complications are rare in Britain. Lawson, Metcalfe and Pampiglione (1965) followed up 64 cases of bacterial and 38 cases of non-bacterial meningitis for periods of 1–8 years. There were no cases of tuberculous meningitis in their series. The mean interval between the illness and reassessment was approximately 4 years. Two children who contracted the disease at 5 and 7 months became severely subnormal. No deterioration in intellectual level was demonstrable in either the bacterial or non-bacterial groups as a whole compared to the general population. However, more children contracting the disease before the age of one year failed to reach an I.Q. of 90 than did those who became ill after that age (35 per cent as compared with 8 per cent). There was striking evidence that delay in the treatment of bacterial meningitis of over 4 days was associated with serious consequences, and it is probably the promptness or delay in treatment of cases which accounts for differences in outcome in various reported series. It thus seems obvious that tuberculous meningitis is an exception and that modern treatment has reduced greatly the rôle of infection as a cause of mental retardation. Many forms of meningitis and encephalitis which used to end often in permanent disablement are now either entirely preventable or rendered more benign. The same is true of other conditions: severe neonatal jaundice, prematurity, certain malformations, and so on. Besides, there is no evidence of a decline in the general level of 'national intelligence' or of a rise in the number of the severely disabled in the community.

The bacteriological pattern of meningitis followed by mental retardation has also changed. Ordinary pyogenic meningitis caused by such organisms as H. influenzae, meningococcus and the gram positive cocci is now usually free from complications, while meningitis secondary to congenital malformations, such as spina bifida cystica, is often caused by other organisms, e.g. B. coli, proteus, and Ps. pyocyanea. These organisms are usually regarded as being of low virulence in somatic tissues but may cause considerable damage and be very difficult to eradicate in the central nervous system.

The graver forms of meningitis followed by retarded mental development probably often involve the brain as well as the meninges; they are virtually cases of *meningoencephalitis*. But the brain may also be damaged by infection in other ways, the commonest being development of hydrocephalus through the formation of adhesions or obstruction of some part of the C.S.F. pathway, such as the cerebral aqueduct (p. 173). Seven of the 22 post-meningitic cases in Berg's series were in fact hydrocephalic. Further, associated inflammation and thrombosis of some of the main arteries may lead to ischaemic changes in the areas supplied by them. This appears to happen relatively frequently in the streptomycin-treated cases of tuberculous meningitis (Fig. 13), but has been also observed in other conditions, e.g. in a case of pneumococcal meningitis treated with sulphonamides, when the arteries were later recanalized (Smith, Norman and Urich, 1957). Thrombosis of the cerebral veins and sinuses is

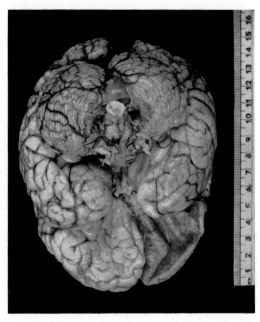

FIG. 13. Infarction of the right frontal lobe caused by obliterative arteritis of the anterior cerebral artery in a case of streptomycin-treated tuberculous meningitis.

P.M.R.—3*

another of the rarer pathogenetic mechanisms of brain damage in meningitis.

Infection of the brain itself—*encephalitis*—seems to be a much rarer cause of mental retardation. One of the commoner forms is, perhaps, brain abscess. This may follow meningitis or infection of one of the air sinuses. Children with cyanotic congenital heart disease are particularly prone to develop this complication as a result of embolism (Campbell, 1957).

Some of the encephalitides mentioned in connection with possible transplacental infection, such as toxoplasmosis, Coxsackie B virus infection, and cytomegalic inclusion body disease, may also occur in the neonatal period. These conditions have been excellently reviewed by Wolf and Cowen (1959), who also discussed herpes simplex, poliomyelitis, equine encephalomyelitis and some of the neonatal bacterial infections. Many aspects of coxsackie virus infection in childhood have been more recently considered by Rentsch (1964). In later infancy any of the viral or bacterial encephalitides may be followed by retarded mental development. All are rare in Britain, but may be commoner in other countries. For example, 40–50 cases of Japanese B encephalitis have been occurring annually in Singapore (Paul, F. M.—personal communication).

Two forms of encephalitis will be mentioned here because of their special interest, although neither appears to be frequent in this country. The first is *subacute inclusion body encephalitis*, also known as subacute sclerosing panencephalitis or subacute sclerosing leucoencephalitis. This condition affects particularly children or adolescents and leads to progressive dementia, hyperkinesis, paralysis and epilepsy. It is usually fatal within a few months but may sometimes last several years and simulate some of the chronic metabolic disorders, such as leucodystrophy and lipidosis. Although the presence of inclusion bodies in many cells in the C.N.S. suggests viral origin, the causative organism has not yet been isolated. It should also be noted that inclusion bodies are not always found in these cases despite thorough search. The E.E.G. records often show 'almost pathognomonic' bursts of repetitive high-voltage complexes. Rhythmic stereotyped 'incomplete' involuntary movements of the limbs, which are synchronous with the above E.E.G. complexes, are also highly characteristic of the condition. However, the motor phenomena may be inhibitory, assuming the form of so-called 'antispasms'. The disease has been well reviewed by Lóránd, Nagy and Tariska (1962). The second condition, occasional instances of which may be encountered among mildly retarded individuals is *postencephalitic parkinsonism*. The patients may show muscular rigidity, particularly of the face, and manifest emotional disturbance with psychopathic tendencies; they were formerly regarded as 'moral defectives'. Many such cases occurred as a sequel to the outbreaks of encephalitis lethargica during and following the First World War, and the disease is believed to have been caused by a virus, which was, however, never isolated. Although epidemic outbreaks of encephalitis lethargica never recurred, sporadic cases of post-encephalitic parkinsonism continue to appear, and it is thought that the acute stage of the disease may now run a very mild or subclinical course. The symptoms of post-encephalitic parkinsonism are a manifestation of severe residual lesions situated chiefly in the substantia nigra, and of milder and less conspicuous changes in the basal ganglia, hypothalamus and elsewhere. One of the fuller texts, such as that of Ford (1960), should be consulted for further details of this and other encephalitides.

The brain may also be involved secondarily in certain extraneural infections. Although such encephalopathy is a rare complication of any of these conditions, the total number of affected cases is by no means negligible since the primary infections themselves are very common.

Infantile gastroenteritis, in its prolonged and intractable form, is an occasional cause of mental retardation (Schlesinger and Welch, 1952). The affected children may show some dementia with marked paralysis and epilepsy. The brain of one such infant presented widespread focal neuronal loss in the superficial cortical laminae and gliosis of the basal ganglia. This may have been caused by the severe dehydration, haemoconcentration and associated electrolyte disturbance (Crome, 1952). Numerically more important are the occasional *encephalopathies—para-infectious encephalomyelitides—*which follow the acute childhood fevers, viz. measles, chicken-pox, rubella, mumps, whooping cough, scarlet fever, and, more rarely, vaccination. While some of these encephalopathies are probably instances of true encephalitis, most are thought to be manifestations of allergy—allergic encephalomyelopathy. The typical cases present demyelination with the formation of a cellular exudate around many of the smaller veins in the white matter of the brain and spinal cord (Fig. 14). Miller, Stanton and Gibbons (1956) have estimated the incidence of neurological complications at 1:5,000 for rubella, 1:1,000 for measles, and 1:800 for scarlet fever. According to them, the immediate and long term prognoses vary with the fevers: the encephalitis in rubella, measles and mumps have a higher mortality (20–25 per cent) than that in scarlet fever (13 per cent) or chicken-pox (10 per cent). On the other hand, sequelae are considerably less common (2–5 per cent) in rubella than in chicken-pox (20 per cent), measles (35 per cent) or scarlet fever (45 per cent). Patients recovering from rubellar encephalitis and showing no further evidence of mental or neurological complications may nevertheless have persistently abnormal E.E.G. records (Pampiglione *et al.*, 1963). Para-infectious encephalomyelitis may also be present in a recurrent form (Alcock and Hoffman, 1962).

Whooping-cough as an occasional cause of mental retardation has been considered by Berg (1961) and by Ladodo and Lebedev (1963), who attributed the cerebral damage in such cases to anoxia. The pathological findings in a 9 year old girl who developed hemiplegia and a severe behaviour disorder following whooping-cough at 18 months have been reported by Wolman (1962). The chief finding was extensive cavitation and gliosis of the cerebral cortex. Inoculation against whooping-cough, but not, apparently, against any of the other infections in infancy, has been also followed by encephalopathy in a few exceptional cases (Berg, 1958).

It is worth mentioning that the suggestion of a fever or some other striking event, such as convulsions or physical trauma, being responsible for mental retardation in a particular case must always be treated cautiously. It is often not possible to be certain of prior normal development in infants or very young children, and the remembered illness or incident ushering in overt retardation is often only the signal of a pre-existent encephalopathy. It is not uncommon, for example, to see records of some immunizing procedure which precedes by a few days or weeks the onset of fits, paralysis and unconsciousness, the diseases later proving to be instances of lipidosis, leucodystrophy, malformation or some other condition entirely unconnected with the suspected cause.

The problem of *febrile fits* as a cause of mental retardation is also exceedingly complex. Febrile fits are common in infancy and are mostly free from lasting

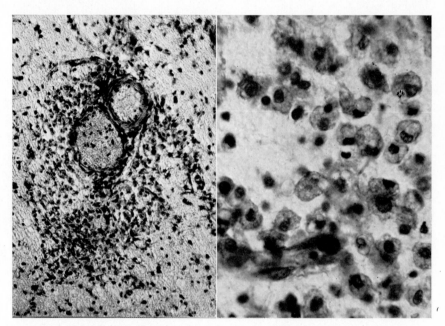

Fig. 14. Perivenous encephalitis. The demyelinated spaces around the blood vessels are filled by lipid phagocytes. Cresyl violet × 125 (left); × 500 (right).

sequelae. However, some may be followed by very severe brain damage (Fowler, 1957), and it was thought by Bourne (1956) that many instances of dementia caused by fits are incorrectly ascribed to encephalitis. However, cause and effect can only be established by a thorough study of all the circumstances in any given case, and the data are seldom fully conclusive. This problem is also considered on p. 73 in relation to epilepsy as a cause of mental retardation.

Kernicterus and its Sequelae

Severe jaundice of the newborn may damage widely scattered areas in the brain and spinal cord. The early lesions are bright yellow in colour—hence the name kernicterus ('Kern' is German for nucleus and is used in reference to the subcortical formations of grey matter). Not all of the earlier workers could demonstrate microscopic changes in the affected areas during the acute stages of kernicterus. These changes are, however, not only constantly present but very severe according to Boreau, Martin, Larroche and Sautriot (1964). The commonest distribution of the lesions is in the basal ganglia, cerebellum, medulla, cerebral cortex (including hippocampus) and substantia nigra, but many other formations can be involved (Crome, 1955; Chen, 1964). Some of the infants survive the acute stage but remain permanently disabled, the typical residual features being athetoid palsy, deafness and mental retardation (Crome, Kirman and Marrs, 1955). Atypical features, such as ataxia, epilepsy or hemiplegia, are, however, not unknown. The deafness is usually perceptive in type with selective high-frequency loss and is believed to result from damage to the primary auditory nuclei in the medulla; there is no evidence of damage to the cochlea itself (Fisch and Osborn, 1954; Fisch and Norman, 1961). Deafness may often be present without the typical athetoid syndrome. The pathological changes in cases presenting as athetoid palsy are considered on p. 320.

Recent work has thrown a good deal of light on the aetiology and pathogenesis of kernicterus (Lathe, Claireaux and Norman, 1958; Brown, 1962). The immediate cause of the jaundice may be severe haemolysis, as in Rhesus factor or ABO group incompatibility or sensitization by one of the rarer blood-group factors, or other rare causes of haemolysis, such as congenital spherocytosis, atypical congenital haemolytic jaundice, hepatitis, some other infections, and exposure to certain drugs. On the other hand, jaundice may also be caused by functional immaturity of the liver, as in prematurity, in some cases of congenital hypothyroidism and, very rarely, in the Crigler-Najjar syndrome (congenital familial non-haemolytic jaundice due to an inherited deficiency of glucuronyl transferase), Gilbert's disease (Schmid, 1966), galactosaemia, and glucose-6-phosphate dehydrogenase deficiency (Doxiadis and Valaes, 1964).

It has been known for some time that bilirubin may react either directly or indirectly with the van den Bergh reagent, and it is now established that this difference depends on whether or not the bilirubin has been conjugated with glucuronic acid by the liver glucuronyl transferase. The conjugated bilirubin reacts directly and the unconjugated indirectly. The latter is more fat-soluble and toxic to neural tissue. *In vitro* studies suggest that this toxicity depends on the inhibition of cellular oxidative phosphorylation and depression of the underlying respiration. The liver of a newborn baby, especially if it is premature, has little reserve of conjugating capacity since its content of glucuronyl transferase is low (Vest, 1958).

In cases of blood group incompatibility excessive breakdown of haemoglobin and the onset of hyperbilirubinaemia in the infant depend, of course, on the presence of antibodies in the mother. It is believed that these are formed in two stages: sensitization and immunization. Since the two stages seldom occur in the same pregnancy, the risk of a primigravida's developing antibodies is negligible unless she has been previously transfused with Rh-positive blood. Further, the risk of antibody formation is diminished if the foetus shows ABO group incompatibility with the mother. It is thought that this is because a considerable number of erythrocytes must enter the maternal circulation in order to produce sensitization. If they are ABO incompatible they are destroyed too rapidly for sensitization to occur. Some events in pregnancy, such as toxaemia and surgical procedure increase the risk of sensitization. Thus whether or not iso-immunization occurs depends on a number of factors which are to some extent predictable in each given case. Some recent work on the prevention of rhesus factor haemolytic disease is based on the vulnerability of the red blood corpuscles of a rhesus positive child to human anti-D gammaglobulin. If these red blood corpuscles could be destroyed as soon as they enter the maternal circulation iso-immunization might be prevented. Preliminary results by this treatment have been encouraging (Clarke, C. A. *et al.*, 1964; Annotation, *Lancet*, 1965).

In utero the foetus is in many cases protected from the excess of its own bilirubin by the placenta and the mother's liver; that is why jaundice often does not set in before birth (Dunn, 1963). Whenever it appears, which may be a few hours or, even, some days later, the infant faces a critical situation until his liver becomes functionally more efficient or the haemolysis ceases. Whether or not kernicterus develops depends therefore not only on the degree of bilirubinaemia, but also on the proportion of unconjugated bilirubin and the maturity of the liver. The immaturity of the blood-brain barrier, as suggested by Ernster, Herlin and Zetterström (1957), is probably a further contributory factor in the development of neural damage.

Recent studies have shown that other factors may be also important in the pathogenesis of kernicterus. Most of the bilirubin in the blood is bound to albumen but some is dissociated from it. According to Odell (1959) it is the dissociated and diffusible form which permeates cell membranes and constitutes the real danger in cases of neonatal jaundice. The amount of such diffusible bilirubin is increased if the albumen content of the plasma is low, as it is in premature babies. The binding power of the plasma can also be lowered artificially and dissociated bilirubin thereby increased by certain substances: haematin, sulphonamides, salicylates and caffeine sodium benzoate, or by increasing the hydrogen ion concentration. It has also been known for some time that large doses of vitamin K or its analogues tend to raise the blood bilirubin levels (Crosse, Meyer and Gerrard, 1955), although some of the newer preparations of this vitamin are said to be free from that action (Asteriadou-Samartzis and Leikin, 1958). An increase in the incidence of hyperbilirubinaemia in newborn infants has also followed administration of 'Novobiocin' (Sutherland and Keller, 1961) and 'Gantrisin' (a salt of sulphasoxazole) (Lathe, Claireaux and Norman, 1958). According to Chen, Lien and Lu (1965) anoxia is an important factor in the production of brain damage in experimental hyperbilirubinaemia.

It follows from the above outline of the pathogenesis of kernicterus that the first aim of treatment must be to flush out as much as possible of the maternal antibodies from the child's circulation and to tide him over the immediate crisis. Exchange blood transfusion is often indicated for this purpose. This treatment has saved many lives and prevented complications in a large number of cases. Nevertheless, instances of residual kernicterus are still relatively frequent. Thus, six such patients have been admitted among 200 consecutive cases of children under the age of 5 years to the Fountain Hospital between 1955–57. All were born after the adoption of the new methods of treatment and some had had exchange transfusions, though perhaps inadequately by the latest standards. Of another 180 infants with Rh haemolytic disease treated at the Maternity Hospital, Birmingham, during 1960 and 1961, 1 case developed evidence of early kernicterus after receiving three full exchange transfusions. The perinatal mortality in that series was 12·7 per cent (Dunn, 1963).

It has been suggested that Rhesus factor incompatibility might be responsible for mental retardation in some cases without previous neonatal jaundice or kernicterus, but evidence supporting this was never convincing. On the other hand, slight impairment of intelligence, usually within the normal range, has been reported in children who had made an apparently full recovery from neonatal jaundice (Gerver and Day, 1950).

Acquired Metabolic Errors and Endocrine Disorders

In addition to the inborn errors of metabolism considered on p. 260 *et seq.* certain 'acquired' metabolic disturbances may be followed by mental retardation. These include, to mention but a few, hypo- and hyperkalaemia, hypoglycaemia, dehydration, acidosis, alkalosis and hyperlipaemia. In some cases the disturbances are secondary to a primary metabolic error elsewhere or to another identifiable condition, such as infection, endocrine deficiency, renal disorder, trauma or burns. In other cases the primary cause cannot be established and the biochemical abnormality is regarded as 'idiopathic'. The relation of these disorders to encephalopathy is complex. Some may cause encephalopathy. On the other hand, neural regulation may be so disturbed by an already established encephalopathy as to cause or contribute to the causation of the metabolic disorder. It is not possible to discuss here all these conditions, but those referred to below are perhaps of special interest.

Hypoglycaemia is important because irreversible brain damage may be prevented in some cases if the condition is recognized and treated in time. Hypoglycaemia is known to damage the brain, the changes resembling, in the main, those of anoxia; the cerebral cortex shows widespread necrosis with sparing of the visual area, and as in anoxia, the Ammon's horn is frequently involved. Of the subcortical formations the striatum and the cerebellum are often affected. Unfortunately, as contrasted with adults, little is known of the neuropathological changes in hypoglycaemic infants and children, but there is no doubt that epilepsy and severe mental retardation may be engendered by hypoglycaemia. For example, neonatal hypoglycaemia in 10 infants has been described by Brown and Wallis (1963). Of the first six, 2 died and 4 survived with evidence of permanent brain damage. The last four cases were treated more effectively and seem to have escaped residual brain damage. The brain of two infants whose neonatal hypoglycaemia had lasted 46 and 55 hours were recently examined by Anderson, Milner and Strich (1966). These workers found evidence of acute degenerative changes in nerve and glial cells throughout the central nervous system. They were impressed particularly by fragmentation of nuclei and granularity of the cytoplasm. Similar changes occur, however, quite frequently in the nerve cells of infants dying from such conditions as neonatal infection with or without secondary hypoglycaemia.

The condition has been reviewed by McKendrick (1962), Gautier-Smith (1965), Neligan (1965) and Marks (1965). Hypoglycaemia has been called 'organic' if an anatomical lesion can be recognised, and 'functional'—if the presence of such a lesion cannot be discovered. Organic causes include islet cell adenoma or hyperplasia, pancreatic hyperplasia, liver disease, pituitary, adrenocortical and hypothalamic lesions, pre-diabetes, some types of glyco-gen storage disease, galactosaemia and fructose intolerance (cf. Chapter 12). Functional causes, which in children are more frequent than the organic ones, include the leucine-sensitive and non-sensitive varieties of idiopathic hypo-glycaemia of infancy, excessive secretion of insulin, as in babies of diabetic mothers or in the Dormandy syndrome (Samols and Dormandy, 1963 a and b), other forms of sensitivity, hypersecretion of insulin, hypoglycaemia due to fructose and galactose sensitivity, defective adrenaline response to hyperglycae-mia (Koegel and Paunier, 1962; Brunjes, Hodgman, Nowack and Johns, 1963; Haas, 1963), prematurity and infection. Hypoglycaemia occurs frequently in babies of low birth weight, e.g. the smaller of twins (Cornblath, 1965) and may be due, at least in part, to immaturity of or damage to the brain centres concerned with glucose homeostasis, and to the low glycogen reserves in these infants. A vicious circle may thus be set up: hypoglycaemia → brain damage → further worsening of glucose homeostasis → additional attacks of hypo-glycaemia. Children who have suffered intrauterine malnutrition and have a low birth weight for gestation, the so-called 'dysmature newborn infants', appear to be particularly vulnerable (Chance and Bower, 1966). The central nervous system, autonomic nervous system, adrenal medulla (and other extramedullary chromaffin tissues) and blood glucose regulation are all inter-related. Brunjes et al., (1963) have commented on the association of hypogly-caemia, adrenal medullary insufficiency and mental retardation, and on the difficulty in deciding which was primary.

Prompt diagnosis is of the greatest importance in idiopathic hypoglycaemia of infancy. Good results have been claimed for treatment with ACTH and steroids. Ephedrine may benefit cases with poor adrenalin response to hypo-glycaemia. Spontaneous remission occurs in a proportion of children with idiopathic hypoglycaemia of infancy before the age of six (see also p. 294).

It has recently been discovered that aspirin ingestion may produce pro-nounced hypoglycaemia in some infants, and possibly other severe metabolic upsets (Limbeck, Ruvalcaba, Samols and Kelley, 1965; Giles, 1965).

Of the other metabolic disorders, several have already been mentioned. Thus, dehydration and the possible electrolyte disturbance associated with infantile gastroenteritis were referred to on p. 67, and hypercalcaemia in Table 4 and p. 307.

It should be mentioned that the distinction between 'inborn' and 'acquired' is by no means clear-cut in all cases of metabolic aberration, and some appear to have both inherited and acquired variants. This may be so, for example, in the case of severe hypercalcaemia of infancy (Schlesinger, Butler and Black, 1956; Crome and Sylvester, 1960) (see p. 307).

The significance of *endocrine disorders* as a primary cause of mental defect was probably exaggerated in the past. The most important of these disorders is hypothyroidism (p. 301), for a full review of which readers can be referred to an issue of the *British Medical Bulletin* devoted to the thyroid gland (Myant, 1960). Some parathyroid disorders may be also associated with mental dysfunction (p. 307). Diabetes insipidus—a hypothalamo-hypophyseal disorder—may lead to encephalopathy by prolonged dehydration with electrolyte shifts. It was also thought that the Laurence-Moon-Biedl syndrome, a condition typically presenting with obesity, hypogenitalism, mental deficiency, retinitis pigmentosa and polydactyly, was a manifestation of a pituitary disorder, but this is unlikely since neither the hypothalamus nor the pituitary have shown any morphological changes in the pathologically examined cases (Ross, Crome and Mackenzie, 1956). Diabetes mellitus is an occasional cause of subnormality, both hyper- and hypoglycaemia being potentially encephalopathic, with hypoglycaemia perhaps the more dangerous of the two. In one of two recently examined unpublished personal cases moderately severe infantile diabetes mellitus was associated with cerebral changes chemically and neuropathologically indistinguishable from Alpers' disease (p. 324). The other case showed marked cerebellar atrophy with bilateral cataracts and retinal atrophy.

On the other hand, endocrine disturbance, such as hypogonadism, may be associated with severe subnormality or gross neurological disease without being causally related to it. This has been mentioned already in the context of the Klinefelter and Turner syndromes (pp. 12–15), and other examples have also been reported (Matthews and Rundle, 1964).

Epilepsy

Epileptics as a group are somewhat less intelligent than non-epileptics, although, as is well known, some are not only normal but intellectually brilliant (Cooper, 1965). On the other hand, seizures of every kind are very frequent in a large proportion of mentally retarded individuals. Since, moreover, the onset of a real or apparent decline in an individual's intelligence may coincide with or follow a period of fits, it is necessary to consider to what extent epilepsy may in itself be a cause of mental retardation.

The belief that convulsions damage the brain is deep-rooted. Many writers have maintained that either the fits themselves or certain processes connected with them, such as anoxia, asphyxia, vascular disturbances—(e.g. ischaemia or vasostasis), or some of the other more imperfectly understood associated chemical phenomena, might permanently injure the brain. If this were so, a vicious circle could be set up, the ictogenic brain lesions causing further fits. This view has been held by many neurologists in the past, and supported particularly by some of the leading German neuropathologists, such as Spielmeyer and Scholz, whose views have recently been restated by Peiffer (1963).

In brief, the characteristic ictal changes in neural tissue are said to be those of 'elective parenchymatous necrosis', i.e. atrophy and ultimate disappearance of neurones with replacement by glial tissue. The lesions are topologically characteristic; certain formations are often involved, the approximate order of frequency being the Ammon's horn, amygdaloid nucleus, cerebellar cortex, thalamus, cerebral cortex, striatum, inferior olives and dentate nucleus. Some of the changes attributed to epilepsy are massive; they include gross atrophy and scarring of the entire cerebrum or marked cerebellar sclerosis. The temporal lobe has also been an object of special interest because of its relation to 'temporal lobe epilepsy'. A formation given particular attention is the Ammon's horn of the hippocampus, where even slight changes are relatively easy to recognize. The area of the Ammon's horn most frequently involved in cases of epilepsy is the Sommer sector (Fig. 15) and the end-folium. Falconer,

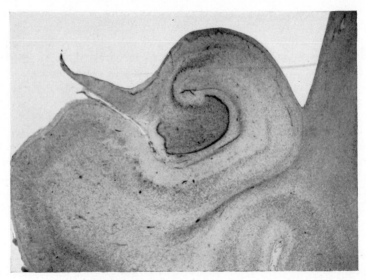

Fig. 15. Loss of nerve cells in the Sommer sector of the Ammon's horn in a case of epilepsy. (Cresyl violet × 6).

Serafetinides and Corsellis (1964) suggest that this characteristic lesion should be referred to as 'medial temporal sclerosis'. They state "In the most minor degrees there is a loss in the Sommer (H_1) sector of the hippocampus (cornu Ammonis) and this tends to be associated with some degree of gliosis of the amygdala. With increasing severity other parts of the hippocampus also show nerve cell loss; the uncus and the amygdaloid region may be similarly affected in a patchy manner, while definite gliosis appears in these structures and in the white matter of the temporal lobe. With further extension of the damage the neuronal loss in all these structures becomes marked and may extend to the adjacent cortex, such as the hippocampal and fusiform gyri, and even to the more lateral temporal gyri. The damage may affect particularly the second and third layers of the cortex and also the whole thickness of the cortex in the depths of sulci." The evidence of Falconer, Serafetinides and Corsellis suggests that medial temporal sclerosis is generally associated with habitual seizures that date from infancy. On the other hand, it is often absent in cases of epilepsy which commence in later life. Furthermore, it may be also present in cases of subnormality not associated with overt epilepsy.

Some of the evidence is pathological. Brains examined at various intervals after particularly severe fits show an evolution of changes which is compatible with ictogenic origin, and this applies perhaps to the relatively easily detectable lesions in the temporal lobe. Furthermore, such lesions resemble to some extent those produced experimentally or attributed in man to anoxia or vascular disturbances. However, as is often the case in neuropathology, the evidence is not conclusive. Lesions, even if coincident in time with fits, are not necessarily the result of the fits; they may equally well be a manifestation of some common underlying cause. Moreover, as far as can be ascertained, the brain remains structurally normal in many cases of epilepsy, even if fits are frequent.

But the argument is not only pathological. Many other aspects of the problem have been considered and the literature is forbiddingly extensive. It is very difficult to estimate accurately the incidence of mental deterioration in epilepsy. There is little doubt, however, that most epileptic individuals do not deteriorate below their initial intellectual level, whatever that may be. For example, in a random sample of 85 adult epileptic institutionalized patients, Falk, Penrose and Clark (1945) failed to detect deterioration in any but 3 patients, and these were psychotic. In another study Chaudhry (1959) found that only 20 (4 per cent) of the children attending the Maudsley Hospital epileptic clinic had shown mental deterioration. He was able to find only 8 similarly deteriorated children at the Fountain Hospital, although that hospital accommodated at the time at least a hundred other epileptic children. The rate of deterioration has been even lower in series comprising non-institutionalized groups of epileptic individuals, although intellectual decline is more frequent in older epileptics when factors connected with ageing begin to play their part.

The case for the prevalence of ictogenic dementia would be strengthened if it were possible to demonstrate normality or a higher level of intelligence before the onset of fits in a significant number of cases. Chaudhry has analyzed a number of factors in his series of 28 deteriorated epileptic children. He found that one of the factors significantly correlated with ensuing mental retardation was the presence of diffuse brain abnormality ascertainable both clinically and by E.E.G. examination. This suggests that active encephalopathy is often present before the onset of fits. The other significant factors in that series were the frequency and type of seizures, their lack of response to medication and disturbed social environment (Chaudhry and Pond, 1961). On the other hand, as indicated already, mental deterioration may occasionally commence more or less simultaneously with the onset of fits in apparently normal children. Twelve such cases were, for example, described by Illingworth (1955). Detailed study showed, however, that in some of them a change in the child's behaviour had preceded the fits. The author presented evidence to show that both fits and deterioration were due to an underlying brain lesion in all his cases.

Some of the children showing real mental deterioration and epilepsy may be cases of one of the progressive encephalopathies, such as leucodystrophy or lipidosis. It is true that Chaudhry has tried to exclude such cases from his series, but this is almost impossible to do, and he cites no criteria for his selection of patients. The cases considered by him were alive at the time of publication and he could thus have had no pathological evidence of 'non-progressiveness'. Nor should it be readily assumed that all progressive encephalopathies are necessarily recognizable even after the fullest pathological investigation.

It would thus appear that epilepsy in itself is not a frequent cause of mental retardation. However, the intelligence of a few epileptic individuals does decline, and much remains to be learned about the real causes of that deterioration.

Nutritional Causes

So long as hunger continues, as it does, to scourge the world, it will be useful to know whether and how it may impede full mental growth. But this is not easy to do. Starvation or malnutrition is only one of many factors in destitution. Furthermore, poverty-stricken areas are usually under-doctored, and the few available specialists have more urgent calls upon their time than the collection of scientific data. On the other hand, the effect of malnutrition on the growth and development of animals has been studied by many investigators. Thus, Platt, Pampiglione and Stewart (1965) have reported on the clinical, electroencephalographic and neuropathological changes in pigs kept on a protein deficient diet.

An interesting report by Stoch and Smythe (1963) has come from South Africa. The authors described two matched groups of Cape Coloured children one of which was severely undernourished. Most of the children were 10 months to 2 years old when first examined and had been followed at the time of publication for periods varying from 2 to 7 years. It was found that the brains of the undernourished children, as measured by the size of the head circumference, remained smaller than those in the control group. There was also a significant difference of 22·6 points in the mean I.Q. as estimated on the Gesell and Amatruda Infant scales and, later, on the Merrill-Palmer scale. The groups were perhaps rather small, comprising 21 children in each and the authors have also considered other reservations. Nevertheless, the trend is plain: severe malnutrition in infancy is associated with retardation of the growth of the brain and of intelligence. Somewhat similar depression of the I.Q. following undernutrition in infancy has been observed in Sarajevo, Yugoslavia, by Cabak and Najdanvic (1965). The whole problem of the effect of malnutrition on mental development has been usefully reviewed by Cravioto, DeLicardie and Birch (1966). In the article these workers also report on their observations on the mental development ('neurointegrative organization' and 'intersensory development') of badly nourished Indian village children in Guatemala. Using height, with appropriate corrections for the height of parents and other factors, as an index of the state of nutrition, a definite connection could be established between malnutrition and retarded intelligence.*

More is known about specific nutritional deficiencies. *Kwashiorkor* is caused mainly by lack of animal proteins, such as milk, in the diet of infants and children. However, the diet of the affected children is usually also deficient in fats, carbohydrates and vitamins (Ivanovsky, 1965). Neurological symptoms developing in some of these cases include tremor, cogwheel rigidity and myoclonus. Learning ability is impaired and the children are apathetic and slow in passing the normal landmarks of development. The mental symptoms are usually reversible, but lasting mental retardation has also been reported. *Beriberi* is caused by thiamine deficiency and its usual nervous manifestation is polyneuritis. However, in infants, it may be associated with *Wernicke's encephalopathy*, as in the 11 undernourished American negro children described by Davis and Wolf (1958). The usual manifestation of nicotinic acid deficiency is *pellagra* with mental and nervous dysfunction in the acute stages and, later, possibly, lasting dementia. Tetany with convulsions may complicate rickets (*vitamin D deficiency*), and subdural haematoma may result from scurvy (*vitamin C deficiency*). Descriptions of all these conditions are contained in fuller texts, such as Ford's (1966).

Primary nutritional deficiencies as a source of mental retardation are probably extremely rare in Britain. But conditioned deficiencies may occur as part of the malabsorption syndrome caused, for example, by coeliac disease, mucoviscidosis and some of the intractable diarrhoeas. The effect of such deficiencies on mental development does not appear to have been studied. Artificially prepared, 'synthetic', diets are increasingly used in the management of certain metabolic disorders, such as phenylketonuria. Imbalance of such diets may result from deficiency of essential constituents, such as vitamins (Wilson and Clayton, 1962). It has been suggested by Calvert, Hurworth and MacBean (1958) and Chanarin *et al* (1960) that the blood level of folic acid may be depressed or the utilization of this substance impaired in some cases by barbiturates and other anticonvulsants, and that megaloblastic anaemia can be induced in this way. Although mental retardation has not yet been attributed to this cause, it is well to bear this danger in mind.

The only known condition dependent on a deficiency of a trace element—iodine—is endemic cretinism (p. 301) (Trotter, 1960).

A substance worth mentioning because of the interest aroused by it in recent years is *gamma-aminobutyric acid (GABA)*. It is an amino-acid formed from glutamates by the enzyme glutamic decarboxylase. Both GABA and this enzyme are present in high concentration in the brain of adults but their level is low in newborn animals. GABA exerts an inhibitory action on nerve cells and there is evidence that its deficiency can be associated with epilepsy. Glutamic decarboxylase has pyridoxal phosphate as its co-enzyme, and seizures associated with pyridoxine deficiency and hypoglycaemia could therefore be related to changes in the GABA concentration in neural tissue (Sinclair, 1962).

* Mean brain weights of malnourished Ugandan infants and children were found to be low by Brown, R. E. (1966). *Develop. Med. Child Neurol.*, **8**, 512.

Some reported cases of epilepsy have in fact been associated with pyridoxine deficiency and appear to have benefited from treatment with that vitamin (Garty, Yonis, Braham and Steinitz, 1962).*

Poisons

Most modern homes abound with poisons, many of which can cause encephalopathy in children. The obvious ones are coal gas, and perhaps, alcohol, but there are many other and more unusual ones in cupboards and drawers. Permanent brain damage is fortunately rare and it is unnecessary to consider this subject in any detail here. Two substances, oxygen and lead, are, however, of special interest.

Oxygen is frequently used in the resuscitation of babies asphyxiated at birth and in the care of premature children. It has been found that such use of oxygen is significantly related to the incidence of *retrolental fibroplasia* (*Brit. med. J.*, 1955). This name is given to an opaque mass in the vitreous formed by the detached retina of newborn and young infants (Fig. 16). The remnants of the

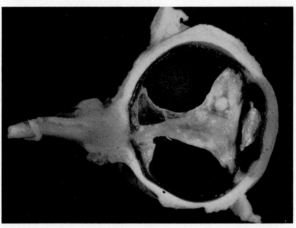

Fig. 16. Retrolental fibroplasia. The retina is detached and scarred. The lens is irregular in shape and shows a cataract. No oxygen has been given in this case.

vitreous itself are displaced forward to form a fibrillary membrane behind the lens. The folds of the detached and disorganized retina undergo gliotic change and may calcify. The affected eye is often small, but there may be buphthalmos and glaucoma, while cataracts may develop and obscure the fibroplastic mass in the vitreous. Other ocular abnormalities, such as coloboma or persistent hyaloid artery may be associated with the condition, or there may be evidence of earlier haemorrhage or inflammation. The condition was previously known under different names, such as pseudo-glioma, or described in association with microphthalmia (Whitnall and Norman, 1940; Macdonald and Dawson, 1954). Associated encephalopathy is common and, although this problem has not been given the attention it deserves, the association of retrolental fibroplasia with mental retardation is well established. Krause (1946) found, for example,

* See also Elliott, K. A. C. (1965). *Brit. med. Bull.* **21**, 70. The rôle of glutamic and aspartic acids in nerve excitation is discussed by Curtis, D. R., and Watkins, J. C. (1965). *Pharm. Rev.*, **17**, 347.

most of the 18 cases he studied to be mentally retarded and suggested the term 'congenital encephalo-ophthalmic dysplasia' for the condition. Williams (1958) observed that at least half of 98 children discharged from Sunshine Homes as 'ineducable' between 1950 and 1956 had suffered from retrolental fibroplasia. He further reports that the condition was present in 14 of 51 mentally retarded children accommodated at an annexe for the blind of the Fountain Hospital. In some of the others it may have been obscured by cataracts, which were present in 10 of the cases.

The observation that the administration of oxygen to newborn infants, particularly the premature, was associated with the development of retrolental fibroplasia has been given wide publicity and oxygen has since been used more sparingly. It is claimed that the incidence of retrolental fibroplasia has consequently greatly declined. However, it is also true that ophthalmologists have become very reluctant to diagnose cases as retrolental fibroplasia unless the child has had oxygen at birth. The untreated cases are often designated differently and the belief in the retinopathic rôle of oxygen remains unbroken. Though there may be some substance in the theory of oxygen causation, there is no doubt that the causes of retrolental fibroplasia are manifold, and may be both congenital or acquired. The condition has been known long before the introduction of oxygen therapy and new cases continue to occur both in oxygen-treated and untreated infants, particularly if they are premature. Three cases of retrolental fibroplasia have been examined pathologically at the Fountain Hospital, and details of two have been published (Crome, 1958). One was premature and received oxygen at birth. The other two were full-term, showed associated congenital encephalopathy and had had no oxygen.

It is fair to add that supporting evidence in favour of the retinopathic action of oxygen has come from experimental work (Ashton, 1954; Ashton, Ward and Serpell, 1954). The retinal vessels of newborn kittens become constricted when the animals are exposed to oxygen, and proliferate excessively, growing into the vitreous, after the animals are returned to air. Somewhat similar changes have been reported in human oxygen-treated infants observed ophthalmoscopically, but it is doubtful whether the pathogenesis and structural features in the kittens and infants with retrolental fibroplasia are fully comparable. Other causes cannot, of course, be excluded in infants developing true fibroplasia. Moreover, oxygen administration does not explain the frequent association of retrolental fibroplasia with mental retardation, which may, however, be partially attributable to a common factor of marked prematurity. It is true that some, rather mild, vascular and cellular changes have been reported in the cerebral cortices of newborn mice exposed to heavy and prolonged concentrations of oxygen by Gyllensten (1959), but these remain as yet unconfirmed by other workers. They are, moreover, in no way comparable with the gross congenital malformations observed in some human cases of retrolental fibroplasia associated with mental defect.

Although the danger of *chronic lead poisoning* in children is well appreciated, cases are still being reported (Gibb and MacMahon, 1955; White and Fowler, 1960; Berg and Zappella, 1964). Forty-six cases of chronic lead poisoning in children were studied in Chicago by Jenkins and Mellins (1957). All presented pica and came from very poor homes. Of the surviving 33 children in that series 27 were mentally retarded, and it was thought that in 20 of these the retardation was directly traceable to lead poisoning. Improved methods have made the estimation of lead in the blood easier and more reliable.* Moncrieff *et al.* (1964) believe that the upper limit of normal blood lead should be regarded as $36\mu g/100$ ml. blood. On that basis they found the level of blood lead abnormally high in 45 per cent of 122 mentally retarded children referred for investigation to Great Ormond Street Hospital. Griggs (1964) found in a house to house survey of 906 children in Cleveland, Ohio, that 27 per cent of those living in old houses but only 3 per cent of similar socio-economic background in a new housing estate had raised urinary lead and coproporphyrin levels. Thirty-eight children in the old houses had clinical evidence of lead poisoning. Flaking lead paint inside the old homes was the most frequent cause of poisoning. The social and public health aspects of the problem have been discussed by Boucher (1965). The experience at the Fountain Hospital, as elsewhere, is that pica may lead to signs of chronic lead poisoning in previously retarded children, and may aggravate an existing mental defect. That lead poisoning must be prevented is obvious, and its early recognition is also important because more effective treatment is now possible with one of the chelating agents, e.g. calcium disodium ethylenediamine tetra-acetic acid—(E.D.T.A.) or D-penicillamine. The prognosis in cases showing evidence of lead encephalopathy remains often rather poor despite treatment.

The pathological and neuropathological findings in cases of acute and chronic lead poisoning, mainly adults, have been reported repeatedly, but as the methods employed were not standardized and the condition was also often complicated by associated and incidental disease, no specially characteristic pathological picture has so far emerged (Meyer, 1963). A relatively frequent and striking change has been the occurrence of eosinophilic intranuclear inclusions in some hepatic and renal cells. In adults, there is frequent peripheral neuropathy with myelin breakdown around many of the nerve fibres. Changes in the central nervous system included various forms of neuronal degeneration and glial proliferation. Vascular changes, such as thrombosis and mural thickening have also been mentioned and are particularly emphasized in a description of six cases of infants and young children by Popoff, Weinberg and Feigin (1963).

Miscellaneous Causes

It would be impossible to mention here all conditions or circumstances occasionally followed by mental retardation. Many must be omitted while others are discussed elsewhere in the book.

Although *head injury* is frequently mentioned as a cause of retardation, it is often difficult to ascertain its true significance. Undue emphasis may be placed on it by parents in an attempt to relieve a feeling of helplessness and responsibility. The difficulty of establishing normality of preceding development in

* The technical problems of estimating lead in the blood and urine are considered on pp. 369–371.

such cases has already been indicated (p. 67). Head injury appears to be only rarely a cause of severe subnormality, but may be more important in the causation of milder intellectual impairment and behaviour disturbances (Berg, 1960). Psychotic states following head injury in children have been described by Selley (1958). In a series of 1,283 cases of cerebral palsy studied by Swinyard, Swensen and Greenspan (1963), 143 (11 per cent) were 'acquired' and of these 17 per cent were thought to have been due to head injury. Other workers have examined this problem prospectively. Thus, for example, of 150 children treated for head injury of varying severity at Edinburgh hospitals 26 developed post-traumatic epilepsy. Thirteen per cent of all cases had 'psychological changes' which persisted in half of these (Harris, 1957). Unhappily, it is also necessary to note the increasing responsibility of car accidents for head injuries and their sequelae. Thus fourteen cases were so caused in the series of Swinyard, Swenson and Greenspan, and ten in a series of 35 cases of acquired cerebral palsy (d'Avignon, 1963). According to Lewin (1965) brain damage in severe head injuries is usually diffuse and affects primarily the white matter. Vascular lesions also occur and may be primary or secondary to cerebral compression caused by blood-clot or oedema. Electrolyte disturbance, anoxia due to obstruction of the airways and cerebral oedema may also produce irreversible changes unless treatment is prompt and effective. A detailed account of the biochemical aspects of head injuries has been given by Matthews (1965). Subdural haematoma in infancy, not necessarily preceded by observed injury—at birth or post-natally, is another cause of cerebral palsy and mental retardation (Russell, 1965).

Vascular factors, the major cause of encephalopathy in adults, are relatively rarely pathogenetic in infants and children. In the already mentioned series of 143 'acquired' cases of cerebral palsy (Swinyard, Swensen and Greenspan) 11 per cent were attributed to cerebro-vascular causes. Many such cases are associated with vascular malformations, such as congenital aneurysms—cirsoid, arteriovenous and capillary (Fig. 17 and 18), and with venous angiomata (Rosner, 1955; Bailey and Woodard, 1959). Gold, Ransohoff and Carter (1965) emphasize particularly the relative frequency of arteriovenous malformation of the vein of Galen. The malformed vessels may bleed, compress or lacerate the neighbouring areas of the brain. Calcification may occur in the vessels and/or surrounding tissue. In other cases arterial thrombosis may take place together with or independently of the vascular malformations, and arteriography may then be diagnostically useful (Byers and McLean, 1962). Arterial obstruction or vascular malformation could be demonstrated before death in most of the 12 cases of childhood hemiplegia with aphasia described by them. However, a word of caution is perhaps indicated since it may not be realised that arteries supplying atrophic parts of the brain are usually narrowed irrespective of the initial cause of the atrophy.

Embolism is another cause of sudden encephalopathy in infancy and childhood. As already mentioned, it is one of the complications of congenital cyanotic heart disease (p. 66). Suddenly developing obstruction of one of the larger cerebral arteries has been described by a number of authors (Stevens, 1959;

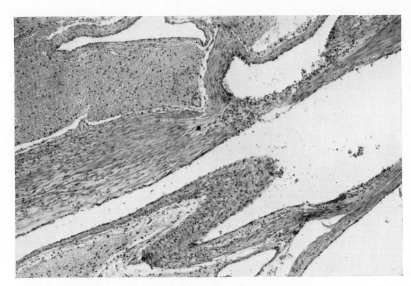

FIG. 17. An arteriovenous malformation embedded deep in the substance of the brain. (Haematoxylin and eosin × 65).

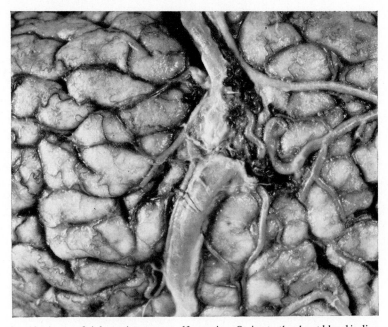

FIG. 18. A superficial arteriovenous malformation. Owing to the shunt blood is diverted from the arteries directly to veins, by-passing the capillaries. The blood pressure in the veins is thereby raised to well above normal, and as a result the veins distend and tend to leak or rupture.

Wisoff and Rothboller, 1961; Fowler, 1962). Venous thrombosis (Fig. 19), particularly if spreading from the dural sinuses, is another cause of residual paralysis and mental retardation (Dekaban and Norman, 1958).

Some of the vascular malformations constitute classifiable syndromes. The best known of these is the *Sturge-Weber syndrome* (encephalo-facial angiomatosis) (p. 192) and so-called 'ataxia telangiectasia', or Louis-Bar syndrome (p. 326).

Anoxic encephalopathy has been referred to already in relation to the possible complications of whooping cough (p. 67). Severe encephalopathy,

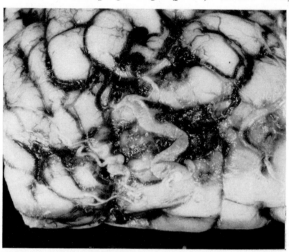

FIG. 19. Some of the veins are bloodless and a few of these are dilated. Others are thin and cord-like. The result of old venous thrombosis which had probably spread from the superior longitudinal sinus.

probably also of anoxic origin, may sometimes complicate bronchopneumonia, as in the cases following scarlet fever reported by Máttyus (1958). One of the newer 'man-made hazards' comes from operations under hypothermia and with cardiopulmonary bypass often performed for congenital heart disease. Cerebral complications, including residual mental defect, have been reported after some of these operations, particularly those complicated by cardiac arrest (*Brit. med. J.*, 1962). An additional risk seems to be incurred if the head of the operating table is tilted up, although this has so far only been observed in operations on adults (Brierley—personal communication).

An interesting and potentially very important observation was recently reported by Schneck and Neubuerger (1962), who described marked deficiency of the cerebellar Purkinje cells and focal pallor of the cerebral cortex in infants dying with *pulmonary hyaline membrane disease*. Since many infants recover from this condition, some of the encephalopathies following neonatal asphyxia may prove to be of similar origin.

Some interest has been shown lately in the encephalopathies complicating *burns in children* which may be associated with severe mental retardation

(Ule and Doose, 1960; *Brit. med. J.*, 1963). The pathogenesis of these encephalo-pathies is debatable but unlikely to be uniform, since the cerebral changes proved to be diverse in the cases examined pathologically.

Some evidence of mental retardation might be expected in children suffer-ing from *cerebral tumour*, but most of these cases are rapidly fatal and the de-tailed clinical picture is usually overshadowed by the more severe manifesta-tions of the condition. However, retardation may be one of the main present-ing signs of the more slowly growing tumours, while in other instances of mental deficiency brain tumours may present additional diagnostic and therapeutic problems (Wolman and Illingworth, 1962). Cases of tuberous sclerosis are sometimes complicated by a malignant transformation of one of the gliotic nodules—usually periventricular, while neoplasms are, by defini-tion, a regular feature of central neurofibromatosis (Crome, 1962).

Psychological Factors

In order to complete the enumeration of the causes of mental retardation we are now compelled to refer reluctantly to the difficult and controversial issue of psychological causes and mental illness. Although forced to grasp this nettle, we can hope to do no more than outline the main dimensions of the problem and direct readers to key sources in the literature.

Protophrenia

The important question in the present context is the extent to which psycho-logical stress can by itself overcome the natural resilience of the human brain so as to produce severe and permanent subnormality. From this standpoint Bourne (1955) studied 155 admissions to the Fountain Hospital. Of these, 138 showed signs of discernible cerebral disease and sixteen—the 'residual' group—did not. A number of possible psychogenic factors in the histories of the above two groups were compared, and it was found that their frequency was significantly greater in the residual group. Thereupon Bourne suggested that such 'residual' cases were instances of a distinct psychogenically induced condition of mental dwarfism—*protophrenia*. This he also defined in terms of psychodynamics as "psychogenic failure of ego formation" and contrasted it with schizophrenia which is characterized by some degree of ego disintegra-tion. Some of Bourne's cases have subsequently died and come to autopsy. One of their brains showed, as anticipated, no change detectable by present methods, but others were abnormal.

The cases studied by Bourne were of low intelligence. He deliberately ex-cluded those with an I.Q. over 50. Psychological stress may be a relatively more important factor in persons of higher intelligence—the feebleminded and the educationally subnormal (*vide infra*).

Schizophrenia

Most psychiatrists would probably tend to regard cases resembling Bourne's 'residual' ones as possible instances of *infantile schizophrenia*. The cause or causes of schizophrenia are unknown but adverse psychological stress is sometimes regarded as a contributory or precipitating factor. The condition usually sets in during the second and third decades of life but occasional rare cases may be present in childhood. Should it commence in infancy, the clinical picture may closely approximate that of severe subnormality or be, indeed, indistinguishable from it. Such early examples of presumed infantile schizophrenia have been also designated as *Heller's dementia*, *dementia praecoccissima* and *infantile autism*.

In adults, schizophrenic states may be a manifestation of an organic brain disease, such as cerebral tumour or syphilis. In an infant such an underlying organic condition may be difficult to recognise, but it is interesting to note that two of the 100 cases of childhood psychosis reviewed by Creak (1963) were subsequently found to be instances of neurolipidosis and that twelve were epileptics. An abnormality of tryptophan metabolism has been detected in some of these children by Heeley and Roberts (1966). Disturbed behaviour can be also caused by deafness or blindness. It is obvious therefore that before accepting the diagnosis of infantile schizophrenia all available clinical and laboratory methods of identifying organic or metabolic disease must be exhausted. Schizophrenia in childhood is certainly a mixed group. Taft and Goldfarb (1964) have shown, for example, that schizophrenic children show a higher incidence of possibly pathogenetic factors in their prenatal and paranatal histories compared with normal controls. This is in agreement with the views of Knobloch and Pasamanick (1963), who state that in none of their series of 67 possibly 'autistic' cases could organic disease be excluded. There is also no doubt that further advance of knowledge will bring to light other metabolic and organic diseases giving rise to this syndrome. A possible mechanism of cerebral dysfunction in schizophrenia is mentioned on p. 91.

The difficulties involved in the diagnosis of infantile schizophrenia have been considered by a special working party which began to meet under the chairmanship of Mildred Creak (Working Party, 1962 and 1964). As a result, nine criteria for diagnosing infantile schizophrenia have been formulated and widely discussed. In a study of Hermelin and O'Connor (1963) the following features were found to be particularly characteristic in the severely subnormal children showing psychotic features: 1. poverty of verbal responses, 2. alternating approach—retreat behaviour in response to social stimuli, and 3. mannerisms, i.e. spontaneous behaviour not apparently related to external stimuli. The above points overlap to some extent with the formulations of the Working Party.

While there is thus still much to be learned about infantile schizophrenia, it is unlikely that its numerical contribution to mental defect is substantial. In England and Wales only 50 children under 10 years were, for example, admitted to mental hospitals during 1958, but others have undoubtedly remained at home or found their way to mental deficiency hospitals or paediatric centres. Looking at the problem in another way, some 10 per cent of the severely retarded children show psychotic features but only a minority of these conform to the picture of infantile schizophrenia.

Psychological Factors as a Contributory Cause of Retardation

There is thus no conclusive evidence that psychological factors themselves can produce severe and permanent mental subnormality. They can, however, aggravate or in favourable circumstances mitigate the effects of an existing defect. Emotional stress, neglect, cruelty, institutionalization, deficient or incompetent mothering, sensory deprivation and poverty of mental stimulation can all interfere with intellectual development and prevent a child from realizing his full potential. It is difficult to measure these environmental factors and to assess them objectively, but it is clear that many are likely to arise and operate more frequently on a background of general social adversity. They are exceedingly difficult to isolate for an assessment of pathogenicity. The importance of the environment is apparent when children are adopted. The quality of the adoptive home and intelligence of the adoptive parents are found to be significant factors in determining the mental level of the children. Intelligence is therefore no longer regarded by some psychologists as an overwhelmingly hereditary quality although the relative contribution of heredity and environment has not yet been fully worked out. It follows that intellectual development cannot be viewed in isolation from emotional relationships with members of the family and with other children and adults. A general survey of this field is outside our scope, but it is appropriate in a book on the pathology of mental defect to mention the following anatomical facts which appear to be relevant particularly to problems of early mental development.

Compared with other species and with human adults the cerebral cortex of a newborn infant is very immature. Only a very small part of it is connected with other areas of the cortex and the subcortical formations by myelinated fibre tracts. No myelination whatever is present, for example, in the frontal lobe anterior to the precentral gyrus. The cortical neurones are everywhere small, poorly differentiated and contain relatively little cytoplasm or cytoplasmic ribonucleic acid, which is now believed to serve as substrate for the storage of memory traces. The substance separating neurones from each other —neuropil, which is formed mainly by neuronal and neuroglial processes, is also very incompletely developed. It thus seems highly improbable that complex mental experiences and organized situations could be registered and stored by an infant's brain in anything like full measure. This would apply particularly to the rather sophisticated conflict situations triggering off mechanisms of repression. These are sometimes postulated as a cause of later mental development and misdevelopment. Some of the extrapolations from adults to infants, particularly by the Kleinian school of psychoanalysts, seem therefore entirely unfounded.*

The position may be quite different in later infancy and childhood, and much has been written, for example, about maternal deprivation (Bowlby, 1951; 1953; and 1961), a concept criticized by some workers (O'Connor, 1956; de Wit, 1964) and elaborated by many others (Foss, 1961 and 1963). The possi-

* The controversial views on the cerebral function of the newborn have been recently reviewed by Robinson, R. (1966). *Develop. Med. Child. Neurol.*, **8**, 561.

bility that an already present defect may be aggravated by psychological causes has been mentioned already. Thus in a group of cerebrally abnormal children with limited cognitive development studied by Woodward (1960) disturbed social responses evident at a later age were found to be significantly related to adverse early development. Moreover, the provision of a more propitious emotional and psychological climate for some of the severely subnormal can certainly result in a distinct improvement in their behaviour and attainments. This has been demonstrated, for example, by the work of Tizard and his colleagues (Tizard, 1960; Lyle, 1959 and 1960; Tizard, 1964). Cases of emotional upset causing temporary or 'pseudo' feeblemindedness have also been observed (Clarke and Clarke, 1958).

Mental defect may, of course, be associated with other forms of mental illness, such as psychosis, neurosis, psychopathy and delinquency (Penrose, 1963; Kirman, 1965) but there is no suggestion that in most of these cases the defect is produced by these abnormalities. Disturbed behaviour simulating psychotic features may be especially common in certain conditions, such as tuberous sclerosis, phenylketonuria or lead poisoning.

GENERAL CONSIDERATIONS

Many causes of mental retardation have been identified and a number have been mentioned in the earlier chapters. Other causes will, no doubt, be added in time to the already formidable list, and more will be learned about the precise chemical mechanisms responsible for neural dysfunction and impairment of mental development. No single cause seems to account for a very large proportion of cases, but many causes share pathogenetic mechanisms, triggering off at some phase of their action a 'common abnormal pathogenetic pathway'. Examples are chromosomal non-disjunction, a change in the structure of the nucleic acids (mutation), obstruction in some part of the C.S.F. pathway leading to hydrocephalus, and other types of malformation or lesions in acquired disease. In addition, certain indirectly-acting factors, e.g. maternal age, prematurity and time of gestation, favour the operation of concrete causes. The action of these factors is usually expressed in epidemiological terms, sometimes as only a very slight rise in the incidence of certain conditions, yet however minor statistically, the result may be disastrous to the affected individual and his family.

The part played by genetic factors, on the one hand, and environmental ones, on the other, has been a hotly, and, at times, acrimoniously, debated issue. Overlapping and excessive claims staked out by both the 'geneticists' and the 'environmentalists' have covered and hidden much of the ground. New knowledge, gained particularly in recent years, has brought greater order and clarity. The elucidation of the rôle of the nucleic acids as the carriers of hereditary information has to some extent obviated the need to operate with hypothetical genetic mechanisms. The discovery of chromosomal anomalies in man has likewise made the understanding of pathogenesis more concrete. At the same time, improved chemical methods have added greater precision to clinical observation, and it has become possible to discuss aetiology in terms of a much larger number of specific conditions. On the other hand, experimental work in animals, particularly during pregnancy (p. 27), as well as human epidemiological studies, have clearly demonstrated the rôle of the environment in many other conditions. General progress has thus been away from generalities towards greater precision.

Heredity or Environment

One of the fallacies has been that of posing the question of either heredity or environment. Taken by themselves, these concepts are mere abstractions. In reality they are inseparable; one is meaningless without the other. Dynamic interaction between the individual or its precursor cells with the environment is the very essence of life. It continues as long as life is maintained. The character of the process, and with it both the individual and his environment, change throughout ontogenesis. In the sex cells and their precursors environmental influences are mediated chiefly by the metabolic and humoral pathways of the ancestors, evidently acting, if radical genetic change occurs, chiefly upon nucleic acids. During gestation, environmental influences are funnelled by the maternal organisms and placenta towards the rapidly growing embryo and foetus. In post-natal life, there is more direct contact with the biological, social and physical agents of the outside world. In some cases, decisive change is brought about by heredity, in others, by the environment; usually perhaps, it is the result of both sets of factors. Causation is thus to be sought neither in heredity nor in the environment, but in their interaction. The manifestations of diseases, even if irrevocably determined by inheritance, are still influenced by the environment. This is always worth stressing, because environmental factors are often modifiable, while the directed production or prevention of a specific mutation is still a distant goal.

It is customary to speak of causes as if they were in themselves sufficient to produce a particular effect, but disease is a complex biological and social phenomenon, and a historical perspective must also be recognized in pathology. Some causes can be decisive in determining disease in individuals with a certain historical background. Others make only a partial contribution towards the end-result by their action at different stages of ontogenesis; their effect is cumulative. The foetus of a diabetic mother, for example, is often large and tends to be delivered with greater difficulty. It is therefore more liable to sustain injury at birth and the newborn infant may also suffer from hypoglycaemia induced by his hyperplastic islets of Langerhans. These events can leave him with lesions in the brain which may be later activated by other still unknown factors to become epileptogenic. Rhesus incompatibility is another example. By operation of the laws of heredity, if the father is Rhesus positive, the infants of a Rhesus negative mother may also be Rhesus positive. Maternal agglutinins may later reach the foetal circulation and haemolysis set in. This, if inadequately treated, may be followed by deafness and permanent neural damage, but the degree of mental defect in these cases will be also modified by educational, domestic and other social factors.

The exciting recent discoveries in chemistry, biophysics and genetics amount perhaps to a revolution in pathology. The rigid distinction between inherited and acquired disease has lost much of its former meaning. Although the final outcome may be vastly different, fundamentally similar causes operate at all stages of ontogenesis. Ionizing irradiation may, for example, induce mutation in germ cells or their precursors to cause, say, phenylketonuria or tuberous sclerosis in the offspring; acting upon the embryo *in utero* it is responsible for micrencephaly, while in the adult it may lead to anaemia, sterility or cancer. Chromosomal abnormality may be associated with Down's disease if it arises in the germ cells or early zygote, and with some forms of leukaemia if it arises in the adult. Similar differences depending on the time of action apply to viruses and poisons, and, probably, many other factors. Some of these diverse causes may have common laws of operation, and one result of the radical change in outlook is that investigations which can be undertaken at only one phase of ontogenesis may also illuminate processes at other, more inaccessible, phases. Another result is that all causes of disease, including the genetic and intrauterine ones, have been shown to be fully knowable and thus, in principle, preventable.

Preventive action is to some extent possible now. The amount of man-made ionizing irradiation need not go on increasing, drugs can be used more prudently during pregnancy, malnutrition can be overcome and a more rational attitude taken to artificial termination of pregnancy. Further, the recent survey of perinatal mortality (Butler and Bonham, 1963) has shown that many of the dangers associated with pregnancy and childbirth can be circumvented by the provision of proper antenatal care and the conduct of confinements in hospitals rather than private homes and general practitioner units. These are but a few of the more obvious implications of the new knowledge. Other practical measures designed to eliminate some of the postnatal causes of mental retardation are more conventional and many of these have been in routine use by public health bodies for some time past.

Gross and Molecular Changes in the Brain

Whatever the initiating cause or causes, the important problem from the viewpoint of mental function is the way structural or chemical changes affect the functioning of neural tissue and of the brain as a whole. Effective prevention and treatment may well depend on answering this question correctly. Similar considerations extend, of course, to much wider fields of adult psychiatry and neurology, for example, the endocrine disorders, vitamin deficiencies, intoxications, neuroses and psychoses. The problems are clearly very complex, but it may be appropriate here to discuss a few of their simpler aspects.

Many of the brains of the mentally retarded individuals are grossly malformed or irreversibly damaged. The obvious and most economical interpretation of mental subnormality in such circumstances is simple qualitative and quantitative inadequacy of the central organ, although this need not necessarily be a full explanation.

P.M.R.—4

In the case of the metabolic disorders there is little apparent difficulty in explaining mental impairment where the brain is obviously damaged at or soon after birth by the abnormal metabolites. Anticipating the account of morphological changes in mental retardation (p. 96 *et seq.*) one may say that the brains of all cases of metabolic abnormality associated with mental subnormality examined so far presented marked structural changes, such as failure of development, malformation or evidence of progressive degeneration (Crome, 1964). It is true that the brains thus examined have been mainly of severe cases, and it may well be that milder instances of similar conditions would not reveal any lesions by the present, rather crude, methods. Even so, future refinements of techniques will no doubt bring to light other and subtler changes. However that may be, the nature of the primary toxic factors remains elusive. Even in the case of phenylketonuria, one of the most-studied of these conditions, the identity of the offending substance is still uncertain (Kleinman, 1964). It is probably not phenylalanine itself, of which there is an excess in the blood, since no correlation between its level and the degree of mental disability has been demonstrated. Rats made phenylketonuric by parenteral administration of phenylalanine show no evidence of 'mental deterioration' on assessment by maze tests (Perez, 1965) although 'oligophrenia' had been observed in experimental phenylketonuric monkeys by Waisman and Harlow (1965). Competitive inhibition of certain enzymes is probably responsible for the neural dysfunction in galactosaemia. It has been shown, for example, that galactose-1-phosphate, an excess of which is present in the tissues of galactosaemic patients, can inhibit such enzymes as phosphoglucomutase and glucose-6-phosphate dehydrogenase. One may, perhaps, also assume that in other conditions belonging to this group neural tissue is irreversibly damaged by the same chemical imbalance which interferes with its function.

In another and more numerous group, which may also be caused by metabolic errors, no consistent chemical deviations from the norm have yet been demonstrated. This group includes such well known entities as Down's disease, tuberous sclerosis, neurofibromatosis, and a number of the system atrophies. As already mentioned, it is possible that the chemical defect is largely time-limited in such cases, acting mainly at certain phases of ontogenesis and remaining quiescent thereafter. At the time of its operation, the defect impedes development; the brain remains abnormal and the result is permanent neural or mental dysfunction, without any specific continuing biochemical abnormality. A similar time-limited mechanism may operate also in the case of other chromosome anomalies.

Occupying the other extreme of the pathological range are conditions in which full recovery is the rule or is, at any rate, possible. These include temporary intoxications by drugs, hypoglycaemia, the toxaemias of infection and some of the neuroses and psychoses. It seems reasonable to assume that the neural changes in these states are reversible, or, in other words, that such neural dysfunction is due only to temporary molecular changes. (One cannot be sure of this, since the immense compensatory power of the nervous system for lost cells should not be underestimated.) Schizophrenic states must also be considered in this context since full recovery is sometimes possible, and it must therefore be assumed that the brain is not irreversibly damaged in such cases. Pavlov had, in fact, suggested that schizophrenia was caused by a state of cerebral inhibition (as understood by him), akin in its nature to sleep but more inert and involving, unlike sleep, fewer of the subcortical areas. On this assumption one would not expect the molecular changes in schizophrenia to differ greatly from those in sleep. However, the clinical features of schizophrenia may be also the result of organic brain disease, and in such cases it is postulated that inhibition is irradiated from the structurally damaged tissues to other extensive cerebral areas. It remains, of course, necessary to demonstrate the chemical basis for all forms of inhibition, including those in 'true' schizophrenia and the schizophrenic organic syndromes.

The occurrence of such combinations of gross and molecular changes, i.e. of the irreversible and reversible changes, may have analogues in the field of mental retardation. To be sure, the incidence of psychosis in general and of schizophrenia in particular, is low in infancy and childhood. But what is entirely possible, is that in many cases of organic brain disease damaged tissues project dysfunction well beyond their confines in some such way as inert irradiated inhibition. And this may be also true of the reverse process— irradiated excitation, which might be expected to result in epilepsy.

REFERENCES

ALCOCK, N. S., and HOFFMAN, H. L. (1962). *Arch. Dis. Childh.*, **37**, 40.
ANDERSON, J. M., MILNER, R. D. G., and STRICH, S. J. (1966). *Lancet*, **2**, 372.
ASHTON, N. (1954). *Brit. J. Ophthal.*, **38**, 385.
ASHTON, N., WARD, B., and SERPELL, G. (1954). *Brit. J. Ophthal.*, **38**, 397.
ASTERIADOU-SAMARTZIS, E., and LEIKIN, S. (1958). *Pediatrics*, **21**, 397.
D'AVIGNON, M. (1963). *Develop. Med. Child Neurol.*, **5**, 626.
BAILEY, O. T., and WOODARD, J. S. (1959). *J. Neuropath. exp. Neurol.*, **18**, 98.
BERG, J. M. (1958). *Brit. med. J.*, **2**, 24.
BERG, J. M. (1960). *Arch. Pediat.*, **77**, 207.
BERG, J. M. (1961). *Wld. Neurol.*, **2**, 56.
BERG, J. M. (1962). In 'Proc. London Conf. on the Sci. Study of Mental Deficiency, 1960, London: May and Baker, p. 160.
BERG, J. M., and ZAPPELLA, M. (1964). *J. ment. Defic. Res.*, **8**, 44.
BOREAU, TH., MARTIN, L., LARROCHE, J. -C., and SAUTRIOT, G. (1964). *Gynéc. et Obstét.*, **63**, 289.
BOUCHER, C. A. (1965). *Mth. Bull. Minist. Hlth. Lab. Serv.*, **24**, 48.
BOURNE, H. (1955). *Lancet*, **2**, 1156.
BOURNE, H. (1956). *Amer. J. ment. Defic.*, **61**, 198.
BOWLBY, J. (1951). Wrld. Hlth. Org. Monogr. Ser. No. 2.
BOWLBY, J. (1953). 'Child Care and Growth of Love,' Penguin Books, London.
BOWLBY, J. (1961). In Foss, B. M. 'The Determinants of Infant Behaviour,' London: Churchill, p. 301.
BRITISH MEDICAL JOURNAL. (1955). Annotation, **2**, 110.
BRITISH MEDICAL JOURNAL. (1962). Annotation, **2**, 1523.
BRITISH MEDICAL JOURNAL, (1963). Annotation, **2**, 1350.
BROWN, A. K. (1962). *Pediat. Clin. N. Amer.*, **9**, No. 3, p. 575.
BROWN, R. J. K., and WALLIS, P. G. (1963). *Lancet*, **1**, 1278; **2**, 147.
BRUNJES, J., HODGMAN, J., NOWACK, J., and JOHNS, V. J. (1963). *Amer. J. Med.*, **34**, 168.
BUTLER, N. R., and BONHAM, D. G. (1963). 'Perinatal Mortality.' Edinburgh: Livingstone.

BYERS, R. K., and MCLEAN, W. T. (1962). *Pediatrics*, **29**, 376.
CABAK, V., and NAJDANVIC, R. (1965). *Arch. Dis. Childh.*, **40**, 532.
CALVERT, R. J., HURWORTH, E., and MACBEAN, A. L. (1958). *Blood*, **13**, 894.
CAMPBELL, M. (1957). *Lancet*, **1**, 111.
CARTER, C. H. (1965). In 'Medical Aspects of Mental Retardation,' Springfield: C. L. Thomas.
CHANARIN, I., LAIDLOW, J., LOUGHBRIDGE, L. W., and MOLLIN, D. L. (1960). *Brit. med. J.*, **1**, 1099.
CHANCE, G. W. and BOWER, B. D. (1966). *Arch. Dis. Childh.*, **41**, 279.
CHAUDHRY, M. R. (1959). Thesis, University of Punjab.
CHAUDHRY, M. R., and POND, D. A. (1961). *J. Neurol. Neurosurg. Psychiat.*, **24**, 213.
CHEN, H. C. (1964). *J. Neuropath. exp. Neurol.*, **23**, 527.
CHEN H., LIEN, J.-N., and LU, T.-C. (1965). *Amer. J. Path.*, **46**, 331.
CLARKE, A. M., and CLARKE, A. D. B. (1958). In 'Mental Deficiency. The Changing Outlook,' London: Methuen, p. 115.
CLARKE, C. A., FINN, R., MCCONNELL, R. B., WOODROW, J. C., LEHANE, D., and SHEPPARD, P. M. (1964). *Brit. med. J.*, **1**, 1110.
COOPER, J. E. (1965). *Brit. med. J.*, **1**, 1020.
CORNBLATH, M. (1965). *Lancet*, **1**, 524.
CRAVIOTO, J., DELICARDIE, E. R., and BIRCH, H. C. (1966). *Pediatrics*, **38**, 319.
CREAK, E. M. (1961). Working Party. *Develop. Med. Child Neurol.*, **3**, 501.
CREAK, E. M. (1963). *Brit. J. Psychiat.*, **109**, 84.
CREAK, E. M. (1964). Working Party. *Develop. Med. Child Neurol.*, **4**, 530.
CROME, L. (1952). *Arch. Dis. Childh.*, **27**, 468.
CROME, L. (1955). *J. Neurol. Neurosurg. Psychiat.*, **18**, 17.
CROME, L. (1958). *J. Path. Bact.*, **75**, 163.
CROME, L. (1962). *Arch. Dis. Childh.*, **37**, 640.
CROME, L. (1964). In Holt, K. S., and Milner, J., 'Neurometabolic Disorders in Childhood,' Edinburgh: Livingstone, p. 31.
CROME, L., KIRMAN, B. H., and MARRS, M. (1955). *Brain*, **78**, 514.
CROME, L., and SYLVESTER, P. E. (1960). *Arch. Dis. Childh.*, **35**, 620.
CROSSE, V. M., MEYER, T. C., and GERRARD, J. W. (1955). *Arch. Dis. Childh.*, **30**, 501.
DAVIS, R. A., and WOLF, A. (1958). *Pediatrics*, **21**, 409.
DEKABAN, A. S., and NORMAN, R. M. (1958). *J. Neuropath.*, **17**, 461.
DEWIT, J. (1964). *Acta paedopsychiat.*, **31**, 240.
DOXIADIS, S. A., and VALAES, T. (1964). *Arch. Dis. Childh.*, **39**, 545.
DUNN, P. M. (1963). *Arch. Dis. Childh.*, **38**, 596.
ERNSTER, L., HERLIN, L., and ZETTERSTRÖM, R. (1957). *Pediatrics*, **20**, 647.
FALCONER, M. A., SERAFETINIDES, E. A., and CORSELLIS, J. A. N. (1964). *Arch. Neurol. (Chic.)*, **10**, 233.
FALK, R., PENROSE, L. S., and CLARK, E. A. (1945). *Amer. J. ment. Defic.*, **49**, 469.
FISCH, L., and OSBORN, D. A. (1954). *Arch. Dis. Childh.*, **29**, 309.
FISCH, L., and NORMAN, A. P. (1961). *Brit. med. J.*, **2**, 142.
FORD, F. R. (1966). 'Diseases of the Nervous System in Infancy, Childhood and Adolescence,' Oxford: Blackwell.
FOSS, B. M. (1961). Determinants of Infant Behaviour. Proc. of a Tavistock Study Group of Mother-Infant Interaction, September, 1959. London: Methuen.
FOSS, B. M. (1963). Determinants of Infant Behaviour II. Proc. of the 2nd Tavistock Seminar on Mother-Infant Interaction, September, 1961, London: Methuen.
FOWLER, M. (1957). *Arch. Dis. Childh.*, **32**, 67.
FOWLER, M. (1962). *Arch. Dis. Childh.*, **37**, 78.
GARTY, R., YONIS, Z., BRAHAM, J., and STEINITZ, K. (1962). *Arch. Dis. Childh.*, **37**, 21.
GAUTIER-SMITH, P. C. (1965). In Cumings, J. N., and Kremer, M. 'Biochemical Aspects of Neurological Disorders,' Oxford: Blackwell, p. 159.
GERVER, J. M., and DAY, R. (1950). *J. Pediat.*, **36**, 342.
GIBB, J. W. G., and MACMAHON, J. F. (1955). *Brit. med. J.*, **1**, 320.
GILES, H. MC. (1965). *Lancet*, **1**, 1075.
GOLD, A. P., RANSOHOFF, J., and CARTER, S. (1964). *Acta neurol. scand.*, suppl. 11, **40**, 1.
GRIGGS, R. C. (1964). *J. Amer. med. Ass.*, **187**, 703.
GYLLENSTEN, L. (1959). *Acta. neerl. Morph.*, **2**, 289 and 311.

HAAS, L. (1963). *Develop. Med. Child Neurol.*, **5**, 517.

HARRIS, P. (1957). *Arch. Dis. Childh.*, **32**, 488.

HEELEY, A. F., and ROBERTS, G. E. (1966). *Develop. Med. Child Neurol.*, **8**, 708.

HERMELIN, B., and O'CONNOR, N. (1963). *Brit. J. soc. clin. Psychol.*, **2**, 37.

HEYCOCK, J. B., and NOBLE, T. C. (1964). *Brit. med. J.*, **1**, 658.

ILLINGWORTH, R. S. (1955). *Arch. Dis. Childh.*, **30**, 529.

IVANOVSKY, YU. S. (1965). *Pediatriya*, **44**, No. 3, p. 34.

JENKINS, C. D., and MELLINS, R. B. (1957). *Arch. Neurol. Psychiat. (Chic.)*, **77**, 70.

KIRMAN, B. H. (1965). In Hilliard and Kirman's 'Mental Deficiency,' London: Churchill, p. 396.

KLEINMAN, D. S. (1964). *Pediatrics*, **33**, 123.

KNOBLOCH, H., and PASAMANICK, B. (1963). Prelim. draft read at Xth Internat. Congr. of Pediatrics, Lisbon. (Personal communication.)

KOEGEL, R., and PAUNIER, L. (1962). *Helv. paediat. Acta*, **17**, 185.

KRAUSE, A. C. (1946). *Arch. Ophthal.*, **36**, 387.

LADODO, K. S., and LEBEDEV, B. V. (1963). In Klosovskii, B. N. 'The Development of the Brain and its Disturbances by Harmful Factors,' Oxford: Pergamon, p. 136.

LANCET (1965). Annotation, **1**, 1311.

LATHE, G. H., CLAIREAUX, A. E., and NORMAN, A. P. (1958). In Gairdner, D. 'Recent Advances in Paediatrics,' London: Churchill, p. 87.

LAWSON, D. N., METCALFE, M., and PAMPIGLIONE, G. (1965). *Brit. med. J.*, **1**, 557.

LEWIN, W. (1965). In Cumings, J. N., and Kremer, M. 'Biochemical Aspects of Neurological Disorders,' Oxford: Blackwell, p. 182.

LIMBECK, G. A., RUVALCABA, R. H. A., SAMOLS, E., and KELLEY, V. C. (1965). *Amer. J. Dis. Child.*, **109**, 165.

LÓRÁND, B., NAGY, T., and TARISKA, S. (1962). *Wld. Neurol.*, **3**, 376.

LYLE, J. G. (1959). *J. ment. Defic. Res.*, **3**, 122.

LYLE, J. G. (1960). *J. ment. Defic. Res.*, **4**, 1 and 14.

MACDONALD, A. M., and DAWSON, E. K. (1954). *Edinb. med. J.*, **61**, 297.

MARKS, V. (1965). In Cumings, J. N., and Kremer, M. 'Biochemical Aspects of Neurological Disorders,' Oxford: Blackwell, p. 169.

MATTHEWS, W. B., and RUNDLE, A. T. (1964). *Brain*, **87**, 463.

MATTHEWS, D. M. (1965). In Cumings, J. N., and Kremer, M. 'Biochemical Aspects of Neurological Disorders,' Oxford: Blackwell, p. 199.

MÁTTYUS, A. (1958). *Arch. Psychiat. Nervenkr.*, **196**, 443.

McKENDRICK, T. (1962). *Develop. Med. Child Neurol.*, **4**, 328.

MEYER, A. (1963). In Greenfield's 'Neuropathology,' London: Arnold, p. 267.

MILLER, H. G., STANTON, J. B., and GIBBONS, J. L. (1956). *Quart. J. Med.*, **25**, 427.

MONCRIEFF, A. A., KOUMIDES, O. P., CLAYTON, B. E., PATRICK, A. D., RENWICK, A. G. C., and ROBERTS, G. E. (1964). *Arch. Dis. Childh.*, **39**, 1.

MYANT, N. B. (1960). *Brit. med. Bull.*, **16**, 89.

NELIGAN, G. A. (1965). In Gairdner, D. 'Recent Advances in Paediatrics, 3rd. ed., Churchill: London, p. 110.

NYHAN, W. L., and RICHARDSON, F. (1963). *Annual Review of Medicine*, **14**, 263.

O'CONNOR, N. (1956). *Acta psychol. (Aust.)*, **12**, 174.

ODELL, G. B. (1959). *J. Pediat.*, **55**, 268.

PAMPIGLIONE, G., YOUNG, S. E. J., and RAMSEY, A. M. (1963). *Brit. med. J.*, **2**, 1300.

PEIFFER, J. (1963). 'Morphologische Aspekte der Epilepsien. Pathogenetische, pathologisch-anatomische und klinische Probleme der Epilepsien,' Berlin: Springer.

PENROSE, L. S. (1963). 'The Biology of Mental Defect,' London: Sidgwick and Jackson. p. 248.

PEREZ, V. J. (1965). *J. ment. Defic. Res.*, **9**, 170.

PLATT, B. S., PAMPIGLIONE, G., and STEWART, R. J. C. (1965). *Develop. Med. Child Neurol.*, **7**, 9.

POPOFF, N., WEINBERG, S., and FEIGIN, I. (1963). *Neurology (Minneap.)*, **13**, 101.

RENTSCH, M. (1964). *Praxis*, **53**, 2, 38, 161, 232, 270, 337.

ROSNER, S. (1955). *J. nerv. ment. Dis.*, **122**, 276.

ROSS, C. F., CROME, L., and MACKENZIE, D. Y. (1956). *J. Path. Bact.*, **72**, 161.

RUSSELL, P. A. (1965). *Brit. med. J.*, **2**, 446.

SAMOLS, E., and DORMANDY, T. L. (1963a). *Lancet*, **1**, 478.
SAMOLS, E., and DORMANDY, T. L. (1963b). *Lancet*, **1**, 1160.
SCHLESINGER, B., and WELCH, R. G. (1952). *Gt. Ormond St. J.*, **3-4**, 14.
SCHLESINGER, B. E., BUTLER, N. R., and BLACK, J. E. (1956). *Brit. med. J.*, **1**, 127.
SCHMID, R. (1966). In Stanbury, J. B., Wyngaarden, J. B., and Fredrickson, D. S. 'The Metabolic Basis of Inherited Disease,' New York: McGraw-Hill, p. 871.
SCHNECK, S. A., and NEUBUERGER, K. T. (1962). *Acta neuropath. (Berl.)*, **2**, 11.
SELLEY, J. (1958). *Acta psychiat. (Kbh.)*, **33**, 208.
SINCLAIR, L. (1962). *Develop. Med. Child Neurol.*, **4**, 620.
SMITH, H. V., NORMAN, R. M., and URICH, H. (1957). *J. Neurol Neurosurg. Psychiat.*, **20**, 250.
STEVENS, H. (1959). *Pediatrics*, **23**, 699.
STOCH, M. B., and SMYTHE, P. M. (1963). *Arch. Dis. Childh.*, **38**, 546.
SUTHERLAND, J. M., and KELLER, W. H. (1961). *Amer. J. Dis. Child*, **101**, 447.
SWINYARD, C. A., SWENSEN, J., and GREENSPAN, L. (1963). *Develop. Med. Child Neurol.*, **5**, 615.
TAFT, L. T., and GOLDFARB, W. (1964). *Develop. Med. Child Neurol.*, **6**, 32.
TIZARD, J. (1960). *Brit. med. J.*, **1**, 1041.
TIZARD, J. (1964). 'Community Services for the Mentally Handicapped,' London: Oxford University Press.
TODD, R. M., and NEVILLE, J. G. (1964). *Arch. Dis. Childh.*, **39**, 213.
TROTTER, W. R. (1960). *Brit. med. Bull.*, **16**, 92.
ULE, G., and DOOSE, H. (1960). *Arch. Kinderheilk.*, **161**, 155.
VEST, M. (1958). *Arch. Dis. Childh.*, **33**, 473.
WAISMAN, H. A., and HARLOW, H. F. (1965). *Science*, **147**, 685.
WHITE, H. H. and FOWLER, F. D. (1960). *Pediatrics*, **25**, 309.
WHITNALL, S. E., and NORMAN, R. M. (1940). *Brit. J. Ophthal.*, **24**, 229.
WILLIAMS, C. E. (1958). *Brit. J. Ophthal.*, **42**, 549.
WILSON, K. M., and CLAYTON, B. E. (1962). *Arch. Dis. Childh.*, **37**, 565.
WISOFF, H. S., and ROTHBOLLER, A. B. (1961). *Arch. Neurol. (Chic.)*, **4**, 258.
WOLF, A., and COWEN, D. (1959). *J. Neuropath. exp. Neurol.*, **18**, 191.
WOLMAN, L. (1962). *Brit. med. J.*, **2**, 775.
WOLMAN, L., and ILLINGWORTH, R. S. (1962). *J. ment. Defic. Res.*, **6**, 1.
WOODWARD, M. (1960). *Brit. med. J. Psychol.*, **33**, 123.

CHAPTER 5

PATHOLOGICAL ASPECTS: GENERAL

Sources of Information

MUCH of the morphological knowledge in the field of mental retardation has accumulated from case reports published because of their authors' interest not so much in the retardation itself as in some other aspect of the clinical and pathological picture. Intellectual impairment was often mentioned only in passing. Most subnormal individuals have attracted no such attention, and this is an important reason for the persistence of wide gaps in the neuropathology of subnormality. Few attempts have been made to investigate comprehensively unselected groups of mentally retarded persons, but some information is available in the accounts by Schob, 1930; Ashby and Stewart, 1932 and 1933; Berry, 1938; Christensen and Vestergaard, 1949; Benda, 1952; Minkowski, 1952; Jacob, 1956; and Gross and Kaltenbäck, 1959a. Other authors have studied similar material from a different but closely related standpoint, for example, that of cerebral palsy (Hallervorden and Meyer, 1956) or epilepsy (Scholz and Hager, 1956; Peiffer, 1963). The grosser examples of congenital malformations of the central nervous system have been described at great length in the classical German texts, e.g. that of Ostertag (1956).

Changes in the brains of patients investigated at the Fountain Hospital, most of whom were severely subnormal, have been studied by Crome (1954 and 1960). These and subsequent studies form the background of the present account. It seems useful to preface it with a comment on the application of anatomical methods to problems of mental retardation.

The importance of normal and pathological anatomy in general is beyond question. It has been recognized for centuries that physiology and anatomy constitute the twin pillars of modern medicine. The definition, identification and classification of diseases (nosology) is the first step in any scientific study in medicine, and this cannot be done without knowledge of structural changes. The character and distribution of the latter often determine the presenting signs and symptoms, and information on pathological changes is useful in searching for the causes of disease. Morphological study in the field of mental retardation has been restricted, however, by special difficulties.

In the first place, the structure of the central nervous system is more complex than that of any other organ. The shape and arrangement of neurones vary at different levels, and variability in normal brains can likewise be substantial. Moreover, marked changes take place during ontogenesis, both before and after birth, and these are by no means fully known. A morbid anatomist, who can only make certain of an abnormality by comparing the examined tissue with the normal, is therefore frequently handicapped, particularly in the case of infants and children.

In addition to the macroscopic examination of the brain and the weighing of some of its parts, a neuropathologist relies on histological techniques. Some of these, especially those designed to detect the more subtle changes, e.g. the silver impregnation methods, are difficult to standardize for human material. Neuropathological assessment tends therefore to be unduly subjective, and is often unreliable. The literature abounds with artefacts presented as lesions, the normal misinterpreted as abnormal, and instances of failure to recognize the changing appearances of normal development.* These shortcomings are not fully compensated for by the newer techniques, e.g. histochemistry, neurochemistry and electron microscopy, which remain somewhat esoteric and unreliable in the hands of all but whole-time specialists. It is true, of course, that much new knowledge has been won by these methods and many of the findings will be described below. Some of the newer methods can be usefully combined with older ones, and a few may possibly be simplified in the future for routine laboratory use. Basically however, the problem is one of manpower. There were never anything like enough specialists in the field, and though the ranks are fuller now, they are still much too thin to exploit fully the new openings.

As matters stand, the grosser abnormalities, such as micrencephaly or marked neuronal loss, are, if present, seldom in doubt, but the commoner and milder changes, demonstrable only by some of the more delicate methods, often remain uncertain. Moreover, most of the hitherto studied brains have been those of the severely subnormal. The considerably more numerous persons of relatively higher intelligence, viz. the feebleminded and the educationally subnormal, die much later in life and, often, outside special hospitals. The brains of most of these individuals are not investigated. The issue is further complicated by the development of acquired incidental lesions in their brains.

It may be supposed that the brains of many mildly retarded individuals would present fewer and less severe lesions than those of the severely subnormal. If so, the changes would be difficult to detect. For example, a reduction by as much as 20 per cent in the number of cortical neurones might be expected to depress intelligence appreciably, but it is by no means certain that a loss of that order would be histologically recognizable unless accompanied by other and more conspicuous changes. Counts can only be reliable if made in both test and control tissues, and this remains insurmountably difficult. The number of neurones in a field of the microscope depends on the age of the subject. Cortical neurones are small and lie close to each other in the newborn infant. They enlarge for some time during infancy and also become sparser on account of the development of the so-called 'neuropil', i.e. the neuronal and neuroglial processes which, together with capillaries, form the tissue between the cells. Thus, up to a certain age, which varies for the different areas and laminae of the cortex, development is towards increasing neuronal sparseness; excessive density is pathological. This form of pathological density occurs, for example, in hypothyroidism, a condition in which the

* Some morphological and chemical parameters of brain growth and maturation will be found in the Appendices, on pp. 377 *et seq.*

neuropil fails to develop fully (Eayrs, 1960 *vide infra*). On the other hand, pathological neuronal sparseness, caused by hypoplasia or atrophy, is more usual. Furthermore, in the mature brain neuronal density varies greatly in different areas and laminae of the cortex and one can never be certain that the studied tissue and controls are correctly matched. Another difficulty is that neurones may vanish at a different rate in the course of terminal illnesses, and, as mentioned already, allowance must also be made for normal variations.*

Quality as well as quantity must be considered. The post-natal enlargement of nerve cells results mainly from accumulation of cytoplasmic proteins and ribonucleic acid (Nissl substance); the nuclei remain relatively small. Hence, a pathologically 'immature' cell preserves a higher nucleus to cytoplasm ratio, but such immaturity is difficult to establish in a cellular population normally as pleomorphic as that of the cerebral cortex. Again, retardation in the development of the neuropil, as in hypothyroidism, suggests that pathological change may affect neuronal and glial processes rather than their cell bodies. It has been shown experimentally, for example, that lack of thyroid hormone impedes the development of neuropil (Eayrs, 1960). Similarly, Hicks, Cavanaugh and O'Brien (1962) were able to demonstrate that newborn rats and mice subjected to anoxia show subsequently retardation in the development of the neuropil and the production of ribonucleic acid without any apparent reduction in the number of neurones. However, the quest for such abnormalities in human material has scarcely begun.

It is not surprising therefore that the few attempts that have been made to determine quantitatively the cellular changes in the brains of mentally retarded individuals have yielded inconclusive and, in some respects, contradictory results (Bolton, 1914; Stewart, 1935; Norman, 1938).

Some cases of mental retardation fit into one of the recognized syndromes or diseases, such as Down's disease, phenylketonuria, residual kernicterus and tuberous sclerosis. Most cannot yet be so classified. It is therefore convenient to consider the two groups separately. The changes associated mainly with the unclassifiable group are discussed in this chapter and those with recognized diseases in the following ones. This does not mean that the character of the lesions is necessarily different. On the contrary, similar anomalies are often present in the brains of cases belonging to either group.

It is worth mentioning another, 'quantitative', aspect of pathology related to the lack of specificity of neural tissue reactions. The all-or-none principle seems not to apply to any of the neuropathological changes. Manifold lesions are often present in the same brain. If mild and small, a given lesion may contribute little to the pathological and clinical picture; it will tend to be overshadowed by the other changes. If more severe, constant or widespread, the same change will tend in its turn to dominate the disease profile (influencing incidentally the name chosen for the disease). It is then said to be characteristic of the condition. This principle seems to hold good for all the changes discussed below, such as micrencephaly, gliosis, leucodystrophy, cavitation, calcification and lipidosis. For example, some calcification is common (p. 134),

---

* Neuropathological techniques are discussed on pp. 371–374.

but in a few instances it becomes extensive. If its cause remains undetermined, the condition is regarded as a disease in its own right, and sometimes referred to as Fahr's disease. Similarly, scarring occurring together with cavitation is frequent, but when the cavitation is very extensive and dominates the picture, and if its cause is unknown, it can be referred to as encephalomalacia and treated as a disease *sui generis*. It is thus possible to consider each anomaly twice; firstly, in its diluted form and, secondly, in its extensive and dominant form, i.e. as a specific disease. However, to avoid repetition, some of the rarer syndromes will be mentioned only once—in this or the other chapters.

Micrencephaly

Smallness of the head—microcephaly, and of the brain—micrencephaly, are the commonest abnormalities in the severely subnormal. In a series of 117 brains examined at the Fountain Hospital up to 1952, 107 were abnormally small (Fig. 20). Other workers have measured the head size of mental de-

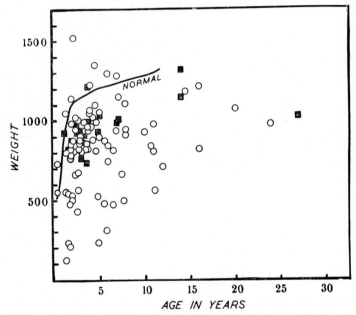

FIG. 20. Brain weights in grams of cases of Down's disease ■, and other mental defectives ○, compared with those of normal children.

fectives and correlated the results with mental age. They found that the head size decreased with intelligence and that the reduction was greatest in the 'idiot' range (Ashby and Stewart, 1932).

With small brains thus the rule, the term micrencephaly is understandably loose. Some workers restrict it to cases below a certain arbitrarily chosen weight, e.g. 900 g. in the adult. Microcephaly has been defined by some workers as a head circumference smaller by three standard deviations than the mean for the age and sex (Brandon, Kirman and Williams, 1959)*. Reduction in brain weight forms a continuum from normality to the smallest recorded. For example, the brain of one 14 year-old severely microcephalic girl, who died at the Fountain Hospital, weighed 110 g. (Fig. 21), (normal about 1,300 g.). The ventricles were not enlarged in this case. It is quite possible that the atrophic solid tissue would weigh even less in some grossly hydrocephalic or hydrencephalic brains.

Many rather unsuccessful attempts have been made to subdivide and classify micrencephaly. Almost all the known causes of mental retardation may

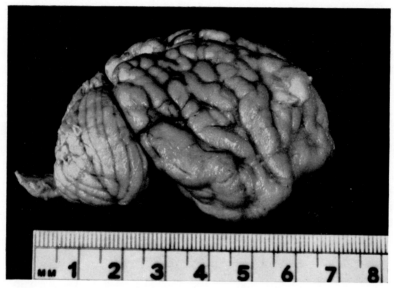

Fig. 21. A micrencephalic brain weighing 110 grams from a patient aged 14 years. The gyral pattern is 'simplified': there is a dearth of tertiary sulci.

impede brain and skull growth, so that no inferences as to aetiology can be drawn from the presence of micrencephaly alone. Some workers have suggested that the term 'true micrencephaly' be applied to brains showing only smallness with no evidence of degeneration and scarring, and that the others be designated as 'secondary micrencephaly', but it is difficult to see the advantage of such classification. It is doubtful whether a 'lilliput' type of smallness can ever be the sole cerebral abnormality. Certainly in most cases smallness is associated with many of the diverse changes listed below, some pointing to an earlier, and others to a later origin of the disturbance. Gliotic micrencephaly may be caused, for example, by such different conditions as phenylketonuria, Tay-Sachs disease, prenatal toxoplasmosis, or postnatal encephalitis.

* Brain weights and those of other organs together with head circumferences for individuals of different ages are tabulated in the Appendices on pp. 377 *et seq.*

'True microcephaly' is considered by Penrose (1963) to be a recessively inherited defect. He states that it is highly characteristic, the patients having a long small head and a dwarfed though well-developed body. The face is not so much reduced in size as the head, so that a relatively normal nose, chin and large ears may contrast with a receding forehead and low vertex in a manner reminiscent of the popular idea of a criminal type. It is difficult, however, to endorse this view fully. All transitional forms from the above picture to the normal head shape and size can be found. Morphologically, the brains of cases conforming to the description of 'true microcephaly' present diverse changes in addition to smallness. These include gliotic encephalopathy, porencephaly, arhinencephaly, prosencephaly, one of the system atrophies, or disorders of cellular migration. Brandon, Kirman, and Williams (1959) also concluded, on clinical and psychological grounds, that it is not possible to isolate a group of cases with 'true microcephaly' from other microcephalies.

Under the heading of 'recessive familial microcephaly' Norman (1963) described a characteristic anatomical picture of a brain weighing usually 500–600 g. with a simplified convolutional pattern "resembling that of the higher anthropoid apes" and with numerous minor architectonic abnormalities. This condition is apparently synonymous with Penrose's "true microcephaly". But the pathological findings mentioned by Norman are rather common in all clinical types of microcephaly, and seem insufficient to demarcate a specific group of cases of like aetiology. (The columnar arrangement of cortical neurones mentioned as being characteristic of 'true microcephaly' seems a normal architectonic feature of certain cerebral areas.)

It is sometimes assumed that microcephaly and micrencephaly are apparent already at birth. This is by no means so. The head may at first be well within the normal range and then lag permanently behind the proper rate of growth.

The reduction in size in micrencephaly may be fairly even, (Fig. 21), but, more commonly, some parts are affected more than others. When the frontal and temporal lobes are particularly small, the insula remains uncovered. Concomitant or secondary atrophy or hypoplasia may be present in areas connected with each other by fibre tracts. Thus the ventro-lateral thalamic nuclei may be small in association with lesions in the parietal lobe. Contra-lateral cerebellar atrophy or hypoplasia may be present in combination with large lesions or agenesis of the opposite cerebral hemisphere. Sometimes the cerebellum remains relatively large, in other cases it may be more affected than the cerebrum (Fig. 22). The pattern of convolutions is often 'simplified' in the smaller brains by the absence of some of the shortest, 'tertiary', sulci and gyri. On the cut surface, the cerebral cortex is frequently too thick in relation to the white matter. Another feature may be the large size of the basal ganglia. This phenomenon has been attributed to the phylogenetic priority of the subcortical structures. The concept of 'hypergenesis' or compensatory enlargement of phylogenetically older formations following the arrest of development of the newer parts originated in the Monakow school of embryo-logical neuropathology in Zürich, but has not been proven experimentally.

The brainstem is often small and the pyramids rudimentary or absent.

Smallness of the spinal cord, micromyelia, is usually more difficult to demonstrate. This was done, however, as long ago as 1866 by Steinlechner-Gretschischnikoff, and also by Kossowitch in 1892. These ladies were able to confirm by careful measurement the smallness of the spinal cords in many cases of micrencephaly. The reduction was mainly at the expense of the white matter.

Ventricular Dilatation. A micrencephalic brain is often smaller than appears from the external examination or, even, weighing, since its ventricles can be dilated, and the fluid remaining within tends to be weighed with the brain.

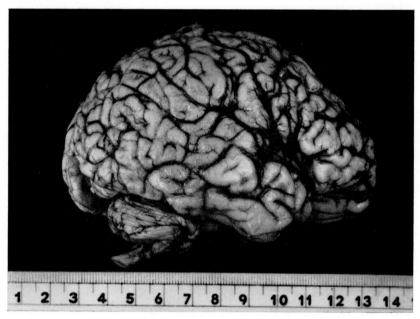

Fig. 22. The brain shows cerebellar atrophy. The whole brain of a boy aged 10 years weighed 450g., and the cerebellum with the brain-stem 20g. The frontal lobes are also relatively small, as is often the case in cerebellar atrophy.

For example, of 176 brains from unclassifiable cases examined by Crome (1960), 106 weighed less than 80 per cent of the average normal. Ventricular dilatation was present in 103 cases. This was classified as follows: slight (ventricles dilated but do not exceed a quarter of the total brain area in the skiagram), 33 cases; moderate (not exceeding half of the total brain area), 33 cases; and marked (over half of total brain area), 37 cases. The ventricular dilatation (or compensatory hydrocephalus) is in such circumstances the result of atrophy or agenesis of the overlying solid parts of the brain. In localized cortical atrophy or agenesis, ventricular dilatation is more marked in the affected area; thus the anterior horns of the lateral ventricles are particularly large in cases of atrophy or agenesis of the frontal lobes; the inferior horns are dilated when the temporal lobes are small; and only one of the lateral ventricles is enlarged in cases of cerebral hemiatrophy. The third ventricle is dilated in cases of atrophy of the basal ganglia and in generalized micrencephaly, and the fourth in cerebellar atrophy. The lateral and third ventricles may be enlarged and abnormal in cases of prosencephaly (Fig. 23), arhinencephaly and absence of the corpus callosum.

This compensatory, or *ex vacuo*, form of hydrocephalus can be distinguished from the hypertensive variety (p. 172) by absence of head enlargement or other evidence of past or continuing rise in intracranial pressure. But this distinction is not always easy. In cases of very marked thinning of the cortex, the patho-

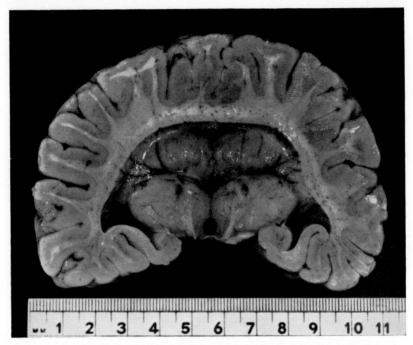

FIG. 23. A prosencephalic brain showing non-separation of the two cerebral hemi-spheres. The corpus callosum, septum pellucidum and fornices are absent. The ventricles form a single cavity.

genesis may remain obscure, particularly if the brain is not enlarged and there is no demonstrable obstruction. Passive ventricular dilatation can be, moreover, occasionally associated with obstructive hydrocephalus as, for example, in cases of micrencephaly complicated by adhesive meningitis or stenosis of the cerebral aqueduct.

Megalencephaly

Contrary to the general rule, the brains of a few severely subnormal in-dividuals can be abnormally large and heavy (Fig. 20). All such hitherto reported *megalencephalic* brains have also shown associated structural changes, such as spongy degeneration of the white matter, microgyria with diffuse hypertrophic gliomatosis (glioblastosis), tuberous sclerosis, ectopic grey matter, lipidosis, or, in some cases, hydrocephalus. In a case studied at the Fountain Hospital, megalencephaly was associated with spongy breakdown and loss of myelin in all parts of the white matter (Fig. 24) together with the presence of numerous hyaline bodies—so-called Rosenthal fibres (Crome, 1953). Megalencephaly can also be partial; confined, for example, to one of the hemispheres (Gross and Uiberrack, 1955). Two cases of megalencephaly have been recently described by Dyggve and Tygstrup (1964) and Laurence

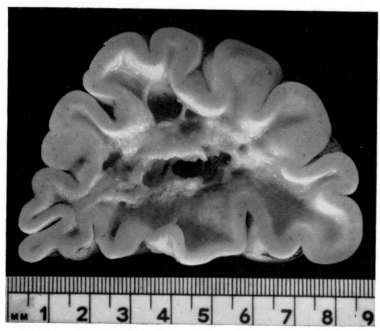

Fig. 24. Coronal block of a frontal lobe showing breakdown of the central white matter. The brain in this case showed megalencephaly and the so-called Alexander type of leucodystrophy: histologically, numerous Rosenthal fibres were present in the white matter.

(1964). In one megalencephaly was associated with syringomyelia and enlargement of the cavum septi pellucidi, and in the other—with unilateral microgyria and gliomatosis. A similar example of unilateral microgyria and gliomatosis has been also seen at the Fountain Hospital (unpublished).

Prosencephaly

Normally, the cerebral hemispheres develop by the transformation of the single prosencephalic vesicle into two telencephalic ones. Interference with this process causes persistence of union between the hemispheres, and this condition is known as *prosencephaly*. In the more pronounced cases the diencephalon is also involved, so that the basal ganglia are partially or completely fused. Since the eyes are formed by outgrowths (optic cups) from each of the diencephalic vesicles, non-separation may result in the formation of only a single eye—*cyclopia*. Fully cyclopic infants do not survive, but cases showing milder forms, viz., some reduction in the interpupillary distance (stenopia) with, perhaps, microphthalmia or anophthalmia, may live, and their brains can be prosencephalic. (Some of the corresponding milder cranio-facial anomalies have been described as *ethmocephaly* and *cebocephaly* by Ernst (1909, quoted by Currarino and Silverman, 1960). The facial anomalies associated with this condition have been also described by Demyer and Zeman (1963).) In extreme cases of prosencephaly the hemispheres are almost completely fused. Such forms have been observed, for example, in association with 13–15 and 17–18 chromosomal trisomy (Fig. 7). More frequently, however, non-separation is limited to the anterior parts of the hemispheres. In the mildest instances, the longitudinal cerebral fissure is present and extends over the entire brain, but the two hemispheres are nevertheless connected with each other at the bottom of the fissure by a plate of grey and white matter (Fig. 25) —a remnant of the so-called telencephalon medium. This formation occupies the usual site of the corpus callosum and may be mistaken for it (Gross and Kaltenbäck, 1958). Prosencephaly in human brains has been described in infants of diabetic mothers, as in Case 5 of the series reported by Dekaban and Magee (1958). It is interesting that cyclopia with prosencephaly occurs in lambs born to ewes grazing on certain alpine pastures in Southern Idaho, where it is caused by a weed—Veratrum californicum (Binns, James, and Shupe, 1962).

The state of the ventricles in prosencephalic brains depends on the degree

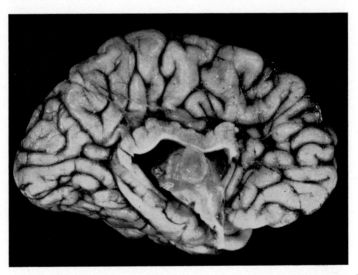

Fig. 25. A 'mild' form of prosencephaly. The hemispheres are partially separate but remain abnormally connected with each other by fused cingulate gyri. The corpus callosum cannot form in such circumstances.

of non-separation. In extreme cases there is only a single cavity (Fig. 23). The third ventricle may be absent or very narrow because of the thalamic fusion. In milder cases however, the posterior and inferior horns of the lateral ventricles and the third ventricle do develop. Usually, the fornices are absent.

Since prosencephaly, like arhinencephaly and absence of the corpus callosum (*vide infra*), can be sometimes diagnosed in life by air encephalography, the shape of the ventricles in these conditions is of practical interest, and it is worth while considering the malformations from this viewpoint, as has been done by Gross, Hoff and Kaltenbäck (1959).

Prosencephalic brains are usually small and often present absence of the olfactory nerves and some of the more central parts of the rhinencephalon, as well as agenesis of the corpus callosum. This is why prosencephaly has been regarded by many authors as synonymous with arhinencephaly and absence of the corpus callosum. However, it seems inadvisable to use these terms interchangeably, since, despite the frequency of association, non-separation of the hemispheres is quite consistent with normal development of the olfactory brain, while the corpus callosum may be entirely absent in some cases showing no evidence of prosencephaly.

Readers should also be aware of many other terms used for these conditions. It is possible, for example, to designate all malformations characterized by midline fusion of normally separate structures by the suffix 'synapsis' (from the Greek for union or liaison), so that prosencephaly becomes 'telencephalosynapsis' and union at lower levels 'diencephalosynapsis', 'mesencephalosynapsis' and 'rhombencephalosynapsis'. On the other hand, certain other malformations are characterized by a failure of normal mandatory midline fusion, and the suffix 'schisis' (from the Greek for rift), can then be added to the name of the formation concerned to form such terms as 'encephaloschisis', 'diencephaloschisis', 'rhombencephaloschisis' and 'rachischisis'. The severest malformation of this series is anencephaly, and the mildest and most familiar —spina bifida. (Since the latter is very frequently associated with hydrocephalus, the whole series of the 'schisis' anomalies is considered on pp. 173 *et seq.*) Other, perhaps more inappropriate, terms for prosencephaly are 'cyclencephaly' and 'holotelencephaly' (Yakovlev, 1959).

Prosencephaly was present in 6 of the 191 unclassifiable cases of severe mental subnormality studied by Crome (1960).

Agenesis of the Corpus Callosum

The corpus callosum—the main commissural connection between the two cerebral hemispheres—can scarcely remain normal in the presence of substantial cerebral anomalies. All forms and degrees of callosal hypoplasia and atrophy do in fact occur in the brains of the severely subnormal. It is usually thin, in whole or in part, and may also be relatively short. Agenesis of the corpus callosum is, however, a term applied to a distinct, somewhat rare, anomaly, in which marked deficiency or complete absence of that body dominates the anatomical picture.

The corpus callosum is phylogenetically a new formation, which is fully developed only in higher mammals. Its precise mode of development in man is still a matter of dispute but it is often stated that the first callosal fibres appear in the upper part of the commissural plate during the third month of embryonic life. They expand by spreading anteriorly and posteriorly, and form the genu, body and splenium of the corpus callosum. Its development is not complete before the eighth month.

Agenesis of the corpus callosum is usually associated with mental defect, but intelligence was said to be normal in some of the recorded cases. Agenesis of the corpus callosum without associated prosencephaly was present in 2 out of 191 unclassifiable cases examined at the Fountain Hospital.

Neurosurgeons have divided the corpus callosum in the course of operations, sometimes without any apparent untoward result. In dogs, tactile salivary conditioned reflexes, established on one side of the body, are reproduced with remarkable precision on similar stimulation of the symmetrical areas on the opposite side (Pavlov, 1949). This effect disappears when the corpus callosum is divided, and the conditioned reflexes have then to be reestablished separately on both sides. The corpus callosum therefore connects symmetrical cortical analyzers of the two hemispheres.

In some cases of agenesis, the entire corpus callosum above the lamina terminalis is replaced by a thin fibrous membrane (Fig. 26), while in others, the third ventricle may open on to the exterior of the brain. In a few recorded instances a lipoma, cyst or meningioma has occupied the site of the absent

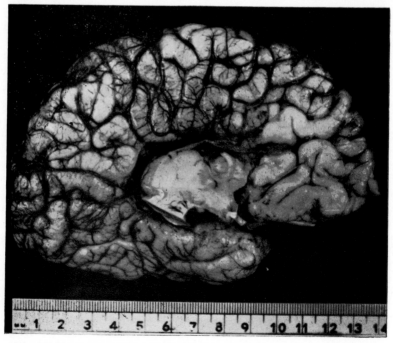

26. The corpus callosum is absent; it is replaced by a thin membrane.

formation. Probably the best morphological description of the changes in both complete and incomplete agenesis of the corpus callosum is that by Gross, Hoff, and Kaltenbäck (1959), and their article should be consulted for fuller details. Associated structural changes include micrencephaly, ventricular dilatation (especially of the posterior horns of the lateral ventricles), prosencephaly, and non-fusion of the calcarine and parieto-occipital sulci. The latter are separated from each other by several abnormal radially arranged convolutions. The cingulate gyrus is often turned under the edge of the sulcus above it. The two leaves of the septum pellucidum and the fornices are widely separated from each other or may, according to some authors, be absent. There may be no trace of the hippocampal commissure but the anterior commissure is usually present and may be enlarged.

Interest has been aroused by the presence in most, if not all, cases of callosal agenesis of the so-called callosal longitudinal bundle ('Balkenlängsbündel'), a structure not recognizable as such in brains with normal corpora callosa. This is a stout bundle of myelinated nerve fibres situated at the upper angle of the lateral ventricles. It originates anteriorly in the white matter of the frontal lobe and terminates posteriorly in the occipital lobe and hippocampus. Its nature is uncertain; it could be a regular component of the corpus callosum which is entirely covered and masked in normal brains by the callosal commissural fibres.

Menkes, Philippart and Clark (1964) described the occurrence of partial agenesis of the corpus callosum and cortical changes in two brothers, two of their male cousins and an uncle, concluding that the anomaly is a hitherto unrecognized sex-linked condition. However, the brain of only one of these cases had been fully examined.

Arhinencephaly

This denotes absence of the olfactory bulbs and tracts. The condition may be bilateral or unilateral. The more central parts of the olfactory brain: the hippocampus, fimbria, induseum griseum and the fornices, may also be absent. The condition is so often associated with prosencephaly and absence of the corpus callosum that, as mentioned already, the terms have come to be used interchangeably. This is unfortunate, since arhinencephaly, like prosencephaly, can certainly occur on its own. Four such cases have been seen, for example, at the Fountain Hospital, but a characteristic anatomical picture of the anomaly has not yet emerged. Another similar case examined recently was an instance of 'cri du chat' syndrome p. 18 and showed partial deletion of one of the No. 5 chromosomes. The brain showed arhinencephaly but no prosencephaly (Fig. 27). An example of arhinencephaly without prosencephaly in an infant born to a diabetic mother has been described by Dekaban (1959).

Anomalies of Shape and Surface

The skulls of mentally retarded individuals are frequently abnormal in shape, as well as size, and in such cases the brains are usually correspondingly anomalous. They may be abnormally round in acrocephaly or brachycephaly, excessively long in scaphocephaly, and asymmetrical in plagiocephaly. The misshapen skull and brain can be a characteristic feature of a distinct syndrome, such as Apert's, Franceschetti's or Crouzon's, but, more frequently the anomalies remain unclassified (pp. 321 *et seq.*).

In some cases, a part of the brain, such as one of its lobes, is abnormal in size, either uni- or bilaterally. The gyral pattern is also often unusual. The relatively common anomaly of simplification caused by a dearth of the smallest 'tertiary' sulci has been mentioned already (p. 100). The configuration of

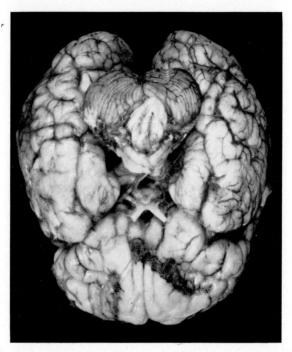

FIG. 27. This brain of a case with 'cri du chat' syndrome shows absence of the olfactory nerves and smallness of the optic nerves and chiasma. The olfactory sulci are present.

the gyri can be atypical, certain sulci being absent and others 'incorrectly' orientated. Gyri may be uneven in width—poikilogyria, or excessively convoluted—polygyria. Other anomalies are discussed elsewhere: ulegyria on p. 119, microgyria on p. 109 and pachygyria on p. 110.

Too much has at times been made of these appearances. A few of the earlier workers thought that many of these brains were significantly atavistic, resembling those of lower animal species, and described them accordingly as 'avian', 'rodent', 'carnivorous' and 'simian'. It is clear, however, that different degrees of micrencephaly and abnormality of shape, combined with an almost infinite range of variations in gyral pattern, offer endless scope for arbitrary grouping, and that any resemblance to the brains of certain animals is entirely fortuitous. It has also come to be realized that normal variations in brain shape and gyral pattern are greater than previously believed, and that it is incorrect to lay undue stress on isolated minor anomalies of this kind.

Disorders of Cellular Migration

In the course of normal embryonic development primitive neuroblasts move outwards to the periphery from the site of their origin and concentration in the paraventricular areas. Disturbances occurring during this period of migration may interfere with this movement, giving rise to distinct types of anomalies: microgyria, pachygyria and nodular ectopia (or 'heterotopia'). These are usually associated with other structural abnormalities, such as micrencephaly, porencephaly and ventricular dilatation.

Microgyria (or micropolygyria) is the commonest. It was present, for example, in 27 of 500 brains of severely subnormal cases examined at the Fountain Hospital. There is usually no difficulty in recognizing this anomaly in the gross specimen. The brain is mostly small, and the normal gyri are replaced in the affected areas by numerous closely-set small convolutions separated from each other by shallow grooves. After the meninges are stripped the appearance varies from a coarse cobble-stone-like surface (Fig. 28), to one reminiscent of Morocco-leather. Microgyria is often bilateral and symmetrical, extending over parts of several lobes. It may sometimes be difficult to distinguish from the scarring of gyri —ulegyria, and from granular atrophy (p. 119).

In stained sections the abnormal pallium is characterized by a four-layer lamination (Fig. 29). The superficial marginal layer contains, as in the normal

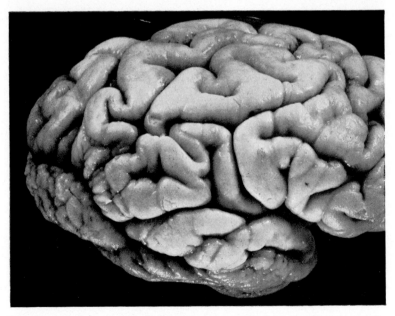

Fig. 28. Microgyria of the occipital and temporal lobes. In the affected areas the surface is cobblestone-like.

cortex, few neurones. The second layer is cellular, and the third, sparsely cellular, is formed chiefly by myelinated nerve fibres, which project at intervals as stout radial sheaf-like bundles into the core of the overlying microgyric convolutions. The deepest, fourth layer, contains, again, nerve cells and a network of nerve fibres. The above pattern may be complicated by infolding and unevenness of development resulting in a gland-like structure, but the typical features can usually be discerned with comparative ease (Crome, 1952).

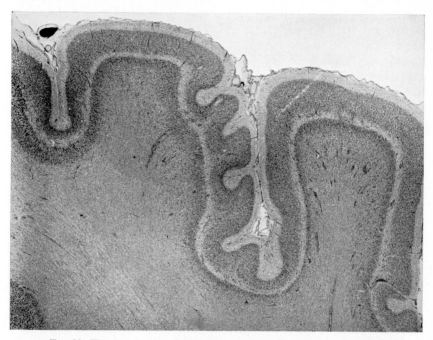

FIG. 29. The characteristic lamination of microgyria. (Cresyl violet × 9).

Furthermore, the typical microgyric lamination may extend beyond the margins of areas occupied by the macroscopically identifiable malformation and be present in the seemingly normal cortex. Cerebellar microgyria is mentioned on p. 145 (Fig. 63).

In cases of *pachygyria*, also called macrogyria, gyri are few and relatively broad and the sulci are short, shallow and straight (Fig. 30). The extreme degree of this condition—total or almost total absence of gyri—is referred to as *agyria* or lissencephaly (Fig. 31). Pachygyria is not nearly so common as microgyria; only two such cases occurred among 500 brains examined at the Fountain Hospital. The pachygyric cortex shows also a four-layered lamination but none of the excessively convoluted gland-like variants which are typical of microgyria (Fig. 32). Ectopic groups of nerve cells may be present in the white matter of the cerebellum (Fig. 37), and ectopic olivary tissue may remain in the tegmentum of the medulla oblongata (Fig. 33), where it develops formations resembling accessory olives (Crome, 1956).

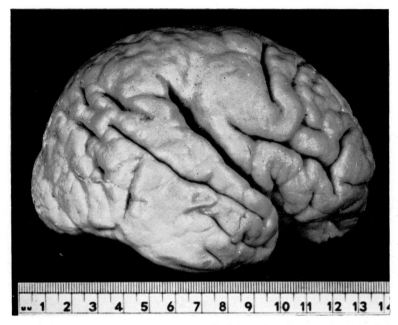

FIG. 30. Pachygyria.

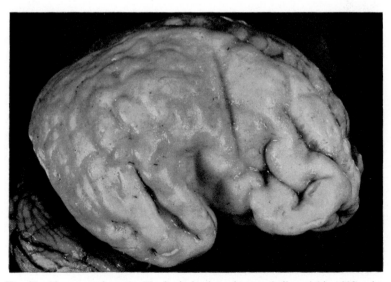

FIG. 31. Almost total agyria. The brain is also micrencephalic weighing 220 g. in a child aged 4 years.

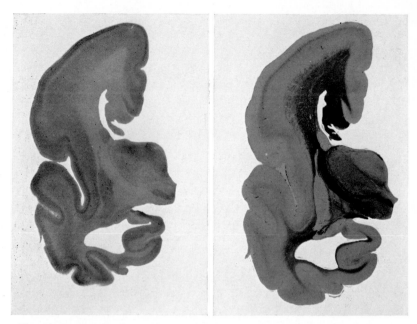

FIG. 32. Pachygyria. The cortex is sparcely convoluted and shows four-layered lamination. The section is stained with cresyl violet stain for cells (left)- to show the 'acellular' layer 3, and by the Heidenhain method for myelin (right)-to show a layer of myelin in the 'acellular' layer 3.

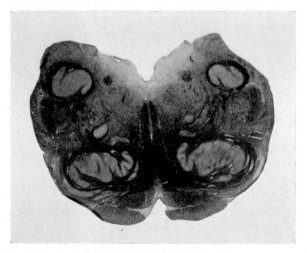

FIG. 33. Ectopic elements of the inferior olives in the posterior part of the medulla in a case of pachygyria. (Heidenhain × 5).

The genesis of the above-mentioned anomalies can be readily understood. Owing to interference with migration, the movement of cells is interrupted at a time when a certain number, represented by layer two, have already reached the cerebral cortex. With further development, axis cylinders of neurones in that layer form the acellular layer three and prevent, when migration is resumed, the remainder of the nerve cells from joining those already in the cortex. The third layer of the anomalous cortex is thus analogous with the subarcuate fibres of the normal brain (Figs. 34 and 35). In animals, analogous

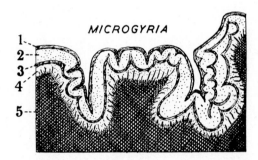

FIG. 34. Schematic representation of the four cortical layers in microgyria.

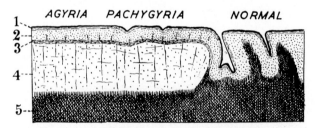

FIG. 35. Schematic representation of the four cortical layers in pachygyria.

conditions have been produced by X-ray irradiation during pregnancy (p. 30), while some human cases of microgyria have been reported in association with maternal carbon monoxide poisoning during pregnancy and with cytomegalic inclusion body disease (pp. 34 and 40). The occurrence of agyria in association with hypertelorism in two siblings has been reported by Reznik and Alberga-Serrano (1964).

Retardation or arrest of cellular migration may result in other anomalies. In *nodular ectopia* nerve cells remain close to their site of origin and form tumour-like nodules which may either project into the ventricles or be 'implanted' deeper in the white matter (Fig. 36). These nodules contain, in addition to nerve cells and neuroglia, capillaries and nerve fibres. They show varying degrees of differentiation and, sometimes, even an indication of cortical lamination. Similar anomalies may occur in the vicinity of the basal ganglia, the brainstem and cerebellum. Thus, elements of the caudate nuclei, inferior olives or cerebellar cortex may be strewn archipelago-wise over a distance from the site of the main formations (Fig. 33). Ectopic cortical elements in the cerebellar white matter (Fig. 37) in brains showing varying degrees of prosencephaly are an almost constant feature of D-trisomy (13–15 group) (vide p. 17). Besides the above forms, other less typical but related anomalies have also been recorded (Kleinsasser, 1955–56; Wiest and Hallervorden, 1958; Bittner, 1959). In many cases the ectopic elements are not cellular groups but single neurones scattered diffusely in the white matter. This is not unusual in

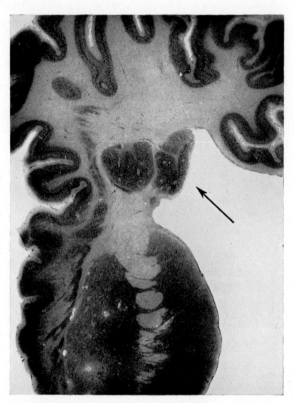

FIG. 36. Coronal section of a brain showing ectopic nodules of grey matter above the caudate nucleus. One of the nodules projects well into the ventricle (arrow). Other, more diffusely arranged, ectopic grey matter is situated closer to the cerebral cortex.

infants but caution is necessary in interpreting the phenomenon. The deepest cortical layer tends to merge gradually with the subjoining white matter in all normal brains of infants, and sections cut tangentially always show many seemingly ectopic nerve cells in the white matter. This is particularly so when the volume of white matter is reduced, as it frequently is in cases of mental retardation.*

* Another rare anomaly not often mentioned in the literature is *brain warts* (Grcvic and Robert, 1960). These are superficial round elevated plaques which range in size from microscopic dimensions to about 5mm. A central core of white matter may sometimes be

Other Cortical Anomalies

In addition to the above well-defined anomalies, the cerebral cortex as well as neurones in many parts of the central nervous system may show manifold less conspicuous changes. The cerebral cortex as a whole can be too wide or too narrow and its lamination incomplete, blurred or interrupted. For ex-

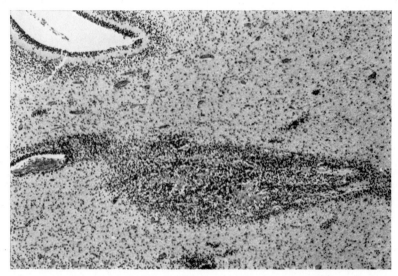

FIG. 37. Ectopic nodule of grey matter in the cerebellar white matter in a case of D-trisomy. The nodule is formed by granular and Purkinje cells. (Haematoxylin and eosin × 65).

ample a curious horizontal, 'foetal', arrangement of the neurones, especially marked in certain areas, has been described by Dodgson (1951). Many anomalies of single neurones have also been reported. Some cells are abnormally large or small. They may be orientated at unusual angles (e.g. 90°) to the normal. Greatly elongated cells, resembling bipolar neuroblasts, and binucleated ones may also be present. Anomalous cells may have unduly conspicuous, undulating processes.

Gliotic Encephalopathy

Scarring is one of the commonest changes in the brains of mental defectives. It occurs frequently in cases of micrencephaly but is not unusual in some of the larger brains.

The way tissues react to injury changes in the course of embryonic development. Although the field of human embryological pathology has not been

seen in these formations. Microscopically, the 'warts' contain glial cells, capillaries and neurones. They are usually surrounded and traversed by numerous glial fibres. They may be associated with microgyria but can also occur in the absence of that anomaly. In a personally studied case they were associated with micrencephaly, periventricular ectopic nodules of grey matter and diffuse fibrous gliosis of the cerebral white matter.

adequately explored, it seems established that in the earliest stages injured tissue simply dissolves. It may be reconstituted later, or leave a cavity in its place. This process may modify the development of the adjoining parts or of the organ as a whole. Malformations of the brain can originate in this way. Inflammatory processes and the formation of scar tissue become possible only during the later stages of foetal life.

Scarring within the central nervous tissue takes the form of gliosis. Its mode of development varies with the nature, extent, and severity of the injury, and, as mentioned already, the maturity of the tissue. A frequent sequence is early proliferation of microglia which can form cellular clusters. Some of the cells may become elongated (rod cells) or mobile and phagocytic. The derivation of these cells is somewhat uncertain but many are certainly haematogenous (Konigsmark and Sidman, 1963). Nerve cells and their processes are partially or completely destroyed and the debris are ingested by phagocytes, which often round-off and are then known as compound granular corpuscles. Astrocytes proliferate in the damaged tissue and around the edges of necrotic foci. They enlarge and develop in time many conspicuous fibrillary processes. Cellular gliosis is in this way gradually replaced by fibrous gliosis (Fig. 38). The end result is a more or less dense network of glial fibres containing a variable admixture of astrocytic cells. New capillaries also form in the course of some reactive processes, but the laying down of collagen, as in somatic tissues, takes place only in the vicinity of the meninges or the larger blood vessels. Since neural tissue, and particularly myelin, contains much lipid, breakdown, however caused, is usually accompanied by the appearance of

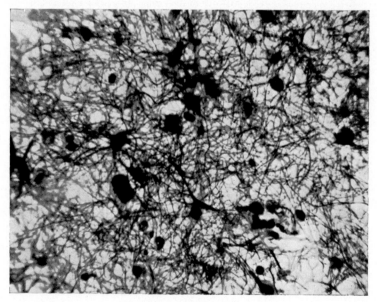

Fig. 38. Gliosis. A network of glial fibres with some cellular hyperplasia. (Holzer × 550).

sudanophil material—cholesterol esters, neutral fat and lipochrome pigment. This material can be seen within the compound granular corpuscles and, also, extracellularly. If the condition is not progressive, the amount of sudanophil material slowly decreases. In 'burnt-out' areas and during the final stages of scar formation lipids may be absent or occur only in the form of minute cytoplasmic granules in some endothelial cells of capillaries and in a few compound granular corpuscles around blood-vessels. On the other hand, clusters of compound granular corpuscles may remain encysted by glial tissue (Fig. 39).

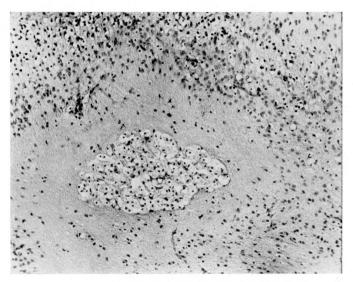

FIG. 39. A 'Virchowian corpuscle'. This is a focal collection of lipid phagocytes in the midst of gliotic tissue. (Haematoxylin and eosin × 110).

Such corpuscles were first described by Virchow in a condition regarded by him as encephalitis of the newborn and may therefore be referred to as 'Virchowian corpuscles'.

The above description is, of course, highly schematic and many variations are possible. Neural tissue may, for example, liquefy rapidly and be absorbed with scarcely any cellular reaction. Slower degenerative processes may be accompanied by little phagocytosis, the most conspicuous change being astroglial overgrowth. In some cases gliosis may follow widespread rarefaction of the tissue—status spongiosus, also called spongiform encephalopathy (p. 139).

It is possible to recognize many abnormal astrocytes in gliotic areas: hypertrophied ones, protoplasmic forms showing cytoplasmic distention with and without inclusions, multinucleated cells, syncytial groupings, and cells with enlarged, elongated, vesicular or horseshoe-shaped nuclei. In general, the greater the hyperplasia the more atypical and pleomorphic the cells.

As in the case of somatic tissues, neural scarring may become 'excessive', causing enlargement of the affected area and reaching, in rare instances, neo-plastic dimension. There is no agreed nomenclature for such changes and, depending on the degree of hyperplasia and cellularity, it may be referred to as hypertrophic astrocytosis, glioblastosis, or diffuse hypertrophic glioblasto-matosis. This change is common in central neurofibromatosis and tuberous sclerosis but may also be encountered in other instances of gliotic encephalo-pathy.

Gliosis is often immediately apparent on examination of the gross specimen (Fig. 40). The affected parts are shrunken and may be as hard as cartilage. On

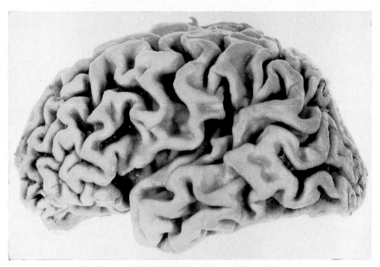

FIG. 40. A micrencephalic brain weighing 315g. of a child aged 7 years. The meninges have been stripped to show generalized atrophy caused by the scarring of gyri (ule-gyria). The sulci are widened.

the cut surface, the normally crisp demarcation between the grey and white matter is blurred or obliterated (Fig. 41). The tissue is discoloured and may have an ivory or bluish tinge. But the smaller gliotic lesions need not be so obvious, and some are only visible microscopically.

Topological Variants of Gliosis

The extent and distribution of gliotic change vary within the widest limits. The whole brain may be involved, as in generalized sclerotic micrencephaly, extreme forms of which have sometimes been described as 'walnut' brains.

Scarring may be more marked in one of the hemispheres—*hemiatrophy*, or in one or several of the lobes—lobar atrophy or *lobar sclerosis*. The gliotic gyri are shrunken, thin and indurated; the sulci between them are widened (Figs. 40 and 42). The cortex of the deeper parts of the gyri is often more shrunken than at their crowns, conferring upon the gyri in histological sections a somewhat mushroom-like appearance.

Gliosis of gyri—*ulegyria* must be distinguished from microgyria, which is described on p. 109. Macroscopically, the essential difference is in the number and position of the gyri. Microscopically, ulegyria shows loss of nerve cells and gliosis whereas microgyria shows a characteristic pallial stratification. The atrophy and scarring may be uneven in some cases of ulegyria, leading to granularity and puckering of the surface—*granular atrophy* (Fig. 43).

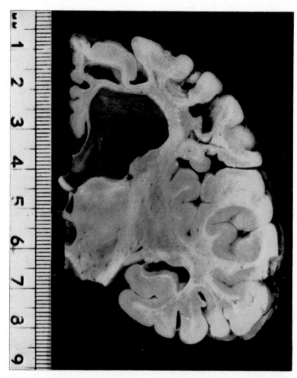

FIG. 41. Atrophy of part of the frontal lobe with ulegyria and cavitation. The demarcation between the grey and white matter is blurred in the sclerotic area. The lateral ventricle is dilated—an instance of compensatory hydrocephalus.

It is difficult to classify gliotic encephalopathy on the basis of the distribution of the changes in the cerebral hemispheres since all or any part of the brain may be affected (*vide infra*). Nevertheless, certain topographical variants have attracted special attention. For example, the area around the occipital poles is often ulegyric even if the rest of the brain is not. Another interesting form is the scarring of one gyrus or a few parallel ones in an otherwise relatively normal brain. Such scarred gyri may be depressed and partially hidden below the surface of the brain, and are often situated somewhere near the central or the calcarine fissures. The anterior extremity of the frontal lobe may be particularly severely affected, especially in cases of cerebral hemiatrophy. Involvement of the temporal lobes and, especially, of the Ammon's horn and amygdaloid complex has been studied very carefully in relation to the problem of epilepsy, in general, and temporal lobe epilepsy, in particular (Meyer, Falconer and Beck, 1954; Crome, 1955; Corsellis, 1957; Falconer and Cavanagh, 1959; Falconer, Serafetinides and Corsellis, 1964).

Many suggestions have been made to explain the above mentioned topological variations of gliotic encephalopathy. For example, some of the lesions have been ascribed to the relative length of the artery supplying the affected areas, e.g. the posterior cerebral in cases of occipital lobe involvement or the anterior choroidal in cases of Ammon's horn sclerosis. However, many of the lesions cannot be explained in this way. Some are situated in what has become known as the 'boundary' zones—i.e. the territory between two areas supplied by major arteries or their branches, such as those of the anterior and middle

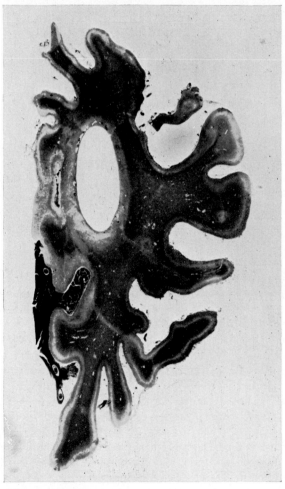

Fig. 42. Lobar atrophy and marked ulegyria. The gyri are narrowed and the sulci widened. (Holzer × 2).

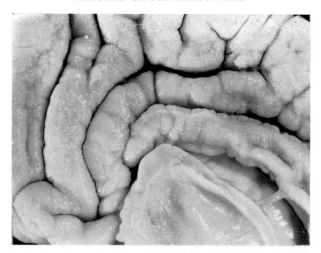

FIG. 43. 'Granular atrophy'. The affected gyrus shows granularity and puckering of the surface.

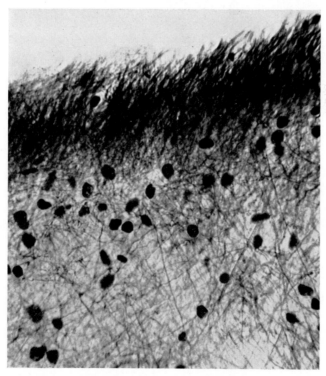

FIG. 44. Marginal or subpial fibrous gliosis. The subjacent areas are also gliotic, but not severely. (Holzer × 375.)

cerebral. It has been suggested that these areas are particularly liable to suffer from ischaemia during episodes of hypotension. It is difficult to accept fully any of the above explanations. They are not usually based on experimental work, and there is often no reason to impugn ischaemia or other vascular factors. The 'boundary zone' theory seems particularly controversial since there is hardly an area of the brain which could not be described as such. Moreover, in theory, a case could be made for a better rather than a worse blood supply in 'boundary' areas, supplied, as they are, by overlapping and anastomosing vessels. In any case, there is no evidence that the blood supply of any area of the brain worsens with the increase in the distance from the origin of its nutrient artery. Many pathologists are, on the other hand, aware that infarction corresponding to the areas of the occluded arteries may occur in the newborn, and Cocker, George and Yates (1965) have recently suggested that in some of the cases showing no obvious cause of the arterial obstruction, this may be due to an embolus derived from the foetal veins of the placenta.

In the gliotic areas, the cerebral cortex may be either completely or partially replaced by scar tissue, and the arrangement of the glial cells and fibres can present certain distinct patterns. For example, gliosis can be mainly superficial, extending also in a more attenuated form into the subjoining cellular layers, and this type is referred to as subpial or *marginal* (Fig. 44). Occasionally gliosis is particularly marked in one or several of the cortical laminae, especially layers two and three. In cases of granular atrophy and 'marbling' of the cortex (p. 136) bundles of glial fibres course perpendicularly to the surface of the brain (Fig. 45).

Atrophic Neuronal Changes

Scarring was described above in terms of changes on the part of glial elements, but the process could be equally well regarded as one of parenchymal atrophy. Generally, there is ample histological evidence of a preceding or concurrent destructive process with loss of nerve cells, although this may be difficult to demonstrate in some cases.

The cortical neuronal loss may be focal, diffuse or laminar (Figs. 46 and 47), and although all layers can be affected, the more superficial ones, the second and third, seem to be particularly vulnerable. The surviving neurones are often distorted in shape and orientation by the scar tissue. Some may be enlarged. Irregularly orientated, polygonal and hypertrophied nerve cells with stout dendritic processes are another, rarer, feature of scarring. These cells resemble those characteristically present in tuberous sclerosis (Crome, 1957; Cravioto and Feigin, 1960). Neurones may show calcification or ferrugination, e.g. incrustation with granules staining positively for calcium, iron or both of these elements. The axis cylinders can undergo focal swelling and degenerate forming characteristic spherical or elongated, granular or homogeneously staining bodies (Fig. 48). These have been discussed recently by Cowen and Olmstead (1963). This change can be very widespread and associated with marked cerebellar sclerosis, as in some cases reported by Cowen and Olmstead as instances of *infantile neuroaxonal dystrophy*. A few of these were

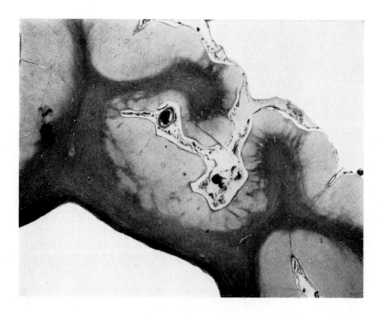

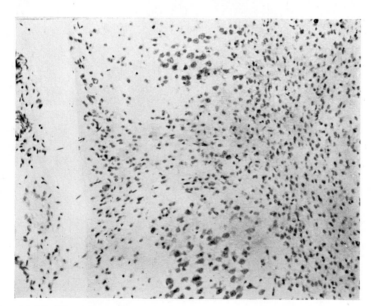

FIG. 45. Marbling of the cerebral cortex. The picture above shows transverse stria-
tions by 'plaques fibromyéliniques'. (Heidenhain × 2). Below, the plaques are seen to
be formed chiefly by astrocytes. They separate groups of surviving neurones. (Cresyl
violet × 200.)

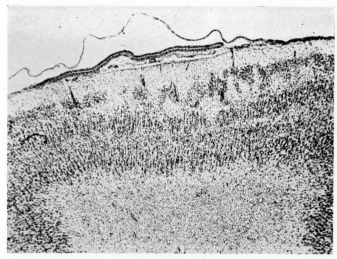

FIG. 46. Multifocal loss of nerve cells in the superficial layers of the cerebral cortex. (Cresyl violet × 20.)

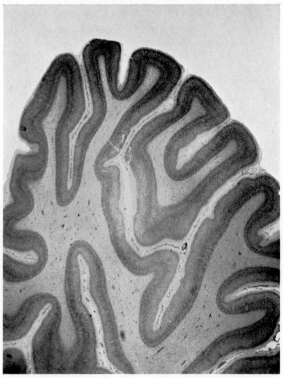

FIG. 47. Diffuse loss of nerve cells in the superficial layers of the cerebral cortex in a case of residual kernicterus. (Cresyl violet × 3.)

familial. Similar lesions have been described in association with lipidosis and with Hallervorden-Spatz disease (Seitelberger, 1957) (cf. p. 321). In a recent communication Sung (1964) reported the presence of similar 'spheroids' in each of the six cases of mucoviscidosis examined by him. He suggested, quoting experimental evidence, that the lesions may be due to vitamin E deficiency. Since it is known, however, that a small number of 'spheroids' can be present in association with a variety of other conditions, there is no reason to suppose

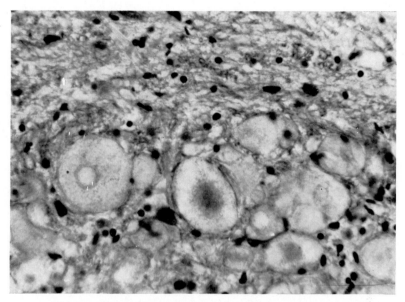

FIG. 48. So-called spheroid bodies—the characteristic change in neuroaxonal dystrophy. (Haematoxylin and eosin × 380.)

that the change is in any way specific. Other recently described cases of infantile neuroaxonal dystrophy include those by Lyon and Sée (1963) and Crome and Weller (1965).

Gliosis of the White Matter

Gliosis of the cerebral cortex is often associated with that of the white matter but the degree of involvement can be very different in the two formations. For example, the cortex may be severely gliotic in cases of lipidosis and of poliodystrophy (Alpers' disease), while the white matter shows only secondary and relatively mild involvement (Blackwood *et al.*, 1963). Selective involvement of the white matter is, perhaps, more common. This occurs particularly in leucodystrophies.

The 'classical' types of leucodystrophy are rare and account for few cases of mental retardation (p. 255), as they often commence in later childhood and can be rapidly fatal. However, the differences between these and other, more frequent, forms of leucoencephalopathy, have certainly been overstressed. For example, in some of the early or congenital cases the white matter is sclerotic but shows no evidence of general progressive demyelination. It is shrunken, often considerably so, and the appearances can be very striking, stained sections showing on naked-eye examination linear scarring which extends 'like the veins of a leaf' into the digital white matter of the gyri. A narrow zone of total myelin loss may be present in the central areas (Fig. 49) and clusters of lipid phagocytes are often 'encapsulated' in the demyelinated zone. As in

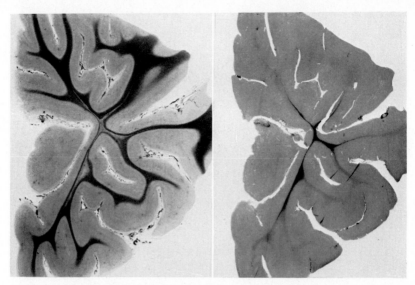

FIG. 49. Sclerosis with marked atrophy of the central white matter. Myelin is absent in the centre. (*Left*, Heidenhain × 2.) The right hand photograph is a Holzer preparation of the same area showing the thin line of gliosis, branching like the 'veins of a leaf'.

the other leucodystrophies, there is often no clear evidence of cortical involvement (Crome and Foley, 1959). Many cases exemplifying transitional stages from such extreme scarring to the generalized progressive demyelination of 'classical' leucodystrophy can be observed (Fig. 50). Other cases may show demyelination of the white matter without sclerosis—the consistency of the tissue being gelatinous or semiliquid (Josephy and Lichtenstein, 1943). Similarly, it is often difficult to distinguish leucodystrophy from some of the leucoencephalitides and other forms of leucoencephalopathy mentioned below and on p. 139. Pursuit of elusive exclusiveness of changes and the influence of the 'all-or-none' principle have been responsible for much confusion over terminology and classification of the leucodystrophies, as, indeed, of many other conditions.

Another somewhat similar form of fibrous gliosis of the white matter which is, however, associated with little or no apparent myelin loss has also been described. The cerebral cortex is not demonstrably abnormal in this condition, and while the white matter may show variable degrees of gliosis, its volume need not be appreciably reduced. This condition was reported as being 'frequent' in the brains of the 22 mental defectives examined by Meyer and Cook (1937). A later study revealed its presence in 10 out of 15 cases of Down's disease (Meyer and Jones, 1939). Similar findings occur in some of the neurometabolic diseases, notably phenylketonuria and galactosaemia, and in many of the still unclassifiable conditions (Crome, 1964). Chemical examination of such gliotic tissue shows a reduction of cerebroside and of total cholesterol. There is usually no chemical or histological evidence of generalized

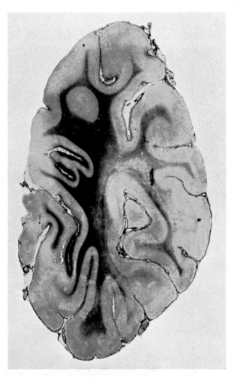

FIG. 50. Fibrous gliosis of the white matter of the occipital lobe. The gliotic areas are stained deep purplish-blue by this method and appear dark in the photograph. (Holzer × 1½.)

and progressive demyelination or of neuronal loss. But the data do not exclude the possibility of a relatively mild, slow and diffuse loss of neurones and of myelin; the available techniques are not sensitive enough to reveal such a change.

Another common form of scarring is periventricular; gliotic tissue can form a thick dense layer beneath the ependyma. (It should be remembered, however, that the presence of a thin subependymal gliotic membrane is quite normal.) In some cases glial tissues may encircle and constrict the cerebral aqueduct causing hydrocephalus. Periventricular gliosis is sometimes associated with the presence of ependymal granulations. These are pinhead-sized or even smaller nodules set upon the ventricular surface. They are formed by pro-

liferated neuroglia in foci denuded of their ependymal lining. In other instances the ventricular surface presents instead a reticular pattern of relief
elevations (Fig. 51)—'*état granulo-réticulé*'. It is often stated that these
changes are evidence of previous infection, but they also occur in cases with
no clear history of it.

Gliosis of Subcortical Nuclear Formations

The basal ganglia are also often gliotic, and in some cases nodularity and
puckering of the thalamic surface are apparent at a glance. Shrinkage of the
basal ganglia is accompanied by a dilatation of the third ventricle and elongation of the connexus thalamicus, if that structure is present. Gliosis is likewise

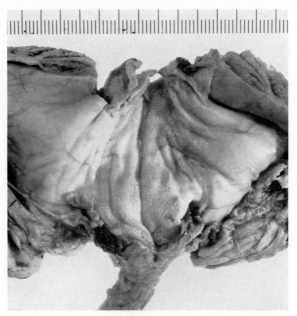

FIG. 51. État granulo-réticulé of the dilated fourth ventricle.

common in the brain-stem. At that level, it is often marginal and periventricular, but can involve more selectively certain nuclear formations and tracts,
especially in cases of system atrophy (*vide infra*). In *cerebellar sclerosis* there is
always partial or complete loss of one or both of the cortical cellular layers,
viz. the Purkinje cells and granular layer (Fig. 52). In these cases there is usually also an overgrowth of Bergmann glia, i.e. astrocytes placed between the
granular and molecular layers. Their long processes rise strikingly in a dense
brush-like manner towards the cerebellar surface (Fig. 53). Gliosis in the
spinal cord may be diffuse, affect the marginal areas, the grey matter or the
area around the grey matter. Parts of the white matter, such as the posterior
or lateral columns may be involved, particularly in the system degenerations.

The term *system degenerations*—or atrophies—is used for a group of rather

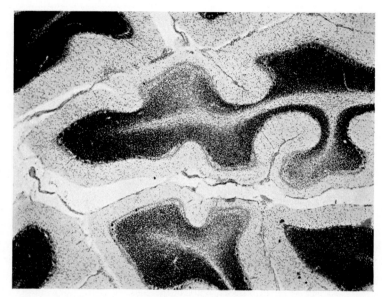

FIG. 52. Multifocal cerebellar atrophy. The affected areas show marked loss of both Purkinje cells and granular layer. (Cresyl violet × 20.)

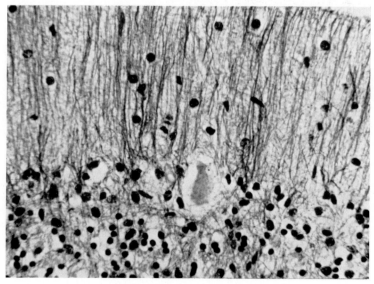

FIG. 53. Fibrous gliosis of the cerebellar molecular layer. (Holzer × 380.)

P.M.R.—5*

ill-defined conditions with a hereditary tendency, characterized, in older patients, by progressive disorder of movement and, frequently, mental deterioration. The pathological changes consist of atrophy and gliosis of several of the subcortical formations and their connecting tracts. Although the adult and juvenile variants of these diseases, particularly Friedreich's ataxia, are better known, the congenital and infantile forms are not uncommon. The clinical picture in such cases is usually overshadowed by the global motor handicap and mental retardation (Norman and Urich, 1958; Gross and Kaltenbäck, 1959b). The formations involved vary in the different conditions. The affected areas can include, for example, the inferior olives, cerebellum and pons, or the posterior and lateral columns of the spinal cord, Clarke's column, parts of the cerebellum and certain nuclei of the brain-stem (Friedreich's ataxia), while the substantia nigra may also be involved in some cases. System atrophies may be associated with other diseases, e.g. the lipidoses (Haddenbrock, 1950), diabetes mellitus, and, in adults, malignant disease.

Cavitation Encephalomalacia

Severe damage may cause rapid breakdown rather than gliosis of the tissues while in other cases repair by scarring can be incomplete. Cavities formed in this way are very common in cases of gliotic encephalopathy. The brains of foetuses and young infants seem to be particularly prone to cavitation, perhaps because they contain more water and less myelin. Their supporting framework of glial tissue and capillaries is also less developed. It is noteworthy in this connection, that in infants the tissue breaks down more readily in the still unmyelinated and 'immature' parts of the brain, such as the centrum semiovale, rather than in the lower and better developed formations.

The size of the cavities varies enormously. The smallest may be microscopic, formed perhaps, by coalescence of vacuoles in initially rarified tissue. A thin linear zone of such rarefaction and breakdown is not uncommon in the middle layers of the cerebral cortex or at its junction with the white matter. Larger cavities are slit-like, round, oval or irregular. Many are multilocular and may be traversed by thin trabeculae. Some cysts are hollow and others, of more recent origin, contain pultaceous or jelly-like material. Most of the older hollow cysts are filled with clear cerebrospinal fluid, but this may occasionally be turbid, blood-stained and contain a deposit. The latter shows phagocytic cells filled with sudanophil material, pigment and other debris (Fig. 54), some of which can be extracellular. The cyst walls and the trabeculae traversing the cysts are formed by glial tissue showing an inconstant proportion of microglia, compound granular corpuscles, astrocytes and capillaries. Particles of calcium may be deposited in the cyst walls, and calcification of nerve cells and capillaries can occur in their vicinity. The cyst lining tends to be rough in the earlier stages, becoming in the course of time progressively smoother. If situated close to the surface, cysts can have only a thin outer wall, consisting, in the grosser instances, of no more than the fused pia and molecular layer of the cortex. Some of the larger cavities communicate with the ventricles but, unless torn by handling, do not usually open into the subarachnoid space.

The Causes of Gliotic Encephalopathy

A good deal has been written about the pathology and the causes of gliotic encephalopathy. Its pathology has, for example, been excellently reviewed by Wolf and Cowen (1956). Allowing for some overlap, they found it possible to group such cases in four categories on the basis of the distribution of the lesions. These groups are: 1, diffuse progressive cerebral cortical atrophy; 2, focal cerebral cortical atrophy and scarring; 3, focal cortical and superficial subcortical encephalomalacia; and 4, multiple cystic encephalomalacia involving chiefly the cerebral white matter. The terms are descriptive and

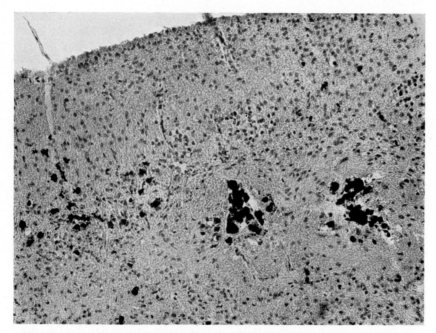

FIG. 54. Loss of nerve cells and cavitation of the cerebral cortex. The cysts contain sudanophil debris. (Scarlet R and haemoloxylin × 160.)

largely self-explanatory. Wolf and Cowen assigned special causal importance to anoxia in all four categories. According to them the anoxia can be brought about in a number of ways, such as asphyxia, local circulatory disturbance, oedema, and epilepsy. It is suggested that the distribution of the lesions depends on the origins of anoxia. "Its varying effect upon the brains, as typified by the four groups of cases presented, would seem to depend on the manner in which it is mediated. The more generalized and uniform the anoxia, the more does relative tissue sensitivity play a part in governing the intensity and distribution of lesions and in producing a picture like that in groups 1 and 2. Even here, associated focal circulatory disturbances lead to localized intensification of the process. One of the seemingly important mechanisms by which anoxia and such localized circulatory disturbances are produced in groups 1 and 2 is that of repeated prolonged and severe convulsive seizures. The causes of these may be varied. It seems more likely that the cystic degeneration of the brain encountered in groups 3 and 4 is due to functional or mechanically induced circulatory disturbances, occasioned in some cases by birth difficulties and resulting in localized anoxia. In group 4 the mechanism, perhaps, may be a stasis in the Galenic system of veins, although this hypothesis is supported only by indirect evidence. That generalized fetal anoxia may produce the same effect seems incontrovertible from one case of intra-uterine carbon monoxide poisoning and from another of maternal shock and hypotension during pregnancy."

Wolf and Cowen do not define anoxia, but they use the term in its broadest sense. Looked at in this way, its rôle in pathogenesis cannot be gainsaid. In combination with other physical and chemical changes, anoxia must be nearly always a factor in disease and injury.

The aetiological importance of epilepsy in the possible genesis of these conditions has been considered on p. 73. Lobar sclerosis following thrombosis of the superior longitudinal sinus has been described by Norman (1936), and similar instances have been also observed at the Fountain Hospital. The rôle of birth injury in relation to this group of conditions has also been discussed very frequently (Malamud, 1959). Many other cases are caused by infection and metabolic disorders; most are probably prenatal in origin, but the pathological changes seldom justify firm conclusions regarding their aetiology.

Porencephaly

Porencephaly is one of the looser pathological terms. As already explained, cerebral cavitation of every kind and extent is common (p. 130) and many authors describe all such cases as porencephalic. It would seem useful, however, to retain a special term, and porencephaly seems a good one, for brains presenting a single, or, at most, a double, large cavity—porus, which communicates with one of the ventricles and is lined by ependyma, unless later partially denuded of it. The condition seems distinct from the cavitation associated with gliotic encephalopathy and from encephalomalacia. It has been described at great length by many writers but none of the classifications proposed so far seems wholly satisfactory. A frequently mentioned subdivision is one by Yakovlev and Wadsworth (1946), according to whom porencephalies fall into two groups: 'schizencephaly', in which the porus is the result of arrested development at the site of one of the primary fissures, and 'encephaloclastic porencephaly', in which previously formed cerebral tissue has been destroyed.

In certain cases the pori are circumscribed roundish holes over which the pallium (i.e. cortex and subjoining white matter) has been replaced by a membrane formed by the fused leptomengines and ependyma. Since this membrane is very delicate, it is often torn in removing the brain, so that the ventricle appears to open directly into the subdural space. The pori are usually situated, bilaterally and symmetrically at about the centre of the outer aspect of the brain. The rim of the cortex at the attachment of the membrane is wedge-shaped in section and is often gliotic. In these cases, there is also an overall dilatation of the lateral ventricles. The defects may be very large and the greater part of the hemispheres is then replaced by the membranes. The areas which tend to be spared in such cases are a crescent-shaped arc at the vertex ('bucket-handle' type of porencephaly) and the parts at the base of the brain (Fig. 55). The larger the porus the more indistinguishable the brain

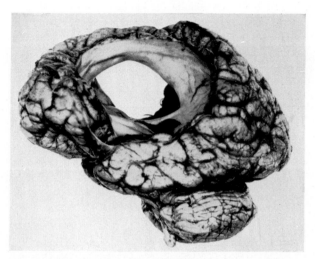

FIG. 55. Porencephaly. Symmetrical large pori with preservation of crescent-shaped areas at the vertex of the brain.

becomes from *hydrencephaly* (p. 181), and it seems possible therefore that the two conditions (this type of porencephaly and hydrencephaly) are quantitative variants of a similarly produced anomaly. It has been suggested that the cause could be arterial occlusion since somewhat similar lesions have been produced in puppies by plugging the common carotid arteries with paraffin (Becker, 1949).

In another group of cases the porus is more tube- or funnel-shaped and opens into a ventricle which is not generally dilated (Fig. 56). These pori may be situated in any part of the brain and the pallium traversed by them is usually relatively normal in thickness. Such cases do not tend to resemble hydrencephaly, but are often combined with other congenital defects, such as microgyria, which is especially common at the margin of the porus (Fig. 57).

Two further groups of cases are often described as porencephaly but they appear to be of a different character. In one, a defect, which can be quite large, is impressed upon the brain surface by an arachnoid cyst. The cavity is not lined by ependyma and does not communicate with the ventricle (Fig. 58). The cortex at the margins of the cyst may show diverse congenital anomalies indicating intrauterine origin of the disturbance. This condition must be regarded as a congenital variant of an arachnoid cyst. In the second group, the cavity is confined to the white matter and is roofed by the corrugations of the overlying cerebral cortex. It may communicate with the ventricle and is possibly formed in some cases as a false diverticulum of the ventricle. It is not lined by ependyma and shows no evidence of ever having been lined by it.

Calcification

Pathological calcification appears to be as common in the brain as in somatic tissues. Calcium can be deposited either in previously abnormal or in seemingly normal structures. The protein matrix upon which it is laid down

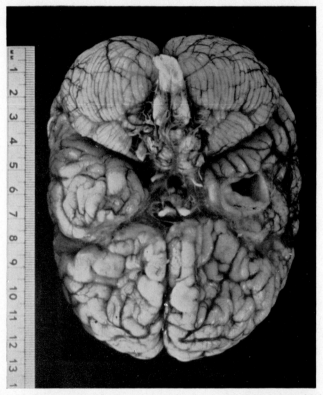

FIG. 56. The opening of a funnel-shaped porus in the right temporal lobe.

is sometimes referred to as pseudo-calcium. It can be demonstrated by dissolving out the mineral salt, and is often seen alongside fully calcified foci in histological preparations. Any part of the brain may be affected. In the early stages, calcium is often deposited in the form of small granules—calcospherites, and these may later coalesce to form deposits of varying size. Calcification often commences in capillaries or larger blood vessels, but may also occur elsewhere: for example, in the choroid plexuses, where the concretions are frequently laminated. An interesting form is encrustation of neurones together with their dendrites and axis cylinders. The latter may be calcified over considerable distances from their site of origin. The periventricular areas are also commonly affected, and the deposits here are often bulky and amorphous. Calcification of the pineal is, of course, a normal phenomenon. As elsewhere, some of the calcified foci in neural tissues may ultimately ossify.

Calcium deposition is initiated and influenced by a complex series of factors, such as the calcium and phosphorus levels of the blood, hydrogen ion concentration, vitamins C and D, and thyroid and parathyroid function (Liebaldt and Descalzo, 1963). Major cerebral calcification is particularly common in certain infections, such as cytomegalic inclusion body disease and

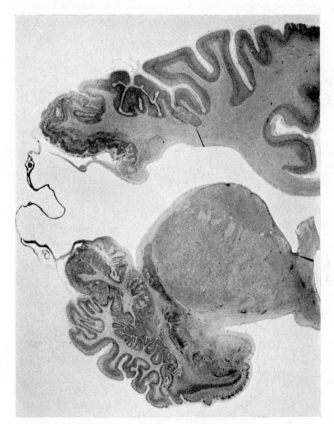

FIG. 57. Porencephaly. The ventricles are continuous with the pori. Microgyria is present at the edge of the defect. (Cresyl violet × 1¼.)

toxoplasmosis (Fig. 59), as well as in the phakomatoses—tuberous sclerosis and Sturge-Weber's disease, some cerebral tumours, hypothyroidism, hypo-parathyroidism and pseudo-hypoparathyroidism (p. 307) (Roberts, 1959). Massive calcification, particularly of the basal ganglia, can also occur without a discoverable cause (Fahr's disease) and can be associated with micrencephaly (Jervis, 1954; Young and Courville, 1961). Other heterogeneous instances of massive calcification of uncertain origin have been reported by Benson (1959) and Dennis and Alvord (1961). The condition can be familial, as in the instances described by Bruyn, Bots and Staal (1964). Cerebral calcification has been reviewed by Erbslöh and Bochnik (1958).

Status Marmoratus

Gliotic brains may display an interesting but not fully understood change —'*marbling*', also referred to as 'état marbré' or 'status marmoratus'. This occurs in the cortex and/or the basal ganglia. In the basal ganglia the macro-

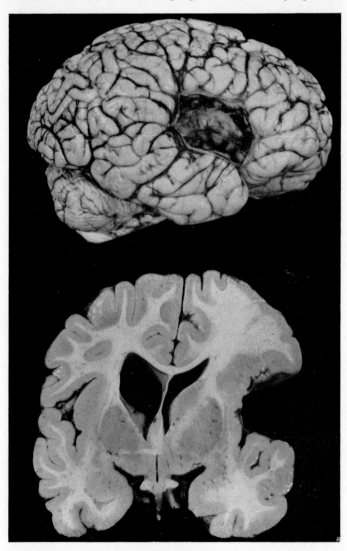

FIG. 58. Congenital arachnoid cyst. The cyst had indented the surface of the brain. The cortex at the margin of the cavity is abnormal. Lateral view, above; coronal block, below.

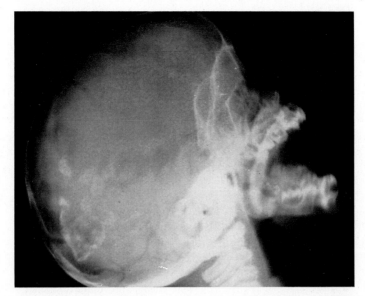

FIG. 59. Intracranial calcification in a case of congenital cytomegalic disease.

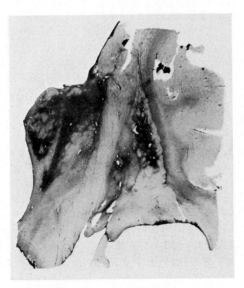

FIG. 60. Status marmoratus of the basal ganglia. Both the putamen and thalamus are affected in this case. (Holzer × 2.)

scopic appearance is that of irregular thin white lines and streaks (like the veins of marble) ramifying upon a background of the gliotic and frequently distorted formation, which can be the thalamus, putamen or globus pallidus. Microscopically, there is always intense fibrous gliosis (Fig. 60) and seemingly, an excess of myelinated nerves, which can be particularly dense around the blood vessels. Some workers distinguish état marbré from *état fibreux*, alleging that in the latter condition myelin fibres are only condensed, in contrast to the état marbré in which there is 'true' hypermyelination. In the cerebral cortex it is usually impossible to be certain of marbling on naked eye examination; the affected areas present only ulegyria or granular atrophy. Microscopically, however, fine radial bundles, 'plaques fibromyéliniques' (Fig. 45), traverse the gliotic cortex separating off islets or larger areas of surviving neurones. These bundles are formed mainly by astrocytes and their fibres, but contain also some myelin sheaths and axis cylinders.

Marbling was first described in the basal ganglia by Cecilie and Oscar Vogt (1920). The patients usually show athetotic palsy, epilepsy and mental retardation, and the clinical picture is sometimes still referred to as 'athétose double' or *Vogts' disease*. However, marbling is not uncommon in other patients. It was present, for example in 14 of 191 unclassifiable cases reported by Crome (1960). The specific feature of bilateral athetosis is, perhaps, submerged in these cases in the gross global motor and mental deficits.

Marbling is usually attributed to aberrant myelin formation or compensatory excessive regeneration of myelin sheaths. But whether the excess of myelin is real is questionable. The appearance could also be interpreted as displacement with condensation of the surviving fibres and, at times, as vagaries of myelin staining (Belloni, 1952; Sylvester, 1960). Whatever the nature of the change, it is widely held that the condition is often caused by anoxia or trauma at birth (Norman, 1949). The history of many cases is consistent with this view. But anoxia is probably not its only cause. It has been suggested by Scharenberg (1957), for example, that these lesions may originate before birth. Marbling of the cortex in adults may also develop following trauma.

Changes in the White Matter

All the main anomalies of the white matter are connected with breakdown of myelin. This may occur, as in Wallerian degeneration of peripheral nerves, as a consequence of neuronal loss or in the distal segments of severed fibres. In such cases, the axis cylinders degenerate concurrently with the myelin sheaths, and the process is usually accompanied by liberation of brightly staining sudanophil debris and proliferation of lipid phagocytes. In other conditions demyelination is primary and in infants there may also be faulty myelin formation. These anomalies are usually considered in the context of the leucodystrophies (p. 250). Scarring and cavitation of the white matter associated with gliotic encephalopathy have been mentioned already on p. 125 and status marmoratus on p. 136. It remains to discuss here a few further changes.

Spongiform Encephalopathy

A relatively frequent change, particularly in infants, is spongiform degeneration of the brain or *status spongiosus*. This is often regarded as a manifestation of chronic oedema. In histological preparations, the tissue, and especially the white matter, is rarified showing numerous vacuoles which may coalesce and cause gross cavitation. Extensive status spongiosus can be associated with lack of myelination and gliotic change. Although spongy degeneration can be ubiquitous, it is often particularly conspicuous at the junction of the cortex and white matter (Fig. 61). Widespread status spongiosus may occur in sib-

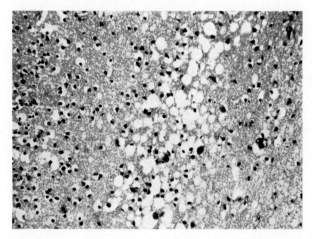

FIG. 61. Spongiform encephalopathy. Vacuolation is particularly marked at the junction of the cortex and white matter. (Haematoxylin and eosin × 200.)

lings and such cases have been described as instances of the so-called Canavan's type of diffuse sclerosis. This commences in early infancy, often after a short period of seemingly normal development, and manifests itself clinically by failure of mental development, increasing paralysis and epilepsy. All laboratory tests have been unspecific. Most of the identified cases were Jewish, reports having come from towns with large populations of Jewish immigrants (vide p. 51). It has been suggested by some workers that the condition is a variant of leucodystrophy (Wolman, 1958; Zu Rhein, Eichman and Puletti, 1960; Bogaert, 1960). The disease has been recently reviewed by Banker, Robertson and Victor (1964) on the basis of 24 previously published cases and seven new ones of their own. However, identical degeneration is certainly seen more frequently than these figures suggest, occurring also in infants suffering from other disorders, such as hydrocephalus and certain metabolic disorders, e.g. maple syrup urine disease (Crome, 1964). Spongiform encephalopathy also occurs in adults and the electron microscopical studies of such cases suggest that the cavities originate in astroglial cytoplasm (Marin and Vial, 1964).

Metachromasia

Material in the tissue clefts, vacuoles and histocytes of sections taken from the brains of certain cases of leucodystrophy, lipidosis, status spongiosus, gliotic encephalopathy and other forms of leucoencephalopathy may stain metachromatically with such dyes as cresyl violet and thionine in a slightly acid solution and give a positive P.A.S. reaction. Other tissues of these cases, such as the kidney (and urine), may also contain similarly staining material. The chemical basis for such metachromatic staining was believed to be hexosamine, but this has been disproved and it is now held that this staining is favoured by a high level of cerebroside sulphatides (Cumings, 1960; Diezel, 1960) or any other compound with evenly spaced negatively charged groups (Pearce, 1960). Despite wide acceptance of this term is seems unprofitable to define metachromatic leucodystrophy solely in terms of staining reactions. Metachromasia in stained sections is a capricious and impermanent phenomenon, and is known to occur in many different conditions as well as in normal persons and animals (Smith, 1949). On the other hand, it may be difficult to demonstrate even in known positive cases. It is therefore fortunate that the rôle of the sulphatides and related compounds in these disorders appears to have been recently confirmed by biochemical studies. *Metachromatic leucodystrophy*, a condition in which presence of metachromatic particles dominates the morphological picture, is described on p. 253.

Other Changes

Gliotic areas, particularly if hypertrophic, often contain homogeneous hyaline bodies—Rosenthal fibres—which resemble fibrin or fibrinoid material in their staining properties. In a few recorded cases of megalencephaly the brains, and particularly the white matter, contained large numbers of these fibres which were particularly concentrated around blood vessels, under the pia and in the subarcuate fibres of the white matter (Alexander, 1949; Crome, 1953; Wohlwill, Bernstein and Yakovlev, 1959; Vogel and Hallervorden, 1962). This condition is now regarded as one of the variants of leucodystrophy (p. 255).

Another form of degeneration is focal destruction of the myelin around blood vessels (Naidoo, 1952). The affected vessels are surrounded by a rarefied zone in which myelin is absent and which is loosely reticulated by a network of fibres which may contain a few lipid phagocytes (Fig. 62). These reticulated areas can be very large and conspicuous in gargoylism (Norman, Urich and France, 1959), but are quite unspecific and occur in many other conditions.

Zones of the white matter particularly vulnerable to such pathological changes as necrosis, rarefaction, demyelination, cavitation and gliosis, are the periventricular areas, especially, perhaps, the upper angle of the lateral ventricles. (This area is also often affected in cases of disseminated sclerosis.) The reason for this vulnerability is not understood. Banker and Larroche (1962) have recently reported on the frequency of such lesions in the periventricular areas ('periventricular leukomalacia') in infants dying during the first month of life, ascribing the change to severe anoxia. Topologically analogous lesions in periventricular areas have been produced experimentally in cats by Abram-owicz (1964) who occluded the basilar and the carotid arteries. He attributes the special vulnerability of these areas to the character of their blood supply, the long penetrating arteries supplying these parts having few collaterals and no authentic anastomoses. An additional element of vulnerability is, according to him, the 'border-zone' character of the periventricular white matter (see however p. 122).

Among the rarer causes of acquired encephalopathy in infancy and child-hood are the so-called *para-infectious encephalomyelitides* (p. 67) which may

FIG. 62. Perivascular reticulation of the white matter. (Haematoxylin and Van Gieson × 120.)

follow some of the exanthemata or, more rarely, vaccination. The neuropatho-logical picture of this condition is very distinctive in the acute and fatal cases. On naked-eye examination the white matter may be purpuric or be studded with numerous pinhead-sized areas of softening and discolouration, which correspond microscopically to perivenous areas of demyelination and pro-liferation of lipid phagocytes (Fig. 14). It is not known, however, what residual changes are left in the milder cases who survive but develop mental retarda-tion.

Evidence of Infection

Although many of the scars and cysts in the brains of mental defectives are probably caused by infection, evidence of continued or past inflammation is less common or certain at autopsy than might be expected. Moreover, damage caused by infection, even if severe enough to result in mental retardation, can remain diffuse and not ascertainable by available methods. On the other hand, such 'inflammatory' changes as perivascular cellular exudate, diffuse or focal increase in leucocytes, and aggregations of neuroglia, are not necessarily evidence of an underlying infection; they may be a reaction to the breakdown of tissue produced by other causes.

Nevertheless, signs of past or continued infection are found in a considerable number of cases. Traces of previous meningitis, such as meningeal fibrosis and opacity, cystic arachnoiditis, granular ependymitis, and occlusion of the foramina or cerebral aqueduct, with, perhaps, obstructive hydrocephalus, are not infrequent. Fresh, supervening and, occasionally, terminal meningitis, following repeated drainage of hydrocephalus or some short-circuiting operation, also occurs.

In certain cases meningitis becomes chronic and can lead to considerable thickening of the leptomeninges and periventricular areas by granulation tissue. Since meningitis frequently commences as an infection of the choroid plexus, it is always worth while searching this structure for such evidence of old infection as interstitial fibrosis, envelopment by a collagenous capsule, calcification and loss of the lining epithelium. Survivors from tuberculous meningitis may show marked chronic arteritis with calcification and ischaemic softening of the brain (Fig. 13).

Encapsulated cerebral abscesses are another of the rarer causes of mental defect. They were noted on four occasions in a series of 500 cases at the Fountain Hospital.

Virus encephalitis, or encephalitides presumed to be caused by viruses, are rare in the United Kingdom. Epidemic or Von Economo's encephalitis may cause post-encephalitic parkinsonism (p. 66), and, anatomically, cellular loss and depigmentation in the substantia nigra together with other lesions in the diencephalon and brain-stem, Perivascular cellular cuffing, Alzheimer's neurofibrillary change and hyaline inclusions in the neuronal cytoplasm have been reported in this condition. However, Greenfield and Bosanquet (1953) did not find inclusion bodies in any of the 10 cases of post-encephalitic parkinsonism examined by them. Neurofibrillary changes were present both in the substantia nigra and the locus coeruleus in 9 of the cases. The histological appearances in another form of encephalitis—the subacute inclusion body encephalitis, can also be very characteristic (Crome and Guthrie, 1963) (p. 66).

A few brains show variously distributed lesions suggestive of encephalitis, i.e. nodes of mononuclear cells of uncertain origin in the cerebral cortex and other formations, together with fairly widespread perivascular cellular exudate. These lesions are sometimes associated with fibrous gliosis and cavitation. They are difficult to interpret without a clear-cut clinical history of encephalitis. However, some sporadic instances of encephalitis have been reported in England and Wales (Conybeare, 1952), and lesions resembling those outlined above have been described in some of these cases by Greenfield (1950).

As already explained, infection occurring during the earlier periods of gestation does not leave specific traces. In later stages, infection may be followed by gliotic encephalopathy and encephalomalacia, while towards the end of gestation the appearances begin to conform to the usual post-natal patterns of inflammatory processes. The changes caused by such infections, including particularly those of toxoplasmosis and cytomegalic inclusion disease, have been reviewed by Wolf and Cowen (1959).

Meningeal Changes

The soft meninges are normally thin and transparent, and the commonest abnormality in the severely subnormal is fibrosis, with some opacity and thickening of the meninges. This is, in most cases, a result of meningitis but may also occur in other conditions. The thickening can be very marked, for example, in cases of gargoylism (p. 232). Extensive meningeal adhesions can lead to hydrocephalus or, if they are localized, to the formation of an *arachnoid cysts*. Such cysts may occasionally form prenatally (p. 133). The meninges can be discoloured, a rusty red or orange tinge indicating old haemorrhage. Subarachnoid haemorrhage may be caused by injury at birth or occur later as a result, for example, of haemorrhagic disease of the newborn. Altered blood may remain encapsulated in the meninges for many years. The underlying tissue may also be lacerated and, in some cases, the haemorrhages break into the brain, or even, into the ventricle. Meningeal neoplasms are very rare in the severely subnormal but may occur in association with neurofibromatosis (p. 192).

The commonest dural change is subdural haemorrhage. A somewhat enigmatic condition—*pachymeningitis haemorrhagica interna*, in which the dura is discoloured, thickened and formed by alternate layers of fibrous and granulation tissue, may also occur, albeit very rarely, prenatally and in infants. One such case was observed at the Fountain Hospital.

Abnormalities of Lower Formations

In cases of mental retardation, lower formations have received even less attention than the cerebral hemispheres. The spinal cord, for example, is not always even looked at by pathologists. Hypoplasia, agenesis or atrophy may, of course, affect the lower levels in the same way as the higher ones, and some of these changes have already been considered. Absence of one or more of the cranial nerve nuclei in the brain-stem has been described under the name of the Moebius' syndrome (Pitner, Edwards and McCormick, 1965). It is difficult to recognize the milder cellular abnormalities in the reticular formation, but the inferior olive is more distinctive in shape and cellular pattern, and anomalies there are more easily discernible. Simplification of its undulate contours is relatively frequent in cases of mental retardation. The inferior olives may be also enlarged in the manner described by Gautier and Blackwood (1961). Lower formations are affected more selectively in the system atrophies (p. 128). Changes not related specifically to mental retardation (e.g. poliomyelitis or syringomyelia), are not considered in this book.

Secondary atrophy of certain subcortical formations and of the long tracts, such as the cortico-pontine and cortico-spinal, is common in cases of mental retardation. Severe retrograde degeneration of the dorso-medial thalamic nuclei following premotor frontal lobe atrophy was described, for example, by Norman (1945). Secondary atrophy may reduce perceptibly the size of the cerebral peduncles, pons, medulla and spinal cord. Shallow vertical sulci develop occasionally upon the ventral surface of the cerebral peduncles, indicating the position of the atrophic cortico-spinal tracts. On account of the smallness of the pyramids, the inferior olives often appear unduly prominent. The relation between the cerebrum, particularly its frontal lobes, and the cerebellum is well known and has been mentioned already. An interesting problem is presented by the spinal cord in cases of extensive cerebral abnormality. In some, the cord shows the 'expected' discrete atrophy and demyelination of areas occupied by the cortico-spinal tracts. In others there is no such discreteness; the spinal cord is instead generally micromyelic showing a reduction in volume of the white matter but no demyelination. It may be that this difference is related to the time of the causative disturbance. If this occurred before the long tracts had properly formed, general micromyelia might follow. The changes in the spinal cord would then represent agenesis rather than atrophy. A disturbance in later ontogenesis could, on the other hand, cause demyelination and atrophy of already formed tracts. There is reason to believe that this explanation was at least partially correct in the series studied at the Fountain Hospital, but this requires further verification. It may well repay the effort, since corroboration of the presumed time of onset of a disturbance is often missing in pathological studies. Fibrous gliosis of the spinal cord has also been observed. Its grey matter can be gliotic without necessarily showing neuronal loss.

Spinal cords of patients with cerebral palsy associated with mental retardation may also show continuous or discontinuous myelin loss in the posterior, lateral and, sometimes, also anterior columns. Such demyelination—*funiculosis*—is in adults characteristic of subacute combined degeneration or vitamin B_{12} deficiency, although it may occur in other conditions. Identical changes are present in cases of Leigh's encephalomyelopathy of children (p. 314), some severe cases of infantile and juvenile diabetes mellitus, and, in our experience, also a few similar cases, in whom no metabolic disease had been established during life. Whether all of these changes indicate primary or secondary disturbances of vitamin B metabolism remains to be answered.

Other changes of the spinal cord, such as micromyelia (p. 101) and those associated with spina bifida (p. 175) are mentioned elsewhere.

The cerebellum is the best studied of the subcortical formations. *Cerebellar hypoplasia* or *atrophy* is not uncommon. In some cases this is uniform and in others either the hemispheres or the vermis show greater involvement. A form of agenesis of the vermis is the so-called *Dandy-Walker syndrome* (p. 176). A cerebellar malformation, 'rhombencephalosynapsis' showing absence of the vermis (but not of its nodule), the superior medullary velum and nuclei fastigii has been described by Gross (1959). Gliotic changes are also frequent in the cerebellum and may present certain characteristic patterns. Atrophy and gliosis may, for example, be either diffuse and general or affect certain of the lobules. The periphery can be more involved than the central parts and vice versa. Some of these cerebellar changes are particularly frequent in cases of epilepsy. The cellular changes may likewise be diverse (Fig. 51). The Purkinje cells are usually the most vulnerable element, but in some conditions, e.g. diabetes mellitus and lipidosis, the granular layer shows greater involvement. Many other instances of cerebellar granular layer atrophy in association with mental deficiency have been described (Norman, 1940; Jervis, 1950; and Ule, 1952). Ule subsequently reviewed the general problem of cerebellar changes (Ule, 1957). Cellular anomalies, presence of ectopic grey matter and cerebellar microgyria (Figs. 37 and 63) are all common in cases of severe subnormality.

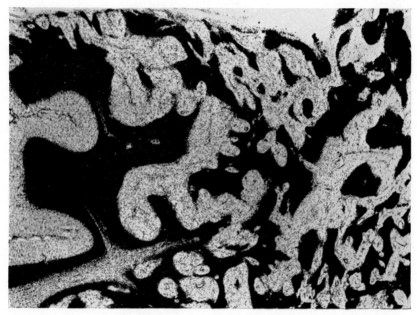

Fig. 63. Cerebellar microgyria. Two normal folia can be seen on the left. (Cresyl violet × 16.)

The Cranial Nerves and the Peripheral Nervous System

The eyes are, for obvious reasons, the most studied part of the extracranial nervous system. Blindness and ocular anomalies are frequent in severe subnormality, the commonest being cataract, microphthalmia (p. 7), retrolental fibroplasia (p. 78), coloboma, choroidoretinitis, and retinal atrophy or hypoplasia with and without pigmentation. Sorsby and Williams (1960) have suggested that certain familial cases of retinal aplasia constitute a distinct clinical entity. Even more common is some degree of hypoplasia or atrophy of the more central parts of the optic pathway, i.e. the optic nerves, chiasma, optic tracts, external geniculate bodies, the optic radiation and the striate cerebral cortex. Complete or partial deafness is probably as prevalent as blindness, but, save for a few studies, such as Vallesi's (1958) on the ear in congenital hydrocephalus, and of Hall (1963) on the effects of asphyxia, regrettably little is known of its underlying pathology because the auditory pathway is anatomically considerably more difficult to examine than the optic one. Hall claims to have demonstrated that in newborn asphyxiated infants the cochlea itself remains normal while the main damage falls upon the dorsal cochlear nuclei and, to a lesser extent, the superior olives and inferior colliculi. He could demonstrate no such damage in kittens subjected to asphyxia. Equally obscure are changes in the autonomic and the peripheral nervous systems. Recent work on the myenteric plexuses and rectal biopsies in suspected cases of lipidosis has shown, however, that neurones and nerves of the autonomic system are frequently affected in such diseases of the central organ as the lipidoses, glycogen storage disease and leucodystrophy. Metachromatic staining has been demonstrated in peripheral nerves in cases of metachromatic leucodystrophy (Hagberg, Sourander and Thorén, 1962). Cases of congenital insensitivity to pain—*sensory syndrome*—some of which are caused by demyelinating peripheral neuropathy, occur occasionally among the severely subnormal, although most patients so far reported appear to have been only mildly retarded (Ogden, Robert and Carmichael, 1959; Wadia and Dastur, 1960; Snyder and Auld, 1962). (See also p. 329).

Somatic Abnormalities

Only neural abnormalities have been considered so far, but mental defectives often present associated visceral and skeletal changes. When marked and relatively constant, these form recognised components of one of the classified syndromes, e.g. the phakomatoses (p. 182). Similarly, the heart is frequently congenitally malformed in Down's disease, and hepato-splenomegaly is an almost constant finding in gargoylism. A characteristic facies has been described in severe hypercalcaemia of infancy, in what is sometimes called the de Lange syndrome, and other conditions (see p. 325). The scalp may be ridged and grooved antero-posteriorly in cases of microcephaly (Berg and Windrath-Scott, 1962). Some conditions, such as acrocephalosyndactyly (Apert's syndrome), naevoid amentia and the Laurence-Moon-Biedl syndrome are, indeed, recognized by these somatic rather than neural changes. It has been suggested that congenital ichthyosis associated with mental deficiency and spasticity constitutes a syndrome (Sjögren and Larsson, 1957; Richards, 1960; Scarabicchi and Martino, 1963), and that another (Rud's syndrome) consists of congenital ichthyosis linked rather loosely and inconstantly with dwarfism, infantilism, mental retardation, epilepsy, anaemia and polyneuritis (York-Moore and Rundle, 1962; Äkesson, 1964). The above and other syndromes are considered more fully in the following chapters (cf. p. 321 *et seq.*). Many other somatic anomalies, such as abnormal head shape, skeletal deformity, skin disease and gonadal hypoplasia seem to be relatively common both in the classified and unclassifiable cases of mental deficiency, but have received little systematic study.

Two general observations will be made here. The first is the frequency of *overall smallness* in the severely subnormal, particularly the lower-grade patients, who are often dwarfed.* Retardation of growth is probably related to lack of trophic regulation; hemiplegic limbs are often smaller than healthy ones. The reduced quality and quantity of response to external stimuli, as well as nutritional and social handicaps are further contributory factors, while in a few cases there may be specific endocrine involvement. Ashby and Stewart (1933) measured the body weight, arm length and foot length of mental defectives of different mental ages, and found that all of these decrease with intelligence, the fall being more rapid towards the lowest mental levels. Experience at the Fountain Hospital has been in keeping with that observation (Fig. 20, p. 98). The skeletal age in the severely subnormal was studied by Pozsonyi and Zarfas (1963) and Pozsonyi, Gibson and Zarfas (1964). It was found that while there was no overall delay of skeletal maturation those with the less common metabolic defects and the severely retarded children with associated multiple handicaps did present delay in bone maturation. Children with Down's disease showed retarded bone growth up to 8 years of age, after which growth accelerated to the 15th year of life. It might be thought that endocrine disturbances could play a leading part in the causation of such reduced growth but apart from certain specific and rare syndromes there is no evidence of primary endocrine deficiency in mental defectives as a group. For example, Sylvester (1964), did not find any marked anomalies of weight in the pituitary and adrenal glands obtained from 100 necropsies on mentally defective subjects. He thought that the thyroid was somewhat reduced in size, but there is no evidence of primary thyroid dysfunction in the vast majority of the mentally retarded.

The second observation relates to expectation of life and the *mode of death*. Mental defectives die, on average, at an earlier age than mentally normal individuals, and the lowest-grade patients die earlier still. Thus, in a series of 117 autopsies at the Fountain Hospital 77 cases were below the age of 5 and 45 of these below 3, even though very few of these children were suffering, on admisson, from any serious acute illnesses. Though most of the patients at the Fountain Hospital were children below the age of 16, similar observations have also been made in institutions for older persons. Sylvester (1961) noted, for example, in his series of mainly adult cases a differential mortality, subjects with smaller brains dying earlier than others. In severely subnormal infants and children the cause of death is often respiratory disease, usually described as bronchopneumonia. The pathology of the condition is, however, unlike that in adult or mentally normal cases. There is little polymorphonuclear exudate in the alveoli or consolidation of the usual type. The lungs present instead a pattern of lobular collapse, infective atelectasis and inhalation pneumonia. This suggests serious impairment in the protective mechanisms against inhalation of food and saliva, and of expectoration of inhaled material and bronchial secretion. This impairment is probably the result of several factors. It is possible that the cough reflex is depressed by the neurological condition. These patients are also more immobile than normal children, and in most hospitals unavoidably have little exercise or individual care

* See Mosier, H. D., Grossman, H. J., and Dingman, H. F. (1965). *Pediatrics*, **36**, 465.

and handling compared with that given by a mother to her child at home. On the other hand, such evidence as is available suggests that tissue and humoral defence reactions at the antigen—antibody level operate in a fairly normal manner in most of these patients. Earlier death can thus be best explained by inadequacy of the biological and social defences against respiratory mishap. Any additional disease, respiratory or other, viz. digestive upset, fits or fever will tend to increase still further the patient's disability and make him an even more likely victim of inhalation. The respiratory system thus becomes the *locus minoris resistentiae*, where adaptation to environment is deficient owing to primary neurological disease and social alienation. The greater expectation of life in the severely subnormal nursed at home compared with similar patients in hospitals can be partly explained on this basis.

Brains Showing no Structural Lesions

Lastly, it is necessary to consider the difficult and unsolved problem of brains showing no detectable abnormality. Their proportion among the mentally retarded in general is unknown; at the Fountain Hospital 8 such cases occurred among 191 unclassifiable ones. This problem has also troubled pathologists in the past and has been briefly considered by Jacob (1956). Many workers in the past have succumbed to the temptation to attach undue weight to minor anatomical anomalies. This must be resisted. Increasing awareness of the surprisingly wide limits of normal variation in brain structure has thrown much doubt on the significance of many of the previously reported findings. Respect is also enjoined by the impressive power of the brain to compensate for lost tissue and function, so that even the grosser anomalies need not necessarily entail mental defect. Minor, circumscribed and questionable histological anomalies are unlikely therefore to account for the gross amentia of the severely subnormal. It would be easier to understand this problem of the 'normal' brains if the cases in question had been nearer the borderline of intellectual normality, but this is not always so. Several characteristics of the 8 cases mentioned above are listed in Table 2 below. All have been examined pathologically and showed no ascertainable change.

Table 2. CLINICAL FEATURES AND PERCENTAGE OF AVERAGE BRAIN
WEIGHT IN 8 CASES WITH NO STRUCTURAL ABNORMALITY

	per cent
1. Low-grade imbecile, possibly psychotic	104
2. Unclassified idiot	107
3. Epileptic	101
4. Spastic and epileptic idiot	90
5. Epileptic idiot	92
6. Educationally subnormal epileptic with cerebral palsy	112
7. Epileptic feebleminded	102
8. Imbecile	90

A suggestion that can be made is the already discussed relative inadequacy of the available anatomical methods. Future refinement of techniques will certainly permit the recognition of many still unknown changes in the brain, particularly those of a submicroscopic kind. In this context the case described by Gonatas and Goldensohn (1965) is of special interest. A biopsy specimen of the brain was obtained from a child aged $2\frac{1}{2}$ years who suffered from mental retardation, epilepsy, and blindness, and whose E.E.G. showed features of hypsarrhythmia (p. 334). The material was examined both by light and electron microscopy. The only 'abnormality' seen by light microscopy was shrinkage, irregularity of outline and increased staining density of some neurones, a finding so common in all specimens as to have no pathological significance. Electron microscopy revealed, however, striking enlargement and other structural abnormalities of many presynaptic axon terminals. The neurons themselves showed no abnormality.

The changes in some cases may be entirely molecular, as are, perhaps, those in schizophrenia (p. 91). Although the problem of the psychoses among the mentally retarded is discussed more fully elsewhere (p. 84), it may be stated here that the few examined brains of patients diagnosed in life as having schizophrenia or Heller's dementia have usually shown no ascertainable change, while a few showed lipidosis. The information in Table 2 does not suggest that many of these cases could be classified with psychoses. It is also clear that they are not a homogeneous group, and that the problem merits further thought and study.

Some interest has been taken over a number of years in the concept of the 'brain-injured child' first outlined by Strauss and Lehtinen (1947). It was suggested by them that *'brain-injured children'*, i.e. those whose defect was caused by structural abnormalities of the brain, constituted a distinct group recognizable by certain clinical and behavioural features, while other cases were the product of familial genetic causes. The theory was never generally accepted (Wortis, 1956) and should now be entirely discarded. It is clear from the data presented in this book that no useful distinction can be made between 'brain-injured' and other defectives on pathological grounds. Conditions due to hereditary causes are often, and perhaps usually, associated with cerebral anomalies, while the rare brains showing no change ascertainable by present-day methods have been of patients presenting a wide variety of clinical signs.

REFERENCES

ABRAMOWICZ, A. (1964). *J. Neurol. Neurosurg. Psychiat.*, **27**, 85.
ÅKESSON, H. O. (1964). *Acta med. scand.*, **175**, 115.
ALEXANDER, W. S. (1949). *Brain*, **72**, 373.
ASHBY, W. R., and STEWART, R. M. (1932). *J. Neurol. Psychopath.*, **13**, 303.
ASHBY, W. R., and STEWART, R. M. (1933). *J. Neurol. Psychopath.*, **14**, 217.
BANKER, B. Q., and LARROCHE, J. -C. (1962). *Arch. Neurol. Psychiat. (Chic.)*, **7**, 386.
BANKER, B. Q., ROBERTSON, J. T., and VICTOR, M. (1964). *Neurology (Minneap.)*, **14**, 981.
BECKER, H. (1949). *Dtsch. Z. Nervenheilk.*, **161**, 407.
BELLONI, G. B. (1952). In Proc. First Internat. Congr. of Neuropathology, Rome: Rosenberg and Sellier, **2**, 235.
BENDA, C. E. (1952). 'Developmental Disorders of Mentation and Cerebral Palsies,' New York: Grune and Stratton.
BENSON, P. F. (1959). *Arch. Dis. Childh.*, **34**, 120.
BERG, J. M., and WINDRATH-SCOTT, A. (1962). *J. ment. Defic. Res.*, **6**, 75.
BERRY, R. J. A. (1938). 'A Cerebral Atlas,' London: Oxford University Press.

BINNS, W., JAMES, L. F., and SHUPE, J. L. (1962). *Arch. environm. Hlth.*, 5, 106.
BITTNER, H. (1959–60). *Zbl. allg. Path. path. Anat.*, 100, 64.
BLACKWOOD, W., BUXTON, P. H., CUMINGS, J. N., ROBERTSON, D. J., and TUCKER, S. M. (1963). *Arch. Dis. Childh.*, 38, 193.
BOGAERT, L. VAN (1960). *Wld. Neurol.*, 1, 396.
BOLTON, J. S. (1914). 'The Brain in Health and Disease,' London: Arnold.
BRANDON, M. W. G., KIRMAN, B. H., and WILLIAMS, C. E. (1959). *J. ment. Sci.*, 105, 271.
BRUYN, G. W., BOTS, G. TH. A. M., and STAAL (1964). *Psychiat. Neurol. Neurochir. (Amst.)*, 67, 342.
CHRISTENSEN, E., and VESTERGAARD, E. (1949). *Acta psychiat. (Kbh.)*, 24, 363.
COCKER, J., GEORGE, S. W., and YATES, P. O. (1965). *Develop. Med. Child Neurol.*, 7, 235.
CONYBEARE, E. T. (1952). *Mon. Bull. Minist. Hlth. Lab. Serv.*, 11, 184.
CORSELLIS, J. A. N. (1957). *Brain*, 80, 193.
COWEN, D., and OLMSTEAD, E. V. (1963). *J. Neuropath. exp. Neurol.*, 22, 175.
CRAVIOTO, H., and FEIGIN, I. (1960). *J. Neuropath. exp. Neurol.*, 19, 572.
CROME, L. (1952). *J. Path. Bact.*, 64, 479.
CROME, L. (1953). *Brain*, 76, 215.
CROME, L. (1954). *J. ment. Sci.*, 100, 894.
CROME, L. (1955). *Lancet*, 1, 882.
CROME, L. (1956). *J. Path. Bact.*, 71, 335.
CROME, L. (1957). *J. Neurol. Neurosurg. Psychiat.*, 20, 117.
CROME, L. (1960). *Brit. med. J.*, 1, 897.
CROME, L. (1964). 'Neuropathological Changes in Diseases Caused by Inborn Errors of Metabolism.' In Neurometabolic Disorders in Childhood. Edinburgh: Livingstone.
CROME, L., and FOLEY, J. (1959). *J. ment. Defic. Res.*, 3, 63.
CROME, L., and GUTHRIE, J. (1963). *Arch. Dis. Childh.*, 38, 301.
CROME, L., and WELLER, S. D. V. (1965). *Arch. Dis. Childh.*, 40, 502.
CUMINGS, J. N. (1960). In Modern Scientific Aspects of Neurology, London: Arnold, p. 330.
CURRARINO, G., and SILVERMAN, F. N. (1960). *Radiology*, 74, 206.
DEKABAN, A. (1959). *J. Neuropath. exp. Neurol.*, 18, 620.
DEKABAN, A. S., and MAGEE, K. R. (1958). *Neurology (Minneap.)*, 8, 193.
DEMYER, W., and ZEMAN, W. (1963). *Conf. neurol. (Basel)*, 23, 1.
DENNIS, J. P., and ALVORD, E. C. (1961). *J. Neuropath. exp. Neurol.*, 20, 412.
DIEZEL, P. B. (1960). In Modern Scientific Aspects of Neurology, London: Arnold, p. 98.
DODGSON, M. C. H. (1951). *J. Neurol. Neurosurg. Psychiat.*, 14, 303.
DYGGVE, H., and TYGSTRUP, I. (1964). *Develop. Med. Child Neurol.*, 6, 581.
EAYRS, J. T. (1960). *Brit. med. Bull.*, 16, 122.
ERBSLÖH, F., and BOCHNIK, H. (1958). 'Symmetrische Pseudokalk—und Kalkablagerungen im Gehirn,' in C. Lubarsch, F. Henke, and R. Rössle's Handbuch der speziellen pathologischen Anatomie und Histologie, 13, ed. W. Scholz, Pt. 2, book B, Berlin: Springer, p. 1769.
FALCONER, M. A., and CAVANAGH, J. B. (1959). *Brain*, 82, 483.
FALCONER, M. A., SERAFETINIDES, E. A., and CORSELLIS, J. A. N. (1964). *Arch. Neurol. (Chic.)*, 10, 233.
GAUTIER, J. C., and BLACKWOOD, W. (1961). *Brain*, 84, 341.
GONATAS, N. K., and GOLDENSOHN, E. S. (1965). *J. Neuropath. exp. Neurol.*, 24, 539.
GRCVIC, N., and ROBERT, F. (1960). *J. Neuropath. exp. Neurol.*, 20, 399.
GREENFIELD, J. G. (1950). *Brain*, 73, 141.
GREENFIELD, J. G., and BOSANQUET, F. D. (1953). *J. Neurol. Neurosurg. Psychiat.*, 16, 213.
GROSS, H. (1959). *Arch. Psychiat. Nervenkr.*, 199, 537.
GROSS, H., and KALTENBÄCK, E. (1958). *Wien. Z. Nervenheilk.*, 15, 91.
GROSS, H., and KALTENBÄCK, E. (1959a). *Wien. med. Wschr.*, 109, 119.
GROSS, H., and KALTENBÄCK, E. (1959b). *Dtsch. Z. Nervenheilk.*, 179, 388.
GROSS, H., and UIBERRACK, B. (1955). *Virchows Arch. path. Anat.*, 327, 577.
GROSS, H., HOFF, H., and KALTENBÄCK, E. (1959). *Wien. Z. Nervenheilk.*, 16, 1.
HADDENBROCK, S. (1950). *Arch. Psychiat. Nervenkr.*, 185, 129.
HAGBERG, B., SOURANDER, P., and THORÉN, L. (1962). *Acta paediat. (Uppsala)*, 51, Suppl. 135, 63.
HALL, J. G. (1963). *Acta oto-laryng. (Stockh.)*, Suppl. 188, 331.

HALLERVORDEN, J., and MEYER, J. -E. (1956). 'Cerebrale Kinderlähmung' (Früherworbene körperliche und geistige Defektzustände) in O. Lubarsch, F. Henke, and R. Rössle's Handbuch der speziellen pathologischen Anatomie und Histologie, 13, ed. W. Scholz, Pt. 4, Berlin: Springer, p. 194.

HICKS, S. P., CAVANAUGH, M. C., and O'BRIEN, E. D. (1962). Amer. J. Path., 40, 615.

JACOB, H. (1956). 'Angeborener erblicher Schwachsinn einschliesslich Befundlose Idiotie, sowie Megalencephalie bei angeborenem Schwachsinn,' in O. Lubarsch, F. Henke, and R. Rössle's Handbuch der speziellen pathologischen Anatomie und Histologie, 13, ed. W. Scholz, Pt. 4, Berlin: Springer, p. 59.

JERVIS, G. A. (1950). J. nerv. ment. Dis., 111, 398.

JERVIS, G. A. (1954). J. Neuropath. exp. Neurol., 13, 318.

JOSEPHY, H., and LICHTENSTEIN, B. W. (1943). Arch. Neurol. Psychiat. (Chic.), 50, 575.

KLEINSASSER, O. (1955–56). Neue öst. Z. Kinderheilk., 1, 235.

KONIGSMARK, B. W., and SIDMAN, R. L. (1963). J. Neuropath. exp. Neurol., 22, 643.

KOSSOWITSCH, B. (1892). Virchows Arch. path. Anat., 128, 497.

LAURENCE, K. M. (1964). Develop. Med. Child Neurol., 6, 585.

LIEBALDT, G., and DESCALZO, C. (1962–63). Dtsch. Z. Nervenheilk., 184, 388.

LYON, G., and SÉE, G. (1963). Rev. neurol. (Paris), 109, 133.

MALAMUD, N. (1959). J. Neuropath. exp. Neurol., 18, 141.

MARIN, O., and VIAL, J. D. (1964). Acta neuropath. (Berl.), 4, 218.

MENKES, J. H., PHILIPPART, M., and CLARK, D. B. (1964). Arch. Neurol. (Chic.), 11, 198.

MEYER, A., and COOK, L. C. (1937). J. ment. Sci., 83, 258.

MEYER, A., and JONES, T. B. (1939). J. ment. Sci., 85, 206.

MEYER, A., FALCONER, M. A., and BECK, E. (1954). J. Neurol. Neurosurg. Psychiat., 17, 276.

MINKOWSKI, M. (1952). Schweiz. Arch. Neurol. Psychiat., 76, 110.

NAIDOO, D. (1952). J. ment. Sci., 99, 74.

NORMAN, R. M. (1936–37). J. Neurol. Psychopath., 17, 135.

NORMAN, R. M. (1938). J. Neurol. Neurosurg. Psychiat., 1, 198.

NORMAN, R. M. (1940). Brain, 63, 365.

NORMAN, R. M. (1945). J. Neurol. Neurosurg. Psychiat., 8, 52.

NORMAN, R. M. (1949). Brain, 72, 83.

NORMAN, R. M. (1963). 'Micrencephaly,' in Greenfield's Neuropathology, London: Arnold, p. 348.

NORMAN, R. M., and URICH, H. (1958). J. Neurol. Neurosurg. Psychiat., 21, 159.

NORMAN, R. M., URICH, H., and FRANCE, N. E. (1959). J. ment. Sci., 105, 1070.

OGDEN, T. E., ROBERT, F., and CARMICHAEL, E. A. (1959). J. Neurol. Neurosurg. Psychiat., 22, 267.

OSTERTAG, B. (1956). 'Missbildungen.' In O. Lubarsch, F. Henke, and R. Rössle's Handbuch der speziellen pathologischen Anatomie und Histologie, 13, ed. W. Scholz, Pt. 4, Berlin: Springer, p. 283.

PAVLOV, I. P. (1949). In 'Lektsii O Rabote Bolshikh Polusharii Golovnovo Mozga,' Moscow: Medgiz, p. 365.

PEARCE, E. G. E. (1960). 'Histochemistry.' 2nd Ed., London: Churchill, 248.

PEIFFER, J. (1963). 'Morphologische Aspekte der Epilepsien,' Berlin: Springer.

PENROSE, L. S. (1963). 'The Biology of Mental Defect,' London: Sidgwick and Jackson, p. 172.

PITNER, S. E., EDWARDS, J. E., and McCORMICK, N. F. (1965). J. Neurol. Neurosurg. Psychiat., 28, 362.

POZSONYI, J., and ZARFAS, D. E. (1963). Canad. med. Ass. J., 89, 1038.

POZSONYI, J., Gibson, D., and ZARFAS, D. E. (1964). J. Pediat., 64, 75.

REZNIK, M., and ALBERGA-SERRANO, K. (1964). J. neurol. Sci., 1, 40.

RICHARDS, B. W. (1960). Brit. med. J., 2, 714.

ROBERTS, P. D. (1959). Brain, 82, 599.

SCARABICCHI, S., and MARTINO, A. M. (1963). Minerva med., 54, 1603.

SCHARENBERG, K. (1957). 'Third Internat. Congr. of Neuropathology, Brussels,' Amsterdam: Excerpta Medica, p. 85.

SCHOB, F. (1930). 'Pathologische Anatomie der Idiotie,' in Bumke's Handbuch der Geisteskrankheiten, 11, Pt. 7, Berlin: Springer, p. 779.

SCHOLZ, W., and HAGER, H. (1956). 'Epilepsie,' in O. Lubarsch, F. Henke, and Rössle's Handbuch der speziellen pathologischen Anatomie und Histologie, 13, ed. W. Scholz, Pt. 4, Berlin: Springer, p. 99.
SEITELBERGER, F. (1957). 'Third Internat. Congr. of Neuropathology, Brussels,' Amsterdam: Excerpta Medica, p. 127.
SJÖGREN, T., and LARSSON, T. (1957). Acta psychiat. (Kbh.), 32, Suppl. 113.
SMITH, M. C. (1949). J. Neurol. Neurosurg. Psychiat., 12, 100.
SNYDER, C. H., and AULD, E. B. (1962). J. Pediat., 61, 894.
SORSBY, A., and WILLIAMS, C. E. (1960). Brit. med. J., 1, 293.
STEINLECHNER-GRETSCHISCHNIKOFF, A. (1866). Arch. Psychiat. Nervenkr., 17, 649.
STEWART, R. M. (1934–35). Proc. roy. Soc. Med., 28, 786.
STRAUSS, A.A. and LEHTINEN, L. E. (1947). 'Psychopathology and Education of the Brain-Injured Child.' New York: Grune and Stratton.
SUNG, J. H. (1964). J. Neuropath. exp. Neurol., 23, 567.
SYLVESTER, P. E. (1960). Acta paediat. (Uppsala), 49, 338.
SYLVESTER, P. E. (1961). J. ment. Defic. Res., 5, 98.
SYLVESTER, P. E. (1964). Internat. Copenhagen Congr. on the Sci. Study of Mental Retardation: Statens Andsvageforsorg, p. 819.
ULE, G. (1952). Dtsch. Z. Nervenheilk., 168, 195.
ULE, G. (1957). 'Die systematischen Atrophien des Kleinhirns,' in O. Lubarsch, F. Henke, and R. Rössle's Handbuch der speziellen pathologischen Anatomie und Histologie, 13, ed. W. Scholz, Pt. 1, book A, Berlin: Springer, p. 934.
VALLESI, R. N. (1958). Boll. Mal. Orecch., 76, 465.
VOGEL, F. S., and HALLERVORDEN, J. (1962). Acta neuropath. (Berl.), 2, 126.
VOGT, C. and O. (1920). J. Psychol. Neurol. (Lpz.), 25, Ergn. 3.
WADIA, N. H., and DASTUR, D. K. (1960). Wld. Neurol., 1, 409.
WIEST, W. -D., and HALLERVORDEN, J. (1958). Dtsch. Z. Nervenheilk., 178, 224.
WOHLWILL, F. J., BERNSTEIN, J., and YAKOVLEV, P. I. (1959). J. Neuropath. exp. Neurol., 18, 359.
WOLF, A., and COWEN, D. (1956). 'The Cerebral Atrophies and Encephalomalacias of Infancy and Childhood,' in Res. Pub. Ass. nerv. ment. Dis., 34, London: Baillière, Tindall and Cox, p. 199.
WOLF, A., and COWEN, D. (1959). J. Neuropath. exp. Neurol., 18, 191.
WOLMAN, M. (1958). Brain, 81, 243.
WORTIS, J. (1956). Amer. J. ment. Defic., 61, 204.
YAKOVLEV, P. I. (1959). J. Neuropath. exp. Neurol., 18, 22.
YAKOVLEV, P. I., and WADSWORTH, R. C. (1946). J. Neuropath. exp. Neurol., 5, 169.
YORK-MOORE, M. E., and RUNDLE, A. T. (1962). J. ment. Defic. Res., 6, 108.
YOUNG, E. F., and COURVILLE, C. B. (1961). Bull. Los Angeles neurol. Soc., 26, 198.
ZU RHEIN, G. M., EICHMAN, P. L., and PULETTI, F. (1960). Neurology (Minneap.), 10, 998.

CHAPTER 6

NON-SPECIFIC BIOCHEMICAL ABNORMALITIES IN THE BODY FLUIDS

HEREDITARY factors and acquired metabolic disorders causing or contributing to the causation of mental retardation exert their influence by means of biochemical processes operating at one stage or another of the individual's existence. The problem is to detect these, and the simplest way has been to use laboratory techniques for the screening of selected and unselected groups of retarded individuals. Important discoveries such as the identification of inborn errors of metabolism in phenylketonuria, homocystinuria and other diseases, have been made in this manner, and further work will no doubt be equally fruitful. Nevertheless, such methods have certain limitations and these are considered below.

As explained elsewhere in this book, biochemical factors are known to be decisive in the causation of only a minority of cases—in the main those with discrete deficiencies of certain enzymes. In conditions of polygenic origin it is more difficult to establish gene-enzyme relationships. Interpretation is rendered still more hazardous by the wide variation of the normal in biochemical parameters, also referred to as 'biochemical individuality' (Williams, 1956). Moreover, the nature of the morphological lesions demonstrable in the brains of retarded individuals suggests that the pathogenetic processes are usually 'burnt out'. Biochemical abnormality in these cases is therefore likely to be secondary or incidental. Nevertheless, the temptation to ascribe aetiological significance to such anomalies has often proved irresistible, and it is therefore necessary to discuss alternative interpretations for the abnormalities detected in the body fluids of mentally retarded individuals.

The environment of retarded patients is always abnormal and often unfavourable. Their world, compared with that of normal people, is always restricted and this must be reflected in their 'biochemical individuality,' although the mechanisms of this process are complex and largely obscure. Long-term nutritional deficiencies and intercurrent infections may result, for example, in liver dysfunction and abnormal serum protein patterns (Griffith, 1965). Plasma viscosity, which is a useful indicator of qualitative and quantitative changes in the plasma proteins, is often abnormal in mentally retarded patients, even those who are apparently fit and well (Eastham and Jancar, 1965). Some patients tend to become dehydrated by diarrhoea, vomiting or inadequate fluid intake. The resultant electrolyte disturbance can be severe. The patients' inability to keep still when receiving intravenous drips aggravates matters still further. Renal damage may ultimately set in from infections or bouts of dehydration and lead to acidosis and proteinuria. Renal tubular dysfunction may be caused by vitamin deficiency or general malnutrition, and, in children with pica, by chronic heavy metal poisoning. Furthermore, it is not always possible to distinguish between acquired and inherited renal lesions. For example, the biochemical findings in Lowe's syndrome (cf. p. 287) are indistinguishable from those produced in a number of other conditions (Richards *et al.*, 1965). In mental defectives non-specific aminoacidurias are found more frequently than those due to specific enzymatic blocks, particularly if cases of phenylketonuria are excluded (Paine, 1960; Gordon and Wilson, 1963; Poser and Bunch, 1963; Carson, 1965).

The effects of immobilisation on the metabolism of patients with cerebral palsy and mental deficiency have not been studied systematically. Patients immobilised with paralytic poliomyelitis or for other reasons, excrete more calcium and phosphate, and the calcium is in some cases deposited in the kidneys, particularly when calcium and vitamin D supplements are given (Fourman, 1960). However, in mentally retarded patients immobilised by cerebral palsy the serum or urine calcium is not usually increased (p. 155), perhaps because the effects of immobilisation are balanced in such cases by a low absorption of calcium and fat-soluble vitamins.

It has long been recognised that metabolic disturbances can cause epileptic fits (Richter, 1960). The reverse problem—of the effects of seizures on the metabolism of the patient—has received much less attention. Epileptic fits are accompanied by disturbances of water and electrolyte metabolism, particularly an excess of sodium and water excretion. Some changes also occur in the C.S.F. proteins and in amino acid excretion (Stemmermann, 1965). The clinical biochemistry of epilepsy has been recently surveyed by Lowenthal (1965).

That the nervous and endocrine systems are interdependent is well established (Michael and Gibbons, 1963; Harris and Donovan, 1966). Serious functional or morphological disturbances of brain activity may thus be expected to interfere with endocrine function. In addition to such impaired neural regulation, the abnormal mode of existence of many mentally retarded patients often involves the endocrine system. As already stated, the range of stimuli perceived by the mentally retarded is always limited, and many are adversely affected by the special stresses of institutional life, which would be readily tolerated by normal individuals. Reiss (1963) went so far as to maintain that practically every mentally retarded patient has endocrine disturbances and that these would be revealed in an increasing proportion of patients with refinement in the analytical techniques for the estimation of hormones in the body fluids. He studied 150 undifferentiated mentally retarded patients aged 9–15 years, most of whom had more than one sign of endocrine disturbance. Gonadal underfunction in conjunction with stunted growth was the most common finding, followed in frequency by the combination of growth, gonadal and thyroid retardation. In some patients the adrenal cortex did not respond to ACTH stimulation. Reiss concluded that these endocrine abnormalities were largely due to anterior pituitary hypofunction. Reduced resting levels of adrenal hormones were found by Mosier, Grossman and Dingman (1966) in most of 97 patients showing severe mental *and* physical retardation. In most of these cases, however, the adrenals responded briskly to stimulation by exogenous ACTH. Iodine uptake by the thyroid was slightly impaired in this group of patients. Rundle and Sylvester (1965) report that in institutionalized mentally retarded girls menarche is delayed and occurs over a wider age range than in normals. This too is evidence of suboptimal hormonal regulation.

Weil-Malherbe (1955) found significantly lower blood adrenaline and nor-adrenaline in mentally retarded patients than in other groups of psychiatric patients. He was also able to show that the blood levels of the two catecholamines correlated with mental activity. In phenylketonuric patients these levels were even lower than in other mentally retarded patients. This however is a specific effect, directly related to the enzymatic lesion of this disease. Pare, Sandler and Stacey (1960) found raised blood 5-hydroxytryptamine in a group of mentally retarded children of mixed aetiology. Its cause could not be established.

A frequent pattern that has emerged from the study of the mentally retarded is one of increased scatter of biochemical parameters (but not necessarily of differences in the mean levels of metabolites), inappropriate response to stress, and inadequate homeostasis. Carbohydrate metabolism is an example. Fasting blood sugar levels are often low and in some cases there is no adrenaline response to hypoglycaemia (cf. pp. 72 and 294).

Malnutrition is frequent in the mentally retarded, even if a balanced diet is offered. Two reasons have been advanced to explain this: unwillingness or inability to eat, and inefficient intestinal absorption. There is good evidence in favour of both factors. The particle size of the diet is of great importance, particularly for patients with cerebral palsy. Culley (1965) quotes a number of reports describing improvement in the nutrition of patients when the consistency of the diet was adjusted to their ability to chew, and our experience has been fully in accord with these observations. Leitner and Church (1956) and Leitner, Moore and Sharman (1964) found low vitamin C, vitamin A and vitamin E levels in institutionalized psychiatric patients supplied with an adequate diet. The authors suggested that these deficiencies were due to the patients' failure to consume the food. The vitamin blood levels rose when a liberal supplement of vegetables and vitamins was given.

That *inadequate intestinal absorption* also contributes to the nutritional imbalance is seen from the low calcium levels in the blood and urine, also referred to elsewhere (p. 154). This occurs frequently, but by no means exclusively, in patients with Down's disease, and is often associated with raised alkaline phosphatase. The absorption of iron appears to be defective in many cases. Nutritional anaemias are frequent in retarded patients, many of whom are slow to respond to oral iron. Further evidence of defective absorption is provided by low xylose absorption in some patients. This may occur in the absence of diarrhoea or evidence of gastrointestinal infection (Chapman, Harrison and Stern, 1966). In other cases it may be variable, i.e. alternately low or normal, in the same patient. It follows from these observations that a diet which is well balanced for a normal child may give rise to biochemical abnormalities in a retarded one. Even more complex, and potentially more dangerous, are the nutritional disturbances which may occur in children maintained on artificial diets, such as those low in phenylalanine or galactose (Mann, Wilson and Clayton, 1965).

Discordant and contradictory results have been reported by authors measuring various metabolites in the blood or urine of groups of mentally retarded patients. This may be due to a number of reasons. The standard of care received by patients varies from hospital to hospital and this is reflected in the incidence of infection and malnutrition. On the other hand, biochemical findings in patients living at home may be affected by poverty or faulty rearing, such as unduly prolonged and unsupplemented bottle feeding.

Grossly misleading results may be obtained when patients are studied too soon in a new environment. The biochemical findings are then influenced by individual differences in adaptation. It is also sometimes overlooked that a measure of 'natural selection' operates among patients. If a disease carries a high mortality, the less severely affected survive longer, and the magnitude of any observed abnormalities will often decrease as the mean age of the patients rises. The same effect is produced if the disease becomes regularly less active after the period of growth and development. Conversely, the biochemical differences between two groups may increase with the age of the subjects if degenerative changes or premature ageing are more pronounced in one of the groups. Contradictory results and age artefacts have been particularly evident in studies on the biochemistry of Down's disease (p. 160) and that of psychotic children. Some of the above factors may have also affected the results of investigations of tryptophan metabolism in children (p. 161), although in this instance the discrepancies are probably mainly due to shortcoming in the analytical techniques and individual variations of the intestinal flora.

Inflammatory and degenerative processes causing cell death or damage are associated with a discharge of *intracellular enzymes* into the extracellular space and circulation. Estimation of enzyme levels in the body fluids can thus help in diagnosis and treatment. However, circulating enzymes rise only during periods of active cell breakdown, so that enzyme assays are of little help in the detection of old or quiescent lesions. Glycolytic enzymes and the transaminases have been most widely used in clinical enzymology, particularly in relation to diseases of the myocardium and liver. These tests have been also applied to diseases of the brain, for example by Green et al., (1957), Aronson et al., (1961) and Landing et al., (1964). But the interpretation of raised enzyme levels in neuropsychiatry is often equivocal, except in the comparatively straightforward situations, such as the aftermath of cerebrovascular accidents (Acheson et al., 1965). The serum or C.S.F. enzyme levels depend on the original content of the affected tissue, the intensity of the pathological process, and on the rate at which the extracellular enzyme is excreted or deactivated. In the later stages of the disease the enzyme level may also be influenced by the progressive decrease in the amount of surviving tissue in the affected organ. In degenerative disorders the combined effect of these factors is that serum and C.S.F. levels are often raised in the early stages of the disease but fall towards the normal as the disease progresses. Concurrently there is a steady decrease in the enzyme levels of the affected organ.

Enzyme studies in degenerative diseases have thus been largely concerned with non-specific changes. Nevertheless, it has been claimed that in some instances, such as metachromatic leucodystrophy, there are changes of specific enzymes in body fluids and that these are (p. 254) diagnostic and directly related to the aetiology of the disease.

Serum and C.S.F. *protein profiles*, i.e., the quantitative or semi-quantitative measurement of the relative amounts of the various protein fractions, have also been used in the diagnosis and control of the progress of neurological diseases. However, the effect of such diseases on the serum proteins may be masked by intercurrent illness, while the C.S.F. abnormalities may reflect changes in the permeability of the blood brain barrier as well as variations in production rate of protein in the C.N.S. Lowenthal (1964) has dealt fully with the application of paper and gel electrophoresis to diagnostic problems in neurology.

Stern and Lewis (1959) observed raised β-lipoprotein to α-lipoprotein ratios in a number of mentally retarded children of mixed aetiology. An increase in β-lipoprotein is often accompanied by an increase in serum cholesterol and phospholipids. These abnormalities are more frequent in the age group of 2–6 years, particularly in those recently admitted to hospital, than in older children, and may be related to the stresses experienced during the period of early hospitalisation. With the exception of α-lipoproteinaemia (p. 311) and abetalipoproteinaemia (p. 310), abnormalities in the serum lipoproteins of mentally retarded patients are thus largely non-specific, as are the changes in the serum and C.S.F. glycoproteins (Saifer and Gerstenfeld, 1962).

From time to time new urine tests have been proposed for the diagnosis of progressive neurological lesions. One of these has been recently introduced in France. It detects the presence in the urine of oxidative enzymes derived from brain tissue by means of the '*Nadi*' *reaction*, that is by the enzymatically catalyzed production of indophenol blue from *p*-phenylene diamine and α-naphthol. The enzyme involved has not yet been identified and the specificity and reliability of the reaction remain to be fully established (Benson, 1964). If validated, this test will clearly have many applications in the field of mental deficiency.

It may thus be concluded that the biochemical changes in undifferentiated mental deficiency, insofar as they are recognizable by present methods, add up to no more of a uniform pattern than the morphological changes considered in the preceding chapter.

REFERENCES

ACHESON, J., JAMES, D. C., HUTCHINSON, E. C., and UESTHEAD, R. (1965). *Lancet*, 1, 1306.
ARONSON, S. M., SAIFER, A., PERLE, G., and VOLK, B. W. (1961). *Amer. J. clin. Nutr.*, 9, 103.
BENSON, P. F. (1964). *Develop. Med. Child Neurol.*, 6, 626.
CARSON, N. A. J. (1965). In Allan, J. D., and Holt, K. S., 'Biochemical Approaches to Mental Handicap in Children,' Edinburgh, Livingstone, p. 3.

CHAPMAN, M. J., HARRISON, P. M., and STERN, J. (1966). *J. ment. Defic. Res.*, **10**, 19.
CULLEY, W. J. (1965). In Carter, C. H., 'Medical Aspects of Mental Retardation,' Springfield: Thomas, p. 88.
EASTHAM, R. D., and JANCAR, J. (1965). *Amer. J. ment. Defic.*, **69**, 502.
FOURMAN, P. (1960). 'Calcium Metabolism and the Bone,' Oxford: Blackwell.
GORDON, N., and WILSON, V. K. (1963). *Develop. Med. Child Neurol.*, **5**, 586.
GREEN, J. B., OLDEWORTEL, H. A., O'DOHERTY, D. S., FORSTER, F. M., and SANCHEZ-LONGO, L. P. (1957). *Neurology (Minneap.)*, **7**, 313.
GRIFFITH, A. W. (1965). *J. ment. Defic. Res.*, **9**, 164.
HARRIS, G. W., and DONOVAN, B. T. (1966). 'The Pituitary Gland,' London, Butterworths.
LANDING, M., SLOBODY, L. B., and MERSTERN, J. (1964). *J. Pediat.*, **65**, 415.
LEITNER, Z. A., and CHURCH, J. C. (1956). *Lancet*, **1**, 565.
LEITNER, Z. A., MOORE, T., and SHARMAN, I. M. (1964). *Brit. J. Nutr.*, **18**, 115.
LOWENTHAL, A. (1964). 'Agar Gel Electrophoresis in Neurology,' Amsterdam: Elsevier.
LOWENTHAL, A. (1965). *Epilepsia*, **6**, 198.
MANN, T. P., WILSON, K. M., and CLAYTON, B. E. (1965). *Arch. Dis. Childh.*, **40**, 364.
MICHAEL, R. P., and GIBBONS, J. L. (1963). *Int. Rev. Neurobiol.*, **5**, 243.
MOSIER, H. D., GROSSMAN, H. J., and DINGMAN, H. F. (1966). *Amer. J. ment. Defic.*, **71**, 230.
PAINE, R. S. (1960). *New Engl. J. Med.*, **262**, 658.
PARE, C. M. B., SANDLER, M., and STACEY, R. S. (1960). *J. Neurol. Neurosurg. Psychiat.*, **23**, 341.
POSER, C. M., and BUNCH, L. (1963). *Arch. Neurol. (Chic.)*, **9**, 35.
REISS, M. (1963). 'The Contribution of Endocrinological Research to the Differentiation of States of Mental Retardation.' In Proc. 2nd Internat. Congr. on Mental Retardation, Vienna, 1961. Basel: Karger, p. 320.
RICHARDS, W., DONNELL, G. N., WILSON, W. A., STOWENS, D., and PERRY, T. (1965). *Amer. J. Dis. Child.*, **109**, 185.
RICHTER, D. (1960). In Cumings, J. N., 'Modern Scientific Aspects of Neurology,' London: Arnold, p. 314.
RUNDLE, A. T., and SYLVESTER, P. E. (1965). *Amer. J. ment. Defic.*, **69**, 635.
SAIFER, A., and GERSTENFELD, S. (1962). *Clin. chim. Acta*, **7**, 467.
STEMMERMANN, M. G. (1965). *Epilepsia*, **6**, 16.
STERN, J., and LEWIS, W. H. P. (1959). *J. ment. Sci.*, **105**, 1012.
WEIL-MALHERBE, H. (1955). *J. ment. Sci.*, **101**, 733.
WILLIAMS, R. J. (1956). 'Biochemical Individuality,' New York: Wiley.

CHAPTER 7

DOWN'S DISEASE

Biochemical Aspects

PATIENTS with Down's syndrome form the largest distinct group amongst the severely subnormal. The disease has been studied for over a century and because of its superficial similarity to cretinism was at first regarded by some workers as a variant of that condition. An endocrinological or other biochemical basis of the disease was hence suspected. Disappointingly, however, in spite of much research, no pronounced or constant biochemical abnormalities have so far been detected. Following the discovery of trisomy 21 in this disease (p. 15), interest has been focused on (1) factors adversely affecting mitosis or meiosis and thus leading to an increased incidence of non-disjunction and related chromosomal aberrations, and (2) the effects of the extra chromosome on the metabolism of cells and the organism.

Autosomal Trisomy

Both environmental and genetic factors can apparently increase the incidence of non-disjunction and thus of trisomy. Compared with the precursors of spermatozoa, oocytes appear to lie dormant in the ovaries for many years prior to their final maturation, ovulation and fertilization, and this may, perhaps, render them more vulnerable to noxious influences interfering with chromosome pairing (Polani, 1962). Experimental work on the production of chromosomal non-disjunction has been mentioned already (p. 22). In humans, advanced maternal age is associated with an increased incidence of chromosomal disorders, probably due to the combined effects of degenerative changes of ageing and the longer exposure to noxious environmental agents. X-ray irradiation of the mother may have occasionally played a part in the pathogenesis of Down's disease, but in no case has this been proven. Attempts to demonstrate abnormal hormonal excretion patterns in the mothers of patients with Down's disease have also been inconclusive.

Thyroid autoantibodies have been found more frequently in the mothers of patients with Down's disease than in controls (Fialkow *et al.*, 1965). Chromosomal nondisjunction may occur more frequently in families with predisposition to autoimmunity (Fialkow, 1964). Viruses have been suggested as agents causing chromosomal abnormalities (Robinson and Puck, 1965; Stoller and Collmann, 1965). Techniques have recently been developed for following the maturation and meiosis of human oocytes in tissue culture (Edwards, 1965). This should make possible the direct study of factors favouring nondisjunction.

Several families are now known in whom there is strong evidence of a genetically determined tendency to chromosomal anomalies. Some of the affected members had 21-trisomy, and some of the others related anomalies of chromosome 21 or of other chromosomes (Lejeune, 1964; Kiossoglou, Rosenbaum, Mitus and Dameshek, 1964).

The actual effects of the extra chromosome on metabolism are not well understood, but any resultant abnormalities are unlikely to resemble those in point-mutational disorders, such as the inborn errors of metabolism (p. 22).

It has been suggested that the trisomy might increase by a factor of 3/2 the concentration of certain proteins or enzymes, but this view has little to commend it (cf. p. 163). A more reasonable assumption is that after the termination of the early embryonic development the presence of a supernumerary chromosome reduces non-specifically the metabolic efficiency of the affected cell. If so, one would expect widespread quantitative rather than qualitative biochemical abnormalities in Down's disease.

Serum proteins

Among the earliest biochemical abnormalities found in Down's disease was an increased serum γ-globulin and decreased albumin (Stern and Lewis, 1957a; Sobel *et al.*, 1958). A number of workers have reinvestigated this problem and their findings have varied in points of detail. Some found that the γ-globulin was raised in institutionalized patients only, some that the γ-globulin level increased with age, and others that it did not, and some that the albumin level was normal (Nelson, 1961; Skanse and Laurell, 1962; Appleton and Pritham, 1963, Pritham; Appleton and Fluck, 1963; Griffith, Rundle and Stewart, 1965).

The above changes in the protein pattern in Down's disease are to some extent age-dependent. Similar, though usually less pronounced abnormalities, are found in other mentally retarded patients. The differences in the results obtained by various investigators can probably be explained by the wide variations in age and state of health of the studied patients and control groups (cf. chapter 6). Patients with Down's disease seem to respond to antigenic and, possibly, other stimuli with an excessive and persistent increase in the serum γ-globulin*. Most questions about the relative rates of synthesis, catabolism and turnover of the γ-globulins in Down's disease remain unanswered. However, this raised γ-globulin is associated with spontaneously occurring milk antibodies (Nelson, 1964). This may be due to absorption of undigested milk protein in the gut or of protein from inhaled milk in the lungs. An increased incidence of thyroid autoantibodies has also been reported (Mellon, Pay and Green, 1963; Saxena and Pryles, 1965).

Fluck and Pritham (1964) have analysed by the Moore and Stein method the peptides obtained by the tryptic hydrolysis of a pooled human globulin fraction, the 7s γ-globulin, and a similar fraction from pooled serum of patients with Down's disease. They claim to have established differences in the peptide pattern which could be due to primary structural changes of a major protein or, and this appears more likely, to differences in the proteins which make up this heterogeneous fraction. Allerhand *et al.* (1963) studied the lacrimal proteins in patients with Down's disease and found an overall increase in

* The immunoelectrophoretic pattern in Down's disease is said to be normal (Rowe, M. J., Agranoff, B. W., and Tourtelotte, W. W., *Neurology* (*Minneap.*), **16**, 714.

proteins of a type otherwise found only in neonates. The a_1-globulin, in particular, was increased. They suggested that abnormalities of protein transport across cell membranes were a possible explanation of their findings.

Calcium Metabolism

It has been known for some years that the serum calcium is reduced in many children with Down's disease (Sobel *et al.*, 1958; Stern and Lewis, 1958). This low serum calcium is associated with a normal total serum protein level, an essentially normal serum phosphate, a normal or slightly raised alkaline phosphatase and a low urinary calcium excretion (Chapman, Harrison and Stern, 1964). The meaning of these findings is not clear. As vitamin A absorption is low in children with Down's disease (Sobel *et al.*), it has been suggested that there may also exist an associated deficiency in the absorption, transport or utilization of vitamin D. Insufficiency of parathyroid activity is an alternative explanation. It may be that this defective transport of the fat-soluble vitamins affects the trisomic organism at all stages of its development and that vitamin deficiencies may occur in the developing embryo. Indeed, Sobel *et al.* have pointed out that the defects of the skeletal and nervous system found in Down's disease resemble some of those produced in the offspring of pregnant animals deficient in the fat-soluble vitamins.

Tryptophan and Vitamin B_6 Metabolism

Gershoff, Hegsted and Trulson (1958) reported that children with Down's disease excrete less xanthurenic acid after an oral tryptophan load than suitably chosen controls (Fig. 64). This was confirmed by Jérôme (1963), who also found a reduced excretion of 5-hydroxyindolylacetic acid (5-HIAA) and indolylacetic acid (IAA), and by O'Brien and Groshek (1962) who, however, failed to confirm the decreased excretion of 5-HIAA. A different approach to this problem was made by McCoy and Chung (1964), who administered the vitamin B_6 antagonist deoxypyridoxine. Their patients with Down's disease excreted significantly more 3-hydroxykynurenine and xanthurenic acid than other mentally retarded patients. In a subsequent study McCoy, Anast and Naylor (1964) found an increase in oxalic acid as well as xanthurenic acid excretion. As the increased urinary excretion of these metabolites was presumably caused by decreased activity of the enzymes 3-hydroxykynureninase, 3-hydroxykynurenine transaminase and glycine transaminase (Fig. 111), which are all vitamin B_6 dependent, these authors concluded that patients with Down's disease are more prone to vitamin B_6 depletion than the controls. They could not confirm the decreased excretion of xanthurenic acid after tryptophan loading in patients not receiving deoxypyridoxine. The data are thus rather inconclusive. Tryptophan load tests are beset with methodological difficulties and the results are notoriously difficult to interpret, particularly because of the marked effects of the intestinal flora on the excretion of tryptophan metabolites. In any case it is difficult to correlate xanthurenic acid excretion with vitamin B_6 deficiency. As the enzyme 3-hydroxykynureninase has a greater B_6 dependency than 3-hydroxykynurenine

P.M.R.—6*

transaminase, excretion of xanthurenic acid may increase or decrease depending on the extent of the deficiency (Coursin, 1964). However, it appears reasonably certain that patients with Down's disease are more readily depleted of vitamin B_6 than controls (McCoy, Anast and Naylor).

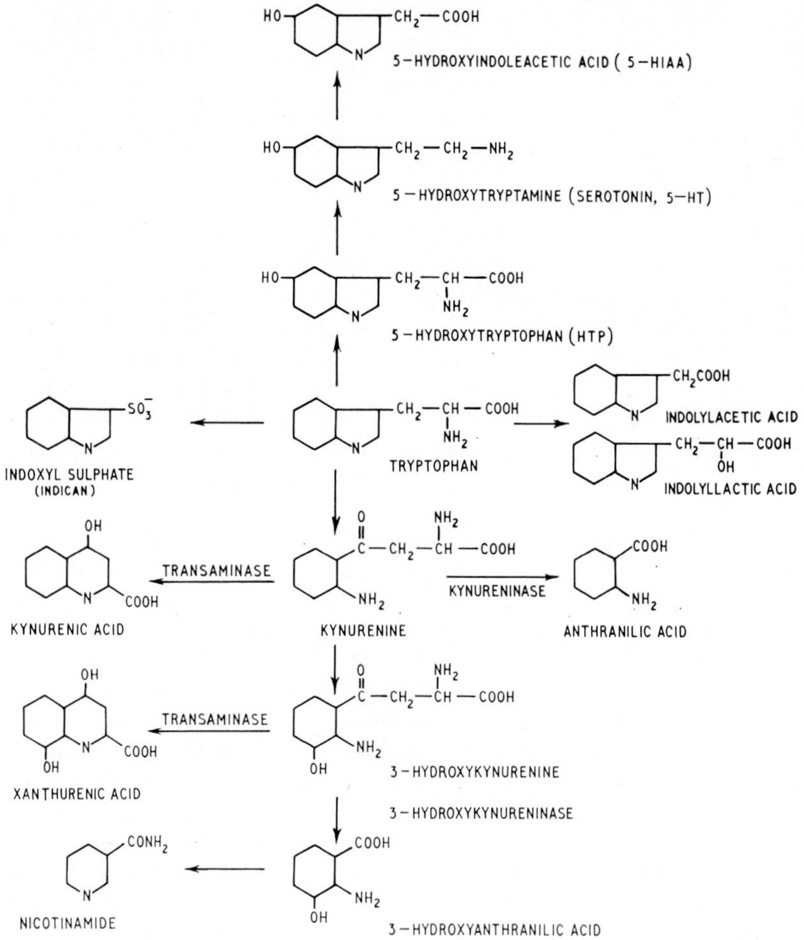

FIG. 64. Tryptophan metabolism.

There is good evidence that in Down's disease the serotonin pathway of tryptophan metabolism is also affected (Fig. 64). Rosner *et al.* (1965a) found low blood levels of serotonin (5-hydroxytryptamine, 5-HT), in patients with trisomic Down's disease compared to healthy controls. Patients with translocation Down's disease had intermediate blood levels. Tu and Zellweger (1965) confirmed these results and showed that while in controls administration of tryptophan produced a rise in blood 5-HT, this did not occur in Down's disease. In cases of Down's disease, but not in the controls, blood 5-HT fell when the vitamin B_6 antagonist DL-penicillamine was given. This fall could be reversed by vitamin B_6. The pyridoxal phosphate-dependent enzyme of the serotonin pathway is 5-hydroxytryptophan (5-HTP) decarboxylase. If the activity of this enzyme is reduced due to a defect in the apoenzyme, or a deficiency in substrate or cofactor (vitamin B_6), 5-HT formation will be impaired. Berman, Justice and Hsia (1965) and Hazra, Benson and Sandler (1965) have in fact demonstrated low 5-HT levels in newborn babies due to functional immaturity of this or other enzymes and a relative deficiency of vitamin B_6. In our view, a reasonable interpretation of the data in patients with Down's disease is that the susceptibility to vitamin B_6 antagonists, and the other abnormalities are caused by defective transport of tryptophan and its metabolites and possibly of vitamin B_6. The reason for the somewhat higher blood 5-HT levels in translocation Down's disease has not yet been satisfactorily explained.

The abnormal results obtained with the tryptophan load test in Down's disease are by no means unique. Given the right conditions, significant differences are shown in Down's disease with almost any load test. As examples one can mention decreased N-methylnicotinamide excretion following a load of niacinamide (Gershoff, Mayer and Kulczycki, 1959), although this was not confirmed when the niacinamide was given parenterally (Careddu, Tenconi and Sacchetti, 1963), and low xylose absorption (Chapman, Harrison and Stern, 1966). Abnormal glucose, insulin, adrenaline and galactose tolerance tests have also been reported (Benda, 1947; Runge, 1959). The abnormal results of these carbohydrate tolerance tests have been interpreted in terms of suboptimal liver function or delayed uptake or release of the carbohydrate by the liver.

Enzymes of the Formed Elements of the Blood

Deletion or duplication of chromosomes has been a useful tool in experimental cytogenetics for detecting genes which show a dosage effect. It is therefore not surprising that an intensive search has been made for markers on the 21 chromosome. A comprehensive review of this field has been published by Lejeune (1964). Much evidence points to chromosome 21 being involved in the regulation of granulocyte production. A small deleted acrocentric chromosome, assumed to originate from a 21 chromosome, has been found in patients with chronic granulocytic leukaemia. The presence of this, the so-called Philadelphia chromosome, is associated with a low level of leucocyte alkaline phosphatase (LAP), and it was tempting to attribute the low levels of LAP to gene dosage and to locate the gene controlling LAP synthesis on chromosome 21. It should follow that in individuals trisomic for chromosome 21 the presence of three doses of the gene in the cell would result, on the average, in the formation of one and a half times more enzyme than normal. A raised level of LAP has in fact been found in Down's disease (Alter, Lee, Pourfar and Dobkin, 1963). Increased levels of the following enzymes have also been reported: in the leucocytes—galactose-1-phosphate uridyl transferase, glucose-6-phosphate dehydrogenase and acid phosphatase (Mellman et al., 1964), and in the red cells—galactokinase, galactose-1-phosphate uridyl transferase (Donnell *et al.*, 1965) and glucose-6-phosphate dehydrogenase (Shih *et al.*, 1965). Of the red cell glycolytic enzymes only phosphohexokinase was found to be raised (Baikie *et al.*, 1965). A puzzling feature is that the level of the leucocyte and erythrocyte galactose-1-phosphate uridyl transferase, leucocyte acid and alkaline phosphatase, leucocyte 5-neucleotidase and erythrocyte glucose-6-phosphate dehydrogenase is apparently raised only in trisomic Down's disease and not in translocation Down's disease (Rosner, Ong, Paine and Mahanand, 1965b). Where the increase in enzyme activity was approximately 50 per cent, it was sometimes suggested that the structural or regulator gene for the enzyme concerned was located on chromosome 21. This interpretation has no firm basis. It is true that simple gene-dosage relationships have been established in some recessively inherited metabolic errors, such as galactosaemia and acatalasia, when the levels of the affected enzymes were compared in homozygotes and heterozygotes (Harris, 1964). In general, however, the control of enzyme synthesis and activity, particularly in higher organisms, is more complex. It involves, in addition to structural and regulator genes, such diverse factors as 'feedback' inhibition, catabolism, inactivation and excretion of enzymes, and humoral and neuroendocrine control mechanisms (Dixon and Webb, 1964; Umbarger, 1964; Brenner, 1965). Simple gene-dosage relationships, while theoretically possible, are therefore unlikely to be demonstrable in practice. The activity of many intracellular enzymes declines as the cell grows older. There is evidence that in Down's disease the mean age of the red cell population is lowered (Naiman, Oski and Mellman, 1965) and some of the raised enzyme levels could be explained on this basis. However, this evidence has been challenged by Galbraith and Valberg (1966). Thus increased enzyme activity in Down's disease cannot, in general, be regarded as a guide to gene location. A more likely explanation of the data is that some genes on chromosome 21 influence blood cell production and turnover. No qualitative differences in the enzymes and isoenzymes of the blood cells in Down's disease have so far been detected (Shih *et al.*, 1965).

Other Biochemical Abnormalities in Down's Disease

Other reported biochemical abnormalities include a decrease in the level of the serum pseudocholinesterase (Stern and Lewis, 1962), and a raised β-aminoisobutyric acid excretion (Lundin and Gustavson, 1962). The serum uric acid level is raised in Down's disease, but this increase is not associated with higher uric acid excretion, as in leukaemia (Chapman and Stern, 1964). This controversial topic is discussed in a recent Ciba colloquium (Study Group No. 25).

Recently Appleton *et al.* (1964) have suggested a causal relationship between raised γ-globulin, lowered vitamin A absorption and raised uric acid levels. They were able to demonstrate increased γ-globulin and serum allantoin (the end-product of purine metabolism in rats) in vitamin A deficient rats. However, this relationship may be indirect. In rats, vitamin A deficiency damages the renal epithelium and greatly increases the incidence of infection.

These two factors may be responsible for the observed increase in the serum allantoin and γ-globulin.

Coburn, Luce and Mertz (1965) found significantly but not pathologically raised levels of blood urea, creatinine and uric acid in Down's disease. Slight impairment of renal function appears to be the most likely explanation of these data.

Non-specific changes are also found in the serum lipoproteins (Simon, Ludwig, Gofman and Crook, 1954; Stern and Lewis, 1959; Nelson, 1961) and serum cholesterol, with a significantly higher incidence of both high and low values* (Stern and Lewis, 1957b).

The endocrinological aspects of Down's disease will not be discussed here, but it seems worthwhile to mention the alleged dysthyroidism in this condition. On the one hand, a significant incidence of thyrotoxicosis has been reported in patients with Down's disease (Kay and Esselborn, 1963; Tips, Weiner, Miller and Meyer, 1964); on the other, frank hypothyroidism (Hubble, 1963). However, thyroid function tests in groups of patients with Down's disease have not shown any significant abnormality (Simon et al., 1954; Pearse, Reiss and Suwalski, 1963; Saxena and Pryles, 1965). The only thyroid function test which is abnormal in Down's disease is the red cell triiodothyronine (T3) uptake test, but this may be due to protein or enzymatic changes in the plasma (Saxena and Pryles, 1965).

According to modern views, hormones exert their action frequently, but not exclusively, by a selective control of messenger RNA synthesis in the nucleus (Karlson, 1965; Colloquium, 1965). The study of how these mechanisms are affected by the presence of a supernumerary chromosome is a difficult but promising field for further research. Reiss et al. (1965) found that urinary 17-ketosteroids and 17-hydroxycorticosteroids were low in Down's disease but that there was a greater than normal response in the metopirone test, which is a measure of pituitary-adrenal responsiveness. The clinical response to human chorionic gonadotrophin was also rapid and striking.

Conclusions

It thus appears that all the hitherto detected biochemical abnormalities in cases of Down's disease are, compared with those of the specific enzymopathies, quantitative rather than qualitative. Analogous, if milder, manifestations of defective homeostasis are shown by many other severely subnormal children. These deficiencies seem aggravated in Down's disease—possibly due to the chromosomal anomaly: children with Down's disease are biochemically just like other severely subnormal children, only more so.

Laboratory Diagnosis.

Biochemical investigations are of little help in the diagnosis of Down's disease. Analysis of the karyotype may be mandatory when the diagnosis is in doubt, but this is seldom the case. Investigation of the chromosomes of the child and his parents may also be required for genetic counselling.

---

* Sodium, calcium and bicarbonate are raised in the saliva secreted by the parotid gland (Winer, R. A. et al., 1965, J. dent. Res., 44, 632).

The haematological aspects of Down's disease have received considerable attention, mainly because of the associated increased incidence of leukaemia (cf. Lahey, Beier and Wilson, 1963, for full references to the relevant literature) and leukaemoid states (Ross, Moloney and Desforges, 1963; Engel *et al.*, 1964). It has also been established that there is a shift to the left in the Arneth count in the disease (Mittwoch, 1957). A shift to the left of a similar degree is, however, sometimes found in normal and severely subnormal females (Kiossoglou, Garrison, Walker and Wolman, 1963).

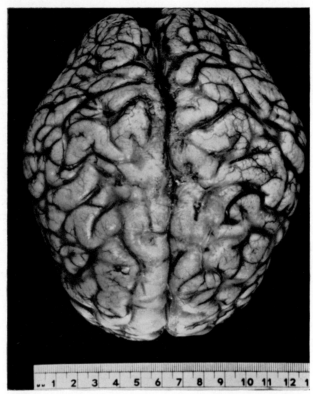

FIG. 65. A brain in a case of Down's disease. It is roundish when viewed from above, and the frontal lobes (lower part of the picture) are small. The gyral pattern is possibly 'simplified', but it is difficult to be certain of this.

Morbid Anatomy

The neuropathological changes in Down's disease are usually diffuse and rather uncertain. This is one of the reasons for many unconfirmed and contradictory statements in the published descriptions of the condition.

In most cases the brains weigh less than normal but are on the average heavier and less variable in weight than those of other low-grade defectives; none show extreme micrencephaly (Fig. 20). Like the skull, the brain is often roundish when viewed from above (Fig. 65 and Fig. 66), and the frontal lobes, brainstem and cerebellum are particularly small. The size of the frontal lobes is reduced in all dimensions and this seems to be the main factor accounting for the smallness of the antero-posterior diameter of the brain and for its overall roundness. Many other minor abnormalities of shape and surface have been described; of these, narrowness of the superior temporal convolution is, perhaps, the most constant.

When the brain is divided from the brainstem at the level of the superior corpora quadrigemina and the two parts weighed separately, the ratio of the weight of the cerebrum to that of the cerebellum with the brainstem is increased (Fig. 67). The brainstem and cerebellum are, in other words, small.

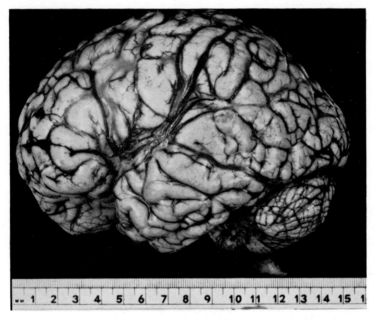

FIG. 66. Lateral view of the same brain as in Fig. 65. The frontal lobes and the cerebellum are small.

Since most of the weight of the cerebellum is accounted for by its middle lobes, and these are, like some of the major tracts in the brainstem, functionally and anatomically related to the frontal lobes (*vide infra*), the size of these formations is interdependent. Ontogenetically, the middle cerebellar and the frontal cerebral lobes are relatively small in the newborn and increase more rapidly than the other parts of the brain in early infancy. Phylogenetically, the expansion of these formations probably reflects the new need in humans for fine control over the movement of the hands and fingers, as well as over that of the lips, tongue and vocal cords, called for by the development of speech. Laterality and cerebral dominance are also specifically human attributes which have developed with the use of the hand for such new work as the making of tools. It may be significant therefore, in relation to the cerebral changes described above, that laterality does not seem to be well established in most cases of Down's disease (Wunderlich, 1965).

Simplification of gyral pattern is another frequently mentioned feature, but this observation rests on rather slender and subjective evidence.

The neurohistological changes are equally uncertain. Some of the older workers could detect none; others described abnormal cells, sparseness of cells—particularly in cortical layer III, or, contrariwise, excessive neuronal density. In a recent report Jelgersma (1963) confirmed the presence of a previously reported, supposedly anomalous, structure in the peduncles of the

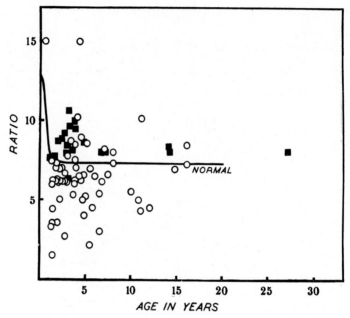

FIG. 67. Ratio of weight of cerebrum over the combined weight of the cerebellum and the brainstem plotted against age in years. Down's disease ■, other mentally retarded children O.

cerebellar flocculi, but since this structure appears to be also present in many normal individuals, the significance of this observation remains obscure. As already indicated, Meyer and Jones (1939) found fibrous gliosis of the white matter without concomitant demyelination in 10 of the 15 brains they examined (p. 127). Various anomalies of the grey matter of the spinal cord have been reported on rather inconclusive evidence by Benda (1947), and many other recorded observations have not been adequately controlled and so must be treated with reserve.

Patients with Down's disease seem to be more liable than other individuals to develop incidental cerebral lesions. Congenital heart disease (*vide infra*) and embolism are responsible for some of these. The embolus may be a fragment detached from a vegetation growing upon a diseased cardiac valve or, more frequently, a thrombus dislodged from a systemic vein and shunted from right to left through a gap in one of the cardiac septa. The infarcted area is often that supplied by the middle cerebral artery (Fig. 68). The risks of developing a cerebral abscess are also increased, particularly in cases showing congenital cyanotic heart disease: two such instances occurred at the Fountain Hospital. It has been further suggested that lesions associated with ageing, such as senile plaques and the Alzheimer neurofibrillary change, are more common and occur at an earlier age in cases of Down's disease (Jervis, 1948; Solitare and Lamarche, 1966).

Gross congenital anomalies of somatic organs and viscera are relatively common in Down's disease (Ingalls, 1947), and the incidence of serious

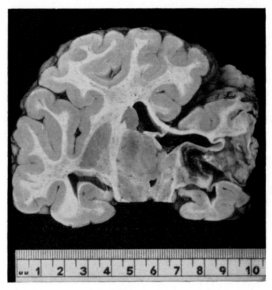

FIG. 68. Infarction of the territory supplied by one of the middle cerebral arteries following embolism in a case of Down's disease complicated by Fallot's tetralogy.

abnormalities is, of course, particularly high in patients dying at an early age. One of these abnormalities, congenital duodenal stenosis, has been described by Bodian *et al.* (1952). The association with congenital heart disease is well known. In a series of 79 pathologically examined hearts of patients with Down's disease Berg, Crome and France (1960) found that the variety of anomalies was as wide as in other children. There were, however, certain quantitative differences, persistent ostium primum, persistent ostium A-V commune, atrial septal defects of the ostium secundum type, and anomalies of the mitral and tricuspid valves being more frequent in Down's disease. On the other hand, Fallot's tetralogy, Eisenmenger's complex, persistent truncus arteriosus, left superior vena cava, coarctation of the aorta of adult type, pulmonary vascular anomalies, anomalies of the aortic and pulmonary valves, and fibroelastosis were less frequent in Down's disease. Miscellaneous anomalies of the skull, teeth and eyes were described by Roche and Sunderland (1960) and by Spitzer, Rabinowitch and Wybar (1961).

Recent advances in Down's disease have been reviewed by Richards (1963 and 1964) and Penrose and Smith (1966), and a full, if somewhat uncritical, review in German of the neuropathological literature on this disease was published by Jacob (1956).

REFERENCES

ALLERHAND, J., KARELITZ, S., ISENBERG, H. D., PENBHARKUL, S., and RAMOS, A. (1963). J. Pediat., 62, 235.
ALTER, A. A., LEE, S. I., POURFAR, M., and DOBKIN, M. (1963). Blood, 22, 165.
APPLETON, M. D., and PRITHAM, G. H. (1963). Amer. J. ment. Defic., 67, 521.
APPLETON, D. M., HAAB, W., CASEY, P. J., CASTELLINO, F. J., SCHORR, J. M., and MIRAGLIA, R. J. (1964). Amer. J. ment. Defic., 69, 324.
BAIKIE, A. G., LODER, P. B., DE GROUCHY, G. C., and PITT, D. B. (1965). Lancet, 1, 412.
BENDA, C. E. (1947). 'Mongolism and Cretinism,' London: Heinemann.
BERG, J. M., CROME, L., and FRANCE, N. E. (1960). Brit. Heart J., 22, 331.
BERMAN, J. L., JUSTICE, P. J., and HSIA, D. Y. -Y. (1965). J. Pediat., 67, 603.
BODIAN, M., WHITE, L. L. R., CARTER, C. O., and LOUW, I. J. M. (1952). Brit. med. J., 1, 77.
BRENNER, S. (1965). Brit. med. Bull., 21, 244.
CAREDDU, P., TENCONI, L. T., and SACCHETTI, G. (1963). Lancet, 1, 828.
CHAPMAN, M. J., and STERN, J. (1964). J. ment. Defic. Res., 8, 119.
CHAPMAN, M. J., HARRISON, P. M., and STERN, J. (1964). Unpublished observations.
CHAPMAN, M. J., HARRISON, P. M., and STERN, J. (1966). J. ment. Defic. Res., 10, 19.
CIBA FOUNDATION STUDY GROUPS (In the press). 'No. 25. Mongolism,' London: Churchill.
COBURN, S. P., LUCE, M. W., and MERTZ, E. T. (1965). Amer. J. ment. Defic., 69, 814.
COLLOQUIUM (1965). Biochem. J., 97, 21P.
COURSIN, D. B. (1964). Amer. J. clin. Nutr., 14, 56.
DIXON, M., and WEBB, E. C. (1964). 'Enzymes,' London: Longmans.
DONNELL, G. N., WONG, G. N., BERGREN, W. R., MELNYK, J., and KOCH, R. (1965). Lancet, 2, 553.
EDWARDS, E. G. (1965). Lancet, 2, 926.
ENGEL, R. R., HAMMOND, D., EITZMAN, D. V., PEARSON, H., and KRIVIT, W. (1964). J. Pediat., 65, 303.
FIALKOW, P. J. (1964). Lancet, 1, 474.
FIALKOW, P. J., UCHIDA, I., HECHT, F., and MOTULSKY, A. C. (1965). Lancet, 2, 818.
FLUCK, E. R., and PRITHAM, G. H. (1964). Amer. J. ment. Defic., 69, 31.
GALBRAITH, P. R., and VALBERG, L. S. (1966). Pediatrics, 37, 108.
GERSHOFF, S. N., HEGSTED, D. M., and TRULSON, M. F. (1958). Amer. J. clin. Nutr., 6, 526.
GERSHOFF, S. N., MAYER, A. L., and KULCZYCKI, L. L. (1959). Amer. J. clin. Nutr., 7, 76.
GRIFFITH, A. W., RUNDLE, A. T., and STEWART, A. (1965). Amer. J. ment. Defic., 69, 805.
HARRIS, H. (1964). In Dyke, S. C. 'Recent Advances in Clinical Pathology,' London: Churchill, p. 83.
HAZRA, M., BENSON, S., and SANDLER, M. (1965). Arch. Dis. Childh., 40, 513.
HUBBLE, D. (1963). J. clin. Endocrinol., 23, 1302.
INGALLS, T. H. (1947). Amer. J. Dis. Child., 73, 279.
JACOB, H. (1956). 'Mongolismus' in O. Lubarsch, F. Henke, and R. Rössle's Handbuch der speziellen pathologischen Anatomie und Histologie, 13, ed. W. Scholtz, Pt. 4, Berlin: Springer, p. 82.
JELGERSMA, H. C. (1963). Psychiat. Neurol. Neurochir. (Amst.), 66, 131.
JÉRÔME, H. (1962). Bull. Soc. Med. Hôp. Paris, 113, 168.
JERVIS, G. A. (1948). Amer. J. Psychiat., 105, 102.
KARLSON, P. (1965). 'Mechanism of Hormone Action,' New York: Academic Press.
KAY, C. J., and ESSELBORN, V. M. (1963). Amer. J. Dis. Child., 106, 411.

KIOSSOGLOU, K. A., GARRISON, M., WALKER, A., and WOLMAN, I. J. (1963). *J. ment. Defic. Res.*, **7**, 69.

KIOSSOGLOU, K. A., ROSENBAUM, E. H., MITUS, W. J., and DAMESHEK, W. (1964). *Blood*, **24**, 134.

LAHEY, M. E., BEIER, F. R., and WILSON, J. F. (1963). *J. Pediat.*, **63**, 189.

LEJEUNE, J. (1964). In Steinberg, A. G., and Bearn, A. G. 'Progress in Medical Genetics,' Vol. 3, New York: Grune and Stratton, p. 144.

LUNDIN, L. -G., and GUSTAVSON, K. -H. (1962). *Acta genet.* (*Basel*), **12**, 156.

McCoy, E. E., and CHUNG, S. I. (1964). *J. Pediat.*, **64**, 227.

McCoy, E. E., ANAST, C. S., and NAYLOR, J. J. (1964). *J. Pediat.*, **65**, 208.

MELLMAN, W. J., OSKI, F. A., TEDESCO, T. A., MACIERA-COELHO, A., and HARRIS, H. (1964). *Lancet*, **2**, 674.

MELLON, J. P., PAY, B. Y., and GREEN, D. M. (1963). *J. ment. Defic. Res.*, **7**, 31.

MEYER, A., and JONES, T. B. (1939). *J. ment. Sci.*, **85**, 206.

MITTWOCH, U. (1957). *J. ment. Defic. Res.*, **1**, 26.

NAIMAN, J. L., OSKI, F. A., and MELLMANN, W. J. (1965). *Lancet*, **1**, 821.

NELSON, T. L. (1961). *Amer. J. Dis. Child.*, **102**, 369.

NELSON, T. L., (1964). *Amer. J. Dis. Child.*, **108**, 494.

O'BRIEN, D., and GROSHEK, A. (1962). *Arch. Dis. Childh.*, **37**, 17.

PEARSE, J. J., REISS, M., and SUWALSKI, R. T. (1963). *J. clin. Endocrinol.*, **23**, 311.

PENROSE, L. S., and SMITH, G. F. (1966). 'Down's Anomaly,' London: Churchill.

POLANI, P. E. (1962). In RICHTER, D., TANNER, S. M., LORD TAYLOR, and ZANGWILL, O. L. 'Aspects of Psychiatric Research'. London: Oxford University Press, p. 154.

PRITHAM, G. H., APPLETON, M. D., and FLUCK, E. R. (1963). *Amer. J. ment. Defic.*, **67**, 517.

REISS, M., WAKOH, T., HILLMAN, J. C., PEARSE, J. J., DALEY, N., and REISS, J. M. (1965). *Amer. J. ment. Defic.*, **70**, 204.

RICHARDS, B. W. (1963). *Develop. Med. Child Neurol.*, **5**, 65.

RICHARDS, B. W. (1964). *Develop. Med. Child Neurol.*, **6**, 175.

ROBINSON, A., and PUCK, T. T. (1965). *Science*, **148**, 83.

ROCHE, A. F., and SUNDERLAND, S. (1960). *J. Neuropath. exp. Neurol.*, **19**, 554.

ROSNER, F., ONG, B. H., PAINE, R. S., and MAHANAND, D. (1965a). *Lancet*, **1**, 1191.

ROSNER, F., ONG, B. H., PAINE, R. S. and MAHANAND, D. (1965b). *New Engl. J. Med.*, **273**, 1356.

ROSS, J. D., MOLONEY, W. C., and DESFORGES, J. F. (1963). *J. Pediat.*, **63**, 1.

RUNGE, G. (1959). *Amer. J. ment. Defic.*, **63**, 822.

SAXENA, K. M., and PRYLES, C. V. (1965). *J. Pediat.*, **67**, 363.

SHIH, L. -Y., WONG, P., INOUYE, T., MAKLER, M., and HSIA, D. Y. -Y. (1965). *Lancet*, **2**, 746.

SIMON, A., LUDWIG, C., GOFMAN, J. W., and CROOK, G. H. (1954). *Amer. J. Psychiat.*, **111**, 139.

SKANSE, B., and LAURELL, C. B. (1962). *Acta med. scand.*, **172**, 63.

SOBEL, A. E., STRAZZULLA, M., SHERMAN, B. S., ELKAN, B., MORGENSTERN, S. W., MARIUS, N., and MEISEL, A. (1958). *Amer. J. ment. Defic.*, **62**, 642.

SOLITARE, G. B., and LAMARCHE, J. B. (1966). *Amer. J. ment. Defic.*, **70**, 840.

SPITZER, R., RABINOWITCH, J. Y., and WYBAR, K. C. (1961). *Canad. med. Ass. J.*, **84**, 567.

STERN, J., and LEWIS, W. H. P. (1957a). *J. ment. Sci.*, **103**, 222.

STERN, J., and LEWIS, W. H. P. (1957b). *J. ment. Defic. Res.*, **1**, 96.

STERN, J., and LEWIS, W. H. P. (1958). *J. ment. Sci.*, **104**, 880.

STERN, J., and LEWIS, W. H. P. (1959). *J. ment. Sci.*, **105**, 1012.

STERN, J., and LEWIS, W. H. P. (1962). *J. ment. Defic. Res.*, **6**, 13.

STOLLER, A., and COLLMANN, R. D. (1965). *Med. J. Aust.*, **2**, 1.

TIPS, R. L., WEINER, F., MILLER, M., and MEYER, D. L. (1964). *Amer. J. ment. Defic.*, **68**, 594.

TU, J. -B., and ZELLWEGER, H. (1965). *Lancet*, **2**, 715.

UMBARGER, H. E. (1964). *Science*, **145**, 674.

WUNDERLICH, CHR. (1965). *Pädiatrie und Grenzgebiete*, **4**, 79.

CHAPTER 8

HYDROCEPHALUS. THE PHAKOMATOSES

HYDROCEPHALUS

MAN's unhappy familiarity with hydrocephalus goes back to earliest history (Wells, 1964) and interest in the condition has been always maintained. Understanding of its pathology is accordingly greater than that of most conditions in the field of mental deficiency, even though some questions, and very elementary ones at that, are yet to be answered. For full details readers can be referred to the monograph by Dorothy Russell (1949), whose views have been widely accepted.

It is difficult to estimate the incidence of hydrocephalus among the severely subnormal. The expectation of life is understandably low in the more severe cases, and the incidence varies greatly in accordance with the age-groups studied. However, hydrocephalus is one of the commoner congenital malformations and many cases are also acquired post-natally. Twenty-one of the 282 brains studied at the Fountain Hospital by Crome (1960) were grossly hydrocephalic.

Hydrocephalus can be internal or external. The latter form need not be considered here in any detail, since the term refers, as a rule, only to the passive accumulation of fluid in the subarachnoid space in cases of cerebral atrophy and shrinkage caused by gliotic encephalopathy. The condition usually considered under the heading of *hydrocephalus* is the *internal* form, characterized by excessive accumulation and raised pressure of fluid in the ventricular system.

It is known that cerebrospinal fluid is secreted mainly or wholly by the choroid plexuses and that it 'circulates' slowly through the foramina of Monro and the cerebral aqueduct (the aqueduct of Sylvius), reaching the subarachnoid space by way of the foramina of Magendie and Luschka. How it is absorbed is less certain. A small amount is probably absorbed in the vertebral canal, but most of the fluid percolates towards the vertex of the brain to be absorbed, perhaps, by the capillaries of the subarachnoid space, through the intracerebral Virchow-Robin spaces surrounding some of the veins, or by the arachnoid villi projecting into the dural venous sinuses. It is worth qualifying the term 'circulation' in reference to the movement of the C.S.F. Under normal conditions the flow is very slow and to some extent tidal—i.e. to and fro through the foramina. Nevertheless, free movement is essential, its complete arrest usually being followed by the development of hydrocephalus. In theory, hydrocephalus could develop in one of three ways: by oversecretion of the C.S.F., by mechanical obstruction within the C.S.F. pathway or by failure of C.S.F. absorption. In practice, oversecretion has not been convincingly demonstrated and could, at most, be only a rare cause. The case for failure of absorption rests on better evidence, but, again, this mechanism does not seem to account for many cases. Physical obstruction of the C.S.F. pathway can, on the other hand, often be inferred from the clinical history or demonstrated at operation or autopsy. However, the mechanism remains obscure in a considerable proportion of cases (*vide infra*).

One of the commonest sites for obstruction to occur is at the cerebral aqueduct—the narrowest and most precarious part of the C.S.F. pathway. The minimum size of the aqueduct compatible with free flow is, however, still uncertain (Beckett, Netzky and Zimmerman, 1950). Very narrow channels, and even some apparently completely occluded by a septum or membrane, have been occasionally encountered by us and other workers in non-hydrocephalic brains. Obstruction of the cerebral aqueduct may be caused by a malformation, such as stenosis. In addition to simple narrowing, other forms of aqueductal anomaly have been described by many authors, e.g. Menozzi and Cagnoni (1958). In some cases the aqueduct is 'forked'—i.e. split into several narrow vertical channels, some of which end blindly. It can be also occluded by a septum, granulation tissue, and intra- or periventricular gliotic tissue. Occlusion by neoplasm is infrequent in infancy, but has been reported in a few cases of neurofibromatosis and other tumours. An inherited sex-linked form of hydrocephalus has been described and its pathogenesis attributed to narrowing of the aqueduct (Edwards, Norman and Roberts, 1961; Warren, Lu and Ziering, 1963) (see also p. 8).

Obstruction may also occur at any of the foramina. In the case of the foramen of Monro, this may be due to a cyst or polyp causing unilateral hydrocephalus, but this is rare in the mentally subnormal. Obstruction at the level of the foramina of Magendie and Luschka is more common. It is usually the result of inflammation but may also be caused by a malformation, such as atresia of the foramina of Magendie and Luschka, or by a septum covering the lower part of the roof of the fourth ventricle, as perhaps, in some cases of the Dandy-Walker syndrome (*vide infra*).

At the level of the tentorium cerebelli, upward flow can be obstructed by subarachnoid haemorrhage or post-meningitic adhesions around the basal cisterns—the interpeduncular and the cisterna ambiens. Cystic arachnoiditis can be present in some of these cases.

The subarachnoid space over the cerebral hemispheres can be similarly occluded by post-meningitic adhesions or extravasated blood. It has also been suggested that occlusion at this level may be due to accumulation of adventitious material in proliferated phagocytes, as in gargoylism or Hand-Schüller-Christian disease.

The possibility of hydrocephalus being occasionally caused by sinus thrombosis remains undecided. Sinus thrombosis is usually fatal, but a few cases recover, if only part of the sinusoidal system is affected. The clot is later recanalized. However, the usual cerebral change in these circumstances is gliotic encephalopathy, with or without haemorrhage from the secondarily thrombosed cortical veins, and with only *ex-vacuo* ventricular dilatation p.101.

Congenital hydrocephalus is often associated with one or more anomalies of the *craniorachischisis* series. It will be recalled that the whole of the central nervous system develops from a neural groove by dorsal midline fusion of its neural folds. Mesodermal tissue, giving rise in the course of later development to bone and muscle, insinuates itself between the neural tube and the dorsal surface of the embryo. If this process is interfered with, the development of the whole or part of the nervous system may show evidence of imperfect closure. All the anomalies of the 'schisis' type are characterized by such incomplete midline fusion of the neural canal and the associated imperfect development of the brain or spinal cord is sometimes referred to as *dysraphism*. Bones and soft tissues are often also anomalous over the affected area. (An unorthodox view of the genesis of spina bifida and the related abnormalities is that of Gardner (1961), who believes that the cause is not failure of fusion but rupture of an already formed neural tube.) The 'schisis' anomalies range from the mildest asymptomatic forms of spina bifida occulta to complete anencephaly and total rachischisis. The commonest form in cases of mental subnormality is spina bifida cystica with hydrocephalus, but instances of occipital, and, more rarely, frontal encephalocele also occur. In general, encephaloceles can be classified as occipital, sincipital and basal according to the part of the skull affected (Drettner, 1963). Not all are congenital in origin or associated with mental retardation.*

Spina bifida cystica is usually situated in the lumbar region, and, less frequently, in the thoracic or cervical ones. The sac may be formed by only skin and meninges—meningocele, but contains more often also neural elements, particularly at its margin—myelocele or meningomyelocele (Cameron, 1956 and 1957; Laurence, 1964). In cases of spina bifida cystica associated with hydrocephalus the brain presents another anomaly—the *Arnold-Chiari malformation*, which is characterized by a downward displacement (and distortion) of parts of the medulla and cerebellum through the foramen magnum into the vertebral canal (Fig. 69). The morphogenesis of this malformation has been the subject of a prolonged and still unconcluded debate (Sandbank, 1955; Lichtenstein, 1959; Daniel and Strich, 1958; Greenfield, 1963). In considering the pathogenesis of this malformation it is worth remembering that an Arnold-Chiari malformation is said to occur, albeit very rarely, in the presence of a normal spine (Peach, 1964). The hydrocephalus in some cases of spina bifida cystica can be communicating, i.e. there is free communication between the spinal theca and the ventricles of the brain. When this is so, the circulation of the C.S.F. is obstructed in the subarachnoid space around the foramen magnum or above it, the block being produced, perhaps, by congestion followed by low-grade arachnoiditis or by the plugging action of the herniated parts. In other cases the hydrocephalus is non-communicating, the block being then caused by co-existing 'forking' or stenosis of the cerebral aqueduct, or by adhesions occluding the foramina of Magendie and Luschka.

*It may not be sufficiently known that occipital meningoceles can be very small. On several occasions nodules from the midline of the scalp were removed as warts or naevi and sent to us for histological examination. Microscopically meningeal elements were evident in the specimens and radiography subsequently revealed the presence of a small hole in the occipital bone. These anomalies were symptom-free.

In some cases of Arnold-Chiari malformation a hood-like prolongation of the velum and 4th ventricle extends downwards over the dorsal surface of the medulla and cervical cord. The dorsal wall of this pouch may be perforated by the foramen of Magendie; in other cases this foramen is absent (Peach, 1965).

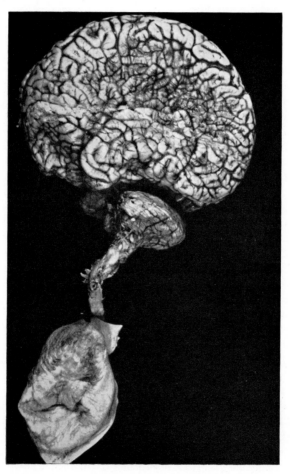

FIG. 69. A hydrocephalic brain with spina bifida cystica and an Arnold-Chiari malformation.

The spinal cord above the level of the main defect is often anomalous. It may show *hydromyelia* (dilatation of the central canal), *syringomyelia* (irregular cavitation and gliosis of areas outside the central canal) and *diastematomyelia* (duplication and flattening of the spinal cord at and below a bony spur protruding in the midline from the dorsal surface of a vertebra above the level of the main defect). The syringomyelic cavity may extend upwards into the medulla (syringobulbia). These and other associated vertebral, cranial and cerebral anomalies have been well reviewed by Cameron (1957) and more recently, by Moes and Hendrick (1963).

A cleft spine need not be always associated with an external deficiency of the skin and soft tissues and a myelocele or meningomyelocele. The overlying soft tissues may be normal or show only minor skin anomalies—*spina bifida occulta*. The spinal cord may, however, be nevertheless abnormal in some of these cases, diastematomyelia being, perhaps, particularly frequent (James and Lassman, 1964).

Hydrocephalus can be associated with yet another anomaly, viz. an imperfect development of the cerebellar vermis, usually referred to as the *Dandy-Walker syndrome*. This can be combined with atresia of the foramina of Magendie and Luschka (D'Agostino, Kernohan and Brown, 1963; Schurr, 1964). The degree of the defect varies. In extreme cases, only the nodule of the cerebellum is formed, and the two hemispheres are widely separated by a greatly ballooned fourth ventricle. However, cases associated with mental retardation usually show somewhat milder defects, such as absence of only the caudal half of the vermis and lesser dilatation of the fourth ventricle. Generalized hydrocephalus is not constant, nor are the foramina of Magendie and Luschka always absent even in the grosser instances of the anomaly. Brodal and Haughlie-Hanssen (1959) have presented evidence refuting the previously accepted view that atresia of the foramina precedes and determines the origin of this malformation.

It has been suggested that hydrocephalus may also be caused by the imperfect development of the subarachnoid space. This space is absent in early embryonic life and is formed later by the horizontal splitting of the single membrane into the arachnoid and pia. Should the splitting be imperfect, the subarachnoid space could remain partially or completely impermeable to C.S.F.

Many cranial and vertebral anomalies can be associated with craniorachischisis. Some vertebrae or parts of vertebrae may, for example, be absent or fused. Certain bony anomalies at the base of the skull, such as platybasia and basilar impression, have been held responsible for the development of hydrocephalus. These conditions were studied by Gátai (1959) and Spillane, Pallis and Jones (1957), who defined *platybasia* as an increase in the breadth (obtuseness) of the basal angle of the skull, which is the angle made by the intersection of the plane of the sphenoid with the plane of the clivus. *Basilar impression* is defined by them as elevation into the cranial cavity of a variable part of the bony rim of the foramen magnum. It has been stated that hydrocephalus could be caused in some of these cases by bony pressure exerted upon the brain-stem, but the problem requires further study since it is difficult to distinguish between cause and effect in such circumstances. Other, certainly secondary, bony defects in cases of hydrocephalus are delayed union of the cranial sutures, formation of accessory bones within the widened interosseous spaces, and craniolacunation. The posterior fossa of the skull is usually flattened, and in cases of Arnold-Chiari malformation the tentorium cerebelli is attached too close to the foramen magnum, thus reducing the volume of that fossa.

Another occasional cause of hydrocephalus is haemorrhage occurring at or soon after birth. Blood can obstruct either the aqueduct or the subarachnoid space and the occlusion may be immediate or delayed, i.e., following later organization of the clot or the formation of adhesions. As already mentioned, two of the largest crania seen at the Fountain Hospital were cases of hydrocephalus following neonatal subarachnoid haemorrhage. The blood had broken into the substance of the brain and the resulting large cysts caused displacement, compression and kinking of the third ventricle and cerebral aqueduct.

Infection is the commonest cause of *acquired hydrocephalus*. Of the 21 cases considered by Crome (1960), 7 were post-meningitic. The pathogenesis can be relatively simple in such cases. In the acute stage, the aqueduct is blocked by pus, and later, by intra- or periventricular gliosis. Similarly, the foramina and the subarachnoid spaces may be obstructed by exudate during the acute stages, or, later, by organized granulation tissue and adhesions. However, it is worth noting that meningitis is frequent in cases of congenital hydrocephalus. Since many of the latter are not recognized as such at birth but develop the first signs only after the onset of infection, the congenital nature of hydrocephalus often remains undetected.

Tumours and cysts are rare causes of hydrocephalus in infancy and childhood. Choroid plexus papillomata provide probably the only instance of hydrocephalus produced by oversecretion of the C.S.F., but even this is somewhat doubtful (Laurence, 1959).

Finally, it must be mentioned that many cases of hypertensive hydrocephalus show no demonstrable obstruction (*vide infra*).

Whatever the cause of hydrocephalus, persistently raised intracranial pressure and progressive ventricular enlargement produce secondary atrophic changes, especially after the sutures have closed and the skull becomes rigid. The pallium over the enlarged ventricles is thinned. The gyri often seem excessively convoluted—*polygyria*, an appearance not to be confused with ulegyria and microgyria. The corpus callosum is always thinned, and the septum pellucidum may be fenestrated or absent. The closure of the fontanelles and cranial sutures is delayed. The base of the skull can be flattened or otherwise distorted. The ventricular lining is often smooth, but may be rough and studded with ependymal granulations. Ventricular diverticula may form irregular, sometimes trabeculated, cavities within the white matter. The basal ganglia are compressed and the alignment of the brainstem and the aqueduct altered. This, together with the virtual obliteration of the subarachnoid space by compression against the skull, if it is no longer yielding, further embarrasses the circulation of the C.S.F. Dilatation of the third ventricle with pressure upon the hypothalamus has been held responsible by some workers for infantilism, or contrariwise, precocious puberty. The cranial nerves are often stretched with resulting ophthalmoplegia and other forms of paresis.

The commonest acute complication is infection, which may be introduced by repeated tapping of the fluid. Sudden rupture of the brain, encephalocele

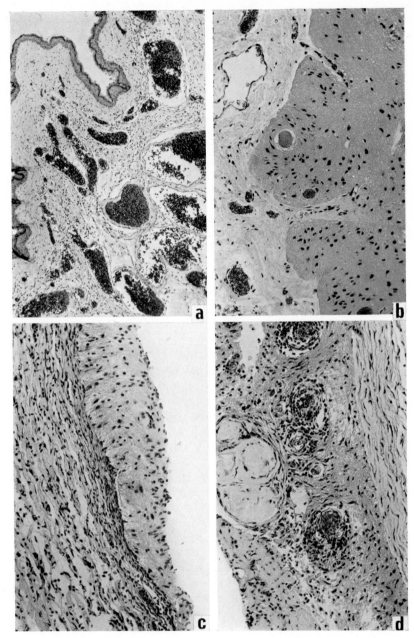

FIG. 70. Structures frequently encountered in the tissue resected prior to the surgical repair of spina bifida cystica. a. plexus of thin-walled blood vessels. b. glial tissue and a few large neurones resembling those normally found in the posterior root ganglia. c. meningeal elements, left, and neural tissue, right. d. a more complex structure containing meningeal elements. (Haematoxylin and eosin × 120).

or myelocele is a possible emergency. Rapid downward displacement of the brain-stem and cerebellum produced, perhaps, by rupture of the sac in cases of spina bifida or improvident lumbar puncture, can also be rapidly fatal. It has further been demonstrated by Lorber and Emery (1964) that needle tracks produced by ventricular puncture frequently enlarge to form cysts within the brain substance.

Pathological Aspects of Surgical Treatment

The management and treatment of spina bifida cystica and hydrocephalus have changed greatly in recent years and patients enjoy now a much higher expectation of life. Many reach late childhood and adolescence, often burdened, however, by physical and mental disability. The pathological implications of the new methods of surgical treatment must hence be considered.

The need for early repair of spina bifida cystica is now widely accepted and the operation is usually performed already on the first day of life. In order to approximate the edges of the defect the membrane covering the cord and a narrow rim of tissue at its margin are first excised. Histologically, the excised membrane is usually formed by epidermis and granulation tissue in the process of epithelialization. The outer part of this tissue as a rule contains skin, skin appendages, fat and meningeal elements. In some cases it also contains neural elements, such as islets of glial tissue, nerve roots, ependymal cells and nerve cells (Fig. 70). The spinal cord in the vertebral gap is flattened, splayed out and parts of it may be embedded in the integument, so that they may be unintentionally removed with the covering membrane. Thus, the malformation, if at all severe, is not a simple gap of the vertebral column and soft tissues. Failure of the neural canal to close over is in such cases always associated with general dysplasia, dysraphism, the constituent tissues presenting many irregularities. Their relation to each other is often abnormal. In transverse sections they often seem broken up into discontinuous columns, islets and fragments which seem intermixed irregularly with each other. The meningeal elements are usually represented by broken strands or whorls of thickened and hyalinized cells and fibres. Blood vessels are frequently arranged in the form of thin-walled cavernous plexuses, and it may be impossible to recognize the topological derivation of the neural elements. Structures resembling the central canal of the spinal cord and smaller tubules lined by ependymal cells may also be present.

It is sometimes said that loss of neural elements during the repair of spina bifida cystica does no harm or that, in other words, the excised neural tissue is as 'redundant' as, say, a supernumerary nipple or a sixth digit of the hand. It is difficult to see, however, how this can be proved, since some paralysis of the lower limbs and bladder almost always complicates the clinical picture in both treated and untreated cases of meningomyelocele or more severe anomalies requiring surgical repair. Additional slight neurological impairment may therefore be easily submerged in the general deficit. Nevertheless, it is possible that the dysplasic neural tissue at the margin of the gap *is* nonfunctioning. The following embryological evidence is relevant (Lopashov and

Stroeva, 1964). When an embryonic eye cup is transplanted or its development otherwise experimentally disturbed, the embryonic fissure (optic) carrying blood vessels may fail, as it should, to close over. If this occurs, adventitious retinal layers, i.e. neural elements, may form and differentiate ectopically at the edges of the abnormally patent fissure. It may be reasonable to infer therefore by analogy and subject to experimental confirmation that the ectopic neural elements at the margins of a spina bifida cystica are 'redundant'. Yet the more marked the dysplasia at the margins of the vertebral anomaly, the greater is also the abnormality of the spinal cord itself. In the more severe cases the spinal cord in the depth of the trough-like cavity may almost entirely disappear or be represented by a slim string- or ribbon-like structure. It seems then that the 'supply' of spinal cord material is limited; the more is used up around the edges of the gap the less is left for the spinal cord in the centre. Furthermore, as mentioned already, the spinal cord above the defect may also be severely abnormal, showing hydromyelia, syringomyelia, micromyelia or diastematomyelia. Some adventitious ectopic structures resembling those at the site of the main defect, e.g. islets of glial tissue, abnormal neural, meningeal, and vascular elements, may also be present dorsally and laterally at all levels of the spinal cord and medulla (Popoff and Feigin, 1964).

Hydrocephalus, incipient or developed, is usually treated by the establishment of an artificial shunt between the lateral ventricles of the brain and the right side of the heart. Sialastic tubes connected by a valve—the Spitz-Holter or Heyer-Pudenz valve, are employed for this purpose, the distal tube being inserted through the jugular vein into the right atrium of the heart. In this way cerebro-spinal fluid is drained and the brain is being continuously 'decompressed'. As a result, the internal and external appearances of the brain change, but not always desirably (Emery, 1964 and 1965). The ventricles of the treated cases may remain within normal range, but the sulci of the cortex may be considerably widened and there may be infolding of the cortex. The arachnoid is often thickened. The subdural space may be widened, the vessels stretched to the point of rupture, and episodes of bleeding lead to the development of pachymeningitis haemorrhagica. The cerebellum is sometimes drawn up, and the movement of the brainstem may, according to Emery, stretch the VI nerve and the pituitary stalk.

Other complications of ventriculo-atrial shunts include thrombosis of the vena cava and right atrium of the heart, and embolization of the lungs. This may be followed in some cases by the development of pulmonary hypertension or pulmonary abscesses, if the emboli are septic. Ulceration of the tricuspid valve has also been seen in a few instances (Erdohazi, Eckstein and Crome, 1966; Crome and Erdohazi, 1966). The cardiac end of the lower tube may perforate the heart wall and drain into the pericardial sac causing cardiac tamponade by cerebro-spinal fluid. Other complications include obstruction of the ventricular end of the tube, usually by tufts of the choroid plexus, tela choroidoea, and, less frequently, by thrombus.*

* A hitherto unrecognized complication encountered here recently was massive chylous pleural effusion caused by surgical damage to a branch of the thoracic duct on the left side of the neck.

Finally, infection is an ever-present danger in both treated and untreated cases of spina bifida cystica and hydrocephalus. Owing to bladder paralysis and development of hydroureter and hydronephrosis, renal infection is particularly common. Similarly, infection of the meninges and choroid plexuses, especially with antibiotic-resistent organisms, such as Ps. pyocyanea and other Gram-negative bacteria, is a problem in the management of these cases.

Hydrencephaly, also called more inappropriately, hydranencephaly, is a rather vague term applied to brains formed largely by thin transparent membranous sacs which replace most of the cerebral hemispheres (Crome and Sylvester, 1958). These sacs are usually ruptured in the course of autopsies, and after the fluid escapes, their interior appears empty, save, perhaps, for the hillocks of the basal ganglia at the base of the skull. Where any solid tissue remains, it is usually found at the base of the occipital and temporal lobes. Parts of the basal ganglia may be also preserved, but they and the midbrain are often degenerate. Formations below that level are usually substantially normal, presenting only agenesis of the long descending tracts. As a rule, there is no evidence of obstruction in the ventricular system and the hemispheres are not enlarged; indeed, the brains are often micrencephalic. In other cases, there is some impediment to the circulation of the C.S.F. caused by aqueductal stenosis and, possibly, absence of the subarachnoid space. It has been suggested that the chief factor in the genesis of hydrencephaly is destruction and resorption of pre-formed tissue and the relation of this malformation to certain forms of porencephaly has been mentioned already (p. 132). Extreme forms of hydrencephaly are incompatible with prolonged survival, but infants with partial or unilateral forms may live long enough to present clinical evidence of severe subnormality.

Remaining Problems

Lest it be thought that the above facts are sufficient for the full understanding of hydrocephalus, the following are a few of the unsolved problems.

First, it is well known that not all cases of hydrocephalus progress unremittingly to fatal termination. Spontaneous stabilization, and, even, occasional reduction in the size of the head can be expected in some cases. This relative unpredictability of individual prognosis makes assessment of the results of various surgical procedures undertaken for the relief of hydrocephalus rather uncertain (Laurence, 1958). The natural arrest may be the result of spontaneous restoration of the flow of C.S.F. by the formation of a new channel or the re-opening of a previously closed one. In many instances, however, it is impossible to demonstrate any such event clinically or anatomically. Paradoxical non-development of hydrocephalus in certain cases showing an apparent block of the cerebral aqueduct must be also considered in this context.

Second, and probably the crux of the problem, is the group of cases—the largest in infancy and childhood—formerly known as idiopathic hydrocephalus. In these cases there is gradual enlargement of the head without a history of overt infection. At autopsy most of the brains show no evidence of obstruction in the C.S.F. pathway other than, perhaps, slight meningeal opacity over the basal cisterns, and possibly, limited circumscribed loculations of fluid in the subarachnoid space. Dorothy Russell suggested in her monograph that such cases are, despite the inconclusiveness of the evidence, also post-meningitic, because she could demonstrate similar unimpressive changes in a few of her cases which had suffered from definite low-grade meningitis. These conclusions appear somewhat strained. Some of the changes considered by Professor Russell can be seen quite frequently in brains showing no hydrocephalus, and could, furthermore, be regarded as a sequel and not the cause of the hydrocephalus. Moreover, as already explained, the occurrence of definite meningitis in infancy followed by cranial enlargement does not necessarily establish a causal relationship (*vide supra*).

The results of experimental work are also relevant. Congenital hydrocephalus is one of the commonest malformations obtained by experimental teratologists (p. 28). The genetic varieties of the condition can be easily produced by selective breeding, while other forms occur in the offspring of animals kept before mating and during pregnancy on vitamin-deficient diets. It is usually quite impossible to demonstrate anatomical obstruction of the C.S.F. pathway in these animals, and workers have had to resort to over-production of the C.S.F. as an explanation of the hydrocephalus (Millen, Woollam and Lamming, 1954; Millen, 1956). Yet overproduction by itself could not result in hydrocephalus, without obstruction or failure of absorption of the excessive fluid, and of these there was no direct evidence.

It is clear therefore that time has not yet come to abandon the search for further causes and mechanisms of hydrocephalus.

THE PHAKOMATOSES

The term phakomatosis was introduced by the Dutch ophthalmologist Hoeve, who described in 1921 retinal tumours in cases of tuberous sclerosis. The group of phakomatoses includes four distinct syndromes: tuberous sclerosis, neurofibromatosis, the Sturge-Weber syndrome, the neuro-retinal angiomatosis of Hippel-Lindau, and several other, more vaguely defined, conditions. Only tuberous sclerosis and neurofibromatosis show significant kinship, but it is nevertheless not unusual to discuss all the conditions as a group, as was done, for example, in a symposium the proceedings of which have been recently published (Michaux and Feld, 1963). The approximate prevalence of the phakomatoses among the severely subnormal can be gauged from the small series studied by Berg and Crome (1963). Of some 2,000 severely subnormal children admitted to the Fountain Hospital in the course of 20 years, 15 were cases of tuberous sclerosis, 2 of neurofibromatosis, 2 of the Sturge-Weber syndrome, while 1 other was, probably, an atypical case of tuberous sclerosis. In addition, a few cases with incomplete tuberous sclerosis remained unrecognized until death and full pathological examination.

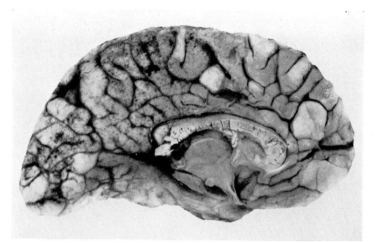

FIG. 71. The brain in a case of tuberous sclerosis after prolonged fixation in formalin. The nodules are more than usually conspicuous.

FIG. 72. A coronal block of a cerebral hemisphere showing large nodules of tuberous sclerosis—pale areas—in the middle frontal and superior temporal gyri. Smaller nodules are present also elsewhere. (Cresyl violet).

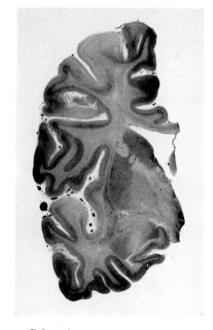

Tuberous Sclerosis

Pathological Anatomy

Few conditions in mental deficiency practice present more striking morphological features than tuberous sclerosis. The disease takes its name from the multiple nodules scattered irregularly through the cerebrum (Figs. 71 and 72), and, to a lesser extent, other parts of the central nervous system. They vary, as a rule, from microscopic dimensions to the size of a cherry, but much larger ones have also been described. In the freshly removed brain the nodules can be palpated better than seen; they become more visible in fixed material, particularly after the meninges have been stripped. The nodules may then be paler than the surrounding tissue and may also appear to be covered by whitish faintly striated or ground-frost-like material. The larger nodules are often indrawn ('umbilicated') in their centre.

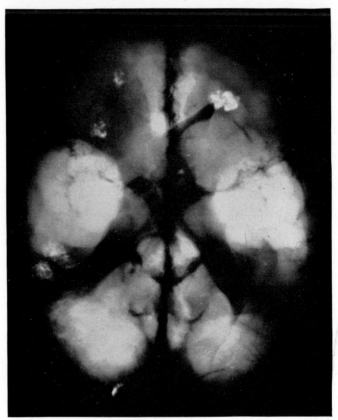

FIG. 73. Calcification of the cerebral nodules in a case of tuberous sclerosis.

The nodules contain glial fibres and cells, many of which are atypical. Some have a large amount of cytoplasm and prominent vesicular or reniform nuclei; others are multinucleate. Mitotic figures may be observed in some areas. The density of the glial fibres can vary even within the same nodule. They are usually densest near the surface of the brain, where some may be condensed to form characteristic brightly staining eosinophil sheaf-like structures. Many nodules contain also a large number of amyloid bodies and calcospherites. Gross calcification is likewise relatively frequent (Fig. 73). Neurones are usually depleted and those remaining are often misorientated. Many are abnormal in shape. Some are thin, elongated and wavy; others are, on the other hand, abnormally small. Many cells stain very faintly. However, the most striking change is, perhaps, the occurrence of giant nerve cells with a large amount of Nissl substance (Fig. 74). They are not specific for tuberous sclerosis; similar neurones may be seen in a few other conditions associated with gliosis (Crome, 1957). Compared with other cells, neurones in general contain more ribonucleic acid (in the form of Nissl substance) and manufacture a larger amount of proteins. This is probably related to the storage of memory traces. It is possible therefore that constriction of the axis cylinder and of dendrites by neighbouring gliosis is followed by excessive accumulation

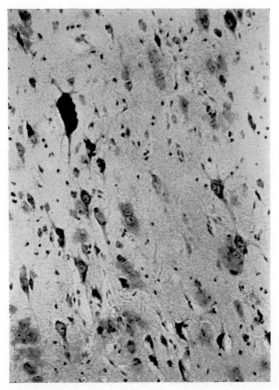

FIG. 74. Nodule of tuberous sclerosis. Many abnormal glial cells and neurones. One is a characteristic 'giant neurone'. (Haematoxylin and eosin × 200).

of proteins within the perikaryon, provided that the affected cell remains viable and 'functionally' active. This could be a factor in the formation of the giant nerve cells. If this were the only cause, however, the change would perhaps be more frequent than it appears to be.

Glial and neuronal irregularity is by no means confined to the recognizable nodules. Milder gliosis and neuronal changes can be very widespread. It is characteristic of tuberous sclerosis that while some of the lesions, like the nodules, are circumscribed, other changes, both in neural and in somatic tissues, are less well-defined and the pathologist is often in doubt whether the area he is examining is or is not abnormal.

The cerebral nodules may be situated in the cortex, basal ganglia, the white matter or periventricular areas, and similar lesions also occur less frequently in the lower formations. The periventricular nodules, formed by rather uniform, elongated glial cells, often project in the form of wax-like elevations into the ventricles, presenting the characteristic appearance of 'candle-guttering' (Fig. 75).

The cellular hyperplasia can occasionally reach neoplastic proportions and malignant transformation to spongioblastoma has been repeatedly described

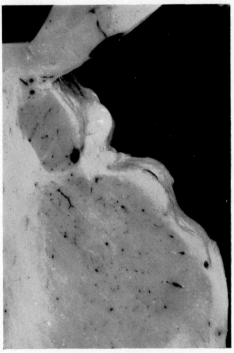

FIG. 75. Periventricular nodules projecting into the ventricle and presenting the appearance of 'candle-guttering'. ($\times$ 1⅞).

In such cases, most of the tumours appear to have been situated in the vicinity of the ventricles, and this suggests that the periventricular nodules are more liable to undergo malignant change than those in other areas. According to Jervis (1954) tumours in some cases of tuberous sclerosis contain not only glial elements but also neurones in various stages of differentiation. They are hence instances of spongioneuroblastoma.

Somatic Involvement

Another characteristic of tuberous sclerosis is somatic and visceral involvement. Almost all tissues and organs can be abnormal, but since it is not easy to recognize minor and marginal changes, it is certain that many anomalies have so far escaped recognition. The better known ones are listed in Table 3,

Table 3. TUBEROUS SCLEROSIS, SOME OF THE LESIONS WHICH MAY BE FOUND IN THIS CONDITION

Brain	Skin	Heart	Kidney	Eye	Lungs	Bones	Other Organs
1. TUBEROUS SCLEROSIS	1. ADENOMA SEBACEUM	1. PURKIN-JEOMA	1. MIXED BENIGN TUMOURS OR HAMARTOMATA	1. PHAKOMA	1. Congenital cysts	1. Periosteal nodules	1. Haemangioma and other benign tumours have been observed in thyroid, spleen, thymus, liver, breast and duodenum.
2. Candle-guttering	2. Peau de chagrin	2. Lipoma	2. Rare malignant tumours, e.g. car-cinoma or sarcoma		2. Alveolar cell adenoma	2. Osteoporosis	
3. Glioma	3. Flat warts	3. Fibroma	3. Polycystic kidney		3. Muscular and fibrous dysplasia	3. Cysts	
4. Secondary changes e.g. demyelination, softening	4. Haemangioma	4. Fibro-elastosis	4. Teratoma			4. Melorheo-stosis	
	5. Fibroma					5. Bony sur-face excrescences	
	6. Subungual fibroma and haem-angioma					6. Spina bifida	
	7. Vitiligo						
	8. Leucoderma					7. Syndactyly, polydactyly	
	9. Café au lait spots						

(The more common lesions are printed in SMALL CAPITALS)

and for further details readers are referred to fuller texts (Critchley and Earl, 1932; Hallervorden and Krücke, 1956; Michaux and Feld, 1963).* A few of the more conspicuous anomalies are described below.

Adenoma sebaceum (Fig. 76), is an acneiform, papular, colourless or brownish rash of the face, which usually appears at the age of 4 to 6 years, and often takes on a reddish tinge after puberty. Histologically, the skin shows moderate hyperplasia and irregularity of most of its elements: sebaceous

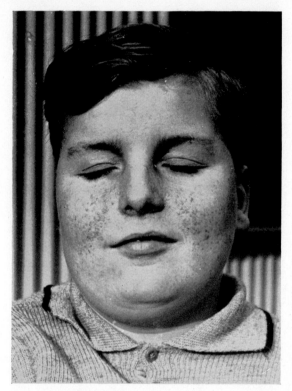

FIG. 76. Adenoma sebaceum.

glands, sweat glands, blood vessels and fibrous tissue in the upper part of the dermis (Fig. 77). There is also hyperkeratosis, thinning of the epidermis and unevenness in the length of the rete pegs.

The cardiac lesion, often referred to as rhabdomyoma, can present as a discrete nodule or tumour, but is more frequently a diffuse hamartomatous structure containing fibrous tissue, fat and a variable number of the character-istic 'rhabdomyomatous' 'spider' cells. These are large polygonal cells, the cytoplasm of which may be coarsely granular in stained sections, or present radial and tangential fibrils, which leave much of the intracellular space 'empty'. Some of these fibrils show the distinct striation of muscle. With appropriate staining, abundant glycogen can be demonstrated in the cyto-

* See also Paulson, G. W., and Lyle, C. B. (1966). *Develop. Med. Child. Neurol.*, **8**, 571.

plasm; the cells are, in fact, structurally similar to those constituting the cardiac conducting system. These were first described by the Czech anatomist, Jan Purkinje, and the malformation could therefore be appropriately described as a *purkinjeoma*. Wolfe and Foley (1963) have studied histochemically the activity of some of the oxidative enzymes in the cells of one of these structures and found increased succinic and isocitric dehydrogenase activity compared

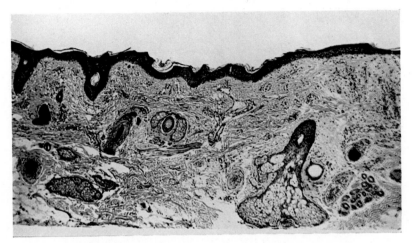

Fig. 77. A histological section of the skin in adenoma sebaceum. Description in the text. (Haematoxylin and eosin × 42.)

with the adjoining normal muscle. Although the purkinjeomata have attracted much interest, lipomata or lipomatosis of the heart with atrophy of the replaced myocardial fibres is probably more common in tuberous sclerosis (Fig. 78). Endocardial fibrosis is also frequent.

The kidney is another of the frequently affected organs. The *renal lesions*, also hamartomata or tumours, can vary in size, number and structure. They may be simple renal adenomata or a complex arrangement of fat, blood vessels, muscle and fibrous tissue. Such mixed structures are usually named after the most prevalent element in them, e.g. fibroma, fibromyoma, myoma, angioma, lipoma and perithelioma, or teratoma. Polycystic disease of the kidneys is also common.

Phakoma is a whitish opaque retinal plaque or nodule, which is often histologically similar to the periventricular gliotic nodules (Fig. 79). The pathological aspects of the phakomata have been recently described by Lund (1960).

Atypical Manifestation

Some individuals present incomplete forms of tuberous sclerosis: for example, only polycystic kidneys and adenoma sebaceum. Furthermore, typical lesions of tuberous sclerosis in several organs can occasionally be found in persons with apparently normal intelligence (Schnitzer, 1963).

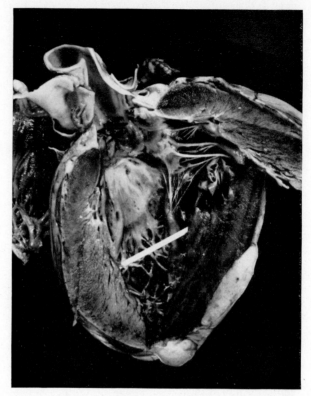

FIG. 78. The heart in this case of tuberous sclerosis shows lipomatosis of the left
ventricle and endocardial fibrosis.

FIG. 79. Phakoma of the retina (Haematoxylin and eosin × 44.)

These *formes frustes* of the disease can occur sporadically or in the parents and relatives of patients suffering from the full syndrome. Again, the somatic manifestations of the disease may be minimal although the neural changes are fully characteristic. In a recently examined personal case, for example, the only discovered visceral change was a renal adenoma measuring 1 mm. in diameter while cerebral changes were widespread and typical. Another case showed typical renal and cardiac changes, but only numerous foci of calcification and not the characteristic cellular anomalies were present in the brain. In other and more atypical cases, it may be impossible to establish the diagnosis even after the fullest pathological examination (Berg and Crome, 1960). Moreover the characteristic lesions of tuberous sclerosis have been usually observed in older infants or children and very few studies deal with the new-

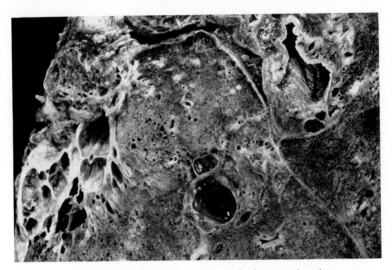

FIG. 80. Pulmonary cysts in a case of tuberous sclerosis.

born. Since most, if not all of the lesions of tuberous sclerosis undergo in time a modicum of change, it must not be assumed that the lesions in the new-born are necessarily as strikingly distinct as those of the older subjects. Thus, in a fifteen-day-old infant reported by Zelman and Wiśniewska (1964) the cerebral cortex was only slightly involved. Tuberous sclerosis is like most of the other conditions not an 'all or none phenomenon'; its manifestations range from the doubtful and not definitely ascertainable to the most wide-spread and characteristic.

The presenting signs are often determined by unusual involvement of particular organs. A case associated with spontaneous hypoglycaemia due to a functioning islet cell tumour of the pancreas has been described, for example, by Gutman and Leffkowitz (1959). The pulmonary changes in tuberous sclerosis (Fig. 80) have been studied very thoroughly by Dawson (1954). The condition was associated with arthrogryposis in a case reported by Sandbank and Cohen (1964).

Comparative Medicine

A complex of changes fully characteristic of tuberous sclerosis has not been reported in animals, but Unterharnscheidt (1964) has recently observed a small gliotic nodule containing tuberous sclerosis-like neurones and glial cells in the brain of a Macaca rhesus. The monkey had no lesions elsewhere, and the author suggested that the case was analogous to the human abortive form of the disease.

Chemical Pathology

Although some neural and somatic lesions in cases of tuberous sclerosis can undergo proliferative change and possess occasional neoplastic potentiality, lesions on the whole are morphologically relatively quiescent. It is not surprising therefore that the few attempted chemical studies of the condition have yielded negative results. In particular, amino acids and protein-bound carbohydrates proved to be normal (Carpenter, Carter, Brinson and Mc-Carty, 1964).

Neurofibromatosis

The resemblance of neurofibromatosis and tuberous sclerosis is interesting. Both can be inherited and transmitted as Mendelian dominants. Both are characterized by focal proliferation of tissues which can become neoplastic. Adenoma sebaceum, which is characteristic of tuberous sclerosis, has been reported in a few instances of neurofibromatosis, and different members of the same family have been known to suffer from either of the two conditions.

Cases of neurofibromatosis show multiple areas of dysplasia and proliferative change in the peripheral nerves, the central nervous system and other tissues. The skin, for example, is often affected, showing patchy brown pigmentation—café-au-lait spots, pigmented naevi, areas of depigmentation, hamartomata, hypertrichosis and haemangiomata. Many other organs may show manifold anomalies (Crome, 1962). Lesions of the peripheral nerves are chiefly neurofibromata. The central nervous system is also invariably involved in cases showing mental retardation. The commonest intracranial and intraspinal lesions are neurofibromata of the nerve roots and nerves, the changes resembling, in the main, those of the peripheral nerves. Within the cranium, the VIII and the V nerves are most frequently affected. The optic and the olfactory nerves can also be involved, but since their structure resembles the C.N.S. rather than peripheral nerves, the changes assume the form of gliosis or gliomatosis (Crome, 1954). Meningiomata or meningiomatosis have been described. From the viewpoint of mental retardation the most important change is, however, multifocal gliosis or glioblastomatosis of the substance of the brain and spinal cord (Fig. 81).

The Sturge-Weber Syndrome (Encephalofacial angiomatosis)

The Sturge-Weber syndrome is another of the rarer conditions associated with mental deficiency. The main pathological changes in this syndrome are

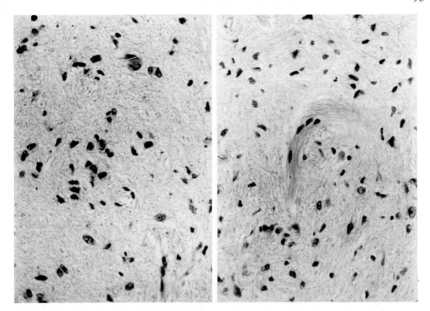

FIG. 81. Two gliotic areas in the cerebral cortex of a case of neurofibromatosis. Most of the cells are astrocytes and spongioblasts, and are arranged diffusely and in clusters. On the right, some of the cells and fibres are arranged in parallel pilocytic bundles. (Haematoxylin and eosin × 400.)

facial haemangioma, often situated in the territory innervated by one or more branches of the trigeminal nerve, and proliferation of dilated, tortuous vessels in the soft meninges (dural involvement has also been reported in at least one case). The meningeal involvement is as a rule restricted to the parietal and occipital lobes on the side of the facial haemangioma. The subjoining cerebral cortex is usually atrophic, and the meninges together with the superficial cortical layers can be calcified. Sudanophil debris are often present in the affected cortex and loss of myelin is manifest in appropriately stained sections.

Many less typical forms of the syndrome have been described. The cutaneous haemangioma may extend, for example, to the opposite side of the face or involve the whole of the ipsilateral side of the body. In such cases it may be associated with hypertrophy of soft tissues and bone (Kramer, 1963). The retina can be involved and the eye may be buphthalmic. The pathological features of the syndrome have been described fully (Wohlwill and Yakovlev, 1957; Alexander and Norman, 1960).

The Hippel-Lindau syndrome is characterized by associated retinal and cerebellar haemangiomatosis (haemangioblastoma) and cysts in different organs—most frequently the kidneys (François, 1963; Goodman, Kleinholz and Peck, 1964).

Neurocutaneous Melanosis is another rare condition which may be associated with mental retardation. The characteristic changes include large areas of cutaneous melanotic naevoid pigmentation with similar changes in the meninges and brain. The lesions tend to become malignant and the patients usually die in early childhood (Fox, Emery, Goodbody and Yates, 1964).

REFERENCES

ALEXANDER, G. L., and NORMAN, R. M. (1960). 'The Sturge Weber Syndrome', Bristol: Wright.
BECKETT, R. S., NETSKY, M. G., and ZIMMERMAN, H. M. (1950). *Amer. J. Path.*, **26**, 755.
BERG, J. M., and CROME, L. (1960). *J. ment. Defic. Res.*, **4**, 24.
BERG, J. M., and CROME, L. (1963). In MICHAUX, L., and FELD, M. 'Les phakomatoses dans la deficience mentale' in Les Phakomatoses Cerebrales, Paris: S.P.E.I.
BRODAL, A., and HAUGHLIE-HANSSEN, E. (1959). *J. Neurol. Neurosurg. Psychiat.*, **22**, 99.
CAMERON, A. H. (1956). *Lancet*, **2**, 171.
CAMERON, A. H. (1957). *J. Path. Bact.*, **73**, 195 and 213.
CARPENTER, D. G., CARTER, C. H., BRINSON, E. M., and McCARTY, D. A. (1964). *J. Pediat.*, **65**, 124.
CRITCHLEY, M., and EARL, C. J. C. (1932). *Brain*, **55**, 311.
CROME, L. (1954). *J. Path. Bact.*, **67**, 407.
CROME, L. (1957). *J. Neurol. Neurosurg. Psychiat.*, **20**, 117.
CROME, L. (1960). *Brit. med. J.*, **1**, 897.
CROME, L. (1962). *Arch. Dis. Childh.*, **37**, 640.
CROME, L., and SYLVESTER, P. E. (1958). *Arch. Dis. Childh.*, **33**, 235.
CROME, L., and ERDOHAZI, M. (1966). *Arch. Dis. Childh.*, **41**, 179.
D'AGOSTINO, A. N., KERNOHAN, J. W., and BROWN, J. R. (1963). *J. Neuropath. exp. Neurol.*, **22**, 450.
DANIEL, P. M., and STRICH, S. J. (1958). *J. Neuropath. exp. Neurol.*, **17**, 255.
DAWSON, J. (1954). *Quart. J. Med.*, **23**, 113.
DRETTNER, B. (1963). *Acta oto-laryng. (Stockh.)*, **57**, 181.
EDWARDS, J. H., NORMAN, R. M., and ROBERTS, J. M. (1961). *Arch. Dis. Childh.*, **36**, 481.
EMERY, J. L. (1964). *Arch. Dis. Childh.*, **39**, 379.
EMERY, J. L. (1965). *Develop. Med. Child Neurol.*, **7**, 302.
ERDOHAZI, M., ECKSTEIN, H. B., and CROME, L. (1966). *Develop. Med. Child Neurol.*, **8**, Suppl. No. 2.
FORD, F. R. (1960). 'Diseases of the Nervous System in Infancy, Childhood and Adolescense,' Oxford: Blackwell, p. 938.
FOX, H., EMERY, J. L., GOODBODY, R. A., and YATES, P. O. (1964). *Arch. Dis. Childh.*, **39**, 508.
FRANÇOIS, J. (1963). 'Angiomatose Retino-Cerebello-Viscerale de von Hippel-Lindau,' in Les Phakomatoses Cérébrales by L. Michaux and M. Feld, Paris: S.P.E.I.
GARDNER, W. J. (1961). *Arch. Neurol. (Chic.)*, **4**, 13.
GÁTAI, G. (1959). *Z. menschl. Vererb. -u. Konstit. -Lehre.*, **35**, 77.
GOODMAN, J., KLEINHOLZ, E., and PECK, F. C. (1964). *J. Neurosurg.*, **21**, 97.
GREENFIELD, J. G. (1963). 'Arnold-Chiari Malformation' in Greenfield's Neuropathology, London: Arnold, p. 337.
GUTMAN, A., and LEFFKOWITZ, M. (1959). *Brit. med. J.*, **2**, 1065.
HALLERVORDEN, J., and KRÜCKE, W. (1956). 'Die Tuberöse Hirnsklerose,' in O. Lubarsch, F. Henke, and R. Rössle's Handbuch der speziellen pathologischen Anatomie und Histologie, **13**, Ed. W. Scholz, Pt. 4, Berlin: Springer, p. 602.
HOEVE, J. VAN DER. (1921). *Albrecht v. Graefes Arch. Ophthal.*, **105**, 880.
JAMES, C. C. M., and LASSMAN, L. P. (1964). *Arch. Dis. Childh.*, **39**, 125.
JERVIS, G. A. (1954). *J. Neuropath. exp. Neurol.*, **13**, 105.
KRAMER, W. (1963). *Psychiat. Neurol. Neurochir. (Amst.)*, **66**, 362.
LAURENCE, K. M. (1958). *Lancet*, **2**, 1152.
LAURENCE, K. M. (1959). *Ann. roy. Coll. Surg. Engl.*, **24**, 388.
LAURENCE, K. M. (1964). *Arch. Dis. Childh.*, **39**, 41.
LICHTENSTEIN, B. W. (1959). *J. Neuropath. exp. Neurol.*, **18**, 3.
LOPASHOV, G. V., and STROEVA, O. G. (1964). 'Development of the Eye. Experimental Studies,' Jerusalem: Israel Program for Scientific Translations.

LORBER, J., and EMERY, J. L. (1964). *Develop. Med. Child Neurol.*, **6**, 125.
LUND, O. -E. (1960). *Albrecht v. Graefes Arch. Ophthal.*, **162**, 369.
MENOZZI, V., and CAGNONI, G. (1958). *Riv. Anat. pat.*, **14**, 1169.
MICHAUX, L., and FELD, M. (1963). 'Les Phakomatoses Cérébrales,' Paris: S.P.E.I.
MILLEN, J. W. (1956). *Proc. roy. Soc. Med.*, **49**, 980.
MILLEN, J. W., WOOLLAM, D. H. M., and LAMMING, G. E. (1954). *Lancet*, **2**, 679.
MOES, C. A. F., and HENDRICK, E. B. (1963). *J. Pediat.*, **63**, 238.
PEACH, B. (1964). *Arch. Neurol. (Chic.)*, **10**, 497.
PEACH, B. (1965). *Arch. Neurol. (Chic.)*, **11**, 609.
POPOFF, N., and FEIGIN, L. (1964). *Arch. Path.*, **78**, 533.
RUSSELL, D. S. (1949). 'Observations on the Pathology of Hydrocephalus,' London: H.M.S.O.
SANDBANK, U. (1955). *Rev. neurol.*, **93**, 529.
SANDBANK, U., and COHEN, L. (1964). *J. Pediat.*, **64**, 571.
SCHNITZER, B. (1963). *Arch. Path.*, **76**, 626.
SCHURR, P. H. (1964). *Develop. Med. Child Neurol.*, **6**, 633.
SPILLANE, J. D., PALLIS, C., and JONES, A. M. (1957). *Brain*, **10**, 11.
UNTERHARNSCHEIDT, F. (1964). *Acta neuropath. (Berl.)*, **3**, 250.
WARREN, M. C., LU, A. T., and ZIERING, W. H. (1963). *J. Pediat.*, **63**, 1104.
WELLS, C. (1964). 'Bones, Bodies and Disease. Evidence of Disease and Abnormality in Early Man,' London: Thames and Hudson.
WOHLWILL, F. J., and YAKOVLEV, P. I. (1957). *J. Neuropath. exp. Neurol.*, **16**, 341.
WOLFE, H. J., and FOLEY, F. D. (1963). *Arch. Path.*, **76**, 197.
ZELMAN, V., and WIŚNIEWSKA, K. (1964). *Polish med. J.*, **3**, 156.

CHAPTER 9

METABOLIC DISEASES

MENTAL defect may be caused by an inborn or acquired error of metabolism but the differentiation of the two is not always simple. Hypoglycaemia may, for example, be either inborn or acquired. In some conditions, like phenylketonuria, the nature of the chemical lesion and, even, its site are known; in others, as the lipidoses, these are still obscure. That the latter are indeed metabolic diseases is inferred from the regular accumulation of abnormal or excessive products in the tissues of patients, their time of onset, and frequent familial incidence.

At one time or another mental impairment has been observed in association with probably all the metabolic diseases, but in this book we consider only conditions presenting more or less constantly with retardation of intelligence. For ease of reference and comparison these are listed alphabetically in Table 4 occupying the bulk of this chapter. Only the most important data are given, but the information is amplified in the succeeding chapters and appendices, page references to which are cited in the appropriate column of the table. Readers are also referred to fuller reviews by Meister (1965), Efron (1965a), Carter (1965), Waisman (1966) and Woolf (1966).

All the metabolic diseases may have to be considered in the differential diagnosis of obscure cases, particularly infants and children, but each one is rare. The relative incidence of some of these in populations of the mentally subnormal has been mentioned on p. 9. However, since many patients die in early infancy, true incidence cannot be fully gauged from figures for institutionalized populations.

Table 4. CONDITIONS ASSOCIATED WITH MENTAL

Serial No.	Designation Synonyms Variants	Main clinical features	Specific Defect	Main abnormal	
				In urine	In blood
1	Abetalipoprotein-aemia. (Bassen-Kornzweig syndrome.)	Steatorrhoea. Atypical retinitis pigmentosa. Acanthocytosis of the erythrocytes. Cerebellar ataxia and mental retardation in some cases.	Probably an inability to form the betalipo-protein molecule.	—	Low serum globulins. Absent betalipo-protein. Low chol-esterol and phospho-lipids. Low vitamin A. No particu-late fat. Microcytic anaemia.
2	Alphalipo-proteinaemia.	Mental and physical retardation.	Not known.	Occasion-ally acetone.	Increase of triglycerides, phospho-lipids, free cholesterol and *a*-lipo-protein.
3	Acyldehydro-genase deficiency.	Neonatal onset of convulsions, lethargy and dehydration. Moderate hepatomegaly. Unusual odour.	Deficiency of green acylde-hydro-genase.	—	Marked acidosis. Increase of butyric acid and hexa-noic acid.
4	Argininosuccinic-aciduria.	Slow onset of mental retardation. Friability of hair. Trichorrhexis nodosa and monilethrix. Convulsions in some patients. Systolic murmur.	Deficiency in arginino-succinase.	Excess of arginino-succinic acid.	Excess of arginino-succinic acid.
5	Cephalin lipidosis.	Progressive mental deterioration in several siblings. Epilepsy. Splenomegaly.	Not known.	—	—
6	Citrullinuria.	Mental retardation in a child at 18 months.	Deficiency in arginino-succinate synthetase.	Excess of L-citru-lline.	Excess of L-citru-lline.
7	Congenital familial non-haemolytic jaundice. (Crigler-Najjar syndrome.)	Severe neonatal jaundice without haemolysis with, possibly, kernicterus. Early death, or, in survivors, ataxia and dystonia, deafness. One patient was later normal save for persistent jaundice.	Impairment or defic-iency in glucuronic acid transferase activity.	No bili-rubin.	Increase in indirectly reacting bilirubin.

RETARDATION AND METABOLIC DISORDER

substances In tissues	Mode of Transmission	Cross Refs.	Key references in literature	Remarks
—	Autosomal recessive.	p. 310.	Wolff (1965). Forsyth, Lloyd and Fosbrooke (1965).	In intestinal biopsies columnar cells covering the villi have unusually clear cytoplasm. Intelligence may remain normal.
—	Described in a pair of siblings.	p. 311.	Bigler, Mais, Dowben and Hsia (1959).	
—	Possibly recessive.		Sidbury, Harlan and Wittels (1962).	
Excess of arginino-succinic acid.	Possibly recessive.	p. 283.	Levin, MacKay and Oberholzer (1961), Dent (1961). Grosfeld, Mighorst and Moolhuysen (1964).	
Excessive storage of a cephalin, inosamine-phosphatide and, probably, an amino-sugar.	Possibly recessive.		Baar and Hickmans (1956).	
Excess of L-citru-lline in C.S.F.	Not known.	p. 283.	McMurray et al. (1962). McMurray et al. (1963).	
—	Possibly recessive.	p. 69.	Schmid (1966).	

Table 4.—

Serial No.	Designation Synonyms Variants	Main clinical features	Specific Defect	Main abnormal	
				In urine	In blood
8	Cystathio-ninuria.	Mental retardation.	Deficiency in cysta-thioninase.	Cystathio-nine, augmented by admini-stration of methionine.	—
9	Diffuse cerebral degeneration of infancy. Alpers' disease. Progressive diffuse degeneration of the grey matter of the cerebrum. Poliodystrophia cerebri progressiva.	Mental retardation commencing in infancy or childhood. Focal or generalized convulsions, myoclonic jerks, occasional blindness, choreoathetosis. Paralysis.	Not known.	Occasional amino-aciduria.	—
10	Familial infantile lactic acidosis.	Hypotonia, mental retardation. Tetany and convulsions in some of the cases.	Probably an obscure metabolic defect of muscle.	—	High lactate level. Acidosis, decreasing with age of the child.
11	Fructosaemia (Fructosuria).	Failure to thrive. Vomiting. Hepatomegaly. Transient jaundice. Retarded growth. Mild mental retardation.	Almost total lack of liver aldolase activity to fructose-1-phosphate and reduced activity to fructose-1:6 di-phosphate.	Fructosuria. Amino-aciduria.	Fructo-saemia after fructose administra-tion. Frequent hypogly-caemia. Low magnesium.
12	Galactosaemia.	Neonatal jaundice. Hepatomegaly followed by cirrhosis. Cataracts. Deafness. Mental retardation.	Lack of galactose-1-phosphate uridyl transferase activity.	Galacto-suria. Protein-uria. Amino-aciduria.	Excess of galactose-1-phos-phate.
13	Gargoylism (Hurler's syndrome. Lipochondro-dystrophy. Hurler-Pfaunder syndrome).	Usually mental retardation. Hepatosplenomegaly. Corneal clouding. Generalized skeletal and cranial changes. Heart changes.	Not known. Suggested abnormality in the metabolism of muco-polysacch-arides.	Excess of chondroit-in sulphate B and of heparitin sulphate.	—

continued

substances In tissues	Mode of Transmission	Cross Refs.	Key references in literature	Remarks
—	Not known.	p. 278.	Frimpter, Haymovitz and Horwith (1963). Harris (1962).	
—	Frequent familial cases.	p. 324.	Blackwood, Buxton, Cumings, Robertson and Tucker (1963).	
—	Not known.	p. 296. p. 314.	Erickson (1965). Worsley *et al.* (1965).	
—	Autosomal recessive.	p. 294.	Levin *et al.* (1963), Froesch, Wolf, Baitsch, Prader and Labhart (1963).	In older children the condition may be symptomless.
Excess of galactose-1-phosphate.	Autosomal recessive.	pp. 291, 357–359.	Holzel (1961), Woolf (1962), Hsia (1965).	Improvement on elimination of lactose from the diet.
Excess of chondroitin sulphate B and of heparitin sulphate. Increase of ganglioside in the brain.	1. Autosomal recessive. 2. Sex-linked, when condition tends to be less severe and there is no corneal clouding.	pp. 226, 362–366.	Maroteau and Lamy (1965). McKusick *et al.* (1965).	The nervous system shows changes histo-logically similar to the other lipidoses.

Table 4.—

Serial No.	Designation Synonyms Variants	Main clinical features	Specific Defect	Main abnormal	
				In urine	*In blood*
14	Gaucher's disease— infantile form.	Physical and mental retardation. Spleno- and hepatomegaly. Hypotonia followed by muscular rigidity. Head retraction. Cachexia. Bulbar palsy.	Deficiency in β-glucosidase (cerebrosidase).	—	—
15	Generalized glycogenosis. (Pompe's disease. Type 2 Cori. Neuromuscular form of glycogen storage disease).	Failure to thrive. Cardiomegaly. Moderate enlargement of liver. Hypotonia. General floppiness. Osteoporosis. Enlargement of the tongue. The appearance may suggest cretinism. Later, signs of cardiac failure.	Probably lack of a $a\ (1 \rightarrow 4)$ glucosidase.	—	Excess of glycogen in the blood and leucocytes.
16	Glycinaemia (Hyperglycinaemia).	Neonatal onset of vomiting. Failure to thrive, convulsions. Lethargy. Mental retardation. Neutropenia. Thrombocytopenia. Osteoporosis.	Not known.	Glycinuria. Ketonuria.	Hyperglycinaemia. Also, general aminoacidaemia. Increase of globulins. Ketosis.
17	Hartnup disease.	Mental retardation with emotional instability. Red, scaly, light-sensitive rash. Ataxia, diplopia and nystagmus in the acute stage.	Possibly a selective disorder of cellular amino acid transport in kidney and intestine.	Aminoaciduria. Indoleacetic acid, indoleacetylglutamic acid and indican.	—
18	Hepatolenticular degeneration. (Wilson's disease).	Hepatic cirrhosis. Progressive athetoid dementia. Occasional epilepsy. Kaiser-Fleischer ring.	Possibly decreased synthesis of caeruloplasmin.	Excess of copper. Aminoaciduria. Glycosuria. Uric acid is raised. Phosphaturia.	Low serum copper. Usually low caeruloplasmin. Low plasma amino acids. Hypoglycaemia. Low serum Phosphate.

continued

substances _In tissues_	Mode of Transmission	Cross Refs.	Key references in literature	Remarks
Excess of gluco- or galacto-cerebrosides (kerasin).	Autosomal recessive Possibly dominant in some cases.	p. 245.	Banker, Miller and Crocker (1962), Bogaert (1962), Aronson and Volk (1965).	There is generalized involvement of the reticulo-endothelial system and the brain may show changes of lipidosis.
Excess of glycogen in all tissues.	Autosomal recessive.	p. 297.	Hers (1964), Crome, Cumings and Duckett (1963).	
—	Not known.	p. 276.	Childs, Nyhan, Borden, Bard and Cooke (1961), Childs and Nyhan, (1964). Gerritsen and Waisman (1965). Menkes (1966)	
—	Autosomal recessive.	p. 285.	Baron *et al.* (1956), Watts (1962). Hooft, Laey, Timmermans and Snoeck (1962). Laey, Hooft, Timmermans and Snoeck (1964), Scriver (1965), Woolf (1966).	
Raised copper in brain, liver, kidney, cornea, spleen, adrenals, and muscles.	Autosomal recessive.	pp. 312, 368.	Walshe and Cumings (1961), Bogaert (1962).	

Table 4.—

Serial No.	Designation Synonyms Variants	Main clinical features	Specific Defect	Main abnormal	
				In urine	*In blood*
19	Homocystinuria.	Mental retardation. Epilepsy. Increasing spasticity. Tremor of the iris. Mottling and dryness of the skin. Hepatomegaly. Dislocation of the lenses. Anaemia. Genu valgum. Pes cavus.	Not known.	Excess of homocystine.	—
20	Hydroxyprolinaemia.	Microscopic haematuria. Mental retardation.	Deficiency of hydroxyproline oxidase.	Excess of hydroxyproline.	Excess of hydroxyproline.
21	Hyperammonaemia.	Episodic vomiting, lethargy and stupor. Mental retardation with decline of vision. Microcephaly. The condition resembles that following Eck's fistula but there is no gross liver damage.	Deficiency in ornithine-transcarbamylase.	Urine persistently neutral or alkaline. Aminoaciduria.	High level of ammonia.
22	Severe hypercalcaemia of infancy.	Characteristic facies. Hypotonia. Failure to thrive. Polyuria. Vomiting. Hypertension. Osteosclerosis. Calcification. Mental retardation.	Not known.	Occasional excess of calcium.	Hypercalcaemia, azotaemia, abnormal vitamin A tolerance. High cholesterol.
23	Hyperhistidinaemia (histidinaemia).	Speech defect. Mental retardation.	Deficiency of histidase.	Excess of histidine and imidazolepyruvic acid.	Excess of histidine.
24	Hyperlysinaemia I.	Mental deficiency. Convulsions. Asthenia. Anaemia.	Not known.	—	Excess of lysine.
25	Hyperlysinaemia II.	Mental deficiency.	Not known.	—	Excess of lysine and arginine.
26	Hyperprolinaemia I.	Renal disease, photogenic epilepsy.	Deficiency of proline oxidase.	Excess of proline, hydroxyproline and glycine.	Excess of proline.

continued

substances *In tissues*	*Mode of Transmission*	*Cross Refs.*	*Key references in literature*	*Remarks*
—	Reported in 2 sisters.	pp. 278, 339.	Carson and Neill (1962), Carson, Cusworth, Dent, Field, Neill and Westall (1963), *Brit. med. J.* (1963).	
—	Autosomal recessive.	p. 274.	Efron *et al.* (1965).	
C.S.F. shows high levels of ammonia and gluta-mine.	Not known. Disease described in two cousins.	p. 283.	Russell, Levin, Oberholzer and Sinclair (1962).	
	Not known.	p. 307.	Lindquist (1962). Jue, Noren and Anderson (1965).	
Excess of histidine in the cerebro-spinal fluid.	Possibly autosomal recessive.	p. 272.	Ghadimi, Partington and Hunter (1961), La Du *et al.* (1963), Davies and Robinson (1963), Holton, Lewis and Moore (1964).	Urine gives green colour with ferric chloride and the condition may therefore be confused with phenylketo-nuria.
—	Not known.	p. 283.	Woody (1964), Ghadimi *et al.* (1964).	
—	Not known.	p. 283.	Colombo *et al.* (1964).	
—	Possibly autosomal recessive.	p. 274.	Efron (1965b).	

Table 4.—

Serial No.	Designation Synonyms Variants	Main clinical features	Specific Defect	Main abnormal	
				In urine	In blood
27	Hyperprolin-aemia II.	Epilepsy. Mild mental retardation.	Deficiency of delta-pyrroline-5-carboxy-late dehydro-genase.	Excess of proline, hydroxy-proline and glycine.	Excess of proline.
28	Hyperuricaemia.	Mental retardation, spastic paralysis, choreoathetosis, biting of lips and fingers.	Not known.	Excess of uric acid.	Excess of uric acid.
29	Hypervalinaemia.	Vomiting, blindness, hyperkinesis.	Possibly deficiency of valine transamin-ase.	Excess of valine.	Excess of valine.
30	Leigh's encephalo-myelopathy (Sub-acute necrotizing encephalomyelo-pathy).	Failure to thrive, lack of movement, hypotonia leading to spasticity, absent reflexes, optic atrophy, nystagmus and, in some cases, con-vulsions.	—	—	High level of pyru-vates (thia-mine resis tant).
31	Leucine-induced hypoglycaemia.	Mental retardation. Epilepsy. 'Blank states.'	Not known.	—	Slight hypogly-caemia. Rapid fall of blood sugar after administra-tion of casein hy-drolysates, leucine and *iso*valeric acid.
32	Leucodystrophies. Diffuse sclerosis, Schilder's disease.	Clinical picture varies with age of onset. Usually, progressive mental deterioration, paralysis and epilepsy.	Not known.	—	—
33	Lowe's syndrome (Cerebrooculo-renal disease).	Mental retardation, glaucoma, cataracts, osteoporosis, rickets. Hypotonia.	Not known.	Amino acid-uria with occasional glycosuria and proteinuria.	Acidosis, azotaemia. Alkaline phosphatase may be raised.

continued

substances	Mode of Transmission	Cross Refs.	Key references in literature	Remarks
In tissues				
—	Possibly autosomal recessive.	p. 274.	Efron (1965b).	
—	Reported in two brothers.	p. 309.	Lesch and Nyhan (1964).	Very high turnover of the uric acid pool.
—			Efron (1965a). Waisman (1966).	
—	Autosomal recessive (possibly atypical dominant).	p. 314.	Richter (1957), Reye (1960).	In one case improvement followed administration of lipoic acid.
—	Familial cases are known to occur.	p. 295.	McKendrick (1962), Efron (1965a).	
—	Often autosomal recessive. Often sex-linked in the Pelizaeus-Merzbacher type.	pp. 250, 374–376.	Poser (1962), Bogaert (1962).	
—	Thought to be sex-linked.	p. 287.	Crome, Duckett and Franklin (1963), Richards *et al.* (1965).	

Table 4.—

Serial No.	Designation Synonyms Variants	Main clinical features	Specific Defect	Main abnormal	
				In urine	In blood
34	Maple syrup urine disease. Branched chain aminoaciduria. Leucinosis.	Failure to thrive. Vomiting. Opisthotonos. Severe mental retardation. Hypertonicity. Characteristic smell of 'maple syrup' in the urine. Convulsions. A late-manifesting variant has also been described.	Probably oxidative co-carb-oxylation of the branched chain amino acids.	Excess of leucine, isoleucine and valine. Ketoacid-uria.	Excess of leucine, *iso*leucine, valine and allo*iso*leu-cine. Occasional hypogly-caemia.
35	Marinesco-Sjögren syndrome.	Mental retardation. Some spasticity as well as signs of cerebellar dysfunction. Occasional epilepsy.	—	—	—
36	Metachromatic leucodystrophy.	Mental retardation, hypotonia, paralysis, epilepsy.	—	Sulphuric acid esters of cerebro-sides.	—
37	Nephrogenic diabetes insipidus.	Polydipsia, polyuria, dehydration. Occasional mental retardation.	Failure of the renal tubules to respond to pitressin.	Low specific gravity. Polyuria.	Hyper-electroly-taemic azotaemia.
38	Niemann-Pick disease.	Occasional early jaundice. Progressive mental deterioration with spleno- and hepatomegaly and wide-spread involvement of the reticulo-endothelial system. Sometimes retinal changes as in Tay-Sachs disease.	Not known.	—	—

continued

substances In tissues	Mode of Transmission	Cross Refs.	Key references in literature	Remarks
—	Autosomal recessive.	pp. 267, 339*et seq.*	Dancis and Levitz (1966), Scriver, (1962), Blattner (1965). Efron (1965a).	The smell in the urine is caused perhaps by the alpha-hydroxy acids of the branched chain amino acids.
—	Autosomal recessive.	p. 324.	Crome, Duckett and Franklin (1963).	Probably not a homogeneous category.
Sulphatides present in brain, peripheral nerves and kidney.	Not known.	pp. 253, 366.	Hagberg, Sourander and Svennerholm (1962), Bogaert (1962). Austin (1965).	
—	Uncertain. Mostly sex-linked.	p. 306.	Ruess and Rosenthal (1963). Woolf (1966)	
Increase of sphingo-myelin and lecithin in brain and some other tissues.	Autosomal recessive.	pp. 243, 375–376.	Bogaert (1962), Aronson and Volk (1962). Aronson and Volk (1965).	The nervous system shows lipidosis as in Tay-Sachs disease. Excess of neuraminic acid has also been found in this condition (Cumings, 1962)

Table 4.—

Serial No.	Designation Synonyms Variants	Main clinical features	Specific Defect	Main abnorma	
				In urine	In blood
39	Non-endemic goitrous familial cretinism.	Mental retardation. Goitre. Signs of hypothyroidism—low metabolic rate. Coarse hair and skin. Stunted growth. Above signs are inconstant.			
	Type 1	As above.	Failure to bind iodine to tyrosine.	Normal.	High cholesterol.
	Type 2	As above but with deafness.	,,		
	Type 3	As Type 1.	Inability to couple iodotyro-sine to form thyroxine.	Increase in mono and diiodoty-rosine.	Increase in mono and diiodotyro-sine. High cholesterol.
	Type 4	As Type 1.	Inability to deiod-inate mono and diiodo-tyrosine due to absence of dehalogen-ase.	,,	,,
	Type 5	As Type 1.	Unknown.		Increase of iodinated polypep-tides. High cholesterol.
40	Oast-house disease.	Mental retardation. Flaccidity, recurrent pyrexia. 'Dry celery' smell of urine.	Not known.	Excess of methionine, α-hydroxy-butyric acid, tyrosine, p-hydroxy-phenylpy-ruvic acid, phenyllactic acid.	—
41	Phenylketonuria.	Mental retardation present in most cases. Epilepsy. Dilution of pigment. Eczema. Frequent micro-cephaly.	Lack of hepatic phenyl-alanine hydroxy-lase.	Excess of phenyl-pyruvic, phenyl-lactic and phenyl-acetic acids.	Excess of phenyl-alanine. Low trypto phanmeta-bolites: e.g. 5-hydroxy-tryptamine. Low cate-cholamines.

continued

substances In tissues	Mode of Transmission	Cross Refs.	Key references in literature	Remarks
		p. 301.	The Thyroid Gland, *British Medical Bulletin* 1960, **16**.	
	Autosomal recessive.			
Thyroid contains mono and diiodo-tyrosines but no iodo-thyronines.	Possibly dominant.		Stanbury (1966).	Differentiation of groups greatly assisted by radio-active iodine studies.
	Autosomal recessive.		Watts (1962).	
	Not known.			
—	Not known.	p. 272.	Scriver (1962).	Related to maple syrup urine disease.
—	Autosomal recessive.	pp. 261, 348–355.	Knox (1966). Lyman (1963), Woolf (1963).	Some improvement on phenyl-alanine low diet.

Table 4.—

Serial No.	*Designation Synonyms Variants*	*Main clinical features*	*Specific Defect*	*Main abnorma*	
				In urine	*In blood*
42	Pseudohypo-parathyroidism.	Mental retardation. Round face. Stubby hands. Widespread calcification. Tetany. Epilepsy. Fragility of nails. Cataracts. Administration of parathyroid extract has no effect.	Not known.	Low calcium.	Hypocal-caemia. Hyper-phosphat-aemia.
43	Spongy sclerosis Canavan's type of diffuse sclerosis. Spongiform ence-phalopathy	Early onset of hypotonia, paralysis and mental retardation.	—	—	—
44	Tay-Sachs disease. (Amaurotic family idiocy) variants according to age and onset: Bielschowsky type, Spielmeyer-Vogt type, Batten's type, Kufs' type.	Progressive mental deterioration. Occasional epilepsy. Progressive paralysis. Macular and later, generalized retinal atrophy with pigmentation.	Not known.	—	—
45	Tyrosinosis.	Neurological disturbances. Evidence of hepatic cirrhosis and renal tubular damage.	Deficiency in p-hydro-xyphenyl-pyruvic acid oxidase.	Excess of tyrosine, p-hydroxy-phenyl-pyruvic acid.	Excess of tyrosine.

continued

ubstances In tissues	Mode of Transmission	Cross Refs.	Key references in literature	Remarks
—	Familial cases are known to occur.		Bartter (1966). Woolf (1966).	A condition showing similar clinical and pathological features but with a normal response to parathyroid hormone is known as pseudo-pseudo-parathyroidism. Cruz and Barnett, (1962).
—	Not known.	p. 139.	Wolman (1958), Bogaert (1962), Banker, Robertson and Victor (1964). Poser (1965).	An unspecific oedematous degeneration of the brain which may occur in different condi-tions of known and unknown aetiology. It occurs, for example, in maple syrup urine disease.
Neuronal increase of neuraminic acid con-taining ganglioside. This sub-stance is also found in cells of the reticulo-endothelial system.	Autosomal recessive.	p. 236.	Bogaert (1962), Aronson and Volk (1962). Volk (1964).	
—	Not known.	p. 270.	François *et al.* (1962), Menkes and Jervis (1961), Halvorsen and Gjessing (1964). Gentz, Jagenburg and Zetterström (1965), Woolf (1966).	Mental retard-ation not a constant or typical feature of the disease.

Table 4.—

Serial No.	Designation Synonyms Variants	Main clinical features	Specific Defect	Main abnormal	
				In urine	*In blood*
46	Undesignated steroid disorder.	Mental retardation. Lack of secondary sex characters. Deaf-mutism and some peripheral muscular wasting.	Not known.	Reduction of oestrogen, pregnandiol and total 17-neutral keto-steroids.	—
47	Undesignated.* ("Kinky hair disease.")	Mental and physical retardation. Lack of pigmentation in hair, pili torti, trichorrhexis nodosa. Epilepsy. Micrencephaly.	Not known.	General slight amino-aciduria.	Excess of glutamic acid.

* Further 9 cases (siblings) of what is regarded as the same condition—'kinky hair disease,' have been recently reported by Aquilar, M. J., Chadwick, D. L., Okuyama, K., and Kamoshita, S. (1966). *J. Neuropath. exp. Neurol.*, **25**, 507. The biochemical findings in these cases have been described by O'Brien, J. S., and Sampson, E. L. (1966). *J. Neuropath. exp. Neurol.*, **25**, 523. The chemical change may involve docosahexaenoic acid (22:6).

continued

substances				
In tissues	Mode of Transmission	Cross Refs.	Key references in literature	Remarks
—	Possibly autosomal recessive.		Richards and Rundle (1959).	
—	Consistent with sex-linked transmission.	p. 327.	Menkes, Alter, Steigleder, Weakley and Sung (1962).	The brains show degeneration of the cerebral grey matter with secondary changes in the white matter. Diffuse cerebellar atrophy.

REFERENCES

ARONSON, S. M., and VOLK, B. W. (1962). 'Cerebral Sphingolipidoses,' New York: Academic Press, p. 375.

ARONSON, S. M., and VOLK, B. W. (1965). In Carter, C. H. 'Medical Aspects of Mental Retardation,' Springfield: Thomas, p. 684.

AUSTIN, J. H. (1965). In Carter, C. H. 'Medical Aspects of Mental Retardation,' Springfield: Thomas, p. 768.

BAAR, H. S., and HICKMANS, E. M. (1956). Acta med. scand., 155, 49.

BANKER, B. Q., MILLER, J. Q., and CROCKER, A. C. (1962). In Aronson, S. M., and Volk, B. W., 'Cerebral Sphingolipidoses,' New York: Academic Press, p. 73.

BANKER, B. Q., ROBERTSON, J. T., and VICTOR, M. (1964). Neurology (Minneap.), 14, 981.

BARON, D. N., DENT, C. E., HARRIS, H., HART, E. W., and JEPSON, J. B. (1956). Lancet, 2, 421.

BARTTER, F. C. (1966). In Stanbury, J. B., Wyngaarden, J. B., and Fredrickson, D. S., 'The Metabolic Basis of Inherited Disease,' New York: McGraw-Hill, p. 1024.

BIGLER, J. A., MAIS, R. F., DOWBEN, R. M., and HSIA, D. Y-Y. (1959). Pediatrics, 23, 644.

BLACKWOOD, W., BUXTON, P. H., CUMINGS, J. N., ROBERTSON, D. J., and TUCKER, S. M. (1963). Arch. Dis. Childh., 38, 193.

BLATTNER, R. J. (1965). J. Pediat., 66, 139.

BOGAERT, L. VAN. (1962). 'Maladies Nerveuses Génétiques D'ordre Métabolique,' Liége: Université de Liége.

BRITISH MEDICAL BULLETIN (1960). 'The Thyroid Gland,' The British Council, 16.

BRITISH MEDICAL JOURNAL (1963). Annotation, 2, 1485.

CARSON, N. A. J., and NEILL, D. W. (1962). Arch. Dis. Childh., 37, 505.

CARSON, N. A. J., CUSWORTH, D. C., DENT, C. E., FIELD, C. M. B., NEILL, D. W., and WESTALL, R. G. (1963). Arch. Dis. Childh., 38, 425.

CARTER, C. H. (1965). 'Medical Aspects of Mental Retardation,' Springfield: Thomas.

CHILDS, B., NYHAN, W. L., BORDEN, M., BARD, L., and COOKE, R. E. (1961). Pediatrics, 27, 522.

CHILDS, B., and NYHAN, W. C. (1964). Pediatrics, 33, 403.

COLOMBO, J. P., RICHTERICH, R., SPAHR, A., DONATH, A., and ROSSI, F. (1964). Lancet, 1, 1014.

CROME, L., CUMINGS, J. N., and DUCKETT, S. (1963). J. Neurol. Neurosurg. Psychiat., 26, 422.

CROME, L., DUCKETT, S., and WHITE FRANKLIN, A. (1963). Arch. Dis. Childh., 38, 505.

CRUZ, C. E., and BARNETT, N. (1962). Amer. J. ment. Defic., 67, 381.

CUMINGS, J. N. (1962). In Aronson, S. M., and Volk, B. W., 'Cerebral Sphingolipidoses,' New York: Academic Press, p. 171.

DANCIS, J., and LEVITZ, M. (1966). In Stanbury, J. B., Wyngaarden, J. B., and Fredrickson, D. S., 'The Metabolic Basis of Inherited Disease,' New York: McGraw-Hill, p. 353.

DAVIES, H. E., and ROBINSON, H. J. (1963). Arch. Dis. Childh., 38, 80.

DENT, C. E. (1961). Bull. schweiz. Akad. med. Wiss., 17, 329.

EFRON, M. (1965a). New Engl. J. Med., 272, 1058 and 1107.

EFRON, M. (1965b). New Engl. J. Med., 272, 1243.

EFRON, M., BIXBY, E. M., and PRYLES, C. V. (1965). New Engl. J. Med., 272, 1299.

ERICKSON, R. J. (1965). J. Pediat., 66, 1004.

FORSYTH, C. C., LLOYD, J. K., and FOSBROOKE, A. S. (1965). Arch. Dis. Childh., 40, 47.

FRANÇOIS, R., QUINCY, CL., RIEDWED, M., LATER, R., BERTRAND AND MANTANUS. (1962). Pédiatrie, 17, 955.

FRIMPTER, G. W., HAYMOVITZ, A., and HORWITH, M. (1963). New Engl. J. Med., 268, 333.

FROESCH, E. R., WOLF, H. P., BAITSCH, H., PRADER, A., and LABHART, A. (1963). Amer. J. Med., 34, 151.

GENTZ, J., JAGENBURG, R., and ZETTERSTRÖM, R. (1965). J. Pediat., 66, 670.

GERRITSEN, T., and WAISMAN, H. A. (1965). Pediatrics, 36, 882.

GHADIMI, H., PARTINGTON, M. W., and HUNTER, A. (1961). New Engl. J. Med., 265, 221.

GHADIMI, H., BINNINGTON, V. I., and PECORA, P. (1964). J. Pediat., 65, 1120.

GROSFELD, J. C. M., MIGHORST, J. A., and MOOLHUYSEN, T. M. G. F. (1964). Lancet, 2, 789.

HAGBERG, B., SOURANDER, P., and SVENNERHOLM, L. (1962). Amer. J. Dis. Child., 104, 644.

HALVORSEN, S., and GJESSING, L. R. (1964). Brit. med. J., 1, 1171.

HARRIS, H. (1962). In Richter, D., Tanner, J. M., Lord Taylor, and Zangwill, O. L., 'Aspects of Psychiatric Research,' London: Oxford University Press, p. 194.

HERS, H. G. (1964). In Levine, R., and Luft, R. 'Advances in Metabolic Disorders,' Vol. I., New York: Academic Press, p. 1.

HOLTON, J. B., LEWIS, F. J. W., and MOORE, G. R. (1964). *J. clin. Path.*, **17**, 621.

HOLZEL, A. (1961). *Brit. med. Bull.*, **17**, 213.

HOOFT, C., LAEY, P. DE, TIMMERMANS, J., and SNOECK, J. (1962). *Acta paediat. belg.*, **16**, 281.

HSIA, D. Y. -Y. (1965). In Carter, C. H. 'Medical Aspects of Mental Retardation,' Springfield: Thomas, p. 596.

JUE, K. L., NOREN, G. R., and ANDERSON, R. C. (1965). *J. Pediat.*, **67**, 1130.

KNOX, W. E. (1966). In Stanbury, J. B., Wyngaarden, J. B., and Fredrickson, D. S., 'The Metabolic Basis of Inherited Disease,' New York: McGraw-Hill, p. 258.

LA DU, B. N., HOWELL, R. R., JACOBY, G. A., SEEGMILLER, J. E., SOBER, E. K., ZANNONI, V. G., CANBY, J. P., and ZIEGLER, L. K. (1963). *Pediatrics*, **32**, 216.

LAEY, P. DE, HOOFT, C., TIMMERMANS, J., and SNOECK, J. (1964). *Ann. paediat.*, **202**, 145, 253 and 321.

LESCH, M., and NYHAN, W. L. (1964). *Amer. J. Med.*, **36**, 561.

LEVIN, B., MACKAY, H. M. M., and OBERHOLZER, V. G. (1961). *Arch. Dis. Childh.*, **36**, 622.

LEVIN, B., OBERHOLZER, V. G., SNODGRASS, G. J. A., STIMMLER, L., and WILMERS, M. J. (1963). *Arch. Dis. Childh.*, **38**, 220.

LINDQUIST, B. (1962). *Acta paediat.* (*Uppsala*), **51**, Suppl. 135, p. 144.

LYMAN, F. L. (1963). 'Phenylketonuria,' Springfield: Thomas.

MAROTEAUX, P., and LAMY, M. (1965). *J. Pediat.*, **67**, 312.

MCKENDRICK, T. (1962). *Develop. Med. Child Neurol.*, **4**, 328.

MCKUSICK, V. A., KAPLAN, D., WISE, D., HANLEY, W. B., SUDDARTH, S. B., SEVICK, M. E., and MAUMANEE, A. E. (1965). *Medicine*, **44**, 445.

MCMURRAY, W. C., MOHYUDDIN, F., ROSSITER, R. J., RATHBUN, J. C., VALENTINE, G. H., KOEGLER, S. J., and ZARFAS, D. E. (1962). *Lancet*, **1**, 138.

MCMURRAY, W. C., RATHBUN, J. C., MOHYUDDIN, F., and KOEGLER, S. J. (1963). *Pediatrics*, **32**, 347.

MEISTER, A. (1965). 'Biochemistry of the Amino Acids,' 2nd Ed., Vol. II., New York: Academic Press, p. 1021.

MENKES, J. H. (1966). *J. Pediat.*, **69**, 413.

MENKES, J. H., and JERVIS, G. A. (1961). *Pediatrics*, **28**, 399.

MENKES, J. H., ALTER, M., STEIGLEDER, G. K., WEAKLEY, D. R., and SUNG, J. H. (1962). *Pediatrics*, **29**, 764.

POSER, C. M. (1962). In Aronson, S. M., and Volk, B. W. 'Cerebral Sphingolipidoses,' New York: Academic Press, p. 141.

POSER, C. M. (1965). In Carter, C. H., 'Medical Aspects of Mental Retardation,' Springfield: Thomas, p. 856.

REYE, R. D. K. (1960). *J. Path. Bact.*, **79**, 165.

RICHARDS, B. W., and RUNDLE, A. T. (1959). *J. ment. Defic. Res.*, **3**, 33.

RICHARDS, W., DONNELL, G. N., WILSON, W. A., STOWENS, D., and PERRY, T. (1965). *Amer. J. Dis. Child.*, **109**, 185.

RICHTER, R. B. (1957). *J. Neuropath. exp. Neurol.*, **16**, 281.

RUESS, A. L., and ROSENTHAL, I. M. (1963). *Amer. J. Dis. Child.*, **105**, 358.

RUSSELL, A., LEVIN, B., OBERHOLZER, V. G., and SINCLAIR, L. (1962). *Lancet*, **2**, 699.

SCHMID, R. (1966). In Stanbury, J. B., Wyngaarden, J. B., and Fredrickson, D. S., 'The Metabolic Basis of Inherited Disease,' New York: McGraw-Hill, p. 871.

SCRIVER, C. R. (1962). In 'Progress in Medical Genetics,' Vol. II, ed. Steinberg, A. G., and Bearn, A. G., New York and London: Grune and Stratton, p. 121.

SCRIVER, C. R. (1965). *New Engl. J. Med.*, **273**, 530.

SIDBURY, J. B., HARLAN, W. R., and WITTELS, B. (1962). *Amer. J. Dis. Child.*, **104**, 531.

STANBURY, J. B. (1966). In Stanbury, J. B., Wyngaarden, J. B., and Fredrickson, D. S. 'The Metabolic Basis of Inherited Disease,' New York: McGraw-Hill, p. 215.

VOLK, B. W. (1964). 'Tay-Sachs Disease,' New York: Grune and Stratton.

WAISMAN, H. A. (1966). *Paediat. Clin. N. Amer.*, **13**, 469.

WALSHE, J. M., and CUMINGS, J. N. (1961). 'Wilson's Disease: Some current concepts,' Oxford: Blackwell.

WATTS, R. W. (1962). *Develop. Med. Child Neurol.*, **4**, 405.

WOLFF, O. (1965). *Develop. Med. Child Neurol.*, **7**, 430.

WOLMAN, M. (1958). *Brain*, **81**, 243.

WOODY, N. C. (1964). *Amer. J. Dis. Child.*, **108**, 543.

WOOLF, L. I. (1962). *Advanc. clin. Chem.*, **5**, 1.

WOOLF, L. I. (1963). *Advanc. clin. Chem.*, **6**, 97.

WOOLF, L. I. (1966). 'Renal Tubular Dysfunction,' Springfield: Thomas.

WORSLEY, H. E., BROOKFIELD, R. W., ELWOOD, J. S., NOBLE, R. L., and TAYLOR, W. H. (1965). *Arch. Dis. Childh.* **40**, 492.

CHAPTER 10

THE LIPIDOSES AND THE LEUCODYSTROPHIES

THE lipidoses and leucodystrophies are characterized by progressive degeneration of neural tissue and accumulation of adventitious material containing an excess or abnormal proportions of lipids and other substances. In the lipidoses degeneration and storage primarily involve neurones; in leucodystrophies—white matter. The rather unsatisfactory classification of these conditions is based on clinical manifestations, morphological changes and the chemistry of the stored material. As the brain normally contains 50–70 per cent of lipids in the dried white matter and 30–45 per cent in the grey, it is not surprising that lipids should loom large in classifications of these disorders, particularly as recognition and measurement of the other constituents of the adventitious material, such as proteins, are still very unsatisfactory.

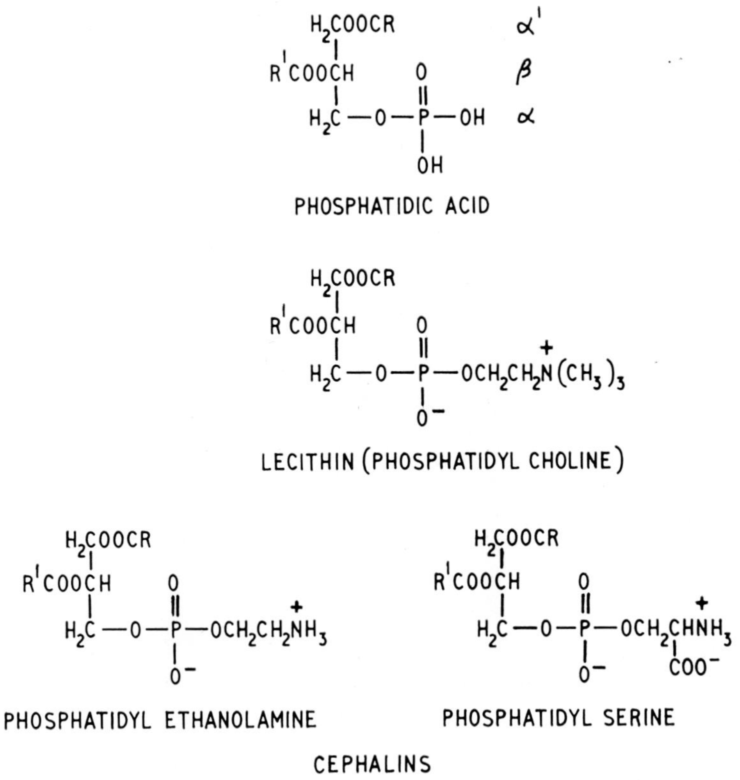

FIG. 82. The glycerophosphatides, R and R^1 are hydrocarbon chains.

The chief lipids of myelin are the phospholipids, especially the sphingomyelins, cholesterol and cerebrosides; the nerve cell and its axon contain less phospholipid and more ganglioside. The structure and metabolic aspects of these substances, insofar as they are relevant to the study of the lipidoses and leucodystrophies, are briefly considered below.

Structure of the Major Lipids

Glycerophosphatides

These compounds are derivatives of phosphatidic acid. Phosphatidic acid itself is derived from the trihydric alcohol glycerol by esterification with 2 molecules of fatty acid and one of phosphoric acid.

In the glycerophosphatides the phosphoric acid part of phosphatidic acid is combined either with choline or with ethanolamine or with L-serine. The resultant compounds are shown on p. 219 (Fig. 82).

In *plasmalogens* the fatty acid in the α' position is replaced by an α,β unsaturated ether (an ether with a double bond between the carbon atoms adjoining the oxygen of the ether). Plasmalogens owe their name to the aldehydogenic nature of the α,β unsaturated ether group (Fig. 83).

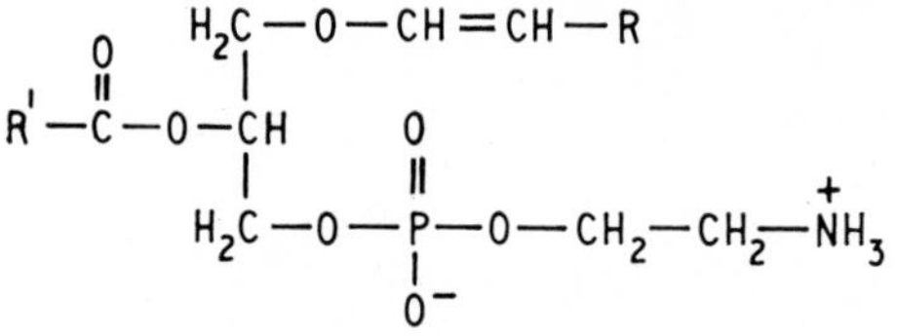

FIG. 83. Phosphatidyl ethanolamine.

Cephalin B is probably a saturated plasmalogen, i.e. a glycerol ether without the carbon-carbon double bond.

In the *phosphoinositides* the phosphate radical of phosphatidic acid is linked to the hexahydric cyclic alcohol inositol (hexahydroxy cyclohexane). Additional phosphate groups may be present in the 4 and 5 position of the alcohol giving rise to di- and triphosphoinositides (Fig. 84).

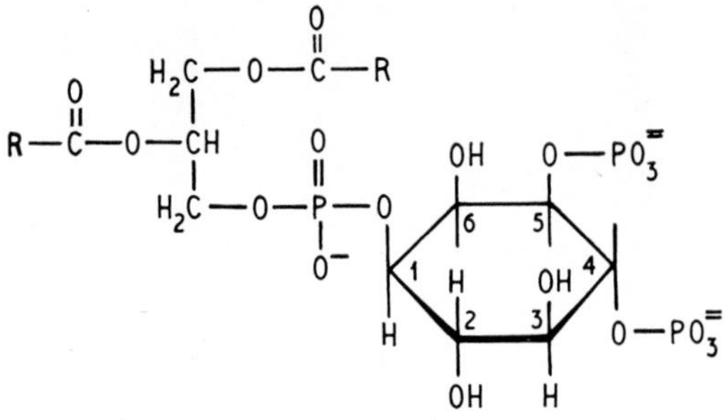

FIG. 84. Triphosphoinositide.

Sphingolipids

The sphingolipids are of particular interest to neurochemists. This group comprises the sphingomyelins, cerebrosides, sulphatides and gangliosides. All, as the name implies, contain sphingosine, an unsaturated amino alcohol or dihydrosphingosine (Fig. 85).

$$CH_3—(CH_2)_{12}—CH=CH—CH—CH—CH_2$$
$$\qquad\qquad\qquad OH \quad NH_2 \quad OH$$

SPHINGOSINE

$$CH_3—(CH_2)_{12}—CH_2—CH_2—CH—CH—CH_2$$
$$\qquad\qquad\qquad\quad OH \quad NH_2 \quad OH$$

DIHYDROSPHINGOSINE

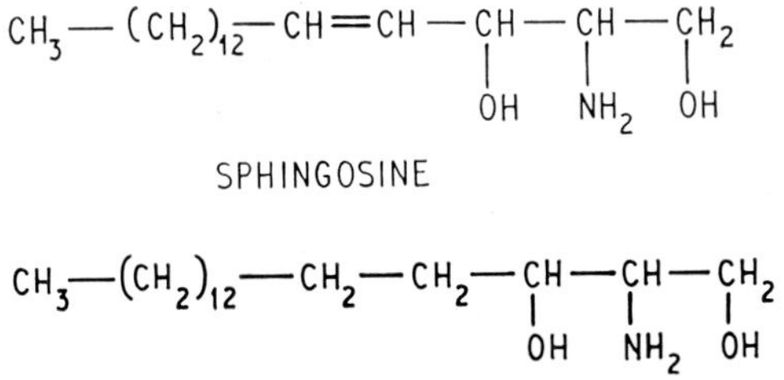

FIG. 85. Sphingosine and dihydrosphingosine.

Sphingosine in which one of the hydrogens of the amino group is replaced by a fatty acid residue is called a *ceramide*. In the sphingomyelins ceramide is combined with phosphorylcholine (Fig. 86). *Sphingomyelin* is therefore a

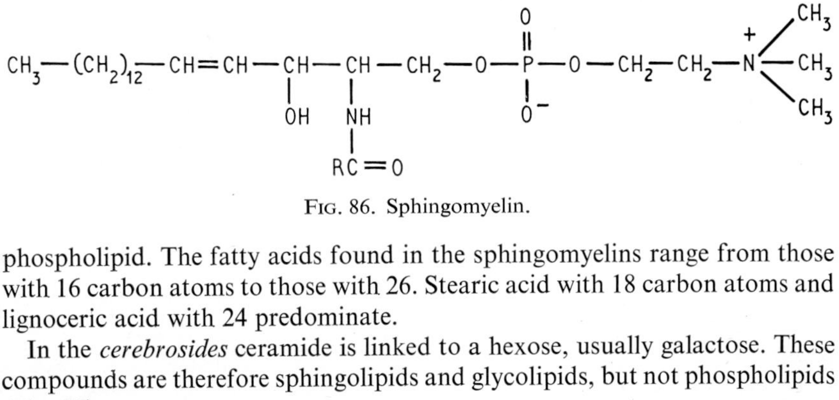

FIG. 86. Sphingomyelin.

phospholipid. The fatty acids found in the sphingomyelins range from those with 16 carbon atoms to those with 26. Stearic acid with 18 carbon atoms and lignoceric acid with 24 predominate.

In the *cerebrosides* ceramide is linked to a hexose, usually galactose. These compounds are therefore sphingolipids and glycolipids, but not phospholipids (Fig. 87).

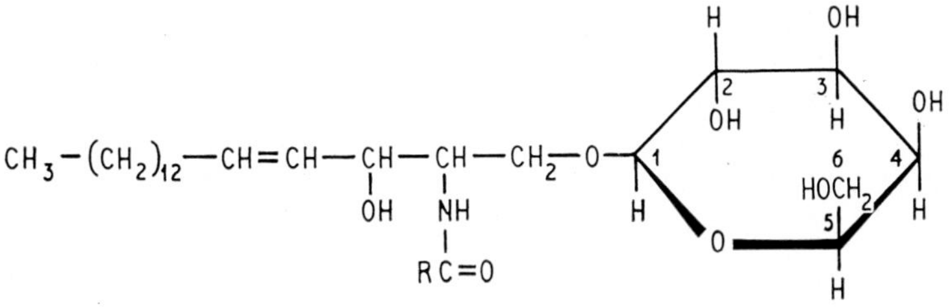

FIG. 87. Cerebroside.

Again the C_{18} and C_{24} fatty acids predominate. Not only does the saturated C_{24} acid, lignoceric acid, occur, but also its hydroxy derivative cerebronic acid, its unsaturated derivative, nervonic acid, and hydroxy oxynervonic acid. Occasionally glucose may replace galactose as the hexose.

If the galactose moiety of a cerebroside is esterified with a sulphate group a *sulphatide* results (Fig. 88). The sulphate group is probably bound to carbon 3 of the hexose.

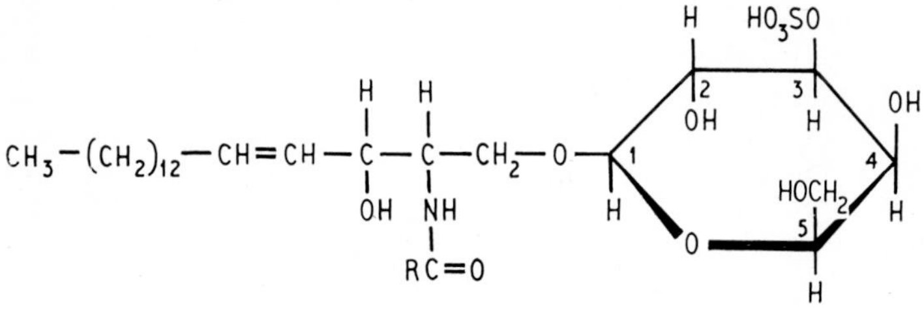

FIG. 88. Sulphatide.

The most complex sphingolipids are the *gangliosides* (Fig. 89). For each molecule of ceramide (acyl sphingosine) they may contain up to 4 molecules

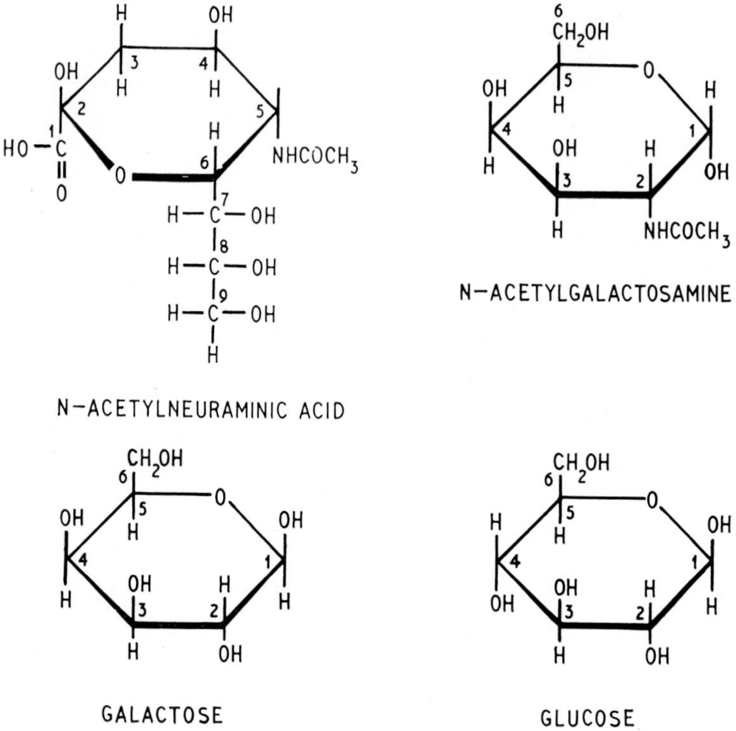

N—ACETYLNEURAMINIC ACID

N—ACETYLGALACTOSAMINE

GALACTOSE

GLUCOSE

FIG. 89. Constituents of ganglioside.

of hexose and 3 of N-acetylneuraminic acid (sialic acid). N-acetylneuraminic acid is a 3-deoxy-5-amino sugar acid and may be envisaged as arising from the condensation of N-acetyl-mannosamine and pyruvic acid. The hexoses include galactose, glucose and N-acetylgalactosamine.

According to current views (Svennerholm, 1964a) the structure of the major *monosialoganglioside*, G_{M1}, is

acyl-sphingosine-glucose-galactose-N-acetylgalactosamine
    (ceramide) | |
                    N-acetylneuraminic acid   galactose
                       (sialic acid)

The sialic acid is linked to carbon-3 of the galactose. Disialogangliosides carry an additional sialic acid group on the terminal galactose, G_{D1a} on carbon 3 and G_{D1b} on carbon 6. The trisialoganglioside G_{T1} carries sialic acid groups in the 3 and 6 position of the terminal galactose, and in the 3 position of the galactose linked to glucose.

Human brain also contains small amounts of two further monosialogangliosides G_{M2} and G_{M3}. G_{M2} has the structure

ceramide-glucose-galactose-N-acetylgalactosamine
                                |
                            sialic acid

and G_{M3} the structure

ceramide-glucose-galactose
                         |
                   sialic acid

In this nomenclature the suffixes 1, 2 and 3 refer to molecules with 4, 3 and 2 molecules of hexose respectively, while the letters M, D and T refer to mono-, di- and trisialogangliosides.

In American publications a different nomenclature is most usual:

$G_{T1} = G_1$, $G_2 = G_{D1b}$, $G_3 = G_{D1a}$, $G_4 = G_{M1}$, $G_5 = G_{M2}$ and $G_6 = G_{M3}$.

German authors have used yet other signs:

$G_{T1} = G_{iv}$, $G_{D1b} = G_{iii}$, $G_{D1a} = G_{ii}$ and $G_{M1} = G_i$.

The lipids of the brain include *cholesterol*, which consists of a phenanthrene and cyclopentane ring and an 8-carbon side chain in position 17 (Fig. 90).

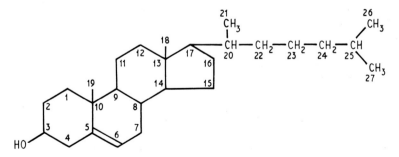

FIG. 90. Structure of cholesterol.

Cholesterol may be esterified in position 3 with fatty acids. Esterified cholesterol is virtually absent from normal adult white matter but is found in demyelinating tissue.

Metabolism of the neurolipids

Progress in understanding the metabolism and function of the neurolipids has been rapid in recent years. Thorough discussions of lipid metabolism will be found in the monographs by McIlwain (1963; 1966), Ansell and Hawthorne (1964), and in the proceedings of a recent symposium (Dawson and Rhodes, 1964).

Analytical problems

Isolation and estimation of the glycolipids is essential for the characterization of the lipidoses and leucodystrophies. The technical difficulties are formidable. Methods of fractionation may include solvent extraction, partition dialysis, thin layer and column chromatography and electrophoresis. The fractions obtained in this way are seldom pure and reproducible. For instance, in partition dialysis gangliosides may be found both in the aqueous and chloroform phases (Korey et al., 1963). Furthermore, as gangliosides contain both lipophilic and hydrophilic groups, they tend to form micelles in aqueous solution and to trap other lipids, peptides and aminoacids (Saifer, 1964).

Glycolipids are usually estimated by the colorimetric reactions of the hexose, hexosamine or sialic acid parts of their molecule. These reactions are not always fully specific. Additional errors will be introduced if contaminants are present containing the constituent estimated. The intensity of the colour is also sometimes affected by the state of combination of the substance. For example, only free sialic acid is determined by the sensitive and specific thiobarbituric acid method for gangliosides but the extent of its release from various gangliosides is not uniform (Svennerholm, 1964a).

Errors may also occur in the chemical separation of lipids. In the fractionation of phospholipids by selective hydrolysis the alkali-resistant fraction was thought for some time to consist exclusively of sphingomyelin. In fact, unless fairly elaborate precautions are taken, this fraction may contain as much as 30–70 per cent of other substances (Bogaert, Seitelberger and Edgar, 1963; Ansell and Hawthorne, 1964). The wide scatter of values reported by various workers for the brain lipids in health and disease is thus in part attributable to differences in techniques and to experimental error.

The Lipidoses

The best defined lipidoses are gargoylism (Hurler's disease), Tay-Sachs disease or infantile amaurotic family idiocy, Batten's disease, Gaucher's disease and Niemann-Pick disease. These and their variants are described below. In addition, cases occur which do not quite fit into any of the above categories, especially if these are defined too narrowly (vide infra). Lipids are not the only substances stored in the lipidoses; abnormal amounts of mucopolysaccharides accumulate, for example, in gargoylism, and this condition is therefore sometimes referred to as mucopolysaccharidosis. Some workers regard Hand-Schüller-Christian disease as a lipidosis, but this seems to be an apparently unrelated granulomatous condition. All lipidoses are rare. The commonest among the severely subnormal is gargoylism; it was present in 6 of 500 brains examined at the Fountain Hospital. The other lipidoses are often dealt with as neurological and paediatric cases and may not be considered in the context of mental retardation. They must, nevertheless, be always included in the differential diagnosis of progressive encephalopathies in children and are hence of practical importance.

The common link in all the lipidoses is neuronal storage of abnormal material (Fig. 91). Sooner or later many neurones perish and their loss is

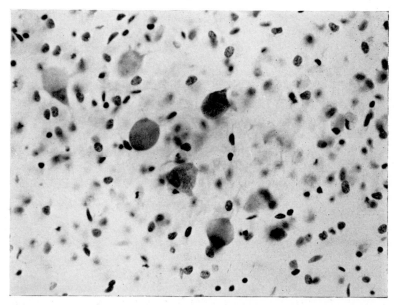

FIG. 91. The cortex in a case of lipidosis (Tay-Sachs disease). There is a great loss of nerve cells and the few remaining ones show distension of the cytoplasm and displacement of the nucleus. (Cresyl violet × 412.)

accompanied by atrophy and sclerosis of the tissue. The intensity and extent of the involvement, like its regional distribution, vary widely. As a general rule, but with many exceptions, the earlier the onset the more widespread the neuronal involvement and the more rapid the course of the disease. Some visceral involvement, particularly of the reticuloendothelial system, is also common. It may be minimal, affecting perhaps only a few cells in the lymph glands and spleen, or, at the other end of the scale, massive, dominating the picture of the disease. In some conditions or cases the nervous system may remain entirely unaffected.

Another common feature of the lipidoses is frequency of familial incidence with Mendelian recessive transmission; a sex-linked form of gargoylism has, however, also been described (p. 227). This suggests that the cause is an inherited enzymopathy in, at least, many of the cases. However, with the possible exception of infantile Gaucher's disease (p. 247), the precise site of the chemical lesion remains obscure. Friede and Allen (1964) have demonstrated, in agreement with earlier work, that oxidative enzymes and acetylcholinesterase in Tay-Sachs disease were displaced in the affected cells by the accumulated adventitious material, but this displacement is probably mechanical. The adventitious material itself shows little or no enzymic activity. Acid phosphatase, by contrast, may be scattered more diffusely in the affected cells, and its activity can be relatively high (Wallace, Volk and Lazarus, 1964). It is localized in various cell organelles, such as small and large vesicles, dense bodies, Golgi cisternae and some membranous cytoplasmic bodies (M.C.B.'s) (*vide infra*). Wallace, Volk and Lazarus have suggested that the M.C.B.'s displaying such activity represent a stage in the degeneration of lysosomes. However, increased acid phosphatase activity is not specific to any particular form of lipidosis, and increased activity has also been demonstrated in various demyelinating diseases.

Histochemistry is not the only experimental approach to the challenging problem of the lipidoses. In a number of centres material is being examined by chemical analysis and electron microscopy, while the older clinical and laboratory techniques continue to be used to good advantage. As a result new and apparently distinct features often emerge in the studied cases. The present stage can perhaps be best described as one of recognizing differences and not similarities. It is a stage of analysis rather than synthesis. Minor differences are sometimes regarded as an indication of a new disease, particularly as few specialists have the opportunity of examining by the same methods more than a small number of cases. Furthermore it is often overlooked that in any disease the result of the basic pathological process may be greatly influenced by the severity and duration of the attack, the patient's age and his individual reactivity.

Much has been and is being written about the lipidoses and the pathological details have been described in many texts. For a useful account of some of the prevailing views readers are referred to the proceedings of a recent symposium (Aronson and Volk, 1962).

Gargoylism and the Mucopolysaccharidoses

The commonest of the lipidoses is, in our experience, lipochondrodystrophy (gargoylism or Hurler's disease). Its manifestations are variable but the following are the usual signs: short stature, short neck, a large dolicocephalic head with coarse hair, thick lips, thick low-set ears, hirsutism, lumbar kyphosis, flexion contractures and limitations of articular movement, claw-like hands, hepatosplenomegaly, cardiac defects, inguinal and umbilical herniae, persistent nasal discharge, corneal clouding and some deafness (Fig. 92). In the past decade gargoylism has been identified as one of the inborn errors of mucopolysaccharide metabolism. At the same time, with the accumulation of clinical, genetic and biochemical data, the heterogeneity of the disease has become apparent. It is believed to be inherited in two ways. It may be transmitted as an autosomal recessive defect. Corneal opacity is common in such patients but deafness is relatively rare. Alternatively, trans-

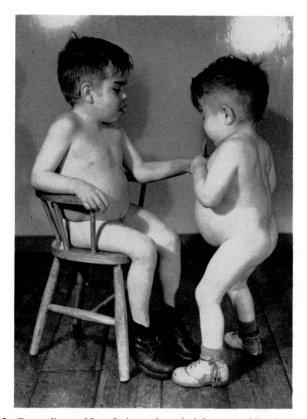

FIG. 92. Gargoylism.   Note facies, enlarged abdomen and lumber kyphosis.

mission may be sex-linked and then corneal clouding does not occur, but many patients are deaf. At least three more mucopolysaccharidoses can be differentiated biochemically, and one of these is also associated with mental retardation (cf. p. 230).

The acid mucopolysaccharides

These mucopolysaccharides are macromolecules with repeating units of hexosamine and hexuronic acid. They are important constituents of connective tissue, particularly in the cornea, blood vessels and cartilage, where they form part of the amorphous ground substance. Many of the clinical features of gargoylism are due to defects in connective tissue metabolism. The sources and constituents of the principal acid mucopolysaccharides are shown in Table 5.

Table 5. THE SOURCES AND CONSTITUENTS OF THE PRINCIPAL ACID MUCOPOLYSACCHARIDES

	Name	Hexosamine	Hexuronic acid	Tissue	Action of Hyaluronidase
Non-sulphated	Chondroitin	Galactosamine	Glucuronic acid	Cornea, embryonic cartilage	++
	Hyaluronic acid	Glucosamine	Glucuronic acid	Synovial fluid, umbilical cord, skin, heart valve, vitreous humour	++
	Keratosulphate	Glucosamine, Galactose	—	Cartilage, cornea, bone, nucleus pulposus, spinal discs	—
	Heparitin sulphate	Glucosamine	Glucuronic acid	Aorta	—
Sulphated	Chondroitin sulphate A	Galactosamine	Glucuronic acid	Cartilage, bone, cornea, embryonic cartilage	+
	Chondroitin sulphate B (β heparin, dermatan sulphate)	Galactosamine	Iduronic acid	Skin, ligaments, heart, aorta	—
	Chondroitin sulphate C	Galactosamine	Glucuronic acid	Tendons, ligaments, heart, aorta	+
	Heparin	Glucosamine	Glucuronic acid	Liver, lung, arterial wall, mast cells	—

It will be noted that keratosulphate, although classed as a mucopolysaccharide, does not contain hexuronic acid. The structure of some of the constituents of the mucopolysaccharides is shown in Fig. 93.

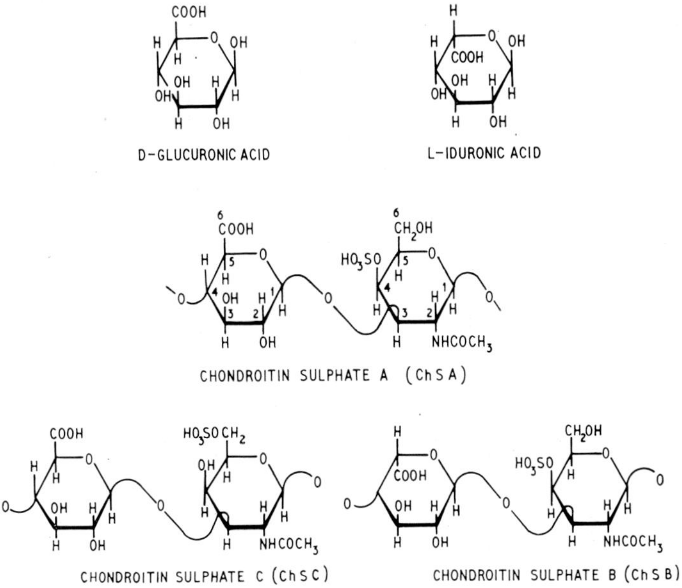

FIG. 93. Repeating units of some mucopolysaccharides.

The structure of chondroitin sulphate A (ChSA) and chondroitin sulphate C (ChSC) differs in the position of the sulphate group which is found in position 4 and 6 of the hexosamine molecule. In chondroitin sulphate B (ChSB) L-iduronic acid replaces D-glucuronic acid.

The biosynthesis of the mucopolysaccharides requires uridine diphosphate and may proceed either by the stepwise addition of monosaccharides or by the interaction of two uridine nucleotides. 3'-phosphoadenosine-5'-phosphosulphate takes part in the sulphation. For a full account of the structure and metabolism of the mucopolysaccharides the reader is referred to the review by Brimacombe and Stacey (1964) and to a recent symposium in the Biophysical Journal (1964).

Chemical Pathology. The currently recognized mucopolysaccharidoses are shown in Table 6 compiled from the reviews by McKusick (1965) and Maroteaux and Lamy (1965). It is the *excessive* excretion of ChSB and heparitin sulphate (HS) which is abnormal in gargoylism: in normal urine ChSA and ChSC predominate, but small amounts of ChSB and HS are also present; in gargoyle urine ChSB and HS predominate but ChSA and ChSC can also be detected (Berggard and Bearn, 1965). The relative proportions of ChSB and HS in gargoylism vary greatly and are of no help in differentiating the sex-linked and autosomal forms.

Table 6. MUCOPOLYSACCHARIDOSES

Name	*Genetics*	*Clinical*	*Mental retardation*	*Excess urinary MPS*
Hurler's syndrome (gargoylism)	Autosomal recessive	Usually severe manifestations, including early clouding of cornea, cardiovascular deficits	$+++$	ChSB and HS
Hunter's syndrome (gargoylism)	Sex-linked recessive	Somewhat milder course, no clouding of cornea, cardio-vascular deficits	$+++$	ChSB and HS
Sanfillipo syndrome (polydystrophic oligophrenia)	Autosomal recessive	Mild growth disorder and so-matic signs, no cardiovascular deficits	$+++$	HS
Scheie syndrome (polydystrophic dwarfism)	Autosomal recessive	Clouding of cornea, stiff joints, characteristic facies, aortic valve disease	$+-$	ChSB
Morquio syndrome	Autosomal recessive	Severe bone changes, clouding of cornea, aortic regurgitation	—	KS

Key to abbreviations : MPS, mucopolysaccharides ; ChSA, Chondroitin sulphate A ; ChSB Chondroitin sulphate B ; HS, heparitin sulphate ; KS, keratosulphate.

The properties of living connective tissue depend in part on the interaction of the mucopolysaccharides with collagen and other proteins. If the bonds between protein and the mucopolysaccharides are weakened due, for example, to faulty protein structure or local hydrolysis, then the mucopolysaccharide may diffuse out of the tissue. Dorfman (1964) suggests that the primary defect in gargoylism lies in such abnormal mucopolysaccharide protein interaction, and that the overproduction of mucopolysaccharide occurs in an abortive attempt to form normal protein-mucopolysaccharide complexes.*

Lipid metabolism in gargoylism

The biochemical abnormalities in gargoylism are not confined to mucopoly-saccharides. Deposits of glycolipids have been demonstrated in the mitral valve (Lagunoff *et al.*, 1962) and, particularly, in the brain (Cumings, 1964). Chemical and histochemical studies show that this glycolipid contains ganglioside (Ledeen *et al.*, 1965) (cf. p. 223). In gargoylism the brain may thus be affected indirectly—via changes in the connective tissue of the meninges and blood vessels—and directly—as a result of the derangement of the metab-olism of nerve cells. It is not clear whether the lipid and mucopolysaccharide abnormalities are causally related, and how the preponderance of one or the other affects intelligence. In some mucopolysaccharidoses, such as poly-dystrophic dwarfism and Morquio's disease (cf. Table 6), the C.N.S. is hardly involved and lipidosis has not been described. On the other hand, in disorders such as 'Pseudo-Hurler disease', also called 'Tay-Sachs disease with visceral involvement' (Norman *et al.*, 1964; O'Brien *et al.*, 1965), the neural lipidosis can be as severe as in Tay-Sachs disease. Wolfe *et al.* (1964) des-cribed two patients with gargoylism, one with normal intelligence, who showed

* According to Rennert, O. W., and Dekaban, A. S. (1966), *Metabolism*, **15**, 419, amino acid metabolism, particularly of serine, is also abnormal.

mucopolysaccharide accumulation only, while the other was mentally retarded with deposits of mucopolysaccharides and lipids in the viscera and
the C.N.S. The authors suggested that the carbohydrate and lipid abnormalities are distinct but frequently occur together, and that the defect in
mucopolysaccharide metabolism is responsible for the classical signs of
gargoylism, and the lipidosis for the mental retardation. According to these
authors the presence of lipid deposits in the ganglion cells of a rectal biopsy
specimen in a case of gargoylism indicates likelihood of intellectual impairment.

The assumption of two independent metabolic disorders in gargoylism is
perhaps unnecessary. It is well appreciated nowadays that not only the
severity of an inherited metabolic disease varies from patient to patient, but
also the extent to which individual organs are affected. Thus, for example, in
the infantile form of Gaucher's disease (cf. p. 245) the brain may or may not
be affected. It may be assumed that the metabolic defect in gargoylism
results in the accumulation of one or more of the acid mucopolysaccharides
but provided that the internal scavenging mechanism of the cell, the lysosomes, deal fully with the excessive material, no substance need be deposited.
If, on the other hand, the lysosomes are overwhelmed, then the excessive
mucopolysaccharides could be retained in the cell. Should this process lead
further to the breakdown of the lysosomes or other intracellular structures,
highly polar glycolipids of comparatively high molecular weight and low
diffusibility, derived from the membranes of the organelles, would accumulate
within the cell. These are demonstrable by appropriate analytical techniques,
particularly if they aggregate to form regular structures (cf. p. 248). This view
is supported by the electron microscopical study of the liver by Hoof and
Hers (1964) and by that of Aleu, Terry and Zellweger (1965) on brain biopsies (p. 239). Non-specific accumulation of lipids is not confined to gargoylism
(p. 225). A minor increase in gangliosides accompanies the deposition of
sphingomyelin in the C.N.S. in cases of Niemann-Pick disease, and a form of
metachromatic leucodystrophy has been described (Austin, 1965) in which
neuronal lipidosis is a minor but constant feature. Similar deposition may
occur in some of the leucodystrophies and the accumulation of lipofuscin in
ageing nerve cells is also a related phenomenon.

Austin *et al.* (1964) have recently reported an increase of lysosomal aryl
sulphatase in gargoylism. The level of the other lysosomal enzymes was not
raised. The significance of this, as indeed of the role of the lysosomes in general, in this disorder, is not yet clear (cf. metachromatic leucodystrophy,
p. 253).

A condition resembling gargoylism occurs in cattle, the affected calves
being known as 'snorter dwarf cattle'. Their urine shows an abnormal pattern
of mucopolysaccharide excretion and some of the lesions resemble human
ones (Lorincz, 1961).

Morbid Anatomy. As already stated, many of the neurones are enlarged
and contain abnormal substances. These are sudanophil, P.A.S. positive and
metachromatic, usually staining red with cresyl violet and thionine in slightly

acid solution. The course of the disease is slower than in most other storage diseases and relatively large numbers of neurones survive to the end of even the most protracted cases.

The brain as a whole is not as small as in some other lipidoses; the meninges, on the other hand, are often thickened, sometimes very considerably. Another characteristic is frequent perivascular reticulation of the white matter (Fig. 94), which can assume gross forms, as in the case reported by Norman, Urich and France (1959).

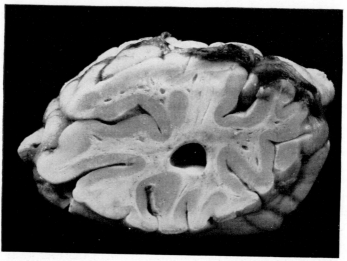

FIG. 94. An occipital lobe in a case of gargoylism. Many small pits are present in the white matter. These are caused by rarefaction of the tissue around blood vessels.

The ultrastructure of the adventitious material has been studied by electron microscopy (Aleu, Terry and Zellweger, 1965). The neurones contain rather pleomorphic transversely striated 'zebra bodies'. These are believed to be similar to the membranous cytoplasmic bodies, M.C.B.'s of Tay-Sachs disease (p. 240) and to contain ganglioside. In addition, neuronal cytoplasm contains granular zones and vacuoles. Large vacuoles are present in the cytoplasm of perithelial cells. Some of the astrocytes show lamellar inclusions resembling the neuronal ones.

Chondroitin sulphate B and heparitin sulphate accumulate in the connective tissue of most organs, especially in the liver and spleen, where they appear as metachromatic deposits if precautions are taken not to dissolve them out during fixation and histological processing. One of the recommended fixatives for this purpose is lead acetate.

The ultrastructure of the liver cells in gargoylism has been studied by Hoof and Hers (1964). Both hepatic and Kupffer cells contain many cytoplasmic vacuoles filled with fine granular material and scarcer pleomorphic inclusions. The authors suggest that the vacuoles are lysosomes containing material which had not been broken down normally.

Mucopolysaccharides are not detectable in all connective and reticulo-endothelial cells of organs, even if they are grossly enlarged. Such appearance of histological quasi-normality in manifestly abnormal tissues is characteristic in gargoylism. On the other hand, storage of the adventitious material seems to provoke fibrous tissue reaction, particularly in certain sites such as the fasciae, endocardium, blood vessels and meninges. Such involvement, if it affects the heart, may impede the coronary circulation, cause fibroelastosis and, ultimately, cardiac failure. Cardiovascular findings in 58 autopsy reports have been collected by Krovetz, Lorincz and Schiebler (1965). Valvular involvement, particularly of the mitral valve, was found in 40 cases, arterial lesions in 28 and endocardial fibroelastosis in 11. Congestive heart failure was the most frequent cause of death noted in 75 autopsy reports collected by the same authors.

The corneal opacities present in many cases of gargoylism are caused by the formation of one or more layers of typical 'clear' cells in the Bowman's membrane (Fig. 95). In stained paraffin sections the cells are vacuolated and

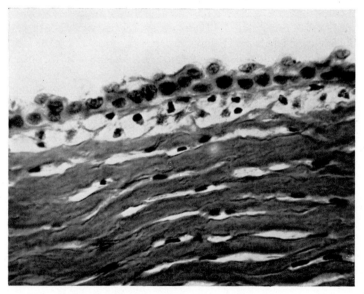

Fig. 95. Adventitious 'clear' cells in the Bowman's capsule of the cornea in a case of gargoylism (Haematoxylin and van Gieson × 550.)

have small dark nuclei with barely visible colourless granules in the cytoplasm. The osseous changes in gargoylism and the related mucopolysaccharidoses do not appear to have been studied fully by histological and chemical methods.

Descriptions of the pathological changes in gargoylism have been recorded by many authors (Henderson et al., 1952; Naidoo, 1953; Bishton, Norman and Tingey, 1956; Máttyus and Jobst, 1958). Further references to pathological changes in gargoylism will also be found in the already mentioned review by Lorincz (1965).

Gargoylism may present incompletely as *formes frustes* (Jervis, 1950). The relationship of gargoylism to Morquio-Ullrich or Morquio-Brailsford disease has been discussed by Robins, Stevens and Linker (1963), Kratter (1964), and Schenk and Haggerty (1964).

Laboratory Diagnosis. The diagnosis of gargoylism and other mucopolysaccharidoses is usually obvious from the clinical and radiological examination (Maroteaux and Lamy, 1965; Lorincz, 1965) but several biochemical and haematological tests are useful (p. 362). Histological examination of the rectal mucosa or of the ganglia of the appendix will confirm the diagnosis. The problem of brain and visceral biopsy in suspected cases of lipidosis is discussed in the Appendix (pp. 374–376).

Biochemical screening tests aim at detecting the excess of mucopolysaccharide excretion by the turbidity produced in the urine by an acidified solution of albumin or a solution of cetyl trimethyl ammonium bromide or similar detergent, or, alternatively, by the filter paper metachromasia test with toluidine blue. The procedure for two of the tests found useful in our laboratories, is given in the Appendix (pp. 362 *et seq.*) These are suitable for preliminary screening but are unfortunately neither quantitative nor fully specific (Muir, 1964). The precipitation of mucopolysaccharides may not be complete in a dilute solution and is affected by the presence of salt and other small molecules. Excretion of 'normal' mucopolysaccharides may also be increased as part of a non-specific mesenchymal reaction (Hauss *et al.*, 1962). To overcome these difficulties some workers use chromatography on columns of 'Dowex' or 'Sephadex' (Maroteaux and Lamy, 1965), and others dialysis, followed by precipitation with acridine and colorimetry, or electrophoresis (Muir, Mittwoch and Bitter, 1963). None of these methods is as yet suitable for the clinical laboratory, except perhaps the recently described electrophoretic method of Manley and Hawksworth (1966). (*vide* p. 363.)

Basophilic granules in the cytoplasm of the polymorphonuclear leucocytes, so-called Reilly-Alder bodies, were the first haematological abnormality described in gargoylism. Unfortunately, these inclusions have seldom been found by other workers. Mucopolysaccharide inclusions and vacuoles in the cytoplasm of the lymphocytes are a much more constant finding. These vacuoles contain characteristic inclusions which stain metachromatically with toluidine blue (Mittwoch, 1959). Such inclusions have not been hitherto observed in the other lipidoses. They are soluble in aqueous and, particularly, in saline solution, so that purely vacuolated cells result by removing the inclusions. Examination of the stained blood films is therefore a useful diagnostic procedure. The methods are simple but certain precautions are necessary. We reproduce in the Appendix (p. 365) the methods used by Mittwoch (1963) together with some of her pertinent observations.

The correlation between the clinical diagnosis of gargoylism and the presence of metachromatic inclusions seems remarkably good. For example, all nineteen cases of gargoylism examined by Mittwoch (1963) were 'haematologically positive'. Furthermore, in a series of eleven patients considered by Muir, Mittwoch and Bitter (1963) every one of the seven patients excreting abnormal amounts of hyaluronidase-resistant sulphated mucopolysaccharides in the urine had also metachromatic inclusions in a proportion of their lymphocytes. Unfortunately, it is not yet possible to be as firm about the quantitative criteria of vacuolation in the other forms of lipidosis since the reported findings vary rather extensively and are, to some extent, contradictory. Thus Rayner (1962) found pathological vacuolation in all his 37 cases of juvenile amaurotic idiocy, an average of about 21 per cent of the lymphocytes being affected. In other forms of lipidosis only about half of his 35 patients were affected, and the average number of vacuolated lymphocytes was 1·2 per cent. Unlike Mittwoch, he found no vacuolation in any of the five cases of gargoylism included in his control series. The occurrence of vacuolation in the infantile and adult forms of lipidosis and in Niemann-Pick disease has also been reported but not confirmed by all observers. Similarly, the significance of a smaller degree of involvement of the lymphocytes, considered by some workers to be an indication of the carrier or heterozygous state of lipidosis, is still debatable. It should be emphasized that vacuoles may be regarded as pathological only if they are sharply defined, as if punched into the cytoplasm. Ill-defined vacuoles seem to be of little significance.

Similar abnormalities have been observed in the peripheral blood cells in the other mucopolysaccharidoses. Histiocytes with numerous, variably-sized metachromatic inclusions and plasma cells with ringlike bodies surrounded by vacuoles (Buhot cells) have been reported in bone marrow preparations in gargoylism and polydystrophic oligophrenia (Pearson and Lorincz, 1964; Maroteaux and Lamy, 1965).

A practical difficulty is the rarity of all lipidoses, so that few haematologists have first-hand knowledge of the appearances in many positive cases. It may be advisable therefore to refer suspected or doubtful cases to one of the few specialists working in this field.

Tay-Sachs Disease and the Amaurotic Family Idiocies

The first of the lipidoses to be described was Tay-Sachs disease (Tay, 1881). It is often said to be the most common, at least in the United States; it is alleged to have an incidence in New York of about 1:10,000 births. In our experience, working with mentally retarded patients, gargoylism is more prevalent, but this may be due in part to the longer survival of patients with this disease. Besides, as explained above, many workers do not include gargoylism among the lipidoses.

The terms Tay-Sachs disease and amaurotic family idiocy are often but not always used interchangeably. The relationship of Tay-Sachs disease to other variants of these conditions, some of which are also referred to as amaurotic family idiocy, or, simply, as amaurotic idiocy, is rather confusing. According to the age of onset it is possible to distinguish several forms: 1. congenital, 2. infantile or Tay-Sachs disease proper, 3. late infantile (Bielschowsky), 4. juvenile (Spielmeyer-Vogt), and 5. adult (Kufs). The late infantile and the juvenile types are aften jointly referred to as Batten's or Batten-Mayou disease, particularly in the English and American literature.

Most writers, however, have abandoned the elaborate classifications of the past, retaining only a distinction between Tay-Sachs disease and juvenile amaurotic disease (Batten's disease). The histological and clinical differences in many of the published cases of the above variants have been very slight and can possibly be accounted for by lack of standardization of methods and other factors, such as individual and age variability, or differences in the severity and duration of the disease process. The neurochemical differences (p. 224) are also often inconclusive. Moreover, many of the cases described correctly from the etymological viewpoint as instances of amaurotic idiocy, because they are severely mentally subnormal and blind, are not really cases of lipidosis. Some of the other recorded cases alleged to have suffered from lipidosis appear to have had only a normal or, at most, an insignificantly raised amount of neuronal lipid storage. It must not be forgotten that neuronal lipid accumulation is a normal phenomenon. The amount of lipid increases with age and in many pathological conditions, most of which are unrelated to the lipidoses in the usual meaning of this term.

Tay-Sachs Disease (TSD), Amaurotic Family Idiocy, Batten's Disease

The classical clinical picture of Tay-Sachs disease is one of lassitude, progressive apathy, mental deterioration and loss of vision, hyperacusis (exaggerated motor response to sound), convulsions, progressive motor weakness, spasticity and paralysis. Retinoscopy will often reveal bilateral macular degeneration—'cherry red spots', which are (wrongly) said to be pathognomonic. Death usually occurs before the age of 24 months. In older children the course is usually slower and the retina may show atrophy with pigmentation.

The alleged racial incidence of the disease has been considered on p. 51.

Morbid Anatomy. In most of the lipidoses the brain is usually small and sclerotic with obvious ulegyria. The cerebellum may also be heavily sclerosed (Fig. 96). A megalencephalic phase has, however, also been described in some cases of Tay-Sachs disease (Volk, 1964). Such cerebral enlargement may be caused in part by spongy oedematous degeneration of neural tissue, and also by swelling of the surviving neurones. The cut surface of the brain shows degenerative changes in both grey and white matter, such as cortical wasting, discoloration, softness or, contrariwise, gliosis, and demyelination of the white matter.

Microscopically the tinctorial properties of the stored lipid material are somewhat variable. The substance is usually granular and sudanophil, staining a dullish red, brown or orange with Sudan III or IV. In many of the younger infants, however, the granules are not sudanophil or only faintly so. The adventitious substance cannot be easily dissolved out of the cells with any of the usual fat solvents. It differs therefore from the bright red, soluble particles of cholesterol esters and neutral fat which are frequently seen both intra- and extracellularly in most conditions, including the lipidoses, associated with destruction of neural tissue. The adventitious substance is always P.A.S. positive. This is a non-specific reaction given by nearly all phospholipids,

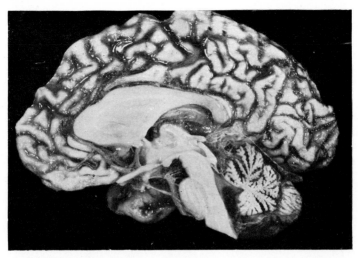

Fig. 96. The brain of a 4-year old child with Tay-Sachs disease weighed 400g. It shows generalized atrophy and well-marked cerebellar sclerosis. (Crome, 1964 in Holt and Milner "Neurometabolic Disorders in Childhood", Edinburgh; E & S. Livingstone.)

glycolipids and unsaturated fatty acids except when masked by proteins or other macromolecules. More specific staining methods suggest the presence of gangliosides and/or ceramide hexosides or cerebrosides (Adams, 1965). The granules of the stored material present on electron microscopy as concentrically laminated cytoplasmic bodies. These have been called 'membraneous cytoplasmic bodies' (M.C.B's) (Fig. 98) by Terry, Korey and Weiss (1962) (p. 239). The affected cells are distended and the nuclei displaced peripherally, often into the apical dendrites. The latter may also be enlarged in a pear-like manner. This is, perhaps, particularly noticeable in the Purkinje cells of the cerebellum. The abnormal cells show chromatolysis, progressive degeneration and gradually perish. The axis cylinders may also display localized swellings—'torpedo bodies', and this, again, is particularly common in the cerebellum.

Neuronal loss is usually accompanied by marked glial overgrowth. Many lipid phagocytes in the cortex and elsewhere contain the same abnormal material as the nerve cells, others show the already mentioned bright-red sudanophil staining of intracellular debris. Astrocytes also proliferate, and in the later stages of the disease there is usually dense fibrous gliosis and shrinkage of the tissue. Indeed, some of the smallest brains encountered among the severely subnormal have been instances of lipidosis (Fig. 96).

The neuronal changes are usually but by no means always diffuse and evident at all levels of the central and peripheral nervous system. They may be more pronounced in certain formations such as the brainstem, particularly in some of the older patients. Following neuronal loss there is secondary demyelination of the white matter and especially of the long descending tracts.

Demyelination of the white matter in the lipidoses has been recently discussed by Fardeau and Lapresle (1963). As mentioned, the cerebellum is often atrophic. Bielschowsky (1920–1921) drew attention to the fact that the cerebellar degeneration in these cases is 'centripetal' in type, with sclerosis and atrophy of the granular layer and of the moss and climbing fibres. The Purkinje cells, although also affected, are better preserved, and basket-cells disappear before them. The appearance contrasts with the more usual 'centrifugal' type of degeneration in other conditions, when Purkinje cells tend to vanish first. In four cases of amaurotic idiocy described by Friede (1964) the cerebellar molecular layer when stained by some methods appeared divided horizontally into rather sharply demarcated outer and inner layers. The outer layer was almost devoid of cells, showed poor vascularization, and lacked oxidative enzyme activity. Friede interpreted this as evidence of arrested cerebellar development.

Among the less constant changes are involvement by lipid storage of cells of the posterior pituitary, and the occurrence of Alzheimer neurofibrillary changes in some neurones.

The reticuloendothelial system may also show storage of adventitious material in cases of Tay-Sachs disease and in the other amaurotic family idiocies, but not to the same extent and not so regularly as in the other lipidoses. For example, a case of Tay-Sachs disease with foam cell formation in the lungs has been recently reported by Norman *et al.* (1964), but, as the authors themselves point out, 'foam cells' in the lung must be interpreted cautiously, since they are quite common and are usually due to inhalation and/ or lipid pneumonia.

Nerve and glial cells in the retina also contain the adventitious material, and there can be much retinal pigmentation in the older infants. The fovea may be unusually wide, a gap being present in the inner nuclear layer while the outer nuclear layer can also be deficient in this area. There are few detailed histological reports on the retinal changes in the lipidoses. Readers are referred for further information and references to the contributions by Greenfield (1951 and 1955). He suggested that in some of these cases degeneration commences in the foveal region and spreads outwards, although isolated areas of retinal change may also be found peripherally.

Several further reports on the retinal changes in amaurotic idiocy have been summarized by Mossakowski (1964), who has also described his histochemical findings in what he regarded as a case of Tay-Sachs disease and in another of Batten's disease. He considered that the adventitious substance in the retinal neurones was virtually identical in both cases. The substance appeared to be also identical with that stored in the cerebral neurones in the case of the older child, while there were distinct histochemical differences between the retinal and cerebral deposits in the younger patient. It is often stated (*vide supra*) that the cherry-red spot is characteristic for the infantile or Tay-Sachs type of the disease while pigmentary degeneration resembling retinitis pigmentosa becomes visible later in older and more protracted cases. However, the basic change in all cases appears to be neuronal lipid storage accompanied by non-specific degeneration of other retinal elements. The whitish halo around the cherry-red spot has been said to be caused by deposition of lipids in the densely arranged nerve cells around the fovea (Wolter and Allen, 1964).

All the retinae examined at the Fountain Hospital have shown very advanced general atrophy, affecting all nuclear layers (Fig. 97). On ophthalmoscopy the cherry-red spot (cf. p. 236), often described as characteristic of Tay-Sachs disease, may be absent, and in many cases retinal atrophy seems as diffuse as it is histologically, the choroid showing through clearly over a wide area. Optic atrophy is a frequent finding. The retinal red spot has been observed in all forms of lipidosis other than gargoylism (Tittarelli, Giagheddu and Spadetta, 1963), so that, contrary to a commonly held view, it is not pathognomonic of Tay-Sachs disease.

Electron microscopy is assuming increasing importance in the study of the lipidoses. As already mentioned, the distinctive feature of Tay-Sachs disease is the M.C.B.'s—membranous cytoplasmic bodies (Fig. 98). These are round or oval, measuring $1-1\cdot5\mu$ in their larger diameter. Other vesicular and tubular inclusions have also been described in the affected neurones (Picó, 1964a). Fewer or none of the typical M.C.B.'s appear to be present in the older cases of lipidosis (Zeman and Donahue, 1963; Picó, 1964b). Most of the ultrastructural inclusions in such older patients are somewhat different, and Gonatas et al. (1963), for example, have referred to them as "membranovesicular cytoplasmic bodies—M.V.B.'s". Conversely, atypical organelles and inclusions other than M.C.B.'s have been found in Tay-Sachs disease (Dyken and Zeman, 1964). The more important cytoplasmic bodies reported

Table 7. ABNORMAL CYTOPLASMIC ORGANELLES IN THE LIPIDOSES

Lipidosis	Predominant cytoplasmic bodies	Reference
Tay-Sachs disease	Membranous cytoplasmic bodies, M.C.B.'s	Terry and Weiss, 1963
Juvenile lipidosis	Membranovesicular bodies, M.V.B.'s; Lysosome-like bodies, L.Y.L.B.'s	Gonatas et al., 1963
Late infantile amaurotic idiocy	Pleomorphic lipid bodies, P.L.B.'s, M.C.B.'s	Volk, Wallace, Schneck and Saifer, 1964
Gargoylism	Zebra bodies	Aleu, Terry and Zellweger, 1965
Niemann-Pick disease	M.C.B.'s and vacuoles, M.C.B.'s lysosomes	Gonatas and Gonatas, 1965 Wallace et al., 1966

in the lipidoses are listed in Table 7. The ultrastructural features of these cytoplasmic bodies are strongly influenced by their lipid composition. The precise relationship of these organelles to the main pathological process in the lipidoses remains to be elucidated (*vide infra*).

FIG. 97. The retina in a case of Batten's disease showing marked cellular loss and focal pigmentation in all layers. (Haematoxylin and van Gieson × 160.)

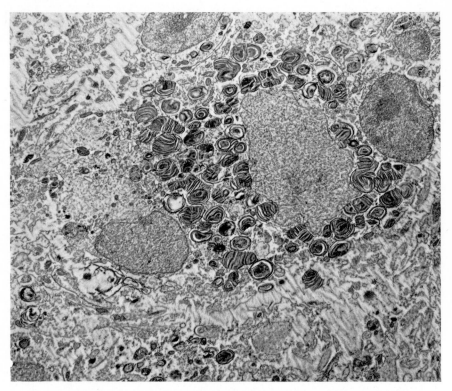

FIG. 98. Membranous cytoplasmic bodies (MCB's) in a case of Tay-Sachs disease.
By courtesy of Dr. S. M. Aronson.

Chemical Pathology. Only a few years ago the biochemical abnormality in the amaurotic family idiocies could be simply and apparently adequately described as an accumulation of ganglioside in the C.N.S. As analytical techniques for the isolation and characterization of the glycolipids improved it became apparent that in the infantile form of the disease there was not only accumulation of ganglioside in the grey and white matter, but that the pattern of the gangliosides was also abnormal (Müldner *et al.*, 1962; Wherrett and Cumings, 1963). In the normal brain G_{M1} and G_{D1a} predominate (see p. 223); in the Tay-Sachs brain it is G_{M2}, while there is a relative decrease in the other gangliosides. G_{M2} has therefore been labelled the 'Tay-Sachs ganglioside' (Svennerholm, 1964a). In other forms of amaurotic family idiocy the increase in ganglioside, which had been at times all too hastily inferred from the histological appearance of the brain, could not always be confirmed by quantitative chemical analysis; the intensity of the staining reactions sometimes depends on the physicochemical state rather than concentration of the lipid (cf. Hagberg *et al.*, 1965). Moreover, other pitfalls in the way of correct histological diagnosis of some of the lipidoses must not be overlooked (p. 226). While in some cases the ganglioside pattern was normal, in other juvenile and adult cases the concentration of the brain lipids was reduced but there was a relative and sometimes small positive increase in gangliosides. Their pattern resembled that of Tay-Sachs disease, although the increase in G_{M2} was less marked than in that condition (Jatzkewitz, Pilz and Sandhoff, 1965). In the condition designated "late infantile systemic lipidosis" by Gonatas and Gonatas (1965), which is probably very similar to or identical with the familial neurovisceral lipidosis of Landing *et al.* (1964) and the 'Sonderform' of late infantile amaurotic family idiocy of Jatzkewitz, Pilz and Sandhoff (1965), there was an absolute and relative increase in ganglioside G_{M1} with a relative decrease in the other gangliosides. In gargoylism, Gonatas and Gonatas (1965) found an increase in the monosialogangliosides and a decrease in the di- and trisialogangliosides. With ganglioside accumulation there is usually also an increase of the corresponding ceramide hexosides, that is asialogangliosides. While a *large* absolute and relative increase in ganglioside G_{M2} is thus associated with Tay-Sachs disease, smaller increases are not diagnostic. For example, Jatzkewitz, Pilz and Sandhoff (1965) found an increase in G_{M2} in a case of Niemann-Pick disease.

An intensive multidisciplinary study of the biochemistry of Tay-Sachs disease has been carried out in the laboratories of the late S. R. Korey (Korey *et al.*, 1963a,b; Samuels *et al.*, 1963; Terry and Weiss, 1963; Terry and Korey, 1963) and those of B. W. Volk (Volk, 1964). Respiration of brain tissue obtained by biopsy was normal in the early stages of the disease, but fell by about half in advanced cases. This depression of respiration may well contribute to the seemingly distinct changes characteristic of the later stages of the disease. Two findings in the infantile form of the disease which have not yet been satisfactorily explained are the low concentration of free amino acids in the brain (however, in a case of juvenile amaurotic family idiocy Samuels *et al.*, 1963, found an increase in free amino acids), and the low concentration in the serum of the glycolytic enzyme fructose-1-phosphate aldolase, which catalyzes the cleavage of fructose-1-phosphate to glyceraldehyde and dihydroxyacetone phosphate.

The site of the enzymatic defect (or defects) in the amaurotic family idiocies has not yet been identified. As there is no evidence of lipid over-production or of structural abnormalities in the brain gangliosides, the fault may lie in some deficiency in one of the catabolic enzymes of ganglioside metabolism, or in abnormal binding of the brain gangliosides to protein which prevents their degradation. Purified brain gangliosides have a mole-cular weight of between 1000 and 2000. In aqueous solution they aggregate into negatively charged polyelectrolytes with a molecular weight of approxi-mately 250,000. These can interact with such substances as proteins and cati-onic dyes (Saifer, 1964). It has therefore been suggested by Korey and his collaborators (Samuels *et al.*, 1963) that the M.C.B.'s in Tay-Sachs disease are formed from excessive ganglioside by physicochemical aggregation with other lipids, proteins and possibly amino acids. Another possibility is that the M.C.B.'s are lysosome-like structures (Lazarus, Wallace and Volk, 1962). Analysis of isolated M.C.B.'s showed that they contain approximately 50 per cent ganglioside, 20 per cent cholesterol, some phospholipid, protein and proteolipid. Samuels *et al.* (1965) have been able to prepare M.C.B.'s *in vitro* from these constituents.

In a case of juvenile amaurotic idiocy Gonatas *et al.* (1963) demonstrated by electron microscopy a number of structures derived from lysosomes, lyso-some-like bodies (L.Y.L.B.'s), lipofuscin and an unusual cytoplasmic organelle, the membranovesicular body (M.V.B.). The M.V.B.'s are similar to but not identical with the M.C.B.'s of the infantile form. The accumulation of lyso-somes and derived structures is probably non-specific and may represent little more than acceleration or accentuation of normal ageing processes.

Abnormal organelles can perhaps be formed in several ways: by physico-chemical aggregation of excess lipids, as in the case of the M.C.B.'s, or as breakdown products of previously formed organelles, such as the lysosomes, as in the case of the M.V.B.'s. It is quite likely that these two mechanisms overlap to some extent. The membranous bodies in Tay-Sachs disease, late infantile amaurotic idiocy, the acid mucopolysaccharidoses and Niemann-Pick disease (*vide infra*) show acid phosphatase and thiolacetate esterase activity (Wallace *et al.*, 1966). Both these enzymes are probably of lysosomal origin. It is, however, impossible to decide with current experimental techniques if the membranous structures are lysosomes which have incorporated accumu-lating lipids, or myelin-like aggregates which have acquired lysosomal characteristics by association with pre-existing cell constituents or organelles.

Thus it is fair to conclude that it is not yet possible to define clearly and dogmatically the difference between Tay-Sachs disease and the other amauro-tic family idiocies. Nevertheless expert chemical analysis is often of consider-able help in classifying cases.

Laboratory Diagnosis. The diagnosis of Tay-Sachs and Batten's disease rests on the clinical features and ophthalmoscopy. The cherry-red spots are often present in Tay-Sachs disease and retinal atrophy with pigmentation in Batten's disease. The cherry-red spots become detectable at about $2\frac{1}{2}$ months (Schneck, 1964) and the characteristic startle reaction to sound (hyperacusis) is also said to be of help in the diagnosis.

The composition of the body fluids shows a number of abnormalities in Tay-Sachs disease. Individually non-specific, they add up to a suggestive pattern. Transaminase and lactic dehydrogenase activity is raised in the C.S.F., as is the level of the aliphatic amino acids in the advanced stages of the disease. The serum total proteins, albumin and γ-globulin levels are depressed. There is a minor elevation of the serum neuraminic acid and an increase in the ratio of globulin neuraminic acid to total neuraminic acid. A transient elevation of serum transaminase, lactic dehydrogenase and fructose-1,6-diphosphate aldolase activity is observed in the early stages of the disease. Serum fructose-1-phosphate aldolase, however, is considerably reduced. Reduced levels are also found in the carriers (heterozygotes), who may therefore be recognized by an assay of this enzyme. A detailed description of serum and C.S.F. changes in Tay-Sachs disease will be found in a review by Saifer (1964).

Biopsy of the cerebral cortex, rectum or appendix will often confirm the diagnosis (p. 374). Peripheral neurones show the characteristic histological and histochemical features of lipidosis but these are not specific to Tay-Sachs disease.

Niemann-Pick Disease

Like Tay-Sachs disease, Niemann-Pick disease often commences in early infancy and presents with failure to thrive, lack of mental development, blindness and epilepsy. Unlike Tay-Sachs disease, the clinical picture is dominated by gross enlargement of the liver, spleen and, sometimes, lymph glands. Macular changes are present in some of the cases. The disease has been subdivided into cerebral infantile, cerebral juvenile and non-cerebral variants. In the non-cerebral forms the disease is of later onset, and runs a milder course.

Morbid Anatomy. The characteristic feature of this disease is accumulation of foam cells (Fig. 99) in many of the affected organs. These cells measure $20-90\mu$ in diameter, are usually round and have a vacuolated honeycombed appearance. With Sudan dyes numerous bright red particles are present in the cytoplasm. Thus the cells stain non-specifically for unsaturated fatty acids and phospholipids (Aronson and Volk, 1965), but using other staining methods it is possible to demonstrate sphingomyelin (Adams, 1965). Although Niemann-Pick cells are always found in cases of this disease, they are not pathognomonic. Similar cells can be found in many other metabolic or infectious diseases, such as the other lipogranulomatoses, Letterer-Siwe disease or histiocytosis.

The neuropathological changes resemble closely those of Tay-Sachs disease, and the two conditions were at one time considered to be identical, showing merely a different range of changes. The clinical and pathological

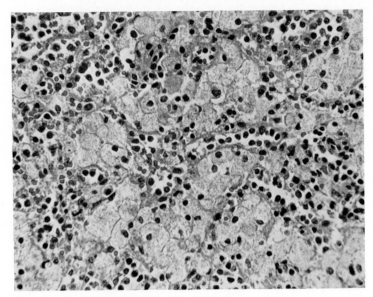

FIG. 99. The spleen in Niemann-Pick disease showing numerous characteristic foam
cells. (Haematoxylin and eosin × 220).

changes in Niemann-Pick disease have been fully described by Crocker and
Farber (1958), Fredrickson (1966) and Aronson and Volk (1965).

Chemical Pathology. Abnormalities reported in the brains of patients with
Niemann-Pick disease include an increase in sphingomyelin, gangliosides,
ganglioside derivatives and cholesterol in the grey matter (Cumings, 1964).
However, the increase in ganglioside is much smaller than in Tay-Sachs
disease. Cerebral sphingomyelin is not increased in all patients and the increase,
if present, is of a much lower order than that in the spleen and liver (Ivemark
et al., 1963). In the brain, sphingomyelin with 24 carbon fatty acids (C_{24}–
sphingomyelin) predominates in the white matter, and sphingomyelin with
18 carbon fatty acids (C_{18}–sphingomyelin) in the grey matter. In a case of
Niemann-Pick disease, in which sphingomyelin was stored in the brain,
Jatzkewitz and Pilz (1964) found that it was C_{18}–sphingomyelin which was
increased. A decrease in the ratio C_{24}–to C_{18}–sphingomyelin without an
absolute increase in sphingomyelin is a non-specific finding in many cases of
dysmyelination, and is not confined to Niemann-Pick disease (Stenhagen and
Svennerholm 1965).

It thus appears that patients with Niemann-Pick disease are unable to
break down sphingomyelin. Little is known about the breakdown of sphingomyelin in mammalian organisms, and the enzyme at fault in Niemann-Pick
disease has not yet been identified, although it has often been assumed that
sphingomyelinase (phospholipase C), which is stated to split sphingomyelin
into ceramide and phosphorylcholine, is involved. It has been suggested that
in addition to a simple deficiency of this enzyme, structural abnormalities in

the lipid, abnormal lipid-protein binding or overproduction of sphingomyelin may also occur in Niemann-Pick disease. There is no conclusive evidence in favour of any of these mechanisms. The extent to which sphingomyelin accumulates in any tissue probably depends primarily on its turnover in the affected organ. Red cell stroma contains significant amounts of sphingomyelin, and it is not surprising therefore that the reticuloendothelial system, where erythrocytes are normally broken down, is also a place of sphingomyelin storage. In the brain sphingomyelin is not confined to the white matter but occurs also in the grey matter, where its turnover is in fact more rapid than in the white matter. This has been offered by Jatzkewitz and Pilz (1964) as an explanation of the preferential accumulation of C_{18}-sphingomyelin in their case. The disturbance of ganglioside metabolism in Niemann-Pick disease may well be nonspecific; it is now recognized that abnormalities in the brain gangliosides occur in many inherited and acquired degenerative diseases of the nervous system (Svennerholm, 1966; cf. p. 248).

Laboratory Diagnosis. In a few cases Niemann-Pick cells may be found in the peripheral blood while the bone marrow usually contains many of these cells. Vacuoles may be seen in the circulating lymphocytes and monocytes (cf. p. 235). There is no increase in the sphingomyelin content of the blood. Techniques for the detection of carriers are not yet available.

The serum acid phosphatase level is raised in a proportion of cases, but this estimation is much less useful than in Gaucher's disease (cf. p. 247). As in the other lipidoses, biopsy of the brain, rectum or appendix will confirm the diagnosis (Appendix 19). Biopsy of a lymph gland, if it is enlarged, is, of course, a simpler procedure.

Gaucher's Disease

Morbid Anatomy. Another of the rare lipidoses occasionally associated with neural change and severe subnormality is infantile Gaucher's disease. The brain, if it is involved, shows severe but patchy loss of nerve cells and neuronophagia. Some neurones store an adventitious glycolipid. The liver, spleen, bone marrow, lymph glands and occasionally the brain contain so-called Gaucher cells. These are large macrophages with central, small, darkly staining, occasionally, double nuclei and a wrinkled cell surface (Fig. 100). The cytoplasm contains granules or fibrils. It is usually P.A.S. positive, Luxol fast blue negative, weakly sudanophilic and metachromatic with thiazine dyes (Aronson and Volk, 1965). Cerebroside may be demonstrable in the affected neurones with more specific stains (Adams, 1965).

Good descriptions of the pathology of the condition are provided by Banker, Miller and Crocker (1962), Inose *et al.* (1964), Aronson and Volk (1965) and Fredrickson (1966). Aronson subdivides the cerebral form of Gaucher's disease into an infantile and a juvenile type. The latter, in addition to its later onset, is said to differ in its neurological manifestations. He includes the case described in detail by Maloney and Cumings (1960) in the juvenile group. The assumption that the infantile and juvenile forms are distinct entities is perhaps premature, as there is as yet no evidence that the enzyme deficiencies or the stored substances differ in the two forms of the disease.

Gaucher's disease may occasionally be transmitted as an autosomal dominant, but is usually inherited as an autosomal recessive. The latter group includes the cases with neurological signs and mental subnormality (Hsia, Naylor and Bigler, 1962).

Chemical Pathology. As one would expect, brain lipids are normal in cases in which there are no neurological signs. In cerebral Gaucher's disease there

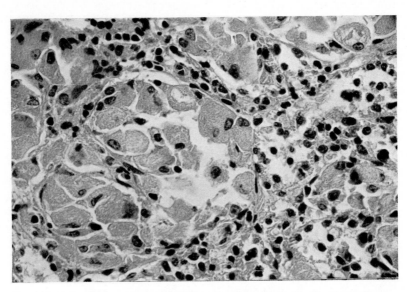

Fig. 100. Adventitious cells in the spleen of a case of infantile Gaucher's disease. (Haematoxylin and eosin × 400.)

is a decrease in some of the myelin lipids and occasionally an increase in cerebroside (ceramide monohexoside) and other ceramide oligosaccharides (Cumings, 1964). While the hexoses of brain cerebroside contain usually 90–95 per cent galactose, in Gaucher's disease the adventitious lipid is largely a glucocerebroside.

With refinement of the analytical techniques for the separation of the gangliosides and the fatty acid moieties of the ceramides, evidence has accumulated that the neurological manifestations in infantile Gaucher's disease are caused by a disturbance of ganglioside rather than cerebroside metabolism (Svennerholm, 1966). The minor gangliosides G_{M2} and G_{M3} are increased in the brain, as are ceramide lactoside and ceramide glucose monohexoside (glucocerebroside). Furthermore, the fatty acid composition of the ceramide glucose monohexoside is that of ganglioside and not that of the normal brain cerebroside. These data can be explained by a deficiency of the enzyme β-glucosidase, and such deficiency has in fact been demonstrated by Brady *et al.*, (1965). The metabolic interrelationships are outlined in Fig. 101. The deposition of glycolipids in other organs probably proceeds by a similar mechanism. Philippart *et al.* (1965) have isolated the glycolipids of the spleen in Gaucher's disease and found an accumulation of glucocerebroside and to a lesser extent of lactocerebroside. From the fatty acid composition of the glycolipids they concluded that the glucocerebroside originated from the gangliosides of erythrocyte stroma, and suggested a block in the conversion of ceramide-glucose to ceramide. Patrick (1965) has since shown that the liver and spleen of patients with Gaucher's disease lack the enzyme β-glucosidase which normally catalyzes this transformation.

Laboratory Diagnosis. Diagnosis during the early stages of the disease depends on demonstrating the typical Gaucher cells. These may be missed in the bone marrow, where they are sometimes very sparse, but will certainly be found on biopsy of a lymph gland or the usually greatly enlarged spleen.

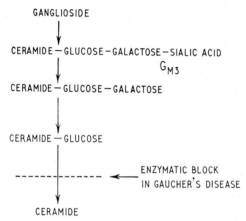

FIG. 101. The degradation of gangliosides in Gaucher's disease. The site of the primary block is probably the bond between glucose and ceramide.

A useful screening test is the estimation of the serum acid phosphatase with phenyl phosphate as substrate. The normal range is up to 4 King Armstrong units while in Gaucher's disease most values are greater than 7 King Armstrong units. The estimation can be refined by testing the inhibition of the enzyme with formaldehyde, tartrate and cupric sulphate (Tuchman *et al.*, 1959). Acid phosphatase, presumably of lysosomal origin, can also be demonstrated histochemically in Gaucher cells (Adams, 1965).

Atypical forms

Not infrequently cases presenting many features of lipidosis cannot be classified correctly even after the fullest clinical and pathological investigation. Some are considered on balance to be examples of one of the recognized conditions (e.g. Maloney and Cumings, 1960). Others are reported as instances of new syndromes or as undesignated cases, as, for example, by Jervis, Harris and Menkes (1962). Neuronal lipidosis was present in three infants showing widespread lipogranulomatosis, described by Farber, Cohen and Uzman (1957).

Two of these were sibs. The visceral lesions were characterized by the presence of lipid-containing macrophages and a granulomatous reaction. The condition described by Wolman *et al.* (1961) as primary familial xanthomatosis with calcification of the adrenals, and by Crocker *et al.* (1965) as 'Wolman's disease', resembles Niemann-Pick disease but the adventitious material contains a greater excess of cholesterol and triglycerides. The condition described by Landing and his colleagues (1964) has been mentioned already (p. 241). It resembles gargoylism but differs from it radiologically and by the chemical nature of the adventitious material. This material, which may be present in the renal glomeruli and lamina propria of the colon, is said to be not a mucopolysaccharide but a relatively soluble glycolipid, probably a ganglioside. Neuronal lipidosis may also occur in association with other conditions, such as tuberous sclerosis, microgyria, blood group incompatibility, Laurence-Moon-Biedl syndrome, Hallervorden-Spatz disease, leucodystrophy and the system atrophies. All this suggests that, like other pathological processes, lipidosis can be regarded as a 'common abnormal' pathway which can be reached by diverse but converging metabolic processes. A disturbance of the ganglioside pattern has been implicated in many of these conditions (Svennerholm, 1966).

Comparative medicine

Lipidosis has been observed in dogs. This will open, perhaps, a way to a fuller range of investigations into the pathology of the condition (Hagen, 1953; Ribelin and Kintner, 1956; Diezel, Koppang, and Rossner, 1965).

The Leucodystrophies

Formation and metabolism of myelin

The metabolic pathways of the biosynthesis of most myelin lipids are now reasonably well established. Little is known, however, about the way in which lipids and proteins combine to form the myelin sheath. It is thought that myelin formation takes place in the Schwann cell or oligodendrocyte, or rather on their surface, by a spontaneous association of lipid molecules into multi-molecular aggregates (Sjöstrand, 1963). Protein and polysaccharide molecules can attach themselves in turn to the surface of the lipid. The myelin sheath is probably formed by spiral winding of myelin layers round the axis cylinders. This gives rise to the characteristic lamellar structure demonstrable by electron microscopy. In the formation of the myelin sheath proteins and enzymes may become denatured at the boundary of the lipid and aqueous phases. If so, myelin is a simplified type of membrane which lacks some of the enzymes and proteins characteristic of other membranes. It is not surprising therefore that most of the myelin sheath lipids undergo only a very slow turnover (Cuzner, Davison and Gregson, 1965). There is, however, a small rapidly metabolizing component in myelin, which includes the phosphoinositides in the form of their calcium or magnesium salts. This component plays a part in controlling the permeability of certain areas of the nerve membrane to univalent ions (Dawson, 1966).

Biochemistry of Demyelination

The biochemical changes in demyelination have been recently summarized by Cumings (1965a) and Adams *et al.* (1965). In the early stages there is a loosening of the regular lamellar pattern of myelin. This may be brought about by diverse factors, such as inflammation, immunopathological processes, anoxia and ischaemia. During this stage lysophosphatides form from phosphatides by the splitting off of a fatty acid molecule, and esterified cholesterol appears. Lysophosphatides are cytolytic and may facilitate further demyelination. However, the brain also contains enzymes for the detoxication and reacylation of the lysophosphatides. The transfer of fatty acid from lecithin to cholesterol has been demonstrated in plasma (Glomset, 1962), and a similar mechanism may well operate in the brain. In the myelin sheath cholesterol probably contributes to the highly organized alignment of the lipid molecules. Esterified cholesterol is much less suitable as a membrane constituent. The Marchi method for detecting degenerating myelin is based on differences in staining properties of free and esterified cholesterol. As demyelination proceeds, there is a concomitant loss of phospholipids (including sphingomyelin), free cholesterol and cerebrosides, and an increase in esterified cholesterol. In certain inflammatory conditions, such as inclusion body encephalitis, sudanophil leucodystrophy and haemorrhagic virus encephalitis, there is, in addition, a raised level of mucopolysaccharides demonstrable by an increase in the total hexosamine content (Cumings, 1965a).

Any factor reducing the viability of the metabolically very active oligodendrocytes, on which myelin depends for maintenance, will also favour the disintegration of the associated myelin sheath. If, as appears likely, the process of myelin formation consists essentially in the aggregation of lipid and protein molecules, then it is clearly important that during myelination and remyelination the right lipids and proteins should be synthesized in proper order and proportions. Interference with the synthesis of myelin proteins or lipids at this stage, due to a deficiency in essential metabolites, enzymes or cofactors, would result in a structurally imperfect myelin sheath (dysmyelination). Such a sheath would be abnormally fragile and prone to degenerate prematurely. This almost certainly occurs in some of the metabolic disorders with extracerebral enzyme deficiencies, such as phenylketonuria, in which toxic metabolites may interfere with brain metabolism or inhibit the passage across the blood brain barrier of essential metabolites which cannot be synthesized in the brain (cf. p. 263).

It is now recognized that almost all the lipids of the C.N.S. form part of the cell membrane or the membranes of the intracellular organelles, such as mitochondria or lysosomes. If for any reason the organized lipid-protein structure of the membrane breaks up, the liberated lipids and proteins can link up to form new complexes. This may alter profoundly the histochemical picture, as the staining properties of lipids depend greatly on their physicochemical state. What is really a rearrangement of molecular aggregates may then appear as an increase in the lipid content of the cell (Hagberg *et al.*,

1965). Lysosomes, which act as intracellular scavengers, are comparatively poor in lipolytic enzymes and this favours intracellular retention of lipid debris. It is possible that the membranous cytoplasmic bodies found in the lipidoses (p. 239) are formed in this way from gangliosides, cholesterol, phosphatides, cerebrosides and amino acids.

The leucodystrophies are characterized by degeneration or abnormal formation of myelin in the white matter of the cerebrum and, more rarely, cerebellum and other formations. Involvement of the grey matter seems to be usually secondary and is relatively mild. The changes are, as a rule, diffuse, symmetrical and widespread. The arcuate fibres (U-fibres) are often spared, especially in the infantile forms of the disease. In other cases the outer limit of the demyelinated areas may fall well short of the cortex and arcuate fibres. Axis cylinders are tougher than myelin sheaths and are often preserved for some time after the breakdown of the myelin. The clinical manifestations of these conditions include progressive dementia, blindness, paralysis and epilepsy, but in the youngest and congenital cases the presenting picture can be one of marked mental retardation without evidence of progressiveness. Some cases are sporadic, but many are familial and the transmission is autosomal recessive. The previously used generic term, Schilder's disease, has been largely discarded (*vide infra*), since many cases can now be classified with greater precision. However, it is still difficult to classify some, and new ones, presenting unusual features, are frequently reported. Hence few experienced neuropathologists have found it possible to leave prevailing classifications unchallenged (Poser, 1962; Peiffer, 1962; Greenfield and Norman, 1963).

A typical case of leucodystrophy should seldom be missed by the examining pathologist. The brain is usually reduced in size and the convolutions are narrowed, although their normal pattern is preserved. Palpation of the hardened sclerotic white matter under the overlying soft cerebral cortex invokes the familiar metaphor of a mailed fist in a velvet glove. On the cut surface, the ventricles are often dilated and large areas of the white matter show a greyish or greyish-blue discoloration with a tendency of the subcortical zone to be spared. These typical appearances, may however, be modified in some of the variants of leucodystrophy listed below, and developing cavitation and calcification may also complicate the pathological picture.

Some workers still retain the original term, *Schilder's disease*, for certain, rather vaguely defined, non-familial cases showing alleged inflammatory change with demyelination and axis cylinder loss in the affected white matter. All other 'degenerative' cases are regarded as leucodystrophies and usually subdivided into: sudanophil, metachromatic, Krabbe type, Alexander type and conditions with mixed sudanophil and 'prelipoid' material. The sudanophil group can be subdivided further into (*a*) simple storage type; (*b*) Pelizaeus-Merzbacher type; (*c*) Seitelberger type; and (*d*) Lowenberg-Hill type. Some workers also include among the leucodystrophies the so-called spongiform type of diffuse sclerosis (p. 255).

According to Poser (1962), leucodystrophies are *dysmyelinating* diseases, caused by inborn errors of metabolism which interfere with the proper anabolism of myelin. This is in contrast with *demyelinating* diseases characterized by breakdown of initially correctly formed myelin. The accumulated adventitious material in cases of leucodystrophy would consist, according to this view, of 'prelipoid' substances which are not properly utilized in the building up of myelin. Poser further suggests that phenylketonuria and the lipidoses might be considered as leucodystrophies.

It is difficult not to oversimplify in attempting to describe briefly the leucodystrophies, but it is nevertheless useful to outline below the salient features in the main forms of these conditions.

Sudanophil Leucodystrophy

As the name indicates, the sudanophil type is characterized by the presence of much distinctly staining sudanophil material in glial cells throughout the affected areas. Chemically, the material consists mainly of cholesterol esters and neutral fat, although hexosamine may also be increased. Nerve cells and axis cylinders are relatively well preserved. There is no metachromatic or 'prelipoid' material (this term is used in this context mainly for the intra- and extracellular substances which stain weakly or not at all with the Sudan dyes). Sudanophil leucodystrophy may be difficult or impossible to distinguish from massive bilateral demyelination that may occur in different conditions, such as, for example, phenylketonuria (p. 265) or adrenal atrophy (Blaw, Osterberg, Kozak and Nelson, 1964).

Pelizaeus-Merzbacher Leucodystrophy

The Pelizaeus-Merzbacher type is characterized by a lengthy clinical course, a much higher incidence in males and, histologically, frequent preservation of myelin islets in the affected areas of the white matter. Axis cylinders are often spared and sudanophil debris can be very scarce. *The Lowenberg-Hill* type is an adult form of the Pelizaeus-Merzbacher disease.

The Seitelberger type, described by Seitelberger, affected three brothers. The disease was congenital and the cerebral white matter showed an almost total absence of myelin.

Globoid Cell Leucodystrophy

Krabbe's or globoid cell leucodystrophy is a disease of young infants. The brain shows very extensive or, even, ubiquitous lack of myelin in the cerebral hemispheres, brainstem and cerebellum, but the arcuate fibres are often spared (Fig. 102). There is little evidence of simple myelin breakdown. Glial cells are overgrown in the affected areas, and a characteristic feature is presence of so-called globoid cells which are arranged in densely packed clusters (Fig. 103). These cells stain only faintly with the Sudan dyes and with P.A.S. In addition, smaller 'epithelioid' cells, resembling those in the clusters, are often grouped around blood vessels. Frequently deformed, tortuous filaments of axis cylinders may be observed in the non-myelinated white matter. Recent instances of the condition have been published by Osetowska *et al.* (1960),

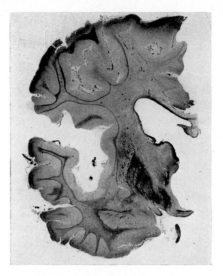

FIG. 102. The cerebral hemisphere in a case of Krabbe's leucodystrophy. There is generalized lack of myelin in the white matter with sparing of the arcuate fibres.

Tingey, Bignami and Torre (1961), Norman, Oppenheimer and Tingey (1961), D'Agostino, Sayre and Hayles (1963), and Cumings and Rozdilsky (1965).

Many attempts have been made to determine the neurometabolic changes in globoid cell leucodystrophy. Anomalous findings have been reported but

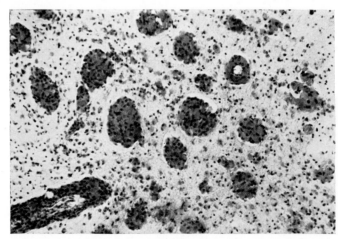

FIG. 103. Tightly packed clusters of globoid cells in a case of Krabbe's leucodystrophy. (Haematoxylin and van Gieson × 230.)

results in different laboratories cannot be readily compared with each other. The chemical lesion remains unknown. Svennerholm (1966) has reported a pronounced increase in the normally less prominent mono- and disialogangliosides G_{M2}, G_{M3}, G_{D2} and G_{D3} in this disease. This is probably a non-specific finding. It may be significant that a globoid-cell-like reaction can apparently be provoked in the white matter of animals by the intracerebral injection of natural or synthetic cerebrosides, such as cerebron and kerasin, while a consistent increase in the cerebroside sulphatide ratio has been reported in human material by Austin (1963) and Austin and Lehfeldt (1965). The previous neurochemical studies of the condition have been reviewed by Austin.

Metachromatic leucodystrophy

Morbid Anatomy. In *metachromatic leucodystrophy* there is macroscopic and microscopic evidence of myelin destruction, which may be variable in degree and topographically selective, and of axonal destruction and gliosis (Austin, 1965). In a personal unpublished case the unfixed white matter of the cerebral hemispheres was ivory white in colour and faintly striated and granular in appearance. It was somewhat soft and there appeared to be no difference in colour between the central and peripheral parts of the centrum semiovale. However, after fixation, the surface exposed to the formalin solution lost its white colour centrally presenting an appearance of obvious demyelination and revealing at the same time a thin white line of myelin preservation of the arcuate fibres. Microscopically, a metachromatically staining substance is present in the affected areas of the white matter, both intra- and extracellularly, and in some neurones, peripheral nerves and myenteric plexuses. In addition, metachromatic material may also be demonstrable in the urine and many somatic tissues, such as the liver, gall bladder, pancreas, lymph glands, kidney, adrenal, tooth pulp*, and ovary (Wolfe and Pietra, 1964). The substance is brown or reddish-brown when stained with cresyl violet or thionine in acid solution and reacts positively with P.A.S. According to Adams (1965), brown metachromasia with cresyl violet in 1 per cent acetic acid is a chemically specific test for sulphatides. Red metachromasia with cresyl violet and thionine, or with toluidine blue, is merely indicative of a certain density of negative charges on the stained substance. Positive P.A.S. staining is difficult to interpret chemically since P.A.S. stains nearly all phospholipids, glycolipids and unsaturated fatty acids, unless blockading methods are used (Adams, 1965). These views are not, however, universally accepted (Austin, 1965).

Some of the material is present in the form of fine granules but the bulk of the metachromatic substance appears usually as coarse homogeneous globules, occasionally in such large quantities that the abnormal colour is easily seen on naked eye examination of the stained section. Metachromatic staining is rather capricious, often impermanent, and the material can be dissolved in the course of the histological processing. It is therefore best searched for in frozen sections as soon as they have been prepared.

Some of the cases of metachromatic leucodystrophy show concomitant disappearance of the oligodendroglia in the white matter (Brain and Greenfield, 1950). These authors therefore suggested that the condition may be due to a primary degeneration of the oligodendroglia, but this view has not been generally accepted. The histological appearances in cases with oligodendroglial fading could perhaps be due to coagulative necrosis or some other necrobiotic process.

* We found, however, brown metachromasia in the pulp of *all* deciduous teeth examined in our laboratory.

In the biopsy material of a case examined electronmicroscopically by Aurebeck *et al.* (1964) the oligodendrocytes were well preserved. They showed, however, according to the authors, numerous diverse osmiophilic inclusions in the cytoplasm.

Chemical Pathology. The main chemical change in cases of metachromatic leucodystrophy is a quantitative reduction of the myelin lipids. There is an excess of hexosamine in the white matter, and esterified cholesterol is present in small amounts (Cumings, 1965a). Sulphatides are increased in all organs with an excretory function, and in the urine and bile. In addition a cerebroside with two hexose molecules—a ceramide-biose-sulphate, also called cytoside— can be demonstrated in the urine (Svennerholm, 1963). It is, therefore, now believed that metachromatic leucodystrophy is a generalized metabolic disorder. A lowered lysosomal arylsulphatase A in autopsy material and urine from cases of metachromatic leucodystrophy has been reported by Austin *et al.* (1963 and 1964). There is evidence of a close relationship of arylsulphatase A to sulphatide sulphatase, the enzyme which is said to hydrolyse the sulphate group of sulphatides (Mehl and Jatzkewitz, 1964). Arylsulphatase B, which differs from arylsulphatase A in electrophoretic mobility, and in optimum pH and substrate concentration, was not decreased. A number of other enzymes were also tested and found to be normal. The interpretation of these findings is uncertain. As other lysosomal enzymes were present in normal amounts, the low arylsulphatase activity cannot be attributed to non-specific degeneration of the lysosomes, but the defect in the lysosomes could be secondary to some other derangement of sulphatide metabolism. Svennerholm (1964b) has suggested that cerebrosides are not the direct precursors of the sulphatides, but that there is a block in the synthesis of the cerebrosides and diversion of metabolites to the synthesis of the sulphatides. It is difficult to see how failure to hydrolyse sulphate esters can be pathological in the absence of an excessive formation of sulphatides, as ^{35}S-sulphate labelled sulphatides can persist in the brain of very young rats for very long periods after the injection of the sulphate. (Svennerholm, 1964b.) This view has to be modified, however, if one accepts that sulphatide turnover is greater in the grey than in the white matter, as suggested by Menkes (1966). Menkes found in two brain biopsy specimens from cases of metachromatic leucodystrophy that the concentration of sulphatides was in fact raised and that the chain lengths of the fatty acids were characteristic of grey rather than white matter.

Laboratory Diagnosis. Diagnosis of the condition depends on the demonstration of metachromatic material in the urine or biopsy material. Metachromasia in urinary deposits is, however, in many cases non-specific, even though newer methods may, perhaps, prove more useful (Austin *et al.*, 1964). A test for the detection of metachromasia in epithelial cells of urinary deposits has been described by Lake (1965) (p. 366). Screening tests should, if possible, be supplemented by thin-layer chromatography of the urinary lipids or assay of the urinary arylsulphatases. A marked reduction in the conduction velocity in peripheral nerves in metachromatic leucodystrophy has been demonstrated by Fullerton (1964).

Biopsy of a peripheral nerve, e.g. the sural, has been used by Hagberg, Sourander and Thorén (1962) and Isler, Bischoff and Esslen (1963). Bodian and Lake (1963) identified metachromatic material in the nerve trunks of the rectum. Brain biopsy (p. 374) has also been successfully used in the diagnosis of the disease (Cumings, 1965b). A recent review of metachromatic leucodystrophy has been published by Austin (1965).

The Alexander Type of Leucodystrophy

The main features in the reported cases of this leucodystrophy were enlargement of the brain (megalencephaly) diffuse demyelination, rarefaction with cavitation of large areas of the centrum semiovale, and the presence of many Rosenthal fibres (p. 140). These were densest around blood vessels and close to the surface of the brain.

Spongiform Encephalopathy

Spongiform encephalopathy, or as it is usually and inappropriately called— spongy diffuse sclerosis—is characterized by rarefaction, vacuolation and, ultimately, breakdown of neural tissue. The cavitation is often most marked at the junction of the white matter and cortex (p. 139 and Fig. 61). Spongiform encephalopathy is not a single disease entity and the condition has already been discussed with other general pathological changes (p. 139).

The Incidence of Leucodystrophies

All forms of leucodystrophy are found in the severely subnormal, but well-defined cases conforming to the descriptions outlined above are exceptional Of 500 brains examined at the Fountain Hospital, 12 could be classified as 'classical' leucodystrophy, of these: 5 were sudanophil, 2–Krabbe type, 2–Pelizaeus-Merzbacher, 1–Alexander type, and 2–spongiform leucoencephalopathy. Many more showed, however, widespread involvement of the white matter without qualifying entirely for any of the above categories. Most of these cases were associated with gliotic encephalopathy (p. 125) and a few of the others showed miscellaneous malformations. A similar case has been described in association with pachygyria by Norman, Tingey, Valentine and Danby (1962). Attention has also been paid to the relation of the leucodystrophies to the lipidoses, some reported cases having shown features common to both groups of conditions (Einarson and Strömgren, 1961). Cases of leucodystrophy may follow or be associated with Addison's disease—adrenocortical atrophy (Turkington and Stempfel, 1966). All this suggest that leucodystrophy may be, like lipidosis, an end-result approachable by diverse aberrant metabolic pathways (p. 248).

REFERENCES

ADAMS, C. W. M. (1965). 'Neurohistochemistry,' Amsterdam: Elsevier, p. 488.
ADAMS, C. W. M., IBRAHIM, M. Z. M., and LEIBOWITZ, S. (1965). In Adams, C. W. M. 'Neurohistochemistry,' Amsterdam: Elsevier, p. 437.

ALEU, T. P., TERRY, R. D., and ZELLWEGGER, H. (1965). *J. Neuropath. exp. Neurol.*, **24**, 304.
ANSELL, G. B., and HAWTHORNE, J. N. (1964). 'Phospholipids,' Amsterdam: Elsevier.
ARONSON, S. M., and VOLK, B. W. (1962). 'Cerebral Sphingolipidoses. A Symposium on Tay-Sachs Disease and Allied Disorders,' New York: Academic Press.
ARONSON, S. M., and VOLK, B. W. (1965). In Carter, C. H. 'Medical Aspects of Mental Retardation,' Springfield: Thomas, p. 684.
AUREBECK, G., OSTERBERG, K., BLAW, M., CHOU, S., and NELSON, E. (1964). *Arch. Neurol. (Chic.)*, **11**, 273.
AUSTIN, J. H. (1963). *Arch. Neurol. (Chic.)*, **9**, 207.
AUSTIN, J. H. (1965). In Carter, C. H. 'Medical Aspects of Mental Retardation,' Springfield: Thomas, p. 768.
AUSTIN, J. H., BALASUBRAMANIAN, A. S., PATTABIRAMAN, T. N., SARASWATHI, S., BASU, D. K., and BACHHAWAT, B. K. (1963). *J. Neurochem.*, **10**, 805.
AUSTIN, J. H., MCAFEE, D. A., O'ROURKE, M., SHEARER, L., and BACHHAWAT, B. (1964). *Biochem. J.*, **93**, 15C.
AUSTIN, J. H., and LEHFELDT, D. (1965). *J. Neuropath. exp. Neurol.*, **24**, 265.
BANKER, B. Q., MILLER, J. Q., and CROCKER, A. C. (1962). In Aronson, S. M., and Volk, B. W. 'Cerebral Sphingolipidoses,' New York: Academic Press, p. 73.
BERGGARD, I., and BEARN, A. G. (1965). *Amer. J. Med.*, **39**, 221.
BIELSCHOWSKY, M. (1920–21). *J. Psychol. Neurol. (Lpz.)*, **26**, 123.
BISHTON, R. L., NORMAN, R. M., and TINGEY, A. (1956). *J. clin. Path.*, **9**, 305.
BLAW, M. E., OSTERBERG, K., KOZAK, P., and NELSON, E. (1964). *Arch. Neurol. (Chic.)*, **11**, 626.
BODIAN, M., and LAKE, B. D. (1963). *Brit. J. Surg.*, **50**, 702.
BOGAERT, L. VAN, SEITELBERGER, F., and EDGAR, G. W. F. (1963). *Acta neuropath.* (Berl.), **3**,57.
BRADY, R. O., KANFER, J. N., and SHAPIRO, D. (1965). *Biochem. biophys. Res. Commun.*, **18**, 221.
BRAIN, W. R., and GREENFIELD, J. G. (1950). *Brain*, **73**, 291.
BRIMACOMBE, J. S., and STACEY, M. (1964). *Advanc. clin. Chem.*, **7**, 199.
CROCKER, A. C., and FARBER, S. (1958). *Medicine*, **37**, 1.
CROCKER, A. C., VAWTER, G. F., NEUHAUSER, E. B. D., and ROSOWSKY, A. (1965). *Pediatrics*, **35**, 627.
CUMINGS, J. N. (1964). In Duncan, G. G. 'Diseases of Metabolism,' Philadelphia, London: Saunders, p. 1405.
CUMINGS, J. N. (1965a). In Cumings, J. N., and Kremer, M. 'Biochemical Aspects of Neurological Disorders,' Oxford: Blackwell, p. 229.
CUMINGS, J. N. (1965b). *Proc. roy. Soc. Med.*, **58**, 21.
CUMINGS, J. N., and ROZDILSKY, B. (1965). *Neurology*, **15**, 177.
CUZNER, M. L., DAVISON, A. N., and GREGSON, N. A. (1965). *Ann. N.Y. Acad. Sci.*, **122**, 86.
D'AGOSTINO, A. N., SAYRE, G. P., and HAYLES, A. B. (1963). *Arch. Neurol. (Chic.)*, **8**, 82.
DAWSON, R. M. C. (1966). *Biochem. J.*, **98**, 19P.
DAWSON, R. M. C., and RHODES, D. N. (1964). 'Metabolic and Physiological Significance of Lipids,' New York: Wiley.
DIEZEL, P. B., KOPPANG, N., and ROSSNER, J. A. (1965). *Dtsch. Z. Nervenheilk.*, **187**, 720.
DORFMAN, A. (1964). *Biophys. J.*, **4**, Suppl., p. 155.
DYKEN, P. R., and ZEMAN, W. (1964). *J. Neurol. Neurosurg. Psychiat.*, **27**, 29.
EINARSON, L., and STRÖMGREN, E. (1961). *Acta jutlandica. Aarsskrift for Aarhus Universitat*, **33**, 1.
FARBER, S., COHEN, J., and UZMAN, L. (1957). *J. Mt. Sinai Hosp.*, **24**, 815.
FARDEAU, M., and LAPRESLE, J. (1963). *Rev. neurol.*, **109**, 157.
FREDRICKSON, D. S. (1966). In Stanbury, J. B., Wyngaarden, J. B., and Fredrickson, D. S. 'The Metabolic Basis of Inherited Disease,' 2nd Ed., New York: McGraw-Hill, p. 586, and 565.
FRIEDE, R. L. (1964). *J. Neurol. Neurosurg. Psychiat.*, **27**, 41.
FRIEDE, R. L., and ALLEN, R. J. (1964). *J. Neuropath. exp. Neurol.*, **23**, 619.
FULLERTON, P. H. (1964). *J. Neurol. Neurosurg. Psychiat.*, **27**, 100.
GLOMSET, J. A. (1962). *Biochim. biophys. Acta (Amst.)*, **65**, 128.

GONATAS, N. K., TERRY, R. D., WINKLER, R., KOREY, S. R., GOMEZ, C. J., and STEIN, A. (1963). *J. Neuropath. exp. Neurol.*, **22**, 557.
GONATAS, N. K., and GONATAS, J. (1965). *J. Neuropath. exp. Neurol.*, **24**, 318.
GREENFIELD, J. G. (1951). *Proc. roy. Soc. Med.*, **44**, 685.
GREENFIELD, et al. (1955). *Neurology*, **5**, 732.
GREENFIELD, J. G., and NORMAN, R. M. (1963). In Greenfield's 'Neuropathology,' London: Arnold, p. 475.
HAGBERG, B., SOURANDER, P., and THORÉN, L. (1962). *Acta paediat. (Uppsala)*, **162**, Suppl. 135, 63.
HAGBERG, B., HULTQUIST, G., OHMAN, R., and SVENNERHOLM, L. (1965). *Acta paediat. (Uppsala)*, **54**, 116.
HAGEN, L. O. (1953). *Acta path. microbiol. scand.*, **33**, 22.
HAUSS, W. H., JUNGE-HÜLSING, G., and KÖNIG, F. (1962). *Med. Welt (Berl.)*, **2**, 2371.
HENDERSON, J. L., MACGREGOR, A. R., THANNHAUSER, S. J., and HOLDEN, R. (1952). *Arch. Dis. Childh.*, **27**, 230.
HOOF, F. VAN, and HERS, H. -G. (1964). *C. R. Acad. Sci. (Paris)*, **259**, 1281.
HSIA, D. Y. -Y., NAYLOR, J., and BIGLER, J. A. (1962). In Aronson, S. M., and Volk, B. W. 'Cerebral Sphingolipidoses,' New York: Academic Press, p. 327.
INOSE, T., INOUE, K., SAWAIZUMI, S., and MATSUOKA, T. (1964). *Acta neuropath. (Berl.)*, **3**, 297.
ISLER, W., BISCHOFF, A., and ESSLEN, E. (1963). *Helv. paediat. Acta*, **18**, 107.
IVEMARK, B. I., SVENNERHOLM, L., THORÉN, C., and TUNELL, R. (1963). *Acta paediat. (Uppsala)*, **52**, 391.
JATZKEWITZ, H., and PILZ, H. (1964). *Naturwissenschaften*, **51**, 61.
JATZKEWITZ, H., PILZ, H., and SANDHOFF, K. (1965). *J. Neurochem.*, **12**, 135.
JERVIS, G. A. (1950). *Arch. Neurol. Psychiat.*, **63**, 68.
JERVIS, G., HARRIS, R. C., and MENKES, J. H. (1962). In Aronson, S. M., and Volk, B. W. 'Cerebral Sphingolipidoses,' New York: Academic Press, p. 101.
KOREY, S. R., GOMEZ, C. J., STEIN, A., GONATAS, J., SUZUKI, K., TERRY, R. D., and WEISS, M. (1963a). *J. Neuropath. exp. Neurol.*, **22**, 2.
KOREY, S. R., GONATAS, J., and STEIN, A. (1963b). *J. Neuropath. exp. Neurol.*, **22**, 56.
KRATTER, F. E. (1964). *Brit. J. psychiat.*, **110**, 257.
KROVErz, L. J., LORINCZ, A. E., and SCHIEBLER, G. L. (1965). *Circulation*, **31**, 132.
LAGUNOFF, D., ROSS, R., and BENDITT, E. P. (1962). *Amer. J. Path.*, **41**, 273.
LAKE, B. D. (1965). *Arch. Dis. Childh.*, **40**, 284.
LANDING, B. H., SILVERMAN, F. N., CRAIG, J. M., JACOBY, M. D., LAHEY, M. E., and CHADWICK, D. L. (1964). *Amer. J. Dis. Child.*, **108**, 503.
LAZARUS, S. S., WALLACE, B. J., and VOLK, B. W. (1962). *Amer. J. Path.*, **41**, 579.
LEDEEN, R., SALSMAN, K., GONATAS, J., and TAGHAVY, A. (1965). *J. Neuropath. exp. Neurol.*, **24**, 341.
LORINCZ, A. E. (1961). *Ann. N.Y. Acad. Sci.*, **91**, 644.
LORINCZ, A. E. (1965). In Carter, C. H. 'Medical Aspects of Mental Retardation,' Springfield: Thomas, p. 638.
MALONEY, A. F. J., and CUMINGS, J. N. (1960). *J. Neurol. Neurosurg. Psychiat.*, **33**, 207.
MANLEY, G., and HAWKSWORTH, J. (1966). *Arch. Dis. Childh.*, **41**, 91.
MAROTEAUX, P., and LAMY, M. (1965). *J. Pediat.*, **67**, 312.
MÁTTYUS, A., and JOBST, C. (1959). *Arch. Psychiat. Nervenkr.*, **198**, 317.
MCILWAIN, H. (1963). 'Chemical Exploration of the Brain,' Amsterdam: Elsevier.
MCILWAIN, H. (1966). 'Biochemistry of the Central Nervous System,' London: Churchill.
MCKUSICK, V. A. (1965). *Circulation*, **31**, 1.
MEHL, E., and JATZKEWITZ, H. (1964). *Hoppe-Seyler Z. physiol. Chem.*, **339**, 260.
MENKES, J. H. (1966). *J. Pediat.*, **69**, 422.
MITTWOCH, U. (1959). *Brit. J. Haemat.*, **5**, 365.
MITTWOCH, U. (1963). *Acta haemat. (Basel)*, **29**, 202.
MOSSAKOWSKI, J. (1964). *Polish med. J.*, **3**, 142.
MUIR, H. (1964). In Hall, D. A. 'International Review of Connective Tissue Research,' Vol. II, New York: Academic Press, p. 101.
MUIR, H., MITTWOCH, U., and BITTER, T. (1963). *Arch. Dis. Childh.*, **38**, 258.
MÜLDNER, H. G., WHERRETT, J. R., and CUMINGS, J. N. (1962). *J. Neurochem.*, **9**, 607.

NAIDOO, D. (1953). *J. ment. Sci.*, **99**, 74.

NORMAN, R. M., URICH, H., and FRANCE, N. E. (1959). *J. ment. Sci.*, **105**, 1070.

NORMAN, R. M., OPPENHEIMER, D. R., and TINGEY, A. H. (1961). *J. Neurol. Neurosurg. Psychiat.*, **24**, 223.

NORMAN, R. M., TINGEY, A. H., VALENTINE, J. C., and DANBY, T. A. (1962). *J. Neurol. Neurosurg. Psychiat.*, **25**, 363.

NORMAN, R. M., TINGEY, A. H., NEWMAN, C. G. H., and WARD, S. P. (1964). *Arch. Dis. Childh.*, **39**, 634.

O'BRIEN, J. S., STERN, M. B., LANDING, B. H., O'BRIEN, J. K., and DONNELL, G. N. (1965). *Amer. J. Dis. Child.*, **109**, 338.

OSETOWSKA, E., GAIL, H., LUCKASEWICZ, D., KARCHER, O., and WISNIEWSKI, H. (1960). *Rev. neurol.*, **102**, 463.

PATRICK, A. D. (1965). *Biochem. J.*, **97**, 17C.

PEARSON, H. A., and LORINCZ, A. E. (1964). *Pediatrics*, **34**, 280.

PEIFFER, J. (1962). *Wld. Neurol.*, **3**, 580.

PHILIPPART, M., ROSENSTEIN, M. D., and MENKES, J. H. (1965). *J. Neuropath. exp. Neurol.*, **24**, 290.

PICÓ, J. E. (1964a). *Acta neuropath. (Berl.)*, **3**, 309.

PICÓ, J. E. (1964b). *Acta neuropath. (Berl.)*, **3**, 289.

POSER, C. M. (1962). In Aronson, S. M., and Volk, B. W. 'Cerebral Sphingolipidoses,' New York: Academic Press, p. 141.

RAYNER, S. (1962). 'Juvenile Amaurotic Idiocy in Sweden with Particular Reference to the Occurrence of Vacuoles in the Lymphocytes of Homo- and Heterozygotes,' Lund.

RIBELIN, W. E., and KINTNER, L. D. (1956). *Cornell Vet.*, **44**, 532.

ROBINS, M. M., STEVENS, H. F., and LINKER, A. (1963). *J. Pediat.*, **62**, 881.

SAIFER, A. (1964). In Volk, B. W. 'Tay-Sachs Disease,' New York: Grune and Stratton, p. 68.

SAMUELS, S., KOREY, S. R., GONATAS, J., TERRY, R. D., and WEISS, M. (1963). *J. Neuropath. exp. Neurol.*, **22**, 81.

SAMUELS, S., GONATAS, N. K., and WEISS, M. (1965). *J. Neuropath. exp. Neurol.*, **24**, 256.

SCHENK, E. A., and HAGGERTY, J. (1964). *Pediatrics*, **34**, 839.

SCHNECK, L. (1964). In Volk, B. W. 'Tay-Sachs Disease,' New York: Grune and Stratton, p. 16.

SJÖSTRAND, F. S. (1963). In Rose, A. S., and Pearson, C. M. 'Mechanisms of Demyelination,' New York: McGraw-Hill, p. 1.

STENHAGEN, S. S., and SVENNERHOLM, L. (1965). *J. Lipid Res.*, **6**, 146.

SVENNERHOLM, L. (1963). *Acta chem. scand.*, **17**, 1170.

SVENNERHOLM, L. (1964a). *J. Lipid Res.*, **5**, 145.

SVENNERHOLM, L. (1964b). In Dawson, R. M. C., and Rhodes, D. N. 'Metabolism and Physiological Significance of Lipids,' New York: Wiley, p. 553.

SVENNERHOLM, L. (1966). *Biochem. J.*, **98**, 20P.

SYMPOSIUM (1964). *Biophys. J.*, **4**, Suppl. 1–255.

TAY, W. (1881). *Trans. ophthal. Soc. U.K.*, **1**, 155.

TERRY, R. D., KOREY, S. R., and WEISS, M. (1962). In Aronson, S. M., and Volk, B. W. 'Cerebral Sphingolipidoses,' New York: Academic Press, p. 49.

TERRY, R. D., and KOREY, S. R. (1963). *J. Neuropath. exp. Neurol.*, **22**, 98.

TERRY, R. D., and WEISS, M. (1963). *J. Neuropath. exp. Neurol.*, **22**, 18.

TINGEY, A. H., BIGNAMI, A., and TORRE, C. (1961). *Riv. Neurol.*, **31**, 712.

TITTARELLI, R., GIAGHEDDU, M., and SPADETTA, V. (1963). *Riv. oto-neuro-oftal.*, **38**, 610.

TUCHMAN, L. R., GOLDSTEIN, G., and CLYMAN, M. (1959). *Amer. J. Med.*, **27**, 959.

TURKINGTON, R. W., and STEMPFEL, R. S. (1966). *J. Pediat.*, **69**, 406.

VOLK, B. W. (1964). 'Tay-Sachs Disease,' New York: Grune & Stratton.

VOLK, B. W., WALLACE, B. J., SCHNECK, L., and SAIFER, A. (1964). *Arch. Path.*, **78**, 483.

WALLACE, B. J., VOLK, B. W., and LAZARUS, S. S. (1964). *J. Neuropath. exp. Neurol.*, **23**, 676.

WALLACE, B. J., VOLK, B. W., SCHNECK, L., and KAPLAN, H. (1966). *J. Neuropath. exp. Neurol.*, **25**, 76.

WHERRETT, J. R., and CUMINGS J. N. (1963). *Trans. Amer. neurol. Ass.*, **88**, 108.

WOLFE, H. J., and PIETRA, G. G. (1964). *Amer. J. Path.*, **44**, 921.

WOLFE, H. J., BLENNERHASSET, J. B., YOUNG, G. F., and COHEN, R. B. (1964). *Amer. J. Path.*, **45**, 1007.

WOLMAN, M., STERK, V. V., GATT, S., and FRENKEL, M. (1961). *Pediatrics*, **28**, 742.

WOLTER, J. R., and ALLEN, R. J. (1964). *Brit. J. Ophthal.*, **48**, 277.

YOUNG, G. F., WOLFE, H. J., BLENNERHASSETT, J. B., and DODGE, P. R. (1966). *J. develop. Med. Child Neurol.*, **8**, 37.

ZEMAN, W., and DONAHUE, S. (1963). *Acta neuropath. (Berl.)*, **3**, 144.

CHAPTER 11

AMINOACIDURIAS

MANY inherited and acquired diseases associated with aminoaciduria have been described in the past few years, and in some of these mental retardation is constant or frequent. Dent was the first to introduce a distinction between 'overflow' and 'renal' aminoaciduria. In the former, the plasma level of certain amino acids is raised and one or more of these 'overflow' into the urine; in the latter, the plasma level is normal or low, but urinary excretion is increased owing to a defect in renal tubular reabsorption. This basic division underlies most of the subsequent classifications (Scriver, 1962; Milne, 1964; Efron, 1965a). Efron classifies aminoacidurias as 'primary', due to an enzymatic defect in intermediary metabolism or amino acid transport, and 'secondary', when the aminoaciduria is produced by interference with the metabolism of the liver or kidney by an endogenous or exogenous toxic substance. Examples of primary aminoacidurias are phenylketonuria (overflow) and Hartnup disease (transport defect). Galactosaemia, Wilson's disease and lead poisoning exemplify conditions associated with secondary aminoaciduria.

In most of the inherited renal aminoacidurias only some of the amino acids are excreted in the urine. The selectiveness is due to the fact that several enzymatic transport systems operate in the kidney. These are distinct, and not uniformly affected in any disease. One transport system is concerned with the basic diamino acids (lysine, arginine, ornithine and cystine); another with the neutral monocarboxylic acids, and yet another with the acidic dicarboxylic amino acids (glutamic, aspartic). The imino acids (proline, hydroxyproline) share at least part of the transport mechanism of glycine, while methionine may have a mechanism of its own (Milne, 1964; Efron, 1965a; Woolf, 1966).

Another useful concept, introduced by Dent, is that of no-threshold aminoaciduria. In some diseases the substance above an enzymatic block does not accumulate in the plasma as there is no renal mechanism for its reabsorption. Such substances normally occur only within cells, and the absence of a mechanism for their reabsorption by the kidney is therefore understandable. Argininosuccinicaciduria and cystathioninuria are examples of no-threshold aminoacidurias.

The above classification is not, of course, rigid. Several types of aminoaciduria may combine. Thus defective deamination of amino acids in the liver may go hand in hand with renal tubular defects, leading to both overflow and renal aminoaciduria. Again, a number of substances may accumulate in the plasma, some with and some without renal transport mechanisms. This will result in a combination of an overflow and no-threshold aminoaciduria.

It is clear therefore that while pure overflow aminoacidurias can usually be detected by one-dimensional chromatography of the serum or plasma, all other types of aminoaciduria require an examination of the urine. It is always best to examine both urine and serum (or plasma) and some suitable screening procedures for this purpose are given in the appendix (p. 338 *et seq.*).

Phenylketonuria

Chemical Pathology

Fölling's discovery in 1934 of mental retardation associated with a constant biochemical abnormality, i.e. the excretion of phenylpyruvic acid in the urine, is a landmark in the history of mental deficiency. No other disease in this field has attracted as much attention. Phenylketonuria was also the first hereditary disease of intermediary metabolism yielding, at least in large measure, to rational therapy. Its clinical features are well recognized (Kirman, 1965; Knox, 1966). They include epilepsy, E.E.G. abnormalities, microcephaly, hyperactivity of reflexes, dilution of hair and iris colour, hyperkinesis, tremor

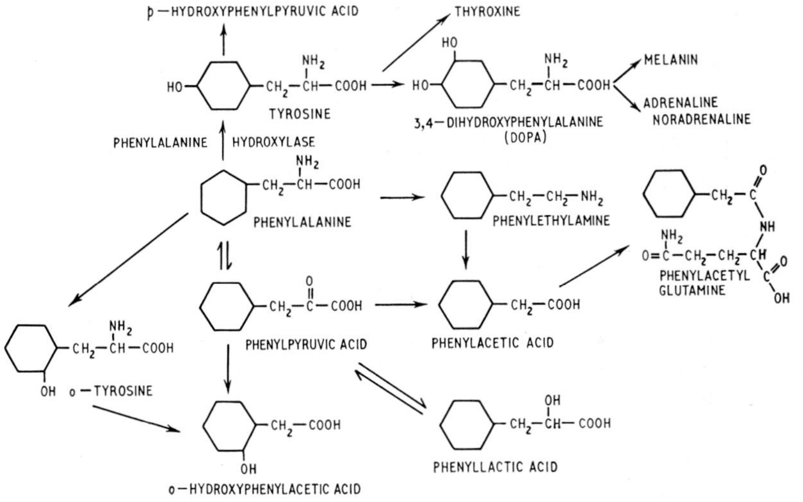

FIG. 104. The metabolism of phenylalanine.

and eczema, but not all of these are present in any one patient. In most patients mental retardation is profound. The disease is transmitted as an autosomal recessive trait; heterozygotes are free from clinical symptoms and are of normal intelligence. It has been estimated that the disease occurs about once in 25,000 births, but recent American surveys suggest an incidence nearer to one in 10,000 births.

The inborn enzymatic defect in phenylketonurics is inability to oxidize, i.e. hydroxylate, phenylalanine to tyrosine. Normally this ability develops soon after birth, and hydroxylation is usually the most efficient pathway of phenylalanine metabolism. Tyrosine is then metabolized further via *p*-hydroxyphenylpyruvic acid and homogentisic acid to carbon dioxide and water (Fig. 104 and 108). A number of quantitatively less important pathways of tyrosine metabolism lead to the production of adrenaline, noradrenaline, thyroxine and melanin.

As a result of the metabolic block phenylalanine accumulates in the body fluids and its excess is diverted into pathways which are of only minor importance in normal individuals. The metabolites in the body fluids of phenylketonurics are thus abnormal only in quantity. The normal blood phenylalanine level is 1–2 mg./100 ml., depending on the method of estimation (cf. p. 348). In the first few days of life, and before the phenylalanine hydroxylase system has fully developed, the blood phenylalanine level rises by 1 or 2 mg./100 ml. In a few babies, particularly those of low birth weight, the levels may rise to 6 mg./100 ml. or even higher, but these peaks are transient and normal levels are soon regained (cf. p. 354). In untreated phenylketonurics the blood phenylalanine continues to rise and may reach 50–100 mg./100 ml. At blood levels greater than about 15 mg./100 ml. phenylpyruvic acid is formed by transamination of phenylalanine and is excreted in the urine. Other metabolites found in abnormal amounts are listed in Table 8.

Table 8. ABNORMAL URINARY METABOLITIES IN PHENYLKETONURIA

Compound	Urinary excretion	Remarks
Phenylalanine	Increased	Level also raised in the blood, C.S.F., and duodenal juice. Levels in the sweat and saliva are almost normal.
Phenylpyruvic acid	,,	Traces found in blood. Not detectable in sweat.
Phenyllactic acid	,,	Detectable in blood.
Phenylacetylglutamine	,,	
N-acetylphenylalanine	,,	
o-Hydroxyphenylacetic acid	,,	
p-Hydroxyphenyllactic acid	,,	Probably derived from p-hydroxyphenylpyruvic acid.
Indolyllactic acid	,,	
Indolylacetic acid	,,	Excretion is decreased when the gut is sterilized.
Indolylpyruvic acid	,,	
Indican	,,	Excretion is decreased when the gut is sterilized.
o-Tyrosine sulphate	Decreased	
5-Hydroxyindoleacetic acid (5-HIAA)	,,	Blood serotonin (5-HT) level is also decreased.
4-Hydroxy-3-methoxymandelic acid (VMA)	,,	Blood catecholamine level is also decreased.

o-Hydroxyphenylacetic acid is excreted in increased amounts in the urine at blood phenylalanine levels well below 15 mg./100 ml. and is therefore useful in the diagnosis of the disease (cf. Appendix, p. 353). Phenylalanine, phenylpyruvic acid, with their derivatives—phenyllactic acid, phenylacetylglutamine and o-hydroxyphenylacetic acid, are the characteristic constituents of phenyl-ketonuric urine.

Studies of liver biopsies have confirmed that the phenylalanine hydroxylase system is almost completely inactive in phenylketonuria, while there is an adaptive increase in enzymes serving the pathways leading to phenylacetyl-glutamine. The low levels of some tyrosine metabolites have been explained by competitive inhibition of some of the relevant enzymes.

Tryptophan metabolism is also disturbed (Table 8 and Fig. 64). Thus intes-tinal absorption of tryptophan (and tyrosine) is inhibited by the high phenyl-alanine levels in the body fluids of untreated patients (Yarbro and Anderson, 1966). Some of the abnormalities are not, however, due to a direct interfer-ence with the patient's metabolism. If the gut is sterilized, for example, with neomycin, the excess of indolylacetic acid normally detectable in phenylke-tonuric urine disappears. Inhibition of some of the enzymes acting along the tryptophan to 5-hydroxyindoleacetic acid (5-HIAA) pathway appears to be responsible for the low levels of blood serotonin and urinary 5-HIAA. Full details of the biochemistry of phenylketonuria will be found in the reviews by Woolf (1963) and Knox (1966).

It is not certain how the above metabolic abnormalities impair intelligence, but tentative suggestions have been made. Phenylethylamine is formed in phenylketonurics when phenylalanine concentrations are high, particularly when the oxidation of phenylethylamine is inhibited by administering an amine oxidase inhibitor. This leads to an exacerbation of the neurological symp-toms. Another possibility is that the mental retardation is due to a deficiency of serotonin (5-hydroxytryptamine, 5-HT) in the brain. This is supported by the recent observation (Woolley and Van der Hoeven, 1964) that serotonin can counteract the toxic effects of artificially produced high phenylalanine levels in mice. A third possibility is that the increased phenylalanine content of the extracellular fluid inhibits the transport of other essential amino acids into cells and across the blood brain barrier and that this may be particularly harmful to the developing brain. Graham-Smith and Moloney (1965) have recently shown that the brain contains a tryptophan hydroxylase, and that this enzyme is inhibited by phenylalanine, probably by inhibiting tryptophan transfer across the membrane of nerve-endings. Any deficiency in serotonin synthesis caused by this inhibition would be serious as serotonin is probably concerned with synaptic transmission in, at least, certain areas of the brain.

Some of the metabolites found in the body fluids of phenylketonurics inhibit in vitro enzymes of tyrosine and tryptophan metabolism, such as L-aromatic amino acid decarboxylase. The significance of these observations is uncertain, as the in vitro concentrations of the inhibitors are many times higher than those which may be expected to occur in phenylketonurics.

More than one mechanism might be responsible for the mental deteriora-tion. Their relative importance may well vary in different patients and depend also on the maturity of the nervous system. Indeed, a few untreated phenylke-tonurics escape the worst consequences of the metabolic defect and are of normal or near normal intelligence.

The phenylketonuric infant is believed to be usually normal at birth as the foetus is protected by the maternal phenylalanine hydroxylase system. The human brain is, however, susceptible to ante-natal damage by high phenylalanine levels. This became known when severely subnormal but non-phenylketonuric children were born to phenylketonuric mothers, who, themselves, were not in all cases mentally subnormal or diagnosed as phenylketonurics at the time of the pregnancy (Mabry *et al.*, 1963). Some phenylketonuric mothers with moderately raised blood phenylalanine levels have, however, borne mentally normal children (Woolf *et al.*, 1961). Waisman (1963) and his collaborators have produced a phenylketonuric state in monkeys and rats by a diet resulting in a persistently elevated phenylalanine in the extra-cellular fluid. This approach could be profitably extended to the study of the effects of high maternal phenylalanine on the foetus.

In view of the known site of the metabolic block in phenylketonuria treatment could be directed towards the following objectives:

(1) Reduction of the tubular reabsorption of phenylalanine, so that more of it is excreted in the urine.
(2) By-pass of the block, viz. by giving supplements of tyrosine.
(3) Increase of the concentration of serotonin by administering its precursor 5-hydroxytryptophan or, alternatively, by raising the level of serotonin and of other biologically active amines by giving amine oxidase inhibitors.
(4) Restriction of phenylalanine intake.

No agent yet found will selectively reduce the tubular reabsorption of phenylalanine; the second and third alternatives have proved ineffective in practice and amine oxidase inhibitors could, as explained, be dangerous by increasing the levels of such substances as phenylethylamine.

A useful advance has undoubtedly been made, however, by restricting phenylalanine intake. Since phenylalanine is an essential amino acid, enough of it must, nevertheless, be provided for growth and development. Some practical details of the dietary treatment are given in the appendix (p. 353). There is no doubt that as a group treated patients fare better, both physically and intellectually, than untreated ones (Kang *et al.*, 1965) (cf. p. 355). Treatment is most effective when started early, preferably during the first few days of life. Just as the severity of the disease varies from patient to patient, so does the response to treatment and the ease with which the blood phenylalanine level can be kept within safe limits i.e. 2–5 mg./100 ml. or, perhaps, 2–7 mg./100 ml. A phenylalanine level below 1 mg./100 ml. may constitute a danger to life, and the presence in the diet of certain essential supplements must be ensured (Mann, Wilson, and Clayton, 1965). The dietary treatment is trying for the patient, parents and doctor, and it is important to establish the earliest age at which it can be safely discontinued and, if early diagnosis is missed, the latest stage at which the diet can be started with a hope of significant benefit. Unfortunately, it is not yet possible to answer these questions definitively. Some children diagnosed and treated early have discontinued the diet after the age of $2\frac{1}{2}$ years with no apparent deterioration over a period of more than a year. We have ourselves seen two such cases. On the other hand, one of our patients diagnosed and treated at 8 months is now $3\frac{1}{2}$. He is severely subnormal (I.Q. 30–35) and shows immediate striking deterioration of behaviour as soon as his blood phenylalanine rises above 7–10 mg./100 ml. Again, while in most cases little intellectual improvement follows treatment delayed by more than a year, one of our cases who was considered hopelessly psychotic when diagnosed at 3 years improved sufficiently on the diet to be admitted to an E.S.N. school 3 years later. Apart from any irreversible damage caused in early infancy, an element of reversible intoxication appears to operate in the disease (Knox, 1966), and this may respond to treatment, particularly in higher-grade patients presenting with behaviour problems and psychotic features. It seems, therefore, that it is never too late to try the diet, particularly if the child is not too severely retarded. Conversely, whenever treatment is discontinued, irrespective of age, patients must be cautiously watched over years for signs of neurological or psychological deterioration.

Morbid Anatomy

The brains of phenylketonurics tend to be small, chiefly, it seems, on account of a reduction in the volume of the white matter, which may show microscopically some astrocytic overgrowth and fibrous gliosis (Crome and Pare, 1960). The number of cortical neurones is, perhaps, also reduced but, if so, the reduction is diffuse and too slight to be ascertained by classical neuropathological methods. Most of the myelin sheaths stain normally (Fig. 105), but, chemic-

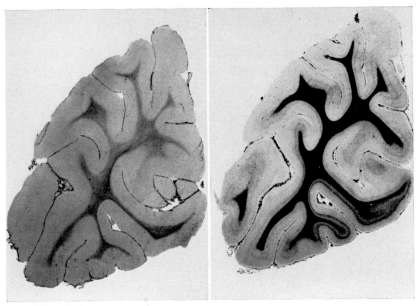

FIG. 105. The occipital lobe in a case of phenylketonuria. Stained by the Heidenhain method for myelin, on the right, and the Holzer method for fibrous gliosis, on the left. The dark hue of the white matter on the left indicates the presence of fibrous gliosis, while the picture on the right shows normally staining myelin. ($\times$ $1\frac{3}{4}$.)

ally, there may be excess of water in the white matter, while the cerebrosides and cholesterol are diminished (Crome, Tymms and Woolf, 1962). These chemical changes may be partly due to the presence of excessive glial tissue, but the findings could also indicate some interference with myelination or, even, gradual, slow demyelination. Small focal areas of frank demyelination and glial scarring have also been encountered. These may be ictal in origin. More or less similar neuropathological changes, ranging from spongiform degeneration to gliosis and demyelination of the white matter have been observed in a series of eight cases by Malamud (1966), who believes that the nature of the lesions can be correlated with the age of the patients and the severity of the process.

Different findings have been reported by Foote, Allen and Agranoff (1965). Samples of the brains of six phenylketonurics examined by them, all of whom were much older than the cases of Crome, Tymms and Woolf, showed normal cholesterol, cerebroside and cerebroside sulphate. On the other hand, major monoenoic acids relative to the major saturated fatty acids were decreased in their material. The brains of their cases are stated to have been normal in weight and showed, apparently, little or no histological change. The discrepancy in the observations is as yet unexplained. No details of the weights of their brains or the histological methods are given in the series of Foote, Allen and Agranoff. The chemical discrepancies may be due to differences in the methods employed, the age of the patients or the sampled areas.

Most, if not all, of the cases examined pathologically had had severe mental defect. The case reported by Bechar *et al.* (1965) was also paraplegic and bilateral degeneration of the pyramidal tracts was present in the spinal cord together with demyelination and gliosis in other parts of the central nervous system. The morphological picture in more intelligent cases or in patients thought to have responded favourably to treatment remains unknown.

Attention has been drawn by Crome (1962) to the fact that some older phenylketonurics develop widespread demyelination with changes indistinguishable from sudanophil leucodystrophy. Such changes appear to have been present in four of the older patients out of a total of 26 cases examined pathologically (at the time of reporting). This frequency of association between two uncommon diseases cannot be fortuitous. Its precise significance is uncertain, but it is likely that leucodystrophy is one of the reactive patterns of neural tissue common to a number of pathogenetic processes. (cf. p. 255)

Laboratory Diagnosis

As the dietary treatment of phenylketonuria is only fully effective if started in earliest infancy, prompt diagnosis is essential. In babies with a family history of the disease periodic blood phenylalanine estimations are mandatory during the first few weeks of life. Any of the methods described in the appendix may be used for this purpose (p. 348).

Different considerations apply when the whole population is to be screened during the first weeks of life, and the problems involved have been fully discussed by Woolf (1963). In earlier surveys urine was tested for phenylpyruvic acid with ferric chloride or 'phenistix', a reagent strip containing buffered ferric ammonium sulphate. False positives may be obtained, for example, in histidinaemia and, particularly, with ferric chloride in tyrosinosis, but this is less important than the false negatives due to decomposition of phenylpyruvic acid in alkaline urine, or due to 'occult phenylketonuria', i.e. failure to excrete phenylpyruvic acid at blood levels of about 15 mg./100 ml. We have seen two cases in two years missed by the 'phenistix' test. One gave a negative 'phenistix' test when his blood phenylalanine was 17 mg./100 ml. Tests for o-hydroxyphenylpyruvic acid are more reliable, but these do not appear to have been widely used except as a confirmatory test.

In recent years there has been an increasing tendency to rely on the Guthrie bacterial inhibition test (Guthrie and Whitney, 1965) or one-dimensional chromatography of serum, or preferably serum *and* urine (Scriver *et al.*, 1964; Efron *et al.*, 1964). Details of some of these tests are given in the Appendix (p. 348 *et seq.*).

It is technically difficult to detect heterozygotes, and this is as yet only a research procedure. The most sensitive technique measures the rate of phenylalanine metabolism after the intravenous administration of the amino acid. The rate is considerably higher in normals than in heterozygotes so that 90–95 per cent of tested individuals can be correctly identified (Woolf, 1965). Detection of heterozygotes will become increasingly important in genetic counselling as successfully treated patients of normal intelligence reach childbearing age.

Maple Syrup Urine Disease

This condition, first described by Menkes, Hurst and Craig (1954), owes its name to the peculiar odour of the patient's urine, which is said to be reminiscent of maple syrup. The disease presents with varying severity. In most cases symptoms begin during the first few days of life. Feeding difficulties are followed by progressive involvement of the nervous system evidenced by convulsions, muscular rigidity—which may alternate with flaccidity, opisthotonos and early death. Some children have, however, survived several years, albeit with severe mental retardation.

Chemical Pathology

The disease is the result of failure of the oxidative decarboxylation of the branched chain keto-acids: α-keto*iso*valeric acid, α-keto*iso*caproic acid and α-keto-β-methylvaleric acid (Fig. 106).

The same enzyme system appears to be involved in the decarboxylation of all three keto acids. Coenzyme A is required as a cofactor. According to Efron (1965a), patients with maple syrup urine disease are unable to link the keto-acids into complexes with coenzyme A during the first step of oxidative decarboxylation. As a result, the keto-acids accumulate in the serum, urine and cerebrospinal fluid, and the level of the corresponding amino acids—valine, leucine and *iso*leucine—rises secondarily. Allo*iso*leucine may also be detected in the urine. Increased amounts of the hydroxy acids corresponding to the keto-acids are also excreted in the urine, and these or their derivatives may be responsible for the maple syrup-like odour adhering to the patients. An alternative suggestion is that the odour is due to a polymer of the keto acid of *iso*leucine. Severe hypoglycaemia occurs in some patients. This is attributed

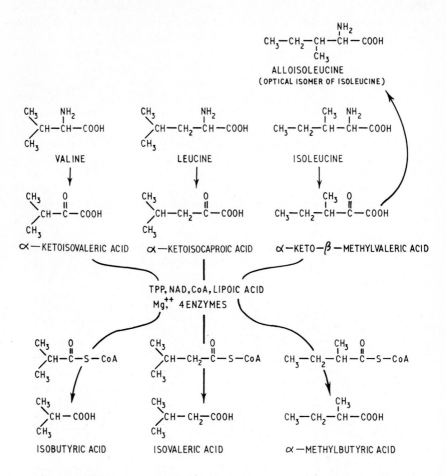

CoA—COENZYME A
NAD—NICOTINAMIDE ADENINE DINUCLEOTIDE
TPP—THIAMINE PYROPHOSPHATE

FIG. 106. The metabolism of the branched chain amino acids.

to the high leucine levels, which are presumed to increase insulin excretion, as they do in leucine-sensitive hypoglycaemia (p. 295). It is probable that the increased plasma leucine concentration is mainly responsible for the neurological symptoms (Efron, 1965a). Leucine, but not valine or *iso*leucine, causes prompt clinical deterioration when fed to a treated infant. Therapy with a diet low in the branched chain amino acids seems effective if started early (Westall, 1964; Snyderman, et al., 1964; Ireland, 1965).

The condition is probably inherited as an autosomal recessive. The presumed heterozygotes have been identified by *iso*leucine, valine or leucine tolerance tests (Linneweh and Ehrlich, 1963), and by the decreased conversion in leucocytes of C^{14} labelled keto*iso*caproic acid to carbon dioxide (Goedde, et al., 1963).

Children with a variant of maple syrup urine disease setting in at a later age are of special interest (Kiil and Rokkones, 1964; Blattner, 1965). Severe symptoms, including convulsions, coma, respiratory distress, severe metabolic acidosis and the characteristic biochemical changes were seen in two sibs aged 15 months and eight years. The older child, who had been of above average intelligence, died; the younger child survived without intellectual impairment after being in coma for three days.

Morbid Anatomy

Neuropathological changes have been described in seven cases of the disease (Crome, Dutton and Ross, 1961; Silberman, Dancis and Feigin, 1961; Diezel and Martin, 1964; Menkes, Philippart and Fiol, 1965). The white

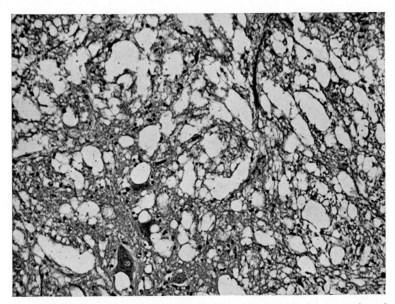

FIG. 107. Spongiform degeneration, mainly of the white matter, in a case of maple syrup urine disease. (Haematoxylin and eosin × 175.) (Crome, 1964, in Neurometabolic Disorders of Childhood, ed. by Holt and Milner. E. & S. Livingstone).

and grey matter of all brains was heavily waterlogged and showed spongy degeneration on microscopic examination (Fig. 107). This was associated with generalized dearth of myelin fibres and some astrocytic overgrowth. Diezel and Martin ascertained that the seemingly empty spaces of the rarefied areas contained a weakly P.A.S.-positive, somewhat water-soluble protein-rich fluid. Crystallized proteins were demonstrated by them in the cytoplasm of glial cells in unfixed or alcohol-fixed material, and somewhat similar protein bodies were present in the vacuoles of certain renal and hepatic cells. Menkes and his colleagues examined the lipids in the formalinized material of their case and found them to be within normal limits*. In another personal unpublished case at Queen Mary's Hospital for Children, who survived longer than some of the others, dying at 18 months, spongiform degeneration was not very marked, but the white matter of the cerebral hemispheres showed uneven fibrous gliosis without perceptible demyelination. Fibrous gliosis was also marked in the white matter of the brainstem and cerebellum. The optic nerves were hypoplastic and showed myelin loss at their periphery.

Laboratory Diagnosis

This condition can, perhaps, be suspected in most infants by the odour of the patient and the positive 2,4-dinitrophenylhydrazine test. The ferric chloride test is often ambiguous. Diagnosis is difficult during the first few days of life. By the time the above tests are clearly positive the health of the child may have been gravely prejudiced. Estimation of the branched-chain amino acid metabolism in leucocytes by means of labelled carbon (see above) may yet prove the most useful procedure in early cases. The raised levels of the branched chain amino acids should be seen on one-way chromatography by about the 5th day (p. 341). Diagnosis of the late-manifesting cases is likely to prove more difficult. Kiil and Rokkones (1964) found in their cases severe metabolic acidosis with normal serum sodium and chloride levels. This electrolyte pattern appears to be characteristic of the condition. According to the authors, the diagnosis should be entertained in all cases of acute acidosis in children, particularly when it is associated with coma.

Tyrosinosis and Related Disorders

Chemical Pathology

Tyrosinosis or tyrosinaemia is the name given to a disorder characterized biochemically by a high urinary excretion of tyrosine and its derivatives, particularly p-hydroxyphenylpyruvic acid, p-hydroxyphenyllactic acid and p-hydroxyphenylacetic acid, high plasma tyrosine levels†, cirrhosis of the liver and multiple renal tubular defects. These renal changes may affect to a greater or lesser extent the reabsorption of amino acids, glucose, phosphate, protein, uric acid, water, potassium and bicarbonate. Of these, aminoaciduria and phosphaturia are always present, except, perhaps, during the first week of life; the other tubular defects are variable and inconstant. Clinically, the course of the disease may resemble that of galactosaemia with the patient dying from liver failure during the first week of life, but some cases have survived for months or years. Mental retardation is present in only a proportion of cases and is usually mild. The disease is, however, of considerable importance in the differential diagnosis of inborn errors of metabolism in the neonatal period.

* See p. 355.
† See also Prensky, A. L., and Moser, H. W. (1966). J. Neuro-chem., 13, 863.

The clinical and biochemical aspects of the disorder have been fully described by Gentz, Jagenburg and Zetterström (1965); Efron (1965a); Woolf (1966); Halvorsen *et al.* (1966); LaDu (1966a); and Gjessing and Halvorsen (1966).

The basic defect in tyrosinosis is a deficit of the enzyme *p*-hydroxyphenyl-pyruvic acid oxidase. This has been proved by enzyme studies on biopsies of the liver and kidney (Gentz *et al.*, 1965; Taniguchi and Gjessing, 1965). The relevant metabolic pathways are shown in Fig. 108.

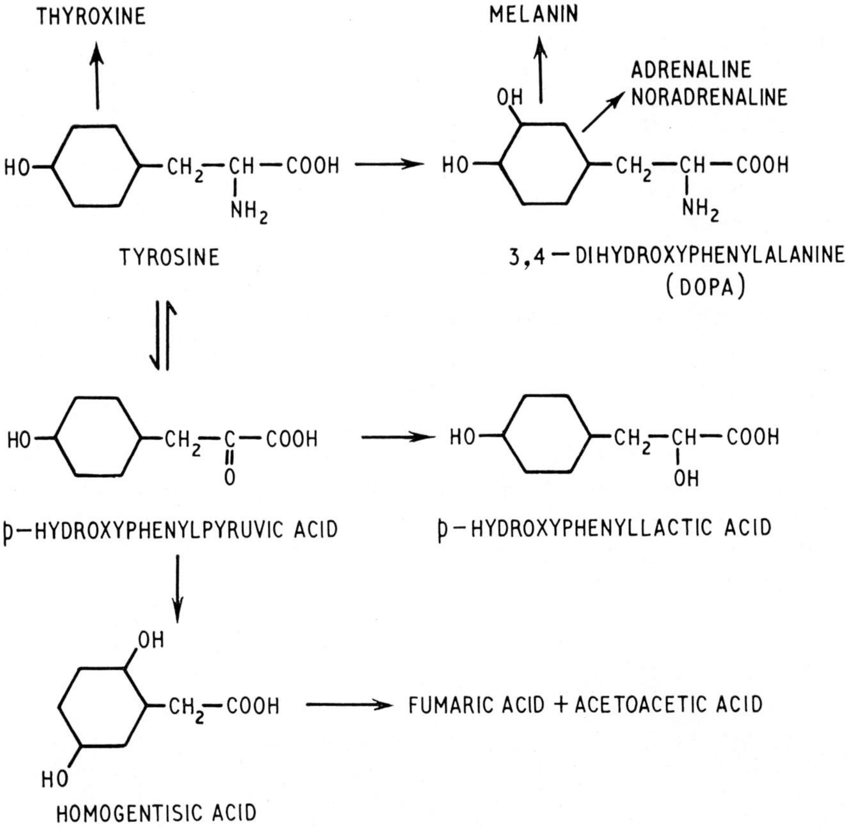

FIG. 108. The metabolism of tyrosine.

Treatment with a diet low in tyrosine and phenylalanine can normalize the plasma tyrosine level and reverse the other biochemical abnormalities (Halvorsen and Gjessing, 1964). Assessment of the results of treatment is complicated by the fact that about 1 per cent of newborn babies show delay, sometimes of many weeks, in the development of *p*-hydroxyphenylpyruvic acid oxidase, without coming to harm. In ascorbic acid deficiency and, particularly, in severe liver disease, tyrosinosis may also result from impairment of *p*-hydroxyphenylpyruvic acid oxidase, and this acquired defect cannot be readily distinguished from the hereditary deficiency of the enzyme (Woolf,

1963). *Hypermethioninaemia* may be found in the terminal stages of cases of tyrosinosis which progress rapidly to hepatic failure (Perry *et al.*, 1965; Gjessing and Halvorsen, 1965; Scriver *et al.*, 1966).

Diagnosis is exceedingly difficult in the young infant in whom liver and kidney damage, and, occasionally, malabsorption, may be superimposed on an inborn error of metabolism. In such cases analysis of blood, urine and C.S.F. and, where possible, histochemical and enzymological studies on biopsy material are necessary to establish the diagnosis. Thus, it has not yet been possible to identify the metabolic block in *oast house disease*, a condition showing certain similarity to tyrosinosis, phenylketonuria and maple syrup urine disease (Smith and Strang, 1958; Jepson, Smith and Strang, 1958). The affected infant excreted an excess of methionine, tyrosine, branched chain amino acids, p-hydroxyphenylpyruvic acid and *p*-hydroxyphenyllactic, and indolyllactic acid. α-Hydroxybutyric acid, derived from methionine by the action of the intestinal flora, was also detected in the urine. The ferric chloride test was positive. The patient suffered from convulsions, hyperpnoea and oedema and died before it could be established whether the basic defect was one of phenylalanine, tyrosine or branched chain amino acid metabolism. Methionine malabsorption may have also been present (Hooft *et al.*, 1964; Effron, 1965a).

Morbid Anatomy

The liver and kidney have been examined in a number of cases and changes, usually minor or marginal, reported. However, gross hepatic cirrhosis has been found in some patients. Changes in the brain have not been described.

Laboratory Diagnosis

The urine of children with tyrosinosis gives a positive test with dinitrophenylhydrazine and ferric chloride; 'phenistix' (Ames) gives a fleeting colour. It is of course most important that tyrosinuria, particularly the benign transient form, should not be confused with phenylketonuria (Woolf, 1963; Efron, 1965a). The chromatographic screening test and the Guthrie test should satisfactorily distinguish between the two conditions, as will, of course, the snake venom and fluorimetric tests if properly carried out (cf. Appendix, p. 348 *et seq.*)

Histidinaemia

Chemical Pathology

This disease, discovered in 1961, is unusual in that the first five cases were of normal intelligence, although four of them had speech defects. However, patients with severe subnormality have been reported later, and some suffered also from convulsions and progressive ataxia (p. 204).

The metabolism of histidine is shown in Fig. 109. It is generally accepted that in normal individuals the most important pathway is via urocanic acid and formiminoglutamic acid (FIGLU). In patients with histidinaemia this pathway is blocked at the point of transformation of histidine to urocanic acid, normally brought about by the enzyme histidase (histidine deaminase). In consequence histidine accumulates in the blood and there is raised excretion

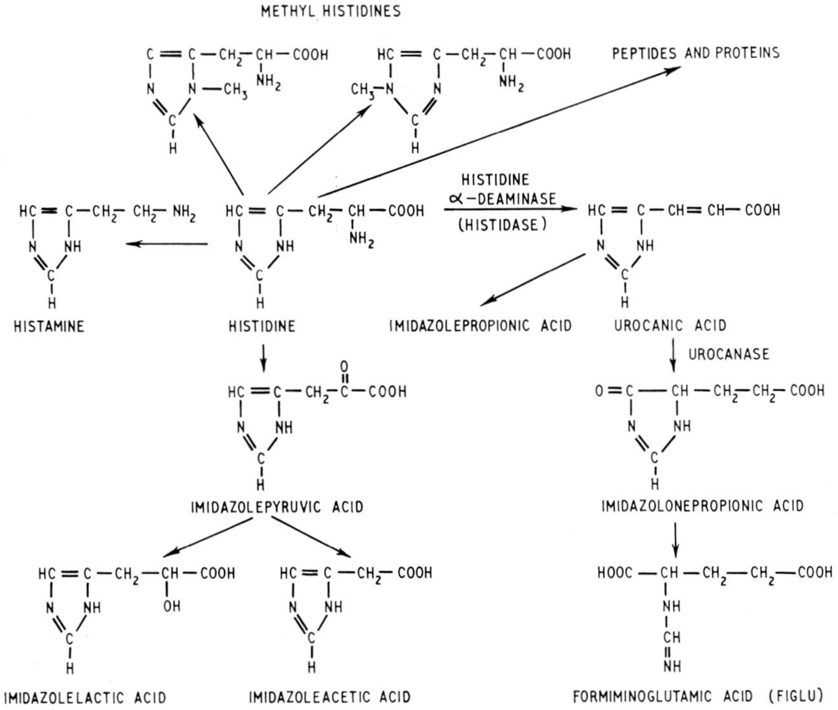

METHYL HISTIDINES

PEPTIDES AND PROTEINS

HISTIDINE
α-DEAMINASE
(HISTIDASE)

HISTAMINE   HISTIDINE   IMIDAZOLEPROPIONIC ACID   UROCANIC ACID

UROCANASE

IMIDAZOLEPYRUVIC ACID   IMIDAZOLONEPROPIONIC ACID

IMIDAZOLELACTIC ACID   IMIDAZOLEACETIC ACID   FORMIMINOGLUTAMIC ACID (FIGLU)

FIG. 109. The metabolism of histidine*.

of histidine and its derivatives in the urine. These abnormalities are accentuated by increased protein intake or histidine loading. The mode of inheritance of the disease appears to be recessive. In a proportion of the patients' parents, who are presumably carriers, the histidine load test is abnormal. The following experimental evidence suggests that histidase is the deficient enzyme in histidinaemia. First, patients with histidinaemia do not excrete FIGLU after a histidine load, but do so after a load of urocanic acid, while some carriers excrete abnormally small amounts of FIGLU after histidine loading. Second, absence of histidase can actually be demonstrated in the skin biopsies of patients while the skin of normal subjects and carriers (heterozygotes) invariably shows epidermal histidase activity.

The biochemical findings in histidinaemia and phenylketonuria show some analogies. In both disorders pathways which are normally of minor importance assume major significance. In phenylketonuria it is phenylpyruvic acid which is excreted, and in histidinaemia a similar substance, imidazolepyruvic acid, although excretion of that substance is intermittent and depends on the intake of histidine. Excess of imidazoleacetic and imidazolelactic acid and of

* A metabolic block above FIGLU, *cyclohydrolase deficiency* (Arakawa, 1966, *Tohoku J. Exp. Med.* **88**, 341), and one below FIGLU, *formimino-transferase deficiency* (Arakawa, 1965, *Ann. Paediat.*, Basel, **205**, 1) have been described. Both are associated with mental subnormality.

other histidine derivatives is also excreted in histidinaemia, just as phenyllactic acid, phenylacetic acid and other derivatives are excreted in phenylketonuria. The striking difference in the consequences of the metabolic lesions
in the two conditions is the still unexplained lower incidence of severe subnormality in histidinaemia. The reason for this is not known. A possible
explanation might be the much higher renal clearance of histidine compared
to phenylalanine (Cusworth and Dent, 1960). In histidinaemic infants the
blood level of histidine is about ten times the normal; in the untreated phenylketonuric infant the serum phenylalanine is usually twenty to over fifty times
the normal.

It is likely that affected children would, if treated early, benefit from a
diet low in histidine, and such a diet is now available commercially. Full
details of all aspects of this disease will be found in the papers of Ghadimi
et al., (1962); Holton *et al.*, (1964); Woody *et al.*, (1965); and LaDu (1966b).

Morbid Anatomy
No autopsy findings have as yet been reported.

Laboratory Diagnosis
The problem here is primarily one of detection. Histidinuria is sometimes
found during pregnancy, in certain vitamin deficiencies, in kwashiorkor and,
occasionally, following treatment with anticonvulsants (*vide* p. 77). It is a
frequent non-specific finding in severely subnormal children. Misdiagnosis is
therefore likely. Furthermore, some histidinaemic patients are of normal intelligence and abnormalities in their amino acid metabolism may not be suspected. A proportion of cases will be found with the routine 'phenistix' or
ferric chloride tests given by health visitors to most babies. However, as already mentioned, these tests are only intermittently positive in histidinaemia.
Possibly the best hope of detecting the disease is with the chromatographic
screening test described by Scriver *et al.* (1964) (cf. p. 341) and by the use of
the Pauly diazo stain on urinary chromatograms. This may disclose a number
of imidazoles in addition to histidine. The presence of histidase activity in the
skin does not exclude histidinaemia; Woody *et al.*, (1965) found such activity
in some of his cases.

Hyperprolinaemia and Hydroxyprolinaemia

Chemical Pathology
Hereditary disorders of imino acid metabolism are rare even compared
with the other conditions in this chapter, but they are of considerable theoretical importance. Until recently it was believed that proline and hydroxyproline,
which differ only by one hydroxy group, were metabolised by the same enzymes (Fig. 110).

However, Efron and her colleagues (Efron, 1965b; Efron *et al.*, 1965) have
established that the enzymes are not identical. Metabolic blocks have been
identified in three positions: at the levels of proline oxidase, hydroxyproline
oxidase, and that of Δ^1-pyrroline-5-carboxylic acid dehydrogenase. Hyperprolinaemia with proline oxidase deficiency has been described by her in two

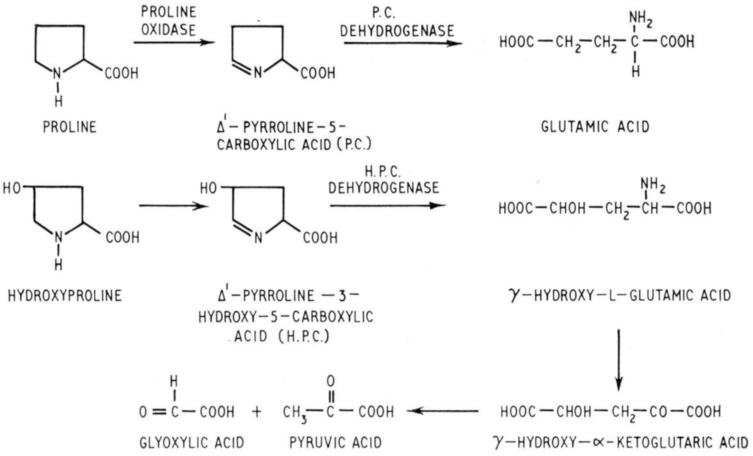

PROLINE OXIDASE → P.C. DEHYDROGENASE → $HOOC-CH_2-CH_2-\underset{\underset{H}{|}}{\overset{\overset{NH_2}{|}}{C}}-COOH$

PROLINE Δ^1-PYRROLINE-5-CARBOXYLIC ACID (P.C.)   GLUTAMIC ACID

H.P.C. DEHYDROGENASE → $HOOC-CHOH-CH_2-\overset{\overset{NH_2}{|}}{CH}-COOH$

HYDROXYPROLINE Δ^1-PYRROLINE − 3 − HYDROXY−5−CARBOXYLIC ACID (H.P.C.) γ−HYDROXY−L−GLUTAMIC ACID

$O=\overset{\overset{H}{|}}{C}-COOH$ + $CH_3-\overset{\overset{O}{||}}{C}-COOH$ ⟵ $HOOC-CHOH-CH_2-CO-COOH$

GLYOXYLIC ACID   PYRUVIC ACID γ−HYDROXY−α−KETOGLUTARIC ACID

FIG. 110. The metabolism of the imino acids.

families affected by hereditary renal disease*. In one family the affected child suffered also from nerve deafness and epilepsy. The mildly mentally retarded propositus in the second family presented malformation of the kidney and died in uraemia. Renal disease and haematuria but not the aminoaciduria seem to be transmitted from parent to child. Some sibs of the affected subjects displayed hyperprolinaemia without signs of renal dysfunction other than haematuria, and were of normal intelligence.

The child with hyperprolinaemia due to Δ^1-pyrroline-5-carboxylic acid dehydrogenase deficiency showed mild mental retardation and convulsions during a febrile illness, but no evidence of renal disease. His blood proline level was higher than in the cases with proline oxidase deficiency, and he also excreted Δ^1-pyrroline-5-carboxylic acid.

Yet another mentally retarded child, the only case described so far of *hydroxyprolinaemia*, was found to have blood hydroxyproline levels 20–50 times higher than normal. This was due to a deficiency in hydroxyproline oxidase. No hydroxyproline was detected in his C.S.F. (Efron et al., 1965). Hydroxyproline constitutes 14 per cent. of collagen and has no other known rôle in mammalian metabolism. However, the patient with hydroxyprolinaemia gave no indication of a disturbance of collagen metabolism. The plasma level did not fall when the child was placed on a diet low in hydroxyproline. This illustrates the difficulty of devising dietary treatment for a disorder of a non-essential amino acid which can be readily synthesized in the body, in contrast to disorders of essential amino acids, when the blood level can be lowered by dietary restriction. The origin of the accumulated hydroxyproline and its relationship to the mental retardation are unknown.

As proline, hydroxyproline and glycine share at least part of the same renal tubular reabsorption mechanism, all three amino acids may be found in excess in the urine in both hyperprolinaemia and hydroxyprolinaemia.

* See also Kopelman, H., Asattoor, A. M., and Milne, M. D. (1964). *Lancet*, **2**, 1075.

Morbid Anatomy

The autopsy findings in one case of prolinaemia have been reported by Efron (1966a). The brain showed absence of the ventral portion of the inferior olive and diffuse neuronal loss in the cortex. Patchy loss of ganglion cells was present in the organ of Corti.

Laboratory Diagnosis

Chromatography of the urinary amino acids is not a reliable method for diagnosing hyperprolinaemia. In normal children proline is not found in the urine after the first few months of life. It can be detected in the urine of some hyperprolinaemics but not in those whose serum proline is not high enough to be excreted. Conversely, some patients with renal tubular disease may have prolinuria. Cases are more reliably detected by testing the serum and urine concurrently (cf. Appendix 2). These screening tests are particularly sensitive in detecting hydroxyproline when isatin is used as an amino acid stain followed by Ehrlich's reagent (Smith, 1960).

In view of the association of hyperprolinaemia with renal malformation and haematuria in two families, Efron (1965b) recommends that the blood of any patient with renal malformations and unexplained familial renal disease should be screened for raised plasma proline levels.

Hyperglycinaemia

Chemical Pathology

Only nine patients with this condition have been reported so far. This may be partly due to the severity of the neonatal manifestations of the disease and frequent early death; it has indeed been suggested that some cases die *in utero*. Clinically, the disease may simulate maple syrup urine disease. Its most prominent features are vomiting, metabolic and respiratory acidosis, and acetonuria. The urine may also contain methyl ethyl ketone and 5 and 6 carbon ketones (Menkes, 1966). Extreme hypotonia and an abnormal E.C.G. have also been noted. Patients who survived the first few months showed osteoporosis, thrombocytopenia and neutropenia. The family histories suggest a hereditary metabolic disease, but the underlying enzymatic defect is not known.

The more important metabolic pathways of glycine are shown in Fig. 111. There is some evidence that the conversion of glycine to serine is defective in hyperglycinaemia. Failure to incorporate glycine into the porphyrin pathway has also been considered because iron-containing pigment was found in the reticuloendothelial cells of the liver, spleen and bone marrow of an affected child who died aged 2 months. The significance of this observation is, however, uncertain since such pigment is relatively common in the reticuloendothelial system of young infants. It has also been suggested that the defect involves the enzyme glycine oxidase. The position is thus still unsettled and, indeed, one cannot exclude the possibility that the disturbance of glycine metabolism is a secondary and not a primary phenomenon.

Some clinical improvement can be obtained by a low protein diet (<0.5 g./kg./day). Of the dietary amino acids *leucine* in particular is liable to precipitate symptoms without, however, producing hypoglycaemia (cf. leucine induced hypoglycaemia, p. 295). Various aspects of this disease have recently been

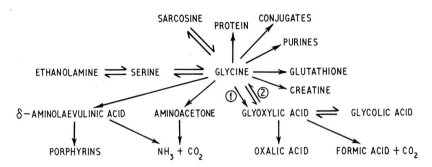

① GLYCINE TRANSAMINASE. INHIBITION OF THIS ENZYME ENHANCES
   FORMATION OF OXALATE

② GLYCINE OXIDASE

Fig. 111. The metabolism of glycine*.

discussed by Visser, Veenstra and Pik (1964) and Wyngaarden and Segal (1966). A variant of this condition with hyperglycinaemia and hypooxaluria has been described by Gerritsen, Kaveggia and Waisman (1965), who consider that their patient had a deficiency of glycine oxidase.

Morbid Anatomy

Necropsies so far carried out have failed to reveal significant abnormalities. No neuropathological studies have been reported.

Laboratory Diagnosis

Diagnosis is not easy since most patients die soon after birth. The disease should be suspected if the family history is positive, and if acetone is present in the urine, since acetonuria is otherwise unusual in the first days of life. Clinically, the disorder may be confused with maple syrup urine disease (cf. p. 267), but in hyperglycinaemia there is, of course, no excess of the branched-chain amino acids in the blood and urine, and no branched-chain keto acids have been found in the urine. The excretion of the straight chain keto acids may be raised threefold. Chromatography shows pronounced hyperglycinaemia with a lesser elevation of other plasma amino acids, and increased excretion of glycine in the urine (p. 341). These findings confirm the diagnosis and also differentiate the disease from the renal tubular glycinurias, in which the plasma glycine level is normal. The ferric chloride test is negative in hyperglycinaemia.

* A family with *hypersarcosinaemia* has been described by Waisman, H. A. (1966). *Pediat. Clin. N. Amer.*, **13**, 469. The block is between glycine and sarcosine.

Homocystinuria and Cystathioninuria

Chemical Pathology

Homocystinuria and cystathioninuria are inborn errors of the metabolism of the sulphur-containing amino acid methionine (Gerritsen and Waisman, 1966) (Fig. 112). Over 25 cases of *homocystinuria* have been diagnosed in Great Britain and the U.S.A. within the space of 2 years; of the neuro-metabolic disorders it is therefore probably second only to phenylketonuria in incidence. Homocystinuria is also remarkable because at least some of the cases can almost be diagnosed on clinical grounds alone: ectopia lentis accompanied by tremor of the iris, fine fair hair, a malar flush, and skeletal deformities, which include long, thin limbs, genu valgum and kyphoscoliosis strongly suggest the diagnosis. The long, thin limbs of the patients have suggested Marfan's syndrome to some authors, and Brenton *et al.* (1966) report that the radiological appearances in one of their patients were somewhat reminiscent of those found in acromegalic gigantism. Thromboembolic accidents occur, even in young patients. The electroencephalogram may show generalised dysrhythmia, and some patients suffer from major fits. More than half the patients are mentally retarded. Cystathioninuria is much rarer and the patient reported by Harris *et al.*, (1959) was mentally subnormal; the psychiatric symptoms in another case reported by Frimpter, Haymovitz and Horwith (1963) were stated to be those of a paranoid psychosis.

It has been established by Mudd *et al.*, (1964) and by Brenton, Cusworth and Gaull (1965 a and b) that patients with homocystinuria are deficient in the enzyme cystathionine synthetase which normally occurs both in the liver and brain. It is of interest, however, that the deficiency of this enzyme does not appear to be ubiquitous. A homocystinuric patient was found, for example, to possess this enzyme in the optic lens (Gaull and Gaitonde, 1966). In cystathioninuria the enzyme cystathioninase is affected (Fig. 112). In patients with homocystinuria the level of cystathionine in the brain and other tissues is low while homocysteine accumulates. Some is methylated back to methionine and some is oxidised to homocystine which can be detected in the plasma and is excreted in the urine. As one might expect, there is delay in the disappearance of methionine from the blood of patients after methionine loading, and increased homocystine excretion. The pattern of inheritance is almost certainly recessive. In many recessively inherited diseases, such as phenylketonuria, it is possible to identify heterozygotes by appropriate load tests (p. 267) but the results of methionine loading in the parents of homocystinurics have not been clear-cut. The condition has been recently studied and described by Brenton, Cusworth, Dent and Jones (1966).

In *cystathioninuria*, where the enzymatic block occurs at the cystathioninase level, cystathionine accumulates in the tissues*. Elevated blood levels cannot be detected because of the rapid renal clearance of cystathionine. Large quantities of cystathionine are excreted in the urine. The mechanism of the mental

* A variant with thrombocytopenia and urinary caluli has been described in a mentally normal child by Mongeau, J.-G. *et al.*, (1966). *J. Pediat.*, **69**, 1113.

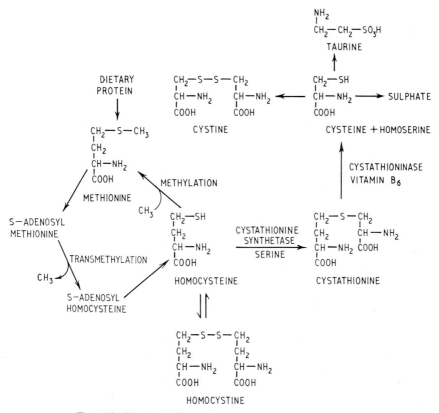

FIG. 112. The metabolism of homocystine and cystathionine.

defect in cystathioninuria is not known. In homocystinuria the mental defect could be due to a deficiency of cystine or cystathionine, or to an excess of methionine. It is not yet clear what rôle is played by cystathionine other than that of an intermediary in the formation of cysteine. Cystine is clearly an essential amino acid for homocystinurics. Direct measurement of its level in the tissues of two untreated patients failed to show any deficiency. It is therefore more likely that excess of methionine or some of its metabolites is responsible for the brain damage (Carson, Dent, Field and Gaull, 1965). If this is so, affected infants should benefit from a diet low in methionine*. Such a diet should also protect patients from the already mentioned frequent thromboembolic accidents. McDonald et al. (1964) have shown that there is an increased platelet adhesiveness in homocystinuria, and that this is due to homocystine, which is present in the blood of these patients in amounts of 1–3mg./100ml. This level should decrease in patients on a methionine low diet.

It has recently been shown that in cystathioninuria the inactive enzyme

* See Komrower, G. M. et al. (1966). Arch. Dis. Childh., 41, 666.

cystathioninase can be activated by massive doses of vitamin B_6 (Frimpter, 1966; Efron, 1965a). At least one case benefited from vitamin B_6 treatment. The basic defect may thus be in the binding of the vitamin to the apoenzyme.

Morbid Anatomy

Thromboembolic and cardiovascular disease are frequent causes of death in homocystinurics. Necropsy findings have included patchy fibrosis of the intima and general degenerative changes of elastic tissue. Severe fatty change in the liver, unassociated with cirrhosis, is also a constant if non-specific finding (Carson *et al.*, 1965; Gibson, Carson and Neill, 1964). A brain examined by Gibson, Carson and Neill showed partial atrophy with brown discolouration and gliosis of one of the cerebral hemispheres, and this was considered to be the result of infarction. The superior sagittal sinus also showed evidence of thrombosis and recanalization. Three of the four cases described by Gibson, Carson and Neill presented features which were regarded by the authors as evidence of associated Marfan's syndrome but such association was not fully confirmed by other workers. In another of their cases the kidney had been removed during life for hypertension. The smaller renal vessels presented irregular proliferation of fibrous and elastic fibres of the intima, and metachromatic staining of the media. The anatomical changes indicate therefore recurrent episodes of thrombosis in many vessels. A case regarded as one of homocystinuria by Chou and Waisman (1965) showed 'thromboembolism' of the right major pulmonary artery, microgyria and widespread spongiform encephalopathy. The ocular changes in one and the neuropathological changes in 3 cases of homocystinuria are reported in greater detail by White *et al.*, (1965). The eye showed dislocation of the lens, atrophy and fibrosis of the ciliary muscle, scarring of the cornea, focal epithelial abrasion and anterior stromal keratitis. The brains showed numerous infarcted areas (encephalomalacia) and thrombosis of numerous veins and arteries.

The brain of a homocystinuric patient aged 9 years was examined at Queen Mary's Hospital for Children (unpublished personal observation). In addition to terminal ante-mortem changes, which included thrombosis of the vena terminalis, the cerebral cortex showed mild neuronal depletion. Neuronal loss and fibrous gliosis were present in the Ammon's horn and its end-folium. The most conspicuous lesions were seen, however, in the posterior part of the thalamus close to its junction with the pulvinar. These were focal areas of incomplete necrosis with disappearance of nerve cells and proliferation of microglia (Fig. 113). The myelin was degenerate and a small amount of fibrous gliosis was demonstrable in some of the affected foci. The thalamus and brainstem also showed areas of tissue rarefaction without glial reactive change, and other areas of diffuse gliosis were present in the midbrain and around the third and fourth ventricles. Some rarefaction of tissue without glial response was seen in a few areas of the grey matter in the tegmentum of the pons. The cerebellum showed slight loss of Purkinje cells with preservation of the basket fibres. Some of the above changes may have been caused by thrombosis but this could not be conclusively demonstrated.

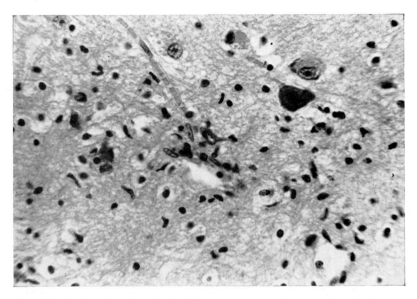

FIG. 113. A necrotizing focus in the thalamus in a case of homocystinuria. (Haematoxylin and eosin × 200.)

Laboratory Diagnosis

It has been mentioned already that the appearance of the patient and the characteristic ocular lesions will often lead to the diagnosis of homocystinuria (Schimke *et al.*, 1965). A simple urine test with nitroprusside is useful in screening suspected cases (cf. Appendix, p. 341). The diagnosis may also be made by paper chromatography of the urine (p. 343). It is not, however, easy to separate homocystine from cystine by the chromatographic methods employed in most laboratories, and cystine may be present in small amounts in the urine of normal children. Also, according to some workers, the amounts of homocystine excreted may be quite small: of the order of 50 mg./day, and sometimes much less. In cystinuria, by contrast, cystine excretion rates of 500–1000 mg./day are quite common. The diagnosis should therefore be confirmed in all cases by an oral or intravenous methionine load test. The plasma methionine usually returns to normal levels within 24 hours; in homocystinurics it remains elevated for at least 3 days. No clear-cut pattern has been established for heterozygotes (Brenton *et al.*, 1965a).

Cases of cystathioninuria are most likely to be detected chromatographically by the very large amounts of cystathionine excreted in the urine. High urinary concentrations of cystathionine are also found in some patients with adrenal neuroblastoma and the excretion of cystathionine may be slightly elevated in cases of thoracic and cervical neuroblastoma, but these conditions are readily distinguishable from cystathioninuria by the raised levels of the catechol amines and their metabolites.

Disorders Involving the Krebs-Henseleit Urea Cycle

Chemical Pathology

Mammals excrete as urea most of their superfluous amino acids. The sequence of the enzymic reactions—the Krebs-Henseleit cycle (not to be confused with the Krebs citric acid cycle)—is shown in Fig. 114. Urea is produced

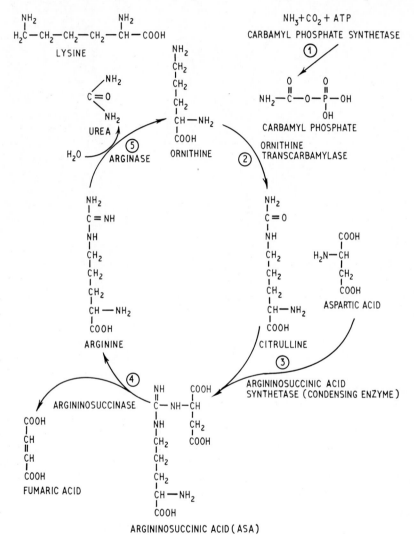

FIG. 114. The Krebs-Henseleit urea cycle.

from ammonia, carbon dioxide and aspartic acid. The enzymes responsible for reactions 1, 2, 3 and 4, i.e. carbamyl phosphate synthetase, ornithine transcarbamylase, argininosuccinic acid synthetase and argininosuccinase are widely distributed in the tissues. Arginase, reaction 5, on the other hand, is largely confined to the liver, which is therefore the major site of urea formation. Urea is also produced in the brain and kidney, but at a much slower rate. Disturbances of amino acid metabolism and accumulation of ammonia may follow a defect at any point of the urea cycle.

Four disorders of the Krebs-Henseleit cycle are in most cases associated with mental subnormality. The first to be discovered was *argininosuccinic-aciduria* (Allan *et al.*, 1958; Levin *et al.*, 1961, p. 198). It is generally accepted that in this disease there is a defect in reaction 4 normally catalysed by the enzyme argininosuccinase. As a consequence large amounts of argininosuccinic acid accumulate in the body fluids. The levels in the cerebrospinal fluid are, surprisingly, higher than those in the plasma. Argininosuccinic acid cannot be detected in the body fluids of normal subjects by routine clinical chemical methods.

In *citrullinuria* (McMurray *et al.*, 1963) citrulline is found in large amounts in the body fluids, but in this condition the plasma level of citrulline is higher than that in the cerebrospinal fluid. The presumed enzyme deficiency is of argininosuccinic acid synthetase (reaction 3). The excretion of argininosuccinic acid in argininosuccinicaciduria and of citrulline in citrullinuria is influenced by the intake of protein and of the amino acids involved in the urea cycle, but there is no clear-cut quantitative relationship between these factors. High blood ammonia levels have been found in citrullinuria.

In *hyperammonaemia*, the third of these disorders, the chief and only major biochemical abnormality is, as the name implies, excess of blood ammonia (p. 204). This can arise in two ways: due to a deficiency of the enzyme ornithine transcarbamylase—reaction 2 (Russell *et al.*, 1962), or of the enzyme carbamyl phosphate synthetase—reaction 1 (Freeman *et al.*, 1964). These defects could, in fact, be demonstrated in the affected children by liver biopsy. It must be mentioned that the apparently uniovular twin of one of the cases with the ornithine transcarbamylase defect was clinically well but had a high normal blood ammonia level. In both types of hyperammonaemia a low protein diet reduces blood ammonia.

It is probable that the fourth disorder, *hyperlysinaemia*, also comprises more than one disease entity. In the child reported by Colombo *et al.*, (1964) the plasma lysine level was raised on a normal or high protein intake. The plasma arginine and ammonia were also raised. Urinary amino acids were normal. The plasma amino acid pattern was normal when the child was on a low protein diet. The enzymes of the urea cycle were present in normal amounts in a biopsy of the liver, which showed histologically slight fatty infiltration but no cirrhosis. The authors concluded that there was an impairment of lysine metabolism which resulted in its accumulation in the body fluids. Lysine is well known as a potent competitive inhibitor of arginase, and it is this inhibition which is believed to limit the effectiveness of the urea cycle and to slow down ammonia detoxication.

The child with hyperlysinaemia studied by Woody (1964) differed in many important respects. In this case evidence did not support a fault in the urea cycle (cf. Ghadimi *et al.*, 1964). Lysine levels were raised in the plasma, cerebrospinal fluid and urine. The blood ammonia level was not recorded. Ornithine, γ-aminobutyric acid and, sometimes, arginine and cystine were also increased in the urine. The biochemical abnormalities were not affected by changes in the diet, but reduction of lysine intake was followed by some improvement in the patient's normocytic normochromic anaemia. A similar pattern of urinary abnormalities was detected in an ostensibly normal cousin. The author suggested that in this disorder there existed some defect in the incorporation of lysine into protein because the clinical picture of convulsions, weakness of the muscles and ligaments, and of anaemia was not unlike that seen in experimental animals on a lysine deficient diet.

Certain features are common to all four disorders. All patients have suffered from vomiting, convulsions or other neurological symptoms, such as hyperreflexia, tremor or stupor. Liver dysfunction was present in some cases. All these disorders are rare. At the time of writing six families with argininosuccinicaciduria have been described, one with hyperammonaemia type 1, one with hyperammonaemia type 2, three with citrullinuria and three with hyperlysinaemia (Efron, 1966b). The age of onset of some of these conditions is variable and the same may be true of their severity. The uniovular twin of a child with hyperammonaemia who was clinically well and the ostensibly normal cousin of a child with hyperlysinaemia, who had the same abnormal urinary amino acid pattern as the propositus, have already been mentioned. It may well be that these children were suffering from a mild form of the disease. On the other hand, in the family described by Freeman *et al.* (1964) the propositus died at 5 months with severe ketosis and acidosis. Two of his sibs had also died in infancy with severe neurological symptoms and there had been three miscarriages in the family.

It is strange that the blood urea should be normal in all four diseases in spite of the enzyme deficiencies. (Raised blood urea levels do occur in argininosuccinicaciduria after a meal). This could mean that the block is partial and only becomes apparent during accelerated ammonia metabolism. Alternatively, the block could be extrahepatic and specific for certain organs such as the brain. This second alternative has been mooted, in particular, for argininosuccinicaciduria, as in this disorder argininosuccinic acid is higher in the C.S.F. than in plasma.

Again, it is reasonable to infer a causal relationship between the neurological signs, which are often like those observed in hepatic coma, and the raised ammonia levels found in some of these disorders. The combination of ammonia with α-oxoglutarate to glutamic acid could deplete the Krebs citric acid cycle of its substrate and impair the aerobic metabolism of the brain. However, according to modern views on the mechanism of hepatic coma summarized by Sherlock (1964), this is an oversimplification. While the hepatic syndrome may be produced in some people by administering ammonium salts, experimental evidence now favours the proposition that the high ammonia levels are an indication of disturbed brain metabolism rather than its cause, and that the high concentration of ammonia reported in uraemia is not toxic to the normal brain. On the other hand, it must be pointed out that the levels reported in hyperammonaemia, citrullinuria and hyperlysinaemia are even higher than those found in hepatic coma, and that, moreover, the developing brain may be specially susceptible to toxic damage by ammonia.

Morbid Anatomy

No neuropathological studies of any of these diseases appear to have yet been published.

Laboratory Diagnosis

Argininosuccinicaciduria being a no-threshold aminoaciduria is best detected by chromatography or high voltage electrophoresis of the urine and C.S.F. The blood levels are too low for the routine screening methods. On urinary chromatograms argininosuccinic acid may show up in the form of two of its anhydrides (p. 343).

Citrullinuria and hyperlysinaemia are probably best detected by serum chromatography (p. 341). The colour reaction given by citrulline with Ehrlich's reagent will help in its detection, but care must be taken not to confuse it with the homocitrulline of dietary origin found in the urine of some bottle-fed infants (Efron, 1966b).

Biochemical estimations other than that of blood ammonia are of little help in the diagnosis of hyperammonaemia. Increased glutamine levels in the urine and C.S.F. may provide a clue to the raised ammonia levels.

Hartnup Disease

Chemical Pathology

This disorder was discovered in a family of eight children born to first-cousin parents. Two of the children had intermittent cerebellar ataxia, a pellagra-like rash and gross aminoaciduria; two others showed mild skin changes and aminoaciduria, and the remaining four were normal (Baron *et al.*, 1956). About another dozen cases have since been described. Mental retardation is by no means constant. Some patients show instead periodic psychiatric disturbance, and others are asymptomatic for long periods. Neuropsychiatric symptoms may be precipitated by febrile illness, gastrointestinal disorders or inadequate diet. Family studies suggest autosomal recessive transmission of the disease.

While the clinical picture is thus variable, massive aminoaciduria is constant. As the plasma amino acid levels are normal or low the aminoaciduria is of renal tubular origin. The reabsorption of only the neutral amino acids is affected; the reabsorption of the basic and acidic (dicarboxylic) amino acids, glycine, the imino acids and methionine is normal. The transport defect has also been observed in the small intestine and, since it is likely that the same enzymatic mechanisms for the uptake of amino acids operate in most cells, the defect is probably also present in other organs. Malabsorption of tryptophan is of special significance. This amino acid is metabolised by intestinal microorganisms to indole, indolylacetic acid, tryptamine and other derivatives, which are absorbed, metabolised further, and excreted in the urine. In Hartnup disease excessive amounts of indoxyl sulphate, indolylacetic acid, indolylacetylglutamine and other indole derivatives are often detected in the urine. The abnormal indole pattern can be almost completely suppressed by sterilizing the gut with antibiotics, thus indicating the bacterial origin of the excessive urinary indoles. Some of these indoles inhibit the enzymes (Fig. 64) of the major metabolic pathway of tryptophan to nicotinamide. Three factors thus contribute to nicotinamide deficiency; low absorption of tryptophan, its excessive loss in the urine and inhibition of the *in vivo* synthesis. The poor absorption of most of the other essential amino acids retards the weight and height gain of the children.

As many of the clinical features stem directly from nicotinamide deficiency, dietary supplementation of this vitamin is indicated. Fuller clinical and biochemical details of the condition will be found in the publications by Milne *et al.* (1960); Scriver (1965); Jepson (1966); and Woolf (1966).

In Hartnup disease the defect of tryptophan metabolism is, as stated, one of transport. Nicotinamide deficiency can, however, also be caused by a block in tryptophan metabolism. Komrower *et al.* (1964) have studied a child who probably had a deficiency of the enzyme kynureninase and who developed signs of nicotinamide deficiency while on a milk diet. This patient excreted excessive amounts of kynurenine, 3-hydroxykynurenine and xanthurenic acid in the urine, and did not respond to pyridoxine therapy. Administration of nicotinamide was followed by marked clinical improvement. The patient was not mentally retarded, her verbal I.Q. at eight years being 96. Komrower *et al.* suggest the name *hydroxykynureninuria* for this disorder. Jepson (1966) refers to a case of *tryptophanuria with dwarfism*. In this condition failure of enzymic conversion of tryptophan to kynurenine is associated with ataxia and a pellagra-like rash.

Morbid Anatomy

No information as to morphological changes in this disease is available.

Laboratory Diagnosis

Nutritional vitamin B deficiency is exceedingly rare in this country. Hartnup disease or kynureninase deficiency should therefore be suspected whenever pellagra-like signs are associated with mental retardation or psychiatric disturbance. The diagnosis is easily confirmed by any of the published chromatographic screening tests for aminoaciduria (Appendices 2 and 3). These will also detect the disease in its quiescent, symptom-free stage. Excretion of indoles may be normal at this stage. Kynureninase deficiency can best be confirmed by a tryptophan load test (O'Brien and Ibbott, 1962; Walsh, 1965) (p. 347).

Cerebrooculorenal Syndrome (Lowe's Syndrome)

Chemical Pathology

This syndrome, first described by Lowe, Terrey and MacLachlan (1952), is characterized, as the name implies, by lesions of the eyes, viz. congenital cataracts and buphthalmos, neurological abnormalities, such as hypotonia with absent or reduced tendon reflexes, mental retardation, and multiple progressive renal tubular defects. Available evidence favours sex-linked transmission. The presumed heterozygous carriers are clinically normal, but some show renal tubular aminoaciduria and in others slit lamp examination reveals opacities of the crystalline lens (Richards *et al.*, 1965; Woolf, 1966).

Disturbance of proximal tubular function is the cardinal feature of the disease. Its severity varies from patient to patient, and from time to time in the same case. Proteinuria is persistent but often mild and 'tubular' in type, that is with globulin rather than albumin predominating. The urine shows reduced tubular reabsorption of phosphate and a generalized aminoaciduria which is, however, less severe than in, for example, the Fanconi syndrome. Glucose reabsorption is also impaired, but the glycosuria is often too slight to reduce Benedict's solution. Mild or moderate hyperchloraemic acidosis is almost constant. Ammonium chloride loading lowers urinary pH, but for a given serum bicarbonate level the urinary pH is above normal and in most cases the ability of the renal tubules to form ammonia is somewhat impaired. A reduced creatinine clearance, indicating glomerular damage, may be found in the later stages of the disease.

Richards *et al.* believe that the renal tubular defects are secondary rather than primary, being caused by the deposition of a proteinaceous material in the lumina of the tubules. This leads to their eventual destruction, glomerular damage and fibrosis.

It may be reasonably asked whether the cerebrooculorenal syndrome constitutes a separate disease entity. Congenital cataracts, renal tubular dysfunction due to a combination of environmental factors, such as vitamin deficiency, chronic lead intoxication or intercurrent infection, and neurological signs as in Lowe's syndrome are not very rare in the mentally retarded and could well occur by chance in the same patient. It is noteworthy in this connection that a number of variants of Lowe's syndrome have been described. In at least one of these the brain changes appeared to be antenatal in origin (McCance *et al.*, 1960).

Nevertheless, cerebrooculorenal syndrome is probably a reasonable concept. The term should perhaps be reserved for cases with evidence of a sex-linked recessive mode of inheritance in addition to the clinical and biochemical features of the disease. The number of such cases is likely to prove exceedingly small.

Morbid Anatomy

Some rather brief and incompletely documented observations on the pathological findings in material from cases of Lowe's syndrome have been reported by Richards *et al.* (1965). The kidneys showed changes ranging from tubular dilatation to destruction of tubular epithelium, interstitial fibrosis and hyalinization of glomeruli. The seminiferous tubules of the testes were narrowed and there was some fibrosis. The posterior halves of two eyes were examined and these are said to have shown irregularity in the shape of the retinal nerve cells. Two brains were studied. One was small and said to have shown pachygyria, pontine atrophy and, possibly, cerebellar hypoplasia. The only macroscopic change presented by the other was meningeal thickening. Histologically, both brains showed rarefaction of the molecular layer with vacuolization of the subpial parenchyma, some perivascular rarefaction and proliferation of arterial endothelium. The authors also mention an unspecified abnormality in cortical lamination and foci of 'acute demyelination' in one of the cases.

Widespread spongiform degeneration of the white and grey matter, neuronal depletion, cerebellar dysplasia, cataracts and renal tubular necrosis were present in two infant sisters, who could have been atypical instances of Lowe's syndrome (Crome, Duckett and Franklin, 1963).

Laboratory Diagnosis

The diagnosis will be suggested by the neurological and ophthalmological findings in association with acidosis and manifold tubular dysfunction. The two-way urinary amino acid chromatogram will show increased amounts of the 'central cluster' amino acids, such as glycine, serine, alanine, glutamine, histidine, methyl histidine, threonine and, occasionally, increased amounts of citrulline, ornithine, proline, lysine, arginine, leucine, isoleucine, valine and phenylalanine (p. 343). The findings vary from case to case and depend to some extent on the patient's diet and the sensitivity of the laboratory methods used. Ingestion of ornithine is said to intensify the abnormal amino acid pattern (Schwartz, Hall and Gabuzda, 1964). The concentration of glucose and protein in the urine is usually less than 100 mg./100 ml.

REFERENCES

ALLAN, J. D., CUSWORTH, D. C., DENT, C. E., and WILSON, V. K. (1958). *Lancet*, **1**, 182.
BARON, D. N., DENT, C. E., HARRIS, H., HART, E. W., and JEPSON, J. B. (1956). *Lancet*, **2**, 421.
BECHAR, M., BORNSTEIN, B., ELIAN, M., and SANDBANK, U. (1965). *J. Neurol. Neurosurg. Psychiat.*, **28**, 165.
BLATTNER, R. J. (1965). *J. Pediat.*, **66**, 139.
BRENTON, D. P., CUSWORTH, D. C., and GAULL, G. E. (1965a). *Pediatrics*, **35**, 50.
BRENTON, D. P., CUSWORTH, D. C., and GAULL, G. E. (1965b). *J. Pediat.*, **67**, 58.
BRENTON, D. P., CUSWORTH, D. C., DENT, C. E., and JONES, E. E. (1966). *Quart. J. Med.*, **35**, 325.
CARSON, N. A. J., DENT, C. E., FIELD, C. M. B., and GAULL, G. E. (1965). *J. Pediat.*, **66**, 565.
CHOU, SH. -M., and WAISMAN, H. A. (1965). *Arch. Path.*, **79**, 357.
COLOMBO, J. P., RICHTERICH, R., SPAHR, A., DONATH, A., and ROSSI, E. (1964). *Lancet*, **1**, 1014.
CROME, L. (1962). *J. Neurol. Neurosurg. Psychiat.*, **25**, 143.
CROME, L., and PARE, C. M. B. (1960). *J. ment. Sci.*, **106**, 862.
CROME, L., DUTTON, G., and ROSS, C. F. (1961). *J. Path. Bact.*, **81**, 379.
CROME, L., TYMMS, V., and WOOLF, L. I. (1962). *J. Neurol. Neurosurg. Psychiat.*, **25**, 143.
CROME, L., DUCKETT, S., and FRANKLIN, A. W. (1963). *Arch. Dis. Childh.*, **38**, 505.

Cusworth, D. C., and Dent, C. E. (1960). *Biochem. J.*, **74**, 550.
Diezel, P. B., and Martin, K. (1964). *Virchows Arch. path. Anat.*, **337**, 425.
Efron, M. L. (1965a). *New Engl. J. Med.*, **272**, 1058 and 1107.
Efron, M. L. (1965b). *New Engl. J. Med.*, **272**, 1243.
Efron, M. L. (1966a). In Stanbury, J. B., Wyngaarden, J. B., and Fredrickson, D. S. 'The Metabolic Basis of Inherited Disease,' New York: McGraw-Hill, p. 376.
Efron, M. L. (1966b). In Stanbury, J. B., Wyngaarden, J. B., and Fredrickson, D. S. 'The Metabolic Basis of Inherited Disease,' New York: McGraw-Hill, p. 393.
Efron, M. L., Young, D., Moser, H. W., and MacCready, R. A. (1964). *New Engl. J. Med.*, **270**, 1378.
Efron, M. L., Bixby, E. M., and Pryles, C. V. (1965). *New Engl. J. Med.*, **272**, 1300.
Fölling, A. (1934). *Hoppe-Seylers Z. physiol. Chem.*, **227**, 169.
Foote, J. L., Allen, R. J., and Agranoff, B. W. (1965). *J. Lipid Res.*, **6**, 518.
Freeman, J. M., Nicholson, J. F., Masland, W. S., Rowland, L. P., and Carter, S. (1964). *J. Pediat.*, **65**, 1039.
Frimpter, G. W. (1966). In Stanbury, J. B., Wyngaarden, J. B., and Fredrickson, D. S. 'The Metabolic Basis of Inherited Disease,' New York: McGraw-Hill, p. 409.
Frimpter, G. W., Haymovitz, A., and Horwith, M. (1963). *New Engl. J. Med.*, **263**, 333.
Gaull, G., and Gaitonde, M. K. (1966). *J. med. Genet.*, **3**, 194.
Gentz, J., Jagenburg, R., and Zetterström, R. (1965). *J. Pediat.*, **66**, 670.
Gerritsen, T., Kaveggia, E., and Waisman, H. A. (1965). *Pediatrics*, **36**, 882.
Gerritsen, T., and Waisman, H. A. (1966). In Stanbury, J. B., Wyngaarden, J. B., and Fredrickson, D. S. 'The Metabolic Basis of Inherited Disease,' New York: McGraw-Hill, p. 420.
Ghadimi, H., Partington, M. W., and Hunter, A. (1962). *Pediatrics*, **29**, 714.
Ghadimi, H., Binnington, V. I., and Pecora, P. (1964). *J. Pediat.*, **65**, 1120.
Gibson, J. B., Carson, N. A., and Neill, D. W. (1964). *J. clin. Path.*, **17**, 427.
Gjessing, L. R., and Halvorsen, S. (1965). *Lancet*, **2**, 1132.
Gjessing, L. R., and Halvorsen, S. (1966). 'Symposium on Tyrosinosis,' Oslo: University Press.
Goedde, H. W., Richter, E., Stahlmann, C., and Sixel, B. (1963). *Klin. Wschr.*, **41**, 953.
Graham-Smith, D. G., and Moloney, L. (1965). *Biochem. J.*, **96**, 66P.
Guthrie, R., and Whitney, S. (1965). 'Phenylketonuria Detection in the Newborn Infant as a Routine Hospital Procedure,' U.S. Dept. of Health, Education and Welfare Administration, Washington.
Halvorsen, S., and Gjessing, L. R. (1964). *Brit. med. J.*, **2**, 1171.
Halvorsen, S., Pande, H., Aagot, C. L., and Gjessing, L. R. (1966). *Arch. Dis. Childh.*, **41**, 238.
Harris, H., Penrose, L. S., and Thomas, D. H. H. (1959). *Ann. hum. Genet.*, **23**, 442.
Holton, J. B., Lewis, F. J. W., and Moore, G. R. (1964). *J. clin. Path.*, **17**, 621.
Hooft, C., Timmermans, J., Snoeck, J., Antener, I., Oyaert, W., and Hende, Ch. van der. (1964). *Lancet*, **2**, 20.
Ireland, J. T. (1965). In Allan, J. D., and Holt, K. S. 'Biochemical Approaches to Mental Handicap in Childhood,' Edinburgh: Livingstone, p. 71.
Jepson, J. B. (1966). In Stanbury, J. B., Wyngaarden, J. B., and Fredrickson, D. S. 'The Metabolic Basis of Inherited Disease,' New York: McGraw-Hill, p. 1283.
Jepson, J. B., Smith, A. J., and Strang, L. B. (1958). *Lancet*, **2**, 1334.
Kang, E. S., Kennedy, J. L., Gates, L., Burwash, I., and McKinnon, A. (1965). *Pediatrics*, **35**, 932.
Kiil, R., and Rokkones, T. (1964). *Acta paediat. (Uppsala)*, **53**, 356.
Kirman, B. H. (1965). In Hilliard, L. T., and Kirman, B. H. 'Mental Deficiency,' London: Churchill, p. 486.
Knox, W. E. (1966). In Stanbury, J. B., Wyngaarden, J. B., and Fredrickson, D. S. 'The Metabolic Basis of Inherited Disease,' New York: McGraw-Hill, p. 258.
Komrower, G. M., Wilson, V., Clamp, J. R., and Westall, R. G. (1964). *Arch. Dis. Childh.*, **39**, 250.
LaDu, B. N. (1966a). In Stanbury, J. B., Wyngaarden, J. B., and Fredrickson, D. S. 'The Metabolic Basis of Inherited Disease,' New York: McGraw-Hill, p. 295.
LaDu, B. N. (1966b). *Ibid.* p. 366.

LEVIN, B., MACKAY, H. M. M., and OBERHOLZER, V. G. (1961). *Arch. Dis. Childh.*, **36**, 622.
LINNEWEH, F., and EHRLICH, M. (1963). *Klin. Wschr.*, **41**, 255.
LOWE, C. U., TERREY, M., and MACLACHLAN, E. A. (1952). *Amer. J. Dis. Child.*, **83**, 164.
MABRY, C. C., DENNISTON, J. C., NELSON, T. L., and SON, C. D. (1963). *New Engl. J. Med.*, **269**, 1404.
MALAMUD, N. (1966). *J. Neuropath. exp. Neurol.*, **25**, 254.
MANN, T. P., WILSON, K. M., and CLAYTON, B. E. (1965). *Arch. Dis. Childh.*, **40**, 364.
McCANCE, R. A., MATHESON, W. J., GRESHAM, G. A., and ELKINGTON, J. R. (1960). *Arch. Dis. Childh.*, **35**, 240.
McDONALD, L., BRAY, C., FIELD, C., LOVE, F., and DAVIES, B. (1964). *Lancet*, **1**, 745.
McMURRAY, W. C., RATHBUN, J. C., MOHYUDDIN, F., and KOEGLER, S. J. (1963). *Pediatrics*, **32**, 347.
MENKES, J. H. (1966). *J. Pediat.*, **69**, 413.
MENKES, J. H., HURST, P. L., and CRAIG, J. M. (1954). *Pediatrics*, **14**, 462.
MENKES, J. H., PHILIPPART, M., and FIOL, R. E. (1965). *J. Pediat.*, **66**, 584.
MILNE, M. D. (1964). *Brit. med. J.*, **2**, 327.
MILNE, M. D., CRAWFORD, M. A., GIRDO, C. B., and LOUGHRIDGE, L. W. (1960). *Quart. J. Med.*, **29**, 407.
MUDD, S. H., FINKELSTEIN, J. D., IRREVERE, F., and LASTER, L. (1964). *Science*, **143**, 1443.
O'BRIEN, D., and IBBOTT, F. A. (1962). 'Laboratory Manual of Pediatric Micro- and Ultramicro-Biochemical Techniques,' New York: Hoeber, p. 301.
PERRY, T. L., HARDWICK, D. F., DIXON, G. H., DOLMAN, C. L., and HANSEN, S. (1965). *Pediatrics*, **36**, 236.
RICHARDS, W., DONNELL, G. N., WILSON, W. A., STOWENS, D., and PERRY, T. (1965). *Amer. J. Dis. Child.*, **109**, 185.
RUSSELL, A., LEVIN, B., OBERHOLZER, V. G., and SINCLAIR, L. (1962). *Lancet*, **2**, 699.
SCHIMKE, R. N., McKUSICK, V. A., HUANG, T., and POLLACK, A. D. (1965). *J. Amer. med. Ass.*, **193**, 711.
SCHWARTZ, R., HALL, P. W., and GABUZDA, G. J. (1964). *Amer. J. Med.*, **36**, 778.
SCRIVER, C. R. (1962). In Steinberg, A. G., and Bearn, A. G. 'Progress in Medical Genetics, Vol. II,' New York: Grune and Stratton, p. 83.
SCRIVER, C. R. (1965). *New Engl. J. Med.*, **273**, 530.
SCRIVER, C. R., DAVIES, E., and CULLEN, A. (1964). *Lancet*, **2**, 230.
SCRIVER, C. R., CLOW, C. L., and SILVERBERG, M. (1966). *Lancet*, **1**, 153.
SHERLOCK, S. (1964). 'Diseases of the Liver and Biliary System,' Oxford: Blackwell.
SILBERMAN, J., DANCIS, J., and FEIGIN, I. (1961). *Arch. Neurol. (Chic.)*, **5**, 351.
SMITH, A. J., and STRANG, L. B. (1958). *Arch. Dis. Childh.*, **33**, 109.
SMITH, I. (1960). 'Chromatographic and Electrophoretic Techniques,' Vol. I., London: Heinemann, p. 82.
SNYDERMAN, S. E., NORTON, P. M., ROITMAN, E., and HOLT, L. E. (1964). *Pediatrics*, **34**, 454.
TANIGUCHI, K., and GJESSING, L. R. (1965). *Brit. med. J.*, **1**, 968.
VISSER, H. K. A., VEENSTRA, H. W., and PIK, C. (1964). *Arch. Dis. Childh.*, **39**, 397.
WAISMAN, H. A. (1963). In Lyman, F. L. 'Phenylketonuria,' Springfield: Thomas, p. 265.
WALSH, M. P. (1965). *Clin. chim. Acta*, **11**, 263.
WESTALL, R. G. (1964). *Arch. Dis. Childh.*, **38**, 485.
WHITE, H. H., Rowland, L. P., Araki, S., Thompson, H. L., and Cowen, D. (1965). *Arch. Neurol. (Chic.)* **13**, 455.
WOODY, N. C. (1964). *Amer. J. Dis. Child.*, **108**, 543.
WOODY, N. C., SNYDER, C. H., and HARRIS, J. A. (1965). *Amer. J. Dis. Child.*, **110**, 606.
WOOLF, L. I. (1963). *Advanc. clin. Chem.*, **6**, 97.
WOOLF, L. I. (1965). Personal communication.
WOOLF, L. I. (1966). 'Renal Tubular Dysfunction,' Springfield: Thomas.
WOOLF, L. I., OUNSTED, C., LEE, D., HUMPHREY, M., CHESHIRE, N. M., and STEED, G. R. (1961). *Lancet*, **2**, 464.
WOOLLEY, D. W., and VAN DER HOEVEN, T. (1964). *Science*, **144**, 1593.
WYNGAARDEN, J. B., and SEGAL, S. (1966). In Stanbury, J. B., Wyngaarden, J. B., and Fredrickson, D. S. 'The Metabolic Basis of Inherited Disease,' New York: McGraw-Hill, p. 341.
YARBRO, M. T., and ANDERSON, J. A. (1966). *J. Pediat.*, **68**, 895.

CHAPTER 12

OTHER NEUROMETABOLIC DISEASES

Galactosaemia

Chemical Pathology

Galactosaemia was probably first observed almost sixty years ago (Reuss, 1908). Many case reports have followed and some authors put its incidence as high as 1 in about 20,000 births (Hansen *et al.*, 1964); it is fortunate therefore that the condition is one of the few metabolic errors which respond to treatment.

Symptoms usually commence during the first few days of life. Patients may die rapidly if untreated. However, the disease may also be milder, the patients presenting later with cataracts and mental retardation. A few cases remain virtually symptomless and are mentally normal. On the other hand, some show signs of cataract and hepatic cirrhosis at birth, and the lesions then are not fully reversible. The clinical and metabolic aspects of the disease have been fully considered by Woolf (1962) Hsia (1965) and Isselbacher (1966).

The metabolic block in galactosaemia is now well understood: the enzyme galactose-1-phosphate uridyl transferase is virtually inactive (Fig. 115).

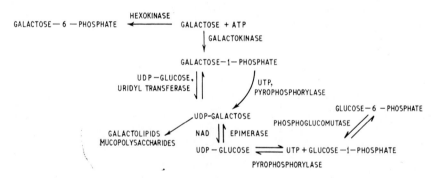

Fig. 115. The metabolism of galactose. ATP—Adenosine triphosphate, UTP—uridine triphosphate, UDP—uridine disphosphate, NAD—nicotinamide adenine dinucleotide.

As a result the blood galactose level rises and galactose-1-phosphate accumulates in cells and tissues. Multiple renal tubular defects develop and interfere with the reabsorption of amino acids, glucose and protein. The proteinuria is usually mild and shows a 'tubular pattern', but occasionally it is more severe, and then the electrophoretic pattern of the urine proteins resembles that of plasma (Woolf, 1966).

UDP-galactose is one of the precursors of the cerebrosides and mucopolysaccharides. However, UDP-galactose-4-epimerase remains active in galactosaemia, and enough UDP-galactose can be synthesized *in vivo* by the galactosaemic infant for myelination and mucopolysaccharide synthesis.

Another enzyme of galactose metabolism, UDP-galactose pyrophosphorylase, is normally present in the liver. Although virtually absent at birth, in older subjects it exerts as much as 20 per cent of the activity of uridyl transferase. This enzyme may account, at least in part, for the increasing tolerance to galactose shown by some older patients. An alternative pathway via galactose-6-phosphate may also operate in some of them. Part of the improvement may, however, be spurious, since older patients habitually consume less galactose. Moreover, many are known to remain completely intolerant to it throughout life.

Galactosaemia is inherited as an autosomal recessive trait. The level of galactose-1-phosphate uridyl transferase is reduced in heterozygotes, on the average, by about half, with however a sizeable overlap with the normals. Beutler *et al.* (1965) have described the so-called 'Duarte variant'. Individuals with this condition have reduced galactose-1-phosphate uridyl transferase levels but are not galactosaemic and are not heterozygotes for galactosaemia. Some authors have also suggested that patients with well developed alternative pathways of galactose metabolism and the asymptomatic cases constitute genetically distinct groups (Baker *et al.*, 1966).

The direct causes of the clinical signs and mental defect in galactosaemia remain to be worked out. Clinical observation, animal experiments and *in vitro* studies suggest, however, that the accumulation of galactose-1-phosphate may be directly or indirectly responsible for the toxic manifestations. Galactose-1-phosphate inhibits the enzyme phosphoglucomutase, which mediates the interconversion of glucose-1-phosphate and glucose-6-phosphate, and suppression of this process has been incriminated as a possible cause of some of the biochemical abnormalities. For example, inhibition of phosphoglucomutase could retard the utilization of glycogen, the conjugation of bilirubin and the synthesis of cerebrosides (Sidbury, 1961). There may also be a deficiency of adenosine triphosphate (ATP) in the disease. Dulcitol, a sugar formed by the enzymatic reduction of galactose, has been implicated in the cataract formation (Egan and Wells, 1966). It is worth mentioning that in *galactokinase deficiency* (Gitzelmann, 1965), a metabolic error associated with *failure* to form galactose-1-phosphate, cataract formation is part of the clinical picture. Hypoglycaemia, which often accompanies galactosaemia, is not now thought to be of importance in the causation of the mental defect.

Treatment with a lactose-free diet has dramatically improved the outlook for galactosaemic patients. If started during or not much later than the first week of life, the lesions can be largely reversed and intellectual development safeguarded. Children treated at a later stage still improve, but the cataracts, mental retardation and cirrhosis may then be irreversible. Nevertheless, in one study 4 of 6 children first treated at the age of 6 months to 1 year, and 3 of 5, in whom treatment was delayed by a year or more, ultimately reached I.Q.'s of 90 and over (Hsia and Walker, 1961). All authors agree that firm dietary control is essential. Argument is still afoot on the risks of trace amounts of galactose contained in such foodstuffs as peas or soya bean products.

As galactose-1-phosphate is an intracellular substance which, once formed, cannot be readily detoxicated, and as there is some evidence that the brain of the foetus may sometimes be damaged before birth, there is a good case for putting known heterozygous women on a lactose-free diet during pregnancy.

Morbid Anatomy

The organs affected in untreated cases are the liver, eyes and brain. The liver shows fatty degeneration and, sometimes, Laennec's cirrhosis. Evidence of an old adrenal haemorrhage and of anomalous pancreatic secretion has been reported in one case (Choremis, Vlachos, Katerelos and Karpouzas, 1962). The usual ocular condition is cataracts. Neuropathological findings have been reported in only one case (Crome, 1962). The patient died at 8 years, having had severe neonatal jaundice, hepatomegaly and lenticular opacities, from which he recovered after the withdrawal of most of the lactose from his diet. However, mental retardation persisted. The main change in the brain was slight micrencephaly with fibrous gliosis of the white matter. There was marked deficiency of total phospholipids in the white and grey matter, and of cerebroside in the white matter. The globus pallidus showed globules of sudanophil material. Some Purkinje cells and, to a lesser extent, granular cells had perished in the cerebellum, and the cerebellar molecular layer presented focal 'trellis-work' gliosis (Fig. 116). Most of the larger neurones

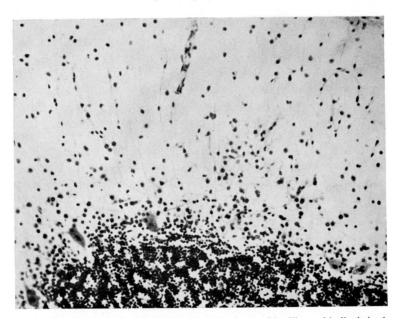

FIG. 116. Loss of cerebellar Purkinje cells and a focus of 'trellis-work' gliosis in the molecular layer in a case of galactosaemia (Cresyl violet × 190) (Crome, 1964 in Holt and Milner; Neurometabolic Disorders in Childhood. E. & S. Livingstone).

throughout the central nervous system contained a slight excess of cytoplasmic lipofuscin.

Laboratory Diagnosis

Many aspects of the laboratory differential diagnosis of galactosaemia are dealt with by Woolf (1962) and Hsia (1965). Ultimately, the diagnosis must rest on demonstrating absence of the enzyme galactose-1-phosphate uridyl transferase in erythrocytes, preferably in cord blood. In Britain most Hospital Regions are served by one or two centres where this test can be carried out at short notice.

In the acutely ill newborn galactosaemia will be suggested by the clinical signs and the presence of a reducing substance in the urine. In some cases a positive Benedict's test, coupled with a negative test for glucose by 'clinistix', will point to the correct diagnosis. However, renal tubular reabsorption of glucose is often reduced and enough glucose may therefore be present in the urine to give a positive 'clinistix' test. Chromatography or the recently introduced galactose oxidase tests, which are specific for galactose, will confirm its presence.

Hypoglycaemia may be detected if a glucose oxidase method is used for blood sugar estimations. Aminoaciduria of the renal type, proteinuria, which is usually mild, and abnormal liver function tests will be found by routine tests. The initial electrolyte disturbance has to be corrected, usually by intravenous therapy, and if the child has been on a glucose saline drip for some time with no milk given by mouth, galactose may not be present in the urine.

Galactose loading is dangerous and this method has in any case been superseded by the enzyme tests. Some of the laboratory tests for galactosaemia are described in the appendix (p. 357).

Most heterozygotes can be identified by an assay of their red cell galactose-1-phosphate uridyl transferase, but this is still only a research procedure.

Hypoglycaemic Disorders

The role of hypoglycaemia in the aetiology of mental deficiency has been discussed on p. 71. Here we mention a few specific disorders which may be associated with mental deficiency. These include *fructosaemia* (hereditary fructose intolerance), the *Dormandy syndrome* (galactose and fructose intolerance), *leucine-induced hypoglycaemia, and ketotic hypoglycaemia.*

Fructosaemia

This condition manifests itself at the time when fructose, usually as sucrose, is first introduced into the baby's diet. The signs are vomiting, hepatomegaly, albuminuria, aminoaciduria and failure to thrive. Raised blood fructose and fructosuria are, of course, detectable only after the ingestion of the hexose. The rise in the fructose level goes hand in hand with a severe fall in blood glucose. The basic defect has been identified by Froesch (1966) and coworkers as greatly reduced activity of the liver fructose-1-phosphate aldolase, while the level of fructose-1,6-diphosphate aldolase is much less affected. Fructose-1-phosphate aldolase catalyses the transformation of fructose-1-phosphate to glyceraldehyde and dihydroxyacetone phosphate; fructose 1,6-diphosphate aldolase converts fructose-1,6-diphosphate to glyceraldehyde-3-phosphate and dihydroxyacetone phosphate. It is still undecided whether the human liver contains two aldolases, one of which is inactive in fructosaemia, or one aldolase which is abnormal in the disease, showing reduced activity with one of its substrates (see also p. 201).

The condition will be suspected from the clinical signs and the presence of fructose in the blood and urine after the ingestion of fructose-containing foods. Fructose is fermentable by yeast, is not attacked by glucose oxidase, is laevorotatory and gives a positive Seliwanoff test with resorcinol. On paper chromatograms fructose is best identified by naphthoresorcinol (cf. Appendix, p. 360). The diagnosis should be confirmed by an intravenous fructose tolerance test which will provoke typical signs of hypoglycaemia and a fall in the plasma inorganic phosphate. It is not known what causes the hypoglycaemia, but impairment of glucose output by the liver rather than an increase in insulin secretion is the more likely explanation (Marks and Rose, 1965).

As in galactosaemia and glycogen storage disease, the children do not suffer as much brain damage from the hypoglycaemia as might be feared. Nevertheless, 4 out of 12 cases reviewed by Levin et al. (1963) were mildly mentally retarded.

Dormandy syndrome

Hypoglycaemia can be produced in the same person by more than one hexose, as in the Dormandy syndrome (Samols and Dormandy, 1963; Marks and Rose, 1965; Froesch, 1966), in which either fructose or galactose induces hypoglycaemia. One of two affected sisters suffered from epilepsy and mental impairment. Her blood insulin rose up to 2,000-fold after ingestion of glucose, but fell precipitately during the period of fructose-induced hypoglycaemia. The mechanism of this disorder is not yet understood but it probably involves an abnormal tissue response to insulin.

In a case described by Evans (1965) hypoglycaemia was provoked by either lactose or galactose. The patient, aged 17 months, was somewhat retarded and had developed hemiparesis. His galactose-1-phosphate uridyl transferase was normal; the insulin levels and response to fructose were not reported.

Leucine-induced hypoglycaemia

Leucine-induced hypoglycaemia is better known and probably more common than fructosaemia and the Dormandy syndromes. The condition may be inherited or acquired, the acquired form being usually associated with a tumour of the pancreas—an insulinoma (Marks and Rose, 1965). The patients present with epilepsy, mental retardation and failure to thrive. Hypoglycaemia may occur on fasting, but characteristically blood glucose falls rapidly and severely following the ingestion of leucine or leucine-containing food (see p. 360). The condition is diagnosed by the leucine tolerance tests described in standard textbooks. The exact mechanism of its production is unknown, but leucine has been shown to have an insulin releasing action. Leucine may also directly inhibit hepatic gluconeogenesis (Greenberg and

Reaven, 1966). Diazoxide, a non-diuretic drug structurally related to the chlorothiazide type diuretics, has been recently used with success in the treatment of leucine-sensitive hypoglycaemia in a child (Drash and Wolff, 1964). Steroids, glutamate and long-acting adrenaline preparations have also been used in treatment.

Ketotic hypoglycaemia of childhood

This form of non-leucine sensitive hypoglycaemia is associated with ketonuria, acidosis, and high plasma non-esterified fatty acid levels. It is induced by a low-calorie ketogenic diet (Colle and Ulstrom, 1964).

The main danger in all forms of persistent and severe hypoglycaemia are convulsions which may be followed by brain damage. This complex and unresolved problem has been mentioned on page 73. (See also Samols, E., and Marks V., 1966. *Proc. roy. Soc. Med.*, **59**, 811.)

Infantile Lactic Acidosis

Transient lactic acidosis with a raised ratio of lactic to pyruvic acid is a well-known finding in the anoxic newborn. Adult levels and ratios are normally established in a few days. Recently, however, five children have been described in whom severe lactic acidosis persisted to a much later age (Erickson, 1965). All five were mentally retarded; one suffered from Down's disease and two were siblings. Clinically, the most significant findings were signs of acidosis, i.e. rapid respiration and hypotonia, convulsions and tetany with carpopedal spasms attributed to the interaction of lactic acid with calcium and magnesium.*

The raised lactate and pyruvate levels and the raised lactate/pyruvate ratio in such cases result in metabolic acidosis. The glucagon test is normal but the response of the blood sugar to adrenaline is exaggerated. Glucose tolerance, muscle phosphorylase and serum lactic dehydrogenase are usually within normal range. The muscle lactic dehydrogenase isoenzymes may show a shift towards the foetal pattern. It is reasonably certain that muscle is the site of the metabolic defect in lactic acidosis but its precise mechanism and the cause of the mental retardation remain unknown. An abbreviated scheme of pyruvate metabolism is shown in Fig. 117.

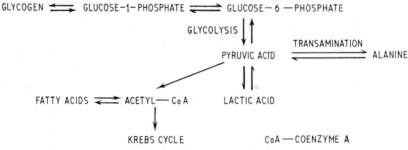

FIG. 117. The metabolism of pyruvate.

* The cases reported by Worsley *et al.* (1965), *Arch Dis.Childh.*, **40**, 492, showed also renal aminoaciduria and a lowered serum phosphate concentration. Post-mortem findings in one of their cases were those of Leigh's encephalomyelopathy (p. 314).

Chronic hypoxia, renal disease, hypoglycaemia, glycogen storage disease and diabetes could be excluded in all the published cases. Erickson (1965) has suggested the following possible explanations of the disorder: abnormal control of phosphorylase activity leading to excessive glycogenolysis and glycolysis, an abnormality in the interconversion of lactate and pyruvate, such as might be due to a shortage of cofactor NAD (nicotinamide adenine dinucleotide; synonym—DPN, diphosphopyridine nucleotide), a block between pyruvate and the Krebs cycle, or excessive conversion of fatty acids to acetyl CoA (acetyl coenzyme A, 'active acetate') and thence to lactic acid.

Glycogenosis

Chemical Pathology

Primary disorders of glycogen metabolism occur as the result of blocks at seven so far identified sites in the pathway of glycogen formation or degradation shown in Fig. 118 (Field, 1966). The known forms of glycogen disorders are listed in Table 9.

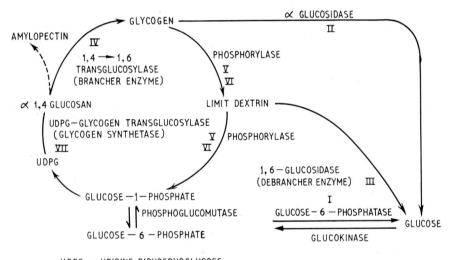

FIG. 118. The metabolism of glycogen.

Only two are associated with mental retardation: type II—a-glucosidase deficiency, and type VII—glycogen synthetase deficiency.

Deficiency of a-glucosidase causes *generalized glycogenosis*, sometimes referred to as Pompe's disease. Deposition of glycogen is particularly heavy in muscle, heart (Fig. 119), liver and brain. In view of Hers's (1963) demonstration that the deficient glucosidase is lysosomal, it is possible that glycogen is initially deposited in lysosomes, There is, however, electron microscopical evidence of an extralysosomal defect in the disease (Cardiff, 1966). Whatever the mechanism, the cytoplasm, and to a lesser extent the nuclei, of the affected cells are in time converted to little more than miniature bags of

Table 9. THE GLYCOGEN DISORDERS*

Cori Type	Designation	Organ involved	Enzymatic Defect	Intelligence	Hypo-glycaemia	Glucagon response	Other tests
I	Von Gierke's disease	Liver, kidney	Glucose-6-phosphatase	Normal	Present	Absent or diminished	I.V. fructose tolerance test abnormal
II	Pompe's disease	Generalized	α-Glucosidase (acid maltase)	Retarded	Absent	Normal	E.C.G. changes
III	Forbes' disease	Liver, heart, muscle, leucocytes	Amylo-1,6-glucosidase (debrancher enzyme)	Normal	Present	Diminished; normal after meals	I.V. fructose tolerance test normal. Blood glycogen raised
IV	Andersen's disease	Liver	Amylo-(1,4→1,6)-trans-glucosidase (brancher enzyme)	Normal	Absent	Diminished	Abnormal liver function tests
V	McArdle-Schmid-Pearson disease	Muscle	Myophosphorylase	Normal	Absent	Normal	No rise in lactate in ischaemic muscle after exercise
VI	Hers' disease	Liver, leucocytes	Hepatophosphorylase	Normal	Present	Absent or diminished	Leucocyte phosphorylase low
VII	Glycogen synthetase deficiency disease	Liver, muscle	UDPG-glycogen transglucosylase (glycogen synthetase)	Retarded	Present	Normal after meals	

* Glycogen storage diseases, VIII and IX, have been described more recently (Hug *et al*, 1966).

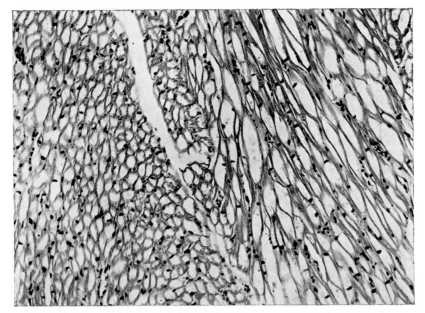

FIG. 119. The myocardium in generalized glycogenosis. (Haematoxylin and eosin
× 150.)

glycogen, and their function is correspondingly depressed. The patients present extreme hypotonia, enlargement of the heart and, occasionally, of the liver, and neurological and mental deficits. The tongue is often large.

The second disorder of glycogen metabolism which may be associated with mental retardation is *glycogen synthetase deficiency* (Lewis, Spencer-Peet and Stewart, 1963; Parr, Teree and Larner, 1965). In this condition the liver and muscle phosphorylase levels are also reduced, but this may be secondary to the synthetase defect. Glycogen is absent from the liver, muscle, kidneys and adrenals. The symptoms and signs include severe hypoglycaemia, acidosis, apnoea and convulsions. Four of the six cases described so far died in early infancy, the others were mentally retarded. The metabolic block is not complete—small amounts of glycogen are formed following a meal.

Occasionally no enzyme deficiency may be demonstrable in glycogen storage disease. Briggs and Haworth (1964) described a case of 'idiopathic glycogen storage disease', otherwise resembling van Gierke's disease, but without glucose-6-phosphate dehydrogenase deficiency. Again, in a child studied by Résibois-Grégoire and Dourov (1966) glycogen deposition was confined to the brain. Glycogen was not seen in the lysosomes, the disease was therefore probably distinct from Pompe's disease. The enzymatic defect was not identified.

Morbid Anatomy

Histologically, much glycogen is demonstrable in cases of generalized glycogenosis at all levels of the central and peripheral nervous system (Crome,

Cumings and Duckett, 1963; Mancall, Aponte and Berry, 1965). Nerve cells in the dorsal root ganglia and Schwann cells of the peripheral nerves also show glycogen deposition. In the brain and spinal cord both neurones and glial cells are affected by the storage (Fig. 120). There may be a variable

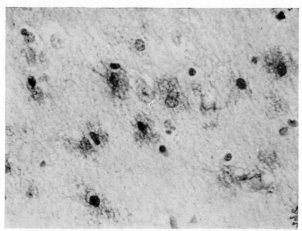

FIG. 120. Glycogen deposition in astrocytes in a case of generalized glycogenosis. (P.A.S. after treatment with diastase × 300.) (Crome, 1964 in Holt and Milner, Neurometabolic Disorders in Childhood, E. & S. Livingstone Ltd.)

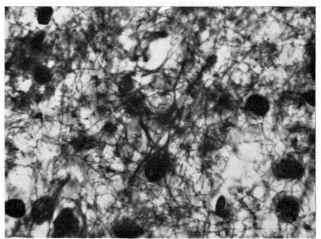

FIG. 121. Fibrous gliosis and astrocytic hyperplasia in the white matter of a case of generalized glycogenosis. (Holzer × 1,000.) (Crome, 1964 in Holt and Milner, Neurometabolic Disorders in Childhood, E. & S. Livingstone Ltd.)

degree of neuronal loss and the white matter shows fine fibrous gliosis (Fig. 121). Chemically, there is a marked deficiency in total phospholipids, cholesterol and cerebrosides of the white matter. The cholesterol esters are normal—this indicates absence of active demyelination. Glycogen deposition is also marked in the heart, liver and skeletal muscle.

The findings in the brain of one case of glycogen synthetase deficiency were thought to be consistent with a diffuse, non-specific degeneration of cerebral white matter of a type found after prolonged hypoglycaemia or anoxia. Glycogen was not demonstrated in the liver, skeletal muscle, kidneys and adrenal glands. Diffuse fatty changes were found in the liver and kidney (Parr, Teree and Larner, 1965).

Available information fits autosomal recessive transmission of the glycogen storage diseases. It is curious that more than one of these exceedingly rare conditions have been observed in the same person (Eberlein, Illingworth and Sidbury, 1962) and that in some families affected sibs showed evidence of dissimilar enzymic defects of glycogen metabolism (Eberlein, Brown and Sidbury, 1961).

Laboratory Diagnosis

Some of the tests differentiating the various forms of glycogen storage disease are indicated in Table 9. Ideally, the lack of the affected enzyme should be demonstrated in a biopsy specimen, but only a few centres are equipped to do so. In routine laboratories investigations are normally confined to the glucagon and adrenaline tolerance tests, and estimation of serum uric acid, lactic acid and lipid. These tests help in excluding glycogen storage disease type I. Various aspects of the diagnosis of glycogen metabolism disorders are discussed by Marks and Rose (1965), Spencer-Peet (1965) and Field (1966).

Generalized glycogenosis is diagnosed by the demonstration of massive glycogen deposits in muscle. The word 'massive' is stressed since moderate amounts of glycogen in muscle are present in many conditions. A few laboratories are able to measure quantitatively the glycogen in blood cells and muscle biopsies. It is also important to differentiate primary from symptomatic glycogenosis which may occur in diabetes (Middleton and Hockaday, 1965), galactosaemia and other metabolic disorders. The glycogenosis in such conditions is usually transient, reversible and milder than in the primary forms.

Hypothyroidism

Cretinism occupies a special place in mental deficiency because it was long regarded as the main if not the only cause of backwardness. Indeed, the words 'cretin' and 'idiot' were once synonymous in the French and German languages. One of the first scientific studies of cretinism was by Virchow (1852), who was at the time of writing undergoing a form of banishment in Wüzburg for his part in the 1848 revolution. He founded there a journal to which he contributed amongst other major studies one on cretinism, written in his characteristic style. As always, he championed in this paper the underprivileged and handicapped and showed, for the first time, that cretinism was a disease rather than an anthropological deviant of mankind, and suggested that it was due to some environmental factor. He was proved right later when it was learned that iodine deficiency was an important cause of endemic cretinism. Nowadays endemic cretinism has largely disappeared in the economically advanced countries but is still prevalent in parts of India (Raman and

Beierwaltes, 1959) and New Guinea (Gajdusek, 1962). The forms which need to be considered here are not the endemic ones but those caused by inborn errors of metabolism and instances of thyroid hypoplasia or agenesis. (Evidence has been adduced by Blizzard *et al.* (1960) that hypoplasia or agenesis of the thyroid may be due to maternal thyroid autoimmunization).

Chemical Pathology

The metabolism of iodine in man is shown in Fig. 122. Metabolic blocks have been identified at five sites, as indicated in the diagram, based on the recent review by Stanbury (1966). Iodide is absorbed in the gut, taken up by the thyroid, transformed to iodine (I_2) and introduced into the benzene nucleus to form monoiodotyrosine (MIT) and diiodotyrosine (DIT). The iodotyrosines can either be deiodinated back to iodide (I^-) or coupled enzymatically to form triiodothyronine (T_3) and thyroxine (T_4). Metabolic blocks have been identified at sites I, II, III, IV and V in Fig. 122. The characteristic features of the corresponding syndromes are indicated in Table 10.

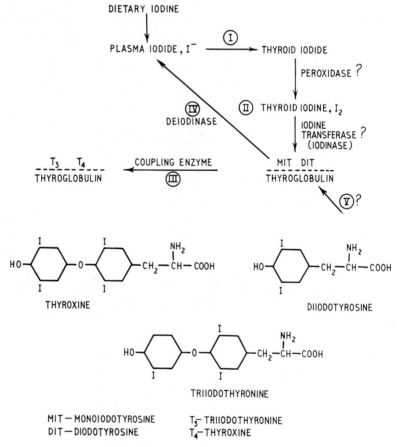

FIG. 122. The metabolism of iodine.

Table 10. FAMILIAL HYPOTHYROID SYNDROMES

Site of defect	Metabolic Defect	Intelligence	PBI	Aids to Diagnosis
I	Iodide transport	Normal	Low	Low uptake of labelled iodine by the thyroid. Inorganic iodide level in saliva approximately the same as in plasma. (Normally the salivary iodide level is much higher.)
II	Iodide organification (a) Iodide peroxidase defect	Retarded	Low	Rapid uptake of labelled iodine is followed by its rapid discharge from the gland. The discharge is accelerated by perchlorate and thiocyanate. No organically bound iodine found in thyroid biopsy.
	(b) Iodine transferase defect. (Pendred syndrome.)	Usually normal	Low	
III	Coupling of iodotyrosines	Retarded	Low or normal	Rapid uptake of labelled iodine by the thyroid, followed by moderately increased rate of discharge. High levels of labelled DIT and MIT found in biopsy 72 hours after iodine administration.
IV	Deiodination of iodotyrosines	Retarded	Low	Rapid uptake of labelled iodine by the thyroid, followed by variable rate of discharge from the gland. MIT and DIT found in the blood and urine. Administered DIT excreted largely unchanged in the urine.
V	Thyroglobulin synthesis	Retarded	High	Demonstration of butanol-insoluble iodine in acidified serum.

MIT—monoiodotyrosine;   DIT—diiodotyrosine;   PBI—protein bound iodine.

The deficit at site I is deficiency in iodide transport. This variant is very rare and mental retardation was not a feature of the recorded cases.

Backwardness seems to be more frequent in the next condition, due to a defect at site II—the organification of iodine. The so-called Pendred syndrome is probably due to a deficiency in iodine transferase and thus also to a block at site II (Stanbury, 1966). In this syndrome intelligence is normal but the patients have goitre and nerve deafness.

A block at site III, failure of coupling mono- and diiodotyrosines to triiodothyronine and thyroxine, is characterized by goitre and mental retardation.This block is not complete since T_4 levels which are low in the thyroid may be normal in the peripheral blood.

The block at site IV—failure of iodotyrosine deiodinase activity—was first observed in a family of tinkers by McGirr and Hutchison (1953). The affected patients were mentally retarded and had goitres. The deficiency of thyroid hormone is in this case attributed to a leakage of the hormone precursor and depletion of body iodine stores.

In the 5th form the site of the block is less definite. Iodinated peptides are found in the blood. The patients are mentally retarded but not always goitrous.

Owing to the rarity of all these conditions information on their incidence and genetics is still fragmentary. The available data have been reviewed by Stanbury (1966).

It will be seen that in cretinism mental deficiency is a frequent but not constant finding. According to Blizzard and Coon (1963) more than half the patients with congenital cretinism remain mentally retarded in spite of early diagnosis and treatment.

While the results of treatment are thus disappointing, the outlook is better if a correct diagnosis is made at birth.

It is known from animal experiments that protein synthesis of the immature but not the mature brain is dependent on adequate supplies of thyroxine (Gelber et al., 1964). Studies on the placental transfer of thyroid hormones have so far not been conclusive (Schultz et al., 1965; Pickering, 1962 and 1964; French and Van Wyk, 1964; Marks and Man, 1965; Marques, 1965). Reported observations suggest that thyroid hormones cross the placenta only slowly and in small amounts, and that the foetal thyroid begins to release thyroxine only close to term. Puppies thyroidectomized in utero need thyroid hormone replacement within hours of birth in order to survive, although they are apparently normal at birth.

Morbid Anatomy

Considering the long interest in the condition, data on the morphological changes in cretinism and myxoedema are disappointingly scanty. The thyroid may be hypoplastic, or, indeed, absent—in the athyreotic forms. In goitrous cases there is a diffuse colloid hyperplasia of the thyroid in the early stages, followed later by development of nodular hypertrophy. Enlargement of the pituitary with loss of the eosinophil cells and proliferation of large cells, interpreted as chromophobes, has also been reported (Anderson, 1961).

The main neuropathological change in experimental hypothyroidism is lack of neuropil development (p. 96), although nerve cells are probably also lost. Various regressive neuronal changes have been described, mainly by older authors, who also mentioned slight and possibly equivocal architectonic disturbances. These reports have been reviewed by Erbslöh (1958). Reports of defective myelination in the brain of athyroid cretins have been reviewed by French and Van der Wyk (1964). In a personal unpublished case of a middle-aged woman, who was alleged to have been hypothyroid from birth and had not benefited much from thyroid treatment, the most striking change was widespread calcification, particularly in the cerebellum.

Laboratory Diagnosis

The diagnosis of cretinism rests on clinical and laboratory findings. Although the word cretinism conjures up a picture of stunted growth, coarse skin and hair, large tongue, characteristic facies, prominent abdomen and mental deficiency, all these signs need not be present, and many of them are also found in other mental defectives (Kirman, 1965). Perusal of the literature on sporadic hypothyroidism due to specific inborn enzymatic defects suggests that the clinical picture of these cases often does not conform to the classical description of cretinism.

Diagnosis and treatment of the newborn are urgent. In the athyreotic cretin the diagnosis may be suggested by persistence of 'physiological' jaundice, poor temperature control, lethargy, and perhaps, the facies. X-ray examination of the skeleton will show delayed ossification. The diagnostic problems in cretinism have been fully discussed in a recent symposium (Stuart-Mason, 1963).

Of the laboratory tests, estimation of the serum cholesterol is useful in the untreated older patient, in whom it is usually raised to 300–600 mg./100 ml., but not in the hypothyroid newborn, in whom the level is often normal. Estimation of the serum protein-bound iodine (PBI) or butanol-extractable iodine (BEI), which is more specific for the thyroid hormones, is probably the most informative single test. In the normal baby the level rises within hours of birth and remains higher than in adults at the age of 1 month (Marks, Hamlin and Zack, 1966). Low values are therefore highly significant, but may be masked by iodine medication of the mother. After the intake of inorganic iodine (e.g. in a cough mixture) by the mother, the baby's PBI may be raised; after the intake of organic iodine (e.g. contrast media) the BEI as well as the PBI may be falsely elevated.

Radioactive tracer studies are likely to come into greater use now that I^{132} is replacing the more dangerous I^{131} as tracer. Another recently developed test is the estimation of labelled triiodothyronine uptake by erythrocytes or ion exchange resins (Goolden *et al.*, 1965). The relative merit of these and other thyroid function tests, and the problems arising out of their use, are admirably discussed by Staffurth (1964). As considerable experience and expertise are necessary for reliable results, suspected cases should whenever possible be referred to specialized centres.

Nephrogenic Diabetes Insipidus

Chemical Pathology

Hereditary inability to concentrate urine, diabetes insipidus, is usually due to a deficiency of the posterior pituitary hormone vasopressin. Occasionally, however, it may be caused by the renal tubules failing to respond to the hormone. Affected infants excrete large volumes of very dilute urine, the specific gravity of which hardly ever reaches 1·010 and is usually below 1·006. The polyuria leads to severe hypertonic dehydration, which, if untreated, is rapidly fatal. The survivors are often but not always mentally retarded (Ruess and Rosenthal, 1963). The mental retardation is said to arise in two ways: (1) the extreme hypertonicity and hypernatraemia of the extracellular fluid leads to intravascular stasis in the cerebral vessels with consequent brain damage; (2) the need of the affected young children to drink almost continuously leaves little time for learning. There is definite evidence in cases described by Kirman *et al.* (1956) and Ruess and Rosenthal of the first of these mechanisms; the extent to which the second contributes to the mental retardation is difficult to assess.

How vasopressin acts is still being discussed (Woolf, 1966; Orloff and Burg, 1966). According to one theory the antidiuretic hormone releases the enzyme hyaluronidase into the urine which, in its turn attacks the acid mucopolysaccharides of the tubular membrane, increasing its permeability. Dicker and Eggleton (1963) found that patients with nephrogenic diabetes insipidus do not excrete hyaluronidase when vasopressin is administered. An alternative view is that vasopressin promotes the formation of the nucleotide adenosine-3,5-phosphate, which enhances tubular permeability to water (Orloff and Handler, 1964). In nephrogenic diabetes insipidus there may be failure to form adenosine-3,5-phosphate.

Treatment was until recently entirely symptomatic. Lately, significant improvement has been achieved with chlorothiazide and hydrochlorothiazide (Schotland, Grumbach and Strauss, 1963). How these two aldosterone antagonists promote the reabsorption of water and decrease that of sodium is not yet understood. Another diuretic which is being tried with some success is ethacrynic acid, an α,β unsaturated ketone derivative of an aryl oxyacetic acid (Brown *et al.*, 1966).

The disease is transmitted as a sex-linked recessive trait. Female carriers may show minimal impairment of the ability to concentrate urine.

Laboratory Diagnosis

In the classical form of vasopressin resistant diabetes insipidus inability to concentrate urine is the only renal defect, and the diagnosis is readily made by establishing failure to respond to vasopressin. In practice, the situation is usually more complex because repeated bouts of dehydration may result in secondary glomerular and tubular deficits. Moreover, the kidney in primary renal diseases of varied aetiology may in the late stages fail to respond to vasopressin (Orloff and Burg, 1966). Psychogenic polydipsia and prolonged administration of vasopressin and water apparently also reduce renal response to the hormone, and cases of pituitary diabetes insipidus may be confused with mild cases of the vasopressin resistant variety.

Pseudohypoparathyroidism

Chemical Pathology

This syndrome, also called Albright's hereditary osteodystrophy, resembles idiopathic hypoparathyroidism. Patients may suffer from tetanic convulsions and have fragile nails, thick skulls, occasionally cataracts, and hypoplasia of the enamel and roots of the teeth. Additional features are short stature, round face and short neck. Ectopic bone may form in the skin and soft tissues. Occasionally, calcification occurs in the basal ganglia. This may cause epilepsy and mental retardation in some patients. The metacarpal and metatarsal bones are short and thick and show changes comparable to those in achondroplasia. Biochemically, the syndrome resembles idiopathic hypoparathyroidism; serum calcium tends to be low and serum inorganic phosphate high. However, in pseudohypoparathyroidism the parathyroids are normal or, even, hyperplastic. The severity of the clinical and biochemical manifestations is extremely variable. Milder forms without hypocalcaemia have been referred to as pseudo-pseudohypoparathyroidism. The basic defect in pseudohypoparathyroidism is the failure of the renal tubules to respond to parathyroid hormone with an increased excretion of phosphate. Bone may also be insensitive to the hormone. Transmission is, perhaps, sex-linked. Detailed descriptions of the various aspects of the disease will be found in the reviews of Bartter (1966), Aurbach and Potts (1964), and Woolf (1966).

Laboratory Diagnosis

The diagnosis is confirmed by the failure of injected parathyroid hormone to increase the urinary excretion of phosphate and raise the serum calcium level. In practice, technical difficulties are considerable, particularly since some hormonal preparations are insufficiently active. The tests are therefore best carried out in departments specializing in calcium metabolism.

Severe Hypercalcaemia

Idiopathic hypercalcaemia occurs in mild and severe forms and these merge into each other. The two forms are stated to be aetiologically distinct but this is unproven. The severe form is frequently but not inevitably complicated by mental deficiency.

The mild form affects infants abnormally sensitive to vitamin D who are maintained on a diet rich in calcium and vitamin D. Cow's milk contains, for example, three times as much calcium as breast milk, and excessive vitamin D supplements may also be given. Recovery follows promptly treatment with a low calcium, low vitamin D diet and cortisone. There are no psychiatric complications.

In the much smaller group of infants suffering from the severe form of the disorder, sensitivity to vitamin D is thought to be so great that hypercalcaemia develops even on a diet low in calcium and vitamin D. Thus in the carefully documented case of Simmons and Hawkins (1965) a serum level of 36 mg./100 ml. of calcium was recorded in a 7 week-old breastfed child on a vitamin D intake of only about 200 units. Some symptoms in this disease, such as hypotonia, vomiting, constipation and polyuria, are directly traceable to the hypercalcaemia. In addition, some of the following signs may be present: dwarfism, osteosclerosis, cerebral palsy, epilepsy and an 'elfin-like' facies. Calcification occurs in the soft tissues and excessive calcium may be deposited in the pulp of the deciduous teeth. According to Jue, Noren and Anderson (1965) the condition may also be associated with supravalvular aortic stenosis and/or peripheral pulmonary stenosis.

The only constant biochemical finding is the raised serum calcium, which ranges from just above normal to well over 30 mg./100 ml. The serum urea, inorganic phosphate and chloride are initially normal but may rise as renal function deteriorates, with a concomitant decrease in the serum bicarbonate. The serum cholesterol is increased and the albumin globulin ratio is often decreased, but these are probably non-specific findings. Hypercalciuria occurs in the early stages of the disease.

It has been suggested that the inborn error in severe hypercalcaemia is defective inactivation of vitamin D. Mental deficiency has been a feature of almost all published cases. However, there is no reason why the mental retardation and renal failure should not prove to be preventable even in the severe form if the serum calcium is kept within normal range by a careful control of the calcium and vitamin D intake. Fuller descriptions of the disorder are contained in the papers by Kenny et al. (1963), Arnim and Engel (1964) and Simmons and Hawkins (1965).

Morbid Anatomy

While nephrocalcinosis and glomerular fibrosis have been repeatedly described in this condition, neuropathological findings have been so far reported in a single case (Crome and Sylvester, 1960). This patient was a microcephalic idiot with quadriplegia and epilepsy who died at 2 years and 10 months. His brain was somewhat small and showed general paucity of cortical neurones. A small vascular anomaly was present in the cerebral cortex and a pea-sized tumour—infundibuloma—was discovered behind the optic chiasma.

Laboratory Diagnosis

The biochemical findings are unequivocal in the severely affected child, but the condition in milder cases might be confused with hyperparathyroidism, vitamin D intoxication or renal tubular acidosis. However, in contrast to idiopathic hypercalcaemia, in hyperparathyroidism serum phosphate is low and alkaline phosphatase high. The bone lesions can also be readily distinguished. The absence of hyperchloraemic acidosis, except in the late stages, differentiates idiopathic hypercalcaemia from renal tubular acidosis. In vitamin D intoxication the bones may show decalcification in the late stages.

Hyperuricaemia

Chemical Pathology

Gout was known already to the ancient Greeks and Romans, and the condition was fully described by Thomas Sydenham in the late eighteenth century. In 1854 A. B. Garrod demonstrated raised uric acid in this condition. Since then much has been learned about purine and uric acid metabolism in gout (Seegmiller *et al.*, 1963; Wyngaarden, 1966), but the basic biochemical fault causing hyperuricaemia is still unknown. Hyperuricaemia develops in 1 or 2 per cent. of the population, predominantly males, and almost invariably after puberty. As a group, patients with hyperuricaemia probably have an enlarged miscible uric acid pool and show enhanced incorporation of glycine or other precursors into uric acid (cf. Fig. 123). About a third of them excrete abnormally large amounts of uric acid in the urine. In adults hyperuricaemia has no adverse effects on intelligence; in fact, intellectually outstanding men, amongst them Newton, Goethe and Darwin, are said to have suffered from the disease.

A simplified diagram of uric acid formation is given in Fig. 123.

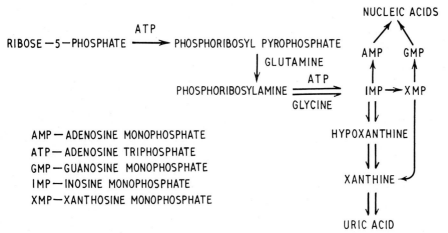

FIG. 123. The formation of uric acid.

Wyngaarden (1966) suggested that in hyperuricaemia there is defective regulation of the synthesis of phosphoribosylamine, the first specific purine precursor, and that this leads to excessive uric acid production via IMP, along the pathway marked with double arrows in Fig. 123.

In recent years Catel and Schmidt (1959), Riley (1960), Hoefnagel (1965) and particularly Lesch and Nyhan (1964), and Nyhan, Oliver and Lesch (1965) have described cases of hyperuricaemia which differ from classical gout by a much earlier onset and involvement of the C.N.S. In these cases hyperactive deep tendon reflexes have been reported as early as the 5th week of life, and urinary uric acid calculi and blood uric acid levels of 25 mg./ 100 ml. were observed at 4 months. This is more than 5 times the normal. Symptoms include generalized spasticity with hyperactive tendon reflexes, athetoid movements, dysarthria, dysphagia and profound mental retardation. Another strange feature has been destructive biting of the lips and fingers.

The metabolic defect is more severe in the children with hyperuricaemia and cerebral palsy than in adults with gout. When the data are expressed per kilogramme of body weight, the former excrete some 5 times as much uric acid as the latter and their uric acid turnover is 6 times greater. Incorporation of labelled glycine into uric acid amounted in 7 days to over 2 per cent. of the administered dose in a child with hyperuricaemia and cerebral palsy (Nyhan, Oliver and Lesch, 1965), compared to an average figure of approximately 0·75 per cent. found in adults with gout and raised urate excretion (Wyngaarden, 1966). While no causal relationship has so far been established between hyperuricaemia and C.N.S. involvement, it is not unreasonable to postulate that uric acid and/or one of its precursors or derivatives may be toxic to the developing nervous system and capable of passing the immature blood brain barrier (Nyhan et al., 1965). It is generally accepted that the blood brain barrier in adults is relatively impermeable to urates. The uric acid in the C.S.F. of adults is usually only about 20 per cent. of that in the serum, but it is somewhat higher in children. Even in advanced cases of adult gout the C.N.S. is not affected. Hoefnagel's patient had a normal C.S.F. uric acid at 11 years, with a serum level of about 12·5 mg./100 ml.

Morbid Anatomy

The brains of two brothers with hyperuricaemia, aged 11 months and 4 years at death, were examined at this hospital. Both were somewhat micrencephalic, showed cortical neuronal loss and astrocytic hyperplasia in the molecular layer of the cortex. The lobulus simplex of the cerebellum of one of the cases presented multiple foci of necrosis. The somatic tissues of one of the cases were also examined. These showed no distinctive abnormality.

Laboratory Diagnosis

In addition to the characteristic clinical signs, patients may present, even at an early age, arthritis, haematuria, crystalluria or uric acid stones. The diagnosis can be readily confirmed by estimating the blood uric acid, preferably by the specific enzymatic method utilizing uricase.

Abetalipoproteinaemia

Chemical Pathology

A new syndrome comprising retinitis pigmentosa, progressive ataxic neuropathy and the presence of irregularly shaped erythrocytes was first observed in an 18-year-old girl by Bassen and Kornzweig (1950). Because of their thorny appearance the red cells came to be called acanthocytes (akantha = thorn). Ten years later Salt, Wolff, Lloyd, Fosbrooke, Cameron and Hubble (1960) observed virtual absence of serum β-lipoproteins in the serum of a patient with such a syndrome. At the time of writing about 20 cases have been reported (Wolff, 1965; Farquhar and Ways, 1966). In this condition steatorrhoea, hypocholesterolaemia, with serum levels below 70 mg./100 ml., and low serum phospholipids are invariably present. About a third of the cases have been children of consanguineous parents, and most of these children were mentally retarded. An autosomal recessive mode of inheritance is suggested by the high rate of consanguinity, the familial incidence, and low serum β-lipoprotein in some of the presumed heterozygotes. However, in most families no clinical or haematological abnormalities could be detected in the presumed heterozygotes, and in some relatives serum β-lipoprotein is actually increased (Forsyth, Lloyd and Fosbrooke, 1965). It is therefore possible that, like agammaglobulinaemia, abetalipoproteinaemia is aetiologically and genetically heterogeneous.

The ocular and neurological symptoms develop in childhood or, sometimes, as late as early adulthood, but acanthocytosis and steatorrhoea are present from birth. It has been shown by Salt *et al.* that after the ingestion of fat chylomicrons do not appear in the blood while triglycerides accumulate in the intestinal mucosal cells. Intraluminal emulsification and the appearance of the villi are normal. Infusion of β-lipoprotein does not improve fat absorption. Ways, Reed and Hanahan (1963) have shown that the phospholipid composition of the membrane of the acanthocytes is altered: it contains more sphingomyelin and less lecithin. They also found similar changes in the serum phospholipids. Since phospholipids are involved in the formation of the membrane of chylomicrons (Hübscher, Smith and Gurr, 1964) failure to form these particles might be attributable to a membrane defect. The lipids of the red cell membrane and of the myelin sheath are not inert. A slow turnover and exchange of lipids with those in serum takes place. Forsyth *et al.* have made the interesting suggestion that *prolonged* exposure to serum deficient in one of the major lipid-carrying proteins may play a part in producing the changes in the red cells, retina and nervous tissue. It is true that acanthocytes retain their abnormal shape when incubated in normal serum, and that the serum of a patient with acanthocytosis does not transform normal red cells into acanthocytes. However, these short term *in vitro* tests do not rule out of court the above hypothesis. Farquhar and Ways (1966) have tentatively attributed the neurological symptoms of the disease to deficient transport of essential lipids to the central nervous system.

Another condition showing a striking decrease in β-lipoprotein on paper electrophoresis is *alphalipoproteinaemia* (Bigler *et al.*, 1959). Only two cases have been described. They were brothers presenting hepatomegaly, stunted growth and mild mental retardation. The serum cholesterol was normal but triglycerides and phospholipids were increased. On fractionation, a considerably raised proportion of cholesterol, total phospholipids and triglycerides was found in the α_2-lipoprotein fraction. No significant abnormalities were present in the bone marrow and peripheral blood. Clinically and biochemically this condition is thus distinct from abetalipoproteinaemia, nor does it appear to fit any of the established forms of idiopathic hyperlipaemia (Fredrickson and Lees, 1966).

Morbid Anatomy

The pathological findings have been reported in a 36-year old woman with abetalipoproteinaemia who died in heart failure (Sobrevilla, Goodman and Kane, 1964). This patient presented cystic ovaries and scarring of the renal cortices. Her spinal cord showed extensive demyelination of the posterior columns and spinocerebellar tracts. Neuronal loss was present in the anterior horns of the spinal cord and cerebellar cortex. The peripheral nerves showed focal demyelination.

Laboratory Diagnosis

The diagnosis of this disease is not difficult. The serum lipid changes, when found in conjunction with acanthocytes in fresh blood films, retinitis pigmentosa, ataxia, neuropathy and steatorrhoea, will point to the correct diagnosis. In intestinal biopsy material the columnar cells covering the villi have been reported to possess unusually clear cytoplasm. Microcytic anaemia is frequent. Impaired renal function and a generalized tubular aminoaciduria were present in one severely affected infant who died at 17 months (Becroft, Costello and Scott, 1965) but this may not have been causally related to the syndrome. Becroft *et al.* discuss in detail the differentiation of acanthocytes from crenated red cells, microspherocytes and pyknocytes.

Wilson's Disease (Hepatolenticular Degeneration)

Dementia rather than mental retardation is the usual consequence of Wilson's disease, which therefore need hardly be considered here from viewpoints other than those of differential diagnosis. The typical clinical picture of Wilson's disease comprises extrapyramidal neurological signs, such as rigidity, tremor and athetosis, as well as paralysis, increasing dementia, nodular cirrhosis of the liver and the presence of corneal Kayser-Fleischer rings. Usually Wilson's disease commences in late childhood or adolescence. Cases of Wilson's disease in early childhood may, however, remain unrecognized, the patients dying from cirrhosis and liver failure before involvement of the brain becomes apparent. The main neuropathological changes consist of degeneration, usually spongiform, of the striatum. Characteristic cells, so-called Alzheimer II and Opalski cells, are present in the obviously degenerate areas and other parts of the brain. For recent reviews of the condition readers are referred to Bearn (1966) and Woolf (1966).

It is believed that the fundamental fault in Wilson's disease is a disorder of copper metabolism. Its absorption from the alimentary tract and excretion in the urine are high while excretion in the bile is low. Synthesis of the copper-carrying protein—caeruloplasmin—is impaired, and its level is usually low.

In the few patients with normal caeruloplasmin levels its linkage to copper is weak. The serum copper is normal or low, but the fraction of non-caeruloplasmin copper (albumin bound) is greatly increased. Since copper is held by albumin more loosely than by caeruloplasmin the metal is more easily deposited in the tissues*. It is believed that this excessive deposition leads ultimately to cirrhosis of the liver and to proximal tubular defects in the kidney. The renal lesions impair the reabsorption of amino acids, peptides, protein, glucose, bicarbonate (acid excretion is diminished), uric acid, calcium and phosphate. Aminoaciduria and proteinuria are thus common in the later stages of the disease. Loss of calcium and phosphate may cause rickets, osteomalacia and pathological fractures.

Estimation of copper in the urine and serum, or of serum caeruloplasmin, and tests of liver and kidney function, help in the diagnosis of doubtful cases. Unfortunately, urinary excretion of copper may occasionally be increased and serum caeruloplasmin decreased in hepatic cirrhosis of other origin, particularly, biliary cirrhosis. The copper content of the plasma and urine may also be abnormal in other diseases. This complicates the diagnosis.

It should also be noted that copper in the body fluids and tissues is only present in minute quantities. Any contamination such as, for example, the impurity from the metal of a steel knife used in cutting a biopsy specimen, may be enough to give misleading results. The need for care in the handling of specimens and interpreting results calls for no other comment.

Muscular Dystrophy

It is not proposed to discuss here the general pathology of muscular dystrophy. Some of the patients with progressive muscular disease of the Duchenne type are, however, mentally retarded and the reason for this is not yet understood (Dubowitz, 1965). No significant changes have been observed by us in the brains of such cases at Queen Mary's Hospital for Children, and none have been reported in the literature. Results of E.E.G. studies have so far also been equivocal (Rutter, 1966).

Mental retardation may be more frequent in other myopathies. Thus Calderon (1966) considers that 43 of 55 published cases of *myotonic dystrophy* (Steinert's disease) were mentally retarded, their intelligence being mostly in the educationally subnormal range. These conditions are, however, very rare.

Werdnig-Hoffmann disease is not a form of muscular dystrophy but a secondary, neurogenic degeneration of muscle following loss of neurones in the anterior horn of the spinal cord and in the medulla. The patients die in infancy and are not usually considered in the context of mental deficiency practice.

Laboratory Diagnosis

Much research in many centres has so far failed to clarify the aetiology and fundamental enzymic defect in the Duchenne type of muscular dystrophy (Tyler, 1966; Symposium, 1963, Symposium, 1965). The condition mostly affects males, and gives rise to definite biochemical changes in the plasma and urine. The serum creatine kinase is raised sometimes more than a hundred-

* For the estimation of serum copper oxidase see p. 368.

fold, even before the onset of clinical signs. This enzyme is also raised in about two-thirds of the female carriers. Serum aldolase and the transaminases are increased, but to a lesser extent. Because of the breakdown of muscle, the urinary excretion of creatine exceeds that of creatinine.

Electromyography and muscle biopsy are useful in the diagnosis of doubtful cases. In the Duchenne type of muscular dystrophy the muscle shows generalized degeneration with fat replacement and fibrosis. This contrasts with neurogenic atrophy, such as Werdnig-Hoffmann disease, in which focal groups of fibres degenerate amongst other groups of surviving and unaffected muscle fibres. In the later stages of Duchenne dystrophy almost the entire muscle is replaced by fat, and the serum creatine kinase may then return to near normal values (cf. pp. 156 and 367).

Some histological changes in the muscle fibres can also be detected in the female 'carriers' of Duchenne muscular dystrophy, and Pearce, Pearce and Walton (1966) suggest that muscle biopsy may be useful in carrier detection.

Leigh's Encephalomyelopathy
(Subacute Necrotizing Encephalomyelopathy)

Since this condition was first described by Leigh (1951) a number of cases have been reported in many parts of the world and it seems likely that the disease will prove to be not uncommon, since at least two pathologists have each been able to collect up to 4 cases within a relatively short time. The familial incidence of the disorder is very pronounced, conforming to the pattern of Mendelian recessive transmission (Feigin and Wolf, 1954; Richter, 1957; Reye, 1960; Tuthill, 1960; Tom and Rewcastle, 1962; Ebels, Blokzijl and Troelstra, 1965). Its metabolic basis is obscure but the histological resemblance to Wernicke's encephalopathy has at once suggested some form of vitamin B deficiency and this view has been sustained by later morphological studies. In particular, lesions in the spinal cord (*vide infra*) are reminiscent of vitamin B_{12} deficiency, although similar changes have been observed in other metabolic diseases. Moreover, the pyruvate levels have been shown to be high in some cases. Assays of vitamin B_{12} have not yet been reported in this condition. The syndrome may well prove to be the result of different metabolic aberrations in infancy. Thus, neuropathological changes characteristic of Leigh's disease were present in two sibs showing in life lactic acidosis and renal aminoaciduria (Worsley *et al.*, 1965). In one case treated at Great Ormond Street Hospital by administration of lipoic acid the patient's condition improved. He was still alive 3 years after the onset of the disease but was mentally retarded*.

The disease commences in infancy, the chief signs being failure to thrive, lack of movement, hypotonia or spasticity, absent reflexes, optic atrophy, nystagmus and, in some cases, convulsions.

Most of the recorded cases of Leigh's disease have run a subacute and fatal course, but it has been suggested that a chronic form may also occur (Christensen, Melchior and Plum, 1963).

* This patient died recently, about four years after the apparent onset of the disease.

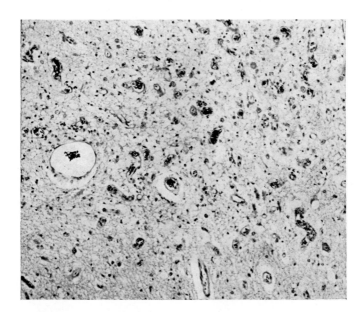

FIG. 124. Rarefaction in the tegmentum of the brainstem with marked capillary proliferation in a case of Leigh's encephalomyelopathy. Many neurones survive, apparently intact, in the affected area. (Haematoxylin and eosin × 112.) (Crome, 1964, in Holt and Milner, Neurometabolic Disorders in Childhood, E. & S. Livingstone Ltd.)

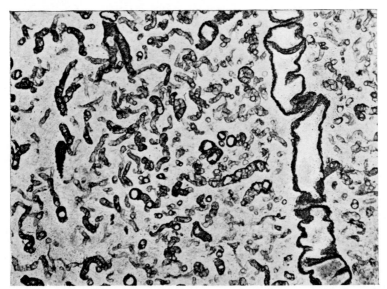

FIG. 125. Capillary proliferation in a lesion in a case of Leigh's encephalomyelopathy. The newly formed capillaries impregnate faintly with silver, while the older ones stain more heavily. (Foote's reticulin stain × 112.) (Crome, 1964, in Holt and Milner, Neurometabolic Disorders in Childhood, E. & S. Livingstone Ltd.)

Morbid Anatomy

Pathologically, the lesions are bilateral symmetrical areas of rarefaction with differing gradation of cellularity. Some foci are rather acellular (Fig. 124), showing only spongiform degeneration or breakdown of tissue, others contain reactive cells. Some lesions present marked capillary proliferation—another

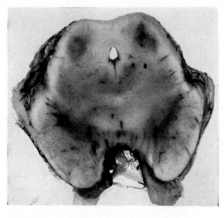

Fig. 126. The midbrain of a case of Leigh's encephalomyelopathy shows macroscopically visible lesions in the substantia nigra and corpora quadrigemina.

feature linking the condition with Wernicke's encephalopathy (Fig. 125). The topological pattern is distinctive. The optic nerves, chiasma and tracts and the basal ganglia are often involved. However, the most striking changes are usually found in the brainstem, viz. the substantia nigra, red nuclei, corpora

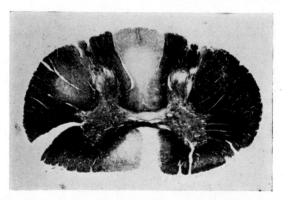

Fig. 127. The spinal cord in a case of Leigh's encephalomyelopathy shows loss of myelin in the posterior, lateral and anterior columns. Similar changes may be present in cases of subacute combined degeneration (Heidenhain × 8).

quadrigemina, tegmentum and inferior olives (Fig. 126). The cerebellar dentate nuclei may be also affected. The spinal cord presents almost invariably loss of myelin in the posterior, lateral and anterior columns in a manner similar to that of subacute combined degeneration (Fig. 127). Rarefaction, neuronal loss and gliosis have been observed in the anterior horns of the spinal cord. The peripheral nerves have shown, when examined, foci of myelin loss (Reye, 1960).

Clinical Pathology

It is not yet possible to diagnose the condition in life unless a sib has died from this disease and been studied pathologically.

REFERENCES

ANDERSON, N. A. D. (1961). In 'Pathology,' St. Louis: Mosby, p. 1002.

ARNIM, G. V., and ENGEL, P. (1964). *Develop. Med. Child Neurol.*, **6**, 366.

AURBACH, G. D., and POTTS, J. T. (1964). *Advances in Metabolic Disorders*, **1**, 45.

BAKER, L., MELLMAN, W. J., TEDESCO, T. A., and SEGAL, S. (1966). *J. Pediat.*, **68**, 551.

BARTTER, F. C. (1966). In Stanbury, J. B., Wyngaarden, J. B., and Fredrickson, D. S. 'The Metabolic Basis of Inherited Disease,' New York: McGraw-Hill, p. 1024.

BASSEN, F. A., and KORNZWEIG, A. L. (1950). *Blood*, **5**, 381.

BEARN, A. G. (1966). In Stanbury, J. B., Wyngaarden, J. B., and Fredrickson, D. S .'The Metabolic Basis of Inherited Disease,' New York: McGraw-Hill, p. 761.

BECROFT, D. M. O., COSTELLO, J. M., and SCOTT, P. J. (1965). *Arch. Dis. Childh.*, **40**, 40.

BEUTLER, E., BALUDA, M. C., STURGEON, P., and DAY, R. (1965). *Lancet*, **1**, 353.

BIGLER, J. A., MAIS, R. F., DOWBEN, R. M., and HSIA, D. Y. -Y. (1959). *Pediatrics*, **23**, 644.

BLIZZARD, R. M., CHANDLER, R. U., LARDING, B. H., PETTIT, M. D., and WEST, C. D. (1960). *New Engl. J. Med.*, **263**, 337.

BLIZZARD, R. M., and COON, W. T. (1963). *Clin. Proc. Child Hosp. (Wash.)*, **19**, 207.

BRIGGS, J. N., and HAWORTH, J. C. (1964). *Amer. J. Med.*, **36**, 443.

BROWN, D. M., REYNOLDS, J. W., MICHAEL, A. F., and ULSTROM, R. A. (1966). *Pediatrics*, **37**, 447.

CALDERON, R. (1966). *J. Pediat.*, **68**, 423.

CARDIFF, R. D. (1966). *Pediatrics*, **37**, 249.

CATEL, W., and SCHMIDT, J. (1959). *Dtsch. med. Wschr.*, **84**, 2145.

CHOREMIS, C., VLACHOS, J., KATERELOS, C., and KARPOUZAS, J. (1962). *Ann. paediat.(Basel)*, **1**, 198.

CHRISTENSEN, E., MELCHIOR, J. C., and PLUM, P. (1963). *Acta paediat. (Stockh.)*, **52**, 304.

COLLE, E. D., and ULSTROM, R. A, (1964). J. Pediat., *64*, 632.

CROME, L. (1962). *Arch. Dis. Childh.*, **37**, 415.

CROME, L., and SYLVESTER, P. E. (1960). *Arch. Dis. Childh.*, **35**, 620.

CROME, L., CUMINGS, J. N., and DUCKETT, S. (1963). *J. Neurol. Neurosurg. Psychiat.*, **26**, 422.

DICKER, S. E., and EGGLETON, M. G. (1963). *Clin. Sci.*, **24**, 81.

DRASH, A., and WOLFF, F. (1964). *Metabolism*, **13**, 487.

DUBOWITZ, V. (1965). *Arch. Dis. Childh.*, **40**, 296.

EBELS, E. J., BLOKZIJL, E. J., and TROELSTRA, J. A. (1965). *Helv. paediat. Acta*, **20**, 310.

EBERLEIN, W. R., BROWN, B. I., and SIDBURY, J. B. (1961). *Amer. J. Dis. Child.*, **102**, 491.

EBERLEIN, W. R., ILLINGWORTH, B. A., and SIDBURY, J. B. (1962). *Amer. J. Med.*, **33**, 20.

EGAN, T. J., and WELLS, W. W. (1966). *Amer. J. Dis. Child.*, **111**, 400.

ERBSLÖH, F. (1958). 'Endemischer Kretinismus,' in O. Lubarsch, F. Henke, and R. Rössle's Handbuch der speziellen pathologischen Anatomie und Histologie, **13**, ed. W. Scholz, Pt. 2, book B, Berlin: Springer, p. 1758.

ERICKSON, R. (1965). *J. Pediat.*, **66**, 1004.

EVANS, P. R. (1965). *Lancet*, **1**, 721.

FARQUHAR, J. U., and WAYS, P. (1966). In Stanbury *et al.* 'The Metabolic Basis of Inherited Disease,' New York: McGraw-Hill, p. 509.

FEIGIN, I., and WOLF, A. (1954). *J. Pediat.*, **45**, 234.

FIELD, R. A. (1966). In Stanbury *et al.* 'The Metabolic Basis of Inherited Disease,' New York: McGraw-Hill, p. 141.

FORSYTH, C. C., LLOYD, J. K., and FOSBROOKE, A. S. (1965). *Arch. Dis. Childh.*, **40**, 47.

FREDRICKSON, D. S., and LEES, R. S. (1966). In Stanbury *et al.* 'The Metabolic Basis of Inherited Disease,' New York: McGraw-Hill, p. 429.

FRENCH, F. S., and VAN WYK, J. J. (1964). *J. Pediat.*, **64**, 589.
FROESCH, E. R. (1966). In Stanbury *et al.* 'The Metabolic Basis of Inherited Disease,' New York: McGraw-Hill, p. 124.
GAJDUSEK, D. C. (1962). *Pediatrics*, **29**, 235.
GELBER, S., CAMPBELL, P. L., DEIBLER, G. E., and SOKOLOFF, L. (1964). *J. Neurochem.*, **11**, 221.
GITZELMANN, R. (1965). *Lancet*, **2**, 670.
GOOLDEN, A. W. G., GARSIDE, J. M., and OSORIO, C. (1965). *J. clin. Endocr.*, **25**, 127.
GREENBERG, R., and REAVEN, G. (1966). *Pediatrics*, **37**, 934.
HANSEN, R. G., BRETTHAUER, R. K., MAYES, J., and NORDIN, J. H. (1964). *Proc. Soc. exp. Biol.* (*N. Y.*), **115**, 560.
HERS, H. G. (1963). *Biochem. J.*, **86**, 11.
HOEFNAGEL, D. (1965). *J. ment. Defic. Res.*, **9**, 69.
HSIA, D.Y.-Y. (1965). In Carter, C. H. 'Medical Aspects of Mental Retardation,' Springfield: Thomas, p. 596.
HSIA, D.Y.-Y., and WALKER, F. A. (1961). *J. Pediat.*, **59**, 872.
HÜBSCHER, G., SMITH, M. E., and GURR, M. I. (1964). In Dawson, R. M. C., and Rhodes, D. N. 'Metabolism and Physiological Significance of Lipids,' New York: Wiley, p. 229.
HUG, G., GARANCIS, J. C., SCHUBERT, W. K., and KAPLAN, S. (1966). *Amer. J. Dis. Child.*, **111**, 457.
ISSELBACHER, K. J. (1966). In Stanbury *et al.* 'The Metabolic Basis of Inherited Disease,' New York: McGraw-Hill, p. 178.
JUE, K. L., NOREN, G. R., and ANDERSON, R. C. (1965). *J. Pediat.*, **67**, 1130.
KENNY, F. M., ACETO, T., PURISCH, M., HARRISON, H. E., HARRISON, H. C., and BLIZZARD, R. M. (1963). *J. Pediat.*, **62**, 531.
KIRMAN, B. H. (1965). In Hilliard, L. T., and Kirman, B. H. 'Mental Deficiency,' London: Churchill, p. 516.
KIRMAN, B. H., BLACK, J. A., WILKINSON, R. W., and EVANS, P. R. (1956). *Arch. Dis. Childh.*, **31**, 59.
LEIGH, D. (1951). *J. Neurol. Neurosurg. Psychiat.*, **14**, 216.
LESCH, M., and NYHAN, W. L. (1964). *Amer. J. Med.*, **36**, 561.
LEVIN, B., OBERHOLZER, V. G., SNODGRASS, G. J. A. I., STIMMLER, L., and WILMERS, M. J. (1963). *Arch. Dis. Childh.*, **38**, 220.
LEWIS, G. M., SPENCER-PEET, J., and STEWART, K. M. (1963). *Arch. Dis. Childh.*, **38**, 40.
MANCALL, E. L., APONTE, G. E., and BERRY, R. G. (1965). *J. Neuropath. exp. Neurol.*, **24**, 85.
MARKS, A. N., and MAN, E. B. (1965). *Pediatrics*, **35**, 753.
MARKS, V., and ROSE, F. C. (1965). 'Hypoglycaemia,' Oxford: Blackwell.
MARKS, J. F., HAMLIN, M., and ZACK, P. (1966). *J. Pediat.*, **68**, 559.
MARQUES, M. G. (1965). 'Interrelations of the Thyroid Gland in Human Pregnancy, Infancy and Childhood,' Nat. Inst. of Neurological Diseases and Blindness, Bethesda, Md.
MCGIRR, E. M., and HUTCHISON, J. H. (1953). *Lancet*, **1**, 1117.
MIDDLETON, G. D., and HOCKADAY, T. D. R. (1965). *Diabetologia*, **1**, 116.
NYHAN, W. L., OLIVER, W. J., and LESCH, M. (1965). *J. Pediat.*, **67**, 257.
ORLOFF, J., and HANDLER, J. S. (1964). *Amer. J. Med.*, **36**, 686.
ORLOFF, J., and BURG, M. B. (1966). In Stanbury *et al.* 'The Metabolic Basis of Inherited Disease,' New York: McGraw-Hill, p. 1247.
PARR, J., TEREE, T. M., and LARNER, J. (1965). *Pediatrics*, **35**, 770.
PEARCE, G. W., PEARCE, J. M. S., and WALTON, J. N. (1966). *Brain*, **89**, 109.
PICKERING, D. E. (1962). *Pediatrics*, **29**, 692.
PICKERING, D. E. (1964). *Amer. J. Dis. Child.*, **107**, 567.
RAMAN, G., and BEIERWALTES, W. H. (1959). *J. clin. Endocr.*, **19**, 221.
RÉSIBOIS-GRÉGOIRE, A., and DOUROV, N. (1966). *Acta neuropath.* (*Berl.*), **6**, 70.
REUSS, A. V. (1908). *Wien. med. Wschr.*, **58**, 799.
REYE, R. D. K. (1960). *J. Path. Bact.*, **79**, 165.
RICHTER, R. B. (1957). *J. Neuropath. exp. Neurol.*, **16**, 28.
RILEY, I. D. (1960). *Arch Dis. Childh.*, **35**, 293.
RUESS, A. L., and ROSENTHAL, I. M. (1963). *Amer. J. Dis. Child.*, **105**, 358.
RUTTER, M. (1966). *Develop. Med. Child Neurol.*, **8**, 85.

SALT, H. B., WOLFF, O. H., LLOYD, J. K., FOSBROOKE, A. S., CAMERON, A. H., and HUBBLE, D. V. (1960). *Lancet*, **2**, 325.

SAMOLS, E., and DORMANDY, T. L. (1963). *Lancet*, **1**, 478.

SCHOTLAND, M. G., GRUMBACH, M. M., and STRAUSS, J. (1963). *Pediatrics*, **31**, 741.

SCHULTZ, M. A., FORSANDER, J. B., CHEZ, R. A., and HUTCHINSON, D. L. (1965). *Pediatrics*, **35**, 743.

SEEGMILLER, J. E., LASTER, L., and HOWELL, R. R. (1963). *New Engl. J. Med.*, **268**, 712, 764 and 821.

SIDBURY, J. B. (1961). In Gardner, L. I. 'Molecular Genetics and Human Disease,' Springfield: Thomas, p. 61.

SIMMONS, R. L., and HAWKINS, B. W. (1965). *Tex. St. J. Med.*, **61**, 407.

SOBREVILLA, L. A., GOODMAN, M. L., and KANE, C. A. (1964). *Amer. J. Med.*, **37**, 821.

SPENCER-PEET, J. (1965). *Proc. Ass. clin. Biochemists* (Great Britain), **7**, 253.

STAFFURTH, J. S. (1964). In Dyke, S. C. 'Recent Advances in Clinical Pathology,' Series IV, London: Churchill, p. 128.

STANBURY, J. B. (1966). In Stanbury *et al.* 'The Metabolic Basis of Inherited Disease,' New York: McGraw-Hill, p. 215.

STUART-MASON, A. (1963). 'The Thyroid and its Diseases.' Proceedings of a Conference at the Royal College of Physicians of London, London: Pitman Medical.

SYMPOSIUM (1963). Research in Muscular Dystrophy. Proceedings of the 2nd Symposium, Muscular Dystrophy Group, London: Pitman Medical.

SYMPOSIUM (1965). Research in Muscular Dystrophy. Proceedings of the 3rd Symposium, Muscular Dystrophy Group, London: Pitman Medical.

TOM, M. I., and REWCASTLE, N. B. (1962). *Neurology (Minneap.)*, **12**, 624.

TUTHILL, C. R. (1959–60). *Arch. Psychiat. Nervenkr.*, **200**, 520.

TYLER, F. H. (1966). In Stanbury *et al.* 'The Metabolic Basis of Inherited Disease,' New York: McGraw-Hill, p. 939.

VIRCHOW, R. (1852). *Verh. phys. -med. Ges. Würzb.*, **2**, 230.

WAYS, P., REED, C. F., and HANAHAN, D. J. (1963). *J. clin. Invest.*, **42**, 1248.

WOLFF, O. H. (1965). *Develop. Med. Child Neurol.*, **7**, 430.

WOOLF, L. I. (1962). *Advanc. clin. Chem.*, **5**, 1.

WOOLF, L. I. (1966). 'Renal Tubular Dysfunction,' Springfield: Thomas.

WORSLEY, H. E., BROOKFIELD, R. W., ELWOOD, J. S., NOBLE, R. L., and TAYLOR, W. H. (1965). *Arch. Dis. Childh.*, **40**, 492.

WYNGAARDEN, J. B. (1966). In Stanbury *et al.* 'The Metabolic Basis of Inherited Disease,' New York: McGraw-Hill, p. 667.

CHAPTER 13

MISCELLANEOUS CONDITIONS

Birth Injury

The rôle of birth injury has been considered at length in an earlier chapter (p. 57). It was concluded that while its incidence remains uncertain, some of the previously expressed views regarding its prevalence have been exaggerated. Nevertheless, birth injury could perhaps account for as much as 5 per cent of severe subnormality associated in most cases with epilepsy and cerebral palsy. In this book birth injury and its sequelae are not presented as one syndrome. The possible pathogenetic mechanisms include such diverse factors as mechanical injury, anoxia, circulatory collapse, oedema, acidosis, various forms of haemorrhage, congestion, thrombosis and ischaemia. The resulting changes are, understandably, manifold and diverse. Certain recognition of the cause is also usually impossible years after the event. It does not appear useful therefore, in the present state of knowledge, to unify under a single heading the clinical and pathological data relating to birth injury. It is probably true, however, that in many cases residual changes of birth injury conform to the patterns outlined in the discussion on gliotic encephalopathy (e.g. ulegyria, marbling and cavitation), even though similar lesions could also follow other causes (p. 131). Some authors prefer to deal with the subject under one heading. For such an aproach readers can be referred to the accounts of Schwartz (1961) and Norman (1963). The experience derived from experimental attempts to reproduce the effects of 'birth injury' in monkeys has been summarized by Windle (1963). Most of the experimental procedures were based on the induction of anoxia in newborn animals. 'Mental retardation' could be successfully induced in some animals, but as already explained (p. 61), corresponding neuropathological changes, insofar as they have been reported, seem rather unlike those usually attributed to birth injury in children.

Residual Kernicterus

Neonatal jaundice and its sequelae have also been discussed in an earlier section (p. 68). The syndrome of residual kernicterus consists usually of mental retardation, athetoid cerebral palsy and deafness, but atypical variants with such signs as ataxia, epilepsy and hemiplegia, may also occur. The morphological changes in both the acute and the residual stages of the condition have been described and summarized by a number of authors (Crome, 1955a). In brief, the characteristic lesions in the residual cases consist of atrophy and gliosis of the globus pallidus and the subthalamic nucleus, and it is noteworthy that the globus pallidus may show evidence suggestive of continuing degeneration years after birth. Atrophic lesions have been reported in the hippocampus, caudate nucleus, putamen and inferior olives, while diffuse cortical neuronal depletion could be also detected in a few cases, particularly those associated with severe subnormality.

Hallervorden-Spatz Syndrome

This condition is characterized by progressive rigidity with or without athetosis. Many, perhaps most, of the recorded cases have been mentally retarded and some have had epilepsy. The most striking pathological change is enlargement and rusty brownish discolouration of the globus pallidus and the anterior part of the substantia nigra. Microscopically, there is considerable increase of the pigment which is present normally in the substantia nigra. Some of the accumulated material gives a positive reaction for iron. In addition, there is widespread neuroaxonal dystrophy, a change already referred to on p. 122. A masterly summary of the condition is that by Meyer (1963), and the character of neuroaxonal changes has been discussed by Seitelberger and Gross (1957) and by Cowen and Olmstead (1963). The patients examined by Környey (1964) showed increased urinary excretion of copper and high blood caeruloplasmin. The gamma globulins in the blood and C.S.F. were also increased. The copper content of the blood, brain and liver in one of their cases coming to autopsy was normal.

Acrocephalosyndactyly and Related Conditions

Acrocephalosyndactyly or Apert's syndrome is, if fully expressed, a very striking condition. The patient's skull is acrocephalic, i.e. high and shortened anteroposteriorly (Fig. 128). The eyes are prominent and widely set, sloping downwards and outwards in a so-called 'antimongolian' slant (Fig. 129). The palate is high and sometimes cleft, showing, in some instances, a shelf-like bony outgrowth of the alveolar margin. The obvious anomaly of the hands and feet is fusion of digits—syndactyly. However, the changes are more complex. In addition to the failure of some of the developing digits to separate transversely, there is frequent absence of the terminal phalanges (failure of vertical separation) and of some metacarpal and metatarsal bones. The distal phalanges of the fingers are often joined to each other by bony arches and may have a single common nail; this is particularly so in the case of the three middle fingers, which usually form a 'mid-digital' mass. The cranial sutures are anomalous. The lambdoid, sagittal, coronal, metopic and squamous sutures, usually easily distinguishable in the crania of children and young adults, may not be seen. The mobility of some of the larger joints, such as the shoulders and elbows, may be impaired by flattening of the articular surfaces, epiphyseal fragmentation or ankylosis. The bodies and arches of some of the vertebrae are frequently fused.

The cranial and facial features of patients with *Crouzon's syndrome* resemble those described above but all or most of the other associated skeletal changes are lacking.

It is not known how often patients with either of the above syndromes are mentally retarded, but subnormality is a feature in many of the recorded cases.

Relatively little is known of the neuropathological changes in Apert's and

Crouzon's syndromes (Crome, 1961). Gliotic infiltration of the meninges, especially at the base of the brain, and astrocytic gliosis of the median thalamic nuclei, the raphé of the midbrain, part of the red nuclei and corpus Luysii, and of the emboliform cerebellar nuclei have been recently reported in a case of Crouzon's syndrome by Hariga (1963). Ventricular dilatation was present in a few other cases, and some showed absence of the corpus callosum.

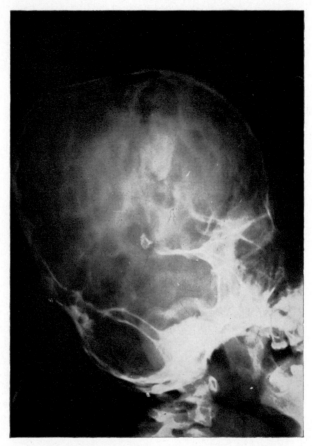

FIG. 128. Lateral X-ray of the skull of a child with acrocephalosyndactyly showing the characteristic shape and the 'digital' markings. Tantalum foil had been inserted during the surgical attempt to disunite the sutures.

Apart from the anomalous shape conditioned by the characteristic contours of the skull, some of the brains were apparently normal.

It is thought by some workers that the cerebral changes and associated mental subnormality in cases of acrocephaly are caused by craniosynostosis or 'craniostenosis', viz. premature closure of the sutures followed by compression of the growing brain by the unyielding skull. Various surgical procedures have been accordingly designed to prevent or relieve such an effect. The concept is open, however, to serious objections.

A condition partially resembling Apert's and the Laurence-Moon-Biedl syndrome has been discussed by Temtamy (1966). The salient features of the case presented by him were acrocephaly, 'peculiar' facies, brachysyndactyly of the fingers, preaxial polydactyly and syndactyly of the toes, hypogenitalism,

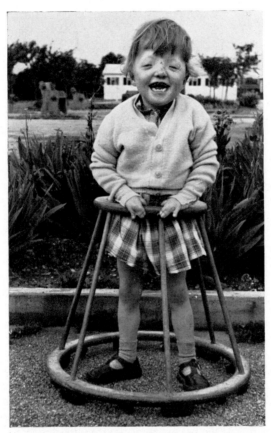

FIG. 129. A child with acrocephalosyndactyly (Apert's syndrome) Note the widely set eyes, their 'antimongolian' slant, and the syndactyly.

obesity and mental retardation. Twelve comparable cases had been previously recorded, and ten of these were familial. Autosomal recessive transmission is therefore a possible aetiological factor. The author suggests that this condition should be designated *acrocephalopolysyndactyly* or *Carpenter's syndrome*.

There are several other syndromes characterized by cranial and facial malformation and, occasionally, mental retardation, although their pathology is still obscure. *Hypertelorism* is characterized by excessive width in the spacing of the eyes. The great wings of the sphenoid are disproportionately small, and the small wings—large (Gross, 1965). *Scaphocephaly* denotes marked antero-posterior elongation of the head. In the *Franceschetti syndrome* or mandibulo-facial dysostosis there is an 'antimongolian' slant of the eyes, hypoplasia of the zygomata and mandible, malformation of the outer, and less frequently, the middle and inner ears, colobomata in the outer parts of the lower eyelids, a big mouth with a high palate, misplacement of the teeth, and a sinus between the ears and the mouth. A rare disease occasionally mentioned in relation to this group of conditions is *cleidocranial dysostosis of Marie and Sainton* (Stewart, 1928–29), in which, however, intelligence is usually normal (Levin and Sonnenschein, 1963). Mandibulofacial dysostosis and some related conditions can be considered as manifestations of maldevelopment of the first visceral arch—*first arch syndrome* (McKenzie, 1966).

Another condition somewhat similar to the Franceschetti syndrome is *oculoauriculovertebral dysplasia* or Goldenhar's syndrome (Gorlin, Jue, Jacobsen and Goldschmidt, 1963; Smithells, 1964a). It is characterized by conjunctival dermoids, colobomata, microphthalmia, skin tags and sinuses in front of the ears, microtia, micrognathia, fused, bifid or supernumerary vertebrae, anomalous ribs, frontal bossing, low anterior hair-line, hemi-facial microsomia and congenital heart disease. Mental retardation has been present in 10 per cent of the recorded cases, but many of the remainder were perhaps too young for a reliable psychological assessment. The chief features of the *orofaciodigital syndrome* comprise hypertrophy of the lingual and gingival frenulae, cleft tongue, midline pseudo-cleft of the upper lip, lateral displace-ment of the medial canthi, clinodactyly, syndactyly, and brachydactyly (Smithells, 1964b). Mental retardation was present in 50 per cent of the recorded cases and some also showed trembling of the extremities. The *mandibulooculofacial dyscephaly* (Hallerman-Streiff syndrome) denotes the association of mental retardation, brachycephaly, dwarfism, partial alopecia, low-set ears, small and beaked nose, micrognathia, ocular anomalies (such as microphthalmia and cataract), and dental anomalies, including the presence of erupted teeth at birth (Hoefnagel and Benirschke, 1965).

The Marinesco-Sjögren Syndrome is a rather vaguely defined condition, the chief features of which are mental retardation, signs attributed to cere-bellar, and, sometimes, to pyramidal involvement, and cataracts (Garland and Moorhouse, 1953; MacGillivray, 1957; Calvi, 1963; Norwood, 1964). Associated neuropathological changes remain obscure. In a case considered an instance of this disease Todorov (1964) observed profound cerebellar changes comprising massive cortical atrophy which did not involve, however, the nodulus, flocculus and paraflocculus ventralis. Some of the surviving Purkinje cells were vacuolated and binucleate. The author is inclined to re-gard the Marinesco-Sjögren syndrome as an infantile variant of Pierre Marie's disease.

Alpers' disease or diffuse cerebral degeneration of infancy has been men-tioned already (p. 200). This is a seemingly rare disease characterized by progressive dementia which sets in after a period of apparently normal early development. Associated signs may include focal or generalized con-vulsions, occasional blindness, choreoathetosis and tremor. The main pathological findings are diffuse degeneration of grey matter in many parts of the brain, particularly in the cerebral cortex, cerebellum, and basal ganglia. Neurones are depleted in these areas and there is associated microglial and astrocytic proliferation. The white matter shows gliosis with loss of myelin sheaths and axis cylinders (Blackwood, Buxton, Cumings, Robertson and Tucker, 1963). Since the precise onset of a supposedly acquired progressive cerebral disease may well be blurred in early infancy, the differentiation of Alpers' disease from generalized congenital gliotic encephalopathy (lobar sclerosis) may prove impossible in certain cases. The neuropathological findings can also remain equivocal.

It is certain that Alpers' disease is not an aetiologically homogeneous group. Identical cerebral changes have been observed, for example, in Addison's disease,* Cockayne's syndrome (*vide infra*) and juvenile diabetes mellitus. In a case reported by Dreifuss and Netzky (1964) cerebral and cerebellar degeneration was extreme, assuming a spongiform, cystic character in many areas. The condition had apparently commenced as an encephalitis. Alpers' disease has been reviewed by Greenhouse and Neubuerger (1964).

The Refsum syndrome (heredopathia atactica polyneuritiformis) presents usually as a combination of polyneuritis, cerebellar ataxia, retinitis pigmentosa, hemeralopia, anomaly of the pupils, deafness and albuminocytological dissociation of the cerebrospinal fluid (i.e. a rise in the C.S.F. protein without a corresponding increase in the number of cells) (Refsum, 1960). Although mental impairment has not been recorded in the earlier cases, the findings in a recent one (Richterich, Kahlke, Mechelen and Rossi, 1963) suggest that the condition may in some cases be associated with lipidosis. The lesions in the peripheral nerves are identical with those of interstitial hypertrophic neuritis of Dejerine-Sottas (Dereux, 1963).

Excessive amounts of 3,7,11,15-tetramethyl hexadecanoic acid have recently been isolated from the liver, kidney and serum of patients with Refsum's disease (Kahlke and Richterich, 1965). This branched chain fatty acid is formed from the chlorophyll derivative phytol and can be further metabolized to the cholesterol precursor, mevalonic acid. When phytol is given to patients with Refsum's disease, 3,7,11,15-tetramethyl hexadecanoic acid (phytanic acid) accumulates in the body fluids; this does not happen in normal subjects. Similar abnormalities of lipid metabolism have been detected in the cases reported by Rake and Saunders (1966) and Alexander 1966). Serum cholesterol levels are, however, normal in the disease, suggesting that mevalonic acid metabolism is not unduly disturbed. The rôle of the fatty acid in the pathogenesis of the disease is not yet known. The results of treating patients with a diet low in chlorophyll are awaited with interest.

The De Lange syndrome comprises mental deficiency in combination with a number of somatic anomalies. The patients are usually dwarfed and show some micro- and brachycephaly. The forehead is low and covered with fine lanugo-like hair. The eyes show an 'antimongolian' slant. Prominent veins are present in the lateral parts of the forehead. The eyebrows are prominent

* See Gordon, N. S., and Marsden, H. B. (1966). *Develop. Med. Child. Neurol.*, **8**, 719.

and heavy and are often confluent over the bridge of the nose. The eyelashes are long and delicate. The nose is small and depressed, and the nostrils are flaring. The mandible is usually small. The ears are low-set. There is hypertrichosis of the back. The limbs are somewhat short and the elbows cannot be fully extended. Many cases show incurving of the little finger, and the thumb is usually short and implanted more proximally than normally. The feet are small and about half the cases show partial webbing between the second and third toes. Other less constant anomalies have also been described. Although the complete syndrome appears to be rare, many of the signs enumerated above occur relatively frequently in patients suffering from other conditions as well as in unclassifiable cases of mental retardation (Jervis and Stimson, 1963). The brain appears to have been examined in only two instances, the only significant findings being micrencephaly and deficiency of myelination (Ptacek et al., 1963).

The chromosomes have been studied in many cases of De Lange syndrome. Some karyograms are normal (Schlesinger, Clayton, Bodian and Jones, 1963; Aberfeld and Pourfar, 1965). Other karyograms showed an extra small chromosomal fragment (Jervis and Stimson, 1963; Dodge, 1965). More recently Falek, Schmidt and Jervis (1966) described a family of three affected sibs and their relatives. They found that some of the relatives were 'carriers' who were phenotypically normal but whose karyograms showed translocation of the major portion of one of the G chromosomes to a part of chromosome A3. The affected children showed, on the other hand, an excess of chromosome A3 material. For a useful recent review of the condition readers are referred to Karpati et al. (1965).

Another syndrome characterized even more vaguely by allegedly distinctive facies goes by the name of leprechaunism (Kálló, Lakatos, and Szijártó, 1965). The reported laboratory data in seven published cases of this condition have been considered by Dekaban (1965). None of the chemical findings appeared to be significant but the brain of one of the cases showed cerebral agyria and rudimentary cerebellar development.

In ataxia-telangiectasia (Louis-Bar syndrome) there is cerebellar ataxia or choreoathetosis with later development of telangiectases in the conjunctivae, ears, eyelids, bridge of the nose, neck, dorsum of the hands and feet, and folds of the knees and elbows. The condition appears to be frequently associated with hypogammaglobulinaemia (Gutmann and Lemli, 1963) and in all the reported familial cases was consistent with autosomal recessive inheritance (Paine and Efron, 1963). The cases observed by Thieffry and his colleagues (1961) presented also alcaptonuria and aminoaciduria. The few cases examined pathologically showed rather equivocal abnormalities of the meninges as well as cerebral and cerebellar changes (Ford, 1966; Hansen, 1962; Annotation, 1963). Atrophy of the cerebellar granular layer, and, to a lesser degree, of the Purkinje cells has been observed in a number of cases (Osetowska and Traczynska, 1963), but the interpretation of these changes is somewhat uncertain.

Data relating to a possible new rare syndrome, relatively often associated with mental deficiency, have been presented by Hallgren (1959). Its main features are retinitis pigmentosa and congenital deafness. Vestibulo-cerebellar ataxia was present in some cases.

A combination of supravalvular aortic stenosis, characteristic facies, identical dental anomalies and mental retardation observed in 10 cases has been reported by Beuren et al. (1964).

Börjeson, Forssman and Lehman (1962) have described a seemingly new syndrome in three brothers who suffered from mental deficiency, epilepsy, infantilism, low metabolic rate and dwarfism. Another similar but non-familial case has been reported by Baar and Galindo (1965). This boy had large breasts, hypogonadism, and hemiatrophy with cavitation of the brain. His karyogram was normal.

A condition numbered 47 in Table 4 on p. 214 is an undesignated disorder described by Menkes and colleagues (1962) which was observed in 5 males in two generations of a single family. The patients had white abnormal hair (pili torti, monilethrix and trichorrhexis nodosa) and severe mental retardation. An excess of plasma glutamic acid is said to have been present in some of the cases but not all of the quoted figures are abnormal. Pathologically, there was widespread focal degeneration of the cerebral cortex and basal ganglia, secondary degeneration of the white matter, and cerebellar atrophy.*

The incidence of *cleft palate* and, probably, of other skeletal anomalies is also relatively high in the severely subnormal. Thus in a series of 1,915 cases of severe mental defect in children there were 19 instances of obvious cleft palate, a proportion of 0·992 per cent. This compared with an incidence of 0·057 per cent in children examined in general hospitals (*Brit. med. J.*, 1957).

It is not possible to mention here all the numerous reports dealing with more unusual cases associated with mental retardation. Some may be the first descriptions of newly recognized syndromes and others of atypical variants of known diseases. There is much scope, of course, for the grouping of cases into yet further syndromes by certain, often arbitrarily selected characteristics, many of which are rather common among retarded individuals. Thus, Smith, Lemli and Opitz (1964) have recently reported a new syndrome in three unrelated children. This consists of microcepahly, mental defect, hypertonicity, retardation of growth, a short nose with anteverted nostrils, broad maxillary alveolar ridges, mild micrognathia, hypogenitalism, abnormal upper palmar creases, and foot anomalies. The so-called *Rubinstein-Taybi syndrome* is constituted by mental deficiency, unusual facial features, broad thumbs and first toes, retardation of skeletal growth, and incomplete or delayed descent of the testes (Jancar, 1965).† All of the above signs are, however, common among the severely subnormal. The usefulness of grouping cases into these and other syndromes, not mentioned here, is doubtful.

Cockayne's Syndrome denotes dwarfism with disproportionately long limbs, a prematurely senile appearance (progeria), prognathism, sunken eyes, mental deficiency, light sensitivity, retinal degeneration with pigmentation, optic atrophy and cataracts (Neill and Dingwall, 1950; Macdonald, Fitch and

* See also footnote on p. 214.
† See also Berg, J. M. et al. (1966). *J. ment. Defic. Res.*, **10**, 204.

Lewis, 1960). One of the recorded cases died aged 12 years. His brain was examined by us. It weighed 919 g. and showed marked active cerebral atrophy with conspicuous capillary proliferation. Atrophic changes were present in the basal ganglia and substantia nigra. The white matter showed demyelination, rarefaction and some gliosis.

Some cases of mental retardation may be associated with *hemi-* or *bi-ballismus* and show atrophy of the subthalamic nuclei and other formations, e.g. mamillary bodies, dorsomedial nuclei and pulvinaria of the thalamus, and the periaqueductal grey matter (Malamud and Demmy, 1960). Severe degeneration of the lateral thalamic nuclei has been described in three infants by Rosales and Riggs (1962). After normal birth, the patients showed failure to thrive, paralysis, opisthotonos and convulsions. A case presented by Jervis (1957) showed progressive severe dementia with paralysis which commenced at 15 months. He died aged $5\frac{1}{2}$ years and the main neuropathological changes were diffuse cerebral cortical degeneration with glial overgrowth, cerebellar atrophy, and degeneration of the basal ganglia with accumulation in them of large quantities of sudanophil material, most of which contained cholesterol.

Special Problems

It remains to discuss in this concluding section certain specific aspects in the relationship of dysfunction to cerebral pathological changes, which have not been covered elsewhere.

The Neonatal Manifestation of Subnormality

Marked contrasts may be observed during the neonatal development of the severely subnormal. Some of these babies scarcely weather a stormy neonatal period marked by convulsions, paralysis, coma and feeding difficulties. In other cases, early development is tranquil and seemingly normal: according to reports, the infants feed well, respond to touch, react appropriately to pain and pleasure, and may show the semblance of a smile. The subnormality may become obvious at only about 10 weeks or even later and then just to trained observers or mothers with previous experience of children. Yet, subsequent pathological examination can disclose in some of these cases profound anomalies, including an all but total absence of the telencephalic structures. Such early 'normality' can occur, for example, in many cases of hydrencephaly; an instance reported in considerable detail by Gamper (1926) was that of an infant with arhinencephaly and encephalocele, whom he called 'Mittelhirnwesen' (a mesencephalic creature).

Such contrasts merit more study than they have received. However, it is perhaps justifiable to regard a newborn infant as a clinically subcortical being, who lives mainly on unconditioned reflexes of the subcortical formations. The cerebral cortex is still very 'immature' in the human newborn, and its absence need occasion little disturbance of observable function provided that the disease is 'burnt-out' or quiescent.* The first serious manifestations of cerebral deficiency can be expected later, at a time when the cortex normally assumes greater regulating control over the lower levels of the central nervous system.

* Cerebral function in the newborn has been recently considered by Robinson, R. (1966). *Develop. Med. Child. Neurol.*, **8**, 561.

The Problem of Mild Subnormality

As explained already, accumulated pathological knowledge has been derived almost entirely from the study of low-grade cases. Information on pathological changes in higher-grade persons is very scanty. For example, only 9 cases in the series studied by Crome (1960) were feebleminded or educationally subnormal. These are listed in Table 11. Some of the milder cases show changes similar to but less severe than those in the low-grade ones, and in other instances no changes are detectable by available methods. In a further large group of mild cases the retardation might be explained by the cumulative effect of several adverse pathogenetic factors, none of which is decisive on its own. These might include, for example, indifferent cerebral endowment, educational deprivation, domestic difficulties, illegitimacy, frequent illness, and so on.

Specific Deficits

Besides impaired intelligence, subnormal persons often display a variety of more specific disabilities and neurological signs. These include all forms of epilepsy, paralysis, disorders of muscle tone and of sensation, athetosis, tremor, ballismus, strabismus, nystagmus, blindness, and deafness, and some of these signs have been mentioned with the descriptions of the lesions and syndromes in the foregoing parts of the text. In general, the correlation of these signs with the structural lesions is very incomplete compared with that in mentally more normal individuals. This is due partly to relative lack of study but also to the inherent complexity of the problems involved. It is usually impossible, for example, to ascertain the central cause of a squint in a brain showing severe and widespread gliotic encephalopathy.

Some severely subnormal persons show typical correlation of lesions and clinical signs, but in many cases specific manifestations are overlaid by the associated global motor and sensory defect. Apart from blindness and deafness, the causation of which is usually readily understandable, cerebral palsy and epilepsy are the two most important of the specific deficits in cases of severe subnormality.

Sensory Syndromes (Insensitivity to Pain)

It is sometimes suggested (Popper, 1920) that idiots do not always respond to painful stimuli. In fact, a survey of some 600 severely retarded children (Stengel *et al.*, 1955) showed a normal pattern of wincing and withdrawal from pin prick. However, like mentally normal individuals, a few of the severely subnormal may suffer from selective insensitivity to pain and this may or may not be associated with anhydrosis (Swanson, 1963; Pinsky and Di-George, 1966). These patients often develop deep and infected ulcers, osteo-myelitis, arthropathy and may lose their terminal phalanges. Amyloid disease may supervene. The syndrome may be due to different causes. In some cases there is progressive or non-progressive sensory radicular neuropathy mani-fested by severe neuronal degeneration in the dorsal root ganglia (Denny-

Table 11. FINDINGS IN NINE MILDLY SUBNORMAL PATIENTS

Age	Clinical Features	Brain weight expressed as per cent of average normal	Pathological Findings
5	Epilepsy. Borderline E.S.N. level. Binet I.Q. 54.	76	Slight micrencephaly.
20	Laurence-Moon-Biedl syndrome.	79	Laurence-Moon-Biedl syndrome.
35	Dull normal to low average. Wechsler I.Q. 79. Matrices 83. Educational deprivation.	80	Slight micrencephaly. Moderate ventricular dilatation.
53	Feebleminded.	82	Marked ventricular dilatation. Gliotic encephalopathy.
20	Feebleminded epileptic.	102	No structural abnormality.
3	Educationally subnormal, possibly due to social causes.	85	Slight micrencephaly.
9	Epileptic, at least E.S.N. level, probably in the dull range.	88	Slight micrencephaly.
4	Epilepsy. Cerebral palsy. Familial. E.S.N. level.	112	No abnormality.
64	Average intelligence. Wechsler I.Q. 90 per cent. Matrices 105.	74	Slight microcephaly.

Brown, 1952). Loss of myelinated nerve fibres in peripheral nerves has been reported in such patients by Ogden, Robert and Carmichael (1959) and Snyder and Auld (1962). Wadia and Dastur (1960) reported marked paucity of terminal nerve fibres in the skin and reduction in the number of fibres in the ulnar nerve. In another case Swanson, Buchan and Alvord (1965) described, perhaps not altogether convincingly, absence of small neurones in the dorsal root ganglia, deficiency of small fibres in the dorsal nerve roots, absence of the Lissauer's tracts, and reduction in the size of the spinal tract of the V nerve. In other cases no relevant anatomical change could be demonstrated despite thorough search (Baxter and Olszewski, 1960). The condition was associated with retinitis pigmentosa in a case described by Landwirth (1964). Sensory syndromes may occur in siblings (Swanson, 1963). Two unrelated affected boys described by Johnson and Spalding (1964) each had consanguineous parents.

Anatomical peripheral neuropathy can, if present, be confirmed by biopsy of one of the comparatively unimportant nerves, such as the interdigital of the foot or the sural. The resected nerve is best divided transversely into two parts, one being fixed in formalin for ordinary paraffin embedding, and the other placed between two thin sheets of filter paper in osmium tetroxide (osmic acid) for myelin staining. As mentioned elsewhere, dissection of a minute nerve in a child calls for skill and experience on the operator's part and it is unfortunately not unusual for a pathologist to receive material containing no nerve whatever.

Cerebral Palsy

Different patterns of motor disorder and of epilepsy seem to depend more on the topological features of the neural anomalies than on their origin and histological character. As with mental retardation in general, some cases of cerebral palsy are caused by birth injury but many stem from pre- or post-natal events. The absolute and relative incidence in each category is not known.

The results of an important study covering the pathological, clinical and aetiological aspects of cerebral palsy associated with severe subnormality has been reported by Malamud *et al.* (1964) from the Sonoma State Hospital in California. The authors studied 508 such patients of whom 68 had come to autopsy at the time of reporting and had been fully examined by pathological methods. As a result the brains could be placed in one of four main groups: 1. malformations—24 cases; 2. presumed sequelae of perinatal trauma—25 cases; 3. presumed sequelae of such post-natal causes as infection, trauma and fits—13 cases; and 4. sequelae of kernicterus—6 cases. The pathological criteria for placing cases into the group of malformations and that of residual kernicterus are those generally accepted and require no comment here (p. 95). As sequelae of perinatal trauma the authors regard the presence of 'primary subcortical pathology', which is characterized, according to them, by diffuse sclerosis or cystic degeneration of the white matter, status marmoratus of the basal ganglia and sclerotic ulegyria (granular atrophy) (*vide* p. 115). If present, the cortical lesions are situated on the dorsal aspect of the cerebral hemispheres. The sequelae of post-natal damage are, on the other hand, characterized by a 'primary cortical pathology', i.e. uniform atrophy of the cerebral convolutions with widening of the sulci and, microscopically, diffuse neuronal loss and reactive gliosis, which is often laminar in pattern. Unlike the 'perinatal' changes, the postnatal cortical lesions are not restricted to the dorsal parts of the hemispheres. It was not considered that enough cases were available in groups 3 and 4, i.e. postnatal causes and sequelae of kernicterus, for a full statistical analysis. Many clinical and historical factors were treated statistically and their significance compared in relation to the other two groups: those of malformations and of birth injury. The tabulated results are discussed in some detail. They are believed to have con-firmed the validity of the initial pathological classification. The only specific-ally significant factor in the group of malformations was vaginal bleeding during the earlier part of pregnancy. Factors of statistical significance in the birth injury group were a prolonged second stage of labour, use of a combina-tion of different anaesthetics and drugs during the confinement, and signs of maternal and neonatal distress. There was a raised incidence of prematurity in both groups, without a statistically significant difference between them. These results are interesting. As such studies go, this one was well-planned and documented. Nevertheless, the large proportion of cases attributed to birth injury is surprising, and this prevalence can only partially be explained by the deliberate exclusion from the series of such conditions as hydrocephalus, craniostenosis, tuberous sclerosis, the lipidoses, leucodystrophies and tumours. It should, perhaps, be said that the number of fully examined cases in this study is rather small, and many of the factors considered are difficult to esti-mate objectively. We do not find it as easy to assign cases pathologically to the 'perinatal', 'postnatal' or 'malformation' groups. To the extent that this can be done, scrutiny of such information and clinical data at the Fountain Hospital suggests that birth injury can be excluded in something like 90 per cent of all the severely subnormal paretic cases.

It is sometimes possible to relate the character of the paralysis to the topology of the lesions. Thus, hemiplegia is often associated with cerebral hemiatrophy, lobar sclerosis, porencephaly or microgyria, affecting predom-inantly the contralateral cerebral hemispheres. But the second hemisphere, basal ganglia and subcortical formations are seldom entirely spared, and this makes hemispherectomy a doubtful method of treatment in such cases of epilepsy and cerebral palsy. Similarly, patients with cerebellar types of dis-turbance may show corresponding atrophy or hypoplasia, but, again, the lesions are seldom, if ever, entirely confined to that formation. It may be mentioned in passing that the subject of the cerebellum and cerebral palsy has been very usefully discussed in a recent symposium (Walsh, 1963).

A problem worth commenting upon is the greater frequency and degree of paralysis in the legs of the patients as compared with their arms. This does not appear to depend simply on the topological character of the lesions, being manifest even in cases of global cerebral involvement, such as hydrocephalus (Hagberg, 1962). The phenomenon is, however, readily explicable by reference to the Pavlovian concept of the space-relationship of the motor analysers in the cerebral cortex. Analysers, according to him, consist of a nucleus and a periphery. The nucleus has a relatively fixed topological situation while the peripheral elements are topologically less constant and are widely distributed throughout the brain overlapping with other centres and analysers. It may be expected, and this has been amply confirmed, that both nucleus and periphery of cortical representation of the arm, and particularly the hand, would occupy a much larger area than those of the leg, and that it would be accordingly much more difficult to fully erase its function.

Patients with choreoathetosis usually show lesions in the basal ganglia. The changes may be those of atrophy, cavitation or marbling, and due to residual kernicterus, birth injury, Hallervorden-Spatz disease, Alpers' disease, or indicate, perhaps, an occasional early case of hepatolenticular degeneration. Mostly, however, the lesions are ill-defined and their causes are not ascertainable. Hemi- and biballismus can be associated with lesions in the subthalamic nuclei. But it is not unusual to find similar changes in the brains of cases who had manifested no specific athetotic or ballistic tendencies. Further, such lesions are not restricted to the basal ganglia. Topologically related lesions have been frequently discussed in the context of the so-called extrapyramidal diseases (Christensen, 1963).

Epilepsy

The morphological changes in the brains of mentally retarded epileptics appear to be similar to those of cases of cerebral palsy, and this is not surprising in view of the frequent association of the two conditions (Table 12).

Table 12. DATA ON EPILEPSY AND CEREBRAL PALSY IN 800 CONSECUTIVE ADMISSIONS OF THE SEVERELY SUBNORMAL TO THE FOUNTAIN HOSPITAL (By courtesy of Dr. J. M. Berg)

	Numbers with epilepsy observed in hospital	Numbers with cerebral palsy	Numbers with epilepsy and cerebral palsy
Patients without Down's disease (625 cases)	228	225	97
Patients with Down's disease (175 cases)	4	2	1
Total of patients (800 cases)	232 (29 per cent)	227 (28 per cent)	98 (12 per cent)

Thus, all the brains of 61 epileptic children examined at the Fountain Hospital showed structural change (Crome, 1954), and in most of these the lesions were as widespread as in cases of palsy. Subsequent study, however, has shown that occasionally brains of epileptic subnormal patients show no demonstrable structural abnormalities. It is not yet known to what extent the different forms of epilepsy, such as grand mal, petit mal or myoclonic epilepsy, depend on special topographical patterns of lesions. All one can say is that parts of the cerebral hemispheres, particularly the cortex, are nearly always abnormal and that the subcortical formations are also often involved.

Certain lesions may be the result rather than the cause of the epilepsy. This applies particularly to focal loss of nerve cells in the cerebral cortex, thalamus, amygdaloid nucleus, and the cerebellar cortex. Neuronal loss in the so-called Sommer sector of the Ammon's horn (Fig. 15), with fibrous gliosis of the hippocampus and the subpial cerebral layer are also often considered to be caused by epilepsy. This subject is, however, very complex and some of the difficulties have been partly considered in an earlier chapter (p. 73).

Special attention has been paid lately to lesions of the temporal lobe in connection with temporal lobectomy—a recommended treatment for cases of intractable *psychomotor epilepsy*. It has long been recognized that the temporal lobe can be the seat of certain distinct lesions, such as tumours, cysts, hamartomata and scars, and that some of these may cause epileptic fits and vague psychological and emotional disturbances. It has been claimed more recently, however, that psychomotor epilepsy and mental deficiency may also be significantly associated with other, less easily defined, histological changes in the temporal lobe, viz. meningeal fibrosis, cellular proliferation in the white matter, sclerosis and loss of nerve cells in the Ammon's horn and amygdaloid nucleus, cortical atrophy and subpial gliosis (see also p. 74). This has served as a rationale for the resection of the temporal lobe even in cases with such vague changes. For a full discussion of the pathological aspects of this problem and results of surgical intervention in carefully selected cases readers are referred to the account of Falconer, Serafetinides and Corsellis (1964).

Study of the brains of mental defectives with all forms of epilepsy at the Fountain Hospital has confirmed that the changes indicated above were, indeed, common in the temporal lobe. They were not, however, commoner there than elsewhere in the brain, and whenever indisputable abnormality was found in one temporal lobe, lesions were also present in other parts of the brain, and often, in the opposite temporal lobe (Crome, 1955b). There is hence no morphological basis for a concept of temporal lobe epilepsy as a common cause of mental deficiency. Nevertheless, the rôle of the medial temporal areas in relation to mental activity and mental retardation raises problems requiring further study, and for a useful account of this difficult problem readers are referred to the work of Margerison and Corsellis (1966).

Interest was also attracted in recent years to another form of epilepsy occurring in infants and children—the so-called *salaam* or *flexion spasm epilepsy*, which is often associated with an electroencephalographic abnormality referred to as hypsarrhythmia, viz. high voltage slow waves and spikes recurring randomly in different cortical areas (Jeavons and Bower, 1964). It was thought at one time that this pattern indicated that the origin of the convulsions was in 'centrencephalic' areas. The pathological changes in cases showing hypsarrhythmia and flexion spasms studied at the Fountain Hospital were, however, as diverse and widespread as in other forms of epilepsy, and this has also been the experience of Bignami, Zappella and Benedetti (1964), who have studied seven new cases of infantile spasm and reviewed thirty previously published ones.

The association of progressive dementia, convulsions and myoclonic jerks, with a tendency of such cases to occur in families, is believed to constitute a distinct disease—*hereditary myoclonus epilepsy* or *Unverricht syndrome*. The pathological changes are dominated by widespread dissemination in the central nervous system and, sometimes, other organs, of Lafora bodies, structures which closely resemble or are identical with the more familiar amyloid bodies. Some of these are intraneuronal. In addition, atrophy and gliosis have been observed in subcortical formations, such as the dentate nuclei, the olives, substantia nigra, red nuclei and thalami (Meyer, 1963). However, all the features mentioned above are not uncommon among the severely subnormal epileptics. Furthermore, cases with the clinical signs of familial myoclonic epilepsy may show other diverse and manifold neuropathological changes, such as lipidosis, leucodystrophy, gliotic encephalopathy or tuberous sclerosis.

REFERENCES

ABERFELD, D. C., and POURFAR, M. (1965). *Develop. Med. Child Neurol.*, 7, 35.
ALEXANDER, W. S. (1966). *J. Neurol. Neurosurg. Psychiat.*, 29, 412.
ANNOTATION. (1963). *Develop. Med. Child Neurol.*, 5, 63.
BAAR, H. S., and GALINDO, J. (1965). *J. ment. Defic. Res.*, 9, 125.
BAXTER, D. W., and OLSZEWSKI, J. (1960). *Brain*, 83, 381.
BEUREN, A. J., SCHULZE, C., EBERLE, P., HARMJANZ, D., and APITZ, J. (1964). *Amer. J. Cardiol.*, 13, 471.
BIGNAMI, A., ZAPPELLA, M., and BENEDETTI, P. (1964). *Helv. paediat. Acta*, 19, 326.
BLACKWOOD, W. B., BUXTON, P. H., CUMINGS, J. N., ROBERTSON, D. J., and TUCKER, S. M. (1963). *Arch. Dis. Childh.*, 38, 193.
BÖRJESON, M., FORSSMAN, H., and LEHMANN, O. (1962). *Acta med. scand.*, 171, 13.
BRITISH MEDICAL JOURNAL. (1957), 2, 56.
CALVI, L. A. (1963). *Sist. nerv.*, 3, 211.
CHRISTENSEN, E. (1963). *Acta neurol. scand.*, 39, 119.
COWEN, D., and OLMSTEAD, E. V. (1963). *J. Neuropath. exp. Neurol.*, 22, 175.
CROME, L. (1954). *Proc. roy. Soc. Med.*, 47, 850.
CROME, L. (1955a). *J. Neurol. Neurosurg. Psychiat.*, 18, 17.
CROME, L. (1955b). *Lancet*, 1, 882.
CROME, L. (1960). *Brit. med. J.*, 1, 897.
CROME, L. (1961). *J. ment. Sci.*, 107, 459.
DEKABAN, A. (1965). *Arch. Dis. Childh.*, 40, 632.
DENNY-BROWN, D. (1952). *J. Neurol. Neurosurg. Psychiat.*, 14, 237.
DEREUX, J. (1963). *Rev. neurol.*, 109, 599.
DODGE, J. A. (1965). *Develop. Med. Child Neurol.*, 7, 31.
DREIFUSS, F. E., and NETSKY, M. C. (1964). *Amer. J. Dis. Child.*, 107, 649.
FALCONER, M. A., SERAFETINIDES, E. A., and CORSELLIS, J. A. N. (1964). *Arch. Neurol. (Chic.)*, 10, 233.
FALEK, A., SCHMIDT, R., and JERVIS, G. A. (1966). *Pediatrics*, 37, 92.
FORD, F. R. (1966). 'Diseases of the Nervous System in Infancy, Childhood and Adolescence,' Oxford: Blackwell.
GAMPER, E. (1926). *Z. ges. Neurol. Psychiat.*, 102, 154.
GARLAND, H., and MOORHOUSE, D. (1953). *J. Neurol. Neurosurg. Psychiat.*, 16, 110.
GORLIN, R. J., and JUE, K. L., JACOBSEN, U., and GOLDSCHMIDT, E. (1963). *J. Pediat.*, 63, 991.
GREENHOUSE, A. H., and NEUBUERGER, K. T. (1964). *Arch. Neurol. (Chic.)*, 10, 47.
GROSS, H. (1965). *Ophthalmologica (Basel)*, 131, 137.

GUTMANN, L., and LEMLI, L. (1963). *Arch. Neurol. (Chic.)*, **8**, 318.
HAGBERG, B. (1962). *Develop. Med. Child Neurol.*, **4**, 583.
HALLGREN, B. (1959). *Acta psychiat. scand.*, **34**, Suppl. 138.
HANSEN, E. (1962). *Acta neurol. scand.*, **38**, 188.
HARIGA, J. (1963). *Rev. neurol.*, **108**, 435.
HOEFNAGEL, D., and BENIRSCHKE, K. (1965). *Arch. Dis. Childh.*, **40**, 57.
JANCAR, J. (1965). *J. ment. Defic. Res.*, **9**, 265.
JEAVONS, P. M., and BOWER, B. D. (1964). 'Clinics in Developmental Medicine,' No. 15, London: Heinemann.
JERVIS, G. A. (1957). *J. Neuropath. exp. Neurol.*, **16**, 308.
JERVIS, G. A., and STIMSON, C. W. (1963). *J. Pediat.*, **63**, 634.
JOHNSON, R. H., and SPALDING, J. M. K. (1964). *J. Neurol. Neurosurg. Psychiat.*, **27**, 125.
KAHLKE, W., and RICHTERICH, R. (1965). *Amer. J. Med.*, **39**, 237.
KÁLLÓ, A., LAKATOS, I., and SZIJÁRTÓ, L. (1965). *J. Pediat.*, **66**, 372.
KARPATI, G., EISEN, A. H., ANDERMANN, F., BACAL, H. L., and ROBB, P. (1965). *Amer. J. Dis. Child.*, **110**, 57.
KÖRNYEY, S. (1964). *Arch. Psychiat. Nervenkr.*, **205**, 178.
LANDWIRTH, J. (1964). *Pediatrics*, **34**, 519.
LEVIN, E. J., and SONNENSCHEIN, H. (1963). *N.Y. St. J. Med.*, **63**, 1562.
MACDONALD, W. B., FITCH, K. D., and LEWIS, I. C. (1960). *Pediatrics*, **25**, 997.
MACGILLIVRAY, R. C. (1957). *Amer. J. ment. Defic.*, **61**, 719.
MALAMUD, N., and DEMMY, N. (1960). *J. Neurol. Neurosurg. Psychiat.*, **33**, 207.
MALAMUD, N., ITABASHI, H. H., CASTOR, J., and MESSINGER, H. B. (1964). *J. Pediat.*, **65**, 270.
MARGERISON, J. H. and CORSELLIS, J. A. N. (1966). *Brain*, **89**, 499.
MCKENZIE, J. (1966). *Develop. Med. Child Neurol.*, **8**, 55.
MENKES, J. H., ALTER, M., STEIGLEDER, G. K., WEAKLEY, D. R., and SUNG, J. H. (1962). *Pediatrics*, **29**, 764.
MEYER, A. (1963). 'The Hallervorden-Spatz Syndrome,' in Greenfield's 'Neuropathology', London: Arnold, p. 412.
MEYER, A. (1963). 'Myoclonus Epilepsy', in Greenfield's 'Neuropathology', London, Arnold, p. 615.
NEILL, C. A., and DINGWALL, M. M. (1950). *Arch. Dis. Childh.*, **25**, 213.
NORMAN, R. M. (1963). 'Cerebral Birth Injury,' in Greenfield's 'Neuropathology', London: Arnold, p. 382.
NORWOOD, W. F. (1964). *J. Pediat.*, **65**, 431.
OGDEN, T. E., ROBERT, F., and CARMICHAEL, E. A. (1959). *J. Neurol. Neurosurg. Psychiat.*, **22**, 267.
OSETOWSKA, E., and TRACZYNSKA, H. (1964). *Acta neuropath. (Berl.)*, **3**, 319.
PAINE, R. S., and EFRON, M. L. (1963). *Develop. Med. Child Neurol.*, **5**, 14.
PINSKY, L., and DIGEORGE, A. M. (1966). *J. Pediat.*, **68**, 1.
POPPER, E. (1920). *Neurol. Zbl.*, **1**, 13.
PTACEK, L. J., OPITZ, J. M., SMITH, D. W., GERRITSEN, T., and WAISMAN, H. A. (1963). *J. Pediat.*, **63**, 1000.
RAKE, M., and SAUNDERS, M. (1966). *J. Neurol. Neurosurg. Psychiat.*, **29**, 417.
REFSUM, S. (1960). *Wld. Neurol.*, **1**, 334.
RICHTERICH, R., KAHLKE, W., MECHELEN, P. VAN, and ROSSI, E. (1963). *Klin. Wschr.*, **41**, 800.
RICHTERICH, R., MECHELEN, P. VAN, and ROSSI, E. (1965). *Amer. J. Med.*, **39**, 230.
ROSALES, R. K., and RIGGS, H. E. (1962). *J. Neuropath. exp. Neurol.*, **21**, 372.
SCHLESINGER, B., CLAYTON, B., BODIAN, M., and JONES, K. V. (1963). *Arch. Dis. Childh.*, **38**, 349.
SCHWARTZ, P. (1961). 'Birth Injuries of the Newborn,' Basel: Karger.
SEITELBERGER, F., and GROSS, H. (1957). *Dtsch. Z. Nervenheilk.*, **176**, 104.
SMITH, D. W., LEMLI, L., and OPITZ, J. M. (1964). *J. Pediat.*, **64**, 210.
SMITHELLS, R. W. (1964a). *Develop. Med. Child Neurol.*, **6**, 406.
SMITHELLS, R. W. (1964b). *Develop. Med. Child Neurol.*, **6**, 421.
SNYDER, C. H., and AULD, E. B. (1962). *J. Pediat.*, **61**, 894.
STENGEL, E., OLDHAM, A. J., and EHRENBERG, A. S. C. (1955). *J. ment. Sci.*, **101**, 52.
STEWART, R. M. (1928–29). *J. Neurol. Psychopath.*, **9**, 217.

SWANSON, A. G. (1963). *Arch. Neurol. (Chic.)*, **8**, 299.

SWANSON, A. G., BUCHAN, G. C., and ALVORD, E. C. (1965). *Arch. Neurol. (Chic.)*, **12**, 12.

TEMTAMY, S. A. (1966). *J. Pediat.*, **69**, 111.

THIEFFRY, ST., ARTHUIS, M., AICARDI, J., and LYON, G. (1961). *Rev. neurol.*, **105**, 390.

TODOROV, A. (1964). 'Le Syndrome de Marinesco-Sjögren. Première Étude Anatomo-Clinique.' Thesis University of Sofia. Genève. Editions Médecine et Hygiène.

WADIA, N. H., and DASTUR, D. K. (1960). *Wld. Neurol.*, **1**, 409.

WALSH, G. (1963). 'Cerebellum, Posture and Cerebral Palsy,' in Little Club Clinics in Developmental Medicine, London: Heinemann, No. 8, p. 31.

WINDLE, W. F. (1963). *Science*, **140**, 1186.

APPENDICES

1: The Screening for Neurometabolic Disorders

The neurometabolic disorders form only a small proportion of cases of mental retardation. However, it is with some of these conditions that the chances of successful treatment are greatest, and clinicians therefore rightly look to the laboratory for help in their detection. Three groups of patients in particular may be referred to the laboratory for screening.

The first group are all newborn babies whom some authorities would like to see screened for a number of diseases, especially those in which delay of early treatment is dangerous. Inborn errors of metabolism, rare amongst the mentally retarded, are rarer still in the general population. A great many samples have to be tested to detect a few affected babies. Planning a screening programme is thus largely an administrative and economic problem. A committee of the American Academy of Pediatrics (1965) concluded that all babies should be tested for phenylketonuria, preferably by determination of their blood phenylalanine levels. The urine of every baby should also be tested for reducing substances. The committee did not recommend that testing should be at present extended to other disorders (cf. also Holt, 1965). Frequent testing by the best available methods is, of course, obligatory for babies with a family history of metabolic disorders, however rare.

The second group comprises all the mentally retarded patients in institutions and in the community. Urine specimens may be collected from every patient, preserved or frozen, and analysed in batches, usually by paper chromatography. Again, administrative problems are formidable and the volume of laboratory work daunting. Inevitably, the preponderance of negative results is disheartening to the laboratory staff, the more so since many abnormalities which at first appear to be due to a metabolic error turn out on further investigation to be caused by drugs, diet or other environmental factors. While a number of neurometabolic disorders have been discovered by such mass screening, e.g. cystathioninuria (p. 278) and citrullinuria (p. 283), the undertaking does not appear attractive in today's conditions when most clinical laboratories have difficulties in dealing with a rising work load, and are unlikely to be in a position to undertake chromatographic investigations of hundreds or even thousands of specimens.

Most cases of neurometabolic disorders are discovered amongst the third group, namely children referred to paediatricians or psychiatrists for retarded physical or mental development or intellectual deterioration. The number of such children seen in hospital at any time is usually small enough to allow for a number of tests to be carried out on the blood and urine of each patient. It should be possible to screen 15–20 cases per week by the methods described below without interfering unduly with the routine of most clinical laboratories.

The methods which we have selected are largely based on the recommendations of Scriver* et al. (1964), Efron et al. (1964), Menkes and Philippart (1965) and Holt (1965). Most of them require no special skills or equipment. It is impossible to devise a practicable scheme for screening which will not miss a few potentially detectable cases, but their number will be reduced by cooperation between ward and laboratory, so that samples are collected correctly and reach the laboratory in good condition with full clinical details of the patient. Reference to Table 4, Chapter 9, will often aid in selecting further appropriate investigations.

We suggest that the following tests should be available.

* See also Scriver (1965). *Ped. Clin. N. Amer.*, **12**, 807.

(1) One-dimensional chromatography of amino acids in the urine and serum, and urine tests with ferric chloride, sodium nitroprusside and dinitrophenylhydrazine, should be done in all cases. Facilities should also be available for further examination of samples by two-dimensional paper chromatography, or two-dimensional thin-layer chromatography, or thin-layer electrophoresis in one dimension followed by chromatography in the 2nd dimension. The most reliable quantitative analysis of amino acids is by the amino acid analyser of Moore and Stein. Because of its high cost this type of equipment is not generally available, but it is desirable that laboratories should be able to refer occasional samples for a full analysis to a centre specialising in this technique.

Phenylketonuria, by far the most common of the aminoacidurias, presents a special problem. The laboratory should not only have facilities for the detection of the disease, but must also be prepared to help in the control of dietary treatment p. 353. The other disorders of amino acid metabolism are so rare that the average clinical chemist will see very few cases in the course of his career. It is not practicable to give adequate experimental details of all the methods and investigations which are necessary to establish the diagnosis. A biochemist, having spotted one of these rare disorders, will clearly want to consult reviews and original papers, some of which are quoted in Chapter 11.

(2) The clinical laboratory should offer diagnostic tests for galactosaemia. Methods for the identification of reducing substances in the urine by paper chromatography and for the specific enzymatic estimation of blood glucose and galactose should likewise be available.

(3) Diagnostic tests for gargoylism are now sufficiently reliable to be of real help in the diagnosis of this disease. Unhappily, the validity of the screening tests for metachromatic leucodystrophy is not so secure. It is nevertheless worth while doing these tests provided that care is exercised in the interpretation of results.

(4) The laboratory may occasionally be asked to exclude or confirm the diagnosis of Wilson's disease or muscular dystrophy of the Duchenne type. Simple screening tests are available for these conditions. Owing to the current interest in lead poisoning as a cause or complication of mental subnormality, blood lead estimations are frequently required by clinicians. The average laboratory should be able to undertake this analysis, except if it is carried out by automated methods in special centres.

References

COMMITTEE ON FETUS AND NEWBORN of the AMERICAN ACADEMY OF PEDIATRICS. (1965). *Pediatrics*, **35**, 499.

EFRON, M., YOUNG, D., MOSER, H. W., and MACCREADY, R. A. (1964). *New Engl. J. Med.*, **270**, 1378.

HOLT, K. S. (1965). *Develop. Med. Child. Neurol.*, **7**, 689.

MENKES, J. H., and PHILIPPART, M. (1965). *J. neurol. Sci.*, **2**, 108.

SCRIVER, C. R., DAVIES, E., and CULLEN, A. (1964). *Lancet* **2**, 230.

2: Screening Tests for Aminoacidurias

I. Qualitative Tests

Ferric chloride test. The test is carried out as follows (Woolf, 1963). A solution of 5 per cent ferric chloride is added drop by drop to a little urine in a test tube, shaking after each addition till a colour appears or half as much reagent has been added as there is urine. The tube should be observed for five minutes, as the blue-green colour characteristic of phenylketonuria may take one or two minutes to reach maximum intensity. The colour fades in a period varying from a few minutes to several hours. Urine containing much phosphate gives at first a greyish-white precipitate of ferric phosphate, making it necessary to add more ferric chloride. The colour produced by phenylpyruvic acid is then blue-grey. Phenistix (Ames) consists of a heavy absorbent paper impregnated at one end with ferric ammonium sulphate and cyclohexylsulphamic acid buffer, pH 2·3. This is the optimum pH for the reaction of ferric chloride and phenylpyruvic acid. Magnesium ions are also added to minimize interference by phosphates. The strips are briefly dipped into urine or moistened by pressing against a wet napkin. 30 seconds later any colour formed is compared with a scale printed on the container of the strips so that a semiquantitative estimate of any phenylpyruvic acid present may be obtained.

While the ferric chloride test has been extremely useful in detecting phenylketonurics, cases are occasionally missed because of the instability of phenylpyruvic acid, particularly in alkaline urine, or if the test is carried out before the blood phenylalanine has reached the level at which phenylpyruvic acid appears in the urine. The sensitivity of the test is also reduced if carried out at a pH significantly below 2.

A number of compounds other than phenylpyruvic acid react with Phenistix and ferric chloride and differences in shade, intensity and permanence of the colour produced in the test tube or on the strip provide useful clues to a number of metabolic disorders (Table 1). It is evident that the specificity of the test is so low that supplementary tests, e.g. by chromatography, are obligatory whenever a positive result is obtained with ferric chloride or Phenistix.

Table 1. REACTIONS OF PHENISTIX AND FERRIC CHLORIDE*

	Phenistix	Ferric chloride
Phenylketonuria (phenylpyruvic acid)	Blue-green, or grey-green, max. 30 sec.–1 min., fading slowly.	Green or blue-green, fades slowly.
Histidinaemia (imidazolepyruvic acid)	Grey-green or blue-green, in most cases	Green or blue-green colour develops in most cases
Tyrosinosis (p-hydroxyphenylpyruvic acid)	Ephemeral green, fading in 2–3 seconds	Blue-green, yellow with excess ferric chloride
Maple syrup urine disease	Nil	Blue to grey with greenish tinge, but results are inconsistent
Alcaptonuria (homogentisic acid)	Nil, brown with strong solution	Fleeting blue-green, brown with stronger solution
Acetoacetic acid	Nil	Red or red brown
Bilirubin	Nil	Blue-green
Phenothiazines	Purple or green	Purple or green
Sodium salicylate	Purple	Purple
p-Aminosalicylic acid	Red-purple	Red-brown
Lysol	Nil	Green
Phenol	Nil	Violet-blue

2,4-Dinitrophenylhydrazine Test. A saturated solution of *2,4*-dinitrophenylhydrazine in 2N hydrochloric acid is added drop by drop to urine until half as much reagent has been added as there is urine. The test is positive if a yellow precipitate forms within five minutes (Woolf, 1963). Any ketone will give this test, so that the test is positive in phenylketonuria, histidinaemia, maple syrup urine disease and tyrosinosis, and in children with hyperglycinaemia, who excrete acetone. The presence of diabetic ketosis must, of course, be excluded.

* Test also positive in formimino transferase deficiency.

Sodium Nitroprusside Test

REAGENTS

(1) N Hydrochloric acid.
(2) 5 per cent sodium cyanide, freshly prepared.
(3) 0·5 per cent sodium nitroprusside.
(4) 25 mg./100 ml. cystine.

PROCEDURE

5 ml. of urine are acidified with 0·5 ml. of hydrochloric acid. 2 ml. of sodium cyanide solution are added and after 30 minutes 1 ml. of sodium nitroprusside solution. 5 ml. of the cystine solution are similarly treated. A pink to purple colour is given by cysteine, and by cystine and homocystine after reduction by cyanide to cysteine and homocysteine.

This test is strongly positive in cystinuria, occasionally positive in cystinuric heterozygotes, and usually positive in homocystinurics, particularly after a loading dose of 100 mg./kg. of L-methionine.

II. One-Dimensional Paper Chromatography

The screening method in use in our hospital is a modification of the procedures of Efron *et al.* (1964) and Scriver *et al.* (1964).

REAGENTS AND MATERIALS

(1) *n*-Butanol-acetic acid-water, 120: 30: 50 (v/v/v).
(2) 0·2 per cent ninhydrin in acetone containing 1 per cent pyridine.
(3) 0·2 per cent isatin in butanol containing 5 per cent acetic acid.
(4) Ehrlich's reagent. 10 per cent *p*-dimethylbenzaldehyde in concentrated hydrochloric acid is diluted 1:4 with acetone just before use.
(5) Pauly's reagent.
   (a) 9 grams of sulphanilic acid are dissolved in 90 ml. of concentrated hydrochloric acid and made up to one litre with water. To diazotize this solution 1 volume is mixed with 1 volume of 5 per cent sodium nitrite in the cold, and allowed to stand for 15 minutes.
   (b) 10 per cent sodium carbonate in water.
(6) Equipment for ascending paper chromatography.

PROCEDURE

Heparinized plasma or serum is obtained from a heel or finger prick. Urine is collected preferably 1–2 hours after a meal. Chromatography is carried out on duplicate 10 in. × 10 in. Whatman No. 1 papers. 0·01 ml. of urine and 0·01 ml. of plasma or serum are applied in $\frac{1}{2}$ in. streaks, at right angles to the direction of the solvent flow, 1$\frac{1}{2}$ inches from the bottom edge of the paper. Each sheet can accommodate 3 samples of urine and blood. Haemolysed serum may give rise to brown streaking which makes the chromatogram impossible to interpret. If this happens, 0·05 ml. of serum are treated with 0·2 ml. of ethanol to precipitate the proteins, and after centrifugation 0·05 ml. of the supernatant are applied to the paper in volumes of 0·01 ml., drying after each application. The papers are developed overnight with butanol-acetic acid-water and dried at room temperature in a stream of air. The approximate Rf values of the more important amino acids are shown in Table 2.

The first sheet is stained with ninhydrin. This stain will detect marked excess of all amino acids, and in particular will readily show increases in the concentration of

Table 2. Rf VALUES OF AMINO ACIDS

Amino acid	Rf
Leucine	70
*Iso*leucine	67
Phenylalanine	60
Valine	51
Methionine	50
Tryptophan	50
β-Amino*iso*butyric acid	49
Tyrosine	45
Proline	34
Alanine	30
Glutamic acid	28
Threonine	26
Glycine	23
Serine	22
Hydroxyproline	22
Taurine	20
Citrulline	18
Glutamine	17
Arginine	15
Lysine	12
Histidine	11
Cystine	5

amino acids of Rf values greater than proline, as this part of the chromatogram is less crowded than that of lower Rf values. The paper is then cut half-way between the spot for glutamine and that for histidine, lysine and the other basic amino acids, which overlap. The top section is dipped in Ehrlich's reagent. The purple ninhydrin spots fade, but citrulline if present in a concentration greater than 10 mg./100 ml. gives a pink spot. Urea stains yellow with Ehrlich's reagent, and the intensity of the staining gives a measure of the concentration of the urine. Efron *et al.* stain filter paper soaked in urine with a 1 per cent solution of picric acid in 55 per cent alcohol, followed by 5 per cent potassium hydroxide in 80 per cent alcohol. In this way an estimate of the relative concentration of creatinine in the urine specimens may be obtained.

The bottom part of the paper is sprayed with diazotized sulphanilic acid, and, when the ninhydrin colours have faded, with sodium carbonate. Histidine in excess of 10 mg./100 ml. stains orange-red. This test is often positive for urine but not for serum, except in cases of histidinaemia. The second sheet of paper is stained with isatin, which is more sensitive for the detection of the imino acids than ninhydrin. Proline stains bright blue, hydroxyproline stains less intensely, but when the paper is overstained with Ehrlich's reagent hydroxyproline in concentrations of 4–5 mg./100 ml. gives a red purple colour.

The following disorders in which elevated blood levels of amino acids occur should be detectable by this method: phenylketonuria, maple syrup urine disease, tyrosinosis, histidinaemia, hyperprolinaemia, hydroxyprolinaemia, hyperglycinaemia and citrullinuria.

Running urine samples side by side with serum from the same patient extends the range of the test to include the renal tubular and no-threshold aminoacidurias, although it is not, of course, capable of resolving minor differences in excretion patterns. The method should detect no-threshold aminoacidurias such as argininosuccinicaciduria and cystathioninuria, in which the no-threshold substance is excreted in large amounts. Homocystinuria on the other hand could be missed, as some patients apparently excrete amounts of homocystine unlikely to be detectable by this method. Most cases of homocystinuria have in fact been diagnosed following the finding of subluxation of the lens (p. 281), or by the nitroprusside test.

The four qualitative tests and one-dimensional chromatography have been in use in our hospital for 18 months. On the average about 15 cases are screened every week. In this period we have found two cases of phenylketonuria and one case of hyperprolinaemia. A mild case of Lowe's syndrome, which had been diagnosed elsewhere, was reported by us as 'non-specific tubular aminoaciduria'.

References

EFRON, M. L., YOUNG, D., MOSER, H. W., and MACCREADY, R. A. (1964). *New Engl. J. Med.*, **270**, 1378.

SCRIVER, C. R., DAVIES, E., and CULLEN, A. (1964). *Lancet*, **2**, 230.

WOOLF, L. I. (1963). In Lyman, F. L. 'Phenylketonuria', Thomas: Springfield, p. 251.

3a: Two-Dimensional Paper Chromatography of Amino Acids

Two-dimensional paper chromatography is still the most widely used method of investigating aminoacidurias. When carried out in its most sophisticated form (Dent, 1948; Woolf and Norman, 1957) this technique is demanding of the operator's skill and time. An even room temperature and freedom from draughts are required for reproducible results, and such conditions are not always readily realizable in the clinical laboratory. On the other hand, when the technique is oversimplified and, say, 20–30 µl. of undesalted urine are chromatographed on 20 cm. square sheets of paper, the information gained barely exceeds that obtainable from one-dimensional screening. Furthermore, if desalting is omitted, amino acids often show up on the chromatogram as streaks rather than discreet spots, and interpretation is then unreliable. The technique of Smith (1960), as used in our hospital, is a compromise. It gives less detailed information than the more elaborate methods of Dent or Woolf and Norman, but is adequate for most clinical purposes. This technique will be described in outline only. Readers requiring fuller details, particularly those venturing into this field for the first time, are advised to consult the monograph by Smith (1960).

MATERIALS AND REAGENTS

(1) Equipment for ascending chromatography. This includes glass tanks, aluminium or polythene frames for holding 10 inch square sheets of Whatman No. 1 filter papers, solvent trays, micropipettes for the application of samples, and dipping trays or spray bottles for staining the chromatograms. Five two-way chromatograms can be run simultaneously on one frame. This type of equipment is supplied by a number of firms, e.g. The Shandon Scientific Company, London.

(2) Equipment for desalting urine electrolytically or with ion-exchange resins (Smith, 1960).

(3) Solvents
   (a) *n*-Butanol-acetic acid-water (12:3:5 v/v/v), BuA.
   (b) *n*-Butanol-pyridine-water (1:1:1 v/v/v), BuP.
   (c) Phenol-0·880 ammonia (100:0·5 v/v), Ph Am.

(4) 0·2 per cent ninhydrin in acetone. 1 per cent of pyridine is added just before use.

(5) 0·2 per cent isatin in acetone or *n*-butanol. 4 per cent acetic acid is added to the solvent.

(6) Amino acid marker solution. 5 mg. alanine, 20 mg. cystine, 10 mg. histidine, 10 mg. glycine, 10 mg. phenylalanine, 10 mg. proline and 15 mg. tyrosine are dissolved in 10 ml. of 10 per cent *iso*propanol in water and stored at 4°C. A little hydrochloric acid has to be added to dissolve the amino acids.

PROCEDURE

An appropriate amount of urine (*vide infra*) is applied by micropipette to the bottom right hand corner of the paper, approximately 3 cm. from each edge. The chromatograms are run in butanol-acetic acid-water or butanol-pyridine-water overnight, dried in warm air, and run in phenol-ammonia at right angles to the first direction of flow over the following night. After blowing off the phenol, which takes several hours, the papers are dipped in or sprayed with ninhydrin. The chromatogram is inspected after 3 hours at room temperature, again on the following day, and finally after heating for 5 minutes at 105°C. The conditions for staining with isatin are the same as for ninhydrin. The sequential staining procedures with Ehrlich's and Pauly's reagents (p. 341) may also be used.

COMMENT

A major difficulty in this field is that results obtained in different laboratories are not readily comparable. It is very confusing to the clinician when, as so often happens, a child's case history contains a number of reports on the urinary amino acids in which the number and identity of the amino acids stated to be present differ widely. To make matters worse, it is often not explained if the chromatogram is considered normal or abnormal. Some of these discrepancies are due to differences in technique. In some chromatographic solvents the sulphur amino acids decompose, and desalting may lead, for example, to losses in taurine. Diet may also affect the urinary chromatogram. A major source of confusion is that the amount of urine applied to the paper varies widely from laboratory to laboratory. Thus on a normal chromatogram prepared by the method of Woolf and Norman up to 16 amino acids may be seen, while when the technique of Smith is used 5–9 amino acids are usually detected.

Many workers calculate the amount of urine to be applied from the creatinine content or nitrogen content of a random specimen. This may be a valid procedure for normal children. It is not, however, safe to assume that creatinine excretion is constant in sick or mentally retarded patients. For example in our hospital an 11-year-old girl produced within one week 24 hour specimens containing 800 mg. of creatinine in 580 ml., and 300 mg. in 1,250 ml. of urine respectively. It is often satisfactory to apply a volume of urine containing 250 μg. of nitrogen but a drawback to this approach is that, depending on the diet, urea may account for anything from 20–90 per cent of the urine nitrogen.

In our laboratory we apply a 6 second fraction of a 24 hour specimen. Thus for a sample of 500 ml. of urine, 0·035 ml. are chromatographed, and as most 24 hour specimens received in this laboratory are between 500 ml. and 1 litre, the amount of urine applied is usually of the order of 0·05 ml. We use the same volume of urine when only a random specimen of urine is available, unless this appears very dilute. This greatly limits the usefulness of the test, as it is clearly impossible to detect any but the most obvious renal tubular defects when applying a constant volume of a random specimen.

According to Smith, glycine usually stands out as the strongest spot in the normal urine chromatogram, followed by alanine, serine and glutamine; histidine, methylhistidine, taurine and β-amino*iso*butyric acid are also occasionally seen. The last two amino acids are excreted in considerable amounts by a small proportion of normal subjects.

Using the same technique, our results differ in points of detail. We always find a spot for histidine which frequently exceeds that of glycine in intensity. Glycine and serine, not well separated, are also invariably present, and usually glutamine and alanine. β-Amino*iso*butyric acid does not react with ninhydrin in the cold but does so when the chromatogram is heated to 105°C. In this way the substance can be often identified on chromatograms from our patients. Taurine, cystine and threonine are only rarely detected. We normally use the system BuA/PhAm except when trying to separate cystine and the basic amino acids. In this case we treat 1 ml. of urine with 0·1 ml. of 30 per cent hydrogen peroxide in the cold and use the system BuP/PhAm.

Useful information is gained if proline, hydroxyproline, citrulline, arginine or methionine are seen on chromatograms, as these amino acids are not normally detectable. When the method of Smith is used, only traces of amino acids show up with Rf values in BuA greater than that of proline, so that an excess of phenylalanine, or of the branched chain amino acids, is readily detectable. In interpreting chromatograms it must be borne in mind that during the first few weeks of life proline, hydroxyproline, the branched chain amino acids, cystine, tyrosine, methionine and ethanolamine are excreted in increased amounts. Moderate variations in the concentration of glycine, glutamine, alanine and histidine have no clinical significance.

References

DENT, C. E. (1948). *Biochem. J.*, **43**, 168.
SMITH, I. (1960). 'Chromatographic and Electrophoretic Techniques', Vol. I, London: Heinemann, p. 82.
WOOLF, L. I., and NORMAN, A. P. (1957). *J. Pediat.*, **50**, 271.

3b: Separation of Urinary Amino Acids by Thin Layer Chromatography

Both cellulose and silica gel layers have been used in the separation of urinary amino acids. Turner and Redgwell (1966) have recently introduced a mixed cellulose-silica layer which is superior to layers prepared from either component alone. Urine can be chromatographed without prior desalting.

REAGENTS AND EQUIPMENT

(1) Cellulose, MN 300 (Macherey Nagel).
(2) Silica gel H or G (Merck's Kieselgel H or G, Stahl) or Whatman SG 41 silica gel.
(3) High speed homogenizer capable of 20,000 r.p.m., e.g. of type 'Virtis' or 'Atomix' (M.S.E., London).
(4) Equipment for thin layer chromatography.
(5) Phenol-water (80:20 w/v).
(6) *n*-Butanol-acetic acid-water (5:1:4, v/v/v, top phase) or the equivalent single solvent system *n*-butanol-acetic acid-water (12:3:5, v/v/v).
(7) 0·5 per cent ninhydrin in 95 per cent. ethanol.

PROCEDURE

A mixture of 10 g. of cellulose, 4 g. of silica gel and 80 ml. of distilled water is blended for 30 seconds at approximately 20,000 r.p.m. Efficient blending is essential. The uniform suspension is spread over 20 × 20 cm. glass plates to a thickness of 250 μ. The plates are gently warmed under a radiant heater until set and then dried overnight at 40°C. A volume of urine containing 10 μg. creatinine or, if a 24 hour specimen is available, the volume excreted in 2 seconds is applied 3 cm. from the corner. The authors use Drummond microcaps. Shandon disposable micropipettes available in sizes from 1 μl. upwards are also satisfactory. The diameter of the spot should not exceed 3 mm., and each sample application is dried at a temperature not exceeding 40°C. The plates are developed in phenol-water, 6 hours, dried overnight at 40°C to remove the phenol and then run twice in butanol-acetic acid-water in the second dimension, allowing 4 hours for each run. The amino acids are located by spraying with ninhydrin.

A suitable solution of amino acid markers may be run at the same time. A standard mixture of 18 amino acids is available from the Shandon Company, London. It contains lysine, arginine, histidine, glycine, alanine, proline, valine, *iso*leucine, leucine, methionine, phenylalanine, serine, threonine, glutamic acid, tyrosine, tryptophan, aspartic acid, hydroxyproline and cystine. 1 μg. quantities of these amino acids can be detected with ninhydrin. This marker solution may be supplemented by glutamine and β-amino*iso*butyric acid.

The mixed layer is suitable for other solvents and stains.

Reference

TURNER, N. A., and REDGWELL, R. J. (1966). *J. Chromatog.*, **21**, 129.

3c: Separation of Urinary and Plasma Amino Acids by Two-Dimensional Thin-Layer Electrophoresis and Chromatography

Walker and Bark (1966) have described a rapid two-dimensional method for the separation of the urinary and plasma amino acids.

MATERIALS AND REAGENTS

(1) Electrophoresis tank.—A standard horizontal tank is modified so that the 10 × 10 cm. glass plates carrying the thin layer rest on a perspex cooling block through which tap water is circulated. Filter paper wicks are made from 4 thicknesses of Whatman 3 MM paper. These overlap the thin-layer plate by about 1 cm. A clear glass plate is placed on the wicks forming a thin moist chamber above the thin layer. The upper edge of the wicks, which lies between the glass plates, is sheathed with a 4 cm. strip of cellophane.

(2) Thin-layer plates.—A 250 μ layer of cellulose (Whatman CC 41 or Macherey Nagel MN 300) is applied to 10 × 10 × 2·5 mm. glass plates.

(3) Buffer for electrophoresis.—78 ml. of glacial acetic acid and 25 ml. of formic acid (98 per cent.) are made up to 1 litre with deionized water.

(4) Solvent for chromatography.—*n*-Butanol-acetic acid-water (3:1:1 v/v/v).

(5) Ninhydrin reagent.—0·25 per cent ninhydrin in acetone. 0·5 per cent of pyridine is added immediately before use.

(6) Universal Indicator (British Drug Houses, Poole, Dorset).

PROCEDURE

0·1 ml. of plasma or serum is pipetted into 0·3 ml. of absolute alcohol. After centrifugation the protein-free alcoholic extract is mixed with three times its volume of chloroform. The chloroform extracts the alcohol leaving an aqueous layer at the top of the chloroform alcohol mixture. 10 μl. of deproteinized plasma or a volume of urine containing 6 μg. of creatinine is applied as a spot not more than 3 mm. in diameter 1·5 cm. from each edge. 0·5 μl. of Universal Indicator is applied over the sample spot and in small volumes at intervals along the anodal side of the plate to provide a visual check of the uniformity of the electrophoretic separation. The plate is evenly sprayed with buffer until it acquires a uniform matt sheen. The appearance of minute bubbles on the surface of the cellulose, which immediately precedes waterlogging, must be avoided. Drifts of the sample due to uneven spraying can be seen by the accompanying drift of the Universal Indicator.

A potential difference of 300 V is applied across the 10 cm. plate (350–400 V across the electrodes, depending on the design of the tank) and a current of approximately 10 mA is passed for 25 minutes. At the end of this period the fastest red component of the indicator should have advanced 1·5 cm. ahead of the yellow component. The plate is then dried under a stream of hot air. Electrophoresis separates the amino acids from salts, urea and sugar, so that desalting is not necessary. The cooling of the plates and the cellophane coating of the wicks minimize loss of fluids by evaporation, and prevents streaking of the solutes due to a capillary flow of the electrolytes.

Chromatography is carried out at right angles to that of the electrophoresis, using butanol-acetic acid-water as solvent. The solvent front should rise 9 cm. in about 35 minutes. The plates are then dried and sprayed with ninhydrin. The colours reach maximum intensity in about 3 hours.

In normal adult urine the following amino acids are commonly found by this method: glycine, serine, histidine, glutamine, alanine, β-amino*iso*butyric acid, aspartic acid, tyrosine, taurine and cystine, and in infants, in addition, proline, hydroxyproline, tryptophan and asparagine. The position of these amino acids should be checked against standard mixtures of amino acids.

Amino acids which may be detected by this technique in normal plasma include glutamine, glycine, alanine, ornithine, lycine, arginine, histidine, threonine, serine, glutamic acid, leucine, valine, phenylalanine, tyrosine, cystine, proline and taurine.

Reference

WALKER, W. H. C., and BARK, M. (1966). *Clin. chim. Acta.*, **13**, 241.

4: Tryptophan Load Test

This test is at times requested in cases of epilepsy to exclude pyridoxine deficiency or dependency. Some of the older techniques were not altogether satisfactory. Recently Walsh (1965) has described a method which is suitable for the separation and estimation of four important metabolites of the tryptophan-nicotinic acid pathway.

REAGENTS AND EQUIPMENT

(1) Ehrlich's reagent.
    (a) for location: 1 volume of 10 per cent *p*-dimethylaminobenzaldehyde in concentrated hydrochloric acid mixed with 4 volumes of acetone.
    (b) quantitative: 1 per cent *p*-dimethylaminobenzaldehyde in 50 per cent glacial acetic acid.
(2) 0·2 M sodium acetate buffer, pH 5·4.
(3) Diazotized sulphanilic acid. 1 volume of 1 per cent sulphanilic acid in 10 per cent hydrochloric acid is mixed before use with 1 volume of 5 per cent sodium nitrite and 2 volumes of 10 per cent anhydrous sodium carbonate.
(4) Standard solution. This contains 1 μg. in 5 μl. of distilled water of each of the following: xanthurenic acid, kynurenine, 3-hydroxykynurenine and anthranilic acid.
(5) Equipment for thin-layer chromatography including a Hamilton microsyringe, an ultraviolet lamp (e.g. 'chromatolite', Hanovia), and a spectrophotometer.

PROCEDURE

A 300 μ layer of cellulose (Macherey Nagel MN 300) is applied to 20 × 10 cm. glass plates. Three samples are spotted 2 cm. from the edge of the plate: 5 μl of neat urine, 5 μl of standard solution and 5 μl each of standard solution and urine. The chromatogram is developed in the acetate buffer, preferably at 4°C, the solvent being allowed to rise nearly to the top of the layer. The chromatogram is then dried at 80°C.

The thin layer is observed in ultra-violet light and the position and colour of the fluorescent spots noted. The thin layer is then sprayed first with Ehrlich's reagent, and, after blowing away residual hydrochloric acid fumes, with diazotized sulphanilic acid. Urea sometimes interferes with anthranilic acid but may be removed by incubation of the urine sample with urease. The approximate Rf values and colour reactions are described by Walsh (1965) as follows:

Xanthurenic acid, Rf 0·40, light blue fluorescence, purple with sulphanilic acid.

3-Hydroxykynurenine, Rf 0·48, faint green fluorescence, faint yellow with Ehrlich's reagent, purple with sulphanilic acid.

Kynurenine, Rf 0·56, bright blue fluorescence, yellow with Ehrlich's reagent, and anthranilic acid, bright purple fluorescence, orange with Ehrlich's reagent.

QUANTITATIVE ANALYSIS

Up to 100 μl. of neat urine is applied to a thin layer in a line parallel to the lower edge, the plate developed and the 4 substances located by their fluorescence. The section of the thin layer containing each substance is scraped from the plate into a test tube.

To the tubes containing xanthurenic acid and 3-hydroxykynurenine are added 1·5 ml. of distilled water, and they are allowed to stand for 1 hour at room temperature. After centrifugation, 1 ml. of the supernatant is transferred to another tube and 2 ml. of diazotized sulphanilic acid (cooled to 10°C) are added. The optical density of xanthurenic acid is read immediately at 510 mμ and that of 3-hydroxykynurenine after 10 minutes at 450 mμ.

Kynurenine is estimated by adding 1 ml. of distilled water to the tube, which is then allowed to stand at room temperature before adding 2 ml. of the quantitative Ehrlich's reagent. After a further 10 minutes the tube is centrifuged, and the optical density of the supernatant read at 450 mμ.

Anthranilic acid is estimated in the same way as kynurenine, but it is essential to remove all the urea by incubation with urease. The optical density is read at 370 mμ.

Optical density plots are linear over the range 0–30 μg. except for anthranilic acid for which the linear range is 0–10 μg. Recoveries are about 90 per cent, except of anthranilic acid, for which recoveries are between 85 and 90 per cent.

After a dose of 70 mg./kg. body weight of L-tryptophan the upper limits of normal are (Walsh, 1966):

xanthurenic acid	—	4·5 μ moles/kg. 7 hours
3-hydroxykynurenine	—	5 μ moles/kg. 7 hours
kynurenine	—	11 μ moles/kg. 7 hours

In pyridoxine deficiency oral L-tryptophan loading is followed by excessive excretion of xanthurenic acid and 3-hydroxykynurenine. The test may be vitiated by the action of intestinal bacteria on the ingested tryptophan, particularly in cases of malabsorption.

References

WALSH, M. P. (1965). Clin. chim. Acta., 11, 263.
WALSH, M. P. (1966). Proc. Assoc. clin. Biochemists (Great Britain), 4, 22.

5: The Estimation of Phenylalanine in the Blood

Estimation of serum phenylalanine is an essential part in the control of treatment of phenylketonuria since failure of dietary restriction in a child can be detected before the C.N.S. is damaged. Should a phenylketonuric infant fail to thrive it is vitally important to establish if the blood phenylalanine level is too high or too low.

Quantitative or semi-quantitative paper chromatography, the method first used for estimating blood phenylalanine, is not without difficulties, particularly at low levels. Column chromatography by the Moore and Stein technique is at present too costly for routine use. Most workers therefore employ one of the following three methods.

(1) The *snake venom* method is based on the fact that when mixtures of phenylalanine and tyrosine are treated with L-amino acid oxidase in a borate buffer, enol-borate complexes are formed with strong absorptions in the ultraviolet, sufficiently distinct for quantitative spectrophotometry. If the serum is ultrafiltered, tryptophan, which also forms enol-borate complexes, does not pass into the filtrate, and this simplifies spectrophotometry.

(2) The *fluorimetric method* utilizes the observation that the fluorescence developed when ninhydrin reacts with phenylalanine is greatly enhanced in the presence of the peptide L-leucyl-L-alanine. The method is quite specific, the fluorescence due to the other amino acids being of a much lower order than that due to phenylalanine.

(3) A *microbiological assay* (Guthrie method) is based on the inhibition of the growth of *Bacillus subtilis* (ATCC 6051) in a minimal agar medium (*vide infra*) by β-2-thienylalanine, a phenylalanine antagonist. If a paper disc is soaked in blood, dried and placed on the medium, the growth inhibition is counteracted to an extent which depends on the level of phenylalanine in the blood.

Of these methods the microbiological assay is widely used in the U.S.A. for the screening of newborn infants. It has also been used in the control of the dietary treatment, but for this purpose it is probably inferior to the other two methods. The snake venom method is more specific than the fluorimetric method but requires more blood. A further point in favour of the fluorimetric method is that it is suitable for use with the Technicon Autoanalyzer.

The techniques given are that of Woolf and Goodwin (1964) for the snake venom method, those of Wong, O'Flynn and Inouye (1964) and O'Brien and Ibbott (1962) for the fluorimetric method, and that of Guthrie and Susi (1963) for the microbiological assay. The normal range for fasting adults is 0.93 ± 0.27 (S.D.) mg./100 ml. by the snake venom method, and 1.55 ± 0.34 (S.D.) mg./100 by the fluorimetric method. In newborn infants the normal range by the latter method is 2.2 ± 0.5 (S.D.) mg./100 ml., and in low birthweight newborns-4.3 ± 0.54 (S.D.) mg./100 ml.

Snake Venom Method

REAGENTS

(1) Arsenate-borate buffer pH 6·5, 2·0 M in arsenate, 1·0 M in borate. Dissolve 312 g. $Na_2HAsO_4.7H_2O$ and 30·9 g. H_3BO_3 in 400 ml. of water, adjust pH to 6·5 and make up to 500 ml.

(2) 0·2 M phosphate buffer, pH 6·5 (19·8 g. Na_2HPO_4 and 8·36 g. NaH_2PO_4 in 1,000 ml.).

(3) Enzyme reagent. Lyophilized *Crotalus adamanteus* venom (100 mg.) is stirred into 10 ml. water and centrifuged. The clear supernatant is added to a mixture of 50 ml. arsenate-borate buffer and 30 ml. 0·2 M phosphate buffer. 0·2 ml. catalase (150,000 U/ml.) is then added, the solution made up to 100 ml. with phosphate buffer, and mixed. The mixed reagent is allowed to stand, then filtered through a Whatman 42 filter paper. It is stable for many weeks in the refrigerator.

(4) Blank reagent. 50 ml. arsenate-borate buffer plus 10 ml. water are made up to 100 ml. with phosphate buffer and filtered.

PREPARATION OF THE BLOOD SAMPLE:

Serum or heparinized plasma is ultrafiltered at about 4°C using prewashed Visking tubing and a positive pressure of about 10 pounds per sq. inch. For near normal blood levels the minimum volume required is 0·35 ml.

PROCEDURE

To 0·5 ml. portions of the reagent in small test tubes are added 0·05 ml. portions of the plasma ultrafiltrate. To further 0·5 ml. portions of the reagent are added 0·05 ml. portions of several standard solutions of phenylalanine and tyrosine. After standing for about ½ hour at room temperature the contents of the tubes are introduced into silica microcuvettes and the optical density determined at 308 and 330 mμ, using 0·5 ml. reagent plus 0·05 water as blank. Then 0·05 portions of the plasma ultrafiltrate are added to 0·5 ml. portions of the blank reagent and these are read against 0·5 ml. blank reagent plus water, also at 308 mμ and 330 mμ. This blank determination gives a correction reading for the small amount of ultraviolet-absorbing material present in the blood ultrafiltrate. The correction readings are subtracted from the ultrafiltrate-reagent readings at the same wavelength. The corrected readings are used to calculate the concentrations of phenylalanine and tyrosine using the simultaneously determined absorbencies of the pure amino acids.

CALCULATION:

Let T_{308}, T_{330}, T_{308} and P_{330} be the optical densities of solutions of tyrosine and phenylalanine with a concentration of 1 mg./100 ml. at 308 and 330 mμ. These parameters are calculated using Beer's law from optical densities obtained with more concentrated (e.g. millimolar) solutions. Let D_{308} and D_{330} be the optical density for the unknown. The phenylalanine concentration in the serum is then given by the expression

Phenylalanine concentration $=$

$$\frac{D_{308} \times T_{330} - D_{330} \times T_{308}}{P_{308} \times T_{330} - P_{330} \times T_{308}} \text{ mg./100 ml.}$$

or with slightly lower accuracy by the expression

$$\frac{D_{308} - 1\cdot75 \times D_{330}}{P_{308} - 1\cdot75 \times P_{330}} \text{ mg./100 ml.}$$

The tyrosine concentration in plasma or serum can be calculated from the expression

Tyrosine concentration $=$

$$\frac{D_{330} - \text{phenylalanine concentration} \times P_{330}}{T_{330}} \text{ mg./100 ml.}$$

Fluorimetric Method

REAGENTS

(1) Ninhydrin-peptide reagent. Prepare daily by mixing 5 volumes of 600 mM succinate buffer pH 5·88 with 2 volumes of 30 mM ninhydrin and 1 volume of 5 mM L-leucyl-L-alanine.

(2) Copper reagent. Prepare daily by mixing 3 volumes of a solution 25 mM in Na_2CO_3 and 0·4 mM in $KNaC_4H_4O_6$ (Rochelle salt) with 2 volumes of 0·8 mM $CuSO_4.5H_2O$.

(3) 0·6 N trichloracetic acid (TCA).

(4) Phenylalanine standards. Prepare solutions containing 1, 5 and 15 mg./100 ml. of phenylalanine in 0·6 N TCA. Mix equal volumes of the phenylalanine solution and a 6·5 g./100 ml. solution of bovine serum albumin. Allow to stand for 10

minutes, centrifuge at 5,000 g. for 5 minutes and separate the supernatant. Re-centrifuge if necessary.

(5) Blank. Mix equal volumes of TCA and 6·5 g./100 ml. albumin solution. Separate the supernatant as above.

The L-leucyl-L-alanine solution is stored frozen, all other reagents are kept at 4°C.

PROCEDURE

Add 0·1 ml. TCA to 0·1 ml. of serum, mix well, allow to stand for 10 minutes and centrifuge at 5,000 g. for 5 minutes. Add 0·05 ml. each of the supernatant, of the 3 phenylalanine standards and of the blank to 0·75 ml. portions of ninhydrin-peptide reagent in stoppered test tubes. Mix and incubate at 60°C for 2 hours. Cool in tap water to about 20°C, then add 5 ml. of copper reagent. Read within 1 hour in a spectrophotofluorimeter* at 515 mμ using an activating wavelength of 365 mμ, or in a fluorimeter† with a Chance OX1 filter on the primary side and an OB2 and OY8 filter on the secondary side.

The fluorimeter readings for the 3 standards and the blank when plotted against concentration yield a straight line from which serum phenylalanine levels can be readily obtained. To avoid errors due to fluorescent compounds in the serum, not derived from the reaction of phenylalanine, ninhydrin and leucyl alanine, it is sometimes advisable to include a serum blank, that is serum incubated with ninhydrin-peptide reagent from which the leucyl alanine has been omitted.

Microbiological Assay

REAGENTS:

(1) Modified Demain's Medium

Substance	Grams
Dextrose	10·0
K_2HPO_4	30·0
KH_2PO_4	10·0
NH_4Cl	5·0
NH_4NO_3	1·0
Na_2SO_3	1·0
Glutamic acid	1·0
Asparagine	1·0
L-alanine	0·5

Salt solution (10 ml.)	Grams/litre
$MgSO_4.7H_2O$	10·0
$MnCl_2.4H_2O$	1·0
$FeCl_3.6H_2O$	1·0
$CaCl_2$	0·5

The above are dissolved in 900 ml. of water

(2) 10 per cent dextrose

(3) 3 per cent agar

(4) Inoculum. Bottles or petri dishes containing a potato infusion agar medium (e.g. Difco Bacto B51) are prepared. The agar surface is inoculated heavily with a *Bacillus subtilis* ATCC 6051 cell suspension from overnight cultures grown on Difco Heart Infusion agar slopes. During incubation for one week at 30°C the growth is examined microscopically at intervals for the presence of spores. These are scraped

---

* Aminco-Bowman, American Instrument Co., Maryland.

† Locarte fluorimeter, Locarte Company, London, W.14.

and washed off the agar into 0·9 per cent NaCl, and washed 3 times with 0·9 per cent NaCl by centrifuging (e.g. 11,000 r.p.m. in a Serval Model SS3). A final suspension is made in distilled water to give an optical density of 0·9 measured in a colorimeter at a wavelength of 550 mμ. 0·3 ml. portions are dispensed into screw-capped vials, dried on a shaking machine at 60°C and stored in a refrigerator with the caps tightly closed.

(5) β-2-thienylalanine. 0·3 ml. portions of a 0·01 M solution are pipetted into screw-capped vials, dried, and stored at room temperature.

Assay Medium

90 ml. of solution (1) are sterilized and 10 ml. of the 10 per cent glucose solution (sterilized separately) are added. 100 ml. of sterile 3 per cent agar are melted and cooled to 55°C and mixed with 100 ml. of the medium. Inoculum and β-2-thienyl-alanine from one vial each are dissolved in 1–2 ml. of the medium and added to 200 ml. of the culture medium. The final inhibitor concentration is thus $1·5 \times 10^{-5}$ M.

Collection of Specimens

A small amount of fresh blood is applied to a piece of thick absorbent filter paper (e.g. Schleicher & Schnell 903). The spot after air drying should be not less than $\frac{3}{8}$ in. and not more than $\frac{1}{2}$ in. in diameter, and the appearance of the spot must be the same on both sides of the paper. Before assay the papers should be autoclaved with dry steam at 15 lbs. pressure for 3 minutes. This prevents interference by blood pigments. Prolonged autoclaving will, however, destroy the phenylalanine. A disc, $\frac{1}{4}$ in. in diameter, is then punched from the centre of the blood spot.

Preparation of Controls

L-phenylalanine is added to outdated blood from a blood bank of known phenyl-alanine content to give a series of concentrations of 2, 4, 6, 8, 10, 12 and 20 mg./100 ml. The blood is spotted on filter paper as above, and, after drying, the control spots are stored in a desiccator at 2°–5°C. The controls are autoclaved simultaneously with the unknowns before discs of each spot are punched out for use. An alternative set of eight control discs, particularly useful for screening is of 2, 4, 4, 4, 6, 6, 6 and 8 mg./100 ml. These values are selected because a result of 6 mg./100 ml. or above is generally considered as positive.

Test Procedure

After combining the culture medium, agar, inhibitor and spore powder, all constituents are thoroughly mixed by pouring back and forth and placed in a flat 8×12 inch dish. After the agar is hardened, controls and unknown samples are placed on the agar 25 mm. apart when screening or 35 mm. apart when high values are expected. The agar dish is then incubated at 35°–37°C for 16–18 hours. Zones of growth are obtained around the standard discs, and the zone size of the test may be compared with those of the controls. Alternatively the diameters of the zones for the controls may be plotted against their concentration on semi-logarithmic graph paper, and the phenylalanine levels for the unknown samples read off the graph. Complete kits for carrying out this assay are available from Scientific Hospital Supplies Ltd., Liverpool.

References

Guthrie, R., and Susi, A. (1963). *Pediatrics*, **32**, 338.

O'Brien, D., and Ibbott, F. A. (1962). 'Pediatric Micro and Ultramicro Biochemical Techniques', 3rd ed., New York: Hoeber, p. 242.

Wong, P. W. K., O'Flynn, M. E., and Inouye, T. (1964). *Clin. Chem.*, **10**, 1098.

Woolf, L. I., and Goodwin, B. L. (1964). *Clin. Chem.*, **10**, 146.

5a: Problems in the Diagnosis and Treatment of Phenylketonuria

As explained elsewhere, the diagnosis of phenylketonuria must be made at once. Delay in instituting treatment can jeopardize the baby's intellectual development while a phenylalanine-low diet is very dangerous for a normal infant. The diagnosis may not be simple, however, during the first weeks of life, if the blood alanine of a baby is over 4 mg./100 ml. The data which may be encountered in such circumstances have been considered by Berry, Sutherland and Umbarger (1966) and are summarized in Table 1 on p. 354.

Benign tyrosinosis (II) occurs in about 1 per cent of normal babies, and elevated blood tyrosine levels may persist for several months because the tyrosine oxidizing system is slow to develop. The screening tests described on p. 339 should reveal an excess of tyrosine in the blood and urine of these cases. Woolf (1963) describes the following screening test for p-hydroxyphenylpyruvic acid, which is excreted in tyrosinosis.

Urine is acidified with acetic acid and creatinine is removed with Lloyd's reagent (Fuller's earth). Protein, if present, is precipitated with trichloracetic acid added to a final concentration of 10 per cent. To 2 ml. of urine are added 5 ml. of 4 per cent potassium dihydrogen phosphate and 5 ml. of a 2·5 per cent solution of sodium molybdate in 5 N sulphuric acid (Briggs' reagent). The mixture is immediately diluted to 50 ml. and the optical density determined at room temperature at 700 mμ after 5 minutes, and again after 3 hours. Suitable standards are read at the same time. Ascorbic acid and indolylpyruvic acid, if present, reduce Briggs' reagent within a few minutes. The colour due to p-hydroxyphenylpyruvic acid reaches near maximum intensity in 3 hours. In benign tyrosinosis the concentration of p-hydroxyphenyl-pyruvic acid in urine may amount to 25 mg./100 ml.

In liver disease (III) other serum amino acids, particularly methionine, will be elevated in addition to tyrosine and phenylalanine. The urine will often show generalized aminoaciduria and glycosuria.

The findings in IV and V may indicate atypical phenylketonuria, but, also, delayed development of phenylalanine hydroxylase, as, for example, in some heterozygotes.

In untreated homozygous phenylketonurics o-hydroxyphenylacetic acid is usually present in the urine in concentrations exceeding 2 mg./100 ml. The following screening test may be used (Berry, Umbarger and Sutherland, 1965). 25 μl. of urine are chromatographed overnight with butanol-ethanol-ammonia (4:1:1). The dried chromatogram is sprayed with a 1 per cent solution of 2,6-dichloroquinone chlorimide in 95 per cent ethanol. After 5 minutes the paper is lightly sprayed with an aqueous solution of 0·5 per cent sodium tetraborate. o-Hydroxyphenylacetic acid gives a blue spot (Rf 0·72) when present in amounts exceeding 0·2 μg. Diazotized sulphanilic acid (p. 341) may also be used as a stain.

Control of Treatment

Several detailed accounts have been recently published of the management of the phenylketonuric infant on a phenylalanine-low diet (Berry, Umbarger and Sutherland, 1965; Berry, Sutherland and Umbarger, 1966; Clayton, Francis and Moncrieff, 1965; Medical Research Council Report, 1963; Sutherland, Umbarger and Berry, 1966; Umbarger, Berry and Sutherland, 1965; Woolf, 1963). Our comments will therefore be confined to those aspects of the treatment which directly concern the biochemist.

The amount of essential biochemical information required for treatment varies with each patient and depends on the child's age and state of health. It may be advisable to estimate the serum phenylalanine as often as two or three times during the

Table 1. GUIDES FOR THE DIAGNOSIS OF PHENYLKETONURIA (BERRY ET AL., 1966)
(The results tabulated are for specimens obtained following a positive screening test)

	I	II	III	IV	V	VI*
Blood phenylalanine	>15 mg./100 ml.	5–15 mg./100 ml.	5–20 mg./100 ml.	5–15 mg./100 ml.	>15 mg./100 ml.	<5 mg./100 ml.
Urine phenylalanine	>10 mg./100 ml.	2·5–15 mg./100 ml.	5–30 mg./100 ml.	<10 mg./100 ml.	<10 mg./100 ml.	<2·5 mg./100 ml.
Blood tyrosine	<5 mg./100 ml.	>5 mg./100 ml.	>5 mg./100 ml.	<5 mg./100 ml.	<5 mg./100 ml.	<5 mg./100 ml.
Urine o-hydroxyphenylacetic acid	present	absent	absent	absent	absent	absent
Other urinary findings	phenylpyruvic acid	p-hydroxy-phenylpyruvic acid	p-hydroxy-phenylpyruvic acid, sugar, etc.†			
Probable diagnosis	phenylketonuria	benign tyrosinosis	liver disease†	'atypical phenylketonuria'	'atypical phenylketonuria'	?
Recommended action	dietary treatment	ascorbic acid and folic acid supplements	treatment as appropriate	repeat assessment after 2 weeks	dietary treatment for trial period, then reassessment	increase dietary intake by 100 mg. ph.al. a day, assess daily

* patient with suspected but unconfirmed phenylketonuria who is receiving a phenylalanine-low diet.
† e.g. tyrosinosis (hepato-renal dysfunction), galactosaemia, acute yellow atrophy.

first week of treatment, weekly during the first two months, fortnightly during the first year, and thereafter at monthly intervals. More frequent determinations are often necessary if the child is ill, as insufficient food intake may lead to a breakdown of tissue proteins and this raises blood phenylalanine.

Estimations of serum phenylalanine are usually sufficient to control treatment. Berry, however, advocates that the urinary excretion of phenylalanine and *o*-hydroxy-phenylacetic acid should also be checked at frequent intervals, preferably by semi-quantitative methods. This is certainly useful in the more difficult cases. According to Berry, random specimens of urine will have phenylalanine levels in the range 2·5–7·5 mg./100 ml. if the dietary intake of phenylalanine is adequate but not excessive. *o*-Hydroxyphenylacetic acid will not be detected in the urine if the serum level of phenylalanine is below 7 mg./100 ml.

There is no general agreement on the safe range of serum phenylalanine in children under treatment. Most workers would probably agree that the level should not exceed 7 mg./100 ml. and not fall much below 2 mg./100 ml. Levels below 1 mg./100 ml. can be extremely dangerous.

Height, weight, bone age, and intellectual progress should be recorded at regular intervals. Sutherland *et al.* (1966) present data to show that with adequately controlled treatment started before 3 months, phenylketonurics do not differ significantly from their unaffected sibs in physical and mental development. Some of these cases have been treated for up to $4\frac{1}{2}$ years.

References

BERRY, H. K., UMBARGER, B., and SUTHERLAND, B. S. (1965). *J. Pediat.*, **67**, 609.

BERRY, H. K., SUTHERLAND, B. S., and UMBARGER, B. (1966). *Pediatrics*, **37**, 102.

CLAYTON, B., FRANCIS, F., and MONCRIEFF, A. (1965). *Brit. med. J.*, **1**, 54.

Medical Research Council Report on Treatment of Phenylketonuria. (1963). *Brit. med. J.*, **1**, 1691.

SUTHERLAND, B. S., UMBARGER, B., and BERRY, H. K. (1966). *Amer. J. Dis. Child.*, **111**, 505.

UMBARGER, B., BERRY, H. K., and SUTHERLAND, B. S. (1965). *J. Amer. med. Ass.*, **193**, 784.

WOOLF, L. I. (1963). *Advanc. clin. Chem.*, **6**, 98.

6: The Estimation of Tyrosine in the Blood

Tyrosine reacts with α-nitroso-β-naphthol in the presence of nitrite and nitric acid to form a fluorescent product (Udenfriend, 1962). Excess of the reagent can be removed with ethylene dichloride. This reaction forms the basis of a sensitive and specific assay of tyrosine.

REAGENTS

(1) α-nitroso-β-naphthol reagent. Dissolve 200 mg. of the naphthol in 100 ml. of 95 per cent ethanol, filter if necessary. Before use mix 2 volumes with 3 volumes of 3 N nitric acid (18·9 per cent v/v) and 3 volumes of 0·1 N sodium nitrite (6.9 g./litre).
(2) Ethylene dichloride.
(3) 0·6 N trichloracetic acid (TCA).
(4) Tyrosine standards of 2·5, 5 and 10 mg./100 ml. of water.
   All reagents are stored at 0–4°C.

PROCEDURE

Add 0·1 ml. each of TCA to 0·1 ml. of serum or heparinized plasma, to 0·1 ml. of standard, and to 0·1 ml. of distilled water (blank). Mix well, allow to stand for 10 minutes, then centrifuge at approximately 5,000 g. for 5 minutes. To 0·05 ml. of supernatant add 0·5 ml. of α-nitroso-β-naphthol reagent, mix and incubate at 33°C for 20 minutes. Add 2·5 ml. of water and 7·5 ml. of ethylene dichloride, mix and centrifuge. Transfer the upper aqueous layer to another test tube and incubate at room temperature (app. 25°C) for 40 minutes.

Measure fluorescence within 30 minutes in a spectrofluorimeter at 570 mμ using an activating wavelength of 460 mμ, or in a fluorimeter with a Corning filter 5–74 on the primary side and a Chance filter OY2 on the secondary side.

The procedure given is essentially that of Wong, O'Flynn and Inouye (1964). These authors found a mean normal level for adults of 1·06 ± 0·24 (S.D.) mg./100 ml. In newborn infants the level was 2·5 ± 1·1 (S.D.) mg./100 ml., and in low birth weight newborns 15·8 ± 8·9 (S.D.) mg./100 ml.

References

UDENFRIEND, S. (1962). 'Fluorescence Assay in Biology and Medicine', New York: Academic Press, p. 129.
WONG, W. K., O'FLYNN, M. E., and INOUYE, T. (1964). *Clin. Chem.* **10**, 1098.

7: The Estimation of Tryptophan in the Blood

This method, introduced by Udenfriend and collaborators (Udenfriend, 1962), has been widely used for the estimation of tryptophan in the blood.

REAGENTS

(1) 0·6 N sulphuric acid.
(2) 10 per cent (0·3 M) sodium tungstate.
(3) 0·25 M barium hydroxide.
(4) 2 M sodium carbonate.
(5) Tryptophan standards. 0, 1, 2 and 5 mg./100 ml. in a solution containing 7·5 g./100 ml. of bovine albumin.

PROCEDURE

0·5 ml. each of plasma and of the standard solutions are diluted with 2 ml. of water and acidified with 0·25 ml. of sulphuric acid. 0·25 ml. of tungstate are added and the precipitated proteins removed by centrifugation. Tungstate ion has a quenching effect on tryptophan fluorescence and has to be removed by the addition of 0·5 ml. of barium chloride solution to 1·5 ml. of the clear supernatant. The resultant precipitates of barium sulphate and barium tungstate are removed by centrifugation. 1 ml. of the supernatant is added to a tube containing 0·25 ml. of sodium carbonate and the precipitated barium carbonate is removed by centrifugation. The fluorescence of the supernatant is determined at 350 mμ with an activating wavelength of 287 mμ. In the Locarte fluorimeter a liquid filter of cobalt and nickel sulphate (iron free!) is used on the primary side (filter LFM/H/1), and a Chance filter OX1 on the secondary side. The fasting plasma tryptophan level is approximately 1 mg./100 ml. After a dose of 100 mg./kg. body weight of L-tryptophan levels of 8–14 mg./100 ml. are reached, usually within 2 hours.

A more sensitive fluorimetric assay based on the condensation of tryptophan with formaldehyde followed by oxidation to norharman has been described by Hess and Udenfriend (1959).

References

HESS, S., and UDENFRIEND, S. (1959). *J. Pharmacol. exp. Ther.*, **127**, 175.
UDENFRIEND, S. (1962). 'Fluorescence Assay in Biology and Medicine', New York: Academy Press, p. 163.

8: The Estimation of Galactose in the Blood

While many methods are available for the enzymatic estimation of glucose (Free, 1963), the enzymatic estimation of galactose has only recently become possible with the marketing of galactose oxidase preparations. Methods for the enzymatic estimation of galactose have been given by Roth *et al.* (1965) and by Hsia and Inouye (1966), whose method is described here with minor modifications.

REAGENTS

(1) Galactose oxidase reagent. 5μ moles of *o*-dianisidine, 500 µg. of horseradish peroxidase and 5 mg. of galactose oxidase (Ames) are dissolved in 10 ml. of 0·01 M Tris buffer, pH 7·5. If another preparation, galactose oxidase X9 (Hughes and Hughes), is used, 10 ml. of the reagent should contain 0.2–1 mg. of the enzyme.
(2) 12 M sulphuric acid.
(3) Galactose standards: 0, 40, 80 and 120 mg./100 ml. of galactose dissolved in a solution containing 7·5 g. of bovine albumin and 200 mg. of sodium benzoate in 100 ml. of water. The pH is adjusted to 7·4.
(4) 0·18 M zinc sulphate.
(5) 0·18 M barium hydroxide.

PROCEDURE

Collect capillary blood into heparinized tubes and separate the plasma as soon as possible. To 0·1 ml. each of the galactose standards add 0·1 ml. of zinc sulphate and 0·1 ml. barium hydroxide. Mix and centrifuge. The protein-free supernatant should have a pH of 7·4. To 0·1 ml. of each of the clear supernatant solutions add 1 ml. of the galactose oxidase reagent and incubate at room temperature for 20 minutes, then add 0·3 ml. of sulphuric acid. Determine the optical density at 527 mμ.

References

FREE, A. H. (1963). *Advanc. clin. Chem.*, **6**, 67.
HSIA, D. Y.-Y., and INOUYE, T. (1966). 'Inborn Errors of Metabolism, Part 2, Laboratory Methods', Chicago: Year Book Medical Publishers, p. 116.
ROTH, H., SEGAL, S., and BERTOLI, D. (1965). *Analyt. Biochem.*, **10**, 32.

9: The Detection of Galactosaemia with Galactose-1-C^{14}

The simple microdiffusion test of London, Marymont and Fuld (1964) appears best-suited for the detection of galactosaemia in laboratories with facilities for radioactive work. It is based on the inability of the red cells of galactosaemics to metabolise galactose to carbon dioxide.

REAGENTS AND EQUIPMENT

(1) The test is performed in a 25 × 35 mm. bottle fitted with a single-bore rubber bung. The end of a solid glass rod ($\frac{1}{8}$ in. × 2 in.) is heated in a flame to form a bulb about $\frac{1}{4}$ in. in diameter. The surface of the bulb is roughened with fine sandpaper. The glass rod is inserted in the rubber bung so that when the bung is applied the bulb is near the centre of the bottle.
(2) A rotator for turning the bottle at 20–40 r.p.m.
(3) A windowless gas-flow counter.
(4) Stock radioactive galactose solution. Galactose-1-C^{14} is obtainable in Europe from the Radiochemical Centre, Amersham, specific activity 2–4 mc/mM, and in the U.S.A. from the Volk Radiochemical Company, Illinois, specific activity 1 mc/mM.

50 μ curies are dissolved in 5 ml. of saturated benzoic acid. This solution is stored in the refrigerator. Periodic checks (e.g. by paper chromatography) should be made of the radiochemical purity of the solution, as labelled carbohydrates are liable to radiation self-decomposition (Bayly and Weigel, 1960). The solution must also be checked for the absence of glucose.

(5) Dilute galactose solution. Dilute the stock solution 1:20 with 0·9 per cent saline. Prepare fresh daily.

(6) Methylene blue-phosphate buffer: 93 mg. of methylene blue are dissolved in 500 ml. 0·1 M potassium phosphate buffer, pH 7·4.

(7) 20 per cent sodium hydroxide.

(8) 2 N sulphuric acid.

PROCEDURE

Blood is collected from fasting patients into heparinized tubes, and 0·1 ml. is pipetted into the bottle, followed by 0·1 ml. of buffer and 0·1 ml. of dilute galactose solution. The roughened end of the glass rod is moistened with 20 per cent sodium hydroxide, the excess alkali removed by touching the side of the sodium hydroxide container and the rubber bung replaced in the bottle, which is then rotated for 60 minutes at 20–40 r.p.m. The rubber bung is withdrawn, 3 drops of 2 N sulphuric acid are added, the bung is replaced, and the bottle rotated for a further 45 minutes. All $C^{14}O_2$ formed is thereby released and absorbed by the sodium hydroxide.

The alkali is washed from the rod into a planchet with approximately 1 ml. of water. The solution is evaporated to dryness with an infra-red heat lamp and counted in a gas-flow counter for one minute.

RESULTS

As used by London *et al.*, that is with an incubation of 60 minutes and galactose preparation of specific activity of 1 mc/mM, well over 1,000 counts/minute were recorded for normals and heterozygotes and counts of less than 50 for known galactosaemics. Elevated blood galactose levels can significantly depress the counting rate, and the authors therefore recommend the use of blood from fasting patients. It is also important to record the specific activity of the galactose preparation used as this affects the amount of $C^{14}O_2$ formed.

References

LONDON, M., MARYMONT, J. H., and FULD, J. (1964). *Pediatrics*, **33**, 421.
BAYLY, R. J., and WEIGEL, H. (1960). *Nature*, **188**, 384.

10: Assay of Galactose-1-Phosphate Uridyl Transferase

The detection of excessive galactose in the blood or urine is not sufficient for the diagnosis of galactosaemia, as urine and blood levels may be raised in disorders of lactose absorption and in liver disease. Conversely, galactosaemics excrete significant amounts of galactose only after the ingestion of lactose or galactose so that false negative results may be obtained, for example, with infants fed parenterally. Ultimately, the diagnosis must rest on the demonstration of grossly reduced levels of the enzyme galactose-1-phosphate (Gal-1-P) uridyl transferase. The uridyl diphosphate glucose (UDP-glucose) consumption test, carried out with the patient's red cells, described, amongst others, by Hsia and Inouye (1966) is suitable for the detection of galactosaemics, and will also correctly identify most heterozygotes.

$$\text{Gal-1-P} + \text{UDP-glucose} \xrightarrow{\text{uridyl transferase}} \text{UDP-galactose}$$

The UDP-glucose remaining is estimated by the reaction

$$\text{UDP-glucose} + \text{nicotinamide adenine dinucleotide (NAD)} \xrightarrow[\text{dehydrogenase}]{\text{UDP-glucose}}$$
$$\text{UDP-glucuronic acid} + \text{NADH}$$

utilizing the difference in absorbance at 340 mμ of NAD and NADH.

REAGENTS

(1) 0·2 M Tris buffer, pH 8·1.
(2) 1·0 M glycine buffer, pH 8·7.
(3) UDP-glucose, 1·0 M in Tris buffer.
(4) Gal-1-P, 4 mM in Tris buffer.
(5) UDP-glucose standards. 0·1μ moles/ml. and 0·25 μmoles/ml. in glycine buffer.
(6) NAD (DPN) 10 μmoles/ml. glycine buffer.
(7) Cysteine, 0·1 M in glycine buffer.
(8) UDP-glucose dehydrogenase (Sigma), 200 units/ml. in glycine buffer.
(9) Haemolysate, 0·1 ml. of packed red cells are mixed with 0·4 ml. of water. The haemoglobin concentration of the haemolysate is determined by a suitable method.

The above reagents are available commercially—for example, from the Sigma Company, London or St. Louis.

PROCEDURE

Cool 3 tubes in crushed ice and add reagents as follows:

	A	B	C
Haemolysate	0·1	0·1	0·1
UDP-glucose	0·15	0·15	—
Gal-1-P	0·05	—	—
Tris buffer	—	0·05	0·2

Incubate at 37°C for 20 minutes, add 0·5 ml. of cold, deionized water, mix and heat in boiling water for 5 minutes. Shake vigorously and centrifuge.

Prepare immediately before use a mixture of 2·4 ml. glycine buffer, 0·4 ml. cysteine, 0·4 ml. of NAD and 4·0 ml. of UDP-glucose dehydrogenase. Add 0·9 ml. of this mixture to 0·2 ml. each of the clear supernatants of tubes A, B and C, to 0·2 ml. of each of the UDP-glucose standards, and to 0·2 ml. of water for the blank. Incubate at 25°C (room temperature) for 30 minutes, and determine the optical density (O.D.) at 340 mμ and 400 mμ. In all cases subtract the optical density at 400 mμ from that at 340 mμ, and use the corrected optical densities in the calculation.

UDP-glucose consumed = 0·15 μmoles — 4 × UDP-glucose determined in 0·2 of the supernatant (corresponding to one quarter of the original reaction mixture). UDP-glucose consumption/hour/gm.Hb = 3 × UDP-glucose consumed/tube in 20 minutes divided by the haemoglobin in 0·1 ml. of haemolysate. The UDP-glucose control tube, B, should have values of approximately 2 μmoles/hour/gm. Hb.

Interpretation: Normals: 25·2 ± 5·3 μmoles/hr./gm. Hb.
     Heterozygotes: 13·1 ± 4·2 μmoles/hr./gm. Hb.
     Galactosaemics: 1·8 ± 3·3 μmoles/hr./gm. Hb.

There is some overlap between the values for normals and heterozygotes: 10–12 per cent of heterozygotes have values greater than 17 μmoles/hr./gm. Hb. and about 20 per cent of normals values of 21 μmoles/hr./gm. Hb. or less.

Reference

HSIA, D. Y.-Y., and INOUYE, T. (1966). 'Inborn Errors of Metabolism, Part 2, Laboratory Methods', Chicago: Year Book Medical Publishers, p. 114.

11: Test for Leucine Sensitivity

Leucine-induced hypoglycaemia is a rare cause of mental retardation (cf. p. 295). While spontaneous remission has not been described, gradual amelioration of the hypoglycaemic tendency occurs sometimes (Marks and Rose, 1965). Periodic reassessment of the severity of leucine sensitivity is, therefore, desirable, lest a child be kept indefinitely on steroids, which are liable to induce a number of complications if given over long periods.

PROCEDURE

The patient is fasted overnight. With the patient resting in bed fasting blood samples are first taken followed by others 15, 30, 45 and 60 minutes after an oral dose of 150 mg./kg. body weight of L-leucine. The leucine may be given mixed with water into a paste or as a suspension in a cup of suitably flavoured water. Glucose is determined in the blood samples, preferably by a specific enzymatic method. Leucine-sensitive subjects usually show a drop of 30–40 mg./100 ml. of glucose 20–40 minutes after taking the dose, and may also show clinical signs of hypoglycaemia. Glucose, glucagon and cortisone must be available for emergency use whenever this test is performed.

Reference

MARKS, V., and ROSE, F. C. (1965). 'Hypoglycaemia', Oxford: Blackwell, p. 285.

12: Paper Chromatography of Sugars

Chromatography of the urinary sugars is often requested in the course of investigation of mentally retarded children. As explained elsewhere, abnormalities in intestinal absorption or renal tubular reabsorption are sometimes only revealed after a suitable loading dose. If only urinary sugars are to be investigated, 20 g. of sucrose in 200 ml. of milk is given to the fasting child, and the urine collected for 5 hours. If lactose or sucrose malabsorption is suspected, 2 g./kg. body weight, up to a maximum of 50 g., of one of the disaccharides is given instead as a 10–15 per cent solution in suitably flavoured water. Blood is collected fasting and 15, 30 and 45 minutes after the loading dose, the urine is collected for 5 hours. In alactasia and in invertase deficiency the rise in glucose is less than 20 mg./100 ml. Glucose should be estimated by glucose oxidase, e.g. Fermcotest S.F.G. (Hughes & Hughes). These load tests are contra-indicated in galactosaemia (p. 291) and hereditary fructose intolerance (p. 294). In some forms of disaccharide intolerance sucrose and/or lactose are absorbed before they can be hydrolysed, and excreted unchanged in the urine. Increased blood levels of sucrose and lactose can be detected by chromatography (*vide infra*). An increase in blood lactose, but not of blood sucrose, will also be shown by analytical methods based on the reducing properties of sugars. The chromatographic methods described below are based on the work of Woolf and Norman (1957), O'Brien and Ibbott (1962) and Seakins (1964).

REAGENTS AND MATERIALS

(1) Equipment for ascending or descending paper chromatography.
(2) Exchange resin for desalting: 'Biodeminrolit' in the acetate form.
(3) Chromatographic solvents: (a) *Iso*propanol-water, 160:40 (v/v); (b) Ethyl acetate-pyridine-water, 120:50:40 (v/v/v).
(4) Stains:

(a) Aldoses. 1·5 ml. of aniline are added to 100 ml. of a saturated solution of phthalic acid in acetone. Dip or spray the chromatogram, and when dry heat at 100°C for 5 minutes.

(b) Ketoses. 100 mg. of naphthoresorcinol are dissolved in a mixture of 85 ml. of acetone and 15 ml. of a 50 per cent solution of trichloracetic acid in water. Dip or spray the chromatogram, heat at 100°C for 5 minutes.

(c) Glucose oxidase reagent, e.g. Fermcotest S.F.G. (Hughes and Hughes) and 12 M sulphuric acid.

(5) Picric acid. Analytical grade reagent is stored under water and dried between filter papers just before use.

(6) Standard solutions are made up in 10 per cent *iso*propanol, as follows:

   (a) Aldoses. Lactose,   300 mg./100 ml.
              Galactose, 100 mg./100 ml.
              Glucose,   100 mg./100 ml.
   (b) Ketoses. Sucrose,   200 mg./100 ml.
              Fructose,   100 mg./100 ml.

Procedure for Urine

About 5 ml. of urine is desalted by shaking for 15 minutes with half its volume of 'Biodeminrolit'. We carry out chromatography by a one-dimensional ascending technique on 10 in. × 10 in. Whatman No. 1 papers. 0·05 ml. of urine, or less if it is gives a positive qualitative Benedict's test, are applied with a micro-pipette in a ½ in. streak, 1½ in. from the bottom of the paper, 5 μl. at a time, drying after each application. Each paper can accommodate six samples, for example, for qualitative examination, 10 μl. each of ketose and aldose standard, and duplicate applications of 50 μl. from two urine specimens. For a semi-quantitative estimate of the sugar concentration one sheet may carry 50 μl. of urine and 10, 20, 30, 40 and 50 μl. of aldose standards, and a second sheet– urine and 5 ketose standards.

We generally use the *iso*propanol-water solvent. The method does not separate glucose and galactose, but this drawback may be overcome by applying a glucose oxidase reagent, Fermcotest S.F.G., to the appropriate area of the chromatogram, followed after 20–30 minutes by 12 M sulphuric acid, when glucose yields a purple spot. A similar test may be carried out with the galactose oxidase reagent (p. 357).

Some authors (e.g. Seakins, 1964) prefer one-dimensional descending chromatography on 55 cm. sheets of Whatman 3MM paper, with ethyl acetate-pyridine-water as solvent, using approximately twice the amount of urine. In this way it is possible to separate glucose and galactose by chromatography alone.

Procedure for Faeces

Stools are collected 3–6 hours after the patient has been given a dose of 2 g./kg. body weight of the disaccharide. The stool is weighed, mixed with a volume of acetone equal to its weight and the mixture centrifuged. The supernatant is shaken with half its volume of 'Biodeminrolit' for 30 minutes to remove the ions and most of the pigments (Seakins, 1964). Chromatography is carried out as described for urine, except that it is sometimes necessary to apply rather larger volumes of the desalted extract. In alactasia, however, 10–20 μl. are usually sufficient.

Procedure for Serum

75 mg. of picric acid are added to 1 ml. of plasma and the mixture is shaken to deproteinize. The supernatant is deionized with 'Biodeminrolit' and chromatographed as described for urine (Seakins, 1964).

NORMAL VALUES

The upper limit of normal for the excretion of sugars in the urine after an oral dose of milk and sugar is as follows: glucose—10 mg./100 ml., fructose—20 mg./ 100 ml., galactose—15 mg./100 ml., sucrose—20 mg./100 ml., and lactose—30 mg./ 100 ml. It must be emphasized that these figures apply to healthy infants and children, and that somewhat higher values are often found in institutional populations.

References

O'BRIEN, D., and IBBOTT, F. A. (1962). 'Laboratory Manual of Pediatric Micro- and Ultra-Micro-Biochemical Techniques', New York: Hoeber, p. 129.
SEAKINS, W. T. (1964). 'Demonstration to the Association of Clinical Biochemists (Great Britain)', London, February 1964.
WOOLF, L. I., and NORMAN, A. P. (1957). *J. Pediat.*, **50**, 271.

13: The Detection of Gargoylism

A number of screening tests have been proposed for the diagnosis of gargoylism, but none is fully reliable. All depend on the presence of excess of sulphated mucopolysaccharide (MPS) in the urine or white cells. Three of these tests are described below. While none of them is conclusive on its own, a positive result in all three strongly suggests mucopolysaccharidosis even in the absence of the full clinical picture. All six cases of gargoylism seen at this hospital in the past 3 years were in fact positive on all three tests. We also describe a method for the electrophoretic separation of the mucopolysaccharides which, being simpler than most fractionation procedures for mucopolysaccharides, should be within the scope of most clinical laboratories.

Cetylpyridinium chloride (CPC) turbidity test

This test, introduced by Manley and Hawksworth (1966), is based on the interaction of the negatively charged mucopolysaccharide with a positively charged detergent. The turbidity produced by the complex formed in this reaction is measured colorimetrically.

REAGENTS

0·1 per cent solution of cetylpyridinium chloride in water.

PROCEDURE

A 24 hour specimen of urine is collected, preserved by the addition of a little thiomersalate and, if necessary, stored at 0–4°C. Unfortunately complete collections are often impracticable with severely subnormal children. Losses in such cases are therefore ignored and the collection continued until 600 ml. have been obtained from an infant or 1,000 ml. from an older child. A representative specimen is thus obtained, but the reliability of the test is naturally somewhat diminished. Random specimens are useless as mucopolysaccharide excretion varies throughout the day.

20 ml. of urine are centrifuged. Two 5 ml. samples of the clear supernatant are pipetted into each of two test tubes. To the first, 'blank', are added 5 ml. of water, and to the second, 'test', 5 ml. of CPC reagent. Both tubes are mixed by inversion, and precisely four minutes later the 'test' is read against the 'blank' in a colorimeter in 1 cm. cells and with an Ilford 625 filter.

CPC Turbidity = Optical density (OD).

The upper limit of normal is 0·5 OD units. The optical density reaches a maximum after four minutes and then decreases. It is important to note that the specified filter and a colorimeter with a barrier layer photo cell has to be used. Narrow band width spectrophotometers give erroneously high optical densities.

Toluidine Blue Test

Sulphated mucopolysaccharides show metachromasia when stained with toluidine blue in acid solution. Berry and Spinanger (1960) have made this the basis of a simple and quick screening test for gargoylism. The following is a modification of their test.

REAGENTS

(1) Toluidine blue solution. 100 mg. of toluidine blue are dissolved in a mixture of 70 ml. of 30 per cent (v/v) acetic acid and 30 ml. ethanol.
(2) Absolute alcohol.
(3) Chondroitin sulphate standard. 10 mg./100 ml. of water.

PROCEDURE

A piece of Whatman No. 1 filter paper is selected to fit a petri dish. With a 5 μl. capillary pipette apply 5, 10 and 20 μl. of urine to the paper. Dry with a hair drier between applications and keep all spots the same size. Also apply 10 μl. of the standard chondroitin sulphate solution, and 10 μl. of urine from an authentic case of gargoylism, if available. When thoroughly dry, immerse the paper in toluidine blue solution in the petri dish for 5 minutes, then wash in several changes of absolute alcohol for about 20 minutes and dry on blotting paper. Sulphated mucopolysaccharides stain purple on a white or light blue background. Each sample of the dye should be tested for suitability in the test with the standard solution of chondroitin sulphate and, if possible, with urine from an authentic case of gargoylism.

Electrophoretic separation of the mucopolysaccharides

Urine is concentrated 100–500-fold by vacuum dialysis and the concentrate fractionated by electrophoresis on cellulose acetate (Manley and Hawksworth, 1966).

REAGENTS

(1) Michaelis' sodium barbiturate-acetate buffer, pH 9·2.
Prepare 500 ml. of a solution of 9·714 g. of sodium acetate trihydrate and 14·714 g. of sodium diethyl barbiturate (sodium barbital) in 500 ml. of distilled water. To 50 ml. of this solution add 20 ml. of 8·5 per cent sodium chloride followed by 0·1 N hydrochloric acid to pH 9·2 (glass electrode). About 20 ml. of acid are required. Make up to 250 ml. with water.
(2) Alcian blue (G. T. Gurr), 1 per cent solution (w/v) in 2 per cent (v/v) acetic acid.
(3) 0·2 per cent (w/v) light green in 3 per cent trichloracetic acid, and
(4) 0·1 per cent azure A in 70 per cent ethanol.

EQUIPMENT

(1) Apparatus for concentrating urine is described in the paper by Manley and Hawksworth (1966). A simple vacuum dialyser used in this hospital by B. A. Saggers consists of a 500 ml. Buchner flask fitted with a single-hole rubber bung, through which is passed a glass tube. The lower end of this glass tube is widened and carries one end of a 6 in. length of Visking dialysis tubing, the other end of which is securely knotted.

The Buchner flask is filled with water to $\frac{1}{2}$ in. below its side-arm, which is connected to a water pump. For vacuum dialysis the bung is pushed firmly into the flask. The dialysing sac containing the urine is then suspended in the water, while the flask is evacuated via its side arm. 10 ml. of urine can usually be concentrated overnight.

(2) Equipment for cellulose acetate electrophoresis is described by Kohn (1960).

(3) A scanner for cellulose acetate electrophoresis strips.

PROCEDURE

Electrophoresis is carried out on 'Oxoid' 20 × 5 cm. cellulose acetate strips which have been allowed to equilibrate for 1 hour in the electrophoresis tank containing the buffer. 10 μl. samples are applied. This is half or more of the residue after dialysis of normal urines. Some urine specimens from patients with gargoylism leave a residue of up to 0·1 ml. after dialysis, and this may have to be diluted before electrophoresis. A potential difference of 20 v/cm. is applied for 80 minutes at 20°C. The strips are then transferred without drying to the alcian blue solution, stained for 30 minutes and washed for 30 minutes. Duplicate strips are stained in light green and azure A stains. After cleaning the alcian blue stained strips are scanned in a suitable instrument. Manley and Hawksworth (1966) use a Chromoscan (Joyce, Loebl & Co.) with a 607 filter and slit 5006. The contribution of each band is expressed as a percentage of the total mucopolysaccharide.

Normal and abnormal urines show several alcian blue positive bands which can be further differentiated by their behaviour with the other stains. The chondroitin sulphate band is fast moving and also shows a metachromatic reaction with azure A, but fails to stain with the protein dye light green. Two (sometimes 1 or 3) more slowly migrating bands which do not stain with azure A but stain intensely with light green are designated 'miscellaneous mucoprotein'. Heparitin sulphate has intermediate mobility, gives a metachromatic reaction with azure A but fails to stain with light green.

Chondroitin sulphate, heparitin sulphate and mucoprotein are found in all urines. In gargoylism the chondroitin sulphate or both chondroitin sulphate and heparitin sulphate fractions are increased. The mucoprotein fraction may be raised in genito-urinary disease. If heavy proteinuria is present it is advisable to remove the protein by heat denaturation before concentrating the urine, as excessive protein interferes both with the vacuum dialysis and electrophoresis.

The Uronic Acid Content of Mucopolysaccharides

The uronic acid carbazole reaction (Bitter and Muir, 1962) appears best suited for the quantitative estimation of mucopolysaccharide excretion. Determination of the hyaluronidase-resistant fraction helps in the characterization of the mucopolysaccharides, particularly when taken in conjunction with the electrophoretic mucopolysaccharide pattern.

REAGENTS

(1) 0·025 M sodium tetraborate in concentrated sulphuric acid.

(2) 0·0125 per cent recrystallized carbazole in ethanol.

(3) 0·015 M acetate buffer, pH 5·0, in physiological saline.

(4) Testicular hyaluronidase, 1500 units/ampoule obtainable from Bengers Ltd. or Evans Medical Ltd.

(5) Glucuronic acid standards.

(6) Cellulose tubing (Visking), heated dry at 85°–90°C to reduce pore size.

PROCEDURE

30 ml. of urine are dialysed at 4°C for 24 hours against 1 litre of acetate buffer. 10 ml. of the dialysed urine are pipetted into a 15 ml. centrifuge tube containing one ampoule of hyaluronidase, the solution incubated at 37°C for 4 hours, and dialysed for a further 24 hours against the buffer. 0·5 ml. samples of the dialysed and hyaluronidase-treated dialysed urine are mixed in stoppered glass tubes with 0·1 ml. of carbazole reagent and 3·0 ml. tetraborate reagent, and heated for 25 minutes at 100°C. It may be necessary to dilute some samples, and to concentrate others at a low temperature under reduced pressure. The optical density is measured at 530 mμ against a urine blank in which only the carbazole reagent is omitted. Standard solutions are treated as urine but read against water blanks. The urine uronic acid content is normally less than 5 mg./litre, while in gargoylism over 20 mg./litre of uronic acid are excreted. This method does not estimate keratosulphate.

Demonstration of Mucopolysaccharide Inclusions in Lymphocytes

Mittwoch (1963) has developed a valuable diagnostic test for gargoylism which is based on the detection of vacuoles and metachromatic inclusions in lymphocytes. Careful attention to detail is necessary to avoid ambiguous or false negative results. The metachromatic inclusions are found in only a proportion of the cells, which may be as low as 2 or 3 per cent. For reliable results it is therefore necessary to scan at least 100 cells.

PROCEDURE

Films are made on cover slips, as films on slides are inferior in the preservation of cytological details and often give ambiguous results. The films must be fixed and stained within 4 hours of being made. Films which have been left longer, whether fixed or unfixed, are unsuitable for the staining of lymphocytic inclusions.

Air-dried and wet-fixed films are prepared. The former are left to dry in small individual paper envelopes, the latter are placed in methanol in glass tubes. The air-dried films are stained with May-Gruenwald-Giemsa; air-dried and wet-fixed films with toluidine blue.

MAY-GRUENWALD-GIEMSA (air-dried films):

(1) Fix in methanol .... 10 minutes
(2) May-Gruenwald (Gurr) diluted 1:1 with distilled water containing 2 per cent (v/v) of a 1:1 mixture of M/15 Na_2HPO_4 and M/15 KH_2PO_4, the pH is 6·8 .... 5 minutes
(3) Giemsa (Gurr R66) diluted 1:14 with solution of pH 6·8, made as in (2) .... 20 minutes
(4) Acetone, 2 changes .... Few seconds
(5) Acetone, xylol, 1:1 .... Few seconds
(6) Xylol, 2 changes .... Few seconds
(7) Mount in distrene-dibutyl phthalate-xylol (DPX).

TOLUIDINE BLUE (air-dried and wet-fixed films).

(1) Fix in methanol .... 10 minutes or longer
(2) 0·1 per cent toluidine blue in 30 per cent methanol .... 30 minutes
(3) Acetone, 2 changes .... Few seconds
(4) Acetone: xylol, 1:1 .... Few seconds
(5) Xylol, 2 changes .... Few seconds
(6) Mount in DPX

Examine 100 lymphocytes each from
    (a) air-dried films stained with May-Gruenwald-Giemsa
    (b) air-dried films stained with toluidine blue.
    (c) wet-fixed films stained with toluidine blue.
Results:

Negative: no lymphocytic inclusions apart from the azurophilic granules of normal lymphocytes stained by (a) only.

Positive: a proportion of the lymphocytes contain abnormal inclusions which are stained by (a), (b) and (c).

(a) *Air-dried films stained with May-Gruenwald-Giemsa:* the inclusions are red to purple. They are distinguished from the azurophilic granules of normal lymphocytes in 4 ways: they are better defined and stain more intensely; they usually occur in clusters, leaving the intervening cytoplasm clear; they tend to be surrounded by well-defined vacuoles; they may be in the shape of dots, commas or small rings. Occasionally one or a few larger inclusions are present instead of a cluster of small ones. The inclusions may be present in lymphocytes of all sizes. Sometimes one sees lymphocytes with cytoplasmic vacuoles. These are interpreted as inclusions which have dissolved.

(b) *Air-dried films stained with toluidine blue:* the inclusions, which show the same range of shapes as in Method a, stain metachromatically. Azurophilic granules are invisible with this stain.

(c) *Wet-fixed films stained with toluidine blue:* usually clusters of granules like pin heads are seen just outside the nucleus, but a few cells show one or two larger inclusions. In wet-fixed films the inclusions are also metachromatic, but the staining is more intense. Since the cells are not as flat as in air-dried films, the inclusions are rarely in the same focal plane as the nuclei and the cells are therefore not suitable for photography. Nevertheless, the characteristic appearance of the inclusions in wet-fixed films and their intense staining make it worth while to use this procedure.

Although the inclusions in films stained with May-Gruenwald-Giemsa have a characteristic appearance, additional staining with toluidine blue is important, because the metachromatic staining will exclude any possibility of confusion with the azurophilic granules which are sometimes of considerable size in normal lymphocytes. Some batches of toluidine blue may not be suitable for metachromatic staining and it is advisable when using this stain on blood films to search for a few basophil cells to make sure that the metachromatic staining is successful.

References

BERRY, H. K., and SPINANGER, J. (1960). *J. Lab. clin. Med.*, **55**, 136.
BITTER, T., and MUIR, H. M. (1962). *Analyt. Biochem.*, **4**, 330.
KOHN, J. (1960). In Smith, I, 'Chromatographic and Electrophoretic Techniques', vol. II, p. 56, London: Heinemann.
MANLEY, G., and HAWKSWORTH, J. (1966). *Arch. Dis. Childh.*, **41**, 91.
MITTWOCH, U. (1963). *Acta haemat.*, **29**, 202.

14: Test for Metachromatic Leucodystrophy

Lake (1965) has proposed a diagnostic test for metachromatic leucodystrophy which is based on the detection of brown metachromasia within the renal epithelial cells or the urinary deposit. Most urinary deposits unfortunately contain much debris and relatively few cells. We therefore use the following modification (Read, 1966).

REAGENTS AND MATERIALS

(1) 1 per cent aqueous solution of cresyl fast violet (Merck). The pH is adjusted to 3·5–3·6 with acetic acid.
(2) Hemming capsules containing Whatman No. 41 filter paper.
(3) Glycerin albumen.

PROCEDURE

The urine, which must be fresh and which should preferably not be an early morning specimen, is centrifuged at about 1,500 r.p.m. for 5 minutes. Most of the supernatant is decanted and the sediment resuspended in the remaining supernatant. The suspension is transferred to a bijou bottle connected to the Hemming's filter with Whatman No. 41 paper. The bottles with the filter are centrifuged at about 2,000 r.p.m. for 5 minutes. This retains particles of diameter greater than 5 μ, including epithelial cells, but allows bacteria and smaller debris, e.g. phosphates, to pass through.

Glycerin albumen is spread thickly on two 3 × 1 in. slides. The filter paper is removed from the Hemming's capsule and an imprint made on the first slide. The imprinted material is relatively fluid and is mixed by means of a slide end with the glycerin albumen on the slide. The mixture is drawn down with the slide edge into several parallel thick transverse lines. The filter paper is then placed firmly on the second slide and the imprinted area ringed on the reverse of the slide with a diamond. The filter paper is then discarded.

The slides are fixed in formalin vapour at 60°C for one hour, washed in water and stained at room temperature for 10 minutes with cresyl fast violet. The smears are finally washed in water and mounted in a watery mounting medium.

References

LAKE, B. D. (1965). *Arch. Dis. Childh.*, **40**, 284.
READ, C. R. (1967). *J. Clin. Path.* (in the press).

15: The Estimation of Creatine Phosphokinase in Serum

This enzyme catalyses the reversible reaction

Adenosine triphosphate (ATP) + creatine
$\rightleftharpoons$ adenosine diphosphate (ADP) + creatine phosphate.

Methods by which the reaction is measured from right to left are more sensitive. The enzyme may be assayed by colorimetric estimation of the creatine formed (Hughes, 1962) or by determination of the ATP formed with glucose, hexokinase, glucose-6-phosphate dehydrogenase and nicotinamide adenine dinucleotide (NAD) (Rosalki, 1966). We have found both methods satisfactory but as all the reagents necessary for the assay in the method of Rosalki (1966) are marketed in capsules which may be stored indefinitely (Calbiochem, Los Angeles and London) the latter is to be preferred in laboratories which perform this test only occasionally.

PROCEDURE

The contents of a capsule are dissolved in 2·90 ml. of water contained in a 1 cm. cuvette. 0·1 ml. of serum is washed in, the contents are mixed gently and allowed to stand at 25°C for 6 minutes. The optical density is then read at 340 mμ against water as blank. Exactly 5 minutes later the optical density is read again. The difference in optical density multiplied by 960 gives the activity of the enzyme in μmoles/litre/minute. In our laboratory the upper limit of normal is 30 μmoles/litre/minute. If the change in the optical density exceeds 0·450, the test is repeated with a 1:10 dilution of serum. The activity of the enzyme increases by about 8 per cent for each 1°C rise in temperature.

Hughes (1962) originally expressed his results in μ moles/ml./hour at 37°C. To convert to μ moles/litre/minute multiply by 16·65. There is a linear relationship between results obtained by the two methods: a sample with an activity of 300 μmoles/litre/ minute at 37°C (Rosalki) will have an activity of approximately 200 μmoles/litre/ minute (Hughes), while a sample recording 300 μmoles/litre/minute at 25°C (Rosalki) will read 30 μmoles/ml./hr. at 37°C (Hughes).

References

HUGHES, B. P. (1962). *Clin. chim. Acta*, **7**, 597.
ROSALKI, S. B. (1966). *Proc. Assoc. clin. Biochemists (Great Britain)*, **4**, 23.

16: The Estimation of Serum Copper Oxidase

The level of serum copper oxidase closely parallels that of caeruloplasmin, and its assay provides a useful screening test for Wilson's disease (Ravin, 1961; O'Brien and Ibbott, 1962; cf. p. 312).

REAGENTS

(1) *p*-Phenylenediamine dihydrochloride. Prepare a saturated solution in boiling water and decolorize with activated charcoal. Filter while hot and recrystallize from the clear, colourless filtrate. Dry the crystals and store under vacuum in the dark. A 0·5 per cent solution is prepared just before use.

(2) 0·4 M acetate buffer, pH 5·5, stored at 4°C.

(3) 0·5 per cent sodium azide in water. This solution is stable at room temperature.

PROCEDURE

Into two 15 ml. tubes (siliconized stoppered glass tubes or polythene tubes), pipette 8 ml. of buffer and add 0·1 ml. of serum. To the first tube, the 'blank', add 1 ml. sodium azide solution and mix. Warm both tubes for 5 minutes in a water bath at 37°C, then add 1 ml. of the phenylene diamine solution to each tube. Mix and incubate for 37°C for 60 minutes. After 60 minutes, add 1 ml. of azide solution to the 2nd tube, the 'test'. After the incubation place both tubes in ice for 30 minutes then read in a spectrophotometer with 1 cm. cells at 530 mμ. Solutions which are too high to read may be diluted with buffer and an appropriate correction made in the calculation. Enzyme activity in optical density units is given by the difference: Optical Density of Test—Optical Density of Blank. The normal range is 0·140–0·570 optical density units. In Wilson's disease the values found are almost always below 0·05 optical density units.

Estimation of serum and urine copper levels is indispensable in the confirmation of the diagnosis and in the management of cases treated with chelating agents. A critical review of methods currently available has been contributed by Sass-Kortsak (1965). A simple, direct extraction method with dibenzyldithiocarbamate has been described by Giorgio *et al.* (1964). This method was originally developed for the estimation of copper in urine, but according to Hsia and Inouye (1966) it is also suitable for serum.

References

GIORGIO, A. J., CARTWRIGHT, G. E., and WINTROBE, M. M. (1964). *Amer. J. clin. Path.*, **41**, 22.

HSIA, D. Y.-Y., and INOUYE, T. (1966). 'Inborn Errors of Metabolism, Part 2, Laboratory Methods', Chicago: Year Book Medical Publishers, p. 50.

O'BRIEN, D., and IBBOTT, F. A. (1962). 'Pediatric Micro and Ultramicro Biochemical Techniques', 3rd. ed., New York: Hoeber, p. 98.

RAVIN, H. A. (1961). *J. Lab. clin. Med.*, **58**, 161.

SASS-KORTSAK, A. (1965). *Advanc. clin. Chem.*, **8**, 1.

17: The Estimation of Lead in Blood and Urine

Moncrieff *et al.* (1964) (cf. p. 80) found raised blood lead levels in 95 of 214 children investigated for mental retardation, severe behaviour disorders, 'encephalitis', or such symptoms as severe unexplained anaemia, abdominal pain, vomiting and general irritability. Many of these cases had a history of pica. In our group of hospitals raised blood lead levels are likewise frequent, and while in our experience lead poisoning is only rarely the cause of mental retardation (Berg and Zappella, 1964), it is a common complication of severe subnormality and occasionally causes further intellectual deterioration. Blood lead estimations are, therefore, often requested for mentally retarded patients. Most assays of lead in the blood are based on the formation of a pink complex with dithizone at alkaline pH. The technique described here is that of Moncrieff *et al.* (1964).

Analytical reagents of the highest attainable purity and of low lead content are used throughout. All reagents are stored in polythene or borosilicate ('Pyrex') glass containers. Glassware is washed in detergent and distilled water, placed in 3 per cent nitric acid for about 16 hours, rinsed in three changes of distilled water, and dried in an oven, making sure that no metal touches the glass. To avoid contamination with lead in the glass, new glassware is submitted to the digestion procedure described below. The glassware is then used for lead estimations only and is kept under cover to exclude dust when not in such use.

REAGENTS

(1) Concentrated sulphuric acid, S.G. 1·835.
(2) Perchloric acid, S.G. 1·53.
(3) Nitric acid, S.G. 1·42.
(4) Ammonia, S.G. 0·880.
(5) Citric acid.
(6) Potassium cyanide.
(7) Chloroform, redistilled from calcium hydroxide.
(8) Dithizone, a 0·1 per cent solution in chloroform is stored under sulphurous acid at 4°C.
(9) 50 per cent ammonium citrate. 500 g. citric acid are dissolved in 300 ml. of distilled water. 450 ml. of ammonia are then added carefully, stirring and cooling. Three drops of phenol red indicator are added followed by more ammonia until the indicator changes from yellow to pink, indicating a pH of 8·5. The solution is extracted in a separating funnel with 10 ml. chloroform and 0·2 ml. dithizone, and the chloroform layer removed. The ammonium citrate is then washed well three times with chloroform, using 45 ml. in all, the final separation being performed after letting the mixture stand overnight. The solution may be stored indefinitely.
(10) 10 per cent potassium cyanide in water, made up fresh each month.
(11) Cyanide-citrate-ammonia solution. 30 ml. of 10 per cent potassium cyanide solution, 3 ml. of 50 per cent ammonium citrate and 10 ml. of ammonia are made up to one litre with distilled water. The solution is stored indefinitely.
(12) Cyanide-ammonia wash solution. This is made up fresh each time. 10 ml. of

10 per cent potassium cyanide and 10 ml. of ammonia are made up to one litre with distilled water.

(13) Standard solution. 183·1 mg. lead acetate trihydrate are dissolved in distilled water, 3 ml. of redistilled acetic acid are added and the solution is made up to one litre. The solution keeps indefinitely. It contains 100 μg. of lead/ml. Lead free reagents are obtainable from B.D.H., Dorset.

Collection of Blood

A solution of heparin, 1:1,000, from a fresh ampoule is drawn into a 10 ml. disposable plastic syringe and expelled, leaving a film of anti-coagulant in the syringe. About 7 ml. of blood, which is enough for a duplicate estimation, is then collected, an air bubble drawn into the syringe, and the needle bent sharply. The blood and anti-coagulant can now be mixed by repeated gentle inversion of the syringe. The blood can be stored in the syringe under refrigeration until analysed. The tip of the bent needle may be plunged into a cork to prevent leakage and to safeguard against accidental injury.

PROCEDURE FOR BLOOD

Using a pipette calibrated 'to contain', 3 ml. of blood are placed in a 50 ml. stoppered borosilicate tube and the pipette washed out with 2 ml. of water. 5 ml. of nitric acid, 3 ml. of perchloric acid and 0·5 ml. of sulphuric acid are added, the tube swirled to mix, and then allowed to stand for 30 minutes to prevent excessive frothing on heating. The tube is boiled on a sand bath until only the sulphuric acid is left (about 90–120 minutes) and heated over a Bunsen until all fuming ceases. After cooling, 3 ml. of 50 per cent ammonium citrate are added, followed by 4 ml. ammonia and 10 ml. cyanide-citrate-ammonia solution. The tube is swirled to mix, and then shaken for 30 seconds after the addition of 0·1 ml. of dithizone solution and 10 ml. of chloroform. The two layers are allowed to separate, and most of the aqueous layer is removed with a Pasteur pipette connected to a filter pump. The chloroform is washed with four successive 20 ml. portions of cyanide-ammonia wash solution. As the chloroform layer is washed its colour changes from green to pink, and the last washing is no longer brown. A roll of 9 cm. Whatman No. 42 filter paper is dropped in the tube to dry the chloroform, and the optical density of the solution is read at 525 mμ against a water blank.

PROCEDURE FOR URINE

A 24 hour sample of urine is collected and stored in plastic containers. 10 ml. of a 50 per cent solution of nitric acid is used as preservative. 25 ml. of nitric acid and 10 ml. of perchloric acid are added to 100 ml. of urine in a 250 ml. beaker, and the mixture is boiled to dryness in a sand bath (4–5 hours). The sample is not left to bake as this may lead to losses of up to 50 per cent. A white crystalline residue is required: a brown residue is treated with a few drops of nitric acid and the mixture reboiled. If the colour persists, a few drops of perchloric acid are added and the mixture is boiled to dryness.

When the sample has stopped fuming it is dissolved in distilled water with slight warming, and the solution is transferred together with two washings of water to a 250 ml. separating funnel. 5 ml. of ammonia, 3 ml. of 50 per cent ammonium citrate and 10 ml. of cyanide-citrate-ammonia solution are added, with swirling to mix the contents, and then 0·2 ml. of dithizone solution and 20 ml. of chloroform. After shaking for 30 seconds and allowing to separate, the chloroform layer is run into a 50 ml. stoppered borosilicate glass tube, and washed with four successive 20 ml. portions of cyanide-ammonia solution. The aqueous layer is removed each time by a

Pasteur pipette connected to a water pump. A roll of Whatman No. 42 filter paper is dropped into the chloroform to remove the last traces of water. The optical density of the solution is measured at 525 mμ against a water blank.

In patients treated with chelating agents, 25 ml. of urine is often a sufficient sample, and in this case 20 ml. of nitric acid and 5 ml. of perchloric acid are used.

Calibration Graph. 10–50 μg. of lead are extracted into 10 ml. of chloroform for blood or 20 ml. of chloroform for urine estimations and a calibration curve is constructed.

Normal Range. Normal children show a blood lead level below 40 μg./100 ml. and excrete less than 80 μg. of lead in 24 hours. These values are not accepted universally.

A partially automated procedure for the determination of lead in whole blood has been recently described by Delves and Vinter (1966).

References

BERG, J. M., and ZAPPELLA, M. (1964). *J. ment. Defic. Res.*, **8**, 44.
DELVES, H. T., and VINTER, P. (1966) *J. clin. Path.*, **19**, 504.
MONCRIEFF, A. A., KOUMIDES, O. P., CLAYTON, B. E., PATRICK, A. D., RENWICK, A. G. C., and ROBERTS, G. E. (1964). *Arch. Dis. Childh.*, **39**, 1.

18: A Note on Neuropathological Methods

Pathologists not familiar with neuropathological methods will find these described in many well-known histological manuals, such as Culling's (1963) and Gasser's (1961). They may nevertheless be interested in the following brief remarks based on long personal experience in the authors' laboratory.

Statutory law, including the Human Tissue Act of 1961, makes it lawful to retain for study any part of the body, such as the brain and spinal cord, provided that certain provisions are complied with. Since the retention of the whole of the central nervous system is essential for neuropathological study, pathologists are advised to consult the Human Tissue Act, 1961, before drafting the customary certificate authorizing the autopsy. This certificate, which must be signed by the person in lawful possession of the body, should conform to the legal requirements.

Even if full measurements have been already recorded in the case documents, we find it useful to re-measure the skull in the post-mortem room. This is particularly necessary because many of the severely subnormal patients are children. The parameters we measure are the head circumference at its widest, the bi-orbital diameter (i.e. the distance between the two outer canthi of the eyes), the parietal diameter (the distance between the two parietal eminences), and the antero-posterior diameter (between the nasion and the external occipital protuberance). The state of the scalp, fissures and fontanelles is noted and the skull is then opened in the usual way. The dura and its sinuses are inspected. The brain is removed, inspected, palpated and weighed. The cranial nerves and blood-vessels are examined, for which purpose it is necessary to separate gently the two frontal and the temporal lobes of the brain. It is best not to section the brain before it is properly fixed, but this may be necessary in coroner's cases. Unfixed deep-frozen tissue also may be required for chemical and histochemical examination, and we then remove a substantial part of the frontal lobe. It is essential that such tissue should include an adequate amount of grey and white matter.

We remove the spinal cord by the posterior route, i.e. by sawing through the vertebral arches. An electrical saw saves a good deal of labour, especially if the spine is deformed. Some workers maintain that the anterior approach is easier. They remove the bodies of the vertebrae in the thorax and abdomen by means of a wide-bladed chisel. We have tried this method but have not persevered with it long enough to obtain consistently satisfying results. The cord must on no account be kinked. The literature contains many examples of artefacts caused by kinking or squeezing the cord, misinterpreted as true lesions by the authors. The spinal cord is removed together with, at least, a few of the spinal root ganglia. The dura around it is slit vertically in front and behind, and the cord is then cut transversely in two or three places. In this way it is possible to inspect the cord at once and to fix and store it in a relatively small container.

We fix the brain in 10 per cent formol saline, suspending it in the solution by a string hooked under the basilar artery. Unlike some other workers, we do not introduce the fixative directly into the ventricles. The period of fixation should not be less than three weeks but it is inadvisable to fix the brain longer than about six months prior to the first cutting as some of the staining may deteriorate after that.

The brain is then dissected, i.e. examined, cut and prepared for histological processing. This 'brain-cutting' is without doubt the most informative single part of the neuropathological examination, and it is therefore advisable to prepare for it by a thorough perusal of the case history, as the choice of the cutting method and the subsequent processing and staining depend in large measure on problems posed by the manifestations of the disease and the somatic pathological findings.

After another external examination and weighing, the brainstem with the cerebellum are separated from the cerebrum by a cut through the upper part of the brainstem. This commences immediately behind the corpora mamillaria and ends posteriorly at the level of the superior corpora quadrigemina, care being taken to leave intact the medial geniculate bodies. The cerebellum and brainstem are then weighed.

As already indicated, the choice of the dissecting procedure and the selection of blocks for histological study must vary in individual cases. Nevertheless, in the absence of special indications, it is advisable to adhere to a relatively constant routine in order to compare the appearances in similar areas. In our laboratory we are interested in pathological rather than purely anatomical problems and do not often require very large blocks or serial sections. If the brain is symmetrical and the clinical data do not suggest unilateral disease, detailed examination is confined in the first instance to a single cerebral hemisphere, the other being left for later study— possibly by different methods. The examined hemisphere is cut coronally at intervals of about 1 cm., and a sagittal block is also taken at the vertex of the brain. This should contain the central fissure and the adjoining parts of the frontal and parietal lobes. After a detailed examination of the cut blocks, parts of the following areas are taken for histological processing: the frontal lobe, the sagittal block containing the central fissure, the occipital lobe, the temporal lobe including the hippocampus and a complete block of the basal ganglia taken at about the mid-level of the thalamus. The cerebellum is then separated from the brainstem. Transverse blocks are embedded of the midbrain, pons and medulla. The cerebellum is cut vertically at a sharp angle to the midline so that the dentate nucleus is included in the embedded block. Blocks are also taken from the cervical, thoracic, lumbar and sacral regions of the spinal cord. These require no labelling as they are easily recognisable in the histological sections. In cases of suspected or manifest spinal disease it may be necessary, of course, to take many more blocks of the spinal cord, and it is then necessary to label and process these separately.

We take careful notes during the brain-cutting and always attempt to arrive at tentative conclusions on the basis of the macroscopic findings and clinical data. It is surprising how often such conclusions remain fully valid, further histological findings calling for no revision of the diagnosis. Unfortunately, naked-eye appearances become meaningful to a pathologist only after prolonged habitual checking against histological findings.

The use of photography at the cutting-up stage (and also, if necessary, in the post-mortem room) saves a good deal of verbal description and provides, of course, a permanent record of the appearances.

The tissue is embedded in celloidin and paraffin, while frozen sections are also used as required. We often use all three methods but it must be remembered that neuropathological techniques are very time-consuming, and it is therefore necessary to restrict oneself to the most economical ones. This calls for knowledge of the limitations and advantages of each of the methods.

Celloidin embedding is useful in neuropathology because very large blocks can be cut without undue difficulty. Furthermore, sections do not crack and it is therefore possible to prepare thick sections, and these are essential for the detection of cytoarchitectonic abnormalities and milder degrees of neuronal loss. Serial sectioning of celloidin-embedded blocks is easy, and intervening unstained sections can be stored indefinitely. On the other hand, celloidin embedding is the longest of the embedding processes. In our laboratory it takes on the average 10 weeks to embed blocks of tissue, and attempts to speed this up often lead to faults. Many cases can however, be embedded, simultaneously and the process itself calls for little inter-vention by technicians. Another disadvantage of celloidin embedding is that it is difficult to cut sections of under 15 μ in thickness. Apart from glassware, the only equipment needed for the preparation and cutting of celloidin-embedded material is a sledge microtome and large plano-concave knives. These are usually available in pathological laboratories. Celloidin embedding and the staining of celloidin-embedded sections are very well described by Gasser.

Paraffin embedding is, of course, familiar to all pathologists and calls for little comment. Some neuropathologists rely entirely on this method, but we find it easier to cut large and thick sections of celloidin-embedded material. Special precautions may, if taken, obviate some of the difficulties with paraffin-embedded material. One is the use of a special mixture of paraffin which we have adopted following a visit to Dr. S. Tariska's laboratory in Budapest. The mixture consists of 15 sheets of dental wax, 5 litres of paraffin wax and 50 g. of cera alba (beeswax). The dental wax is added to the paraffin, the mixture is heated until swirling occurs, and the cera alba is then added to it.

Even pathologists like ourselves, who rely largely on celloidin, also employ fre-quent paraffin embedding. Usually a few blocks are taken for this purpose in all cases, in addition to those for celloidin. Moreover, paraffin embedding is almost imperative when the tissue is very cellular, as in the case of tumours, granulomata and many other inflammatory processes.

The choice of staining methods varies, of course, from case to case and is to some extent a matter of individual preference. In general, the law of diminishing return operates with great force in the field of stain technology, a battery of stains yielding very little in the way of extra information over and above that derived from a few familiar stains. We employ as a routine cresyl violet for staining cells and the Wölke-Heidenhain method for myelin in celloidin processed material, and haematoxylin and eosin, and haematoxylin and van Gieson for paraffin-embedded tissue. Other methods which we use frequently include the Holzer method for fibrous glia, P.T.A.H., luxol-fast blue for myelin and the P.A.S. method.

General pathologists are, perhaps, most apprehensive of the frozen tissue neuro-pathological techniques and, especially, the silver impregnation methods. Many have tried them at one time or another and were disappointed with the results. They can be reassured. These methods are almost as refractory in the hands of neuropatholo-gists. This is particularly so in paediatric neuropathology. The chemical and physi-cal state of the brains of children is more variable than that of adults and im-pregnation methods are therefore more difficult to standardize. Fortunately, examination of frozen sections is seldom decisive, and the use of these techniques need not be extended beyond the most reliable ones. These include the demonstration of soluble sudanophil and metachromatic substances. Axis cylinders are demonstrable by the usually reliable Bielschowsky method. Staining of myelin sheaths by the Kulschitsky-Pal and of fibrous glia by the Holzer methods is also usually very satisfactory.

It should be mentioned, however, that some neuropathologists use the freezing microtome very extensively for cutting large sections and staining them by all the usual methods. In other words, they employ frozen sections in place of celloidin- or paraffin-embedded material. In doing so, they gain a good deal of time and the results, in their expert hands, seem satisfactory.

In recent years histochemical and electron microscopical methods have also been increasingly employed for necropsy material, but such techniques have scarcely been taken into routine use. We have no personal experience of them.

It may thus be concluded that neuropathological examination of cases though laborious and time-consuming is not intrinsically difficult. Any pathologist wishing to study the central nervous system has an abundant choice of methods. He would be well advised, however, to visit himself or ask his technician to visit a neuropathological laboratory, for the success of many methods depends to a considerable degree on minor ways and details in the handling of the material. These are never fully described in manuals.

References

CULLING, C. F A. (1963). 'Handbook of Histopathological Techniques', London: Butterworths.
GASSER, G. (1961). 'Basic Neuropathological Technique', Oxford: Blackwell.

19: A Note on the Use of Biopsies in the Diagnosis of Conditions Associated with Mental Subnormality

Brain Biopsy

The indications for brain biopsy in the mentally subnormal present a somewhat difficult problem. Brain biopsy can contribute little or nothing to the diagnosis or management of the majority of such patients. Although, as has been explained at length in this book, the basis of most, if not all, cases of subnormality is some structural or chemical anomaly of the brain, the encephalopathy is usually 'burnt-out'. In many instances it takes the form of some malformation which need not be associated with any characteristic histological changes in limited areas of the brain. Other cases present only non-specific changes, such as gliosis and neuronal loss, and these can be focal and are often difficult to ascertain in a small piece of tissue. The possible immediate dangers of the operation and remote effects on the neurological and mental status of the patient must also be considered (see below). Furthermore, clinical laboratory methods are constantly improving and many conditions can now be diagnosed without resort to brain biopsy. In some cases, pathological examinations of certain other tissues might prove to be as diagnostic as that of the brain (see below). Nevertheless, there is a place for brain biopsy in certain selected cases and much has been learned by its judicious use. In general, its indications are the impossibility of diagnosing the condition by other means in cases associated with *progressive* dementia, especially where genetic counselling is indicated. When craniotomy is carried out to exclude a focal condition, such as subdural haematoma, brain abscess or tumour, which may be amenable to surgery, a cerebral biopsy may also be undertaken. If the operation is planned carefully little tissue needs to be excised. Indeed, it is astonishing how much information was extracted from specimen weighing less than 1 g.

by some teams of American workers, who used minute amounts of material for combined enzyme studies, histochemistry, neurochemistry, light microscopy and electron microscopy. Such work is a triumph of laboratory organization and methods. The importance of brain biopsies for research is therefore clear.

Several workers have mentioned that they saw no untoward results of brain biopsy in their series of cases. Although this statement is no doubt formally correct, its wider implications cannot be accepted unreservedly. In the first place, no study has yet been made of the possible long-term results of the biopsy on the neurological and mental state of the patients, although a few cases have now been followed up for more than five years and appear to show no ill effects from the biopsy. In the second place, deterioration caused by the operation might be easily submerged in the global dementia. This may not matter greatly in severe and irreversible conditions, but the effects might well be serious and, even, critical in more intelligent or border-line cases.

It seems useful to mention here the experience of some authors with a large number of brain biopsies performed in selected cases of progressive dementia. In a series of 65 patients studied by Blackwood and Cumings (1959) at the National Hospital for Nervous Diseases, Queen Square, London, a definite diagnosis could be made by means of the chemical and histological examination of the tissue in three-quarters of the cases. The conditions thus diagnosed included lipidosis, leucodys-trophy, tuberous sclerosis, and subacute sclerosing encephalitis. Twenty-three specimens showed no abnormality. Later experience of these and other workers has been even more encouraging (Cumings, 1965). As methods, particularly chemical ones, improve, diagnosis becomes more accurate in a larger proportion of cases, and many other conditions can now be diagnosed and studied with the aid of brain biopsy. For example, in a recent verbal communication to the British Neuropatho-logical Society Blackwood and Cumings reported on 178 biopsies. Thirty-five showed no abnormality, 66 were abnormal without being diagnostic of any specific disease and 77 presented evidence of one of the classified diseases.

It may be sufficient to examine the excised material only by light microscopy in cases of focal lesions, such as abscess, tumour, haematoma or malformation, but in all other cases neurochemical study is an essential part of the examination.* Indeed, electron microscopy may soon prove to be as necessary. Since few centres in any country can accumulate sufficient material to establish and standardize the necessary laboratory procedures, or have sufficient resources to undertake the work, the practical result of this new development is its centralization. In this country the work is best done at the Institute of Neurology, Queen Square, London, and doctors planning a brain biopsy are advised to consult one of the pathologists there on questions relating to fixation and transport of the material. The neurosurgeon will resect the material from one of the 'silent areas' of the brain—usually the frontal lobe; the biopsy should include both grey and white matter.

Intestinal Biopsy

Some pathological changes affecting the central nervous system involve also parts of the peripheral nervous system, particularly the myenteric plexuses of Meissner and Auerbach which are situated, respectively, in the intestinal submucosa and between the two layers of the muscularis. It was therefore reasonable to expect that certain encephalopathies, such as lipidosis and leucodystrophies, could be diagnosed by means of a rectal biopsy, and the first reported results of this method have been encouraging (Bodian and Lake, 1963). The resected material is either fixed in forma-

* Details of suitable neurochemical methods are given by Menkes, J. H., Philippart, M., and Fiol, R. E. (1965). *J. Pediat.*, **66**, 584.

lin and sections cut on a freezing microtome, or cut at once on a cryostat. Both methods can, of course, be combined if enough material is available.

Much interest has been aroused by this use of rectal biopsy and the method is now being tried in many centres. Coming years will no doubt witness the publication of the results obtained, and the advantages and drawbacks of the method will be determined. In the authors' laboratory rectal biopsy has been used so far in a dozen cases; all gave negative results. Certain difficulties have become apparent. Rectal biopsy is often used in children's hospitals for the diagnosis of Hirschsprung's disease. For this purpose material containing only the submucosa is sufficient. In order to diagnose generalized nervous disease it is essential, however, to have many more nerve cells and nerves than are normally present in the submucosa. It is known, for example, from the study of autopsy material that only one nerve cell out of many may show such a change as lipidosis. What is really needed is the whole thickness of the muscularis and this must be removed fairly high in the rectum, well above the sphincter ani. It is difficult to avoid bleeding during such an operation and blood transfusion became necessary in a few of our cases. Moreover, some of the rectal biopsies sent to us did not contain enough of the myenteric plexuses for a diagnosis to be made. We have therefore come to the conclusion that appendicectomy may be a better and safer procedure in such cases. The appendix and its mesentery are amply endowed with nervous elements, and provide enough material for all the required control procedures, and for examination by many methods. We have found, however, that the nerve cells and fibres of a child's appendix undergo structural changes in the course of their maturation, and these have not been adequately studied.

Biopsy of other Tissues

On rather rare occasions circumstances call for biopsies of other tissues. The sural nerve has been used in the diagnosis of metachromatic leucodystrophy (p. 255). For this purpose sections were cut on a freezing microtome and stained with toluidine blue or cresyl violet in 1 per cent acetic acid. Only 1 cmm. of peripheral nerve is required for the biochemical ascertainment of metachromatic leucodystrophy in so far as it is present in the tissue. Dr. P. Sourander (verbal communication) has recently observed that peripheral nerve changes, such as degeneration of myelin sheaths and axis cylinders, and fibrosis, were present in cases of globoid cell (Krabbe's) leucodystrophy. The resection of portions of all small cutaneous nerve calls, however, for a good deal of skill on the part of the operator and it is not unusual for a pathologist to receive material which contains little or no nerve tissue.

Examination of enlarged lymph glands may assist occasionally in the diagnosis of lipidosis, particularly Niemann-Pick disease. The same applies to splenectomy, splenic puncture or bone-marrow biopsy. As in the case of brain tissue, it is advisable to submit such material to both chemical and histological examination.

References

BLACKWOOD, W., and CUMINGS, J. N. (1959). *Lancet*, **2**, 23.
BODIAN, M., and LAKE, B. D. (1963). *Brit. J. Surg.*, **50**, 702.
CUMINGS, J. N. (1965). *Proc. roy. Soc. Med.*, **58**, 21.

20: Some Parameters of Brain Development

Table 1. WEIGHTS OF BRAINS AND OTHER ORGANS ACCORDING TO COPPOLETTA AND WOLBACH
(1933)

Age	Body Length	Heart	Lung		Spleen	Liver	Kidney		Brain
			Right	Left			Right	Left	
	cm.	gm.	gm.	gm.	gm.	gm.	gm.	gm.	gm.
Birth–3 days	49	17	21	18	8	78	13	14	335
3–7 ,,	49	18	24	22	9	96	14	14	358
1–3 weeks	52	19	29	26	10	123	15	15	382
3–5 ,,	52	20	31	27	12	127	16	16	413
5–7 ,,	53	21	32	28	13	133	19	18	422
7–9 ,,	55	23	32	29	13	136	19	18	489
2–3 mths.	56	23	35	30	14	140	20	19	516
4 ,,	59	27	37	33	16	160	22	21	540
5 ,,	61	29	38	35	16	188	25	25	644
6 ,,	62	31	42	39	17	200	26	25	660
7 ,,	65	34	49	41	19	227	30	30	691
8 ,,	65	37	52	45	20	254	31	30	714
9 ,,	67	37	53	47	20	260	31	30	750
10 ,,	69	39	54	51	22	274	32	31	809
11 ,,	70	40	59	53	25	277	34	33	852
12 ,,	73	44	64	57	26	288	36	35	952
14 ,,	74	45	66	60	26	304	36	35	944
16 ,,	77	48	72	64	28	331	39	39	1010
18 ,,	78	52	72	65	30	345	40	43	1042
20 ,,	79	56	83	74	30	370	43	44	1050
22 ,,	82	56	80	75	33	380	44	44	1059
24 ,,	84	56	88	76	33	394	47	46	1064
3 years	88	59	89	77	37	418	48	49	1141
4 ,,	99	73	90	85	39	516	58	56	1191
5 ,,	106	85	107	104	47	596	65	64	1237
6 ,,	109	94	121	122	58	642	68	67	1243
7 ,,	113	100	130	123	66	680	69	70	1263
8 ,,	119	110	150	140	69	736	74	75	1273
9 ,,	125	115	174	152	73	756	82	83	1275
10 ,,	130	116	177	166	85	852	92	95	1290
11 ,,	135	122	201	190	87	909	94	95	1320
12 ,,	139	124	..	..	93	936	95	96	1351

Table 2. RELATIVE SIZE OF CEREBRUM, CEREBELLUM AND BRAINSTEM ACCORDING TO KROGMAN
(1941)

Age	Per cent of total brain formed by		
	Cerebrum	Cerebellum	Brainstem
3 lunar months	88·6	3·1	8·3
6 ,, ,,	93·1	3·4	3·5
8 ,, ,,	93·5	4·1	2·4
Birth	92·7	5·8	1·5
3 months	92·1	6·5	1·4
9 ,,	89·0	9·6	1·4
1 year	88·5	10·1	1·4
2 years	88·0	10·4	1·6
5 ,,	88·0	10·2	1·8
10 ,,	88·0	10·1	1·9
20 ,,	88·0	10·1	1·9

Males and females combined.

Table 3. HEAD CIRCUMFERENCE ACCORDING TO VICKERS AND STUART (1943)

Age	Boys	S.D.	Girls	S.D.
0 0	35·3	1·2	34·7	1·0
0 3	40·8	1·2	40·0	1·2
0 6	44·0	1·0	42·9	1·2
0 9	45·8	1·0	44·7	1·2
1 0	47·1	1·1	45·9	1·3
1 6	48·8	1·1	47·4	1·2
2 0	49·6	1·2	48·2	1·4
2 6	50·1	1·2	49·0	1·4
3 0	50·4	1·2	49·3	1·3
3 6	50·7	1·2	49·6	1·4
4 0	51·0	1·2	49·9	1·3
4 6	51·2	1·2	50·2	1·4
5 0	51·3	1·2	50·3	1·3
5 6	51·3	1·1	50·6	1·3
6 0	51·9	1·2	50·8	1·4
8 0	52·7	1·3	51·8	1·4
10 0	53·1	1·1	53·0	1·4

Proportion of children within 1 S.D. of mean either way is 68 per cent.
,,   ,,   ,,   ,,   2 S.D. ,,   ,,   ,,   ,, ,, 95   ,,

Table 4. HEAD CIRCUMFERENCE RELATED TO WEIGHT AT DIFFERENT AGES ACCORDING TO ILLINGWORTH AND LUTZ (1965)

| | Boys | | | Girls | | | Weight | | | |
| | Average Head Circumference | | Regression Coefficient Head Circumference on Weight | Average Head Circumference | | Regression Coefficient Head Circumference on Weight | Boys | | Girls | |
	Inch	Cm.		Inch	Cm.		lb. oz.	g.	lb. oz.	g.
Birth	13·7	34·8	0·343	13·8	35·0	0·231	7 5½	3180	7 5½	3180
6 weeks	15·3	38·9	0·235	14·9	37·8	0·262	10 13	4860	10 0	4500
6 months	17·5	44·4	0·122	17·0	43·2	0·124	18 12¼	8520	17 7¼	7840
10 months	18·4	46·7	0·114	17·9	45·5	0·099	22 2½	10460	20 10½	9380

Table 5. CALCULATION OF EXPECTED HEAD CIRCUMFERENCE FROM AGE AND WEIGHT* AC-
CORDING TO ILLINGWORTH AND LUTZ (1965)

	Boys		Girls	
	Inch	*cm.*	*Inch*	*cm.*
Birth	0·3	0·8	0·25	0·6
6 weeks	0·25	0·6	0·25	0·6
6 months	0·125	0·3	0·125	0·3
10 months	0·1	0·3	0·1	0·3

* The figures show the amount to be added or to be subtracted from the head circumference for each lb. above or below the average weight.

References

COPPOLETTA, J. M., and WOLBACH, S. B. (1933). *Amer. J. Path.*, **9**, 55.
ILLINGWORTH, R. S., and LUTZ, W. (1965). *Arch. Dis. Childh.*, **40**, 672.
KROGMAN, W. M. (1941). *Tabulae biologicae*, **20**, 652.
VICKERS, V. S., and STUART, H. C. (1943). *J. Pediat.*, **22**, 155.

21: Normal Values of Various Brain Constituents

We reproduce below tables indicating normal values of brain lipids and a few
other constituents at different stages of development. Most of these have been published by Professor J. N. Cumings and his colleagues and the source of the infor-

Table 1. LIPID CONTENT OF UNFIXED CEREBRAL WHITE MATTER (g./100 g. FRESH TISSUE)
CUMINGS, GOODWIN, WOODWARD AND CURZON (1958)

Age and maturity	Total phospho-lipid	Sphingo-myelin	Kephalin	Lecithin	Cholesterol		Water
					Total	Esteri-fied	
10 weeks foetus*	1·43	0·32			0·18	0	91·5
28 weeks foetus*	1·07	0·5	0·28	0·34	0·45	0·03	93·7
34 weeks foetus*	2·1	0·2	0·9	1·0	0·65	0	89·7
Full term (38 weeks)	2·1	0·4	1·0	0·7	0·5	0	91·0
Full term (5 cases)	1·95–2·5	0·2–0·8	1·5–1·3	0·7–1·1	0·65–0·87	0·01–0·15	75·8–91·0
1 day	1·0	0·1	1·2	0·7	0·74	0·04	89·0
4 days	3·2	0·3	1·4	1·5	1·15	0	91·8
7 days	2·8	0·5	1·3	0·9	0·55	0	87·7
2 months	2·8	0·3	1·7	0·8	0·9	0·1	89·0
3 months	3·7	1·0	1·6	1·1	1·15	0	86·8
4 months	4·5	0·7	2·5	1·3	1·7	0	82·3
7 months	3·2	0·8	1·1	1·3	1·8	0	81·4
10 months	4·8	1·1	2·5	1·2	2·4	0·1	79·8
2 years	4·9	1·1	2·5	1·3	3·2	0·1	75·7
3 years	3·0	0·7	1·5	0·8	2·1	0	74·9
5 years	4·7	1·2	2·8	0·7	3·7	0·15	71·2
6 years	6·0	1·4	3·2	1·4	4·4	0·05	73·0
7 years	6·6	1·6	3·4	1·6	4·5	0	71·3
12 years	6·3	2·0	2·8	0·5	3·8	0	74·8

* Whole brain

mation is cited with the tables. It should not be assumed that these values will necessarily be the same in all other laboratories. Methods differ considerably and each laboratory usually prepares in the course of time its own controls and tables of normal values.

Table 2. LIPID CONTENT OF UNFIXED CEREBRAL CORTEX (g./100 g. FRESH TISSUE)
CUMINGS, GOODWIN, WOODWARD AND CURZON (1958)

Age and maturity	Total phospho-lipid	Sphingo-myelin	Kephalin	Lecithin	Cholesterol Total	Cholesterol Esteri-fied	Water
34 weeks foetus	1·75	0·25	0·7	0·8	0·5	0	91·5
Full term (38 weeks)	1·8	0·5	0·7	0·6	0·5	0	89·4
Full term (5 cases)	1·8–2·5	0·3–0·4	0·8–1·8	0·2–1·0	0·54–0·67	0·02	85·5–89·2
1 day	1·8	0·1	1·4	0·3	0·53	0	88·9
4 days	3·0	0·3	1·3	1·4	1·0	0	91·4
7 days	2·5	0·5	1·2	0·8	0·47	0·0·92	90·4
2 months	2·7	0·3	1·5	0·9	0·7	0	90·0
3 months	2·7	0·4	1·3	1·0	0·6	0·01	88·5
4 months	2·9	0·3	1·6	1·0	0·7	0	83·3
7 months	2·3	0·6	0·8	0·9	0·8	0	87·0
10 months	2·5	0·5	1·3	0·7	0·8	0	88·5
2 years	2·3	0·5	1·1	0·7	0·9	0	84·7
3 years	2·7	0·5	1·3	0·9	1·1	0	84·1
5 years	2·7	0·7	1·5	0·5	1·0	0	84·9
6 years	3·5	0·6	1·7	1·2	1·0	0	84·2
7 years	3·2	0·7	1·7	0·8	0·9	0	83·7
12 years	4·0	0·8	2·2	1·0	0·9	0·06	78·9

Table 3. CEREBROSIDES IN UNFIXED BRAIN TISSUE (g./100 g. FRESH TISSUE)
CUMINGS, GOODWIN, WOODWARD AND CURZON (1958)

Age and maturity	Cerebral white matter 'Galactose cerebroside'	Cerebral white matter Cerebroside (Radin)	Cerebral cortex 'Galactose cerebroside'	Cerebral cortex Cerebroside (Radin)
Full term (1)	0·54	0·05	0·46	0·04
(2)	0·39	0·03	0·34	0·04
(3)	0·7	0·05	0·5	0·07
(4)	0·7	0·04	0·6	0·03
(5)	0·6	0·09	0·5	0·07
1 day	0·5	0·09	0·6	0·06
4 days	0·48	0·08	0·72	0·06
7 days	0·32	0·07	0·37	0·11
2 months	1·1	0·4	0·9	0·20
3 months	1·15	0·53	0·48	0·04
7 months	2·23	1·3	0·43	0·14
10 months	2·5	2·15	0·48	0·03
2 years	3·6	1·9	0·7	0·14
3 years	3·13	1·23	1·03	0·29
5 years	4·7	3·17	0·61	0·07
6 years	4·6	4·0	0·79	0·20
7 years	5·15	5·02	0·67	0·19
12 years	4·03	3·31	0·91	0·26

Table 4. TOTAL HEXOSAMINE AND NEURAMINIC ACID IN UNFIXED BRAIN TISSUE
(mg./100 g. DRY TISSUE)
CUMINGS, GOODWIN, WOODWARD AND CURZON (1958)

Age and maturity	Cerebral white matter Total hexosamine	Cerebral cortex Neuraminic acid
10 weeks foetus*	410	109
28 weeks foetus	300	208
34 weeks foetus	647	200
38 weeks foetus	622	223
Full term (5 cases)	335–556	217–319
4 days	573	162
7 days	750	270
2 months	612	328
3 months	705	323
4 months	608	347
7 months	410	478
10 months	254	355
2 years	278	377
3 years	232	396
5 years	227	413
6 years	217	351
7 years	239	552
12 years	284	223

* Whole brain

Table 5. PHOSPHOLIPID DISTRIBUTION IN UNFIXED WHITE MATTER OF HUMAN BRAIN (RESULTS EXPRESSED AS mg. LIPIDPHOSPHORUS/100 g. DRY TISSUE BALAKRISHNAN, GOODWIN AND CUMINGS (1961)

	Newborn	3 months	8 months	1 year	6 years	14 years	Adult
Total lipid phosphorus	720	750	770	900	1020	1000	990
Water (%)	89	84	78	77	71	70	70
Phosphatidylcholine	317 (44)	285 (38)	224 (29)	252 (28)	224 (22)	210 (21)	198 (20)
Phosphatidylethanolamine	138 (19)	120 (16)	69 (9)	83 (9)	112 (11)	80 (8)	100 (10)
Phosphatidylserine	115 (16)	105 (14)	138 (16)	143 (16)	160 (16)	170 (17)	149 (15)
Phosphoinositide	29 (4)	30 (4)	24 (3)	29 (3)	30 (3)	30 (3)	29 (3)
Plasmalogens	50 (7)	90 (12)	112 (16)	184 (20)	143 (13)	130 (13)	134 (13)
Sphingomyelin	22 (3)	45 (6)	100 (13)	120 (13)	152 (15)	200 (20)	178 (18)
Unidentified mild alkali and acid stable phospholipids	22 (3)	23 (3)	62 (8)	54 (6)	82 (8)	120 (12)	79 (8)
Recovery (% of total lipid phosphorus analysed)	96	93	96	95	89	95	88

Values in parentheses represent percentage of total lipid phosphorus.

Table 6. CEPHALIN AND SPHINGOMYELIN DISTRIBUTION IN THE WHITE MATTER OF HUMAN BRAIN AT DIFFERENT AGES. (RESULTS EXPRESSED AS g./100 g. FRESH TISSUE) BALAKRISHNAN, GOODWIN AND CUMINGS (1961)

Age	Phosphatidyl-ethanolamine	Phosphatidyl-serine	Phospho-inositide	Plasma-logens	Sphingomyelin
Newborn	0·38	0·32	0·08	0·14	0·06
3 months	0·48	0·42	0·12	0·36	0·18
8 months	0·38	0·76	0·13	0·67	0·54
1 year	0·48	0·85	0·17	1·06	0·70
6 years	0·81	1·16	0·22	1·04	1·10
14 years	0·60	1·28	0·23	0·98	1·50
Adult	0·74	1·11	0·22	1·01	1·30

All phosphorus values multiplied by a factor of 25 for conversion into phospholipid.

Table 7. LIPIDS ESTIMATED IN UNFIXED CEREBRAL CORTEX (g./100 g. DRY TISSUE) CUMINGS, GOODWIN AND CURZON (1959)

Age	Neuraminic acid (N.A.)	'Lipid-soluble' hexosamine (L.H.)	N.A./L.H.	Residual hexosamine	Water-soluble hexosamine	Water (%)
Full term infant	0·27	0·06	4·5	0·37	0·07	88·4
Full term infant					0·10	89·8
3 months	0·32	0·11	2·91	0·29		88·5
10 months	0·35	0·13	2·69	0·38		84·7
2 years	0·38	0·15	2·53	0·49	0·05	84·7
3 years	0·40	0·14	2·86	0·60		84·1
5 years	0·41	0·09	4·55	0·38	0·04	84·9
7 years	0·35	0·12	2·91	0·48		83·7
12 years	0·22	0·08	2·75	0·32	0·03	78·9
26 years	0·20	0·09	2·22	0·32	0·05	84·2
53 years	0·27	0·08	3·37	0·31		81·9
70 years	0·30	0·14	2·14	0·27		84·9

Table 8. LIPIDS ESTIMATED IN UNFIXED CEREBRAL WHITE MATTER (g./100 g. DRY TISSUE) CUMINGS, GOODWIN AND CURZON (1959)

Age	Neuraminic acid (N.A.)	'Lipid-soluble' hexosamine (L.H.)	N.A./L.H.	Residual hexosamine	Water-soluble hexosamine	Water (%)
Full term infant	0·15	0·07	2·14	0·33	0·12	85·5
Full term infant					0·11	82·7
3 months	0·29	0·10	2·9	0·61		86·8
10 months	0·10	0·05	2·0	0·32		79·7
2 years	0·07	0·04	1·75	0·35	0·02	75·7
3 years	0·08	0·05	1·6	0·24		74·9
5 years	0·08	0·03	2·66	0·26	0·03	71·2
7 years	0·07	0·05	1·4	0·25		71·3
12 years	0·09	0·03	3·0	0·19	0·01	74·8
26 years	0·05	0·02	2·5	0·21	0·01	67·9
53 years	0·04	0·02	2·0	0·23		67·4
70 years	0·04	0·04	1·0	0·23		71·7

Table 9. ALTERATION OF PHOSPHOLIPID COMPOSITION IN BRAIN FOLLOWING FORMALIN
FIXATION
CUMINGS (personal communication)

	White Matter		Cortex	
	Fresh Biopsy	*After 5 days fixation*	*Fresh Biopsy*	*After 5 days fixation*
Total Phospholipid	30·6	29·9	28·2	22·4
Sphingomyelin	11·9	12·3	8·5	8·0
Cephalin	13·2	9·1	13·8	8·0
Lecithin	5·5	5·0	5·8	5·8

Results in g./100 g. dry tissue

Table 10. HEXOSAMINE FRACTIONS IN CEREBRAL WHITE MATTER
CUMINGS (personal communication)

Age	*Lipid Soluble*	*Water Soluble*	*Residual*
Full term	0·16	0·11	0·41
Full term	0·07	0·12	0·33
2 months	0·14	0·09	0·48
3 months	0·15	0·05	0·43
8 months	0·08	0·04	0·32
2 years	0·04	0·02	0·35
5 years	0·03	0·03	0·26
6 years	0·04	0·02	0·28
12 years	0·03	0·01	0·19
26 years	0·02	0·01	0·21

Results in g./100 g. dry tissue

For a concise record of brain lipid values in different pathological conditions readers are referred to the account of Cumings (1960).

References

BALAKRISHNAN, S., GOODWIN, H., and CUMINGS, J. N. (1961). *J. Neurochem.*, **8**, 276.
CUMINGS, J. N., GOODWIN, H., and CURZON, G. (1959). *J. Neurochem.*, **4**, 234.
CUMINGS, J. N., GOODWIN, H. WOODWARD, E. M., and CURZON, G. (1958). *J. Neurochem.*, **2**, 289.
CUMINGS, J. N. (1960). *In* 'Modern Scientific Aspects of Neurology', London: Arnold, p. 330.

AUTHORS'* INDEX

*The index contains the names of all authors including those covered in the text by the appellation *et al.* However, the pages given here are only those where these authors are concerned in the text and not the bibliography at the end of the chapters.

SUBJECT INDEX

Subacute inclusion encephalitis, 66
Subacute necrotizing encephalomyelopathy,
   see Leigh's encephalomyelopathy
Subcultural group, 4
Sulphatide, 222
Synthetic diets, 77
Syphilis, 34
Syringobulbia, 175
Syringomyelia, 175
System atrophies, 128

Tay-Sachs disease, 212, 235–243
  chemical pathology, 241
  racial incidence, 52
  morbid anatomy, 236
Telencephalosynapsis, 105
Temporal lobe epilepsy, 74, 334
Teratogenesis, 28
Terminal illness, 147
Thalidomide, 8, 32, 34
Thin-layer chromatography, 345 *et seq*
Thiouracil, 45
Thyroid disorders, maternal, 44
Tolbutamide, 44
Torpedo bodies, 237
Toxaemia of pregnancy, 46
Toxoplasmosis, 35
Translocation, chromosomal, 10
Trauma, maternal, 46
Triphosphoinositide, 220
Triple X females, 12
Triplet code, 20
Trisomy, 10
True microcephaly, 100
Tryptophan, estimation of, 356
Tryptophan load test, 347
Tuberous sclerosis, 8, 183–192
  chemical pathology, 192
  comparative, 192

formes frustes, 191
  somatic lesions, 186
Tumours, 84
Turner's syndrome, 14
Twins, 3, 4, 49, 50
Tyrosine, metabolism of, 271
  estimation of, 355
Tyrosinosis, 212, 270–272

Ulegyria, 119
Undesignated disorders, 214, 327
Unverricht syndrome, 335

Vascular factors, 81
Ventricular dilatation, 101
Ventriculo-atrial shunt, 180
Virchow's corpuscles, 117
Virus infection, maternal, 39
Vitamin A, deprivation, 28
  excess of, 28
Vitamin B deficiency, 29
Vitamin B_{12} deficiency, 144, 314
Vitamin C deficiency, 77
Vitamin E deficiency, 29, 125
Vitamin K, 70
Vogts' disease, 138

Walnut brain, 118
Weights of brains, 377
  cerebrum and cerebellum, 378
Werdnig-Hoffmann disease, 313
Wernicke's encephalopathy, 77, 314
White matter, anomalies of, 138
White matter, gliosis of, 125
Whooping cough, 67
Wilson's disease, *see* hepatolenticular
  degeneration

XYY formula, in delinquency, 13

PRINTED AND BOUND IN ENGLAND BY
HAZELL WATSON AND VINEY LTD
AYLESBURY, BUCKS